Contents

Section 1: Open Games

Section 2: Semi-Open Games

Symbols

+	check
++	double check
#	checkmate
!!	brilliant move
!	good move
!?	interesting move
?!	dubious move
?	bad move
??	blunder
Ch	championship
Cht	team championship
Wch	world championship
Wcht	world team championship
Ech	European championship
Echt	European team championship
Ct	Candidates event
IZ	interzonal
Z	zonal
ECC	European Clubs Cup
OL	olympiad
jr	junior event
tt	team event
1-0	the game ends in a win for White
½-½	the game ends in a draw
0-1	the game ends in a win for Black
(n)	nth match game
(D)	see next diagram

Dedication

To Maura, the Light of My Life

Acknowledgements

Special thanks to Graham Burgess for his patience and help throughout this project.

Bibliography

Periodical Publications
ChessBase Magazine (up to 112)
New in Chess Magazine; New in Chess
Informator (up to 95); Šahovski Informator

Websites
ChessPublishing; Kosten, A.; www.chesspublishing.com
The Week in Chess; Crowther, M.; www.chesscenter.com/twic/twic.html
Jeremysilman.com; Silman, J.; www.jeremysilman.com
ChessCafe.com; Russell, H.; www.chesscafe.com

CDs and DVDs
Bangiev, A.; *Philidor Defence*; ChessBase 2002
Henrichs, T.; *Queen's Gambit Orthodox Defence – Exchange Variation D31/D35-D36*;
    ChessBase 2004
Opening Encyclopaedia 2005; ChessBase 2005
Petronijević, Z.; *Caro-Kann Panov Attack B13-B14*; ChessBase 2004
Ripperger, R.; *Giuoco Piano C50-C54*; ChessBase 2004
Ripperger, R.; *Isolated Queen Pawn*; ChessBase 2003

Books and Articles
Aagaard, J.; *Easy Guide to the Panov-Botvinnik Attack*; Gambit/Cadogan 1998
Alburt, L., Dzindzichashvili, R. & Perelshteyn, E.; *Chess Openings for Black, Explained*;
    CIRC 2005
Baburin, A.; *Winning Pawn Structures*; Batsford 1998
Beliavsky, A. & Mikhalchishin, A.; *The Two Knights Defence*; Batsford 2000
Bosch, J.; *Secrets of Opening Surprises* 1-3; New in Chess 2003-5
Bücker, S.; 'Only a Storm in a Teacup?' (Marshall Attack); ChessCafe 2006
Burgess, G.; *The Taimanov Sicilian*; Gambit 2000
Burgess, G.; Nunn, J.; & Emms, J.; *The Mammoth Book of the World's Greatest Chess Games*;
    Robinson 1998
Chernin, A. & Alburt, L.; *Pirc Alert!*; CIRC 2001
Collins, S.; *Understanding the Chess Openings*; Gambit 2005
Davies, N.; *Play 1 e4 e5!*; Everyman 2005
Dearing, E.; *Play the Sicilian Dragon*; Gambit 2004
de Firmian, N.; *Chess Openings the Easy Way*; Batsford 2003
Donaldson, J. & Silman, J.; *Accelerated Dragons*; Cadogan 1998
Emms, J.; *Play the Open Games as Black*; Gambit 2000
Emms, J.; *Starting Out: The Sicilian*; Everyman 2002
Euwe, M. & Kramer, H.; *The Middlegame*, Books I and II; David McKay 1964
Fine, R.; *The Ideas Behind the Chess Openings* [3rd Edition]; McKay 1989
Flear, G.; *Open Ruy Lopez*; Everyman 2000
Flear, G.; *The Ruy Lopez Main Line*; Everyman 2004
Gallagher, J.; *Starting Out: The Pirc/Modern*; Everyman 2003

Golubev, M.; *The Sicilian Sozin*; Gambit 2001

Hansen, Ca.; *Improve Your Positional Chess*; Gambit 2005

Hillarp Persson, T.; *Tiger's Modern*; Quality Chess 2005

Jacobs, B.; *Mastering the Opening*; Everyman 2001

Jacobs, B.; *Starting Out: The French*; Everyman 2003

Johansson, T.; *The Fascinating King's Gambit*; Trafford 2004

Kallai, G.; *Basic Chess Openings* [1 e4]; Cadogan 1997

Kindermann, S. & Dirr, E.; *Französisch Winawer – Band 1: 7 ♕g4 0-0*; Chessgate 2005

Kindermann, S.; *The Spanish Exchange Variation – A Fischer Favourite*; Olms 2005

Kinsman, A.; *Spanish Exchange*; Batsford 1998

Krnić, Z. (ed.); *ECO B – 4th Edition*; Šahovski Informator 2002

Marović, D.; *Dynamic Pawn Play in Chess*; Gambit 2001

Matanović, A. (ed.); *ECO C – 4th Edition*; Šahovski Informator 2004

Nielsen, P.H. & Hansen, Ca.; *Sicilian Accelerated Dragon*; Batsford 1998

Nunn, J.; Burgess, G.; Emms, J. & Gallagher, J.; *Nunn's Chess Openings*; Gambit/Everyman 1999

Nunn, J.; *Grandmaster Chess Move by Move*; Gambit 2005

Pachman, L.; *Modern Chess Strategy*; Dover 1971 (based upon 1963 English Edition)

Panczyk, K. & Ilczuk, J.; *Ruy Lopez Exchange*; Everyman 2005

Pedersen, S.; *The French: Tarrasch Variation*; Gambit 2005

Pinski, J.; *The Two Knights Defence*; Everyman 2003

Psakhis, L.; *French Defence: Steinitz, Classical and Other Systems*; Batsford 2004

Raetsky, A.; *Meeting 1 e4*; Everyman 2002

Sammalvuo, T.; *The English Attack*; Gambit 2004

Silman, J.; *Amateur's Mind*; Siles 1999

Silman, J.; *Reassess Your Chess Work Book*; Siles 2001

Soltis, A.; *Pawn Structure Chess*; McKay 1995

Taimanov, M.; *Sicilian: Paulsen*; Batsford 1984

Uhlmann, W.; *Winning With the French*; Batsford 1995

Watson, J.; *Play the French* [3rd Edition]; Everyman 2003

Watson, J.; *Chess Strategy in Action*; Gambit 2003

Watson, J. & Schiller, E.; *Survive and Beat Annoying Chess Openings – The Open Games*; Cardoza 2003

Zeller, F.; *Sizilianisch im Geiste des Igels*; Kania 2000

Introduction

The initial moves of a chess game hold a particular fascination for those who play the game. This is reflected in the fact that chess-players at all levels devote the greatest part of their study to what are called 'openings'. Put simply, openings are sequences of early moves; we'll discuss exactly what qualifies as an opening as we go along. Players normally study the openings that may potentially appear in their own games. After all, nobody wants to incur a disadvantage before the game warms up, and every chess-player would like to gain an advantage over his opponent right out of the blocks.

Thus we find in the chess literature vast numbers of books about particular openings and opening systems. More has been written about the initial phase of the game than about any other chess topic, whether the middlegame, endgame, history, strategy, attack or defence. There are also encyclopaedias, magazines, CDs, DVDs, videos, and websites devoted solely to opening moves. We refer to such material in general as 'opening theory' or simply 'theory'. Within most fundamental openings there are seemingly countless subsystems (called 'variations') and still further divisions of material into 'subvariations'. It is not uncommon to see large books devoted exclusively to variations or even subvariations. Fortunately, openings are usually named, so we can communicate about them without explicitly having to restate, for example, the first nine moves played by both sides.

Among these myriad books and products, very few are devoted to explaining the ideas, strategies, and interconnections of chess openings taken as a whole. That is, individual theoretical books concentrate upon a single opening's moves and variations, and most discuss why some of those moves are good or bad. A fair number of these books will also examine basic strategies underlying the opening in question, which is important and beneficial. But few give a feeling for the common threads that underlie opening play or the reasons why opening strategies can differ so radically. In the book before you (and Volume 2 of this project), I seek to provide a durable standpoint from which to view the opening phase of the game. Then, regardless of the uncertainties of theory, you should be able to find your way through many of the problems posed by unfamiliar moves.

As I began work on this book it became obvious that even in two large volumes it wouldn't be possible to cover every opening, nor even the most significant variations of every opening, and still achieve the insights that I hoped to convey. On the other hand, I have sought here to provide a starting-point for players of all strengths to be able to understand these openings. Regardless of what anyone says, that simply can't be done without particulars, i.e. investigation of moves, alternatives, and annotated examples. What's more, those particulars must be comprehensible within some framework of general chess knowledge. In the end, I decided to begin the book with three chapters covering fundamental ideas of opening play. The first chapter presents elementary concepts shared by all openings. In the next two chapters, I incorporate motifs and structures that will inform your study as you proceed to specifics.

The greater part of the book is devoted to a selection of individual openings (king's pawn openings in the case of this book; Volume 2 will focus on queen's pawn openings). These openings are examined from the ground up, which is to say that each chapter begins with an explanation of the very basics of strategy. I shall often show what happens when you play alternatives that are inferior to the generally approved moves. As the chapter progresses, established variations are explored, sometimes in considerable detail, in order to establish the ideas and themes that characterize each opening and to investigate the extent to which they resemble other opening complexes. At the beginning of each section I've paid special attention to move-order issues. Students are often perplexed by move-orders, which frequently determine whether they get the opening position that they're aiming for.

Choosing which systems and variations to investigate proved an extremely difficult task. I decided to concentrate upon the most 'important' openings, that is, the ones which are and have been the centre of theory and practice for decades. Obvious examples are the Ruy Lopez, Sicilian Defence and Queen's Gambit. Within those and other major opening systems, I have selected a limited number of variations that are, I believe, enlightening in strategic terms. I have also examined some less prominent openings which not only have uniquely interesting properties but also lend themselves to comparisons with more popular systems. You may find that structures and ideas from superficially contrasting openings overlap more than you think. Finally, I explore how these openings and their variations fit into the general contours of a chess game. It is important to understand that the games and analysis do not always represent current theory; they are intended to illustrate underlying properties of the opening.

What are the rewards for studying openings and understanding the ideas associated with them? Well, it's always nice to gain an early advantage over your opponent, as I mentioned above. But such study has more valuable and far-reaching effects: it benefits your general chess knowledge in a way that reading abstract books on strategy can't. The more thorough your investigation into openings, the better your understanding of the play that occurs *after* the opening. To begin with, many characteristics of openings, including typical strategies and tactics, endure throughout the middlegame, so your deeper understanding of them will translate to your overall success. In addition, the typical pawn-structures established by an opening will persist as we enter into simplified positions and even endgames.

This book assumes a basic level of playing competence. Nevertheless, those who know the rules, have played a bit, and are willing to put some effort into their chess study will do well. You need not have advanced much beyond the initial playing stage to understand the basic ideas presented here. All of Chapter 1, most of Chapter 2, and the introductions to the chapters on individual openings are designed to help in that regard. I have also woven fundamental ideas into the analysis of specific openings, attempting to begin my presentation at a lower level and then proceed to the more advanced concepts needed for substantial improvement.

After years of exploring the initial phase of the game, I have come to an important and, I think, encouraging conclusion: every well-established opening is playable. That is not to say that all openings lead to full equality, nor that all speculative gambits will lend themselves to acceptable outcomes. But with sufficient study and understanding, any opening *system* that masters play, even on a periodic basis, will serve you well enough to get you to the middlegame in decent shape. Under those circumstances, the result of the game will not be decided by your choice of the first 5-10 moves, whether against a club opponent or in top competition. Players on all levels have an understandable tendency to follow the latest fashions, and that can lead to the notion that openings not currently being played are substandard. It's much more likely that those openings are simply out of favour or running into difficulties against some esoteric move within a complicated variation. There are many variations and even whole opening systems that have been declared inferior but were then taken up again by the world's best players. When in doubt, look up the number of grandmasters who play one 'bad' opening or another. This will encourage you to approach your explorations with an open mind.

I hope that this book will reward your careful study and give you a new perspective on openings and on the game of chess itself.

1 The Nature of Chess Openings: Fundamentals

The first moves of a chess game can be played in random fashion, or they can be organized so as to form a coherent strategy. Chess is above all a game of logic and planning, so the player who coordinates his moves towards an end will almost always defeat an opponent whose moves have no purpose or are inconsistent. This book concerns itself with initial moves that make sense together and attempts to explain the reasoning underlying those moves.

The first order of business will be to clarify the scope of our investigation and to orientate ourselves in the world of openings. Then we shall look at some rudimentary ideas underpinning successful opening play.

What is an Opening?

Generally speaking, an opening is defined by the introductory moves of a chess game. An opening begins on move one. The obvious question that suggests itself is surprisingly difficult to answer: how do we decide on what move an opening ends and the middlegame begins? There is no general agreement among players or authors about this; in many cases it turns out to be a subjective judgement informed by playing experience. In this book I shall define openings (and their variations) as sequences of moves that are specifically *named*, with the name in common chess usage and sometimes referring to a complex of related positions. The advantage of using this convention is that we can know precisely at which move an opening or variation ends. For instance, the 'English Opening' is defined by a single white move: 1 c4. The 'Sicilian Defence' consists of 1 e4 c5. And the variation called the 'Najdorf Variation of the Sicilian Defence' is delimited by the moves 1 e4 c5 2 ♘f3 d6 3 d4 cxd4 4 ♘xd4 ♘f6 5 ♘c3 a6. By defining the word 'opening' to designate

moves with names that are in general usage, we avoid dealing with such near-irrational sequences as 1 a4 e5 2 f3, which do not fall within the category of openings as I have defined them. There are very few *meaningful* openings that are unnamed, but I shall touch upon them if the occasion arises.

Most of this book is divided into major openings which can be identified within four moves or fewer; for example, the Ruy Lopez (1 e4 e5 2 ♘f3 ♘c6 3 ♗b5), or the Grünfeld Defence (1 d4 ♘f6 2 c4 g6 3 ♘c3 d5), each of which then subdivides into 'variations'. Named variations of openings can be of almost any length; for example, the Closed Variation of the Sicilian Defence has just two moves: 1 e4 c5 2 ♘c3; and the Exchange Variation of the Ruy Lopez (also known as the 'Spanish Game') consists of the four moves 1 e4 e5 2 ♘f3 ♘c6 3 ♗b5 a6 4 ♗xc6. Lasker's Variation of the Queen's Gambit is distinguished by the seven moves 1 d4 d5 2 c4 e6 3 ♘c3 ♘f6 4 ♗g5 ♗e7 5 e3 0-0 6 ♘f3 h6 7 ♗h4 ♘e4 *(D)*.

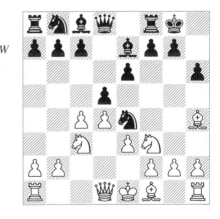

W

But some variations stem from other variations, which can stem from still others, and so forth. For example, the Chinese Variation of the

Dragon Sicilian evolves from this move-order: 1 e4 c5 (this is the 'Sicilian Defence') 2 ♘f3 d6 3 d4 cxd4 4 ♘xd4 ♘f6 5 ♘c3 g6 (the moves thus far are known as the 'Dragon Variation') 6 ♗e3 ♗g7 7 f3 ♘c6 8 ♕d2 (these first eight moves define the 'Yugoslav Attack') 8...0-0 9 ♗c4 (some authors refer to this as the '♗c4 Yugoslav Attack') 9...♗d7 10 0-0-0 and now with 10...♖b8 (D), we have arrived at the 'Chinese Variation of the Dragon Sicilian'.

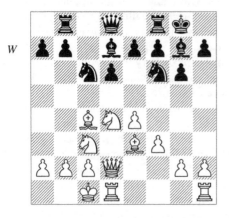

W

If some of this is confusing, you shouldn't worry: it will become clear as we work our way through the book.

In this general scheme the word 'theory' is used to indicate specific moves that have been previously played or analysed, and are known by a significant portion of the chess community, usually via publications or databases. In most but not all cases we can think of theory as representing the end of the opening *phase* of the game but not the opening itself. Theory can therefore extend far into the game because people all over the world repeatedly play the same opening and consistently add to what is known about it. Theoretical discussions sometimes deal with the 20th move of a variation or even further into the game, but most opening theory typically ends on a move in the teens, and the theory of a lesser-known variation may end after only six or seven moves.

The opening has certain characteristics that distinguish it from the other parts of the game, especially from the endgame. In the opening a large majority of the pieces and pawns are still on the board. In this situation, it is quite possible that in each position there are two, three or more moves that are of equal worth, so we cannot decide in practice or even with hindsight whether one move actually achieves more than another. Even if a hypothetical supercomputer could solve the position, the end result of either move would usually be the same – for example, a draw. Thus a player may have a wide choice that is more a matter of taste and playing style than of objective quality. We can contrast this situation with another part of the game – the endgame. In most endgames, particularly those with just a few pieces on the board, we can establish precisely what the ultimate effect of a particular move would be. Consequently, very few moves will be made simply because they suit someone's style of play.

You should also note that players can usually make one or two inaccuracies in the opening and still not be punished with a lost position. By contrast, a single mistake in a king and pawn endgame, for example, may be fatal, and punishment can come quickly for even a small endgame inaccuracy. Thus, many reasonable-looking decisions in the endgame are unambiguously right or wrong and can be demonstrated to be so. In the opening, however, a player has more leeway, which means that he is able to approach positions more creatively, without needing to calculate variations out to a win or loss. This in turn allows players of any strength to come up with worthwhile new opening moves. Openings are also more forgiving with respect to static features of play: the earlier in the game that you take on a bad bishop or pawn weakness, for example, the more likely it is that you can solve the associated problems. Furthermore, there are many opening positions that are chaotic and defy useful generalization.

It should not be surprising that the middlegame shares features with both the opening and endgame. Middlegame play tends to include more immediately critical decisions than opening play and middlegame mistakes are frequently life-threatening. An inaccurate attack or defence can lead to instant defeat and positional problems tend to be harder to resolve. On the other hand, most middlegame moves will not radically alter the strategic character of the position. Even allowing for the heightened possibility of irreparable error, the majority of middlegame positions are still flexible enough to support more than one functional move and, sometimes, more than one strategy.

Setting these details aside, what is extremely important and should be a part of your chess thinking is this: most features of a game, outside of material loss or catastrophic setback, can be changed or will evolve of their own accord as the game goes from opening to endgame. Mastering the opening is to some extent recognition of this fact and adaptation to it.

Elementary Properties of Openings

We now look at just a few fundamental features of opening play. These are presented on a very basic level to provide some tools and vocabulary with which you can advance to the next chapters and at least partially understand specific opening discussions. The experienced player may want to skip this material altogether.

The terms and ideas presented here are used throughout the book. For this first chapter, the assumption is that you know the rules of the game, can follow chess notation, and know basic chess terms such as 'file', 'diagonal', 'pin', and so forth. You should also understand the relative value of the pieces and how much 'material' both sides have in terms of relative strength (counting points is the best way to start). Finally, you should have played enough to be comfortable with a discussion of chess formations. A vast array of ideas and advice for the inexperienced is given by books, electronic material, and web sites; what I'm presenting instead is an extremely abbreviated version of introductory material. Some of what you'll be reading involves definitions of terms, which will probably bore you but are necessary if you're going to understand the fun parts later.

The Centre

Every opening has unique characteristics including pawn-structure, typical tactics, and diverse methods of attack and defence. But all openings have one consideration in common when it comes to organizing one's pieces: central configuration and control. The centre is a primary concern in deciding how to proceed

with your plans, not to mention your next move. I have placed this section about the centre before the one on development of the pieces because it provides a foundation for everything that follows in this book. As you read the chapters on specific openings you will run into more commentary about the centre than about any other subject, so it's important to familiarize yourself with the related concepts.

The four squares in the middle of the board (e4, d4, e5 and d5) are traditionally called the 'centre'. The value of the centre can be seen by imagining a piece on a central square on an otherwise empty board. Queens, bishops and knights all control more points from the centre than if they were placed on a non-central square.

When we then include the bordering squares (e3, d3, c4, c5, d6, e6, f4, f5), we sometimes use the phrase 'extended centre'.

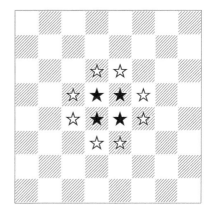

Notice that if pawns occupy the bordering squares they can contribute to control of the centre proper (the middle four squares). Normally when I speak of the 'centre', I'll be referring to the four inside squares, but you may also want to think about the border squares when I speak about 'central control'.

There's more jargon that you'll get used to as you see specific examples. One player's pawns on central squares are said to be '*his centre*'. For instance, we might say that White's centre in the top diagram overleaf consists of the white pawns occupying d4 and e5.

In the position in the lower diagram, Black may be said to have a broad centre (or 'central front'), describing his pawns on c5, d5, e5 and f5.

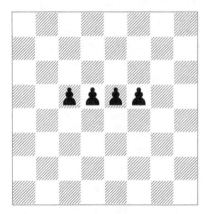

To confuse things a bit more, the phrase 'centre pawns' also denotes pawns that occupy *any* square along the central corridors from e2 to e7 or d2 to d7. Don't worry: none of this need be memorized. It may just help a little as you go along.

On occasion I shall use the phrase 'ideal centre', which refers to having pawns on e4 and d4 when you are playing with the white pieces, or pawns on e5 and d5 when you play Black. We call that the ideal centre because of all the possible first two moves, the advances d4 and e4 as White (or ...d5 and ...e5 as Black) give your pieces the most freedom to move about, and therefore to have the greatest influence on the game. The player with the ideal centre can also more easily add to his control of the four central squares. For instance, he might place his pieces as in the following diagram.

White controls the central square e5 three times (with two pieces and a pawn), d5 three times, d4 twice and e4 once. His pieces are developed and active, with both his bishops and

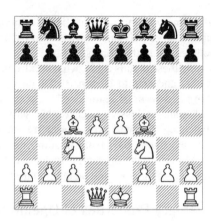

knights controlling many squares in Black's half of the board.

Here are some examples of the ideal centre versus some not-so-ideal centres. Suppose a game begins with these moves:

1 d4 a5

This is a common beginner's move, hoping to bring a rook out via a6.

2 e4

Now if 2...♖a6, White will simply capture the rook.

2...h5 3 ♘c3 ♘a6 4 ♘f3 g6 5 ♗c4 ♖h7 6 ♗f4 ♘h6 (*D*)

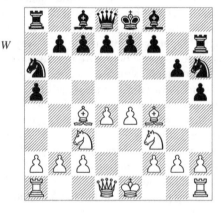

We can see how Black has neglected the centre. In fact, none of his pieces control d4, e4, d5 or e5. White has by far the better position.

Even if Black plays more reasonably and develops his pieces in the centre, he can get in trouble for lack of central *control*. A simple example, again using the ideal centre for White:

1 e4 e6 2 d4 d6 3 ♘f3 ♘f6 4 ♘c3 ♘c6 5 ♗c4 ♗e7 6 ♗f4 ♗d7 (*D*)

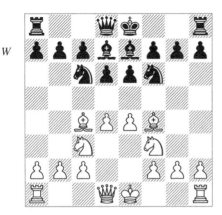

W

At least Black has established some influence over the centre, but neither of his pawns has reached the fourth rank; his pieces are cramped behind their own lines. Compare Black's bishops, which have only two retrograde moves available to them, with White's bishops, which can reach 8 squares apiece. And while Black's knights are actively placed, White's superior centre can chase them away by means of the pawn advances d5 or e5. White has a distinct advantage. What went wrong for Black? He needed to challenge White's centre with his own pawns, bringing one of them to d5 or e5 to break up White's ideal centre and establish territory of his own.

Let's take a look at a variety of common openings with respect to central control. You will see the universal emphasis on controlling central points. For each move of a pawn or piece I have indicated the corresponding central squares that it controls (or helps to control) in brackets:

a) In what is called the Italian Game, note that every move for both sides controls at least one main central square: **1 e4** [controlling d5] **1...e5** [d4] **2 ۚf3** [d4 and e5] **2...ۚc6** [d4 and e5] **3 ۚc4** [d5]. Black typically responds with the 'Giuoco Piano', **3...ۚc5** [d4], or **3...ۚf6** [e4 and d5], the Two Knights.

b) The Ruy Lopez (or 'Spanish') goes **1 e4** [d5] **1...e5** [d4] **2 ۚf3** [d4 and e5] **2...ۚc6** [d4 and e5], and now **3 ۚb5** attacks a piece that controls d4 and e5, thus *indirectly* reducing Black's influence over them.

c) The Queen's Gambit Declined: **1 d4** [e5] **1...d5** [e4] **2 c4** [d5] **2...e6** [d5] **3 ۚc3** [e4 and d5] **3...ۚf6** [e4 and d5]. A traditional line now

runs **4 ۚg5** [indirectly controlling e4 and d5 by pinning the defender of those squares] **4...ۚe7** [indirectly controlling d5 and e4 by unpinning the defender] **5 e3** [d4] **5...0-0** [a useful move, but doesn't control a central square] **6 ۚf3** [d4 and e5] **6...ۚbd7** [e5] **7 ۚc1 c6** [d5] **8 ۚd3** (D) [e4].

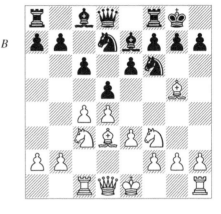

B

d) The Nimzo-Indian Defence: **1 d4** [e5] **1...ۚf6** [e4 and d5] **2 c4** [d5] **2...e6** [d5] **3 ۚc3** [e4 and d5] **3...ۚb4** [indirectly controlling e4 and d5 via a pin on the c3-knight]. One typical line proceeds **4 e3** [d4] **4...c5** [d4] **5 ۚd3** [e4] **5...ۚc6** [d4 and e5] **6 ۚf3** [d4 and e5] **6...d5** [e4] **7 0-0** [unpinning the c3-knight, which regains its influence on e4 and d5] **7...0-0 8 a3 ۚxc3** [eliminating the knight's control of e4 and d5] **9 bxc3** [d4] **9...dxc4 10 ۚxc4** [d5] **10...ۚc7** [e5] **11 ۚd3** [e4] **11...e5** [d4] **12 ۚc2** [e4, indirectly] **12...ۚe8** (D) [e5].

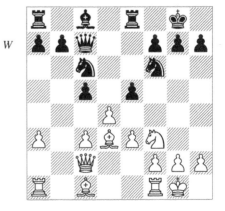

W

In some openings, one or both sides fianchetto their bishops ('fianchetto' means to bring a bishop to g2, b2, g7 or b7); this move is also for the sake of central control; for instance:

e) The English Opening: **1 c4** [d5] **1...e5** [d4] **2 ♘c3** [e4 and d5] **2...♘c6** [d4 and e5] **3 g3 g6 4 ♗g2** [e4 and d5] **4...♗g7** [d4 and e5] **5 d3** [e4] **5...d6** [e5] **6 ♘f3** [d4 and e5] **6...f5** [e4] **7 0-0 ♘f6** [e4 and d5].

To be fair, half of the initial moves of a knight and all those of the middle four pawns control *some* central square, so one might think that central control practically takes care of itself. But the openings above show that the masters who developed them intended to occupy and control central squares in a continuous and harmonious way. To a strong player, a particular central structure calls out to the pieces and indicates where they should go. Then the pawns and pieces control the key squares while they are safely defended and work together. This coordination of pieces leads to the next subject.

Development

Another critical but simpler opening idea is called 'development'. This refers to moving pieces (not including pawns) off their initial squares and putting them 'in play'. Just counting the number of pieces that you have moved is the simplest measure of development. Of course it's essential to consider the 'quality' of development, that is, how well the pieces are placed. There are some principles of good development, which are unfortunately limited by the context of each position, first and foremost by the pawn-structure. Nevertheless, as you first get used to playing chess you will do well most of the time to:

a) get as many pieces developed (off their initial squares) as possible, preferably early in the game;

b) bring those pieces to active squares where they have good scope (without subjecting them to attack, of course); and

c) coordinate your developed pieces with the centre, working with pawns to control as many central squares as you can.

Usually you can't achieve everything that you want to, but by keeping these principles in mind you will have a better chance of gaining the advantage.

In order to develop efficiently, it's often desirable to move each piece only once or twice until they're all in useful positions. Also, be careful about bringing the queen out early in the game, because she is sometimes subject to attack and will have to retreat. The difference between the queen and other pieces in this regard is that the queen can't be exchanged for most other pieces (the exception being for another queen) without losing a lot of material, so in many situations she has to run away from the threat of capture and waste time.

Here's a short game that combines the concepts of centre and development:

Estrin – Libov
Moscow 1944

1 e4 e5 2 ♘f3 ♘c6 3 ♗c4 ♗c5

So far every move has contributed to both development and central control.

4 c3

Now White tries to occupy the centre with pawns. If he succeeds, that will determine the best available squares for his other pieces.

4...♘f6 5 d4 exd4 6 cxd4 *(D)*

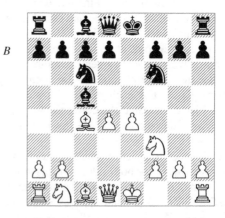

White has achieved the ideal centre, but Black is slightly ahead in development, in the simplest sense of the number of pieces that are out in play.

6...♗b6?

This retreating move allows White's centre to advance. Black needs to gain time to get his king castled into safety. The way to do that is 6...♗b4+!.

7 d5 ♘e7?

Another backward move that allows White to win more time. 7...♘a5 attacks White's bishop on c4, but after White retreats the bishop by 8 ♗d3, Black has to be careful because White is about to play the move b4, winning the trapped knight.

8 e5 ♘e4 9 d6! *(D)*

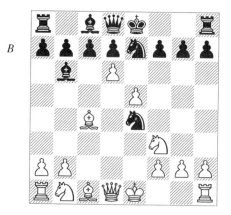

B

The centre is the key to most openings, and White's just keeps moving forward.

9...♘xf2

Black indulges his greed by both taking a pawn and setting up a double attack on White's queen and rook.

10 ♕b3 ♘xh1 11 ♗xf7+ ♔f8 12 ♗g5!

The bishop pins the knight which is already under attack.

12...cxd6 13 exd6 1-0

Black resigns because he will lose his queen after dxe7+ or ♗xe7+. Ouch!

The moral of the story is that Black neglected to challenge White's centre and then had to move his knights too many times in the opening.

King Safety

One of the most important guidelines in chess is to protect your king from harm. This elementary consideration is sometimes forgotten. It can strongly affect the proper conduct of the opening stage of the game.

The most common method of enhancing a king's security is castling, but it should be done with eyes wide open. The goal is usually to provide pawn-cover for the king, as in this skeletal view:

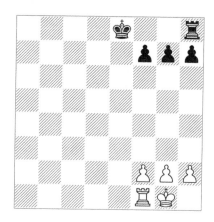

White's king is sheltered and relatively safe. The squares f3, g3 and h3 are all protected from a piece intrusion, nor can the king be directly attacked along diagonals by a bishop or queen, or along files by a rook or queen. If Black does manage to capture one of White's pawns, that reduces the king's safety, but at least the other two pawns are still around for the king to hide behind. Black's uncastled king, however, is subject to checks, perhaps by a knight on d6 or c7, from a bishop on b5 or c6, a rook on e1 or a8, or a queen from several directions.

Nevertheless, pawn-cover for the king may be more than overshadowed by the aggressive placement of the opponent's pieces towards the kingside (or queenside, if that is where castling is contemplated).

A position from a famous game illustrates the point:

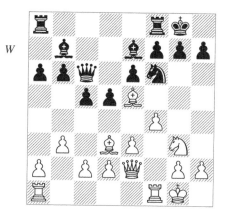

W

Em. Lasker – Bauer
Amsterdam 1889

A lot of White's pieces are pointed towards the king so even its well-positioned pawn defenders can't save it:

14 ♘h5! ♘xh5 15 ♗xh7+!! ♔xh7 16 ♕xh5+ ♔g8 17 ♗xg7! ♔xg7 *(D)*

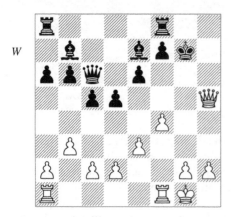

See how White has ripped away Black's protective pawn-cover?

18 ♕g4+ ♔h7

18...♔f6 19 ♕g5# is already checkmate!

19 ♖f3

The last type of piece joins the attack. White's idea is 20 ♖h3+ ♗h4 21 ♖xh4#. Notice how the rook can only have an effect on Black's king when the pawns in front of the king are gone.

19...e5 20 ♖h3+ ♕h6 21 ♖xh6+ ♔xh6 22 ♕d7

This fork finishes off the combination by winning a piece. White is well ahead in material now and even comes back to complete the attack on Black's king:

22...♗f6 23 ♕xb7 ♔g7 24 ♖f1 ♖ab8 25 ♕d7 ♖fd8 26 ♕g4+ ♔f8 27 fxe5 ♗g7 28 e6 ♖b7 29 ♕g6 f6 30 ♖xf6+ ♗xf6 31 ♕xf6+ ♔e8 32 ♕h8+ ♔e7 33 ♕g7+ ♔xe6 34 ♕xb7

and Lasker won shortly thereafter.

Strong players have no fear of leaving their kings in the centre if that is the safest place on the board, or if by doing so the king contributes to the defence of weak or potentially weak squares. Sometimes an opening is even based upon the useful position of the king. Also, when an opening becomes rapidly simplified, the king may remain in the centre to assist with the endgame. Centralized kings will generally be strong pieces in an endgame, but here one must beware.

If only the queens have been exchanged, or if only the queen and one or two pairs of other pieces have been exchanged, then the king can still be hounded before a true ending arrives. This is the sort of decision that comes with experience.

Space and Its Properties

The amount of territory that is under one's control, generally referred to as space, is a concept that is deceptively hard to understand. The first point to be made is that having space is an advantage more often than not. It gives you more room to organize your forces and with luck it will frustrate your opponent, who will have difficulty getting his forces out. When you control more territory you can often move your pieces from one theatre of action to another more quickly than your opponent can, and thus attack on that front before he can defend. Some great players have spent their careers playing openings that emphasized the control of space over any other factor, even the assumption of weaknesses in their position or difficulties with their development.

In many situations I shall simply assume without explanation that the side with space has an advantage, although in other cases space may be a problem that needs to be overcome! For example, the possessor of more territory has more of the board to defend. That may seem trivial, but some positions are well-known for the property that the player with less space ties down the one with more space by constantly threatening to change the pawn-structure in his own favour if his opponent tries to do anything. Several variations of the Sicilian Defence, the most popular opening in chess, include lines in which something of that nature occurs.

Since space is usually defined as a portion of the board that is delineated by pawns, one question that needs to be answered is whether those pawns are true boundaries or simply a temporary construct that can be neutralized. For example, pawns can be overextended in the opening such that the squares behind the pawns are compromised and pawn advances do not correspond to control of space. Consider this position from the King's Indian Four Pawns Attack:

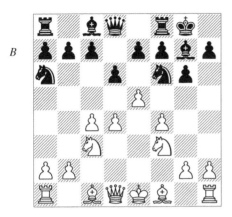

White's pawn penetration into Black's position defines White's territory and he has an indisputable advantage in space. He also occupies more of the centre. But occupation and control are two different things and the possibility of undermining the advanced pawns can make them unstable. For instance, the play from the diagram might continue 7...♘d7 8 h4?! (White stakes out even more territory and tries to attack the king by playing h5; however, he is making too many pawn moves when he should be defending the space that he has grabbed in the centre) 8...c5! (this is referred to as 'undermining White's centre'; regardless of what White does, his pawns will be cleared away) 9 exd6 ♖e8 10 dxe7 ♖xe7+ 11 ♗e2 cxd4 12 ♘xd4 ♘b6 13 ♘f3 ♗f5 14 ♕xd8+ ♖xd8 (D).

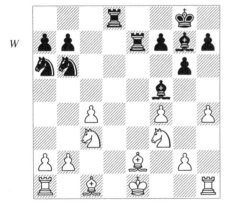

At this point Black controls every central square and threatens ...♘b4, while at the same time White's bishops are running into their own pawns. It turns out that Black has a winning position because, ironically, he controls

the centre. You can see how positively that affects his development and activity.

Regardless of the mediocre quality of play in this example, the lesson remains: if you seize a large hunk of the centre in the first moves of the game, make sure that you can defend the pawns that control that territory. The concept of space advantage is only significant when the pawns and pieces begin to assume more settled positions.

By contrast, look at this example from one of the main lines of the same King's Indian Defence:

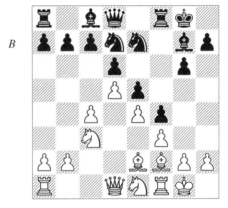

It's already fair to say that Black has staked out territory and has space on the kingside whereas White has space on the queenside. Surely enough, a few moves later we might see something like:

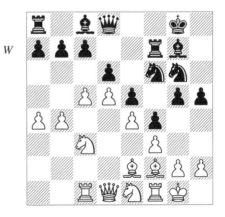

There's no question of who has secured territory on which side of the board.

In numerous openings we'll be talking about who has a space advantage, and what it means in terms of the assessment of the position.

Piece Characteristics

Some fairly elementary terminology disguises much more complex issues that will come up in the next few chapters. But it's worth discussing a few representative terms with respect to pieces.

First of all, we have a couple of terms to describe knights and bishops. They are called 'minor pieces', in contrast to the rooks and queen, which are called 'major pieces'. I shall regularly refer to the advantage of the 'bishop-pair' or 'two bishops' in this book. This reflects the fact that in every stage of the game, including the opening, having two bishops on the board versus two knights or a bishop and a knight *more often than not* constitutes a meaningful advantage. That emphatically qualified statement reflects the fact that, in a considerable minority of cases, the player who possesses two knights or a knight and bishop will have the advantage over, or at least stand equally with, his opponent who possesses two bishops. Nevertheless, those instances are in the minority, and when the bishop-pair is a recognizable advantage I shall often point that out. Likewise, if the bishops are hemmed in and/or the knights are in excellent positions, that will frequently be mentioned. Much of the time, however, I hope that the reader will come to notice all these imbalances on his or her own.

So why are the two bishops so good in tandem? First and foremost, because they cover squares of both colours. The bishop is a powerful, long-range piece that in a sense 'should' be better than the knight because it can attack from afar; but unlike a knight, a bishop can only travel on one colour. With two bishops that disadvantage is partially corrected. But another considerable advantage is that the possessor of the bishops can exchange one or even both of the knights under favourable circumstances, i.e. dictate when and where he can exchange other pieces to advantage. It is difficult for the short-hopping knight to track down and exchange a bishop that is performing magnificently (or fulfilling some essential function), but a bishop of

the right colour can exchange a knight from afar. Thus the two bishops can do more than simply control squares.

There follow some elementary properties of the pieces, and advice regarding their use in the opening. Most readers will find them almost self-evident, but this chapter is primarily designed to help the inexperienced player become comfortable with ideas that we'll be referring to later.

1. **Bishops like open diagonals and should usually be developed accordingly.** You may also use your bishop to pin an enemy piece, or to unpin your own. Exchanging your bishop for a knight is reasonable, but do so only to gain some advantage (or if forced to), otherwise you will be surrendering the advantage of the bishop-pair for no return.

Although there are many exceptions to this in various openings, try not to let your bishops become trapped behind their own pawns without good reason. Having said that, limiting a bishop's activity may be necessary to ensure that your knights, rooks and remaining bishop secure good positions.

2. **Knights also need as much freedom of movement as possible, but only to the extent that they don't unduly interfere with the activity of other pieces.** For that reason, you may see knights developed on the second rank or on the side of the board with their first move, instead of to one of the 'ideal' squares f3, c3, f6 or c6. Knights are particularly fond of outposts, which arise in many openings. An outpost is a place in the opponent's pawn-structure where your piece cannot be attacked by a pawn. To have significance, an outpost should be on at least your 4th rank, and preferably on the 5th or 6th rank. From an outpost on a central file, a knight can exert considerable influence on several squares in the enemy position while maintaining defensive coverage. Here's an example of an outpost that's occupied by a knight (*see upper diagram on following page*):

The defining feature of the outpost is that the knight can't be captured by a pawn. Its influence would be further strengthened by a rook or queen on the d-file, or by another knight on c3 or e3.

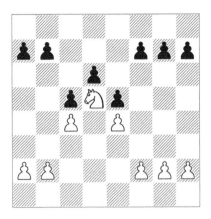

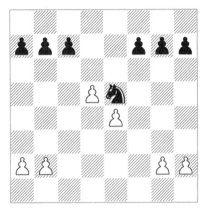

In the lower diagram Black's knight is on an outpost that is unsupported by his own pawns yet not subject to attack by the opponent's pawns. Notice that Black could also occupy this outpost with a dark-squared bishop, rook, or queen. Support for the e5-knight could come from rooks on the open file, another knight, a bishop on f6 or d6, and various placements of Black's queen.

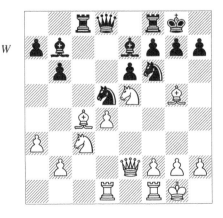

This is a real-world example: Black has an outpost on d5. Some students will say that White's knight has an outpost on e5, but notice that if Black's knight moves from f6, he could then attack the knight with a pawn by ...f6. Instead, the e5-square is sometimes called a 'support-point' because it is supported by his d4-pawn and unlikely to be driven away by a pawn in the near future. Knights are sometimes just as happy to reside on a support-point as they are to occupy an outpost.

The outpost and support-point are examples of structural configurations, a subject that we expand upon in Chapter 2 and still more Chapter 3.

3. **Rooks like to have open files, preferably ones that extend vertically as far as possible into the enemy camp.** Early pawn exchanges will sometimes let rooks breathe and have immediate effect upon the game. In the opening, assuming that you castle in one direction or another, your rooks may well end up on half-open files (ones blocked only by enemy pawns). If they can be centralized so as either to defend your e- or d-pawns or to assist in their advance, that's also not a bad role. Doubling rooks (placing one behind the other on a file) used to be uncommon in the opening stage, but because openings extend further and further into what was previously called the middlegame, you'll definitely run across that situation. Likewise with the placement a rook on the seventh rank, which isn't generally possible until after the opening, but does occur, usually to assist in an attack. Rook-lifts to the third rank, on the other hand, happen relatively frequently; often they will move horizontally to help with an attack on the opponent's king. Another common rook-lift in the opening is to the second rank, because a rook which moves horizontally along the second rank can defend extremely sensitive squares such as the ones immediately in front of the king. This 'second-rank defence' is essential against some attacks, and such rooks may also be able to swing to the e- and d-files to support the centre.

4. **Apart from wide-open games in which the centre pawns are blown off the board early on, the queen tends to stay at home or**

to lurk behind her pawns and pieces in the early stages of the opening. Increasingly, advanced players are bringing the queen out early but in a judicious manner to control more of the board – a practice that you'll see in this book. There's nothing wrong with exchanging queens in the opening, but there's also no reason to go out of your way to do so, as many inexperienced players do.

Activity and Initiative

I shall refer time and again to a player's active pieces and to activity in general. This is a concept that may encompass a coordination of forces, but to a first approximation simply expresses the mobility and reach of one's pieces. Active pieces control more squares. Such pieces aren't necessarily involved in a direct attack but can serve to harass opposing forces, support a pawn advance, and generally accrue more territory. You will see that in opening play the active player tends to get the better game, in part because active pieces tend to force slower ones onto the defensive, resulting in the creation of weaknesses in the enemy camp. The balance that generally exists between attack and defence in chess will break down if one player is working with direct threats and gaining more control of the board. Gathering momentum like this is called 'having the initiative'. As long as the aggressor is able to force his opponent to keep reacting to threats, he will maintain his initiative. Sometimes the initiative peters out, especially if handled poorly; it can even change hands. In this book, you will run across an assessment of mine that reads simply 'Black has the initiative'. While it is ambiguous how *much* advantage that confers on Black, the initiative constitutes an advantage in and of itself.

This chapter has covered terminology and general ideas that I hope will serve you well. Remember that most of what is discussed in these first three chapters will be applied and reinforced in the investigation of specific openings that occupies the larger portion of this book.

2 Opening Ideas and Positional Features

In this chapter we'll begin by considering some general and even philosophical issues about opening play. We'll then turn to special topics involving different types of centres and properties of pieces and pawns. Much of the chapter will be devoted to pawns and weaknesses, opening the investigation of 'positional' chess and setting the stage for its more detailed discussion in Chapter 3.

Black's Goals in the Opening

Chess books have traditionally said that Black's goal in the opening is to obtain equality. A popular variant of this is that Black must first secure equality and only later search for chances to gain the advantage. There are certainly openings in which that is likely to be the case, but in many openings Black also has the choice to play aggressively and endeavour to steal the advantage from White right away. In cases where he falls short of that goal, energetic opening play by Black may still lead to a position so complex and unclear that to speak of equality is meaningless. Sometimes we say 'dynamically balanced' instead of 'equal' to express the view that either player is as likely as the other to emerge from complications with an advantage. This style of opening play has become prevalent in modern chess, with World Champions Fischer and Kasparov as its most visible practitioners.

Both approaches to playing Black are valid, and the distinction between them contributes to the diversity of styles amongst contemporary players. Of course, we should remember that White has always had a better percentage score than Black. But is that due to Black's acceptance of a small disadvantage in the course of playing directly for equality, or does it result from Black becoming overextended in his search for an advantage? Books from the first half of the 20th century particularly stressed the need for equalizing before all else. They often implied that the advanced, mature player would focus on neutralizing White's first-move advantage, whereas the impatient youngster who tried to bowl over his opponent would be punished by a seasoned master. This attitude may have slowly evolved out of experiences with the openings that were played in the middle of the 19th century, openings which gradually lost favour after players became more 'scientific'. Most games of that day began with 1 e4 e5, and the apparent failure of ambitious counterattacks by Black reinforced the philosophy of 'equality first'. For example, interest dropped in the more exotic King's Gambit lines such as that of the famous Andersson-Kieseritzky 'Immortal Game': 1 e4 e5 2 f4 exf4 3 ♗c4 ♛h4+ 4 ♔f1 b5?! *(D)*.

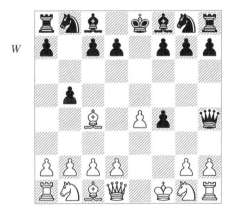

Also pushed to the periphery were 1 e4 e5 2 ♗c4 ♗c5 3 b4 ♗xb4 4 f4 and 1 e4 e5 2 f4 exf4 3 ♘f3 g5 4 ♗c4 g4 5 ♘c3 (maybe not *so* horrid but abandoned nevertheless).

Similarly, the adventurous Evans Gambit stayed around for a while, but after 1 e4 e5 2

♘f3 ♘c6 3 ♗c4 ♗c5 4 b4 ♗xb4 5 c3 ♗a5 6 0-0 the likes of 6...♕f6!? were largely replaced by safer defences such as Lasker's 6...d6 7 d4 ♗b6. In addition, provocative openings such as the Philidor Countergambit (1 e4 e5 2 ♘f3 d6 3 d4 f5), and the Schliemann Defence to the Ruy Lopez (1 e4 e5 2 ♘f3 ♘c6 3 ♗b5 f5) were held to be dubious or were at any rate supplanted by more careful strategies. Lastly, responses to 1 e4 which favoured confrontation over equality also failed to gain a foothold until their playability was established. Most masters didn't take seriously such moves as 1...♘f6, 1...d6 and 1...g6, nor was 1...d5 approved of by the leading masters. In fact, the latter has only been convincingly revived in the last ten years.

As an alternative to 1...e5, the solid Caro-Kann (1...c6) gained popularity after 1900, primarily as an equalizing weapon. In the same 'equality-first' vein, French Defence players employed the unambitious move ...dxe4 (e.g., 1 e4 e6 2 d4 d5 3 ♘c3 dxe4), and the French Defence generally lacked the dynamic character that it later acquired. (To this day, in fact, ...dxe4 systems are chosen by leading grandmasters, often as a way to simplify the play and equalize). When players did essay upon 1 d4 instead of 1 e4, 1...d5 was the overwhelming response by Black, with the various 'Indian' defences (beginning with 1...♘f6) held in low esteem.

Looking back, we can see that the legitimate desire to establish a pawn presence in the centre greatly influenced the choice of and attitudes towards opening play. The Sicilian Defence (1 e4 c5) neglects to move a centre pawn (see the next paragraph), whereas defences to 1 e4 such as 1...♘f6, 1...d6 and 1...g6 all concede the ideal or at least favourable centre to White. So do several of today's dynamic and/or unbalancing replies to 1 d4. For instance, the King's Indian Defence allows White to occupy the centre directly in the main lines after 1 d4 ♘f6 2 c4 g6 3 ♘c3 ♗g7 4 e4 d6 (D).

Compare the related discussion at the beginning of Chapter 3.

The Sicilian Defence (1 e4 c5), which accounts for nearly 20% (!) of all top-level grandmaster games played today, was at first a more ambiguous case, with a curious evolution. Although one sees only a handful of modern-style treatments in top-level games throughout the

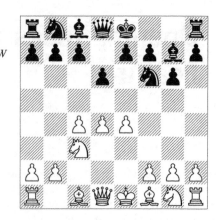

latter half of the 19th century and into the 20th, the Sicilian Defence grew to be played in a respectable 5% of such encounters. At first it was White who failed to play aggressively in the centre, typically choosing the Closed Sicilian (2 ♘c3) or 2 f4. As players then turned to the Open Sicilian with 2 ♘f3 and 3 d4, Black tended to play active, developing moves, until the Scheveningen Variation with its backward central structure (...e6 and ...d6) was brought to general attention in the 1920s by prominent players such as Euwe. Soon, various new interpretations of the Open Sicilian became established as main lines. But the extent to which Black could disrespect the basics of development and space in favour of other factors became apparent only much later. During the 1940s and 1950s new interpretations of the Sicilian Defence ushered in a modern age of dynamism; players and theoreticians developed the fundamental structures and piece-play that are used today by nearly every major player. Dynamic variations of traditional openings also gained popularity; e.g., the Winawer Variation in the French Defence and the Marshall Attack in the Ruy Lopez. The Alekhine Defence and Pirc Defence had accumulated masses of theory and stalwart grandmaster adherents by the time Fischer used both openings in his 1972 World Championship match versus Spassky; today these openings are played less than others in high-level chess but certainly retain their legitimacy.

After that lengthy digression, no one will be surprised to find that either of Black's approaches to the opening is valid, that is, he can play for equality or aspire to achieve a dynamic imbalance. Some players just starting out, however, may not have heard about the latter option.

White's Goals in the Opening

White has choices similar to Black's, assuming that he has the same opportunities. White can work patiently to hold on to his inherent advantage, usually by suppressing his opponent's counterplay and 'accumulating small advantages'. Or White can seek dynamic situations in which he tries to take the initiative and keep Black on his heels. Finally, White can plunge into two-sided slugfests and hope to express his theoretical advantage or superior skills in that environment. Once again all of these methods are admissible. But for White there is a different twist. Curiously, it is sometimes easier for Black to launch an effective attack and to define the quality of early play than it is for White to do the same. Black has the advantage of knowing his opponent's moves ahead of time. If he chooses to play a solid game it may be impossible for White to attack aggressively. Of course the reverse is also true: White can play 1 d4, 2 ♘f3 and 3 ♗f4 against most openings, or, for example, 1 ♘f3, 2 g3, 3 ♗g2, 4 d3 and 5 0-0 against practically anything. But most players aren't interested in giving away the advantage of the first move with such conservative moves and so will choose to play more ambitiously. Paradoxically, this can let Black set the pace in certain openings.

Central Types

Several very important central formations will be explored in detail in the next chapter. Among them will be centres characterized by:
   a) isolated pawns;
   b) majorities and minorities;
   c) restrained central pawns; and
   d) pawn-chains.
   Most other types of centre that have practical significance will be represented somewhere in the main body of the book. It's useful to look at some of those central formations to get a feel for how they can be analysed and assessed. Be aware that the material in this chapter will begin at an elementary level but quickly move into complex areas that are not essential for the inexperienced player to master.

1. The **'vanishing centre'**. As the name implies, all or most of the centre pawns are exchanged or captured. They leave a gap in the middle of the board through which pieces can move in a more-or-less unobstructed fashion. The vanishing centre tends to favour the side with the better development, and tactics can easily dominate the play; for example, in the Danish Gambit with 1 e4 e5 2 d4 exd4 3 c3 dxc3 4 ♗c4 cxb2 5 ♗xb2 d5 6 ♗xd5 ♘f6! 7 ♗xf7+! ♔xf7 8 ♕xd8 ♗b4+ 9 ♕d2 ♗xd2+ 10 ♘xd2, and the game settles down. But if development is about equal and the game hasn't been reduced to disorderly skirmishing, then vulnerable points and pawn weaknesses can be magnified because they are so accessible.

1 e4 e5 2 d4 exd4 3 c3 d5 4 exd5 ♕xd5 5 ♘f3!?

5 cxd4 is the main move.

5...♗g4 6 ♗e2 *(D)*

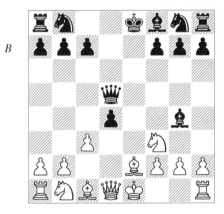

6...d3! 7 ♗xd3 ♗xf3 8 gxf3

White's doubled pawns are a serious disadvantage. His bishop-pair on an open board offers some degree of compensation, but probably not enough, since it's easy for Black to develop his pieces.

Here's an illustration from a d-pawn opening:

1 d4 ♘f6 2 c4 g6 3 ♘c3 ♗g7 4 e4 d6 5 ♘f3 0-0 6 ♗e2 e5 7 dxe5 dxe5 8 ♕xd8 ♖xd8 9 ♘xe5 ♘xe4 10 ♘xe4 ♗xe5 *(D)*

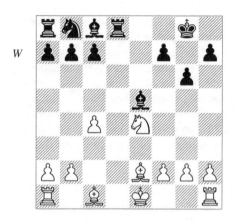

This is a well-known version of the Exchange Variation of the King's Indian Defence where a series of early exchanges has decimated the centre. According to theory, Black stands slightly better. White has weaknesses on d3 and d4 that can be occupied by Black's minor pieces, whereas White can't find good squares other than f6 to exploit in Black's position. If White waits around, Black will occupy the d4-square by ...♘c6-d4, so White should move quickly and play 11 ♗g5 ♗xb2 12 ♗xd8! ♗xa1 13 ♗xc7 ♘c6 14 0-0 ♗g7, when Black has only a small positional advantage.

1 e4 e5 2 ♘f3 ♘c6 3 ♗b5 a6 4 ♗xc6 dxc6 5 0-0 ♗d6 6 d4 exd4 7 ♕xd4 f6 8 ♖e1 ♘e7 9 e5 fxe5 10 ♘xe5 0-0 (D)

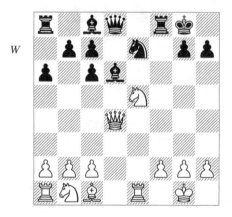

This position and ones like it have occurred regularly in the Ruy Lopez Exchange Variation. The centre pawns have been swept away but static factors are still controlling the play. Black has the weaker pawn-structure but he

also has the bishop-pair. White has a mobile majority on the kingside, which can theoretically be used to create a passed pawn. But that's far down the road and in the middlegame, especially with the vanished centre, one would expect that Black's two bishops would be more effective than the bishop and knight. The problem is that White controls more space and Black has no centre pawn with which to drive White's pieces away. The position is about equal.

The vanished centre shows up in old gambit lines which were popular 100 or more years ago. Some of these lines have never been permanently stowed away. A case in point:

1 e4 e5 2 ♘f3 ♘c6 3 ♗c4 ♘f6 4 d4 exd4 5 0-0 ♘xe4 6 ♖e1 d5 7 ♗xd5 ♕xd5 8 ♘c3 ♕h5 9 ♘xe4 ♗e6 10 ♗g5 h6 11 ♗f6! ♕g6 12 ♘h4 ♕h7 13 c3 dxc3 14 bxc3 (D)

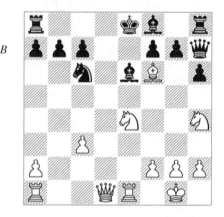

This is all theory, that is, published knowledge. The centre has been cleared out and there's no way to make a simple assessment. Only a lot of brainpower, computer analysis and correspondence chess can solve this sort of thing; in fact, only those things got chess researchers this far! Which brings me to another point: my aim in this book is to have you understand strategy, including typical methods for both sides to handle attacking positions. It's often possible to indicate recurrent themes and some connections among them. However, I shall rarely analyse chaotic positions like this one featuring moment-to-moment variations in tactical events. The correct moves are so unpredictable that they really can't be 'explained' except on a case-by-case basis. You may be able to find out more about them in books that make specific detailed investigations; better yet, you can try to work them out for yourself!

2. We have already seen and discussed cases of the **'ideal centre'** (also known as the 'classical centre'), in which one side has pawns on e4 and d4 (or e5 and d5). Normally the ideal centre constitutes an advantage, but that's only true if it has some positive effect on the position; for example, tying down the opponent's pieces, advancing with tempo, creating a passed pawn, and/or serving as the pivot point from which pieces can launch an attack. Otherwise the opponent might be able to attack the centre pawns from afar with little risk. In a typical situation Black restrains White's ideal centre but can't break it down. This imbalance arises in certain variations of the Queen's Gambit Accepted, Slav, Grünfeld, and this main line of the Semi-Tarrasch:

1 d4 d5 2 c4 e6 3 ♘c3 ♘f6 4 ♘f3 c5 5 cxd5 ♘xd5 6 e4 ♘xc3 7 bxc3 cxd4 8 cxd4 ♗b4+ 9 ♗d2 ♗xd2+ 10 ♕xd2 0-0 11 ♗c4 ♘c6 12 0-0 b6 13 ♖ad1 ♗b7 *(D)*

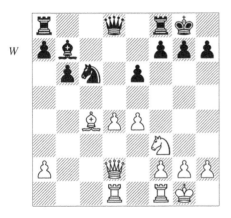

White has won some famous battles from this position, but the moves ...e6 and ...♗b7 in conjunction with ...♘a5 can serve to restrain White's ideal centre, while ...♕d6 covers key squares, so the position is only a little bit better for White.

3. The formation arising from what is called the **'surrender of the centre'** appears in many different openings. It involves a single white central pawn on e4 or d4 facing a lone black

pawn on d6 or e6, respectively. Generally, White has somewhat the better game by virtue of his greater control of space, but Black has a compact structure and an open file aiming at White's 4th-rank pawn, so the advantage can range from tiny to moderately significant.

Here's an illustration taken from the 'classical' Philidor's Defence:

1 e4 e5 2 ♘f3 d6 3 d4 exd4 4 ♘xd4 ♘f6 5 ♘c3 ♗e7 6 ♗c4 0-0 7 0-0 ♖e8 8 ♗f4 ♗f8 9 f3 *(D)*

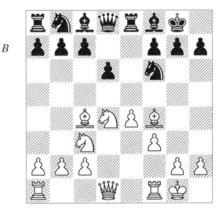

White has a pleasant advantage because he controls more space and has freer development.

A surrender of the centre occurs in the old main line of the Caro-Kann Defence:

1 e4 c6 2 d4 d5 3 ♘c3 dxe4 4 ♘xe4 ♗f5 5 ♘g3 ♗g6 6 ♘f3 ♘d7 7 h4 h6 8 h5 ♗h7 9 ♗d3 ♗xd3 10 ♕xd3 ♕c7 11 ♗d2 e6 *(D)*

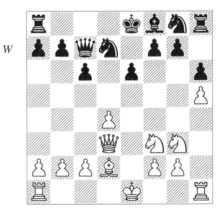

Black has less space but a safe position and no weaknesses. He can also try to break down the d4-based centre with the move ...c5. White has the easier game, but against accurate play he will retain little if any advantage. This type of 'restraint centre' will be discussed at some length in Chapter 3.

Flank versus Centre

It's always hard to assess whether a flank pawn advance in the opening is strong or weak. It's often said that a centre has to be safe in order to justify a pawn advance. That is true in many situations; e.g.:

1 e4 c5 2 ⏄f3 d6 3 d4 cxd4 4 ⏄xd4 ⏄f6 5 ⏄c3 g6 6 ⏄e2 ⏄g7 7 ⏄e3 0-0 8 0-0 ⏄c6 9 ⏄b3 a5 10 a4 ⏄e6 11 g4 *(D)*

This is too early an advance. The centre should be secured by 11 f4 with the idea 11...d5? 12 f5.

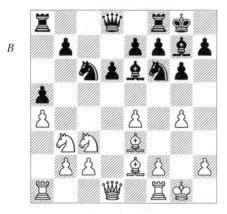

11...d5!

A central counterattack creates a threat on e4 and makes the g-pawn look foolish out there doing nothing.

12 exd5 ⏄xd5 13 ⏄xd5 ⏄xd5 14 c4 ⏄e6 15 ⏄c5 ⏄c8 16 ⏄xe6 ⏄xe6

Black stands better because White's central position is weak and the g4-pawn renders his kingside difficult to defend.

But the reverse is also true: flank pawn moves will frequently drive a piece away from a square on which that piece controls the centre and/or threatens to support a central advance. Another line of the Sicilian Defence is a case in point:

1 e4 c5 2 ⏄f3 d6 3 d4 cxd4 4 ⏄xd4 ⏄f6 5 ⏄c3 a6 6 ⏄e3 e6 7 f3 ⏄e7

A similar illustration of the advance g4 as a disincentive to ...d5 is 7...⏄c6 8 ⏄d2 ⏄e7 9 g4 d5?! 10 g5 ⏄xd4 11 ⏄xd4 ⏄h5 12 f4!. White is threatening 13 ⏄e2, and 12...dxe4 (12...h6 13 exd5 hxg5 14 fxg5 ⏄xg5 15 0-0-0) 13 ⏄xd8+ ⏄xd8 14 ⏄e2 g6 15 0-0-0+ leaves Black struggling.

8 g4 d5!? *(D)*

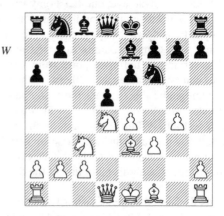

9 g5 ⏄fd7 10 exd5 ⏄xg5 11 ⏄xg5 ⏄xg5

At this point the position doesn't look that bad for Black, but a simple move illustrates how effective it was to drive Black's knight away from f6.

12 ⏄d2! ⏄xd2+ 13 ⏄xd2 ⏄b6 14 ⏄e1

White stands comfortably better. Black will have serious weaknesses after 14...0-0 15 dxe6 fxe6 16 ⏄d3. In these examples, the flank defends the centre.

As long as you're aware that each situation has to be assessed on its own merits, you should always consider responding to a flank attack with a central counterattack, and vice-versa. But neither response should be made into a rule.

Weaknesses

The word 'weakness' refers to problems with pawns and pawn-structures. Some terms relating to pawns still need to be defined, which we'll do presently. First, however, I want to make a broader comment. Pawn weaknesses are to be avoided at any stage of the game if you get nothing in return for them, and understanding *pawn-structures* (a subject much wider than pawn weaknesses) is more important than any other factor in understanding chess. But that insight should not be confused with a general phobia towards weaknesses. Generally they are not as important in the opening as they are later in the game. Tarrasch's dictum 'Before the endgame the gods have placed the middlegame' is part of the explanation, yet it is not the whole story here. As the middlegame progresses and considerable simplification has occurred (or is imminent), a player must be particularly concerned with current weaknesses, and eventually with what an endgame might bring if that pawn-structure persists. Sometimes this calls for radical action. But in the opening stage (particularly within the first 10 moves or so) structural weaknesses are generally more of an immediate defensive problem than one which must be attended to for the sake of the ending. They can be incorporated into an overall approach to a position that works extremely well; e.g., a terribly weak pawn may temporarily provide protection from the opponent's play and allow you to gain the advantage. That holds true because of the ever-changing nature of most openings and middlegames. Especially players who are beginning to gain experience with chess should not overestimate the drawbacks of weaknesses such as doubled, isolated or backward pawns and thus ignore good opportunities for attack or other positive activity. I find that students generally err on the side of caution in this respect, when they could aggressively pursue the initiative. So yes, try to avoid unnecessary weaknesses and take advantage of those in your opponent's position, but don't make decisions that are too focused on just this one aspect of the game. Your pawn-structure may be telling you other important things about how to handle the position as a whole.

There follow some definitions and short explanations of pawn types and properties. In Chapter 3 we investigate and evaluate these in much greater detail.

1. An **isolated pawn** is one that has no pawns of its own colour (i.e. friendly pawns) on any adjacent file. In practice, we are especially concerned with such a pawn when it's on an open file. In Chapter 3 you will find a lengthy

discussion and many examples of isolated pawns. In some very typical situations, their advantages are famously in balance with their disadvantages, which is why so many players rush to take them on and others to play against them.

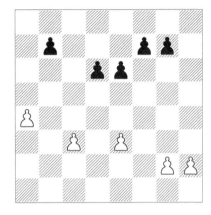

White has three isolated pawns, on a4, c3 and e3. Black has one isolated pawn on b7. The pawns on a4, c3 and b7 are on open files and thus relatively more exposed than the pawn on e3, which is masked by an opposing pawn on the same file.

2. A **backward pawn** is one that has at least one pawn of its own colour on an adjacent file, but that neighbouring pawn is situated one rank or further ahead of its compatriot.

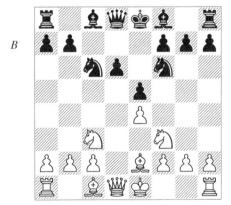

In this well-known position from the Sicilian Defence, Black's d6-pawn is a backward pawn. Often the square in front of the backward pawn serves as an outpost for the opponent, as it does here (see Chapter 1 for a description of the outpost). We care most about backward pawns on a half-open file, as is Black's on d6. Backward pawns are usually weak, but not always so.

3. A **doubled pawn** is one that resides on the same file as another of your pawns. As usual, doubled pawns on an open file are weaker than those that are masked by enemy pawns. Doubled pawns can be weak or strong, but most of the time *isolated* doubled pawns on an open file are a serious disadvantage, both because they are hard to defend and because there is a wonderful outpost in front of the pawns, just asking for an opposing piece to occupy it. Here is a well-known situation in which a knight is stationed in front of doubled f-pawns.

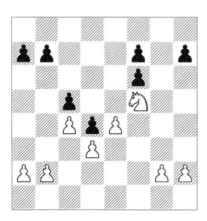

4. **Pawns that block the path of pieces** are always a problem, and the most famous of such problems involve 'good' and 'bad' bishops. I'll be using those terms throughout the analysis section, so I should attempt a definition. A 'bad' bishop is one whose *central* pawns are on the same-coloured squares as the bishop; conversely a 'good' bishop lives on the squares that are of the colour opposite to its central pawns. Notice the emphasis on central pawns. By far the most important pawns in determining the 'goodness' or 'badness' of a bishop are the d- and e- pawns. Adjacent c- and f-pawns can be factored in if they seem relevant to the bishop's overall mobility, but these pawns must be given considerably less weight. Let's look at this situation in the abstract:

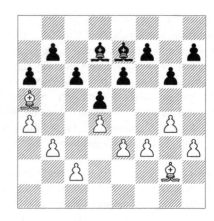

Assessing Black's bishops is the easiest task. Black's pawns on e6 and d5 are on light squares, so his bishop on d7 is 'bad' and the one on e7 is 'good'. It happens that all of Black's other pawns are on light squares as well, but except for the c- and f-pawns, which are of limited importance, they aren't factors in the way we assess whether a bishop is good or bad.

White's light-squared bishop may look useless because it is blocked by pawns on f3, h3 and g4, while even those pawns on c2, b3 and a4 might provide obstacles. But it is a 'good' bishop because White's centre pawns are on dark squares. By contrast, the a5-bishop has two nice open diagonals and can even reach the wonderful outpost on e5. Nevertheless, it is a 'bad' bishop because it is on the same colour as the central pawns. The point is that a 'good' bishop can be a poor or even dysfunctional piece whereas a 'bad' bishop may be the best piece on the board. However, those situations are exceptional. In a considerable majority of cases a 'good' bishop really is the one that serves you the best (and that you don't want to exchange!), while a 'bad' bishop tends to be obstructed and passive. This generalization goes back to the extraordinary importance of the centre.

Bad bishops can serve as decent defenders but they can be particularly unhelpful when opposed by a good knight (*see following diagram*):

13...d5?!

In a fairly conventional Sicilian position, Black plays the standard ...d5 break, thinking to free his pieces. But he may not have considered the full consequences of a general liquidation.

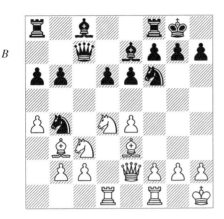

V. Gurevich – Zakharov
Azov 1995

14 exd5 ♘bxd5 15 ♘xd5 ♘xd5 16 ♗xd5! exd5

This is a type of end-position that can result from a number of other openings, such as a French Defence with 3 ♘d2 c5 or a number of Queen's Gambits in which Black plays ...c5. The simplification that has occurred favours White, who now succeeds in getting rid of Black's good bishop.

17 ♗f4! ♗d6

After 17...♕xf4 18 ♕xe7, Black lacks a really good square for his c8-bishop so he has a tough time getting his rooks out. In the meantime, after ♖fe1, all of White's pieces would be actively placed.

18 ♗xd6 ♕xd6 19 ♕d2 ♗g4 20 f3 ♗e6 *(D)*

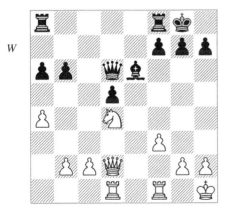

White has achieved the desired 'good knight vs bad bishop' position, which enables him to control play on both sides of the board. This

formation of the d-pawn, knight and bishop is one that frequently arises. Now watch how White exploits the dark squares, his advantage in space, and superior mobility.

21 a5 bxa5 22 ♕xa5 ♖fb8 23 b3 ♕b6 24 ♕d2 a5 25 ♖a1 ♗d7 26 ♖fe1 g6?!

White gains a crucial kingside square after 26...a4 27 bxa4 ♖xa4 28 ♖xa4 ♗xa4 29 ♘f5!. A better try is 26...♕c5.

27 ♕f4 ♖e8 28 h4! ♕b4 29 ♖xe8+ ♖xe8 30 ♔h2 a4 31 bxa4 ♗xa4 32 c3 ♕c4 33 h5! ♗d7 34 h6 ♗f5 35 ♕d6 1-0

There's nothing to be done about ♕f6; e.g., 35...♕xc3 36 ♕f6 ♕c7+ 37 ♔h1 ♔f8 38 ♘c6, etc.

Fianchetto Themes and Prophylaxis

Bad bishops can serve some productive roles that are not always obvious. The word 'prophylaxis' in chess has to do with the prevention of an opponent's plans and desired-for continuations, the latter including freeing moves and moves that serve a productive purpose, whether defensive or aggressive in nature. Although the concept of prophylaxis can also embrace a wider set of meanings, those are the relevant ones for most discussions about openings.

Fianchettoed bishops, for instance, can be bad and still serve prophylactic purposes. By way of illustration, one might wonder why Black spends two moves to fianchetto his bishop in the King's Indian Defence and then plays ...e5 to block it off! And why does Black in that defence often go to lengths to avoid exchanging that bishop? Shouldn't it be considered the epitome of a poorly-placed bishop? To the contrary, King's Indian fans tend to think of that piece as their most precious possession. Let's see a simplified example:

1 d4 ♘f6 2 c4 g6 3 ♘c3 ♗g7 4 e4 d6 5 ♘f3 0-0 6 ♗e2 e5 7 0-0 ♘a6 8 d5 ♘c5 9 ♕c2 a5 10 ♘e1 ♘fd7 *(D)*

Black is planning ...f5. If one's analysis were based solely upon attacking Black's centre, one might play the weak move 11 f4?, leading to 11...exf4 12 ♗xf4 ♘e5, but then the g7-bishop is not only a powerful piece but supports the outpost on e5 in front of White's backward pawn. So one can say that the g7-bishop 'prevents' 11 f4 (and the idea of f4 generally). Or, in

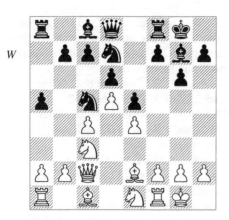

a sequence such as 11 ♘d3 f5 12 ♘xc5 ♘xc5, White shouldn't play 13 exf5?!. He might do this for the sake of avoiding Black's dangerous attack that follows from 13 f3 f4. But 13 exf5?! ♗xf5 14 ♕d1 runs up against 14...e4!, when the g7-bishop has gone from a passive onlooker to a major force. In this and similar positions, the dark-squared bishop serves as a prophylactic measure versus White's exf5, which might otherwise hamper Black's plans. I should add that in some cases where Black replies to exf5 with ...gxf5, that will also allow him to play a favourable ...e4 and free his bad bishop. What's the lesson? That a bad bishop can discourage moves that would otherwise hurt his cause.

It doesn't take a fianchettoed bishop to fill that role, of course. In the Closed Ruy Lopez when White constructs a pawn-structure with e4 and d5 and places his bishop on c2, one might say that White's bad bishop on c2 has a natural prophylactic effect against the move ...f5, because then exf5 brings the bishop into a kingside attack. If Black has a pawn on c7 (with the same piece placement), then the move ...c6 can be answered by dxc6 and ♗b3, taking over the open a2-g8 diagonal. For these ideas see, for example, the Breyer Defence or Zaitsev Variation in the Ruy Lopez (Chapter 8).

Colour Complexes

In a great number of openings, one player or both will concentrate his forces either largely or exclusively on squares of one colour or the other. This is particularly logical in Black's case because he doesn't have time to keep up with White on both colour squares. One case in

point is the Nimzo-Indian Defence, in which the first three moves all control light squares (1 d4 ♘f6 2 c4 e6 3 ♘c3 ♗b4), and several main lines continue with ...b6, ...♗b7 and ...♘e4 (strictly speaking this last move aims at dark squares, although it 'plays on' light squares and prepares another light-square move, ...f5). In doubled-pawn variations such as 4 a3 ♗xc3+ 5 bxc3, we might see Black play ...b6, ...♗a6, ...♘c6-a5 and ...d5, which is truly playing on a colour complex. The following game combines complementary themes of backward pawns, outposts, and playing on a colour complex.

Taimanov – Karpov
Moscow teams 1973

1 d4 ♘f6 2 c4 e6 3 ♘c3 ♗b4 4 e3 c5

Karpov departs for a move from the light-square strategy but he will soon return to it.

5 ♗d3 0-0 6 ♘f3 d5 7 0-0 dxc4 8 ♗xc4 cxd4 9 exd4

Now White has an isolated pawn on d4.

9...b6 10 ♕e2 ♗b7 11 ♖d1 ♘bd7 12 ♗d2 ♖c8 13 ♗a6?! *(D)*

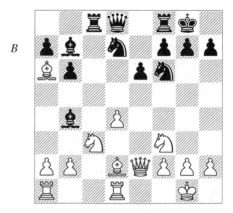

This is the key move to the early part of the opening. A colour complex takes on stronger meaning when a bishop residing on the colour opposite that of the centre pawns (i.e., a good bishop) is exchanged. Thus White risks losing control of the light squares.

13...♗xa6 14 ♕xa6 ♗xc3 15 bxc3 *(D)*

Now White has assumed a backward pawn on an open file (often the only way a backward pawn is defined), and Black has an outpost on c4, in front of that pawn. Instead, 15 ♗xc3?!

would put a very bad bishop on c3 whose potential to be freed by the move d5 is almost non-existent, especially after Black places a knight on the truly powerful outpost on d5.

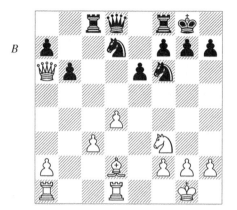

The c3-pawn can be either weak or strong, the latter depending upon two possibilities:

a) the c3-pawn does such a good job of supporting d4 that it allows White the time to organize a kingside or central attack;

b) the pawn can advance to c4.

Taimanov wants to pursue the latter idea, counting upon the superiority of his bishop over Black's d7-knight (which incidentally doesn't have many prospects right now because it is restricted by White's d4-pawn). A favourable change of structure might come about, for instance, if White can play c4 followed by &b4. The problem is that Black strikes first.

15...&c7

Black protects the a-pawn and would like to play ...&c8 followed by ...&d5. He has already set his eyes on light-square weaknesses on c4, a4, and possibly that on d5.

16 &ac1

White aims to make the move c4. Transforming a backward pawn into a hanging pawn is more often than not a good idea. If there's no real possibility of dynamic play, however, it's usually easier to defend a pawn on the third rank than on the fourth.

16...&c8 17 &a4 *(D)*

17 &xc8? &fxc8 fixes the pawn permanently until it can be won, which won't take long to happen.

17...&c4!

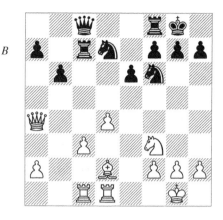

The second key move. Karpov sacrifices a pawn just to occupy the outpost and maintain a blockade! Ripperger offers the insightful line 17...&b7 (protecting a7) 18 c4 &fc8 19 &f4 &c6 20 h3 a6 21 &b3 b5 22 c5 &d5, when Black has restrained White's d-pawn but at the cost of a protected passed pawn on c5. After 23 &d6, the position looks about equal.

18 &xa7 &c6 19 &a3

Black was threatening to trap the queen by ...&a8.

19...&c8 20 h3 h6 21 &b1 &a4 22 &b3 &d5 *(D)*

Light-square domination! This is a particularly good illustration of favourable play on a colour complex.

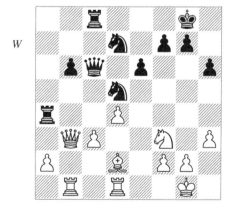

The opening stage is over and Karpov has more than enough positional compensation for a pawn. The rest of the game is very accurately played until the last moves before the time-control and demonstrates the strength of the blockade and associated outpost:

23 罩dc1 罩c4 24 罩b2 f6 25 罩e1 當f7 26 豐d1
勾f8 27 罩b3 勾g6 28 豐b1 罩a8 29 罩e4 罩ca4 30
罩b2 勾f8 31 豐d3 罩c4 32 罩e1 罩a3 33 豐b1
勾g6 34 罩c1 勾xc3 35 豐d3 勾e2+ 36 豐xe2
罩xc1+ 37 象xc1 豐xc1+ 38 當h2 (D)

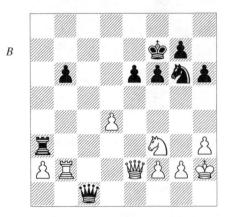

38...罩xf3!?

Certainly an intimidating move when there's
not much time left. Objectively 38...勾f4! would
have left Black with a large positional advantage.

39 gxf3 勾h4 0-1

White should play on (perhaps he lost on
time?) with 40 d5!, although Black still has the
advantage after, for example, 40...豐f4+ 41
當h1 exd5 42 豐e3 豐f5.

This game is typical in that the structure resulting from the opening is indicative of whether
players will be concentrating upon a certain
colour throughout the game.

There are quite a few other openings with a
lasting orientation towards playing on one colour. Consider the main lines of the Dragon
Variation of the Sicilian: Black's central pawns
are situated to control dark squares, and his
most active pieces control dark squares: the all-
important g7-bishop, the c6-knight, his queen
on a5 or c7 (more often than not), and even the
c8-rook has its greedy eye on c3. Black's f6-
knight has a tendency to go to d7 and augment
control of the dark squares e5 and c5. Only the
queen's bishop doesn't participate, but it has inherent difficulties in that respect. White normally castles queenside, when Black's most
devastating attacks seem to land on the squares
c3 and b2.

Nevertheless, when I speak of a position in
which 'Black dominates the dark squares',
there's usually a persistence of structural weakness that I'm referring to. For instance:

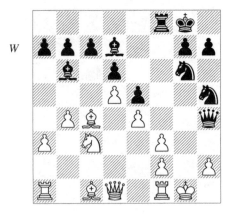

Domination of a colour complex doesn't necessarily mean a winning position but it probably
constitutes a serious advantage, often compensation or more for the exchange, which was sacrificed in this example by capturing a knight on
f3. White still has his dark-squared bishop, but
he has lost the dark squares anyway.

Internal Weaknesses

An important situation arises when one or
both sides have 'internal weaknesses'. This
means that they have unoccupied squares on
their third or fourth ranks that cannot be defended by other pawns. Often these weaknesses are somewhat masked by a pawn-front,
but they can also be exposed when a pawn-
front disappears or breaks down. Generally,
I'll refer to internal weaknesses in the centre
of the board, i.e. White's squares e4, d4, e3
and d3, or Black's on e5, d5, e6 and d6. Weaknesses on the flank squares are normally of
less note, but those created by a pawn advance
in front of one's king are a huge exception; for
instance, an attack by f4-f5, g4-g5 and h4 can
create critical weaknesses on f4, g4, h4, f3, g3
and h3. Players tend to be very careful about
exposing their kings in such a fashion. In my
experience, less advanced players fail to recognize this type of weakness, especially if the
squares in question are not immediately attacked or occupied.

A typical example of a complex of internal weaknesses arises with an advanced centre. In the last chapter we saw a King's Indian Four Pawns Attack in which the front of the centre collapsed and the internal weaknesses were exposed. It's worth taking the time to look back at that example, especially the final diagram. The weaknesses remain regardless of whether the pawns that mask them disappear.

The following game is a classic between two of the greatest players of all time:

Karpov – Kasparov
Moscow Wch (16) 1985

1 e4 c5 2 ᐸf3 e6 3 d4 cxd4 4 ᐸxd4 ᐸc6 5 ᐸb5 d6 6 c4 ᐸf6 7 ᐸ1c3 a6 8 ᐸa3 d5!?

A shocking gambit prepared by Kasparov for this match.

9 cxd5 exd5 10 exd5 ᐸb4 11 ᐺe2 ᐺc5?! 12 0-0? 0-0 13 ᐺf3 ᐺf5 *(D)*

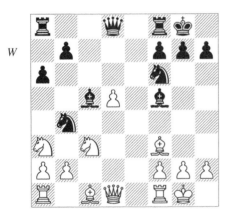

What does Black have for his pawn? Greater activity, to be sure, and White's a3-knight is a very poor piece, but most of all White has serious internal weaknesses in his own camp, d4 and d3. They are both on the closed d-file yet still of major importance.

14 ᐺg5 ᐼe8 15 ᐺd2 b5 16 ᐼad1 ᐸd3 *(D)*

There it is. The d3-square has no protection and the knight will radiate influence from its position almost until the end of the game.

17 ᐸab1 h6 18 ᐺh4 b4 19 ᐸa4 ᐺd6 20 ᐺg3 ᐼc8 21 b3 g5!

More space.

22 ᐺxd6 ᐺxd6 23 g3 ᐸd7

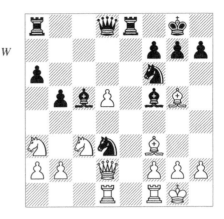

Black is even ready to reinforce d3, which hardly needs it. In nearly every critical variation analysed later it proved to be the difference. The d4-square, which is also weak, isn't occupied by a piece until much later, but White's loss of control over it allowed Black to proceed without impediment.

24 ᐺg2 ᐺf6 25 a3 a5 26 axb4 axb4 27 ᐺa2 ᐺg6 28 d6

The forward guard has to be sacrificed. White is hopelessly tied up, the more so after Black's next move.

28...g4 29 ᐺd2 ᐺg7 30 f3 ᐺxd6 31 fxg4 ᐺd4+ 32 ᐺh1 ᐸf6 33 ᐼf4 ᐸe4 34 ᐺxd3 *(D)*

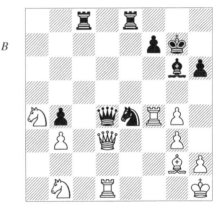

White finally captures the knight that has been on his own third rank for 18 moves! But at this point the damage has been done and it's way too late to save the game.

34...ᐸf2+ 35 ᐼxf2 ᐺxd3 36 ᐼfd2 ᐺe3 37 ᐼxd3 ᐼc1 38 ᐸb2 ᐺf2 39 ᐸd2 ᐼxd1+ 40 ᐸxd1 ᐼe1+ 0-1

3 The Significance of Structure

A Simple Question: Pawns or Pieces?

An inexperienced player, having struggled with a number of opening sequences, might legitimately ask: "Is it more important at the beginning of a game to establish my position with numerous pawn moves, or should I be developing my pieces as quickly as possible?" This question is not so easily answered, perhaps not even by those more familiar with the game.

In chess history, new openings that don't stake a claim to the centre have been regarded with suspicion, and one of the first reactions is to refute such openings with the construction of a large centre, soon to be followed by its advance. Thus the Alekhine Defence was challenged by 1 e4 ♘f6 2 e5 ♘d5 3 c4 ♘b6 4 d4 d6 5 f4, and the King's Indian Defence by 1 d4 ♘f6 2 c4 g6 3 ♘c3 ♗g7 4 e4 d6 5 f4 *(D)*, each called 'the Four Pawns Attack' in their particular opening.

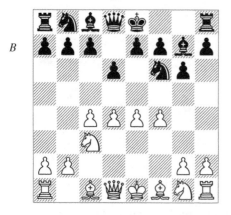

The Modern Benoni faced the pawn onslaught 1 d4 ♘f6 2 c4 c5 3 d5 e6 4 ♘c3 exd5 5 cxd5 d6 6 e4 g6 7 f4 ♗g7 8 e5. In the early days of the Pirc Defence, theory and practice concentrated primarily upon the Austrian Attack, i.e. 1 e4 d6 2 d4 ♘f6 3 ♘c3 g6 4 f4 *(D)*, often with an early e5.

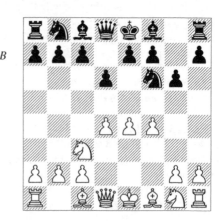

The related Modern Defence, 1 e4 g6 2 d4 ♗g7, was similarly met by 3 ♘c3 d6 4 f4 or 3 c3 d6 4 f4. Even in a uniquely positional opening such as the Benko Gambit, 1 d4 ♘f6 2 c4 c5 3 d5 b5 4 cxb5 a6 you'll find quite a few early games with bxa6 followed by f4 and e4 with the idea of e5. Likewise, when the English Defence began to gain notice, attention was focused on broad-pawn-front variations such as 1 c4 b6 2 d4 e6 3 e4 and 1 c4 b6 2 d4 ♗b7 3 ♘c3 e6 4 e4. Recently the opening 1 d4 ♘f6 2 c4 ♘c6 (the 'Knights' Tango') has become respectable, but it first had to be shown that the uninhibited advance 3 d5 ♘e5 4 e4 e6 5 f4 was not a threat to the entire system. Returning to more conventional openings, it's easy to forget how often early games with the Nimzo-Indian featured 1 d4 ♘f6 2 c4 e6 3 ♘c3 ♗b4 4 a3 ♗xc3+ 5 bxc3 followed by a set-up with e4 (e.g., 5...0-0 6 f3 c5 7 e4 with ♗d3, ♘e2 and f4 to follow, establishing a broad central front). Most of the variations listed above are not bad, and some remain effective weapons to this day, but none are refutations of the openings concerned.

After these impetuous attempts, attention usually turned to a less ostentatious centre and quicker development. In the examples above, we might find White playing, respectively, 1 e4 ♘f6 2 e5 ♘d5 3 d4 d6 4 ♘f3 (versus the

Alekhine Defence) or 1 d4 ♘f6 2 c4 g6 3 ♘c3 (or 3 ♘f3 ♗g7 4 g3) 3...♗g7 4 e4 d6 5 ♘f3 (D) (versus the King's Indian Defence).

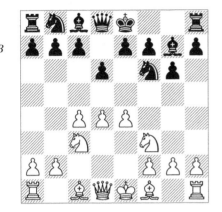

B

There are also 1 d4 ♘f6 2 c4 c5 3 d5 e6 4 ♘c3 exd5 5 cxd5 d6 6 e4 g6 7 ♘f3 (versus the Benoni) and 1 e4 d6 2 d4 ♘f6 3 ♘c3 g6 4 ♘f3 (D) (versus the Pirc Defence).

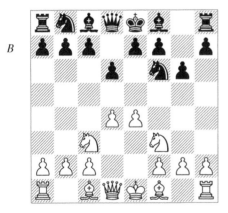

B

Today we see the more modest 1 d4 ♘f6 2 c4 c5 3 d5 b5 4 cxb5 (4 ♘f3) 4...a6 5 bxa6 and ♘f3 followed by ♘c3 and g3 (versus the Benko Gambit); 1 c4 b6 2 d4 e6 3 ♘c3 ♗b7 4 a3 or 4 ♘f3 (versus the English Defence); 1 d4 ♘f6 2 c4 ♘c6 3 ♘f3 e6 4 ♘c3 (versus the Knights' Tango); and 1 d4 ♘f6 2 c4 e6 3 ♘c3 ♗b4 4 ♕c2 (versus the Nimzo-Indian Defence).

Of course these are just a few examples, and many other main-line pawn-structures support fast piece development. In these variations the pieces and pawns seem to be in mutual support and one might easily conclude that this is the ideal situation.

But the distinction between a philosophy of 'pawns-before-pieces' and one assigning equal priority to both has become increasingly more subtle and context-dependent as time has gone by. I already mentioned in Chapter 2 that when the Open variations of the Sicilian were establishing themselves in the first part of the 20th century, there was a tendency on Black's part to get his pieces out reasonably quickly. For instance, you would see 1 e4 c5 2 ♘f3 ♘c6 3 d4 cxd4 4 ♘xd4 ♘f6 5 ♘c3 e6 and ...♗b4 and/or the freeing move ...d5 with rapid development. Systems such as the Dragon Variation became relatively popular; for example, 1 e4 c5 2 ♘f3 d6 3 d4 cxd4 4 ♘xd4 ♘f6 5 ♘c3 g6 6 ♗e2 ♗g7 7 0-0 0-0 8 ♗e3 ♘c6 (D).

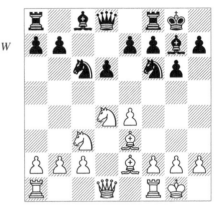

W

In that case four of Black's pieces are developed within the first eight moves. We then often see Black make several more piece moves before touching another pawn (e.g., ...♘xd4, ...♗e6, ...♖c8); this policy is clearly indicated by the initial pawn-structure. In contemporary play, however, we regularly see variations of the Sicilian Defence in which the establishment of pawn-structure swamps rapid development, not least of which is the most popular Sicilian system of them all, the Najdorf Variation: 1 e4 c5 2 ♘f3 d6 3 d4 cxd4 4 ♘xd4 ♘f6 5 ♘c3 a6 to be followed by more pawn moves such as ...e6 and ...b5. Even in the list of 'balanced' variations that I gave two paragraphs back, things will shift dramatically in one direction or another while still in the opening stage. In the King's Indian example, everything follows the harmonious model in the main line 1 d4 ♘f6 2 c4 g6 3 ♘c3 ♗g7 4 e4 d6 5 ♘f3 0-0 6 ♗e2 e5 7 0-0 ♘c6 8 d5 ♘e7 (D).

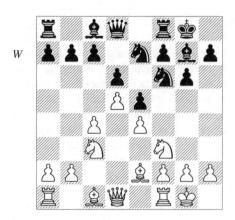

All well and fine, with a nice balance between piece moves and pawn advances. But in this position Black will customarily embark upon a massive pawn advance that, in its determined neglect of piece development, would put a Four Pawns attacker to shame. As you may know, Black plays ...♘d7 first, and then that advance typically consists of ...f5-f4, ...h5 and ...g5-g4 and is frequently accompanied by *undeveloping* moves such as ...♗f8 and ...♘g8. In a large number of lines, Black's a8-rook and c8-bishop will remain in their places until moves 20 to 25 or even longer. So the initial moves of an opening are not always indicative of its balance between pawn moves and development. Naturally there are times in which early piece development and related events will dictate what structure becomes appropriate, but not often.

Furthermore, pawn-structures have primacy in terms of the weaknesses they create, which determine both where the opponent can attack and what squares he can usefully occupy. For crucial periods of time, pawns block the development of pieces, or open lines for them. Whether freeing moves are even available to activate passive pieces is largely dependent upon pawn-structure. Pieces have only secondary roles in these areas of consuming interest for the player.

So the obvious answer to the query in the first paragraph, namely, that 'you should both advance pawns and develop at the same time, in a mutually supportive manner', is simplistic and wanting in content. What's more important, such a statement doesn't serve as helpful advice for most players. I think that the question

should be reframed: which takes precedence in any given position, pawn-structure or piece development? How should we organize our thoughts so as to optimize our understanding? In the examples of openings above, and in the vast majority of opening variations in this book, the pawn-structure is in fact the determinant of appropriate piece placement and not the other way around. The structure sets the overall parameters of development, such that there may be many ways to bring the pieces out but their effectiveness (or lack thereof) depends upon pawn configuration. That relationship is true whether or not you throw all of your pawns forward to begin the game, or only a couple of them; thus it lends itself to a more useful view of opening play. Relevant questions now emerge: is my centre breaking down before I can complete the development with which it was supposed to assist? Am I creating weaknesses and targets of attack for my opponent? Is there any way, given the pawn-structure before me (or the one I am about to construct) that I can arrange all my pieces on useful squares where they don't interfere with each other? Given that my pieces won't be able to reach their desirable squares in time, can I change the structure so as to make their deployment timely and useful? In other words, the pawns usually determine the harmony or lack thereof in your potential piece configurations.

In addition, there is the crucial relationship between pawn-structure, which we tend to think of in static terms, and dynamics. In a sense every attack depends upon the structure the attacker inherits, but that is not a very useful disclosure. What counts is whether we can associate identifiable dynamic elements with known structures. The result may be compared with happily recognizing an old friend (resulting in a combination or tactic that one can easily assess), or running into vaguely familiar but enigmatic companions (when combinative success may depend upon intuition). Ultimately, of course, the most brilliant and original attacks (and defensive miracles) have their own capricious character that can't be anticipated from previous knowledge. In fact, the most awe-inspiring combinations are precisely those that 'shouldn't' work within a particular structural context, and 'shouldn't' work given the pieces and pawns available for action. Nevertheless, the majority of attacks will be informed by describable categories of positions.

Thus the precedence of pawn-structure, and the motivation for this chapter. It is generally agreed now that pattern recognition and the ability to process patterns in context is the foremost determinant in chess strength (putting aside competitive factors). The number of patterns one can recognize and associate with other structures correlates to how well one understands and plays the game. Grandmasters store and process many more pawn-structures with accompanying piece placements than the average player does, if only because of their repeated exposure to them in preparation and over the board. With study alone it's possible for one to master a great number of standard opening positions in the same way, and to understand their interaction with the subsequent play. Appreciation of why a strategy works in one position but not in a similar position is an indispensable part of chess mastery. Furthermore, if you recognize ideas and manoeuvres from other openings that apply to the one that you are playing, it will help you to focus on the issues and inspire you to make better decisions.

How might we improve our knowledge of pawn-structures? Obviously it's not possible to list them all and memorize their unique features. But there are formations and related issues that repeat themselves from opening to opening, very often constituting the basis for the fundamental strategy of each. In this chapter I'll examine some pawn-structures and the issues associated with them, choosing *selected* areas most likely to impact one's understanding of the game, or at least to grasp the common elements of the opening. These are not strange or irregular formations; one idea is to show how one might use the same approach to study other, more complex, structures. Hopefully their usefulness will extend to players of a wide range of skills. This is not a middlegame book, however, and my main goal has been to make the discussion in the forthcoming openings section more readily comprehensible. When presenting individual variations and games, I'll often assume your familiarity with this chapter.

Isolated Pawns

We saw some broad characterizations of positional features in the last chapter. Now I want to look at the structural elements across the board that bear upon the opening stage. We'll begin with the fairly straightforward case of the isolated pawn, also called the 'isolani', which we defined in Chapter 2. Textbooks almost always concentrate upon the isolated d-pawn, also called the 'isolated queen's pawn' (abbreviated as 'IQP'). Most authors do so to the exclusion of isolated pawns anywhere else on the board, writing chapters and even whole books on this specific case. Granted, it's very important to give the IQP its due because it can arise from so many openings, and so early in the game. Why is that? To generate an IQP in the opening, it's generally necessary to have the moves d4 and ...d5 appear early on, and it's extremely likely that one or both of the moves c4 or ...c5 were also played in the first stage of the opening. To show this, let's take a list of several openings that lead to the same, well-known type of isolated queen's pawn position, and sometimes to the very same position:

Queen's Gambit Accepted: 1 d4 d5 2 c4 dxc4 3 ♘f3 ♘f6 4 e3 e6 5 ♗xc4 c5 6 0-0 cxd4 7 exd4 ♗e7 8 ♘c3 0-0 9 ♖e1.

Nimzo-Indian: 1 d4 ♘f6 2 c4 e6 3 ♘c3 ♗b4 4 e3 c5 5 ♘f3 0-0 6 ♗d3 cxd4 7 exd4 d5 8 0-0 dxc4 9 ♗xc4 ♘c6 10 ♗g5 ♗e7 11 ♖e1.

Alapin Sicilian: 1 e4 c5 2 c3 d5 3 exd5 ♕xd5 4 d4 ♘f6 5 ♘f3 e6 6 ♗d3 ♘c6 7 0-0 cxd4 8 cxd4 ♗e7 9 ♘c3 ♕d8 10 ♖e1 0-0.

Caro-Kann: 1 e4 c6 2 d4 d5 3 exd5 cxd5 4 c4 ♘f6 5 ♘c3 e6 6 ♘f3 ♗e7 (6...♗b4 7 cxd5 ♘xd5 8 ♗d2 ♗e7 9 ♗d3 ♘c6 10 0-0 0-0 11 ♖e1 ♘f6 12 ♗g5 would be a typical transposition; White can also play 8 ♕c2 followed by 9 ♗d3) 7 cxd5 ♘xd5 8 ♗d3 (or 8 ♗c4 0-0 9 0-0 ♘c6 10 ♖e1 ♘f6) 8...0-0 9 0-0.

Semi-Tarrasch: 1 d4 d5 2 c4 e6 3 ♘c3 ♘f6 4 ♘f3 ♗e7 5 cxd5 ♘xd5 6 e3 0-0 7 ♗d3 c5 8 0-0 cxd4 9 exd4 ♘c6 10 ♖e1.

This is the basic picture (*see diagram overleaf*):

The most significant difference among these openings is the position of White's light-squared bishop (it's on c4 or d3). Sometimes the queen is already placed upon c2 or e2, and the king's

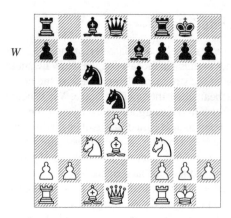

W

rook is usually but not always moved to e1. The basic position and its variants have been played thousands of times and investigated in depth. In fact, more words have been written about the IQP than about any other specific positional feature in chess. Neither side can be said to stand inherently better, which is why both sides are willing to enter into these positions. Without going into detail, here are the basic structural properties and strategies that should be stressed. For ease of discussion, let's assume that White is the possessor of the IQP before we attend to specific examples.

Disadvantages of the isolated d-pawn:

1. The IQP is a relatively easier target than most pawns because it can only be protected by pieces, several of which may be required for the task (as opposed to needing only a single pawn). Also, the d-pawn is almost always on an open file potentially facing Black's rooks and/or queen.

2. Defence of the isolated d-pawn can tie down White's pieces which might be used more effectively elsewhere.

3. Black gains an influential outpost in front of the isolani, which means that it is very difficult to drive his pieces off that spot.

4. The IQP tends to be a more serious weakness in simplified positions, the more so in an endgame. Notice that the mutual possession of the open c-file increases the chances of simplification. Nevertheless, Black must be skilful to make the right kind of simplification that doesn't come with other disadvantages. Often a new equilibrium will result from exchanges.

Advantages of the isolated d-pawn:

1. White will be able to develop more easily and aggressively, having more space and open lines for his bishops.

2. The IQP creates a support-point for a knight (or other piece) on e5.

3. The threat of the d-pawn's advance ties Black's pieces to the defence of d5.

4. Black, with less space, will have difficulty developing actively without making some concession such as creating a weakness or ceding the bishop-pair.

5. White has good kingside attacking chances based upon the support-point on e5, the e-file, and his bishops aimed in that direction.

In terms of strategy, White will have several ways of proceeding. He will usually complete his development by putting his queen on e2 or d3 (less frequently c2 or b3) and queen's rook on d1. Then one of the first goals is to provoke a weakness on the kingside. To do this, he can play ♘e5 and swing a rook to the kingside via e3. Or he can line up his bishop and queen to create a threat on h7. Black will generally defend by keeping a knight on f6 and playing ...g6 if necessary. With that set-up White can attack the dark squares by ♗h6, work to soften up the kingside by h4-h5 and/or play for d5, often by bringing his bishop back to the a2-g8 diagonal.

The safe advance of the d-pawn to d5 betokens success in most cases because it opens lines or broadens potential uses for almost all of his pieces (notably, the rooks on d1 and e1, bishop on a2 and knight on c3) and breaks down the defender at e6; it also liquidates the isolani itself. After d5 White usually has the far superior pieces, and he often has tactical resources that win material. The d5 break is probably the most frequently successful plan. There are also set-ups with the moves ♖e1-e3-g3; or, more commonly, ♘e5, ♗c4 and ♖e1, intending tactics such as ♘xf7, particularly if Black's rook is on e8. These ideas and others only work because White's superiority in space permits him to transfer his pieces rapidly, make threats, and take Black out of his game plan. The more pieces with which to attack, the better.

Black's strategy is not excessively complicated, although implementing it may be. His first goal is to maintain the blockade on d5, usually with a knight. Simply leaving a knight there is often not enough, however, because White may be able to capture the piece at a point where ...exd5 is forced, eliminating the threat to d4 and sometimes transforming the pawn-structure in White's favour. Thus, whether occupied or not, d5 itself needs to be reinforced. Often Black's knights will go to f6 and d5 (via ...♘b4-d5) or to d5 and e7. His c8-bishop will be developed to b7, either by ...b6 or by ...a6 and ...b5. A rook on d8 can also act to support a piece on d5 or restrain White's pawn advance to d5. One of Black's goals is simplification: the more pieces that are exchanged the less likely it is that White can break through. Moreover, the closer that Black can get to an endgame the better his prospects usually are. Exchanging White's minor pieces is a high priority, because they can have considerable range from squares around the isolated pawn. Knights in particular are dangerous when posted on e4, e5 and c5; and even seemingly 'defensive' knights on c3 and f3 can quickly come into action. Exchanging White's light-squared bishop is a real coup for Black; whether on c4, d3, a2 or c2, it is the piece most likely to be involved in a direct attack. By contrast, a rook on d1 defending the isolani is much less likely to do any damage.

For all that, simplification can be double-edged because sometimes it clarifies White's attacking themes, especially if he has support-points along open files in conjunction with pawn advances. A wonderful illustration of this is seen in Chapter 5 on the Giuoco Piano (in the main line with 10...♘ce7).

All that is rather abstract, so here are some examples of strategy by both sides. There are literally thousands of isolated-pawn positions in games between masters, many of which can be found in books on the opening or middle-game. As indicated, these positions will be taken from openings in which an IQP situation is normally created (for instance, in the same openings listed above). What you will eventually find is that isolated pawns are formed in a wide range of positions, many of them appearing *after* the opening stage because of an exchange on d4 or d5.

Here is a brief lesson about the main danger posed by the d-pawn: its advance.

Spassky – Avtonomov
Leningrad 1949

1 d4 d5 2 c4 dxc4 3 ♘f3 ♘f6 4 e3 c5 5 ♗xc4 e6 6 0-0 a6 7 ♕e2 b5 8 ♗b3 ♘c6 9 ♘c3 cxd4? 10 ♖d1 ♗b7 11 exd4 ♘b4

The d5-square is protected by four pieces and a pawn.

12 d5! *(D)*

Anyway! Can this be sound?

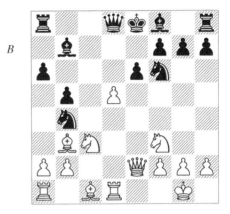

12...♘bxd5

You can confirm that after 12...♘fxd5 13 a3! and 12...♗xd5 13 ♗g5! ♗e7 14 ♗xf6 gxf6 15 a3 White will win material.

13 ♗g5! ♗e7 14 ♗xf6 gxf6 15 ♘xd5 ♗xd5 16 ♗xd5 exd5 17 ♘d4! ♔f8 18 ♘f5 *(D)*

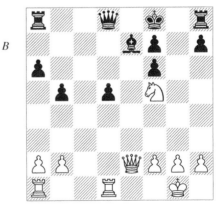

Many a pawn or exchange has been sacrificed to bring a knight to f5. Here it's worth more than a rook.

18...h5 19 ♖xd5 ♕xd5 20 ♕xe7+ ♔g8 21 ♕xf6 1-0

This next game is not as easy to understand, but expresses the same theme.

Yusupov – Lobron
Nussloch 1996

1 d4 ♘f6 2 c4 e6 3 ♘c3 ♗b4 4 e3 0-0 5 ♗d3 d5 6 ♘f3 c5 7 0-0 cxd4 8 exd4 dxc4 9 ♗xc4 b6 10 ♖e1 ♗b7 11 ♗d3 ♘c6 12 a3 ♗e7 *(D)*

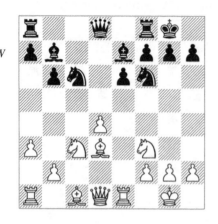

All the moves thus far are customary ones.
13 ♗c2 ♖e8 14 ♕d3 g6!

An instructive combination goes 14...♖c8? 15 d5! exd5 16 ♗g5 (threatening ♗xf6) 16...♘e4 (16...g6? 17 ♖xe7! ♕xe7 18 ♘xd5) 17 ♘xe4 dxe4 18 ♕xe4 g6 19 ♕h4 ♕c7 20 ♗b3 h5 21 ♕e4 (threatening ♕xg6+) 21...♔g7 22 ♗xf7! ♔xf7 23 ♗h6! ♕d6 24 ♕c4+ ♔f6 25 ♖ad1 ♘d4 26 ♕xd4+ ♕xd4 27 ♖xd4 ♖c5 28 h4! 1-0 Petrosian-Balashov, USSR 1974.

15 h4 ♕d6 16 ♗g5 ♖ad8 17 ♖ad1 ♕b8
Unmasking the rook against White's d-pawn.
18 ♗b3 a6? 19 d5! *(D)*

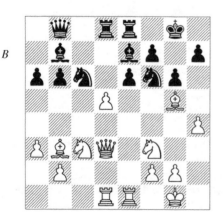

There's the thematic break.
19...♘a5
We're still in the opening! 19...exd5 20 ♖xe7! is a tactical device to remember, while 19...♘xd5 20 ♗xd5!? ♗xg5 21 ♘xg5 exd5 22 ♖xe8+ ♖xe8 23 ♘xd5 ♕e5 24 ♕f3 f5 25 ♕b3 is another typical idea. Now we see a not-so-typical one:
20 dxe6! ♘xb3
Capturing the queen by 20...♖xd3 loses to 21 exf7+ ♔g7 (21...♔h8 22 ♖xd3 ♘xb3 23 ♖xe7! ♖xe7 24 ♗xf6# is pretty) 22 fxe8♕ ♕xe8 23 ♖xd3 ♘xb3 24 ♖de3! and White wins.
21 exf7+ ♔xf7 22 ♕c4+ ♔g7 23 ♘e5! ♘g8 24 ♖xd8 ♕xd8 25 ♕f7+ ♔h8 26 ♕xb3 ♕d4 27 ♖e3! ♖f8 28 ♗xe7 1-0
28...♘xe7 29 ♘f7+ ♔g7 30 ♖xe7 follows.

The next example is a model treatment from Black's viewpoint:

Korchnoi – Karpov
Merano Wch (9) 1981

1 c4 e6 2 ♘c3 d5 3 d4 ♗e7 4 ♘f3 ♘f6 5 ♗g5 h6 6 ♗h4 0-0 7 ♖c1 dxc4 8 e3 c5 9 ♗xc4 cxd4 10 exd4
The isolated queen's pawn arises.
10...♘c6 11 0-0 ♘h5! *(D)*

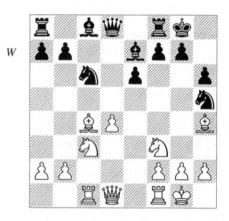

Black's goal is simplification, to draw the sting out of White's attacking chances. The knight went to h5 so that the bishop couldn't escape capture by going to g3. It also looks at f4.
12 ♗xe7 ♘xe7
The knight covers the key square d5.
13 ♗b3

13 ♖e1 would be the usual idea: get all the pieces out. On the other hand, with a pair of pieces off and more to come, the customary d5 advance will only lead to liquidation, and probably not one that White would be happy with; for instance, 13 d5?! exd5 14 ♘xd5 ♘xd5 15 ♗xd5 (15 ♕xd5 ♕xd5 16 ♗xd5 ♘f4 17 ♗c4 ♗e6! runs into the same kind of problems as 15 ♗xd5) 15...♘f4 16 ♗c4 ♕xd1 17 ♖fxd1 ♗g4 and Black already stands slightly better. This is based more on the specifics of this position than a statement about the move d5, however. The h5-knight happens to serve a powerful function due to the possibility of ...♘f4. Usually a move like 13 d5 would lead to equality, which is still a success for Black in opening play.

13...♘f6

Again protecting the crucial d5-square.

14 ♘e5

White does the right thing by occupying the support-point.

14...♗d7!

The normal continuation 14...b6 followed by ...♗b7 would only be tempting sacrificial ideas on f7, as described above.

15 ♕e2 ♖c8 16 ♘e4!?

More simplification. But ...♗c6 was coming anyway.

16...♘xe4 17 ♕xe4 ♗c6 18 ♘xc6 ♖xc6 19 ♖c3

Take a look at 19 ♖xc6 bxc6! (D).

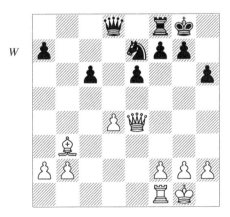

This is our first example of what is a recurring type of position in the openings world. Black takes on an isolated c-pawn at the same time as White has an isolated d-pawn. In the general case, the obvious difference between

the d-pawn and c-pawn is that White has more space; not so obvious is that a third-rank pawn is easier to defend than a fourth-rank pawn! In this instance the pawn on c6 prevents White's isolated pawn from advancing while maintaining an outpost on d5 and the options of ...♕d6, ...♖d8 and ...♘f5. Black also has a useful b-file that is typical of this structure. A lot comes down to activity here; for instance, will a white rook on the outpost c5, with the possible help of a bishop on a4, make up for Black's pressure on the d-pawn? Probably not, but those are the kinds of competing factors that arise. More on the isolated c-pawn will follow in the examples below.

Incidentally, after 19 ♖xc6, 19...♘xc6 20 d5 exd5 21 ♗xd5 is at best equal for Black, because bishop versus knight with pawns on both sides of the board is usually difficult for the side with the knight.

19...♕d6 20 g3 ♖d8 21 ♖d1 ♖b6!

The opening is over and Black has restrained the pawn, while White has no outposts or attack. Thus Black has the advantage. From this point on Karpov plays one of the best technical games in world championship history.

22 ♕e1 ♕d7 23 ♖cd3 ♖d6 24 ♕e4 ♕c6 25 ♕f4 ♘d5 26 ♕d2 ♕b6 27 ♗xd5 ♖xd5 28 ♖b3 ♕c6 29 ♕c3 ♕d7 30 f4 b6 31 ♖b4 b5 32 a4 bxa4 33 ♕a3 a5 34 ♖xa4 ♕b5 35 ♖d2 e5 36 fxe5 ♖xe5 37 ♕a1 ♕e8 38 dxe5 ♖xd2 39 ♖xa5 ♕c6 40 ♖a8+ ♔h7 41 ♕b1+ g6 42 ♕f1 ♕c5+ 43 ♔h1 ♕d5+ 0-1

In the next game, two younger superstars present a different approach to the same type of position:

Kramnik – Anand
Dortmund 2001

1 d4 d5 2 c4 dxc4 3 ♘f3 e6 4 e3 ♘f6 5 ♗xc4 c5 6 0-0 a6 7 ♗b3 cxd4 8 exd4 ♘c6 9 ♘c3 ♗e7 10 ♗g5 0-0 (D)

Pretty much the same position that we're used to.

11 ♕d2!?

This is a somewhat different way of deploying White's forces. Kramnik has ♕f4-h4 in mind.

11...♘a5 12 ♗c2 b5 13 ♕f4 ♖a7

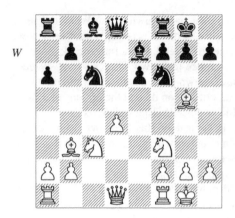

W

Black plans ...Rc7 or if possible ...Rd7, to stop d5.

14 Rad1 Bb7

Since 14...Rd7 allows De5, Anand wants to play ...Bxf3 and then ...Rd7 with at least equality.

15 d5! *(D)*

Again, this sacrifice is intended to cut off Black's pieces and free White's own.

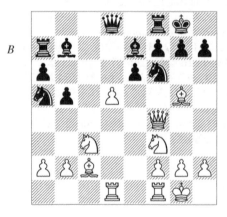

B

15...Bxd5!

From here on Anand defends in heroic fashion. After 15...exd5 16 Wh4 g6 17 Rfe1 White threatens a killing Rxe7, and he wins after 15...Dxd5 16 Dxd5 Bxd5 17 Rxd5! due to 17...exd5 18 Bxh7+ Kxh7 19 Wh4+ Kg8 20 Bxe7 Wxe7 21 Dg5. A pretty combination, perhaps the one that Anand missed when he allowed White to play 15 d5.

16 Dxd5 exd5!

Again, not 16...Dxd5? 17 Rxd5! exd5 18 Bxh7+, etc.

17 Wh4 h5!! *(D)*

An incredible defence! It can't quite save Black, but everything else loses; for example, 17...g6 18 Rfe1 or 17...h6 18 Bxh6 gxh6 19 Wxh6, with Dg5 and Rd3 to follow next.

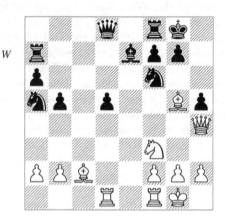

W

18 Rfe1

18 Dd4!? would be a typical tactical idea, looking hungrily at the f5-square.

18...Dc6 19 g4!? Wd6! 20 gxh5 Wb4! 21 h6!

Black has miraculously averted mate, but now a queenless middlegame ensues in which White's attack persists for another 10 moves. Notice the knight getting access to the key f5-square; as Kasparov has shown, this tends to win almost by itself!

21...Wxh4 22 Dxh4 De4 23 hxg7 Rc8 24 Bxe7 Dxe7 25 Bxe4 dxe4 26 Rxe4 Kxg7 27 Rd6! Rc5 28 Rg4+ Kh7 29 Df3! Dg6 30 Dg5+ Kg7 31 Dxf7 Rxf7 32 Rdxg6+ Kh7 33 R6g5 Rxg5 34 Rxg5 Rc7 35 a3 b4 36 axb4 Rc1+ 37 Kg2 Rb1 38 Ra5 Rxb2 39 Ra4! 1-0

Lautier – Karpov
Monte Carlo (rapid) 1995

1 d4 Df6 2 c4 e6 3 Dc3 Bb4 4 Wc2 0-0 5 a3 Bxc3+ 6 Wxc3 b6 7 Bg5 Bb7 8 f3 d5 9 e3 Dbd7 10 cxd5 exd5 11 Bd3 Re8 12 De2 c5 13 0-0 We7 14 Dg3 Rac8 15 Bf5 cxd4 16 Wxd4

There's the isolani; Black really doesn't seem ready for it.

16...Rc4 17 Wd2 Dc5 18 Rad1 h6 19 Bxf6 Wxf6 20 Bb1

Threatening Ba2. White has the better bishop and is restraining the IQP.

20...De6 21 Ba2 Rc5

Lateral defence of the isolani is best if you can maintain the rook's position. That often applies to the endgame as well.

22 ♘e2 ♗a6! 23 ♖fe1 ♗xe2 24 ♖xe2 ♖d8 25 ♕d3 g6 26 ♖ed2 (D)

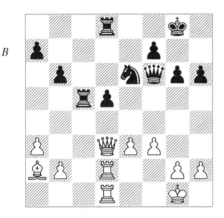

Hasn't Black merely simplified into a rotten position?

26...d4!

His d-pawn is weak so Karpov finds a clever way to liquidate it.

27 ♗xe6 ♕xe6 28 exd4 ♖cd5

Black is a full pawn down but now it's *White* with the IQP, and he can't break down the blockade!

29 ♕e4 ♕f6 30 ♔f2 ♔g7 31 ♖d3 a5 32 a4 b5 33 b3? bxa4 34 bxa4 ♕c6

Hitting c2 and a4. Suddenly White's got some problems.

35 ♖a3? ♕d6!

Black is attacking both the important pawn on h2 and the rook on a3!

36 ♖e3 ♕xh2 37 f4 ♕h4+ 38 ♔g1 ♕f6 39 ♖ed3 h5 40 ♕e3 h4 41 ♕e4 ♖8d6 42 ♖1d2 ♖f5 43 ♖f3 ♖e6 44 ♕d3 ♖xf4 45 d5 ♕a1+ 46 ♔h2 ♖xf3 47 gxf3 ♕e5+ 0-1

Remember that Black can also take on the isolated queen's pawn. In fact, every d-pawn opening above has some kind of reversed case, but particularly the Semi-Tarrasch, which can arise from a number of openings; e.g., 1 c4 ♘f6 2 ♘c3 c5 3 ♘f3 e6 4 e3 d5 5 cxd5 exd5 6 d4 ♘c6 7 ♗e2 ♗e7 8 dxc5 ♗xc5 9 0-0 0-0, or 1 d4 d5 2 ♘f3 ♘f6 3 c4 e6 4 ♘c3 c5 5 e3 ♘c6 6 cxd5 exd5 7 ♗b5 ♗d6 8 dxc5 ♗xc5 9 0-0 a6 10 ♗e2 0-0 and so forth.

But we also have instances of IQPs on Black's side of the board that look somewhat different:

French Defence: 1 e4 e6 2 d4 d5 3 ♘d2 c5 4 exd5 exd5 5 ♘gf3 (or 5 ♗b5+ ♗d7 6 ♗xd7+ ♘xd7 7 ♘gf3 ♘gf6 8 0-0 ♗e7 9 dxc5 ♘xc5) 5...♘c6 6 ♗b5 ♗d6 7 dxc5 ♗xc5 8 0-0 ♘e7 9 ♘b3 ♗d6 (D).

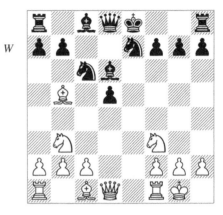

Tarrasch Queen's Gambit: 1 d4 d5 2 c4 e6 3 ♘c3 c5 4 cxd5 exd5 5 ♘f3 ♘c6 6 g3 (6 e3 ♘f6 7 ♗e2 cxd4 8 ♘xd4 would be analogous to our examples from the white side) 6...♘f6 7 ♗g2 ♗e7 8 0-0 0-0 9 ♗g5 cxd4 10 ♘xd4 (D).

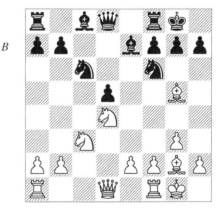

Roughly the same ideas apply to handling these openings: White should maintain close control of d4 and seek *carefully-chosen* exchanges. As mentioned above, he may be better off exchanging minor pieces than rooks, because rooks tend to be passive pieces as defenders. The side with the isolani should follow the reverse approach, exchanging rooks (if anything has to be exchanged) and keeping minor pieces on the board. That's getting into the realm of middlegame theory, however. At any rate, activity is at a premium: rooks on open files, bishops attacking weak points, etc. And of course if you can safely get ...d4 in, your odds of a happy conclusion increase.

Isolated e-Pawns

The IQP isn't the only isolated pawn of interest in chess openings. First, we might ask why we don't see more isolated e-pawns in the opening. That's fairly easy: at some point an f-pawn would have to advance and that's not part of most openings, especially since there would have to be another central capture at some point. However, in the Sicilian Defence we do see a situation that is rare in other openings, i.e. the pawn-structure often leads to isolated e- and d-pawns on adjacent files. There are a great number of lines like 1 e4 c5 2 ♘f3 d6 3 d4 cxd4 4 ♘xd4 ♘f6 5 ♘c3 a6 6 ♗e2 e5 7 ♘b3 ♗e7 8 0-0 0-0 9 ♔h1 ♘bd7 10 ♗e3 ♕c7 11 f4 exf4 12 ♗xf4 *(D)* involving the routine moves ...e5, f4 and ...exf4.

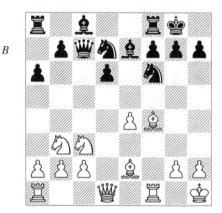

Sometimes Black has his pawn on e6 and the advance f4-f5 can lead to the same structure, that is, if White responds to ...exf5 by capturing with a piece (usually a knight, i.e. ♘xf5), or Black does the same after White's fxe6 (for instance, by ...♗xe6). The characteristics of those positions are fairly consistent and will be discussed in Chapter 11 on the Sicilian Defence.

Isolated c-Pawns

Isolated c-pawns are very common and we shall see them frequently throughout this book. They may arise a little later in the game than in the standard isolated d-pawn openings, partly because they can easily stem from them. The Sicilian Defence offers some examples:

Sicilian Defence, Alapin Variation: 1 e4 c5 2 c3 ♘f6 3 e5 ♘d5 4 d4 cxd4 5 cxd4 d6 6 ♘f3 ♘c6 7 ♗c4 ♘b6 8 ♗b5 dxe5 9 ♘xe5 ♗d7 10 ♗xc6 ♗xc6 11 ♘xc6 bxc6 *(D)*.

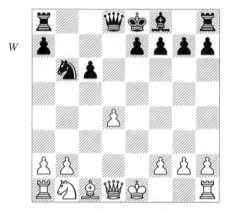

Sicilian Defence, Rossolimo Variation: 1 e4 c5 2 ♘f3 ♘c6 3 ♗b5 e6 4 c3 ♘ge7 5 d4 cxd4 6 cxd4 d5 7 exd5 ♘xd5 8 0-0 ♗e7 9 ♘e5 ♕b6 10 ♗xc6+ bxc6 *(D)*.

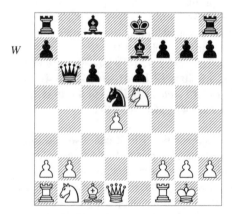

Here are some other examples:
Queen's Gambit Declined: 1 d4 d5 2 c4 e6 3 ♘c3 ♗e7 4 ♘f3 ♘f6 5 ♗g5 h6 6 ♗h4 ♘bd7 7

e3 0-0 8 ♖c1 c6 9 ♗d3 dxc4 10 ♗xc4 b5 11 ♗d3 a6 12 a4 bxa4 13 ♘xa4.

Catalan: 1 d4 d5 2 c4 e6 3 ♘f3 ♘f6 4 g3 ♗e7 5 ♗g2 0-0 6 0-0 dxc4 7 ♘e5 ♘c6 8 ♗xc6 bxc6 9 ♘xc6 ♕e8 10 ♘xe7+ ♕xe7 11 ♕a4 e5 12 dxe5 ♕xe5 13 ♕xc4, a position that has been played repeatedly over decades.

Two Knights Defence: 1 e4 e5 2 ♘f3 ♘c6 3 ♗c4 ♘f6 4 ♘g5 d5 5 exd5 ♘a5 6 ♗b5+ c6 7 dxc6 bxc6 8 ♗e2.

Semi-Slav: 1 d4 d5 2 c4 e6 3 ♘c3 c6 4 ♘f3 ♘f6 5 ♗g5 h6 6 ♗xf6 ♕xf6 7 e3 ♘d7 8 ♗d3 dxc4 9 ♗xc4 g6 10 0-0 ♗g7 11 e4 e5 12 d5 ♘b6 13 ♗b3 ♗g4 14 h3 ♗xf3 15 ♕xf3 ♕xf3 16 gxf3 ♔e7 17 dxc6 bxc6.

Isolated c-pawns are often created in the middlegame. For the most part we won't see that in this book, but the same concepts apply.

Isolated a-Pawns

Few isolated b-pawns arise in the opening, but isolated a-pawns are quite common, because their creation requires only that a b-pawn captures towards the centre. One recurrent situation arises in a number of openings when White plays a4-a5 against Black's pawns on a6 and b7. This is a 'one pawn holds two' situation in the sense that if Black plays ...b5 (or sometimes ...b6), then White captures *en passant* and isolates Black's a-pawn.

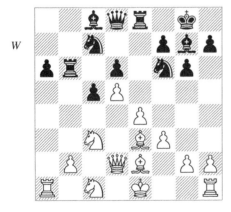

This type of situation occurs repeatedly in the King's Indian Defence and Benoni, for example, but watch for it in other openings. In many cases White's c-pawn will be on c4 or off the board, so his b-pawn will be isolated or backward.

In the Sicilian Defence, the same capture happens but White's b-pawn is in better shape, at least theoretically, because it has the c-pawn in its vicinity. A different way for 'b-pawn versus a-pawn' to arise is in a position with a white pawn on a3. Black plays ...b5-b4, the b-pawn is captured by the a-pawn, and a piece recaptures on b4. Then Black's a-pawn is left isolated, and often White's b-pawn as well. This can occur in the Sicilian Defence, French Defence, King's Indian Defence, or other openings featuring a minority attack. Finally, it sometimes happens that with Black's pawn on b5 and White's on a4, Black will play simply ...bxa4, a common idea in the Ruy Lopez and Sicilian Defence (likewise with Black's pawn on b4 capturing White's on a3).

Because of their distance from the centre of action, isolated and even doubled a-pawns are seldom worthwhile targets in the opening. Their vulnerability shows itself more in the endgame. Certain structures lend themselves to a-pawn raids; e.g., ...♕a5(+) and ...♕xa2 in the Exchange Grünfeld Defence and certain Queen's Gambit Exchange Variations; or, for instance, when Black goes out of his way to capture White's a4-pawn in the Winawer Variation. But usually isolated a-pawns situated on the first two ranks (such as a black pawn on a6 in several openings) tend to be defensible until the middlegame is in full swing. For example, sometimes White captures a knight on a6 with his light-squared bishop and the same issues arise; for example, 1 d4 d5 2 c4 c6 3 ♘f3 ♘f6 4 ♘c3 dxc4 5 a4 ♘a6 6 e4 ♗g4 7 ♗xc4 e6 8 ♗xa6 bxa6 9 ♕d3 ♗xf3 10 gxf3 (now we have two sets of doubled pawns; Black's are weaker, of course, but he is compensated by the b-file and a potentially safer kingside) 10...a5 11 ♕c4 ♕c8 12 ♖g1 ♖b8 13 ♖g5 ♖b4 14 ♕e2 ♖xd4 15 ♖xa5 ♕c7 16 ♗e3 ♕xa5 17 ♗xd4 with approximate equality, Korchnoi-Conquest, Budapest 1996.

The treatment of all these phenomena varies so much from position to position that we'll have to discuss them in context.

Pawn-Chains

When authors give examples of pawn-chains they tend to be pawns adjacent to and facing another pawn-chain, i.e. interlocking. The textbook example is the French Defence Advance Variation, 1 e4 e6 2 d4 d5 3 e5 c5 4 ♘f3 ♘c6 5 c3. The line of pawns from b2 to e5 is called a 'chain', and the directly interlocking pawns are on e6 and d5, but of course Black's pawn on f7 holds up the ones on e6 and d5. Most books on strategy discuss this French Advance Variation when they want an example of pawn-chains, and also the main lines of the King's Indian Defence. Those are excellent starting-points. We don't always think in terms of pawn-chains even if they share classical properties, for instance, in the Slav with 1 d4 d5 2 c4 c6 3 ♘f3 ♘f6 4 e3 a6 5 c5, in which White's pawn-chain is lengthy indeed. But in fact ...e5 is the natural way to attack that chain, and of late we've even seen the arduous b4, a4 and b5 by White to attack the base of Black's pawn-chain at c6 (this has occurred a bit more often in the line that goes 4 ♘c3 a6 5 c5 followed by ♗f4, but that's another matter).

Furthermore, much of what relates to those pawn-chains is relevant to a great number of other 'pawn strings' that aren't fully or directly opposed by other pawns. In accordance with some other sources, I'll call these pawn-chains as well. For example, if you look at the Modern Benoni (1 d4 ♘f6 2 c4 c5 3 d5 e6 4 ♘c3 exd5 5 cxd5 d6 6 e4, especially with 6...g6 7 f3) you see short 'pawn duos' pointing in opposite directions. In several openings only partially overlapping chains emerge but have chain-like properties; for example, things like c3/d4/e5 versus f7/e6 and e4/d5 versus c7/d6, and so forth. We see a truncated chain in some Ruy Lopez variations, when White plays d5, thus forming an opposition of e4/d5 versus c7/d6/e5. Furthermore, pawn-chains with doubled pawns at their base will emerge from exchanges. Almost all of these can be looked at in the same terms as the traditional French and King's Indian chains; for example, in methods of attacking and defending them. Study of their common and contrasting elements will help you to master this part of the game.

Let's start with the traditional examples and see what we can discover. We'll start out with the French Defence, probably the only opening

in which the majority of its main variations have pawn-chains.

1 e4 e6 2 d4 d5 3 e5

The logic behind this move for White is that it claims space on the kingside and cramps the development of Black's pieces. After 3 e5, Black's king's knight cannot go to its 'best' square on f6, and Black's queen's bishop, which was already blocked by its pawn on e6, is further incarcerated by the inability of the e6-pawn to advance. As mentioned, a variation well-suited for a discussion of chains continues:

3...c5 4 c3 ♘c6 5 ♘f3 *(D)*

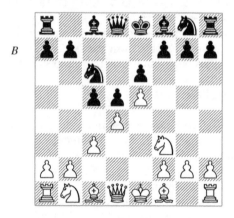

The last two moves are natural in that 4...♘c6 develops and exerts influence upon d4 and e5, whereas 5 ♘f3 defends those points. Note first that if White had played 5 dxc5 he would have broken the chain, which would have weakened the front of the pawn-structure at e5. That pawn would then be subject to a greater threat of capture, like an isolated pawn which can't be defended with other pawns. It also could be exchanged more easily due to insufficient resources for maintaining it. A direct attack could come by the moves ...♕c7 and ...♘ge7-g6. Or the offer to exchange could be pursued via the pawn move ...f6.

This leads to the idea that if Black can break down the d4 point, sometimes called the 'base' of the pawn-chain, he can cripple or destroy the pawn-structure itself. To what end? By getting rid of the pawn on d4 and then winning or exchanging the one on e5, a natural place would appear on f6 for the knight currently doing nothing on g8, and the move ...e5 would be more feasible. With a little luck that advance would lead to the liberation of the c8-bishop, and in the meantime Black would control the action with his own 'ideal centre' of pawns on e5 and d5. This particular fantasy, for the moment out of reach without White's cooperation, motivates Black's desire to break down the chain at its base. As it turns out, locating the base of a pawn-chain is more of a practical than a theoretical determination; if Black played ...b5-b4, then White's pawn on c3 would be called the base of the chain, and in the unlikely event that Black played ...a5-a4-a3, then b2 would be so designated. Essentially it comes down to where one is most likely to succeed in undermining the chain.

Returning to the French Defence and its 'effective' base at d4, we can see why White is interested in maintaining his pawn there rather than playing dxc5 or allowing it to be captured. The two sides' conflicting goals might be played out by a variety of means. An example of the further play is:

5...♕b6

Black attacks d4 again; for the moment the pawn is adequately protected.

6 ♗e2

This develops pieces and prepares to castle. Another theme can arise if White plays 6 ♗d3 ♗d7?! (6...cxd4 is normal) 7 dxc5 ♗xc5 8 0-0, when White gives up his supporting pawn but in return gains the possibility of b4-b5, when he can use the d4-square as an excellent support-point for his pieces.

6...cxd4 7 cxd4 ♘ge7

Already White has to think about the health of his base, the d4-pawn. If he plays the most natural move on the board, 8 0-0?, that pawn is unavoidably lost after 8...♘f5.

Obviously White would not play 8 0-0? but would instead protect the pawn by, say, 8 b3 ♘f5 9 ♗b2 *(D)*.

These moves are not necessarily the best, but they illustrate the basic idea. I've avoided a discussion of move-order subtleties in order to get the point across without unnecessary complications.

The concept of attacking the base, first systematized by Nimzowitsch, rapidly spread throughout the chess world and was treated as sort of a general principle of pawn-chains. It's interesting that what are labelled chains are precisely

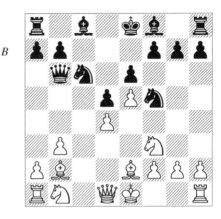

B

those structures that can be attacked following this rule.

For instance, few if any players refer to the lines of pawns from f7 to d5 and f2 to d4 in the Queen's Gambit Declined as pawn-chains, even when White plays c5 (as Steinitz used to do without provocation!). For example, 1 d4 d5 2 c4 e6 3 ♘c3 ♗e7 4 ♘f3 ♘f6 5 ♗g5 h6 6 ♗h4 ♘bd7 7 e3 0-0 8 ♖c1 a6 9 c5 c6 *(D)*.

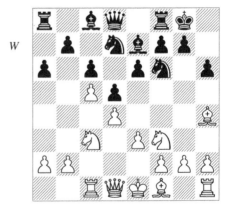

W

Thinking in terms of pawn-chains isn't our habit in this case, because the traditional idea of how to break up a chain, that is, at its 'base', doesn't apply. After 10 ♗d3, it's normally not on the cards for White to play b4-b5 (he's turning his eyes towards the king, a less trivial target). Black can attack in the centre by ...e5 (hardly with the idea of putting pressure on d4, however) or attack the front of the chain by 10...b6 11 cxb6 c5!?, a sound idea although subject to tactical issues.

What is the reality? Even in the French Defence example above, the standard illustration of attacking the base, Black will end up by attacking the protected front of the chain. For example, after White successfully protects his base by 8 b3 ♘f5 9 ♗b2, Black's next step is to attack the front of the pawn-chain by ...f6. For instance, one line goes 9...♗b4+ 10 ♔f1 ♗e7 11 ♘c3 0-0 12 g3 f6 (D) and White will soon surrender the leading pawn by exf6.

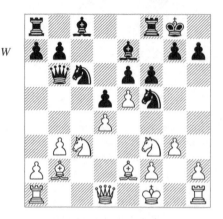

Or, in the same Advance Variation, the phenomenon is illustrated in the variation 3 e5 c5 4 c3 ♘c6 5 ♘f3 ♗d7 6 ♗e2 ♘ge7 7 0-0 ♘g6 with the intention of ...f6 next or soon thereafter; for example, 8 ♘a3 ♗e7 9 ♘c2 (White is still concerned with protecting the base at d4) 9...0-0 10 ♖e1 cxd4 11 cxd4 f6 (D).

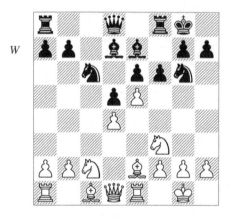

Now the front of the pawn-chain disappears because of the three-way attack: 11 exf6 ♗xf6. This time Black ignored the base and came out fine.

Other French pawn-chain variations are clearer in that respect; e.g.:

1 e4 e6 2 d4 d5 3 ♘d2 ♘f6 4 e5 ♘fd7 5 ♗d3 c5 6 c3 ♘c6 7 ♘e2 cxd4 8 cxd4 f6

The e5-pawn is attacked three times.

9 exf6 ♘xf6 10 ♘f3 ♗d6 11 0-0 (D)

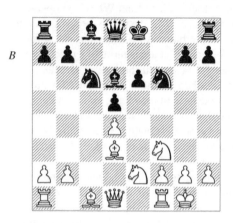

In this instance Black made only a half-hearted attempt to attack the base of the pawn-chain and then successfully attacked the front of it.

So perhaps the procedure should be to attack the base and then the front? But then there's the following unadulterated example of attacking only the front of the chain:

1 e4 e6 2 d4 d5 3 ♘d2 ♘c6 4 ♘gf3 ♘f6 5 e5 ♘d7 6 ♗d3 f6 (D)

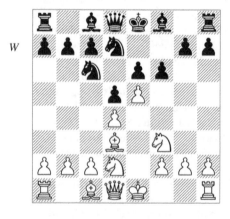

I should note that according to theory Black stands perfectly well in this position. Other openings attack chains in this manner; for example, English Opening variations in which Black plays ...e4 and White eliminates the front pawn by f3. There are also Ruy Lopez variations in which d5 is met by ...c6 (e.g., the

Breyer Defence), and several King's Indian variations as well.

Clearly we need a broader way of looking at this subject. Let's go to the King's Indian Defence example that's always used in the books:
1 d4 ♘f6 2 c4 g6 3 ♘c3 ♗g7 4 e4 d6 5 ♘f3 0-0 6 ♗e2 e5 7 0-0 ♘c6 8 d5 ♘e7 *(D)*

We'll quickly look at two very distinct approaches to this position, but only in terms of pawn-chains.
A: 9 ♘e1
B: 9 ♘d2

A)
9 ♘e1 ♘d7 10 ♗e3 f5 11 f3 f4
Black ignores the first 'effective' base at e4, the one that he attacked in the French Defence situation. Indeed, 11...fxe4 12 fxe4 ♖xf1+ 13 ♗xf1 ♘f6 14 ♗f2 only helps White because Black has no kingside targets to bite upon. By playing ...f4 instead, he extends the chain to f3 in preparation for the march of his g-pawn. These are all normal moves, details of which will be given in the chapter on the King's Indian Defence in the next volume.
12 ♗f2 g5
This pawn is headed for the new base at f3.
13 ♘d3 ♘f6 14 c5 ♘g6 15 ♖c1 ♖f7 16 ♖c2 ♗f8 17 cxd6 cxd6 18 ♕d2 g4 19 ♖fc1 g3 *(D)*
So Black never did attack the base on e4 or on f3, neither of which was ever seriously threatened. In fact, the pawn attack ran right by the chain with ...g3 and puts no pressure whatsoever on it! But in spite of the g2-d5 chain surviving in full health, Black has a

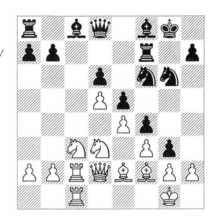

great attack as shown by one game that continued as follows:
20 hxg3 fxg3 21 ♗xg3 ♘h5 22 ♗h2 ♗e7 23 ♘b1 ♗d7 24 ♕e1 ♗g5 25 ♘d2 ♗e3+

B)
9 ♘d2 *(D)*
A very different approach emerges from this move in the same variation.

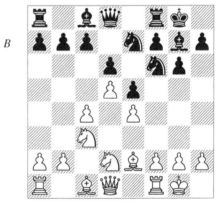

In some games the traditional pawn race ensues:
9...♘e8 10 b4 f5
Attack on the base.
11 c5
Likewise.
11...♘f6 12 f3 f4 13 ♘c4 g5 14 ♗a3 ♘g6 15 b5 ♘e8
White is threatening the base at d6 three times, so Black has to defend it.
16 b6! *(D)*
A nice picture! White transfers the base all the way down to Black's second rank, the

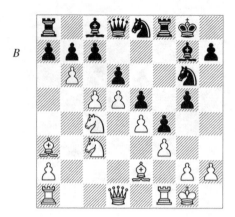

B

ultimate undermining theme. This pure form of attacking the base of such a long chain almost never occurs in any opening.

16...axb6 17 cxb6 cxb6 18 ♕b3 h5 19 ♖ab1 g4 *(D)*

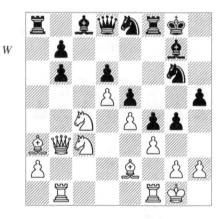

W

Now if only Black could play ...h4-h3, he could duplicate White's achievement!

20 ♘xb6

Having destroyed the very back of the pawn-chain, White has a very good position, though must be careful that the tactics don't get out of control.

This example illustrates how important it is, in a game with pawn-chains, to have at least one file open for a rook to work with in a direct way next to the pawn-chain. Other pieces alone usually can't completely break down the opponent's position.

Since White's pawn-chain is so impervious to assault in the foregoing variation, Black can think about challenging the front of the pawn-chain, even when it's protected to the hilt. As

seen in the French Defence examples, there are benefits to that approach.

9...a5 *(D)*

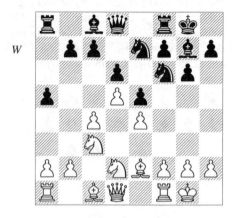

W

First Black defends against b4, in turn preventing the key move c5.

10 a3 ♗d7 11 b3

11 ♖b1 would be answered by 11...a4! (one pawn holding down two, a theme that pops up periodically through this book) 12 b4 axb3 13 ♖xb3 b6 and White will never get c5 in. After 11 b3, however, White is ready for ♖b1, b4 and c5.

11...c6 *(D)*

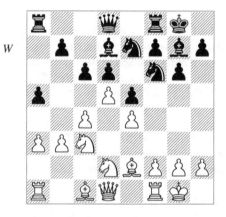

W

A strike against the front of the pawn-chain. The first point is that the leader of the chain on d5 will now be vulnerable if White plays c5.

12 ♖b1 ♕b8!? 13 b4 cxd5

Sometimes Black skips this move and answers b4 with ...b5, a dynamic attack on the entire chain, which is at least interesting if not entirely convincing.

14 cxd5

14 exd5 gives Black a type of kingside majority that we shall see more of as we proceed. ...f5 will follow shortly. Suffice it to say that in general that situation is favourable to Black.

14...♖c8 15 ♗b2 axb4 16 axb4

The pawn-chain has been neutralized, proving that Black needn't only play on the side of the board where he has the undermining moves. The same applies to White. Chess is not so one-dimensional that you aren't permitted to think about more than one theme, at least not in the opening where we have so many pieces on the board.

What's the upshot of all this? Is the practical player left without any guidance whatsoever? Not at all, because the more positions you see and play, the more tools that you acquire. As in any other situation in chess, you have to make an assessment of which positions call for which treatment. For instance, notice that Black addressed the front pawn on the queenside and never attended to the e4 base. How realistic is that in general? Let's imagine a similar position of a type that does arise in the French Defence:

1 e4 e6 2 d4 d5 3 ♘d2 ♘f6 4 e5 ♘fd7 5 f4 c5 6 c3 ♘c6 7 ♘df3 ♗e7 8 g3 ♕a5 9 ♔f2 (D)

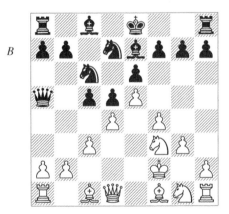

B

Here White has safeguarded his king (it can even go to g2 if necessary) and his pieces are about to spring out to aggressive positions; e.g., ♗d3, ♘e2, with perhaps g4 and f5. How likely is that plan to succeed? The structure is analogous (d4/e5/f4 to c4/d5/e4), so Black's procedure would have to do with ...f6, perhaps preceded by ...h5, connected with ...g5. But

the crucial difference is that this is the side of the board where Black's king resides, so such a plan is unrealistic. A simple analysis (with a little bit of calculation) also tells you an attack on d4 won't get very far: not enough pieces and plenty of defenders. But if you're thinking in terms of pawn-chain experience, you'll see that Black should play to undermine White's pawn-structure by **9...b5!** followed by ...b4 and moves such as ...♖b8, ...bxc3, ...♗a6 and ...♘b6-a4 in some intelligent order. This can be an effective idea as long as Black is alert to the defence of his king.

With those ideas in mind, let's look at examples from the Caro-Kann Advance Variation.

Anand – Karpov
Wijk aan Zee 2003

1 e4 c6 2 d4 d5 3 e5 ♗f5 4 ♘c3 e6 5 g4 ♗g6 6 ♘ge2 ♘e7 7 f4 (D)

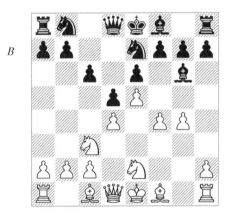

B

7...c5!

As we saw above, once f4 is in, it's less likely that 7...f6?! will do any good. White simply shores up the centre by 8 ♗e3, when 8...fxe5 9 fxe5 gives White f4 for his knight. I should add that in some lines in which White plays h4-h5 instead of f4, ...f6 is the best defence.

8 ♘g3!? cxd4 9 ♘b5 ♘ec6!

A piece sacrifice to win the centre.

10 f5 ♗c5 11 ♘d6+

Black's point is that after 11 fxg6 fxg6 he picks up a second pawn and threatens the total decimation of White's centre by ...♘xe5. Then 12 ♕e2 0-0 prepares ...♘d7 winning the last centre pawn, and then 13 g5 (to get ♗h3 in) runs into 13...♕b6! 14 ♗h3 d3! 15 ♕xd3 (15 cxd3 ♕xb5) 15...♘xe5 and everything falls apart. Notice how this was a consequence of ...c5 and ...cxd4, although by no means a necessary one, and in fact later games improved for White before this point in the game.

11...♗xd6 12 exd6 ♕xd6 13 ♗g2

13 fxg6?! fxg6! is strong (Black has the open f-file, a big centre and three pawns for the piece). In fact, ...fxg6 is usually the correct answer in the French and similar structures. Having said that, even 13...hxg6!? sets up the rogue tactic 14 ♗g2? ♖xh2!.

13...f6

Now Black threatens to escape with the bishop.

14 fxg6 hxg6 15 0-0

White steers clear of ...♖xh2 again.

15...♘d7 16 ♖f2 0-0-0 17 c3 dxc3 18 bxc3 ♘b6! *(D)*

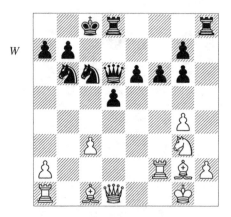

Although Black has only two pawns for the piece, he more than makes up for it with the mobile centre, c4 outpost and kingside attack. White went on to win, but not because of the opening. Attacking the base was the correct decision.

Short – Seirawan
Tilburg 1990

1 e4 c6 2 d4 d5 3 e5 ♗f5 4 ♗e2 e6 5 ♘f3 c5 6 0-0 ♘c6 7 c3 *(D)*

In this Caro-Kann Advance Variation we have the equivalent of the French Advance Variation but with Black's light-squared bishop

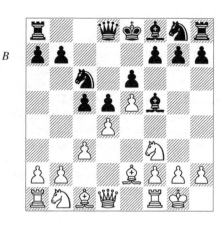

outside the pawn-chain. Notice, however, that Black lost a tempo by playing ...c6-c5, and that he's made an extra move with his light-squared bishop, which doesn't happen in the French. The point is that White is getting extra time to consolidate his space advantage and Black needs to break down the centre in some way before he becomes permanently cramped. Thus:

7...♕b6 8 ♕a4!

This move would be worse than useless in the Advance French because Black would play ...♗d7.

8...c4!?

There springs up another pawn-chain! This takes all the pressure off White's base while forming a new one. The plan is slow (and unusual) but there are special considerations. First, Black has to look at lines like 8...cxd4 9 ♘xd4! intending ♗e3 next, with ♘xf5 another promising idea; e.g., 9...♗c5 10 ♘xf5 exf5 11 b4 ♗e7 12 ♗e3 ♕d8 13 ♖d1. This is almost impossible to prevent without real compromise; for example, a pretty line runs 8...♘h6 9 dxc5 ♗xc5 10 b4 ♗e7 11 ♗e3 ♕c7 12 b5 and here 12...♘b8 13 b6+ ♕d7 14 ♕xa7! or 12...♕a5 13 ♗d1! ♕xa4 14 ♗xa4 ♘a5 15 b6+. There are many other lines with tactical and positional problems. So Seirawan reasons that he'll keep the position closed for a while, and by the time White organizes g4 and f5 he'll be winning on the other side of the board.

9 ♘bd2?!

What do we know about such positions? The base of the enemy pawn-chain is far, far away, so it's not hard to see that the head must be attacked. Short knows this of course, but his timing is bad. 9 b3! is a good move, hitting the vulnerable part of the chain, when Black would cave in if he were to play 9...cxb3 10 axb3 and activate all of White's pieces; e.g., 10...♘ge7 11 ♗a3 ♘g6 12 ♗xf8 ♖xf8 13 ♗b5 a6 14 ♘bd2 and Black is short of good moves.

9...♕a5 10 ♕d1 h6! 11 ♖e1 b5

Back to pawn-chain operations! ...b4 is next, so White tries to do something about it.

12 b4?! (D)

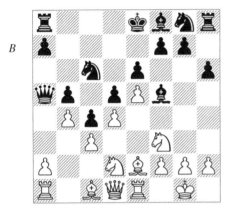

12...♘xb4! 13 cxb4 ♗xb4

As in the last game, Black has two pawns for the piece and the promise of much more after ...♗c3. Short finds an interesting reply in the midst of these threats.

14 ♘f1!? ♘e7

Capturing the rook by 14...♗xe1 15 ♘xe1 allows White to survive the pawn-rush.

15 ♘g3 ♗g6 16 ♖f1

Here instead of 16...♗c3?, as he played, Seirawan gives 16...♘c6 17 ♗e3 ♗c3 18 ♖c1 b4 19 ♘h4 ♗h7 20 ♘h5 ♖g8 21 ♗xh6 0-0-0 22 ♗g5 ♖d7 23 ♘f3 ♕xa2 with an unstoppable mass of pawns.

When faced with a long-term space problem, like the one that Short created for his opponent, waiting around is the worst thing to do. Look at whether attacking the base or front of the pawn-chain has any chance of succeeding, then whether the two in combination can be effective. If not, you must create your own counterchances by hook or by crook, which structurally may amount to a radical advance of your own.

Practically every opening system has its pawn-chain examples. What about some other shorter chains, or ones with outposts? How to assess them? The Benoni complex shows us a little variety. In the Czech Benoni it's fairly easy to see the nature of the pawn-chains:

1 d4 ♘f6 2 c4 c5 3 d5 d6 4 ♘c3 e5 5 e4 (D)

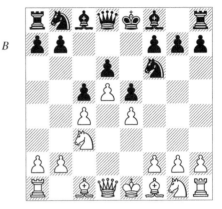

Black would like to play for ...f5 or ...b5, White for f4 or b4. In practice, White's breaks are more likely to succeed because of Black's lack of space *or* good squares for his pieces; e.g., he lacks c5 for his knights, or anywhere active for his king's bishop (which is sometimes reduced to the exotic idea ...h6 and ...♗e7-g5). In particular Black has trouble enforcing ...f5 if White sets up a structure involving ♗d3, ♘f3 and h3.

Notice that the same pawn-structure in the King's Indian Main Line is more bearable for Black because with his bishop better-placed, he can get counterplay with ...f5 before White squelches it.

A Benko Gambit pawn-chain analysis reveals a little about the gambit's strengths. After 1 d4 ♘f6 2 c4 c5 3 d5 b5 4 cxb5 a6 5 bxa6 followed by Black's recapture of the pawn over the next moves, White is very seldom able to enforce an attack at the effective base of Black's pawn-chain at d6, and can only dream of achieving a successful b4 (it does happen, but only rarely). Black on the other hand has already eliminated the base of White's pawn-chain on c4, and the move ...e6, cracking up the front pawn at d5, characterizes most Benko Gambit variations at one point or another.

Take the Alekhine Defence, which actually includes a lot of pawn-chains. Here's the Four Pawns Attack, producing a partial chain after 1 e4 ♘f6 2 e5 ♘d5 3 d4 d6 4 c4 ♘b6 5 f4 dxe5 6 fxe5. Where to attack? Let's see: 6...♘c6 7 ♗e3 ♗f5 8 ♘c3 e6 9 ♘f3 ♗e7 10 ♗e2 0-0 11 0-0 f6!. In front, that's the best plan! These concepts cement themselves with study and experience. Here's a recent high-powered example:

Grishchuk – Ponomariov
Torshavn 2000

1 e4 ♘f6 2 e5 ♘d5 3 d4 d6 4 ♘f3 g6 5 ♗c4 ♘b6 6 ♗b3 ♗g7 7 a4 a5 8 ♘g5 e6 9 f4 *(D)*

This is a solid chain that must be taken care of quickly, or Black must find counterplay elsewhere, which is no easy task.

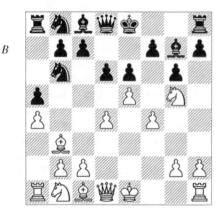

9...dxe5 10 fxe5 c5
Base of the chain.
11 c3 cxd4 12 0-0 0-0 13 cxd4 ♘c6 14 ♘f3 f6
Front of the chain.
15 ♘c3! fxe5
It's a little late to turn around.
16 ♗g5! ♕d7 17 dxe5 ♘xe5?
The best chance is 17...♕xd1! 18 ♖axd1 ♘xe5 19 ♘xe5 ♖xf1+ 20 ♔xf1 ♗xe5 21 ♗e3 ♗xc3 22 ♖d8+ ♔f7 23 bxc3 and the bishops are worth more than a pawn, but Black can at least hope for survival. However, he should avoid 23...♘d7 24 ♔e1! b6 25 ♖h8 ♔g7? 26 ♗xe6! ♔xh8 27 ♗d4+.
18 ♘xe5 ♖xf1+ 19 ♕xf1 ♕d4+
Or 19...♗xe5 20 ♖d1 ♗d4+ 21 ♔h1.
20 ♔h1 ♕xe5 21 ♗d8 ♕c5 22 ♘e4 ♕b4
Black is also dead in the water following 22...♕f5 23 ♗xb6 ♕xe4 24 ♖d1 h5 25 ♖d8+ ♔h7 26 ♕f7.

23 ♘g5 ♔h8 24 ♕f7 ♗d7 25 ♗xe6 ♖xd8 26 ♕g8+! ♖xg8 27 ♘f7# (1-0)
Hopefully this section will give you a feel for what's happening when we encounter cases of pawn-chains in other openings throughout this book.

Doubled Pawns and Related Pawn Captures

Understanding of doubled pawns is essential to playing openings and eventually mastering them. As above, I'll approach this subject with some standard examples and then try to introduce some more complicated ideas for you to chew over. Other structures will be discussed in conjunction with individual openings.

Doubled pawns are a recurring *motif* in the Nimzo-Indian Defence. After 1 d4 ♘f6 2 c4 e6 3 ♘c3 ♗b4, capturing the c3-knight produces doubled pawns, whose structure is such that the forward c-pawn is particularly vulnerable. Without getting into the jargon, you can see that a structure with pawns on c4, c3 and d3 is more secure than one with pawns on c4, c3 and d4. In the former case each pawn can be protected by another, whereas in the latter the c4-pawn is unsupported. Here's a game with several thematic ideas in a typical Nimzo-Indian:

Geller – Smyslov
USSR Ch (Moscow) 1949

1 d4 ♘f6 2 c4 e6 3 ♘c3 ♗b4 4 a3 ♗xc3+ 5 bxc3
White now has doubled pawns on c3 and c4. The forward pawn is the target; note that if White's d-pawn were on d3, his doubled pawns would be protected.
5...♘c6 6 f3
Having secured the advantage of the two bishops in compensation for his doubled pawns at c3 and c4, White wants to build a large centre and use his extra space to help in a kingside attack. The kingside is a particularly good target because Black's dark-squared bishop has been exchanged and can't guard vulnerable squares around the king.
6...b6 7 e4 ♗a6
Black is taking aim at White's weak c4-pawn.

8 ♗g5

And White begins to drift to the right.

8...h6 9 ♗h4 ♘a5

There are more examples of this structure in Volume 2.

10 ♕a4 ♕c8! 11 ♘h3 ♘h7?!

Better is 11...♕b7! 12 ♗d3 ♕c6! *(D)*.

By this means the c-pawn would have fallen, although Black's advantage might not be enough for a win after 13 ♕xc6 dxc6 14 e5 ♘d7 15 ♔f2 ♗xc4 16 ♗c2. Capturing the c4-pawn directly is one theme; what happens in the game is related.

12 ♗d3 0-0 13 e5 ♖e8 14 0-0 ♘f8!? 15 ♘f4!?

White should always maximize his kingside play in such positions and not worry much about a pawn or two on the queenside. Thus 15 f4! d5 16 f5 was called for, attacking the pawn-chain. Notice that White's attack benefits greatly from the lack of Black's dark-squared bishop, which was exchanged off on the fourth move.

15...d5!

Black may not win the c-pawn but he wins the light squares. This is often the result of fighting against doubled pawns: the squares they are on become more important than the pawns themselves. 15...g5? isn't worth it after 16 ♘h5 gxh4 17 ♘f6+.

16 cxd5 ♗xd3 17 ♘xd3 exd5 18 f4 ♘g6!

Smyslov anticipates the idea of ...♘e7-f5.

19 ♗g3 ♕f5!

Now Black begins a series of moves designed to conquer an entire colour-complex. This was discussed in Chapter 2.

20 ♘b4 c6! 21 ♖ae1

21 ♘xc6? ♕d7.

21...h5! 22 ♕c2 ♘e7 *(D)*

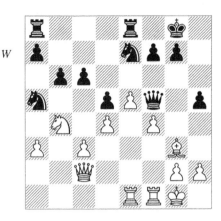

Summing up: every important light square is covered by Black, whose knight will be in a dominating position on c4, with another knight coming to f5. To make things worse for White, his dark-squared bishop is bad and his rooks are inactive. This is all the logical result of the opening, and of 15...d5 in particular. After many ups and downs, the game was eventually drawn, but Black has a winning position at this point.

Next, a classic game that illustrates typical pros and cons of doubled pawns.

Portisch – Fischer
Sousse IZ 1967

1 ♘f3 ♘f6 2 g3 g6 3 c4 ♗g7 4 d4 0-0 5 ♗g2 d6 6 ♘c3 ♘bd7 7 0-0 e5 8 e4 c6 9 h3 ♕b6 10 ♖e1

Oddly enough there's an important main line of this same variation that involves doubled pawns: 10 c5!? dxc5 11 dxe5 ♘e8 12 e6! fxe6 13 ♘g5 ♘e5 (13...♘c7!?) 14 f4 ♘f7 15 ♘xf7 ♗d4+ 16 ♔h2 ♖xf7 *(D)*.

This has arisen in several games. Black is left with doubled c-pawns (resulting from a capture away from the centre), as discussed below, and a masked isolated pawn to boot. Given his extra pawn and reasonable piece placement, however, the position is about equal.

10...♖e8 11 d5 ♘c5 12 ♖b1 a5

All conventional moves so far, except that Black's ...♖e8 leaves him a tempo down compared to some similar variations. Black normally plays ...♗d7 and ...cxd5 to cover a4. This

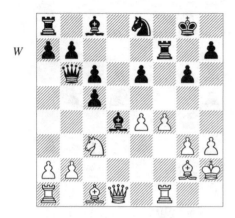

variation is generally another good illustration of how Black can play on the queenside in King's Indian Defence.

13 ♗e3 ♕c7!? 14 ♗xc5!?

The exchange on c5 to get doubled pawns can occur in many, many distinct positions of the King's Indian. White has to decide whether to give up his best bishop in order to cripple Black's pawn-structure. He usually declines the bargain. Here, however, he's a little ahead in time and goes for it.

14...dxc5 15 dxc6 bxc6 (D)

The first point is that 15...♕xc6 would give White a huge and favourable outpost on d5, one that might be reinforced by ♘d2-f1-e3.

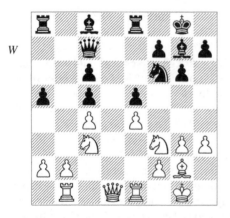

What are the main characteristics of the position? Black's doubled pawns are isolated, and what's more he has an isolated pawn on a5. We've already mentioned, however, that isolated a-pawns are usually not serious weaknesses until the endgame. What is typical about the doubled c-pawns is that they control very

important central squares, both the black outpost on d4 and most importantly White's d5, which is protected from intrusions. On the other hand, Black's dark-squared bishop has very little scope, so the advantage of two bishops is not yet a factor, and he has no pawn-breaks other than ...f5, which White can keep under control.

16 ♘a4

The forward doubled pawn is usually the more vulnerable one. Here White has no prospects of attacking it along an open file because of his own c4-pawn, but he can focus pieces on it in order to tie Black's pieces to its defence. When a player's doubled pawn can be protected by adjacent pawns then his pieces need not be diverted to defend it. That's why isolated doubled pawns are so much worse than connected ones, assuming that other factors aren't at work.

16...♗f8 17 ♕b3 ♘h5 18 ♕e3 ♕a7

Black's pieces are passive and now White could try to transfer his f3-knight to b3, but if necessary Black can bring his knight to e6 or d7. What Portisch does instead is quite clever.

19 h4!

This has the obvious idea of ♗h3, trying to exchange his bad bishop for Black's good one at c8. But White also sees that Black's best plan is the manoeuvre ...♘g7-e6-d4, which will leave his kingside less defended against the moves h5 and hxg6.

19...♘g7 20 ♔h2 f6 21 ♗h3 ♗xh3 22 ♔xh3 ♘e6 23 h5 (D)

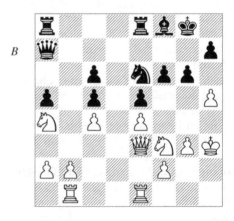

23...gxh5!?

Black takes on yet another set of isolated doubled pawns! And he gives up the valuable square f5. But Fischer realizes that he will be able to cause trouble down the g-file in conjunction with ...♘d4. Normally 23...♘d4 would solve all of Black's difficulties but the opening of the h-file would cause a few problems after 24 hxg6 hxg6 25 ♖h1.

24 ♖h1 ♖ad8 25 ♔g2 ♕g7 26 ♔f1

26 ♖xh5?? loses to 26...♘f4+.

26...♕g4 27 ♖h4 ♕g6 28 ♕e2 ♗h6 29 b3 ♖d7

29...♗g5 30 ♘xg5 fxg5 31 ♖xh5 ♖f8 was also suggested, as in the game. Black is doing fine in any case.

30 ♖d1 ♖xd1+ 31 ♕xd1 ♖d8 32 ♕e2 ♗g5 33 ♘xg5 fxg5 34 ♖xh5 ♖d2! 35 ♕g4!

35 ♕xd2 ♕xh5 threatens ...♘d4. White's knight has served a good function but now looks out of play.

35...h6 36 ♖h2 ♔g7 37 ♘c3 ♖d3 38 ♘d1!?

White is ready to take up an outpost by ♘e3-f5.

38...♕f7 39 ♔g2

But he never gets a chance. At this point 39 ♘e3?? loses to 39...♖xe3.

39...♕d7! 40 ♕f5 (D)

White decides to bail out. 40 ♘e3 ♖xe3 41 ♕f5! (not 41 fxe3?? ♘f4+ 42 ♔f3 ♕d1+) is another way to do so.

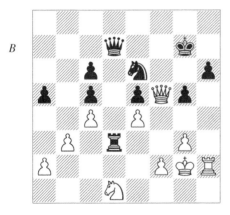

40...♖xd1 41 ♕xe5+ ♔g8?

Perhaps Fischer was trying to win, but this gives White a real attack. Black had a draw by 41...♔g6 42 ♕f5+ ♔g7 43 ♕e5+ with perpetual check.

42 ♖xh6 ♘g7 43 ♖g6?

An error in turn. Good winning chances were to be had by 43 ♕xc5, or by 43 ♕b8+ ♘e8 44

♖g6+ and ♖xg5 with a third pawn and play against Black's exposed king. The game ends with true equality.

43...g4! 44 ♖xg7+ ♕xg7 45 ♕e8+ ♔h7 46 ♕h5+ ♔g8 ½-½

The subject of doubled pawns is boundless but especially for the sake of opening investigation we can narrow our focus considerably and look at cases that significantly influence practical play. Specifically, doubled c-pawns arise more often than any other type and they determine the nature of the play in many of those games. For the sake of clarity I'll concentrate on them, with a brief look first at a particular central situation.

Doubled Centre Pawns

Doubled centre pawns arise much less often in the opening than doubled c-pawns. They are generally produced by exchanges of minor pieces on the third or fourth rank, and usually don't allow of the choice of recaptures that we saw above. Their effects on the position tend to be ambiguous.

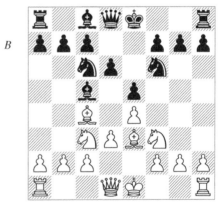

This is a position from Chapter 6 on the Two Knights Defence; similar situations can arise from a number of 1 e4 e5 openings. White plays ♗e3 to challenge the enemy bishop on c5 (likewise with colours reversed, of course). Capturing that bishop on e3 will help White to gain central control (in particular of d4, which was a potential support-point for Black's knight), and he will have the open f-file to work with. But the resulting centre e3/e4/d3 is generally not mobile. What does that mean? After the exchange on e3, White's pawns are initially well-protected; it's usually difficult to get at the single weakness at e3. However, if White plays d4 thereafter, the forward e-pawn will be unprotected by another pawn and therefore vulnerable, just as the c4-pawn was in the Nimzo-Indian example above. And if the d-pawn advances further to d5, the e-pawn may not be able to move for the rest of the game. Both sides have to weigh whether one advantage or the other is more important. If Black isn't going to exchange on e3, one of his options is to leave the bishop where it is on c5. Normally the doubled pawns that Black would get if White·played ♗xc5 wouldn't be harmful (see the discussion of c-pawns below); but that's not always true. The same idea comes up in the Ruy Lopez after 1 e4 e5 2 ♘f3 ♘c6 3 ♗b5 a6 4 ♗a4 ♘f6 5 0-0 ♗e7 6 ♖e1 b5 7 ♗b3 d6 8 c3 ♗e6, as well as in some queen's pawn variations; e.g., 1 d4 d5 2 ♘f3 e6 3 ♗f4 ♘f6 4 e3 ♘bd7 5 ♗e2 ♗d6 *(D)*.

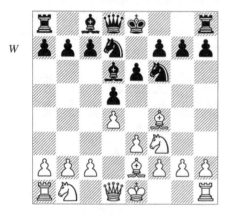

Again the choice arises of whether White should:

a) exchange bishops on d6, allowing ...cxd6 if Black wants to;

b) leave his bishop on f4, inviting ...♗xf4; or

c) retreat to g3.

In master play all three solutions are played. This position is simplified but shows the basic situation that arises in many variations.

Isolated doubled e- and d-pawns are rare when the queens are off the board; nevertheless, an opening line such as 1 e4 d6 2 d4 ♘f6 3 ♘c3 e5 4 dxe5 dxe5 5 ♕xd8+ ♔xd8 6 ♗c4

♗e6!? 7 ♗xe6 fxe6 shows that it's possible to adopt such pawns in that situation. The resulting position is one that current theory indicates is equal. See Chapter 7 on the Philidor Defence, in particular the discussion of early move-orders.

It bears repeating that the exchange of queens by no means betokens entrance into an endgame, because there can be many active pieces remaining on the board producing astonishingly complex positions. The phrase 'queenless middlegame' doesn't appear often enough in chess discussion, written or otherwise. It describes an extremely large set of situations, often lasting for the bulk of the game. The conditions for a decisive result are still there, as shown by literally thousands of games. But for our purposes it's important to note that a lot of queen exchanges such as the one above result in queenless *openings*! Although the boundaries of the queenless opening, middlegame and ending are to some extent a matter of judgement, variations in which the queens have been exchanged within the first 10 moves are routinely analysed by players and theoreticians for another 10 moves, and clearly belong to the territory of the opening proper.

Finally, we run across 5th-rank doubled pawns in just a few openings; for example, 1 c4 c5 2 ♘c3 ♘c6 3 g3 g6 4 ♗g2 ♗g7 5 d3 ♘f6 6 e4 0-0 7 ♘ge2 d6 8 0-0 ♘d4 9 ♘xd4 cxd4 10 ♘e2 *(D)*.

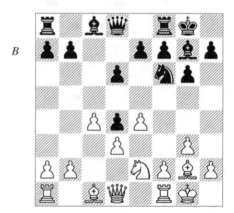

Keene referred to the doubled pawn on d4 as a 'dead point', so called because it has little or no dynamic potential. It makes Black's central play difficult because White will be ready to respond to ...e6 and ...d5 by cxd5 and e5 (especially if the move f4 has been played), whereas Black's move ...e5 would restrict his own bishop and isn't very helpful with respect to mobility. The opponent (in this case White) can play 'around' the pawn by f4, intending f5 and g4, and/or by b4. This is a theme worth remembering as it arises fairly frequently in openings such as the Closed Sicilian, King's Indian and English Opening. It tends to occur in the move sequence above, with a knight on d4 (from White's point of view) being captured by a knight on e2 or f3. In many cases there would be a bishop on e3 in the above case, say, by 8...♘d7 9 ♗e3 ♘d4 *(D)*.

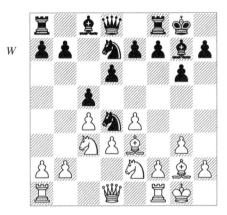

In this instance White's knight can't capture on d4 because of the fork, and most players will avoid giving away their good bishop by ♗xd4, dead spot or not. So you will commonly see players wait until a bishop comes to e3 before occupying the outpost with their knight. It also frequently happens that when a bishop arrives at e3, White is just ready to play d4, so Black's knight jump has a double purpose. Obviously all of this is true with colours reversed as well.

Naturally there are no absolutes and the dead-point structure isn't always bad, but one should be careful that there are compensating factors before adopting it.

Doubled c-Pawns

Now let's move on to doubled c-pawns, which are far more common than central ones. The most frequent exchange in the opening that

leads to doubled pawns is when a knight on c3 or c6 is captured by a knight or bishop. Then a basic decision often presents itself: whether one wants to recapture with a b-pawn ('strengthening' the centre) or with the d-pawn, opening lines for development. There are plenty of situations in which there is no choice; for instance, 1 d4 ♘f6 2 c4 e6 3 ♘c3 ♗b4 4 a3 ♗xc3+ 5 bxc3 or 1 e4 e6 2 d4 d5 3 ♘c3 ♗b4 4 e5 c5 5 a3 ♗xc3+ 6 bxc3, both cases where the precedence of structure is conspicuous. In neither case does either player have many pieces developed, but by their pawn moves both sides have established a structure that will serve and determine their development.

In both of these cases the players were forced to capture 'towards the centre', the advice given to students everywhere. But it's more revealing to look first at recaptures requiring a decision.

Ruy Lopez Exchange Variation

1 e4 e5 2 ♘f3 ♘c6 3 ♗b5 a6 4 ♗xc6 *(D)*.

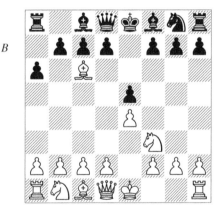

a) One answer is 4...bxc6, but this is rarely chosen. This case has more to do with specifics than with general principles, but that in and of itself adds interest. The usual lines go:

a1) 5 0-0 d6 6 d4 f6 7 ♘c3, when White controls the centre and has a simple lead in development (three pieces to none). Black's f8-bishop can't take part in the action, and his pieces are cramped, not what you want when you have the bishop-pair.

a2) 5 ♘c3 d6 6 d4 exd4 (6...f6 7 ♗e3 threatens 8 dxe5 fxe5 9 ♘xe5!, and otherwise 8 ♕d2 and 0-0-0 will be pretty unpleasant for Black) 7 ♕xd4 with a position much as in the Philidor Defence, but a tempo up for White due to 3...a6. It's a bad sign if Black has to surrender the centre in a centre-strengthening variation!

b) 4...dxc6 is well-known and doesn't require special analysis. What counts is that the recapture away from the centre affords wide-open play for the bishops.

b1) The line 5 d4 exd4 6 ♕xd4 ♕xd4 7 ♘xd4 ♗d7 and ...0-0-0 illustrates Black's ideas. He will gladly play with a pawn-structure such as ...c5 and ...b6.

b2) The generally-approved move 5 0-0 has other attributes, but again the fact that a variation such as 5...♗g4 6 h3 h5 7 d3 ♕f6 even exists shows that Black has dynamic counterplay. In fact, White often plays c3 and d4 versus the ...c5/...e5 structure, allowing the doubled pawns to be liquidated and therefore indicating that they weren't the sole reason for playing 4 ♗xc6. A case in point: 8 ♘bd2 ♘e7 9 ♘c4 ♗xf3 10 ♕xf3 ♕xf3 11 gxf3 ♘g6 12 ♗e3 ♗d6 13 ♖fd1 f6 14 ♔f1 c5 15 c3 ♔f7 16 d4! cxd4 17 cxd4 ♖hd8?! (17...exd4) 18 ♖ac1 ♗e7 19 d5 with an advantage for White, Glek-Winants, 2nd Bundesliga 1997/8.

The Berlin Variation with 3...♘f6 4 0-0 ♘xe4 5 d4 ♘d6 6 ♗xc6 dxc6 7 dxe5 ♘f5 8 ♕xd8+ ♔xd8 also shows that Black is willing to play this pawn-structure. For more on this subject see Chapter 8 on the Ruy Lopez.

Overall, we can say that in this particular opening, Black's choice of developing and activating his bishops by capturing away from the centre leads to better positions than if he decides upon a more compact pawn-structure by capturing towards the centre.

Rossolimo Variation of the Sicilian Defence

This positionally instructive opening is defined by 1 e4 c5 2 ♘f3 ♘c6 3 ♗b5, and has numerous lines with ♗xc6. I'll pick a few.

a) 3...g6 and then:

a1) 4 ♗xc6 and now:

a11) 4...bxc6 5 0-0 ♗g7 6 ♖e1 gives another lead in development which particularly shows up after 6...♘f6 7 e5 ♘d5 8 c4 ♘c7 9 d4! cxd4 10 ♕xd4 with space and the simple idea ♕h4 and ♗h6. Thus 6...♘h6 with the idea ...f6 is

preferred by top masters, when the play seems to favour White slightly but Black has squares for his pieces and the extra centre pawn gives him a certain leeway, so in the hands of a knowledgeable player 4...bxc6 isn't bad. Nevertheless, we can't say that it's fully satisfactory.

a12) Black can equalize by capturing away from the centre: 4...dxc6 5 d3 ♗g7 and 6 0-0 ♘f6 or 6 h3 e5 works out well for him. White is not able to achieve an effective d4 or e5, so Black gets easy development for his pieces.

a2) 4 0-0 ♗g7 5 ♖e1 e5 6 ♗xc6 and then:

a21) 6...bxc6?! 7 c3 ♘e7 8 d4 cxd4 9 cxd4 exd4 10 ♘xd4 0-0 11 ♘c3 (D) is notoriously better for White.

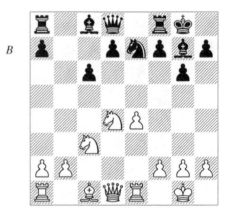

Even in the reversed position from the English Opening, Black usually gets the better of this position with one less move to use. The problem is that 11...d5? gives White too much pressure after 12 exd5 cxd5 13 ♗g5. But otherwise Black's dark squares are weak and 11...d6 presents a target down the d-file. Notice that this Sicilian Rossolimo is similar to the Exchange Ruy Lopez that we just looked at, in that both variations have lines in which the pawn-break d4 is paradoxically strong even though it straightens out the opponent's pawns.

a22) By contrast, 6...dxc6 7 d3 ♕e7 has traditionally been considered equal with careful play. The d-file is handy for Black and White's move d4, a poor one, would only open up the game for Black's bishops.

b) 3...e6 4 ♗xc6 and here:

b1) 4...bxc6 5 0-0 ♘e7 6 ♖e1 (these are hardly forced moves, just illustrations of the play) 6...♘g6 7 c3 ♗e7 8 d4 0-0 9 ♘bd2 cxd4 10 cxd4 f5! and Black has freed all of his pieces.

b2) 4...dxc6 is inferior because White will get a pawn to e5 that cramps Black's game; e.g., 5 0-0 ♕c7 6 e5 and moves such as b3, ♗b2, d3 and ♘d2-c4 can follow. If he had an extra centre pawn (as he does after 4...bxc6), Black could play ...f6 and break up White's centre, but in this case exf6 would expose a weak pawn on e6.

In making a decision how to recapture in the Rossolimo Variation, a major consideration is whether Black can achieve ...e5 after taking with the d-pawn. If so, White has no particular way to gain space, because now c3 followed by d4 merely opens the centre for Black's bishops. But if Black captures with the b-pawn he has to watch out that an early d4 doesn't leave him too far behind in development (he has no open d-file to challenge a white piece on d4). In particular, the variations in which Black fianchettoes his bishop can put his development behind schedule.

Petroff Defence

1 e4 e5 2 ♘f3 ♘f6 3 ♘xe5 d6 4 ♘f3 ♘xe4 5 ♘c3 (this move is fashionable at the moment, but it is not the only example of doubled pawns in the Petroff: 5 c4!? is an interesting move whose very purpose is 6 ♘c3 ♘xc3 7 dxc3!, aiming for active development) 5...♘xc3 6 dxc3 (D).

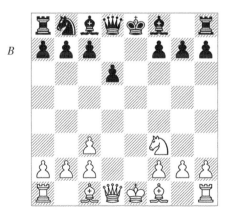

Recapturing with the d-pawn is the very point of 5 ♘c3, to get White's pieces out quickly with additional pressure down the open d-file if 0-0-0

follows. Having pawns on c2 and c3 is easy for White to handle, just as ...dxc6 was in the Ruy Lopez. The difference is that in this Petroff line both sides have two bishops, so it's unlikely that White has anything special in the way of a permanent advantage. Nevertheless, taking with the d-pawn is more promising than 6 bxc3, which would leave White with a restricted centre in which one of his bishops wouldn't be able to assume an active role.

Scotch Game

In the Scotch Game with 1 e4 e5 2 ♘f3 ♘c6 3 d4 exd4 4 ♘xd4 ♘f6 5 ♘xc6, 5...bxc6 is the almost automatic recapture. This is still an unresolved line, but Black's queenside structure doesn't hurt him in most lines. Two examples with this type of structure:

Rublevsky – Bologan
Dortmund 2004

1 e4 e5 2 ♘f3 ♘c6 3 d4 exd4 4 ♘xd4 ♗c5 5 ♘xc6 ♕f6 6 ♕d2 bxc6 7 ♘c3 ♘e7 8 ♘a4 ♗b6 9 ♗d3 0-0 10 0-0 d6 11 ♕e2 ♘g6 12 ♘xb6 axb6 (D)

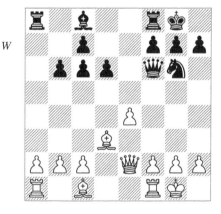

Thus White has given Black a compact structure on the queenside but gained the bishop-pair and a mobile kingside majority as well. But Black has some advantages too. His bishop is good and he has two useful files for his rooks. Right off, ...♘f4 is a positional threat.

13 f4 ♕d4+!

13...♖e8 is also reasonable.

14 ♔h1 f5!

Blockade.

15 ℤd1! ♕f6 16 exf5 ♗xf5 17 ♗xf5 ♕xf5 *(D)*

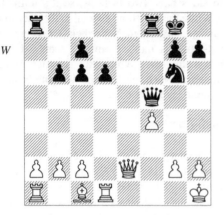

18 ♕c4+

Otherwise, White's bad bishop and weak squares down the e-file will give him a serious disadvantage.

18...ℤf7!?

Alternatively, 18...♕f7 19 ♕xc6 ℤae8! would threaten ...ℤe2, ...♘xf4, etc. The opening has been a success for Black.

19 ♕xc6 ℤa5! 20 ♕e8+ ℤf8 21 ♕e2 ♘xf4!? 22 ♗xf4 ♕xf4 23 ℤf1 ℤe5! ½-½

After 24 ♕d3, 24...♕e4! gets Black's rook to the 7th rank in an ending.

Morozevich – Bezgodov
Russia Cup (Tomsk) 1998

1 e4 e5 2 ♘f3 ♘c6 3 d4 exd4 4 ♘xd4 ♘f6

Another set of choices confronts Black in the main-line variation 4...♗c5 5 ♘xc6 ♕f6! 6 ♕d2 dxc6 7 ♘c3 ♘e7 8 ♕f4. Without getting too theoretical, it's relevant to observe that Black wants to take on another set of doubled pawns after 8...♘g6!? 9 ♕xf6 gxf6, as in Kasparov-Topalov, Las Palmas 1997. How to assess this kind of thing? It takes some experience but also a little calculation. Black has a temporary lead in development and if he could castle queenside and/or exchange off his f-pawn by ...f5, he'd leave White having to defend squares such as c2 and f2. Thus slow moves from White are not dangerous. But 10 ♗d3 isn't much of a solution because it runs into 10...♘h4 11 ♔f1 (11 0-0? ℤg8 12 g3 ♗h3 13 ℤd1 ♘f3+ 14 ♔h1 ♗xf2)

11...ℤg8 12 g3 ♗h3+, which is at least equal. So Kasparov played 10 ♗d2 ℤg8 (10...f5!?) 11 ♘a4 ♗d6 12 0-0-0 ♗e6 13 ♘c3 0-0-0 (it's hard for White to develop) 14 g3! ♗g4 15 ♗e2 ♘e5 16 ♗f4 (16 f4 ♗xe2 17 ♘xe2 ♘g4 18 ℤdf1 ♗c5, targeting weaknesses, is equal) 16...♗h3 (16...♗xe2 17 ♘xe2 ♗c5 with equality) 17 ♗h5 ♗c5 18 ℤxd8+ ℤxd8 19 ♘d1 ♗g2 20 ℤe1 and the game was drawn in short order.

5 ♘xc6 bxc6 6 e5 ♘e4!?

6...♘d5 is the main continuation.

7 ♘d2 ♘c5 8 ♗e2 ♗e7 9 0-0 0-0 10 ♘b3 ♘xb3?! 11 axb3 *(D)*

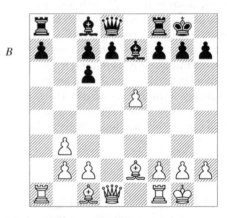

White has foreseen something analogous to the Rossolimo Variation above. Black can't move his d-pawn without one problem or another. White's queenside complex actually protects him from intrusions on the b-file, and his possession of the a-file is a bonus.

11...d5 12 exd6 ♗xd6?

Notice that this is an example of the vanishing centre! Since Black has no attack he has no real compensation for the weak c-pawns. 12...cxd6 must be a little better. On the other hand, Black's centre pawns would still be weak and White could probe the kingside. There might follow 13 ♗d3!? (or 13 ♗f3) 13...d5 14 ℤe1 ♗d6 15 ♕h5 and now 15...f5!? 16 ♗g5 or 15...g6 16 ♕h6. Black's kingside is causing him serious problems. ℤa4-h4 and ♗d2-c3 are productive ideas.

13 ℤa4! *(D)*

13...♗f5 14 ♗d3

This time the theory that simplification helps White makes sense. That's one less piece for Black to defend pawns with.

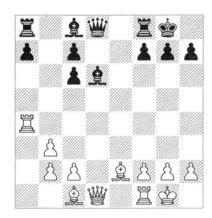

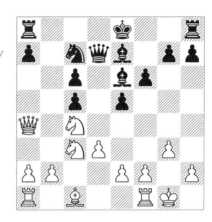

14...♗xd3 15 ♕xd3 ♕f6 16 g3 ♖fe8 17 ♔g2 ♗c5 18 ♖f4 ♕e6 19 ♖d1 ♗d6

Versus ♕d7.

20 ♖c4 c5

Now Black won't be able to defend the c- and a-pawns, especially the former.

21 ♕f3 ♖ab8 22 ♗d2 f6 23 ♖a1 ♖bd8 24 ♗e3 ♕e5 25 ♖c3 ♖a8 26 ♖a5

There goes the c-pawn.

26...♕e4 27 ♗xc5 ♕xf3+ 28 ♔xf3 ♗e5 29 ♖e3 ♗xb2 30 ♖xa7 ♖xe3+ 31 ♔xe3 ♖xa7 32 ♗xa7 ♔f7 33 ♔d3 1-0

Finally, giving up a fianchettoed bishop on g7 for a knight on c3 (or one on g2 for a knight on c6) is a traditional technique that crops up in many variations. The question is always whether the bishop-pair compensates for the doubled c-pawns. By themselves the bishops usually aren't sufficient to offset the pawns, but the capture has also seriously weakened squares on the opponent's kingside. Getting a feel for this trade-off is more a matter of experience, so here's a small selection of a few very lightly annotated games. The first is a win by White in a variation that's arisen hundreds of times:

Korchnoi – H. Böhm
Wijk aan Zee 1980

1 c4 c5 2 ♘c3 ♘f6 3 g3 d5 4 cxd5 ♘xd5 5 ♗g2 ♘c7 6 ♘f3 ♘c6 7 0-0 e5 8 d3 ♗e7 9 ♘d2 ♗e6

Later, 9...♗d7 became the main line, to avoid the doubled pawns:

10 ♗xc6+ bxc6 11 ♕a4 ♕d7 12 ♘c4 f6 *(D)*

Black has battened down the hatches but White has many modes of attack on the weakened c-pawns in these sorts of positions, including ♗e3, ♖ac1, ♘e4, ♕a5 and some cases even b3 and ♗a3.

13 ♘e4 ♗h3 14 ♖d1 0-0 15 ♘a5 ♘b5

The only defence for the c-pawn but the knight also heads for d4, a typical defence.

16 ♗e3 ♘d4 17 ♗xd4 cxd4 18 ♘xc6

As was the case with doubled pawns in the Nimzo-Indian, it's very common to see the one in front be exchanged and the one behind fall.

18...♔h8 19 ♖ac1 ♖fc8 20 ♕a6 ♗f8 21 b4 ♖c7 22 b5 ♖ac8 23 f3 h5 24 ♖c2 ♕d5 25 ♖dc1 ♗d7 26 ♘e7 ♖xc2 27 ♖xc2 ♗xe7 28 ♖xc8+ ♗xc8 29 ♕xc8+ ♔h7 30 ♕e8

White is winning a second pawn, after which the rest was easy for him.

Hamann – Geller
Copenhagen 1960

1 d4 ♘f6 2 c4 g6 3 ♘c3 ♗g7 4 e4 0-0 5 ♗e2 d6 6 ♘f3 ♗g4 7 0-0 ♘fd7 8 ♗e3 ♘c6 9 d5 ♗xf3 10 ♗xf3

10 gxf3!? is definitely worth thinking about. It keeps more queenside options open, and White's king is perfectly safe.

10...♘a5 11 ♕a4

White could also try keeping the position open for the bishops by 11 ♗e2 ♗xc3 12 bxc3 e5!? 13 f4 (13 dxe6 fxe6 14 f4).

11...♗xc3!? 12 bxc3 b6 13 ♗e2 e5 14 g3

14 dxe6 might be better. The rest of the game gets one-sided as the knights dominate the bishops.

14...♘c5 15 ♕c2 ♕d7 16 ♗h6 ♖fe8 17 a4 f6 18 ♔g2 ♖e7 19 h4 ♖ae8 20 ♗e3 ♘ab7 21 h5 g5

Geller closes the kingside. It's hard to believe that he can win on the queenside alone.

22 g4 ♖c8 23 f3 ♘a5 24 ♖fb1 ♘cb7 25 ♖b4 c6 *(D)*

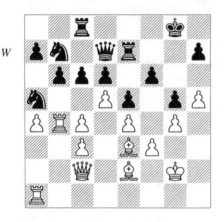

A key concept. In many Nimzo-Indians, this pawn is on c5 and in spite of Black's efforts there is no way to increase the pressure on the doubled pawns. Black should always think about keeping ...c6 in reserve.

26 ♗d2 ♕d8 27 ♕a2 ♖ec7 28 ♖d1 ♔g7 29 ♔g3 cxd5

There it is, the attack on the back pawn that we've talked about. But how can Black break down the defensive structure?

30 cxd5 ♖c5 31 ♖db1 ♖8c7

Black probably intends ...♕c8 before anything else, with the same ideas as in the game; but as events have it he doesn't have to wait.

32 ♖b5? ♖xc3! 33 ♗xc3 ♖xc3 *(D)*

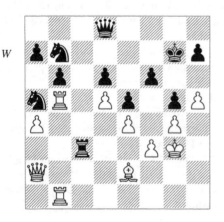

After this exchange sacrifice things are clear. There is no dark-squared bishop remaining to exchange one of Black's mighty knights, Black has control of the c-file, and White's light-squared bishop is awful.

34 ♕d2 ♕c7 35 h6+ ♔f7 36 ♖5b4 ♘c5 37 ♗b5 ♘cb3 38 ♕h2 ♔f8 39 ♕h5 ♕c8 40 ♖f1 a6 41 ♗e2 ♕c5 42 ♖h1 ♘c1 43 ♖h2 ♕e3 44 ♗d1 ♕f4+ 45 ♔f2 ♘d3+ 46 ♔g2 ♕c1 0-1

The coming ...♘f4 is about as strong a knight move as you'll see.

Remember, though, that the fianchettoed bishop is missing. There have been numerous games where the opponent made that count. Here's one example that almost explains itself:

Anikaev – A. Petrosian
Kiev 1973

1 c4 ♘f6 2 ♘c3 c5 3 g3 d5 4 cxd5 ♘xd5 5 ♗g2 ♘c7 6 d3 e5 7 ♕b3 ♘c6 8 ♗xc6+ bxc6 9 ♘f3 f6 10 ♕a4 ♗d7 11 0-0 ♘e6 12 ♘e4 ♕b6 13 ♘fd2 ♕b5 14 ♕d1 ♗e7 15 ♘c4 0-0 16 b3 ♕b8! 17 ♗a3?! f5 18 ♘c3 ♖f6 19 ♖c1 ♖h6 20 ♘a4 f4 21 e3?

It's surprisingly difficult for White to defend. Perhaps 21 ♗b2 ♕f8 22 e4!? is a good idea, to hit the weak e5-pawn and at the same time prevent ...♕f5.

21...♕f8! *(D)*

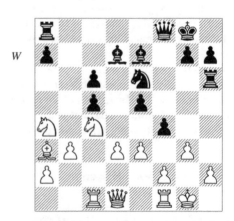

22 f3

It's too late for 22 ♘xe5 ♕f5.

22...fxg3 23 hxg3 ♕f5 24 ♖c2?! ♕h3 25 ♖g2 ♘g5 26 ♕e2 e4! 27 dxe4 ♘xe4 28 fxe4 ♗g4 29 ♖h2 ♗xe2 30 ♖xh3 ♖xh3 31 ♖f4

♗xc4 32 bxc4 ♖xg3+ 33 ♔f2 ♖h3 34 ♗xc5 ♗xc5 35 ♘xc5 ♖f8 36 e5 g5 37 ♖xf8+ ♔xf8 38 ♘e6+ ♔e7 39 ♘xg5 ♖h2+ 40 ♔f3 ♖xa2 41 ♘xh7 a5 0-1

It's worth adding that in the Accelerated Fianchetto Sicilian the capture ...♗xc3 often comes without White having made a move like c4. The best example of this situation occurs after 1 e4 c5 2 ♘f3 ♘c6 3 d4 cxd4 4 ♘xd4 g6 5 ♘c3 ♗g7 6 ♘b3 ♗xc3+ 7 bxc3, a line which usually continues 7...♘f6 8 ♗d3, and now Black has the interesting choice between 8...d6, intending to blockade the c-pawns, and 8...d5 9 exd5 ♕xd5, when Black develops so quickly that White's pieces tend to be tied down. The usual considerations with respect to Black's dark squares on the kingside apply in principle, but there is little chance that they will become a real factor.

If you want to continue investigating the issue of captures away from and towards the centre, there will be instances of both in the openings that you play. The more that you study these and get to experience them, the better a player you'll be in the widest sense.

Hanging Pawns

The term 'hanging pawns' is habitually used to refer to black pawns on c5 and d5 separated from Black's other pawns by at least a file on both sides. The hanging pawns are usually pitted against a white pawn on e3 and open d- and c-files. Of course the same applies with colours reversed.

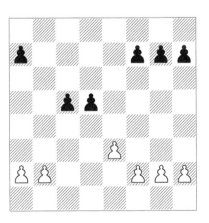

This structure generally arises from two pawn exchanges on c5 and d5, but it can also come about when an isolated pawn is transformed by a piece exchange on c6.

Like 'isolated pawns', the term 'hanging pawns' is defined more broadly, but it doesn't seem to extend beyond this single case when actually being discussed. That is understandable, because so few analogous structures regularly arise, at least in the opening. You could call pawns on e4 and d4 'hanging' under certain circumstances, but that's not conventionally done.

Returning to the basic position, Black's hanging pawns have advantages and disadvantages. Much as is the case with an isolated d-pawn, Black has the persistent possibility of breaking the position up by ...d4, thus extending the range of his pieces, initiating favourable tactics, and/or creating a powerful passed pawn. The hanging pawns also cover key central squares and give Black's pieces somewhat more manoeuvring room than White's. Finally, the e- and b-files can be used to create dynamic chances.

From White's point of view there are many promising ways to attack this structure. Most of them begin by restricting the advance of the d-pawn. White has a pawn, a knight (sometimes two), and a rook or two on an open file to achieve this, with a bishop on b2 for good effect. Once the pawn is 'fixed', White can do one of several things:

a) Attack it with his pieces; e.g., a bishop on g2, knight on c3 and/or f4, and rook(s) on an open file. The queen and rooks are particularly effective attackers of hanging pawns.

b) Advance a pawn to b4 or e4 to force a desirable change in pawn-structure. If White's advancing pawn either captures Black's or vice-versa, an isolated pawn remains in Black's camp. Or, if one of Black's pawns advances, it creates a juicy outpost for White to the side of it. For example: if White attacks with e4 and Black responds with ...d4, then the c4-square is available for a piece.

c) Exchange pieces and simplify the position; as is the case with an isolated queen's pawn, this reduces the pawns' dynamic possibilities and makes them easier to put under pressure.

In the following game White strives to fix the hanging pawns and Black to use them dynamically.

Seirawan – Short
Montpellier Ct 1985

1 d4 ♘f6 2 c4 e6 3 ♘f3 b6 4 ♘c3 ♗b7 5 ♗g5 h6 6 ♗h4 ♗e7 7 ♕c2 c5 8 dxc5 bxc5 9 e3 0-0 10 ♗e2 d6 (D)

This pawn-structure is fine, as has been demonstrated in many games. Black ultimately plays ...d5, which he could also do immediately; e.g., 10...d5 11 cxd5 exd5 12 ♖d1 ♘bd7 followed by ...♕b6 (or ...a6 first).

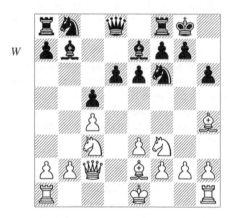

11 0-0 ♘h5!?

Black gets rid of White's most dangerous bishop, the one that could attack him from g3 or capture on f6 at the right moment. This takes an extra move (the knight will return to f6 while Black gets ...♕e7 in) but he seems to have the time to get away with it.

12 ♗xe7 ♕xe7 13 ♖ad1 ♘f6 14 ♖d2 ♘c6 15 ♖fd1 ♖fd8

White has a little space and d-file pressure, but the d6-pawn is typically safe and he has no particular targets of attack.

16 h3 ♖d7 17 a3 ♖ad8

17...♖b8 is the other natural move, to take advantage of the open file and potentially probe the holes left by a3.

18 ♕a4 d5!?

A huge decision, changing the character of the game, although not necessarily to Black's detriment. Preventing b4 by 18...a5 looks equal.

19 cxd5 exd5 (D)

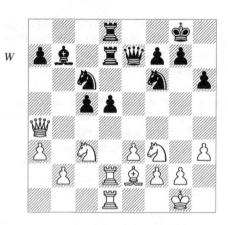

A standard picture of the hanging pawn duo c5/d5.

20 ♗b5 ♖c7 21 ♕f4

Short may have been hoping for 21 ♘xd5 ♖xd5 22 ♖xd5 ♘xd5 23 ♖xd5 ♘d4!, when Black is at least equal.

21...♘a5 22 ♕a4 ♘c6 23 ♗e2 ♖cd7 24 ♕f4 a6!?

24...♘a5 25 ♘e5 ♖d6 is probably OK as well; and 24...a5 would put the idea of b4 to rest for a while.

25 ♗f1 ♕f8

Unfortunately, Black has no ...d4 break and there isn't much positive to do.

26 g3!? ♕e7 (D)

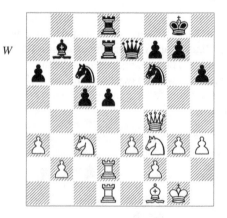

27 ♗g2

White's reorganization is complete. The d5-pawn holds firm, however.

27...♕e6 28 ♔h2

The danger lurking in the background is shown by 28 ♕a4?! ♔h8 29 b4? d4!.

28...♘a5?

Black, trying to win, disturbs the balance and permits simplification. After that, White forces serious positional concessions from Black's position.

29 ♘e5 ♖d6 30 ♕a4! ♕xe5 31 ♕xa5 ♖c8 32 ♘a4! ♖dc6 33 ♖c2 ♕e7 34 ♖dc1 c4 *(D)*

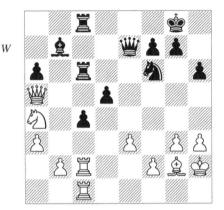

An almost decisive concession. Sometimes this advance is a reasonable trade-off because White's vulnerable pawn on b2 is fixed. But here Black can't even begin to mount an attack on that pawn, and his b7-bishop is too passive to make room for any dynamic compensation. Compare this position from O.Bernstein-Capablanca, Moscow 1914:

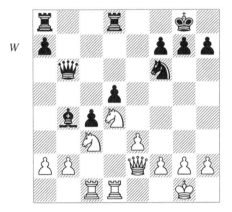

In the Capablanca game Black has full equality because the b-file and b-pawn are just as much a worry to White as the d-pawn and d-file are to Black. The biggest difference is that Black has an active good bishop versus the very bad one in Seirawan-Short. This well-known game (because of its cute finish) continued 18

b3!? ♖ac8 19 bxc4 dxc4 20 ♖c2 ♗xc3 21 ♖xc3 ♘d5! (it turns out that the pawn is not weak; at this point 22 ♖xc4? loses to 22...♘c3) 22 ♖c2 c3 23 ♖dc1 ♖c5 24 ♘b3 ♖c6 25 ♘d4 ♖c7! 26 ♘b5 ♖c5 27 ♘xc3?? ♘xc3 28 ♖xc3 ♖xc3 29 ♖xc3 ♕b2! 0-1.

35 ♖d1

Once again all pieces are to be aimed at d5. White still has to win the overprotected pawn on that square or break through in some other fashion, no easy task.

35...♖d8 36 ♖cd2

This attacks d5; in one more move, every piece will be trained upon it.

36...♖cd6?!

36...♖cc8 keeps the possibility of lateral defence by ...♖c5 alive. The d-pawn is tough to corral, but ultimately the threat of a break by e4 will overload Black; for example, 37 ♔g1 (37 ♘c3 ♖c5!) 37...♘e4 38 ♖d4! ♘c5 39 ♘xc5 ♖xc5 40 ♕b4 a5 41 ♕c3 f5 42 b3! cxb3 43 ♕xb3 and Black is reduced to total passivity.

37 ♘c3 ♕e6 38 ♖d4 ♖6d7 39 ♖1d2 g6 40 ♘a4

Back to c5!

40...♕e7 41 ♘c5 ♖c7 42 ♘xb7

A typical exchange of a horrible piece for a good one in order to eliminate the best defender.

42...♖xb7 43 ♗xd5 ♖xd5 44 ♖xd5 ♘xd5 45 ♕xd5

and wins.

Here's the flip side:

Korchnoi – Karpov
Merano Wch (1) 1981

1 c4 e6 2 ♘c3 d5 3 d4 ♗e7 4 ♘f3 ♘f6 5 ♗g5 h6 6 ♗h4 0-0 7 e3 b6 8 ♖c1 ♗b7 9 ♗e2 ♘bd7 10 cxd5 exd5 11 0-0 c5 12 dxc5 bxc5 *(D)*

13 ♕c2 ♖c8

Obviously ...d4 is on Karpov's mind, in order to exploit White's queen's position.

14 ♖fd1 ♕b6

This is a perfect spot for the queen. It supports ...d4, will attack the b-pawn if ...c4 is needed, and, not least, Black's rooks are connected.

15 ♕b1 ♖fd8 16 ♖c2

Korchnoi would like to double rooks on the d-file, as in Seirawan-Short.

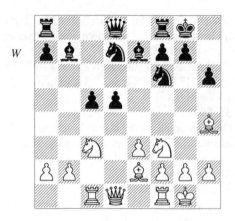

16...♕e6! 17 ♗g3

But now 17 ♖cd2? fails to 17...♘e4! 18 ♘xe4 dxe4 19 ♗xe7 exf3 20 ♗xd8 fxe2 21 ♖xd7 ♕g4! 22 ♖1d5 (the only move) 22...♗xd5 23 ♖xd5 ♕b4 and wins. This gives Black just enough time to rid himself of White's bishop.

17...♘h5 18 ♖cd2 ♘xg3 19 hxg3 ♘f6 20 ♕c2 g6 21 ♕a4

White's pieces begin to assume more active posts.

21...a6 22 ♗d3 ♔g7 23 ♗b1 ♕b6! *(D)*

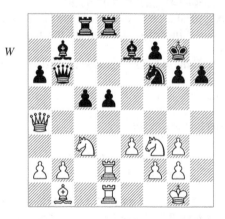

24 a3?

White is trying to avoid ...♕b4, but he underestimates the strength of Black's next move:

24...d4!

Everything depends upon whether Black can get away with this advance.

25 ♘e2

A sad retreat. The idea of 24...d4 is 25 exd4 ♗c6! 26 ♕c2 (26 ♕c4 ♗xf3 27 gxf3 cxd4) 26...♗xf3! 27 gxf3 cxd4 28 ♘a4 ♕b5! and the knight falls.

25...dxe3 26 fxe3

White's pawn-structure is shattered, although simplification would still leave him with some chances. So Karpov takes aim immediately.

26...c4! 27 ♘ed4 ♕c7 28 ♘h4

Hoping for 28...♕xg3?? 29 ♘hf5+.

28...♕e5 29 ♔h1 ♔g8!

There are always issues of accuracy. Karpov avoids 29...♘h5? 30 ♘hf5+ gxf5 31 ♘xf5+ with some play. Now Black wins with ease.

30 ♘df3 ♕xg3 31 ♖xd8+ ♗xd8 32 ♕b4 ♗e4 33 ♗xe4 ♘xe4 34 ♖d4 ♘f2+ 35 ♔g1 ♘d3 36 ♕b7 ♖b8 37 ♕d7 ♗c7 38 ♔h1 ♖xb2 39 ♖xd3 cxd3 40 ♕xd3 ♕d6! 41 ♕e4 ♕d1+ 42 ♘g1 ♕d6 43 ♘hf3 ♖b5 0-1

Majorities and Minorities

The term 'pawn-majority' refers to one player having more pawns than his opponent in a particular sector of the board, that sector being defined by a number of adjacent files. Normally, we only talk about a majority when the pawns in question are connected, i.e. there is no empty file between them. Putting that into a real-world context, here is a Grünfeld Defence in which Black has a queenside majority (2 to 1, henceforth '2:1'), White has a central majority (2:1), and the pawns are evenly divided on the kingside (3:3):

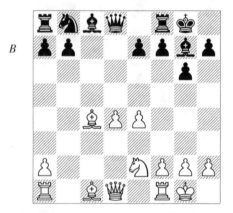

The other way to express this is that there are two connected sets of pawns ('pawn-islands'), so that we have 2:1 on the queenside and 5:4 in the centre and kingside. I think that imparts less information, so I'll divide centre and flank pawns, with the exception that if there is a *single* centre pawn on the board and it is connected with other pawns on the flank, I may group them together, an important case being the 4:3 kingside set-up that we shall run into in the course of discussing openings with that pawn distribution.

One way of thinking about the Grünfeld Defence main line above is that White's centre is under pressure by direct threats and other inconveniences from an enemy who has no targets of attack in his own position. What's more, there aren't even prospective targets of attack in the near future! This sounds one-sided until you take into account that White is protecting a central majority, possibly the most valuable asset in chess in the realm of pawns and structures. How is that? First, two central pawns control more central points than one, in itself an advantage. Then, after a protracted struggle to survive the constant threats to their lives and/or their integrity, a central pawn-majority can sweep across the board and scatter the opponent's pieces, sometimes exacting material tribute along the way. Even more frequently a central majority can be transformed into a passed pawn that is difficult or impossible to stop. That is precisely what happens when things go wrong for Black in many variations of the Grünfeld Defence. Barring such a triumphant journey, a central majority has other advantages. It can advance far enough to grant abundant room for friendly pieces to roam, but can also provide the maximum security to the pieces behind it. There are even advantages to having a central pawn-majority that resides on the third rank. The most important situation in which that occurs is in the Open Sicilian, in which Black *always* has a central majority to begin with, because White has played 3 d4 cxd4 4 ♘xd4, as in this example (*see following diagram*):

The pawns on d6 and e6 protect against threatening incursions by putting all of White's important 5th-rank squares under pawn supervision. They combine that with a threat to advance, when they would give Black's pieces freer play and begin to restrict White's. Such a majority can compensate for a space disadvantage elsewhere, because the main value of a space advantage is the ability to shift forces about more easily, and that can be limited by

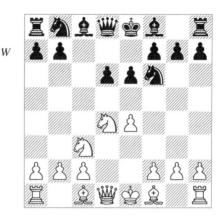

the necessity of keeping White's pieces fairly rigidly poised to prevent Black's central expansion. Even though White's centre pawn in this example is more advanced than Black's are, it can still cover only one central square, namely, d5.

To illustrate this, we might ask why ...b5 is so effective in the Sicilian Defence (when Black has pawns on e6 and d6). A large part of the reason is a well-timed ...b4, of course, to drive away the c3-knight (e.g., to e2) and then either put pressure on White's e-pawn or successfully achieve a pawn-break in the centre.

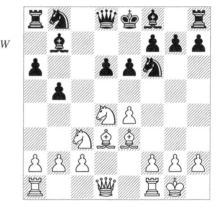

But White often plays g4-g5 himself and drives away the f6-knight (e.g., to d7). Often that has less effect as regards positional considerations in the centre. What's the difference? The central majority. Let's pretend that Black had only a pawn on d6 and White has his usual central pawn on e4. Then driving away White's c3-knight might be of about the same importance as White's driving away the f6-knight. Furthermore, the lack of an e-pawn for Black would mean seriously weakened defence against White's pieces occupying centrally-oriented squares, specifically d5 and f5. For example, if Black's e-pawn were missing, then d5 would be an attractive outpost that would be further weakened if White could force Black's knight off f6 by g4-g5. In that kind of a position a knight on f5 is also notorious for tearing Black's position to shreds. As it is, since Black's pawn *is* on e6, White's limited central pawn presence in the Open Sicilian also allows Black to use influential squares for his purposes, such as c5 and e5 for his knights. Then the knights will have fewer obstacles to reaching c4 or attacking e4.

Of course, in 'extra-positional' terms, White has the opportunity for violent attacks based upon the pawn advances e5 and f5, and/or sacrifices on f5, e6, d5 and b5. With a single inaccuracy by Black (or merely choosing the wrong variation), these attacks can be so powerful as to decimate the defence. Otherwise no one would play White's side of an Open Sicilian. I simply want to demonstrate Black's underlying reason for accepting a cramped position. See Chapter 11 on the Sicilian for other illustrations of how his central majority functions in diverse situations, such as the Paulsen and Dragon Variations.

The next diagram shows another type of central majority in the Open Sicilian arising from 1 e4 c5 2 ♘f3 d6 3 d4 cxd4 4 ♘xd4 ♘f6 5 ♘c3 ♘c6 6 ♗e2 e5 7 ♘b3 ♗e6 (D).

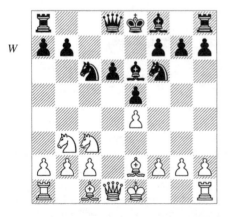

Although by comparison with the previous example, Black has a more vulnerable structure

of pawns (on d6 and e5), White's knights are denied e4 and d4, so that defending d5 is really Black's only practical concern, just as White himself must watch out for ...d5. Again, see Chapter 11 on the Sicilian for various examples.

What are some other common central pawn-majorities? White finds himself with this majority in several variations of the Grünfeld Defence such as the one mentioned above and in the important variation 1 d4 ♘f6 2 c4 g6 3 ♘c3 d5 4 ♘f3 ♗g7 5 ♕b3 dxc4 6 ♕xc4. In the Queen's Gambit Exchange Variation White assumes a 2:1 majority on move four (1 d4 d5 2 c4 e6 3 ♘c3 ♘f6 4 cxd5 exd5), and in the Queen's Gambit Accepted he gets it on move two (1 d4 d5 2 c4 dxc4). White also ends up with an extra centre pawn in many variations of the English Opening in which Black plays ...d5 (an example would be 1 c4 c5 2 ♘c3 ♘f6 3 ♘f3 d5 4 cxd5 ♘xd5). Finally, every Modern Benoni variation has Black accepting a 2:1 deficit from the start (1 d4 ♘f6 2 c4 c5 3 d5 e6 4 ♘c3 exd5 5 cxd5).

There aren't a great many 2:0 central majorities in standard openings, although examples do exist. Take the Nimzo-Indian variation with 1 d4 ♘f6 2 c4 e6 3 ♘c3 ♗b4 4 ♕c2 d5 5 cxd5 ♕xd5 6 ♘f3 ♕f5 7 ♕xf5 exf5 (D).

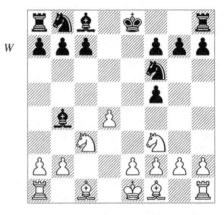

Ironically, this position seems to be perfectly playable for Black. White's difficulty is that when he finally organizes f3 and e4, Black can capture on e4 and will have an f-pawn in reserve to restrain or even attack the centre. There are a growing number of openings in which this structure arises.

In conclusion, whether central majorities are inherent to a specific opening or not, they are extremely important and tend to assert themselves in the long run. Defenders must be sure to have a clear plan for neutralizing them, sometimes by transforming the structure itself before the pawn-majority can do any damage.

The corresponding issue has to do with *queenside* majorities and minorities, since central majorities for one side almost always leave the other side with a queenside majority. Since most majorities can in principle be transformed into a passed pawn, it has been said that a queenside majority is advantageous because the resulting passed pawn will usually be an *outside* passed pawn and thus of special value. That is, in a king and pawn ending, one king will have to go chasing after the queenside passed pawn in order to stop it from promoting, while the other king mops up on the enemy pawns on the kingside. Unfortunately, several considerations interfere with this optimistic scenario.

First, if both kings are centralized (as happens in many endings) neither majority necessarily results in a passed pawn further 'outside' than the other. Secondly, the hypothetical advantage of the queenside majority is reversed if the parties castle queenside. But since kingside castling is the rule, a more compelling issue arises that especially impacts the opening (our area of concern, after all): the relation of majorities to king safety. Since there are more pieces on the board in the opening, the advance of kingside pawns to create a passed pawn carries with it the risk of exposing one's own king; obviously, doing the same with a queenside majority is safer. On the other hand, the results of a kingside advance may be to put the *opposing* king in danger, whereas defence against a queenside majority doesn't require any compromise of the king's position!

These many considerations suggest a sort of theoretical balance between the types of majorities, depending upon concrete features of the position. As a practical matter in the opening stage of the game, one shouldn't pay much attention to the matter of majorities and minorities, apart from their value in beginning to pursue a specific plan. The odds are that the pawn-structure will be transformed prior to the onset of the endgame.

This brings us to the minority attack, which involves two pawns attacking three. It is famously effective in the Sicilian Defence, involving ...b5 and ...b4, sometimes supported by ...a5, driving away White's knight from c3 and/or gaining open files. The exposure of White's queenside renders his majority irrelevant in most cases, at least in so far as creating passed pawns is concerned.

The most famous minority-attack structure is 2:3, 2:1 and 3:3, sometimes called the Carlsbad pawn-structure.

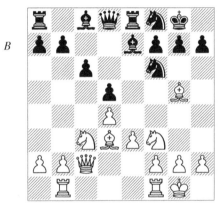

Numerous books discuss the minority attack by b4-b5 in great detail because its application is widespread, although not necessarily in the pure form shown. The most important examples that directly conform to the model in the diagram are in the Queen's Gambit Exchange Variation and a few other variations of the Queen's Gambit Declined. The Carlsbad pawn-structure also emerges in the Nimzo-Indian Defence following 1 d4 ♘f6 2 c4 e6 3 ♘c3 ♗b4 4 ♕c2 d5 5 cxd5 exd5 6 ♗g5 h6 7 ♗xf6 ♕xf6 8 a3 ♗xc3+ 9 ♕xc3. Then Black often feels compelled to play ...c6 in the face of c-file pressure, making White's minority attack by b4-b5 all the more effective. Interestingly, the Caro-Kann has the same pawn distribution with colours reversed after 1 e4 c6 2 d4 d5 3 exd5 cxd5 4 ♗d3 ♘c6 5 c3 ♘f6; in fact, you will find an example of a pure minority attack by Black in Chapter 12. The most thorough discussion of minority attacks in this set of books will naturally be linked to the Queen's Gambit Exchange Variation (covered in Volume 2).

In addition to this there are related positions. For instance, a minority-attack situation comes up in the Grünfeld Defence after 1 d4 ♘f6 2 c4 g6 3 ♘c3 d5 4 ♘f3 ♗g7 5 ♗g5 ♘e4 6 cxd5 ♘xg5 7 ♘xg5 e6 8 ♘f3 exd5. Then White's strategy is based upon b4-b5, whether or not Black gives him a target by playing ...c6. These positions share the same basic ideas but naturally have their own subtleties.

The Modern Benoni provides a good example of a central majority versus a queenside majority:

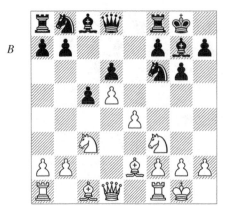

White has the central majority, which sets the stage in and of itself. We know that central majorities are vitally important and generally underrated. Let's think about the King's Indian Defence ('KID') vis-à-vis the Benoni. They both take the same number of tempi to arrive at their basic position, and in the Benoni Black's bishop is on a powerful open diagonal whereas in the King's Indian Black's bishop is blocked by its own pawn. How can the King's Indian as an opening be considered the equal of or superior to the Benoni? I think that the answer rests mostly with the pawn-majority. In the King's Indian Defence, Black and White go on pawn-chain assaults. White's attack consists of, for example, c4, b4 and c5 with ♘d2-c4 and cxd6. What has White accomplished? He has spent all those moves to create a weak pawn on d6, but that pawn is only exposed to attack by pieces, since Black's c-pawn has replaced his d-pawn. However, in the Benoni Black's pawn is already sitting alone on d6 without the expenditure of 6 or more moves by White to get it there! What's more, White's e-pawn is always

threatening to advance to e5, breaking up Black's pawn-structure and opening up the game in favour of White's more aggressively-placed pieces. Naturally that's not the end of the story. Unlike Black in the King's Indian, the Benoni player has the unrestrained bishop on g7 and a clear shot at White's e-pawn along an open file. Moreover, he has a mobile queenside majority that can cause considerable disarray in White's camp. But understanding the role of majorities and minorities explains a lot about these and other openings.

The Light-Square Restraint Structure

Because of their increasing popularity, we'll take a look at structures with ...c6 and ...e6 versus two white pawns, one on d4 and the other on either c4 or e4. I'll call these 'restraint structures' or a 'restraint centre', because their function is to restrain the advance of White's d-pawn. Four of many openings with versions of this set-up are:

a) The Caro-Kann Defence: 1 e4 c6 2 d4 d5. Now several sequences produce the basic structure; for instance, 3 ♘c3 dxe4 4 ♘xe4 and now either 4...♗f5 5 ♘g3 ♗g6 (with ...e6 to come) or 4...♘d7 5 ♘g5 ♘gf6 6 ♗d3 e6 and similar lines. Another example is 1 e4 c6 2 ♘f3 d5 3 ♘c3 ♗g4 4 h3 ♗xf3 5 ♕xf3 e6 6 d4 dxe4 7 ♘xe4 (D). In these lines White retains his c-pawn but not his e-pawn.

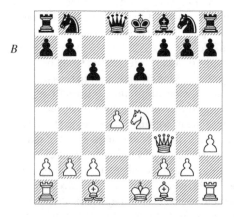

b) The Scandinavian Defence: 1 e4 d5 2 exd5 ♕xd5 3 ♘c3 ♕a5 4 d4 ♘f6 5 ♘f3 ♗f5 6 ♗d2 c6 7 ♗c4 e6. There are numerous variants of this opening with the same structure, including lines with ...♗g4, ...♗xf3 and ...e6. In the Scandinavian, as in the Caro-Kann, White is left with a c-pawn but no e-pawn.

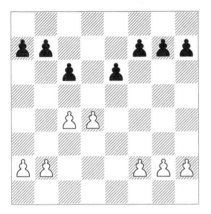

c) The Slav/Semi-Slav: in the traditional Slav lines we have 1 d4 d5 2 c4 c6 3 ♘f3 ♘f6 4 ♘c3 dxc4 5 a4 ♗f5 6 e3 e6 7 ♗xc4, and in the Semi-Slav Meran Variation 1 d4 d5 2 c4 c6 3 ♘f3 ♘f6 4 ♘c3 e6 5 e3 ♘bd7 6 ♗d3 dxc4 7 ♗xc4. These are two of many examples of the basic structure. By contrast with the first two openings, White remains with an e-pawn but no c-pawn.

d) The Queen's Gambit Declined: in the Classical Capablanca and Lasker Variations, we have 1 d4 d5 2 c4 e6 3 ♘c3 ♘f6 4 ♗g5 ♗e7 5 e3 0-0 6 ♘f3 ♘bd7 (or 6...h6 7 ♗h4 ♘e4 8 ♗xe7 ♕xe7 9 ♖c1 ♘xc3 10 ♖xc3 c6 11 ♗d3 dxc4 12 ♗xc4 ♘d7) 7 ♖c1 c6 8 ♗d3 dxc4 9 ♗xc4. In this opening White again ends up with an e-pawn but no c-pawn.

Generally, White's first goal is expansion in the centre, in the one case by c4 and d5, in the other by e4 and d5. These are difficult to achieve given Black's pawn-structure, which is specifically designed to prevent d5, and Black is ready to play ...e5 or ...c5 at the first opportunity. But White also has other resources, including using the support-point at e5 (and sometimes at c5) to make threats and favourably transform the central situation. Or he can expand on the wings.

In some of these variations, Black's light-squared bishop comes out in front of its pawns. Then Black already has some freedom for his pieces and can take more time to play for a transformation of the pawn-structure. When the bishop is stuck behind its pawns, as in the Queen's Gambit or the Caro-Kann with 4...♘d7, Black needs to get ...e5 or ...c5 in as a freeing move, preferably sooner rather than later, if he is to equalize. The ...c5 move not only loosens White's grip on the centre but if followed up by ...cxd4 it claims the c5-square for Black's pieces, often a knight. In that case we have something similar to various French Defence lines with 1 e4 e6 2 d4 d5 3 ♘c3 (or 3 ♘d2 dxe4) 3...dxe4 (or 3...♘f6 4 ♗g5 dxe4) 4 ♘xe4 ♘d7 5 ♘f3 ♘gf6 6 ♘xf6+ ♘xf6, where Black will generally play for ...c5. If Black can play ...e5, he attacks the centre but also frees his light-squared bishop. It's better to show a few examples than to speak in generalities.

Gulko – Lakdawala
USA Ch (San Diego) 2004

1 d4 d5 2 c4 c6 3 ♘f3 ♘f6 4 ♘c3 dxc4 5 a4 ♗f5 6 e3 e6 7 ♗xc4 ♗b4 *(D)*

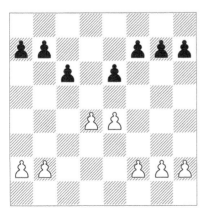

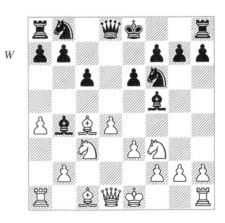

Here's the ...c6/...e6 structure. Thanks to Black's control of the centre via ...♗b4 this may be considered about equal.

8 0-0 0-0 9 ♕e2 ♗g4!?

9...♗g6 is a popular move, preventing e4 for the moment. Then ...♘bd7 and ...♕a5, with the idea ...c5 or ...e5 might follow. But 9...♗g4 has proven quite playable.

10 h3

White grabs the two bishops without delay. This means that Black will have to do something in the centre or simply stand worse. Knights are often the equal of bishops in such positions; it depends upon the timing.

10...♗xf3 11 ♕xf3 ♘bd7 12 ♖d1 ♖c8 (D)

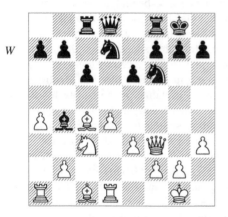

Black plays a subtle move designed to answer a potential d5 by White with ...cxd5. At the same time ...♖c8 lends strength to the advance ...c5.

13 e4 e5

The standard idea: Black doesn't wait around for the centre to become protected and stabilized; rather, he wants to break it up and establish strong points for his pieces. The only other positional solution in such lines is ...c5; one of these pawn-breaks is just about obligatory.

14 ♗e3 ♕a5 15 d5!? (D)

White could delay this thematic push, but then he would have to deal with ...exd4 and ...♘e5.

Now we're in another typical and critical struggle between two bishops with a passed pawn versus immediate pressure by opportunistic knights. The issue is whether the bishops can consolidate.

15...♗xc3?!

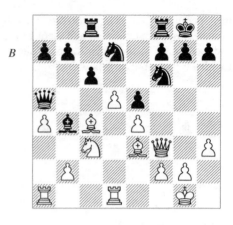

This seems to win something but there are tactical problems. Black could justify his two-knight strategy and ...♖c8 move by playing 15...♘b6!. Then all of Black's pieces combine with tempo and he can capture on d5 to better effect. Still, never underestimate those bishops! For instance: 16 ♗a2 (16 ♗xb6 ♕xb6 17 ♖ab1 keeps more tension, but the opposite-coloured bishops don't really help either side's attacking chances and therefore the position might prove drawish in the end) 16...♗xc3 17 bxc3 cxd5 18 exd5, and now 18...♖fd8 isn't clear because 19 c4!? ♘xc4 20 ♗g5! sacrifices a pawn to maximize the bishops' power. The ambitious 18...♖xc3 19 ♗d2 ♖xf3 20 ♗xa5 ♖f4!? 21 d6 is also hard to assess. The bishops seem to balance out Black's extra pawn. These are raw chess fundamentals at work!

16 bxc3 cxd5 17 ♗xd5 (D)

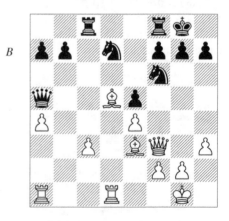

17...♘c5

The first point is that 17...♖xc3? 18 ♗d2! ♖xf3 19 ♗xa5 traps Black's rook. On 17...♘xd5

18 罩xd5 豐c7, White has 19 豐f5! (or 19 a5) 19...公b6 20 罩c5 (20 桌xb6 豐xb6 21 豐xe5) 20...豐d6 21 罩xe5 g6 22 豐f4 with the idea 22...公xa4? 23 豐h6!. These lines show the bishops in their best light.

18 c4 公xd5 19 cxd5

The opening is essentially over and White has won it because the restraint upon his centre broke down. True, Black has the c-file and a comfortable knight on c5 but as is so often the case, the advantage of an ideal centre is transformed into a powerful central passed pawn that wreaks havoc.

19...公xa4

After a slow move the bishop and passed pawn are too much; e.g., 19...罩fd8 20 豐g4 ⬨h8 21 罩ac1 b6 22 罩c4 and 罩dc1.

20 豐f5! f6

Or 20...罩fe8 21 d6 罩cd8 22 罩d5.

21 d6 罩cd8 22 豐e6+ 罩f7?!

Losing, but after 22...⬨h8 23 d7 the pawn is strong, backed up by the advantage of bishop versus knight. 罩ac1-c8 is one problem.

23 罩dc1 ⬨f8 24 罩c8 b5 25 罩ac1 1-0

Bogoljubow – Kramer
Travemünde 1951

1 d4 公f6 2 桌g5 d5 3 公c3 c6 4 e3 桌f5 5 桌d3 桌xd3 6 cxd3 e6 7 公f3 桌e7 8 0-0 0-0 9 罩c1 公bd7 10 e4 *(D)*

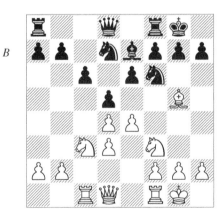

Here's a case of the immobile centre that we see in the mirror-image form of e3/e4/d4 versus a black pawn on e5 in some 1 e4 e5 openings. For example, that situation typically arises in a Giuoco Piano with d3 (1 e4 e5 2 公f3 公c6 3

桌c4 桌c5 4 d3), when Black's bishop is on c5 and White's bishop goes to e3. Then when Black plays ...桌xe3 and White recaptures by fxe3 we have the mirror image. I discuss this at some length in Chapter 6.

Returning to our game, Black soon unnecessarily straightens out White's pawns for him, and creates our restraint centre.

10...h6 11 桌f4 dxe4!? 12 dxe4 豐a5

The ...c6/...e6 centre arises. Since he doesn't face the bishop-pair, as he did in the above example, Black has more time to organize ...c5 or ...e5. Notice that White has no light-squared bishop to enforce d5.

13 豐e2 罩fd8 14 a3

14 罩fd1 罩ac8 would be a typical restraint position. Black can't undertake much but has dynamic counterplay if White tries to make progress. This resilience accounts for the renewed interest in such structures. As this game shows, the drawback is that it's difficult, but not impossible, to get positive chances.

14...公f8!? 15 h3 公g6 16 桌h2

Bishops in many openings are stuck on the side of the board at g3 and h2. This one apparently has good scope but it doesn't defend the d-pawn. Therefore 16 桌e3 looks better, centralizing and intending 16...公h5 17 公e5!.

16...罩d7 17 罩c2 公h7! *(D)*

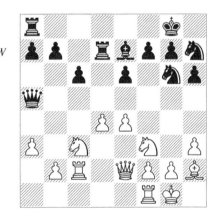

A great idea! Black wants to play ...公g5 and eliminate White's best piece on f3, the defender of the d-pawn.

18 豐e3 罩ad8 19 桌g3 公g5 20 公d2

White's protects his d-pawn indirectly and plans a logical reorganization of the position. He almost achieves it.

20...♕b6

Not 20...♖xd4? 21 ♘b3.

21 ♘e2 c5!

Just in time, Black manages to get this move in with the help of tactics. Of course, the normally dangerous response d5 isn't remotely possible.

22 ♘c4

White cedes a pawn but what else? 22 dxc5 ♗xc5! 23 ♕xc5 (23 ♖xc5 ♖d3!) 23...♕xc5 24 ♖xc5 ♖xd2 threatens e2 and b2.

22...♕c6 23 f3 cxd4

Black's strategy has succeeded. ...♘h7-g5 was quite a blow to White's position.

24 ♕d3 ♘h7 25 f4 ♘f6 26 ♘d2 ♕xc2! 27 ♕xc2 d3 28 ♕c4 dxe2 29 ♖e1 ♖xd2

Black is winning.

G. Lee – Taulbut
British Ch (Morecambe) 1981

1 e4 d5 2 exd5 ♕xd5 3 ♘f3

Instead of the usual 3 ♘c3.

3...♘f6 4 d4 ♗f5 5 ♗e2 e6 6 0-0 c6 7 ♗f4 ♘bd7 8 c4 ♕a5 9 ♘c3 *(D)*

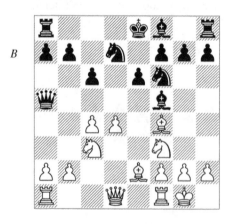

In this situation, White has a c-pawn, not an e-pawn as in the last two examples. Although both configurations arise regularly and have differences, Black's main strategy is still to get ...e5 or ...c5 in, and White would like to play d5.

9...♗b4 10 ♕b3 0-0 11 ♘e5!? ♘xe5 12 ♗xe5 ♘d7 13 ♗g3 e5!

He has to play this way to get counterplay. White will transform the centre in response.

14 a3! ♗xc3 15 bxc3 ♖fe8 16 ♖fe1

♕xb7 is an option here and next move.

16...h6 17 ♕b4 ♕b6 18 c5!? ♕xb4 19 axb4 exd4 20 cxd4 ♖e4 21 ♗f3!?

21 ♖ad1 ♖ae8 22 ♔f1 is solid and equal.

21...♖xd4 22 b5! ♘xc5 23 bxc6 bxc6 24 ♗xc6 ♖c8 25 ♗b5 ♗d3!?

With White's two bishops gone, Black has won a pawn for very little, but White manages to scare up play.

26 ♗xd3 ♘xd3 27 ♖ed1 ♖d7 28 f3 ♖cd8 29 ♔f1 ♘b4 30 ♖xd7 ♖xd7 31 ♗f2 ♘c6 32 ♖a6 ♖c7 33 ♗g3 ♖c8 34 ♗f2 ♖c7 35 ♗g3 ♖c8 36 ♗f2 ♘b4!? 37 ♖xa7 ♖c1+ 38 ♔e2

The game is about equal and was eventually drawn.

Djurić – Larsen
Copenhagen 1979

1 e4 d5 2 exd5 ♕xd5 3 ♘c3 ♕a5 4 d4 ♘f6 5 ♘f3 ♗f5 6 ♗c4 ♘bd7 7 ♕e2 e6 8 ♗d2 ♗b4! 9 a3 0-0 10 0-0 ♗xc3! 11 ♗xc3 ♕b6 *(D)*

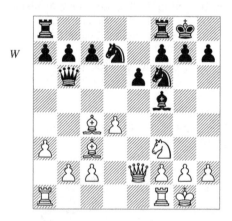

This was a shocking idea at the time: giving up the bishop-pair and accepting less space at the same time! But the ...c6/...e6 structure is very handy for such a position: knights are temporarily as good as bishops and ...c5 or ...e5 is not to be stopped forever.

12 ♗b3 a5 13 ♗a4 c6 14 ♗d2!

Rerouting from a passive square to a nice lengthy diagonal is logical.

14...h6 15 ♗e3 ♖fe8 16 c3

16 c4 is the thematic move. Then Black might think about exchanging off his other bishop by 16...♗g4!? (16...♕c7 would prepare ...e5 and also makes sense) 17 h3 ♗xf3 18 ♕xf3 ♕a6!? 19 ♖ac1 b5 20 cxb5 cxb5 21 ♗c2 ♘d5 and this

IQP position is hard to assess, but I think that Black can be satisfied.

16...♗g4

Now ...♗xf3 is threatened because if the queen recaptures, ...♕xb2 works. In what follows Black makes the ...e5 break and exchanges off a pair of bishops with full equality.

17 ♖ab1 ♕c7 18 h3 ♗h5 19 ♗c2 e5! 20 g4 exd4 21 cxd4 ♗g6 22 ♗xg6 fxg6 23 ♕d3 ♘d5! 24 ♗xh6! gxh6 25 ♕xg6+ ♔f8 26 ♕xh6+ ♔g8 27 ♕g6+ ♔f8 28 ♕h6+ ♔g8 ½-½

Black seemed to stand perfectly well throughout.

There's a better-known version of this c4/d4 structure:

Matanović – Petrosian
Kiev (USSR-Yugoslavia) 1959

1 e4 c6 2 ♘c3 d5 3 d4 dxe4 4 ♘xe4 ♘d7 5 ♘f3 ♘gf6 6 ♘xf6+ ♘xf6 7 ♗c4 ♗f5 8 ♕e2 e6 9 ♗g5 ♗e7 10 0-0-0 ♗g4! *(D)*

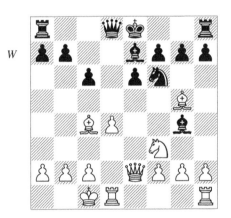

A familiar idea. A knight on d5 becomes as strong as a bishop.

11 h3 ♗xf3 12 ♕xf3 ♘d5 13 ♗xe7

A very important point is that Black will get a great attack if White tries to conserve his bishop-pair: 13 ♗d2 b5 14 ♗b3 a5!.

13...♕xe7 14 ♖he1 0-0 15 ♔b1

15 ♗xd5 ♕g5+ 16 ♔b1 cxd5 is equal.

15...♖ad8 *(D)*

Here we have a d4- and c-pawn versus ...c6/...e6 again. Obviously White needs to play c4 if he's going to claim any advantage, but Petrosian has a way of dealing with that.

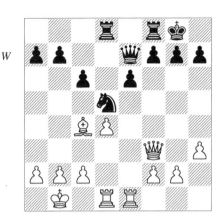

16 ♗b3 ♕f6!?

Considering what happens, there's really no reason for this.

17 ♕e2

White could have admitted to his difficulties and exchanged the knight on d5. But the position seems so innocent.

17...♖d7 18 c3

The advance 18 c4 is way too committal and weakens d4: 18...♘e7 19 ♗c2 ♖fd8 20 ♕d3 ♘g6 and the pawn will fall.

18...b5!

A simple idea designed to prevent c4, and Black also has in mind a minority attack with ...b4.

19 g3 ♖fd8 20 f4!?

White stops ...e5, but that's not the only pawn-break.

20...b4! 21 ♕f3 bxc3 22 bxc3 c5!

Once Black achieves this he already has the advantage.

23 ♖e5

Black penetrates White's position after 23 c4?! ♘b4! 24 dxc5 ♕f5+ 25 ♔a1 ♘d3. And 23 ♗xd5 ♖xd5 threatens the d-pawn. White's king is none too safe either.

23...cxd4 24 ♗xd5 ♖xd5 25 ♖xd5 exd5! 26 ♖xd4 h6 *(D)*

White has managed to exchange down into an isolated queen's pawn position, but his king is too exposed.

27 g4

27 ♖xd5 can be answered by 27...♖b8+ 28 ♔c2 ♕b6! and Black's attack will be too strong.

27...♕e7! 28 ♕f2 ♖b8+ 29 ♔a1 ♕a3 30 ♕c2 ♖e8 31 ♖b4 d4! 32 ♖xd4 ♖e1+ 33 ♖d1

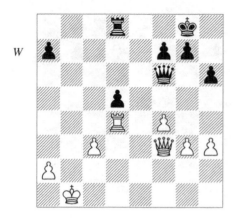

W

♖xd1+ 34 ♕xd1 ♕xc3+ 35 ♔b1 ♕xh3 36 a4 h5! 37 gxh5 ♕f5+ 38 ♔b2 ♕xf4 39 ♔b3 ♕f5 40 ♔c4 ♔h7 41 ♕d2 0-1

The opening of the following game combines this ...b5 idea with our earlier theme of the fight between an isolated d-pawn and isolated c-pawn:

Iordachescu – Wohl
Naujac sur Mer 2002

1 e4 ♘f6 2 e5 ♘d5 3 d4 d6 4 ♘f3 dxe5 5 ♘xe5 c6 6 ♗c4 ♘d7 7 ♘f3 e6 8 0-0

Again we've arrived at the ...c6/...e6 restraint structure, coming from a slightly unusual source. Now Black makes a very committal but logical move:

8...b5!? 9 ♗d3 ♗b7 (D)

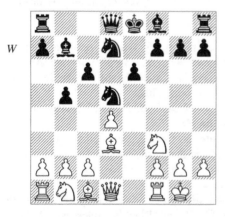

W

The bishop may not seem to be doing much here, but Black wants to play ...a6 and ...c5. If you know the Meran Variation of the Semi-Slav

you might recognize that idea right away and take action against it, as Iordachescu does.

10 a4!

The same technique as in the Meran.

10...a6

Now ...c5 is prevented for a while.

11 ♖e1 ♗e7 12 ♘bd2

White seems to be planning a stock attack by ♘e4 but Black's next move changes his mind.

12...♕b6?! (D)

12...0-0 13 ♘e4 ♕b6 is better since it takes the bite out of c4.

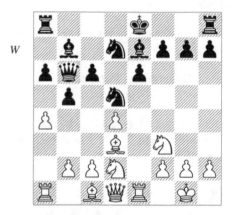

W

13 c4!

White takes on an isolated and fully blockaded pawn on d4. But having seen this d4 versus c6 structure before (hopefully many times) he assesses this as a favourable isolated queen's pawn position. Black is well-developed, and if he gets ...c5 in it will open up the b7-bishop and activate his game. The issue then is whether White can make use of any particular advantages that he has in advance of that freeing move. The dark squares and aggressively-placed pieces look good, so the first question is: where is Black weak? The squares c5, e5 and d6 may be vulnerable, and if you've foreseen the move 15 ♗g5 before playing 13 c4, that should be enough to convince you to go ahead.

13...bxc4 14 ♘xc4 ♕c7 15 ♗g5! (D)

15...c5?!

Black's position is still solid, so he shouldn't allow the exchange of dark-squared bishops. Other moves are 15...♘7f6 16 ♖c1 0-0 and 15...♗b4, just to get castled. The b4-square is a nice outpost for Black, who has a future ...♖b8 in mind.

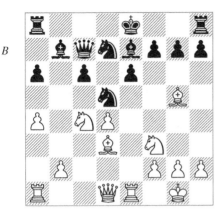

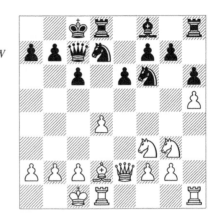

16 ♖c1!? 0-0 17 ♗xe7 ♘xe7 18 ♘ce5 ♖ad8 19 b4

Admirably sticking to his purpose, even though the tactic 19 ♗xh7+ ♔xh7 20 ♘g5+ ♔g8 21 ♘xd7! does ultimately win after complications.

19...♘xe5 20 ♘xe5

Black's c-pawn falls, and the opening is over. Previous knowledge of the properties of ...c6/...e6 restriction and the standard IQP position, as well as recognizing the similarity to the Meran Variation, undoubtedly helped White to find his way in this game. That is an illustration of what I call 'cross-pollination', discussed below.

Rather than trying to fight directly against the ...c6/...e6 complex, it's sometimes better to give up on d5 and transform the structure. In this famous game White does so by using his support-points:

Spassky – Petrosian
Moscow Wch (13) 1966

1 e4 c6 2 d4 d5 3 ♘c3 dxe4 4 ♘xe4 ♗f5 5 ♘g3 ♗g6 6 h4 h6 7 ♘f3 ♘d7 8 h5 ♗h7 9 ♗d3 ♗xd3 10 ♕xd3 ♕c7 11 ♗d2 e6 12 ♕e2! ♘gf6 13 0-0-0 0-0-0 *(D)*

14 ♘e5! ♘xe5 15 dxe5 ♘d7 16 f4

White stands well. He has more space and no worries about the kind of central attacks that we've seen from Black. Of course, White still needs to break through Black's defences; he does so by creating another support-point on c5.

16...♗e7 17 ♘e4 ♘c5 18 ♘c3 f6!?

This creates a weakness on e6 but otherwise White can squeeze Black by expansion on either or both wings.

19 exf6 ♗xf6 20 ♕c4! ♕b6 21 b4 ♘a6 22 ♘e4!

White has the advantage. He can exploit the weakness on e6, or play for a well-timed ♘c5. Spassky went on to win the game.

Space and Structure

The relationship of space to structure is potentially an immense subject, but I just want to make a few comments about it. We know that White is the one who will generally grab more space in the opening (particularly in the major openings discussed in this book). Several situations can arise for Black. In the Closed System of the Ruy Lopez and several other double e-pawn openings, Black's strongpoint on e5 (based upon the pawn-chain c7-d6-e5) and his b5-pawn establish a sufficient command of territory that he doesn't usually feel the need to acquire more. The Chigorin set-up with ...♘a5 and ...c5 is an exception, in that it is clearly aimed at extending Black's territorial reach; but that this policy is not necessary is shown by the popular Breyer, Zaitsev, Møller and Smyslov Variations (see Chapter 8 on the Ruy Lopez for examples). To some extent this is also true with the double d-pawn openings such as the Queen's Gambit Declined and Slav. Nevertheless, in the traditional Queen's Gambit variations Black tends to play for ...e5 at some point, arguably exchanging one type of territorial control (the d5-pawn) for another that also activates his pieces. In the Dutch Variation of the Slav (1 d4 d5 2 c4 c6 3 ♘f3 ♘f6 4 ♘c3 dxc4 5 a4 ♗f5 6 e3), Black is generally in no hurry to play ...e5 or even ...c5, which also true of several of the other ...e6/...c6 restraint openings that we saw above, especially since his queen's bishop is outside his pawn-chain.

By contrast, look at many of the other major d-pawn openings. In the King's Indian Defence main lines (e.g., 1 d4 ♘f6 2 c4 g6 3 ♘c3 ♗g7 4 e4 d6 followed by ...0-0 and ...e5), once White takes space in the centre, Black will seldom be satisfied that the single central pawn on e5 fully represents his interests in that sector. Without further pawn moves he will slowly be strangled by White's central and queenside pawn advances. Therefore you will almost always see a rapid ...f5, or in some cases an attempt to take over territory on the queenside by ...c6 or ...c5. Likewise in the Modern Benoni (1 d4 ♘f6 2 c4 c5 3 d5 e6 4 ♘c3 exd5 5 cxd5 d6 followed by ...g6, ...♗g7, ...0-0, etc.), Black can almost never be satisfied with the central control offered by his c5-pawn. In most variations he is almost compelled to win more space by ...b5 or ...f5 or get strangled by White's pieces and onrushing pawns. In the Semi-Slav, a combination of ...dxc4 and ...b5, or ...dxc4, ...♗d6 and ...e5 is customary before White extends his control over the central squares (note that Black's light-squared bishop is trapped behind his pawns).

What about the Sicilian Defence? In general, if he has the ...e6/...d6 centre, Black is in a remarkable lack of hurry to take on more space. At most he will play ...b5, and if White stops that by playing a4 it is hardly a matter of great concern. But look at White's various strategies against the Sicilian. It seems practically mandatory to expand his reach over the board. Recently there are players who set up with f3, g4, g5 and h4 (and even h5 and g6) against the majority of Sicilian variations. Traditionally, f4 has been a standard way of proceeding, with f5 to follow or perhaps e5 (although the latter is sometimes more of a tactical device, because the pawn will seldom stay on e5 long enough to be a true claimant of territory). These days there are also more combinations of f4 and g4. Barring those kingside moves, White will at least play a4 to stake out some space on the queenside. In the Maroczy Bind and Hedgehog Variations, in which White already has control of space with pawns on c4 and e4, Black finds it a little more urgent to achieve ...b5 or ...d5, or at least threaten to do so.

Almost every opening can be looked at in this way, that is, how vital is it for the side with less space (usually Black) to win space, and how quickly? What about the need for White to take on more space quickly, or can he be patient? If you understand the urgency (or lack of it) in achieving these goals, you will have a much better feel for the logic and timing behind the opening moves.

Cross-Pollination

Sometimes manoeuvres and positional ideas will arise across openings that are not specifically related, a phenomenon that I call 'cross-pollination'. We have seen repeated examples of structures that show up in various openings, and in a way everything that we've seen about structures to this point has involved cross-pollination, that is, every structure has been related to other structures. Here I'll briefly discuss the process that may lead you to recognize such similarities and therefore play an unfamiliar or only partly familiar variation with increased confidence. Grandmasters are very good at seeing this type of relationship in subtle ways. You'll gain a lot from the very process of using your study and experience from one position and then applying it to another. All the more reason to keep your opening knowledge broad and not overspecialized.

As an example, you've probably wondered whether to play with an isolated queen's pawn in a given position. This requires judgements based upon experience. We already know that the isolated pawn offers similar lessons across a wide range of openings. We even see standard IQP positions that are essentially the same in the Nimzo-Indian, Caro-Kann, Sicilian and Queen's Gambit. But you'll consistently be given the option of deciding whether a new IQP position in a foreign position has more good features than defects, and experience with other openings will do more than an author's generalities can.

A more interesting illustration of cross-pollination relates to decisions about when to bring your queen out, and whether you can do so productively at an early stage. If, as Black, you've captured some 'poisoned' pawns on b2 or gambited them as White, you'll certainly get a better feel for when to take the risk in either way. Here are a few examples that you might run into:

1 e4 c5 2 ♘f3 d6 3 d4 cxd4 4 ♘xd4 ♘f6 5 ♘c3 a6 6 ♗g5 e6 7 f4 ♕b6 8 ♕d2 ♕xb2

1 d4 ♘f6 2 ♘f3 e6 3 ♗g5 c5 4 e3 ♕b6 5 ♘bd2 ♕xb2

1 e4 g6 2 d4 ♗g7 3 ♘c3 d6 4 f4 c6 5 ♘f3 ♗g4 6 ♗e3 ♕b6 7 ♕d2 ♕xb2

1 e4 e6 2 d4 d5 3 e5 c5 4 c3 ♘c6 5 ♘f3 ♕b6 6 ♗e2 cxd4 7 cxd4 ♘h6 8 ♗xh6 ♕xb2

1 e4 c6 2 d4 d5 3 e5 ♗f5 4 ♗e3 ♕b6 5 ♘d2 ♕xb2

1 d4 ♘f6 2 ♗g5 c5 3 d5 ♕b6 4 ♘c3 ♕xb2 5 ♗d2

1 d4 ♘f6 2 ♗g5 ♘e4 3 ♗f4 c5 4 d5 ♕b6 5 ♘d2 ♕xb2 6 ♘xe4 ♕b4+ 7 ♕d2 ♕xe4 8 c3

Or, with colours reversed:

1 d4 d5 2 c4 ♗f5 3 ♕b3 e5 4 ♕xb7

1 d4 d5 2 c4 dxc4 3 ♘f3 ♘f6 4 e3 ♗g4 5 ♗xc4 e6 6 ♕b3 ♗xf3 7 gxf3 ♘bd7 8 ♕xb7

1 d4 ♘f6 2 c4 c5 3 d5 e6 4 ♘c3 exd5 5 cxd5 d6 6 e4 a6 7 a4 g6 8 ♘f3 ♗g4 9 ♕b3 ♗xf3 10 ♕xb7 ♘bd7 11 gxf3

They are of differing soundness and strength. If you get a new position in which you are being offered a b-pawn in the opening, you can make a better decision by studying these.

Another question: when do you want to allow your queen to come out with the move ...♕xd5 or ♕xd4 within the first few moves of the game? What about that rule that says the queen shouldn't come out too early? Maybe as a beginner you have seen or read about the Danish Gambit line 1 e4 e5 2 d4 exd4 3 c3 d5 4 exd5 ♕xd5. The c3-square is temporarily occupied and thus there's time for Black to develop before his queen is attacked; for instance, 5 cxd4 ♘c6 6 ♘f3 ♗g4 7 ♗e2 ♘f6 8 ♘c3 ♗b4 (this position also arises in the Göring Gambit) and Black has equality. Later you see similar ideas in the Sicilian Defence, where we have 1 e4 c5 2 c3 d5 3 exd5 ♕xd5 and c3 is occupied so that White can't place a knight there with tempo; often 4 d4 ♘f6 5 ♘f3 ♗g4 will follow. Perhaps the improving student will start to examine the c3-square as one strong criterion in deciding

whether to play ...d5 and/or recapture with the queen on that square. From White's point of view we have such things as 1 c4 e5 2 g3 ♘f6 3 ♗g2 c6 4 d4 cxd4 5 ♕xd4.

Say that you're playing the French Defence and start out 1 e4 e6 2 d4 d5 3 ♘d2 ♘c6, recently a hot variation. Maybe you have some recent analysis on 4 ♘gf3 and 4 ♗b5 that you want to try out. When your opponent plays 4 c3, you don't recognize the move, but search your pattern database and come up with 4...e5! 5 exd5 ♕xd5. Pattern recognition could also be involved if you play the Pirc Defence and are confronted with 1 e4 d6 2 d4 ♘f6 3 ♗d3. Playing 3...e5 is fairly obvious, and then White plays 4 c3. What now? If you're attuned to the way that a pawn on c3 prevents ♘c3, you might see 4...d5!, with the idea 5 exd5 ♕xd5 or 5 dxe5 ♘xe4 (D). This looks fun and worth a try.

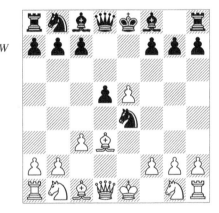

But then you notice 6 ♗xe4 dxe4 7 ♕a4+ followed by ♕xe4, shake your head, and play some other 4th move. This is where the stock of familiar positions comes in. Two weeks later you happen to notice a grandmaster in this position as Black and after a short think he plays 4...d5 anyway. There follows 5 dxe5 ♘xe4 6 ♗xe4 dxe4 7 ♕a4+ ♗d7! 8 ♕xe4 ♗c6 (D) with plenty of compensation (two bishops, light squares, and direct attack on g2).

Our grandmaster didn't give up on the line after he saw 7 ♕a4+; was this due to seeing further than the club player? Probably not, because just about every grandmaster and international master has seen this kind of sequence before. For example, there are a couple of classic games

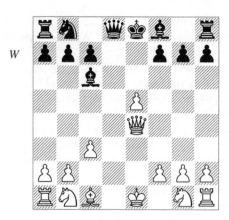

with 1 c4 ♘f6 2 ♘c3 e6 3 e4 d5 4 cxd5 exd5 5 e5 ♘e4 6 ♘xe4 dxe4 7 ♕a4+ ♗d7 8 ♕xe4 ♗c6. The broader your exposure to typical structures, the better you'll be able to handle unfamiliar situations. See Chapter 14 on the Pirc Defence for more details about this variation; the next thing that happens is that it turns into an Open Variation of the Ruy Lopez!

Along the same lines (bringing queens to d4 or d5), a tricky anti-Sicilian variation goes 1 e4 c5 2 ♘f3 d6 3 c3 ♘f6 4 ♗d3!? ♘c6, when some players may not want to face ...♗g4, so they play 5 h3. But with that pawn on c3, 5...d5 should be considered, with the idea 6 e5 ♘d7, and now White can play 7 ♗b5 ♕b6 (a French Defence pattern), or he might enter into the sequence 7 e6!? fxe6 8 ♘g5, a tactical ploy that arises in a good half-dozen other opening variations. With experience in any of those, you may be helped by recognition of associated patterns such as 8...♘f6 9 ♘xh7 (9 ♗xh7 ♘xh7 10 ♕h5+ ♔d7 11 ♘xh7 ♔c7, etc.) 9...♕d6 (or maybe 9...♘xh7 10 ♕h5+ ♔d7 11 ♗xh7 b6, even if you haven't seen that one before). The fact that you've seen and/or played other positions with the e6 move helps you to make more accurate calculations and gives you confidence that the resulting positions should be fine for Black.

There are plenty of other cases of an early ♕xd4 (or ...♕xd5) in which the c3-square (or c6-square for Black) isn't occupied. The simplest of these is the Scandinavian Defence (Centre Counter) 1 e4 d5 2 exd5 ♕xd5, when 3 ♘c3 forces the loss of a tempo with the queen, still out early and subject to further attack. I

think that it's fair to say that the reason that Black can get away with this is that the knight isn't all that well placed on c3, such that Black can play moves like ...♗f5, ...e6 and ...c6 at some point, when White would prefer to have his c-pawn free to advance and increase his central control. Or the queen, when attacked, may use the tempo 'lost' to make a second productive move. A good example comes up in the line 1 c4 e5 2 g3 ♘f6 3 ♘f3 e4 4 ♘d4 ♘c6 5 ♘c2 d5 6 cxd5 ♕xd5 7 ♘c3 ♕h5! intending ...♗h3, when Black has an excellent game.

That leads to many other examples, such as those in which a knight on c3 (or ...c6) is pinned, so that a queen can come to d4 (or d5). A well-known case is the Nimzo-Indian line with 1 d4 ♘f6 2 c4 e6 3 ♘c3 ♗b4 4 ♕c2 d5 5 cxd5 ♕xd5; and a related one is the Chigorin Defence with 1 d4 d5 2 c4 ♘c6 3 cxd5 ♕xd5 4 e3 e5 5 ♘c3 ♗b4. From the white side, we have a Sicilian Defence with 1 e4 c5 2 ♘f3 d6 3 d4 cxd4 4 ♕xd4 ♘c6 5 ♗b5, which we might compare with a Philidor Defence 1 e4 e5 2 ♘f3 d6 3 d4 exd4 4 ♕xd4 ♘c6 5 ♗b5. In both cases the queen is allowed to stand her ground, but often at the cost of the bishop-pair. Do you spot the main difference? In the Sicilian line, Black keeps his central majority intact; in the Philidor Black surrenders the centre. After a while it becomes second nature to look for these situations, and advanced players do so.

Cross-pollination between 1 d4 and 1 e4 is more common than you'd think. The chess-player with some experience may have noticed that the Benoni pawn-chain ...c5/...d6 versus White's e4/d5 will often arise in the King's Indian Defence, after, for instance, 1 d4 ♘f6 2 c4 g6 3 ♘c3 ♗g7 4 e4 d6 5 ♗e2 0-0 6 ♗g5 c5 7 d5 h6 8 ♗e3 e6 9 ♘f3 exd5 10 cxd5 and in several other major lines. But if you're playing the black side of a Ruy Lopez, you might consider heading for this same structure by way of various Closed lines. For example, in the Keres Variation you may arrive at this main position: 1 e4 e5 2 ♘f3 ♘c6 3 ♗b5 a6 4 ♗a4 ♘f6 5 0-0 ♗e7 6 ♖e1 b5 7 ♗b3 0-0 8 c3 d6 9 h3 ♘a5 10 ♗c2 c5 11 d4 ♘d7!? 12 ♘bd2 exd4 13 cxd4 ♘c6 14 d5 ♘ce5 (D).

The Benoni structure has arisen and you already have the move ...b5 in. That's the key move in nearly every Benoni and very often

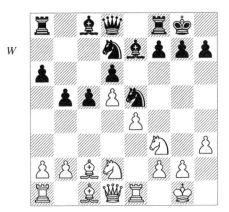

W

White will prevent it. All Black needs to do next is 'fianchetto' his bishop by ...♗f6 and he will obtain an excellent game. White doesn't want to allow this and plays 15 ♘xe5, but as it turns out that frees Black's game or at least gives his pieces places to go.

Cross-pollination will appear in contexts that are not strictly structural, but relate to the scope of plausible structures. I think that a lot of this shows up in the opening preparation of players and their borrowing of ideas from each other. Grandmaster X will see a new move that Grandmaster Y has played on the 18th move of a certain variation of the Sicilian. Then he may apply that move to his 14th move in a closely-related variation. That is an interesting exchange of ideas, of course, but it's more exciting to see players latch on to the same moves or general ideas across the range of openings. The number of older, well-known, positions in which White has recently found and played the move g4 cannot be coincidental. Whole articles have been written about this move appearing in so many new and interesting contexts. The list of openings thus affected includes several variations of the English Opening, the Semi-Slav, the Two Knights Defence, the Bogo-Indian Defence, the Dutch Defence, the Caro-Kann Defence, and just about every variation of the Sicilian Defence! And I could make a similar although shorter list of openings in which Black has begun to use the move ...g5. Obviously, once the idea struck players' imaginations they began to look for it in every position.

Something that has struck me about chess from the last several decades, actually stretching back more than a century but only recently

flowering, is the phenomenon of semi-waiting moves in the opening. That is, moves that serve a definite purpose but only just so, and which seem to need the opponent's cooperation to take on meaning. It is fascinating to see, however, that these moves are a little more effective than my description would imply, i.e. the opponent hasn't really the luxury of doing nothing in return without giving ground. A lot of these ideas are unassuming; for example, development of pieces to the second rank that appear to have five good answers and yet are hard to meet. Or a sequence of moves that seems to lose a tempo but puts the opponent's pieces somewhere they'd rather not be; for instance, in d-pawn and c-pawn openings with an early ...e6 we see many new cases of ...♗b4+ followed by ...♗e7, and ...♗a6 followed by ...♗b7. In the Sicilian Defence and English Opening, Black always seems to be playing ...♗c5 or ...♗b4 followed by ...♗e7.

I find the little rook's pawn moves to be particularly thought-provoking, and I suspect that grandmasters are finding inspiration from such moves' success in some openings to experiment with them in others. These are not necessarily new moves but often obscure older ones which later received general acceptance. For instance, Kasparov's strengthening of Petrosian's little move 1 d4 ♘f6 2 c4 e6 3 ♘f3 b6 4 a3!? led to an explosion of games and investigations, and 4 a3 has been going strong in the Queen's Indian Defence for many years now. Variations such as 1 c4 c5 2 ♘f3 ♘f6 3 d4 cxd4 4 ♘xd4 ♘c6 5 ♘c3 e6 6 a3!? began to appear. Then some years later players got serious about the modest-looking ...a6 within the first four moves in two variations of the Slav: 1 d4 d5 2 c4 c6 3 ♘f3 ♘f6 and here 4 e3 a6 or 4 ♘c3 a6. Not only that, these two moves have now accumulated analysis and playing experience that rival the main lines of some openings! In that case, Black wants to play ...b5 to gain space, or capture on c4 and then play ...b5. He may also want to play his bishop out to g4 or f5 and not worry about ♕b3, answering that move with ...♖a7 in some variations! Another example: the variations with 4...a6 in the Modern Defence are a little insulting to the classical thinker, but refreshing; e.g., 1 e4 g6 2 d4 ♗g7 3 ♘c3 d6 and now 4 ♗e3 a6, 4 f4 a6, 4 ♘f3 a6 or 4 ♗g5 a6, and so forth. These all seem fully playable, in part because ...c5 can follow and 'threaten' to go into a favourable Sicilian Defence, an example of cross-pollination. Recently players started looking at long-established openings and found a new idea or rediscovered it in older literature; for instance, 1 e4 e5 2 ♘f3 ♘c6 3 ♘c3 ♘f6 4 a3!?. This is another waiting move that doesn't do much but achieves a little something; for example, 4...♗c5 5 ♘xe5!, when the resource ...♗b4 isn't available after 5...♘xe5 6 d4. Or in the Pirc Defence, the remarkable 1 e4 d6 2 d4 ♘f6 3 ♘c3 g6 4 f4 ♗g7 5 a3!?, preventing the usual 5...c5 in view of 6 dxc5 ♕a5 7 b4, and otherwise waiting for Black to make a committal move, of which it turns out that many have disadvantages. In the Sicilian Defence, 1 e4 c5 2 ♘f3 ♘c6 3 d4 cxd4 4 ♘xd4 ♘f6 5 ♘c3 e6 became a popular way to avoid major Sicilian theory; after a century of experience with that line players noticed the possibility of 6 a3, preventing 6...♗b4 and again waiting to see what Black is going to do. There's a current interest in 1 e4 c5 2 a3 (not to mention 2 ♘a3!?), and even a monograph devoted to it. Similar things have been going on with Black. In the French Defence with 1 e4 e6 2 d4 d5 3 ♘c3 (and 3 ♘d2), grandmasters have been using 3...h6 (the other rook's pawn!), asking White to commit while preventing ♗g5 and finding the move ...g5 useful in a remarkable number of positions. Likewise, Anand and many others have played 1 c4 e5 2 g3 ♘f6 3 ♗g2 h6.

It seems obvious that these sorts of ideas feed off each other, with each new explorer inspired by the most recent discoveries. But if you look at the details of the newly discovered theory and practice of such lines, you will see that standard structures from other chess openings appear everywhere throughout them. In other words, experiments like these are successful only because of the vast knowledge of traditional openings that lets players find old patterns in new contexts. The moral of the story is not to play the move a3 in every position (or any position!), but to realize that mastery of openings comes from a broader set of structures and techniques that appear across the board. While you study the traditional openings, be sure to look at ideas from every other source to reinforce what you're learning.

Furthermore, you can look at structural themes in the same way, comparing them from opening to opening. The more that you examine and compare outposts and support-points, for example, the more you will find yourself able to work with them. Ask simple questions when you play over games by grandmasters: when are outposts on squares like e5, d5, e4 and d4 similar, and how do they differ? Does the outpost piece radiate influence and make counterplay fruitless? Can the outpost be maintained? Can a piece on the outpost be exchanged off favourably in order to change the pawn-structure? Is there a situation in which the outpost can be 'played around', leaving an impressive-looking but uninvolved piece occupying it? Similarly, is a piece on an outpost in front of doubled or backward pawns so powerful that it's worth a rook, or will it just sit there and block one's own play? Either result is possible.

Cross-pollination turns out to be an unlimited subject and contributes to the fact that we take so strong an interest in chess. There are examples throughout this book and in most sources of chess information. Keep an eye out for them, especially as you study and play openings. You'll find it a fun exercise, and helpful for your chess.

4 Introduction to 1 e4 and the Open Games

Want to play a game of chess? I'll move first:
1 e4 *(D)*

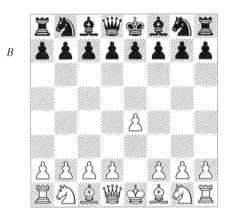

B

Advancing the e-pawn two squares is the oldest and still the most popular way to begin the game. Beginners who know little more than the rules proudly play 1 e4 before they start losing their pieces. Chess in the movies is dominated by e-pawn play. The majority of the world's top ten players use 1 e4 more often than not.

What's so great about this move? On the most basic level, 1 e4 fights for control of the key central square d5, and it frees the f1-bishop to join the fray. Indeed, in the 1 e4 e5 openings that dominated chess practice for so many years, we find the bishop being developed at an early stage. Surprisingly, however, that doesn't hold true for most of Black's other defences to 1 e4. What other advantages stand forth? Well, moving the e-pawn also opens up the d1-h5 diagonal for White's queen to come out on, although she doesn't use that privilege much in the early stages, so as not to become an object of attack. White's queen does prevent or discourage certain uncommon deployments of Black's pieces and pawns, such as rash advances involving ...f6 or ...f5.

These are not exactly compelling reasons for 1 e4 to have ascended to the throne of the openings realm. Maybe we should think on an even more fundamental level. What's the first goal of opening play? To control the centre. And what's the best way to do that? To set up an ideal centre. There are only two moves involved in that project: e4 and d4. To some extent, playing the one creates the threat to play the other. Thus, playing one of these two moves right away narrows Black's set of logical responses and in some sense establishes a degree of control. At that point there are various advantages to either move, and indeed 1 d4 is White's second most popular opening move by a landslide. The overall preference for 1 e4 then comes down to more subtle factors, and I may as well cite the obvious fact that in the great majority of openings, 1 e4 prepares the way for kingside castling more quickly than does 1 d4.

Now things get a little more complicated. Notice that the e4-pawn is undefended. Not surprisingly, Black will often attack it and try to compel White to spend a move protecting his pawn. This immediate vulnerability is not shared by other popular first moves by White such as 1 d4, 1 c4, or 1 ♘f3. Hence Breyer's proclamation that 'After 1 e4, White's game is in its last throes'! That is melodramatic, of course, but it does reflect the direction in which Black's defences will tend to go. He will generally create threats to White's e-pawn, usually by the move ...♘f6 or by ...d5. We find such an attack on White's e4-pawn in most of the major defences to 1 e4, usually within the first two or three moves of the game. For example:

a) The Caro-Kann: 1 e4 c6 2 d4 *d5*;
b) The Alekhine: 1 e4 ♘*f6*;
c) The Petroff: 1 e4 e5 2 ♘f3 ♘*f6*;
d) The French: 1 e4 e6 2 d4 *d5* (and 3 ♘c3 ♘*f6* or 3 ♘d2 ♘*f6*, among other examples);

e) The Scandinavian: 1 e4 *d5*;

f) The Pirc: 1 e4 d6 2 d4 ♘*f6*.

After 1 e4 e5 much the same holds; for example, 2 f4 exf4 3 ♘f3 *d5* (or *3...♘f6*). Or, after 1 e4 e5 2 ♘f3 ♘c6, we have 3 ♗c4 ♘f6, 3 ♗b5 ♘*f6* and many other Ruy Lopez positions with ...♘f6 at a very early stage.

An exception to all this is the Sicilian Defence: after 1 e4 c5, Black's move ...d5 is normally inferior and in the main lines he doesn't usually get to play ...♘f6 until the 4th or 5th move (e.g., 2 ♘f3 d6 3 d4 cxd4 4 ♘xd4 ♘f6), or perhaps later (after 2 ♘f3 e6 3 d4 cxd4 4 ♘xd4 ♘c6 5 ♘c3 a6 6 ♗e2 ♕c7 7 0-0 ♘f6, for example). Nevertheless, attack on White's e4-pawn is a consistent theme of Black's strategy in these Sicilian variations; he very often follows ...♘f6 with moves such as ...♗b7, ...♘bd7-c5 and the like. Finally, one of White's principal alternatives to 1 e4 c5 2 ♘f3 is 1 e4 c5 2 c3, to which Black normally replies 2...d5 or 2...♘f6, both attacking e4.

This observation may seem trivial, but in how many queen's pawn openings (i.e., those stemming from 1 d4) does Black attack the d4-pawn at all? Certainly not early on in openings like the following:

a) The Queen's Gambit Declined: 1 d4 d5 2 c4 e6 and, for example, 3 ♘c3 ♘f6 4 ♗g5 ♗e7 5 e3 0-0, etc.;

b) The Nimzo-Indian: 1 d4 ♘f6 2 c4 e6 3 ♘c3 ♗b4;

c) The major Indian defences that begin with 1...♘f6 and 2...e6 or 2...g6, with the exception of the Benoni (1 d4 ♘f6 2 c4 c5). This is not universally the case, but for the most part it holds true.

After 1 ♘f3, of course, White's knight is exempt from direct attack by Black; in practical terms, so is White's pawn after 1 c4. We therefore have a fundamental difference between 1 e4 and other first moves.

The Open Games

It is interesting that 1 e4 is commonly thought to be an 'attacking' move. To some extent that derives from the very exposure of the e4-pawn to attack, which can lead to early confrontation and the kind of dynamism often associated with king's pawn openings. But the characterization

of 1 e4 as an 'attacking' opening, and of 1 d4 as a 'positional' opening doesn't really follow. The openings arising from 1 e4 e5 are called the 'Open Games' because pieces tend to come out rapidly and at least part of the pawn-centre tends to evaporate. In particular, the association of 1 e4 with aggressive play stems in large part from the tradition of tactically-based annihilations that spring from 1 e4 e5. Openings deriving from 1 e4 e5 *(D)* are also combative from at least one perspective, namely that even within the first few moves the players so often make threats to pawns, pieces, or even the king.

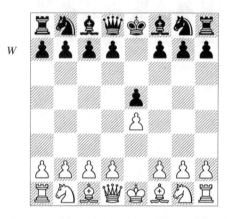

We can see this reputation illustrated by numerous standard variations. The move 2 ♘f3 immediately threatens the e-pawn, and after 2...♘c6 3 ♗c4 ♘f6, 4 ♘g5 already attacks the king! Such things don't happen after 1 d4 d5.

It might be useful to look at some of the more traditional openings after 1 e4 e5. We have 2 f4 (the King's Gambit, an opening ubiquitous in master chess of the 19th century). After 2...exf4 White tries to attack the king down the f-file in conjunction with ♗c4, ♘f3 and 0-0. 2 d4 is another way to attack the pawn, and after 2...exd4 3 c3, White is already trying to blast open the centre with tempo (after 3...dxc3, 4 ♗c4!? cxb2 5 ♗xb2 is the Danish Gambit, and 4 ♘xc3 is the Göring Gambit). The Vienna Game with 2 ♘c3 ♘f6 3 ♗c4 ♘xe4 4 ♕h5 has all the elements of attacking chess. Even the generally calm Giuoco Piano main line, 2 ♘f3 ♘c6 3 ♗c4 ♗c5 4 c3 (don't forget 4 b4, the Evans Gambit) 4...♘f6 5 d4 exd4 6 cxd4 ♗b4+, can result in violent play after 7 ♘c3!? ♘xe4 8 0-0 ♗xc3 9 d5 and similar variations. There are plenty of other examples such as the wild Max Lange with 2 ♘f3 ♘c6 3 ♗c4 ♘f6 4 d4 exd4 5 0-0 and after 5...♗c5 6 e5 (a typical advance; see below) 6...d5 7 exf6 dxc4 8 ♖e1+ ♗e6 9 ♘g5 ♕d5 10 ♘c3 or 5...♘xe4 6 ♖e1 d5 7 ♗xd5 ♕xd5 8 ♘c3 there are things being attacked all over the place!

In all of these examples the centre opens up quickly with short-term tactical consequences. So isn't it clear that the Open Games are dominated by attacking chess? There's something missing from this argument; you could make it in the year 1900 but not today. In contemporary chess, most of the above variations are rarely seen (although they are instructive and worth experimenting with), partly because the quality of dynamism can easily peter out when accompanied by too many exchanges. In fact, all of them put together aren't played nearly as often as the Ruy Lopez (1 e4 e5 2 ♘f3 ♘c6 3 ♗b5). That is significant because in the most important variations of the Ruy Lopez it frequently occurs that not a single pawn is exchanged until well into the middlegame, nor do the pieces get near each other if they can help it. Looked at from that perspective, the king of e-pawn openings doesn't act like an Open Game at all! To be sure, the variations described in this manner are 'Closed' Ruy Lopez systems and do not encompass the entire opening. Nevertheless, in most games with the Ruy Lopez the dynamic action is delayed until after some serious manoeuvring has occurred, a type of play that becomes increasingly fascinating as you become a better player. A similar statement can be made about the Petroff Defence (1 e4 e5 2 ♘f3 ♘f6), the next most popular 1 e4 e5 opening at the international level. The Petroff shouldn't be described as non-confrontational, but it tends to lead to fairly stable half-open structures in which tactics play a lesser role. The Giuoco Piano (1 e4 e5 2 ♘f3 ♘c6 3 ♗c4 ♗c5) and the Scotch Game are examples of double e-pawn openings that can produce either tactical or positional struggles. I think that it's fair to characterize 1 e4 e5 as neither exceptionally dynamic nor sedate.

It might be argued, in fact, that the Open Sicilian (1 e4 c5 2 ♘f3 with 3 d4) has inherited the mantle from double e-pawn openings in producing romantic attacking chess. Not with

disappearing centres, to be sure – the centre is remarkably stable in most Sicilian variations when you consider what's going on around it – but in the exuberant activity of the pieces. White's energetic knights on c3 and d4 are often complemented by bishops on g5, e3, d3 and/or c4; his queen goes to d2, e2 or f3; his rooks to central files, and his pawns rush forward to attack from squares such as f4, f5, g4, g5, h4, h5, etc.

1 e4 versus 1 d4

So which is *objectively* better, 1 e4 or 1 d4? The short answer is that it depends upon the preferences of the individual player. To go any further, we should address the state of theory. Many of us will remember that for some time 1 d4 was Garry Kasparov's main opening move, played in order to generate attacks. Indeed, a significant portion of his most brilliant and aggressive games begin with 1 d4. Attackers like Shirov also used d-pawn openings, as did a younger and more aggressive Kramnik. Korchnoi rarely deviates from his adherence to 1 d4/1 c4 openings and of course many other top-level grandmasters use 1 d4 almost exclusively. Nevertheless, at this moment we see a distinct preference for 1 e4 among most of the world's strongest grandmasters. Is that because 1 d4 isn't an exciting move? Would you say that the Exchange Variation of the Grünfeld, the Botvinnik Variation of the Semi-Slav, the Exchange Variation of the Queen's Gambit Declined, the Taimanov Variation of the Benoni, and any number of King's Indian lines, are not aggressive attacking systems? In reality, what happens is that in different eras, *individual* defences prove to be temporary barriers to the general use of 1 e4 or 1 d4 at the very highest levels. At this moment in time I would say that the Nimzo-Indian (1 d4 ♘f6 2 c4 e6 3 ♘c3 ♗b4) is such a defence, with Black complementing its use with the Queen's Indian Defence or Queen's Gambit Declined when confronted by 3 ♘f3. Recently, however, White has done reasonably well against the Queen's Indian and it has traditionally been possible to create chances against the Queen's Gambit. Furthermore, White's score against the Nimzo-Indian is somewhat better than his score against other openings, including those beginning with 1 e4. In the Ruy Lopez, on the other hand, we currently see White avoiding the Marshall Attack with, for example, an early h3 followed by moves such as d3, a3, ♘c3 and ♗a2 (see Chapter 8). Given the unambitious appearance of this method of play (although it's faring tolerably well so far), one wonders if the pendulum might swing back to 1 d4. Or perhaps players will amend their tastes some years hence, for unrelated reasons. That is part of the fun of following opening theory. At any rate, the average player (and even 'ordinary' master) need not worry about such matters; either first move will produce games with plenty of opportunities for victory.

Don't worry if the recital of names in the last few paragraphs befuddles you. My point is to present 1 e4 from a broad perspective. It can be as much an option for positional players as for attacking players. There are ways to fight for very small and lasting advantages against nearly every defence to 1 e4, and there are ways to try to decimate the opponent with slash-and-burn tactics. Most of the latter methods come up short of their goal against proper defence, or in the face of counterattack by Black. Still, once the smoke has cleared, a bold attack may be just as effective as any other approach at producing a small but durable advantage.

Rather than measuring degrees of aggression, a dispassionate investigation of e-pawn openings turns up a more interesting distinction between 1 e4 and 1 d4. This has to do with the acquisition of space by the pawn advance e5, which is prominent in the Semi-Open Games (defences other than 1...e5), but can also occur in double e-pawn openings. Consider that White can play e5 on the third move of both the Caro-Kann Defence (1 e4 c6 2 d4 d5 3 e5) and French Defence (1 e4 e6 2 d4 d5 3 e5), and on the second move of the Alekhine Defence (1 e4 ♘f6 2 e5). Against the Pirc Defence, e5 is a common move in the variation 1 e4 d6 2 d4 ♘f6 3 ♘c3 g6 4 f4, and played in several lines with 4 ♘f3

and 4 ♗c4. Just a bit further on in French Defence games, we have 1 e4 e6 2 d4 d5 3 ♘c3 ♗b4 4 e5, 1 e4 e6 2 d4 d5 3 ♘c3 ♘f6 4 ♗g5 ♗e7 5 e5, and so forth. After 1 e4 e5, there are moves such as 2 ♘f3 ♘c6 3 ♗c4 ♘f6 4 d4 exd4 5 e5, or the more complex 2 ♘f3 ♘c6 3 d4 exd4 4 ♘xd4 ♘f6 5 ♘xc6 bxc6 6 e5, the latter revived and brought into prominence by World Champion Kasparov.

Where do you find similar advances in the practice of 1 d4 d5, or in any line beginning with 1 d4? In a d-pawn opening, White seldom plays d5 with a threat within the first six moves. In fact, only in a few openings (such as 1 d4 ♘f6 2 c4 c5 3 d5) does the d-pawn even reach the fifth rank, whether there is a threat or not. It's true that d5 will fairly often occur in the King's Indian Defence (e.g., 1 d4 ♘f6 2 c4 g6 3 ♘c3 ♗g7 4 e4 d6 5 ♘f3 0-0 6 ♗e2 e5 and now 7 d5 or 7 0-0 ♘c6 8 d5); and similarly in a few lines of the Grünfeld. However, such d5 advances don't occur often after 1 d4 d5 and will usually happen well past the first several moves of the opening. In e-pawn openings, an analogous situation would be the advance d5 in the Ruy Lopez, normally played after the 10th move.

What does that mean? That by using 1 e4, at least in some openings, White has the option of staking out a significant space advantage early on. This is indeed an aggressive stance, but not one that involves open centres and multiple exchanges – quite the contrary. And keep in mind that when pawns are advanced they can become vulnerable; again we hark back to Breyer's 'last throes'. If you are an e-pawn player, you have to take that possibility into account when you advance your pawns. Failure to tie your opponent down or make other difficulties for him can sometimes leave you on the defensive. On the other hand, an aggressive pawn presence in the enemy camp can reward you with a winning advantage. You will see examples of both of these results throughout the book.

5 Giuoco Piano

1 e4 e5 2 ♘f3 ♘c6 3 ♗c4 *(D)*

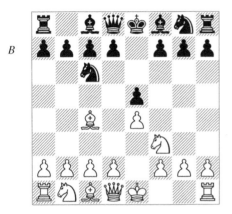

The move 3 ♗c4 has been used consistently since the early days of chess in its modern form. Although far behind the Ruy Lopez (3 ♗b5) in popularity, 3 ♗c4 is White's second favourite continuation. Placing the bishop on c4 agrees with the principles of development and centralization, and prepares to castle quickly. It is also the move that most directly attacks Black's position, in particular the sensitive f7-square. In addition, White wants to control the central d5-square and thus prevent Black's freeing move ...d5. In this respect 3 ♗c4 fulfils a positive positional role that, for instance, 3 ♗e2 doesn't.

As always, there are drawbacks, not obvious at first. Because the bishop on c4 makes no threat, Black himself is able to develop freely. That would also seem to be true of 3 ♗b5, which also has no direct threat; but the latter move discourages a number of black set-ups that ♗c4 doesn't, by virtue of the potential threat of ♗xc6 and ♘xe5. In the Giuoco Piano, moreover, we shall see that if Black *does* achieve the move ...d5, White may lose a tempo or suffer some positional disadvantage. These considerations are rather abstract, and can only be shown by example.

I should mention that the Bishop's Opening, 1 e4 e5 2 ♗c4, is a respectable choice that

will sometimes transpose to 3 ♗c4, for instance after 2...♗c5 3 ♘f3 ♘c6. The independent line 2 ♗c4 ♘f6 3 d3 c6 4 ♘f3 d5 5 ♗b3 ♗d6 can lead to complex play, and of course Black can play ...♘c6 on one of the first few moves. One of the problems with 2 ♗c4 is that Black has various ways to control the direction of play. That interferes with some players' desire to be in command as White, particularly when facing a symmetrical variation such as 1...e5.

3...♗c5 *(D)*

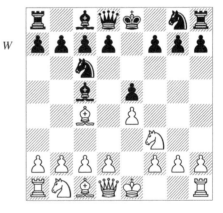

This development of Black's bishop is the oldest well-analysed response to 3 ♗c4. I'll use the generally accepted name 'Giuoco Piano' for 3...♗c5; it is also called 'the Italian Game' in recognition of the Italian players who published analysis of the move in the late 16th and early 17th centuries.

With 3...♗c5, Black attends to White's move d4, the idea of which is to form an ideal centre. Moreover, the move ♘g5 is lurking in the background; since that would attack the f7-square twice, Black wants to be ready to defend against the threat by castling. The straightforward position after 3...♗c5 contains a majority of the basic classical ideas about development, centre and attack. That should motivate us to examine it in some depth.

4 c3

I shall concentrate upon this continuation as representing the purest intent of the opening: to establish an ideal centre and drive Black's pieces away with tempo. 4 c3 leads to play that resembles other openings and is therefore of general value. For organizational reasons, the line 4 d3 ♘f6 is discussed in Chapter 6 about the Two Knights Defence. It will arise via the move-order 1 e4 e5 2 ♘f3 ♘c6 3 ♗c4 ♘f6 4 d3 ♗c5. The similar 4 c3 ♘f6 5 d3 is placed at the end of this chapter.

4...♘f6

With this move Black develops a piece and counterattacks. Other moves allow White to execute his plan; for example, the line 4...d6?! 5 d4 exd4 6 cxd4 ♗b4+ *(D)* illustrates White's central superiority.

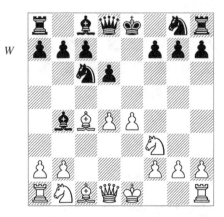

Then White has several good continuations:

a) 7 ♔f1!? (this is the fancy way to get out of check; White threatens 8 d5, and when the knight moves, 9 ♕a4+ picks up the bishop) 7...♗a5 8 d5 ♘ce7 9 b4! (9 ♕a4+ c6 protects the a5-bishop) 9...♗b6 10 ♗b2 and the bishops are dominating the board. One can compare the Evans Gambit (1 e4 e5 2 ♘f3 ♘c6 3 ♗c4 ♗c5 4 b4 ♗xb4 5 c3), in which something like this can arise but with Black having an extra pawn by way of compensation.

b) Naturally 7 ♘c3, developing a piece, can't be bad: 7...♘f6 8 d5 ♗xc3+ (again, watch out for 8...♘e7?? 9 ♕a4+, winning a piece; this is a common trick in many openings, including those stemming from 1 d4) 9 bxc3. The resulting position favours White because of his dominating centre.

c) 7 ♗d2 ♗xd2+ 8 ♕xd2 gives White superior development in terms of quantity *and* quality.

We now return to 4...♘f6 *(D)*:

5 d4

Certainly the most challenging continuation. A less aggressive but also interesting alternative is 5 d3. I'll discuss that more technical move at the end of the chapter.

White has the instructive option of playing 5 0-0, when Black does best to capture by 5...♘xe4 and meet 6 d4 with 6...d5! (file this move away in your memory! Black should almost always play ...d5 when allowed to do so, that is, if it's tactically sound) 7 dxc5 dxc4 8 ♕xd8+ ♔xd8. From White's point of view, this endgame is at best equal, and more likely he will end up with a somewhat inferior position.

5...exd4 6 cxd4

The seemingly assertive 6 e5 can again be answered by 6...d5! (6...♘e4?!, with 7 ♕e2 d5 8 exd6 0-0 in mind, is strongly answered by 7 ♗d5) 7 ♗b5 (7 exf6? dxc4 8 fxg7 ♖g8 leaves all of Black's pieces active and ready to spring into action, whereas White is underdeveloped and losing badly in the centre; Black will castle queenside in order to safeguard his king) 7...♘e4 8 cxd4. Now Black can play either 8...♗b4+ or, more commonly, 8...♗b6. In the latter case play might go 9 0-0 0-0 10 ♗xc6?! (this slightly dubious capture is given in the books; the rationale is that Black was planning ...♘e7) 10...bxc6 *(D)*.

At first it may look like the bishop is badly placed on b6 and Black suffers from weak

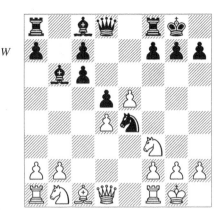

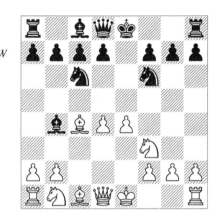

pawns on the open c-file. However, he has the bishop-pair and is ready to assault White's centre by ...c5. There's little White can do about that; for example, 11 b4!? (to stop ...c5; some other moves are 11 ♕c2 ♗g4! and 11 h3 c5! 12 ♗e3 cxd4 13 ♘xd4 ♕e8!, having in mind ...♕xe5, or ...c5 and ...f6; lastly, 11 ♗e3 ♗a6 12 ♖e1 c5 13 dxc5 ♘xc5 is good for Black) 11...a5 12 ♗a3 axb4 13 ♗xb4 c5 14 dxc5 ♗xc5 15 ♗xc5 ♘xc5 16 ♕c2 ♘e6 17 ♖d1 c5; then Black has two passed pawns and a nicely centralized position.

Notice the combination of 13...c5 and 17...c5. This double-hammer with the c-pawns with the intent to destroy White's centre is a common theme. White should take that possibility into account when playing ♗xc6. This type of position will frequently arise in other opening variations.

6...♗b4+ *(D)*

It's worth a look to see how powerful the possession of an unopposed ideal centre can be: 6...♗b6? 7 d5! ♘e7 8 e5 ♘e4 9 0-0 0-0 10 ♕e2 ♘c5 11 b4 ♘a6 12 d6 cxd6 13 exd6 ♘g6 14 ♗g5 ♕e8 15 ♗e7 ♔h8 16 ♘c3 ♘xb4 17 ♖ae1 ♘c6 18 ♗xf8 ♕xe2 19 ♖xe2 ♘xf8 20 ♖e8 ♔g8 21 ♘d5 g6 22 ♘e7+ 1-0 Euwe-Jutte, Amsterdam 1927. See also the sample game in Chapter 1.

7 ♗d2

The tactics that follow 7 ♘c3 ♘xe4 8 0-0 ♗xc3 9 d5 lead to some 20 moves of theory and are not dealt with here. Various books will supply the details. 7 ♔f1, the 'Krakow Variation', should be met by the standard counterthrust 7...d5! 8 exd5 ♘xd5 and it's not clear what the king is doing on f1.

7...♗xd2+

Recently the older 7...♘xe4 8 ♗xb4 ♘xb4 9 ♗xf7+ ♔xf7 10 ♕b3+ has again been tried for Black, often leading to 10...d5 11 ♘e5+, when 11...♔e6!? 12 ♕xb4 c5 results in complex play. This line is unresolved; many players will not trust it because Black's king comes to the centre, and others will embrace its adventurous character. In any event, it's refreshing that long-discarded variations can spring to life again.

8 ♘bxd2 d5 9 exd5 ♘xd5 *(D)*

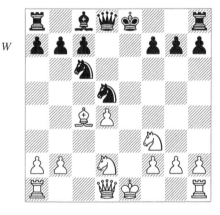

10 ♕b3

White usually plays this immediately, in order to attack Black's blockading knight on d5 before it is fully secured and before Black's king reaches safety. There are two instructive alternatives, the second of which keeps the game interesting for both players:

a) 10 0-0 is playable but allows Black more options after 10...0-0, when 11 ♕b3?! ♘a5! eliminates White's c4-bishop without compromise. A demonstration of how White can pit his activity against Black's static advantages went 11 ♘e5!? (objectively, the move 11 ♕c2! is doubtless better; compare 10 ♕c2 in variation 'b') 11...♘xd4!? (11...♘xe5 12 dxe5 ♗e6 13 ♕b3 ♖b8 is equal, but White's pawns are reconnected in that case) 12 ♘b3! ♘xb3 13 ♗xd5! ♘xa1? (13...♕f6 is best) 14 ♗xf7+ ♔h8 15 ♕h5! *(D)* with a terrific attack, Kluxen-Capablanca, Hamburg simul 1911.

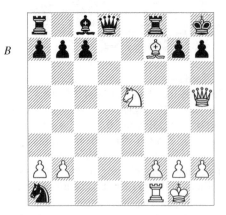

The game continued 15...♗f5 (15...h6 16 ♖d1) 16 ♕xf5 ♕f6 17 ♘g6+! ♕xg6 (17...hxg6 18 ♕h3+ is a trick worth knowing) 18 ♗xg6 ♖xf5 19 ♗xf5 g6 20 ♗e4 1-0, since the a1-knight will fall. If this hadn't been a simultaneous exhibition (as opposed to a serious tournament game), Kluxen's name would have gone down in history for beating the mighty Capablanca! As it stands, the game shows the appeal of the Open Games.

b) The other alternative with a durable character is 10 ♕c2; for example, 10...♘ce7 (if 10...♕e7+, then 11 ♔f1 is good for White; likewise 10...♗e6 11 0-0 0-0 12 ♖fe1 ♘db4 13 ♕b3 ♗xc4 14 ♘xc4) 11 0-0 0-0 12 ♘e4 ♗g4 13 ♖ac1 ♗xf3!? 14 ♘g5 g6 15 ♘xf3. So White has more than one way to maintain active play on the board.

Now let's return to 10 ♕b3 *(D)*:

This venerable position is characterized by a balance of classic positional factors: White's greater activity and space, including pressure down the c- and e-files, versus Black's firm blockade of a potentially weak isolated pawn on d4. In Chapter 3, I discuss numerous other isolated queen's pawns in chess openings. How does this IQP compare with those? As always,

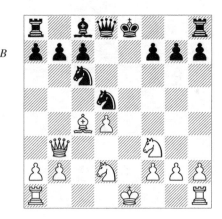

Black's blockade of d5 is a key element in his attempt to keep the position under control. In the position before us, White can't break the blockade but can 'play around' that knight to create threats. The exchange of dark-squared bishops should favour Black, because simplification makes it harder for White to muster forces for an attack. This raises the interesting question of what degree of simplification tends to negate the more active party's compensation for his isolated pawn weakness. In this particular situation White still has significant resources, as we shall see. Although some further exchanges will seriously cut into his chances, others can increase his pressure! It all depends upon piece-play. For instance, isolated queen's pawn positions from other openings like the Queen's Gambit Accepted, Nimzo-Indian, Caro-Kann, etc., allow Black options of expanding on the queenside by ...a6 and ...b5 or fianchettoing with ...b6 and ...♗b7. That sort of thing doesn't apply to our current variation, nor does Black appear to have a way to disturb the equilibrium. If that's true, Black may have to leave his opponent alone for a while, giving White crucial time to try to improve his position. On the other hand, Black has no weaknesses to attack and will only permit a weakness to be created if he can gain something in return.

After 10 ♕b3, Black has two basic plans: reinforcing his blockade by 10...♘ce7, or trying to force events by 10...♘a5. We'll examine both.

Blockading the Pawn

10...♘ce7 *(D)*

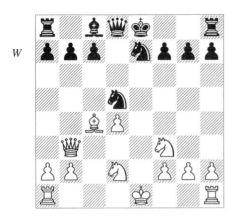

W

In this situation, the battle between piece activity and positional factors revolves specifically around the isolated pawn and its blockader. Some samples of the play follow.

O'Kelly – Euwe
Amsterdam 1950

11 0-0 c6 12 ☖fe1 0-0

Black has shored up d5 with no obvious difficulties. However, White has energetic minor pieces and can create significant problems. First, he stakes out some territory.

13 a4

Gaining space is often the best policy when there are no direct targets. White operates against ...b5, but also plans a5, serving the double function of preparing an attack on b7 and keeping a knight from b6. The other strategy is to emphasize piece-play, for instance by 13 ☖e4. White can also develop immediately by 13 ☖ac1, as he has done in a few games; for example, 13...a5!? (or 13...♛b6 14 ♛a3 ♝e6 15 ☖e4, with nagging pressure involving moves like ☖d6, ☖c5 and ☖fg5, Rossolimo-O'Kelly, Amsterdam 1950; Black would most likely do better to play 13...☖b6 14 ♝d3 ♝f5 15 ☖e4 ♛c7 with some kind of dynamic equality) 14 ☖e4 a4 15 ♛a3 ☖f5, Renner-Gabriel, 2nd Bundesliga 2000/1; at this point White had the opportunity for the transformation 16 ♝xd5!? ♛xd5 17 ☖c5 ♛d8 18 ♛b4 when Black is tied down; e.g., 18...☖e8 19 ☖e5!.

13...♛b6!

Euwe's continuation is probably the most logical response. Simplification should help the defender and Black avoids weaknesses as

well. The irritating effect of the pawn-push a5 shows up in the beautiful game Rossolimo-Reissman, Puerto Rico 1967: 13...b6 14 ☖e5 ♝b7 15 a5! ☖c8?! (15...f6! 16 ☖d3 ♚h8 is the consistent strategy, guarding d5; Black should use his own strengths) 16 ☖e4 ♛c7 17 a6 ♝a8 18 ♛h3 ☖f4 19 ♛g4 ☖ed5 20 ☖a3!. Now Black's king is under serious attack before he has the chance to play ...c5 and free his a8-bishop. The game continued 20...☖e6? (a poor move, but 20...c5 21 g3 ☖g6 22 ☖xg6 hxg6 23 ♛h4 is also good for White, with ideas including 24 ☖g5 ☖f6 25 ☖ae3!) 21 ♝xd5 cxd5 22 ☖f6+ ♚h8 23 ♛g6!! *(D)*.

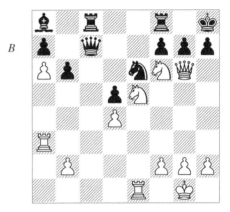

B

Naturally the brilliance of this move strikes one first (reminiscent of the famous Levitsky-Marshall ...♛g3!! game) but an eye for detail will also pick up Black's bishop stuck behind the d5-pawn. That was of course the blockading square which was the pride and joy of Black's position. The game continued 23...♛c2 (mate on h7 is threatened, but accepting the queen sacrifice loses instantly: 23...fxg6 24 ☖xg6+ hxg6 25 ☖h3#; 23...hxg6 24 ☖h3#; or 23...gxf6 24 ♛xf6+ ☖g7 25 ☖g3 ☖g8 26 ☖xf7+) 24 ☖h3! 1-0. Either the rook or queen threatens to capture on h7 with checkmate on the next move, but 24...♛xg6 25 ☖xg6+ fxg6 26 ☖xh7# is checkmate.

Instead of 13...♛b6 or 13...b6, a defence which avoids weakening the queenside and maintains the bishop on the h3-c8 diagonal is 13...☖b8; for example, 14 a5 f6!? *(D)*. Any move of Black's f-pawn is double-edged: why would he allow a hole on e6? The answer is that, by protecting e5, Black prepares ...♝g4 without fear of ♘e5. He can also play ...♔h8 without worrying about a knight attack on f7. Black thinks that he can afford the weakness on e6 for the sake of quick development. Another, apparently safer, move is 14...h6, preparing ...♗e6 or ...♗f5, but then 15 a6! b5 16 ♗xd5 ♘xd5 17 ♘e4 ♖b6 18 ♘c5 ♘c7 19 ♕c3! ♘xa6 20 b4 establishes a huge clamp that is worth more than a pawn.

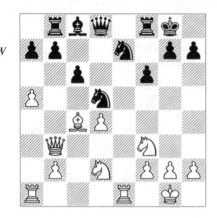

Garcia Fernandez-Korneev, Madrid 2002 continued 15 ♘e4 (15 a6 b5 16 ♘e4 ♗g4!) 15...♔h8 16 ♕a3 ♗g4 17 h3 ♗h5 18 ♘c5 ♖e8 19 ♘e6 (a huge square but there are no targets!) 19...♕d7 20 ♘c5 ♕c8 21 ♗xd5 ♘xd5 22 ♖xe8+ ♕xe8 23 ♖e1 ♕d8. Black has achieved the desired simplification and preserved the precious blockade on d5. Now the re-entry of the knight by 24 ♘e6 is met by 24...♕g8 threatening ...♖e8, ...♗f7, etc. It takes courage to play this way, however.

14 a5!? *(D)*

Rossolimo presses on with a remarkable idea. It's amazing that White can permit Black to exchange queens, which in theory should be all that Black needs to consolidate his d5 outpost and attack the d4-pawn. Here we have a lesson about isolated queen's pawns: although it's not the rule, a great deal of simplification can be suffered by their owner if his pieces get to favourable squares. Instead, 14 ♕a3 is thematic, yet the black pawn-structure remains unchallenged following 14...♗e6 (14...♘f5 has been played but 15 ♗xd5! cxd5 16 ♘b3 should give White a small advantage due to his good knights and Black's bad bishop) 15 a5?! (15 ♘e4 is double-edged) 15...♕c7 16 ♘e4 (16

♘g5 ♗f5) 16...♖ad8 17 ♘c5 ♗c8!. Here White is running out of ideas whereas the d5-square is the axis of the game. This line serves as a good model for Black's play.

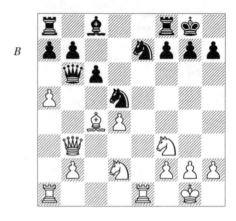

14...♕xb3 15 ♘xb3 ♗f5

Although developing the bishop is probably satisfactory, it is not as clear as 15...♖d8, when if White gets too ambitious we can see all of Black's pieces coordinate to his benefit; e.g., 16 ♘c5!? ♖b8! 17 ♘e5 (White can try 17 ♖ac1 b6 18 ♘d3!, but Black will equalize after 18...♗d7 19 axb6 axb6; for example, 20 ♗xd5! ♘xd5 21 ♘fe5 ♘e7 22 ♘b4 f6! 23 ♘xd7 ♖xd7 24 ♘xc6 ♘xc6 25 ♖xc6 ♖xd4 26 f3 ♖b7 with an equal position) 17...♔f8 (17...f6? 18 ♘ed7!) Rossolimo-Unzicker, Heidelberg 1949; now if White plays 18 ♖a3? (18 ♘f3 is equal; that's the best that White can do) 18...b6 19 axb6 axb6 20 ♘e4, Black repulses White by 20...f6 21 ♘f3 ♗d7!.

16 ♘e5

With the idea 17 a6.

16...♘b4!?

16...♖fe8 gives a more solid impression. Black is probably close to equality hereabouts but it's hard to counter White's queenside pressure. 16...a6? would create a strongpoint on c5 which White could immediately occupy to good effect.

17 ♖ac1

After 17 ♘xf7, Black's trick was 17...♘ed5! with the threats of ...♖xf7 and ...♘c2.

17...♘ed5 18 a6! *(D)*

White destroys the foundation of Black's light-square bulwark.

18...b5 19 ♗xd5 cxd5 20 ♘c6 ♘xc6 21 ♖xc6 ♖fe8 ½-½

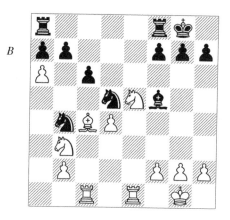

Pachman analysed this position and showed that White stands much better, confirming the general idea that White's knight is superior to Black's bishop: 22 ♖xe8+ ♖xe8 23 f3 (23 h3 is also good) 23...♖e1+ (23...♖c8 24 ♖d6 ♗e6 25 ♘c5) 24 ♔f2 ♖b1 25 ♘c5 ♖xb2+ 26 ♔g3 g5 27 ♖c7 ♔g7 28 ♖xa7 ♖a2 29 ♖b7 ♗c8 30 ♖xb5 ♗xa6 31 ♘xa6 ♖xa6 32 ♖xd5 with a technically winning game.

All this material is terribly instructive for the developing player, and even masters might find the ideas intriguing.

Chasing the Pieces

10...♘a5 11 ♕a4+ *(D)*

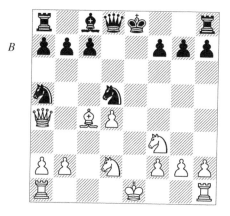

11...♘c6
This has long been thought to provide Black with a drawing option, or at least an extremely drawish one. Instead, 11...c6? defends d5 but fails for concrete reasons, because after 12 ♗xd5! ♕xd5 13 ♖c1 White threatens both

♖c5 and b4. Then 13...♕b5! is forced, but White dominates after 14 ♕a3! (threatening ♖c5 and ♘e4) 14...b6 15 ♘e4 ♘b7 16 ♘e5 ♗d7 17 ♘c4 ♕d5 18 0-0 0-0-0 19 ♕xa7! ♕xe4 20 d5! with utter destruction of Black's position to follow.

After the text-move, ...♘b6 is threatened, to rid White of his best attacking piece, the c4-bishop. There follows an illustration of the play.

Kupreichik – Aleksandrov
Bad Wörishofen 2001

12 0-0!? *(D)*
Castling is the most interesting continuation. Quite a few games have continued 12 ♕b3 ♘a5 13 ♕a4+ ♘c6 14 ♕b3 ♘a5 with a draw, an outcome that must have been satisfactory to both players, probably even before the game started. This indicates that in order for Black to try for a win, he should play 12...♘ce7 (see the previous section on 10...♘ce7). However, White doesn't have to take this draw and can keep the play alive by 12 0-0. He also had the earlier option of 10 0-0-0-0 11 ♕c2, mentioned above in the note to White's tenth move.

White's other options are 12 ♗b5, which is playable but not so convincing after 12...♗d7; and 12 ♘e5?!, which runs into surprising problems after 12...0-0! 13 ♘xc6 ♕e8+! 14 ♔f1 ♘b6! 15 ♕b3 (15 ♕b5 bxc6 16 ♕c5 ♘xc4) 15...♕xc6, Karkocha-Swerin, corr. 1985. Black has a big advantage in view of White's terrible king position.

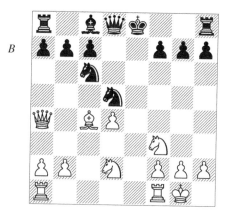

12...0-0

The problem with 12 0-0 is supposed to be that 12...♘b6 forks queen and bishop, but then there can follow 13 ♖fe1+ ♗e6 14 ♕a3!, after which White prevents Black from castling and 14...♘xc4 (what else?) 15 ♘xc4 gives White extremely well-placed pieces and Black still can't bring his king to safety. A simple plan is ♖ad1 followed by d5. If Black captures the d-pawn by 15...♘xd4, he is subject to a typical open-position attack after 16 ♖ad1 ♘xf3+ 17 ♕xf3. After 17...♕c8?! 18 ♕a3 White has prevented castling and threatens f4-f5. Black should play the active 17...♕h4, though 18 ♕xb7 keeps an edge.

13 ♗xd5!?

Slightly passive. In the spirit of avoiding simplification, White should try 13 ♕c2! ♗e6 (13...♘b6 14 ♗d3 h6 15 ♕c5!?) 14 ♖fe1 ♘db4 15 ♕c3, and the struggle between White's space and Black's pressure on the IQP continues, a sample line being 15...♗xc4 16 ♘xc4 ♘d5 17 ♕b3 ♘b6 18 ♖ac1!? ♘xd4 19 ♘xd4 ♕xd4 20 ♘a5 with an edge for White. This kind of play resembles our 10 ♕b3 ♘ce7 main line above.

13...♕xd5 14 ♖ac1 ♕d8

Also 14...♗e6 is sensible, to blockade on d5; e.g., 15 ♖c5 ♕d8! (15...♕xa2 16 ♕xa2 ♗xa2 17 b3) 16 ♖e1 ♗d5.

15 ♘e4 (D)

15 ♘b3 intending ♖fe1 and ♘c5 is a more complex route. Then play might go 15...♘e7 16 ♖fe1 ♘d5 17 ♘c5 c6 with unclear prospects.

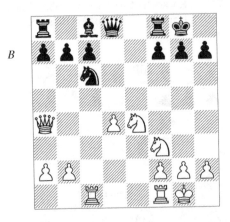

15...♘e7! 16 ♖fe1 ♘d5

The opening is over and the chances appear about equal. In spite of White's significant lead in development, Black's grip on d5 and absolute

lack of weaknesses protect him from immediate attack.

The older lines of the Giuoco Piano can still challenge the chess understanding of both players. No other opening serves better as a model for classical double e-pawn chess. Those of little or moderate playing experience will find careful study and practice of this opening particularly valuable, and even experienced players could do worse than to investigate its unique properties.

A Technical Approach: 5 d3

What if White doesn't want to engage in the kind of open struggle just described? Let's take a look at what happens if he doesn't go in for the relatively forced moves that follow 5 d4 and plays 5 d3 instead:

1 e4 e5 2 ♘f3 ♘c6 3 ♗c4 ♗c5 4 c3 ♘f6 5 d3 (D)

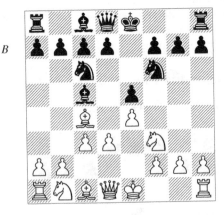

This is the kind of slow move that White typically makes in order to play it safe and engage Black in a battle of positional skills. His ideas by setting up this structure are:

   a) to protect his e4-pawn;

   b) to cover the d4-square against intrusions by Black's pieces (in particular ...♘d4); and

   c) to hold off on the move d4 until his pieces are more developed, thereby avoiding the forcing variation that we saw in the main variation after 5 d4 exd4 6 cxd4 ♗b4+, which was soon followed by the centre-clearing move ...d5.

On the other hand, Black now has much more freedom to develop his pieces. Without fear of d4 he can do so actively and should secure equality. But don't expect the play to be easy for either side.

Now I'm going to show one game out of the many that have been played, with the goal of including some general ideas that will be applicable to similar positions.

Karpov – Korchnoi
Merano Wch (8) 1981

5...d6

Black secures the e5-pawn against threats such as b4-b5. Here is a general warning for Black: you shouldn't be in too great a rush to play the tempting ...d5, because your centre can become too vulnerable; for instance, 5...d5?! 6 exd5 ♘xd5 7 b4 (7 ♕b3 is also dangerous) 7...♗b6 8 b5 ♘a5 9 ♘xe5. Notice that the pin on the knight by 9...♕e7?! means nothing after 10 0-0!, because 10...♕xe5?? loses to 11 ♖e1. Also weak would be 5...0-0 6 0-0 d5?! 7 exd5 ♘xd5 8 b4! followed by 9 b5. These lines show one of the benefits that White gets by playing c3.

6 0-0 0-0

6...♗g4 is also possible, with more or less the same kind of position that we shall discuss in Chapter 6 when we look at 4 d3 in the Two Knights Defence.

7 ♘bd2 *(D)*

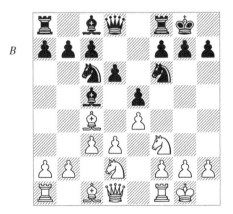

7...a6!?

Advancing the a-pawn so modestly has two ideas: to put the bishop on the safe square a7 and to be able to play ...♘a5 and capture the c4-bishop. That exchange would gain Black the

advantage of the bishop-pair with no concession on his part. Note that 7...♘a5 right away would have allowed 8 ♗b5! a6 9 ♗a4 b5 10 ♗c2, which saves White's bishop from exchange and threatens b4. So we can see another advantage of White's move c3. After the textmove, the positional threat of 8...♘a5 is real, so play can continue as follows:

8 ♗b3 ♗a7 9 h3!? *(D)*

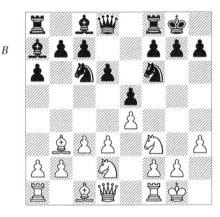

Karpov's move. It prevents ...♗g4 in some situations, but mainly it prepares ♖e1 without having to worry about ...♘g4. White is now ready to reorganize by moving his knight to c4 and e3, or to play ♖e1 followed by ♘f1, in turn followed by ♘g3 or ♘e3. Perhaps you're familiar with this sequence of moves, but if not, it must look rather odd. In fact, the knight manoeuvre ♘bd2-f1-g3/e3 is standard practice. I won't go into detail at this point, but the principle here is that if the centre is stable, players may be able to embark upon long trips with their pieces without being punished. From g3, White's knight lusts after the wonderful square f5 and protects e4; and after ♘e3, the knight sets its eyes upon both d5 and f5 (at the cost of blocking off his queen's bishop). We shall see a lot of this manoeuvre ♘bd2-f1-g3/e3 in the Ruy Lopez chapter, and it's good to be introduced to it now.

9...♗e6

9...h6 is a good option. You will see a lot of these 'little moves' in variations with d3 and ...d6. The idea is to prevent ♗g5 after White's knight moves. After 10 ♖e1, there can follow 10...♘h5!. Compare the game and comments below.

9...d5!? is also playable at this point, although 10 罝e1 is curiously solid for White and asks Black what he's going to do next.

10 皇c2 d5!? 11 罝e1 dxe4

Ripperger gives the fascinating line 11...d4 12 ᐠc4 dxc3 13 bxc3 皇xc4 14 dxc4, when White's pawn-structure is thoroughly damaged, but he has the bishop-pair and play down the b- and d-files.

12 dxe4 ᐠh5! *(D)*

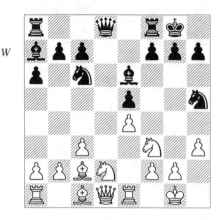

W

This isn't the only move by any means, but it follows a 'mini-rule' that can apply to any opening in which there are pawns on e4 and e5: if White plays h3, the move ...ᐠh5 should be strongly considered. The reasoning is that after ...ᐠf4, the knight can't be kicked out by g3 since ...ᐠxh3 will follow. But if White's bishop captures that knight (皇xf4), he will have ceded the bishop-pair; that is hardly disastrous but usually not a good thing for White (remember how important it is to possess the two bishops). Notice that in the note above about 9...h6, the d-file was closed. This time we're about to get an exchange of queens.

Of course this sort of technical guidance only fits in certain situations, but it can also apply to the Ruy Lopez and Philidor Defences, and the same idea quite frequently occurs in the King's Indian Defence, a very different opening indeed!

13 ᐠf1 豐xd1 14 罝xd1 罝ad8 15 皇e3 f6 16 皇xa7 ᐠxa7 17 ᐠe3 ᐠf4 18 h4 皇f7 19 ᐠe1

At this point Polugaevsky suggests 19...ᐠe6 20 皇b3 ᐠc5, which looks equal.

6 Two Knights Defence

1 e4 e5 2 ♘f3 ♘c6 3 ♗c4 ♘f6 *(D)*

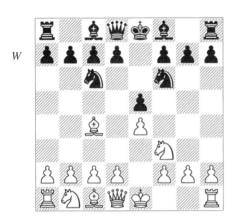

This is the Two Knights Defence. Its main lines are definitely more ambitious and tactical than those after 3...♗c5. I shall focus on the two main continuations, 4 ♘g5 and 4 d4, and we'll also examine 4 d3 at some length due to its popularity and its instructive nature.

But first, let's briefly glance at a few rare continuations:

a) 4 c3?, as in the Giuoco Piano, is mistimed here due to 4...♘xe4 and White won't even get his pawn back without severe disadvantage; for example, 5 ♕e2 d5 6 ♗b5 f6! 7 d4 ♕d6 or 7...♗g4.

b) 4 0-0 ♘xe4 5 ♘c3!? is the maverick Boden-Kiezeritsky Gambit (some inferior moves are: 5 ♖e1 d5 6 ♗b5 ♗c5!, 5 d4 d5 and 5 ♕e2 d5 6 ♗b5 ♗g4! 7 d3 ♗xf3 8 gxf3 ♘f6). A traditional main line goes 5...♘xc3 (Black can also spoil White's fun by 5...♘d6 6 ♗d5 ♗e7 or 5...♘f6 6 ♖e1 ♗e7 7 ♘xe5 ♘xe5 8 ♖xe5 d6 9 ♖e1 d5 10 ♗f1 0-0, with equality in both cases) 6 dxc3 f6 (interesting is 6...♕e7!? 7 ♘g5 ♘d8) 7 ♘h4 g6 8 f4 ♕e7 (threatening ...♗c5+) 9 ♔h1 d6, when Black has a solid game and is still a pawn up, but some players would relish the challenge facing White!

c) 4 ♘c3 *(D)* can be unique, especially because it can transpose from the Vienna Game

with 2 ♘c3 ♘f6 3 ♗c4 ♘c6 4 ♘f3 (to avoid 4 d3 ♗b4!?):

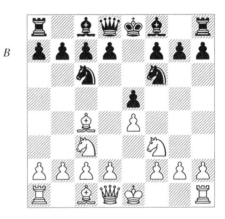

Black can opt for 4...♗c5, of course, probably heading back to lines below; but he can also play more decisively by 4...♘xe4!? 5 ♘xe4 (5 0-0 is the Boden-Kiezeritsky Gambit again; as usual, Black's centre is more important than his king position after 5 ♗xf7+? ♔xf7 6 ♘xe4 d5! 7 ♘eg5+ ♔g8 with ...h6 coming next) 5...d5, and we enter some fun and unresolved territory:

c1) 6 ♗b5? dxe4 7 ♘xe5 ♕g5! is a standard tactical trick of the kind that we also see in the Ruy Lopez. In this particular case White is in big trouble because of the attack on g2 and unfortunate placement of the knight and bishop along the same rank. There follows 8 ♘xc6 (8 d4 ♕xg2 9 ♖f1 a6 10 ♗xc6+ bxc6 will win for Black) 8...♕xb5 9 ♘d4 ♕e5 10 ♘e2 ♗f5 and Black stands very well.

c2) 6 ♗d3! dxe4 7 ♗xe4 *(D)*.

Now:

c21) The traditional 7...♗d6 8 ♗xc6+ (8 d4 exd4 9 ♗xc6+ bxc6 transposes) 8...bxc6 9 d4! exd4 10 ♕xd4 0-0 11 0-0 is complicated with an unclear imbalance, perhaps favouring White slightly; e.g., following 11...c5 12 ♕c3 ♗b7 with two bishops versus better structure.

c22) 7...♘e7!? (Black plays ambitiously, threatening to win a piece by 8...f5 and at the

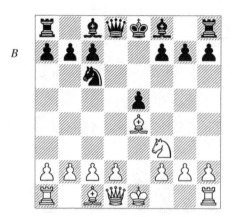

B

same time sidestepping ♗xc6+) 8 ♗d3 (not 8 ♘xe5?? ♕d4) 8...♗g4 9 h3 ♗h5 10 ♗b5+! (denying Black's knight access to the key c6-square; 10 0-0?! ♕d5! and 10 g4?! ♗g6 are definitely worse) 10...c6 11 ♗c4 ♕d6 12 ♕e2 f6 13 0-0 0-0-0 with equality.

The Calm 4 d3

4 d3 *(D)*

This move quietly protects the e-pawn with a minimum of risk.

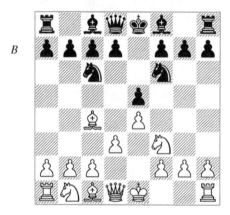

B

It is not dangerous for either side but White's modest pawn-push brings up some important positional points. Instead of doing a systematic analysis I want to emphasize a few characteristic types of positions that one should know to understand this variation.

Before I even get to that, very inexperienced players might want take a look at 4...♗e7 (a slow move, but not a bad one) 5 ♘g5?! 0-0 6 ♘xf7? ♖xf7 7 ♗xf7+ ♔xf7. Few players who

have built up playing experience with 1 e4 e5 would even consider such a trade for White, but those just starting out are often attracted to this ♘g5/♘xf7 idea (which appears in many 1 e4 e5 openings, such as the Giuoco Piano, Göring Gambit and Ruy Lopez). It's important to know that in most chess openings, two pieces are better than rook and pawn, and usually the equal or better of a rook and *two* pawns, until there arises an ending or a considerably simplified position. Of course, that claim contradicts simple point-count chess (White has 6 or 7 points versus Black's 6). The explanation is that the minor pieces enter the action earlier and co-ordinate better in attack and defence, especially on a crowded board. Keep in mind that rooks tend to get developed later and, more importantly, to get blocked off if there are too many pawns and pieces around. There are few exceptions to this. Thus 5 ♘g5 and 6 ♘xf7 are mistakes.

However, you should know that in an *endgame* with a rook and pawns versus bishop and knight, the latter will often have trouble defending each other at the same time as they attempt to hold off the pawns. The bishop and knight may do reasonably well if pawns are on the same side of the board, but if the rook is escorting a pawn or two far from the opponent's king, the minor pieces will normally have a very hard time of it.

4...♗c5 5 ♘c3

The position after 5 c3 is examined in Chapter 5 as part of the Giuoco Piano.

5...d6 *(D)*

We have arrived at a completely symmetrical position.

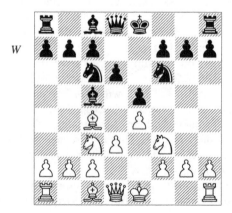

W

It's surprising how much chess content there can be in such a simple position. We'll now look at a number of instructive continuations and themes:

6 ♘a4 can be met by 6...♗b6 7 ♘xb6 axb6, which grants Black a solid game and an open a-file; but that may not be what he wants. There is another way to give up the bishop-pair: 6...♕e7 7 ♘xc5 dxc5. This sequence changes the pawn-structure, and along with it the character of the game. In return for the bishop-pair Black gets an open d-file and freedom of development. White's wished-for move d4 will be next to impossible to organize. This kind of exchange varies from position to position, and crops up in the King's Gambit Declined (1 e4 e5 2 f4 ♗c5 3 ♘f3 d6 4 ♗c4 followed by d3 and ♘a4) and even the English Opening, via, for instance, 1 c4 e5 2 ♘c3 ♘f6 3 ♘f3 ♘c6 4 g3 ♗c5 5 ♗g2 d6 6 0-0 0-0 7 d3 ♗g4 8 ♘a4, etc. In these cases most experts would tend to regard the trade as an equal one, giving no exceptional advantage to either player.

6 ♗e3 ♗xe3 (of course, 6...♗b6 or 6...h6 is also possible; in the latter case the exchange on c5 is not particularly effective) 7 fxe3 *(D)*.

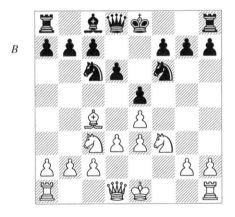

We talked about this in Chapter 3. White gains two important advantages from this trade: he has opened his f-file and prevented Black's knight from hopping to d4 (normally a main theme of the opening). That means that White might want to move his forces to the kingside; e.g., ♘h4-f5 is a good idea. But White's centre pawns have also lost their ability to advance successfully; for example, 7...0-0 8 d4 ♗g4. Then Black can simply let the pawn sit on d4,

when White has the choice of exchanging on e5, when his remaining e-pawns are doubled and isolated, or advancing to d5, which hampers his own pieces and does nothing positive. There are a number of versions of this exchange with varying results: sometimes the advantages of the doubled pawns will outweigh their disadvantages, but just as often the reverse will be true. What counts is to be aware of the issues.

It's very important to know when the move ♗g5 (or ...♗g4) is useful and when it is detrimental. Although that's a very complex question here are two types of positions that frequently arise:

In Case 1, White's bishop pins Black's knight *before* Black castles by **6 ♗g5** *(D)*.

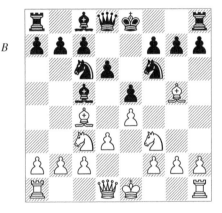

Then the harassment of the bishop by 6...h6 7 ♗h4 g5 is successful in so far as 8 ♘xg5? hxg5 9 ♗xg5 ♖g8 fails to give White compensation (the best try, 10 h4, is answered by 10...♗g4! and White's attack is at an end). So White plays 8 ♗g3, but then his bishop is a little uncomfortable running into a brick wall of pawns. Black can play 8...♗e6, for instance, and prepare to castle queenside with a fine game.

Let's compare Case 2, in which White plays **6 a3**, a handy move so that the bishop can be tucked away on a2. On an average level of play Black might respond with 6...0-0?!. But now White has 7 ♗g5! *(D)*.

Then he threatens ♘d5, and the pin is bothersome anyway. By analogy with Case 1, Black might try 7...h6 8 ♗h4 g5?, but this time 9 ♘xg5! hxg5 10 ♗xg5 is a whole different story. Black has to prevent ♘d5, for example by

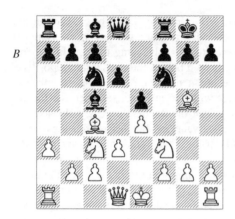

B

10...♗e6, when 11 ♘d5 ♗xd5 12 exd5 ♘b8 13 ♕f3 lands him in big trouble. For instance, 13...♔g7 14 h4 ♘bd7 15 ♗b5 (or 15 ♖h3 ♖g8 16 ♕f5, etc.) 15...♘b6 16 ♖h3 (there are plenty of options; e.g., 16 c4 ♗d4 17 ♖h3) 16...♘bxd5 17 ♖g3 ♔h8 18 ♕f5.

Without the opponent castling, this sacrificial idea doesn't work, so you can see why both sides tend to play h3 and ...h6 *before* castling! The old saw about not moving pawns in front of your king has many exceptions. In almost any opening, with 1 e4 or 1 d4, there are plenty of cases where either h3 or g3 will frustrate your opponent's attack. The same applies to ...h6 or ...g6, of course.

White targets f7: 4 ♘g5

4 ♘g5 (D)

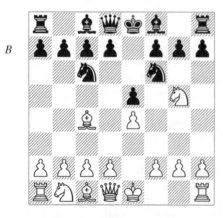

B

With this sortie White immediately breaks the rules about moving a piece twice in the opening before the other pieces are developed

(and in this case most of White's pieces aren't). For that reason, 4 ♘g5 has been called a beginner's move. Nevertheless, there have been thousands of master games with 4 ♘g5 for over a century, and several whole books have been devoted to precisely this position (not to mention lengthy parts of other books and countless articles). The main point is that, principles notwithstanding, Black has a difficult time defending f7 without making some kind of concession. White's philosophy is simple: if it works, play it!

4...d5

Black cuts off White's bishop with tempo while dramatically helping his central situation and freeing his c8-bishop for action. There are a number of alternatives over the next few moves that I won't be considering. One is the chaotic 4...♗c5!?, which has the idea 5 ♘xf7 ♗xf2+!?. This has been analysed in excruciating detail, often past 20 moves, by players and theoreticians. Several experts seem to feel that playing 5 ♗xf7+ instead of 5 ♘xf7 grants some advantage. We'll leave the whole mess to them. In spite of the fascinating play that stems from this and other highly tactical sidelines, I shall mainly devote my attention to the main lines and in general the more strategic (and popular) continuations. Naturally the course of events after, say, 4 ♘g5 ♗c5 or the wilder 4 d4 lines are instructive in the broader sense, conspicuously so in the realm of attack. They are, however, singular in their nature, and the purpose of this book is not to pursue particularities of forcing play but rather to broaden understanding of openings and tie them together wherever possible.

5 exd5 ♘a5! (D)

Black continues to gain time for development by attacking the c4-bishop. He is willing to sacrifice a pawn to that end. The disorderly 5...b5 and 5...♘d4 (sometimes transposing) fall into the same category as 4...♗c5. A more familiar line to inexperienced players is 5...♘xd5, when 6 ♘xf7!? ♔xf7 7 ♕f3+ ♔e6 is known as the 'Fried Liver Attack'. According to theory this line, if properly played, can be defended by Black. White's other try, 6 d4!, has the similar idea 6...exd4 7 0-0 ♗e7 8 ♘xf7!, this time leading to an extremely strong attack, at least according to the older theory. That's because White has more open lines. A lot of study will be required of anyone interested in these variations.

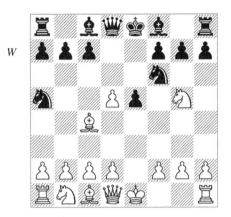

But we're going to look at 5...♘a5 because most good players choose that move, and because the resulting variations are marked by numerous defined strategic and tactical themes that can teach us about the Open Games.

6 ♗b5+

This is White's point: he will stay a pawn ahead, having no pawn weaknesses himself. His knight may look a little funny out there on g5, but so does Black's on a5. Black has two moves here: 6...c6 and 6...♗d7. Be forewarned that what follows is not a complete overview of the latest theory, but examples that will hopefully illuminate the issues involved.

Interposition with the Pawn

6...c6!?

Black sacrifices a pawn, but he gains another tempo by attacking White's bishop and thereby takes the initiative.

7 dxc6 bxc6 8 ♗e2 h6 9 ♘f3 e4 10 ♘e5 ♗d6 (D)

Of course there are legitimate alternatives for both sides along the way. For instance, White could have played Steinitz's 9 ♘h3 or, instead of 10...♗d6, both 10...♕d4 and 10...♗c5 have fairly good reputations.

But the position after 10...♗d6 arises more frequently than any other. Black wants to use his space advantage and develop quickly by attacking the e5-knight. Whatever happens, he's a pawn down and has to keep making active and/or forcing moves before White gets his

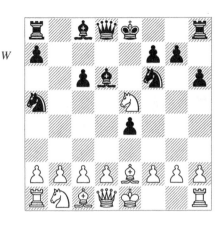

pieces out. Black's first goal is to attack the king, with the hope that the cramping role of his e4-pawn will render White's defence difficult. If that pawn is exchanged, he will develop pressure down the d- and e-files. His only real problem is the wayward knight on a5, which he hopes to reposition by ...♘b7 followed by ...♘c5 or ...♘d6.

For his part, White wants to eliminate the e4-pawn. If he can't do that he can bypass the pawn and put his pieces on more active posts, for instance by playing d4, ♗e3, ♘c3 (or ♘d2), and perhaps ♕d2. In a real game all of these plans conflict. You can only get a feel for the ideas by looking at examples. Because of Black's open lines and pressure down the d-file, White will probably have to keep his pieces on passive squares while he unwinds.

Estrin – Levenfish
Leningrad 1949

11 f4!?

This pawn advance has a poor reputation because it weakens White's kingside, but the resulting play is fairly balanced. One advantage is that White keeps his d-pawn; compare 11 d4 in the games that follow this one.

11...exf3

It's not strictly necessary to make this capture, but Black craves space and open lines in return for his pawn.

12 ♘xf3 0-0 13 0-0 ♕c7 14 d4 c5!

We've arrived at a position that can arise from other move-orders. Black wants to break up White's centre and bring his rooks to the centre files as fast as possible. White simply needs to get his pieces out, secure his position, and prove that the extra pawn means something in the long run. Both sides have won their share of points.

15 ♘c3 a6 *(D)*

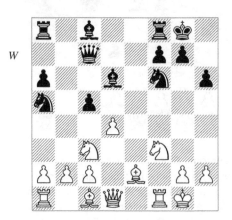

A move designed to prevent ♘b5.

16 d5!?

This pawn can become a target or it can provide cover for White's pieces. Against other moves Black will most likely play ...♗b7 and ...♖ad8.

16...♖e8

16...♗b7 17 ♔h1 ♖ad8 is an alternative, hoping to put pressure on the d-pawn by direct means.

17 ♔h1!?

17 h3 would prevent Black's plan. Again, 17...♗b7 and ...♖ad8 would probably follow and White might answer in the same manner as he employs in the game.

17...♖b8 *(D)*

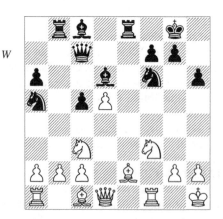

18 a3!?

18 ♕d3 ♘g4 19 h3 is obviously risky, yet plausible. Then 19...c4 20 ♕d4! ♗c5? 21 ♗f4! is good for White. This variation is in general double-edged, and neither side can afford to sit passively by.

18...♘g4

Attacking h2 but focusing upon the weakness on e3.

19 h3 ♘e3 20 ♗xe3 ♖xe3 21 ♖b1 ♕e7

Or 21...♗f4!?. Black is putting extra pressure on the dark squares and limiting White's plans. He certainly has enough for his pawn by virtue of his bishop-pair and activity.

22 ♕d2? ♗f4 23 ♕d1 ♖b6 24 ♘d2!

Having messed up once, White finds the right way to reorganize his pieces.

24...♗c7 25 ♖f3 ♕e5 26 ♘f1 ♖xf3 27 ♗xf3 *(D)*

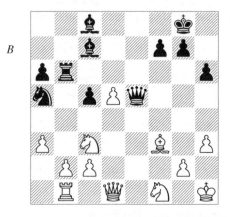

By a clever reorganization White has defended his d-pawn and has some control over most key squares. He's not out of the woods yet, but things are looking better. It's interesting that in this game Black never achieved a full central liquidation.

27...♘c4 28 ♘a4 ♖b5?!

28...♖f6! is better. It's important to keep some pressure on White's king.

29 ♕d3 ♘d6 30 ♕e3 ♕d4!?

The next few moves don't work out but Black is in trouble anyway.

31 b3! ♗f5 32 ♖d1 ♕f6? 33 c4 ♖b7 34 ♘xc5 ♗b6 35 b4

White is two powerful pawns up. The last tactic 35...♖e7? can be met by 36 ♘d7!. Estrin went on to win, but of course Black's opening was not the cause.

Although White had success in that game he was under significant pressure, in part because 11 f4 created an internal weakness on the sensitive e3-square. Most players would prefer to have no weaknesses, even if it means having no centre pawns!

11 d4

This is the most popular continuation, getting White's pieces out as fast as possible.

11...exd3

As was the case with 11 f4, Black doesn't have to capture, but again he needs open lines to pursue his attack, so why not create them now?

12 ♘xd3 ♕c7 *(D)*

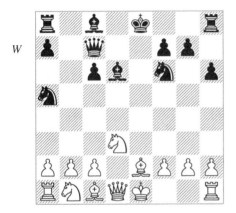

A key position. Note that this is the 'vanishing centre' that we talked about in the introductory chapters. The Open Games (1 e4 e5) have a number of these because the move d4 is so basic to White's play, as is the move ...d5 to Black's. Obviously that results in a greater likelihood that the entire centre will be eliminated. Such a position is naturally characterized by open lines and tactical play. In this case the tactics don't usually arise for a while as both players jockey to achieve their most effective formations. Then the action starts.

At this juncture we'll look at two games.

Beshukov – Malaniuk
Kstovo 1997

13 b3 *(D)*

The fianchetto is widely approved although there are many options here. Getting a piece out certainly feels right. Nevertheless, White was more successful with 13 h3 in the next example.

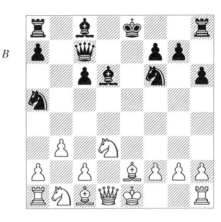

13...c5

A double-purpose move that plans ...c4 and prepares to bring Black's bishop to b7 along a strong diagonal. Black has other strategies as well:

a) 13...♗f5 14 ♗b2 0-0-0!? 15 ♘d2 ♖he8 is a distinctive plan – maximum activity! Of course Black's king won't be much better-placed than White's because it lacks pawn-cover: 16 ♔f1 (16 h3 ♗xd3 17 cxd3 ♗e5 18 ♗xe5 ♕xe5 19 ♔f1 ♘d5 with an attack worth at least a pawn) 16...♔b8 17 b4 (17 ♘f3 ♘e4!?) 17...♘b7 18 a3 (18 h3) 18...♗xh2 and, having regained his pawn, Black prospects aren't that bad, Short-Van der Sterren, Wijk aan Zee 1987.

b) The aggressive 13...0-0 14 ♗b2 ♘e4 was tried in Morozevich-Nenashev, Alushta 1994: 15 ♘c3 f5 16 h3 ♗a6!? 17 0-0 ♖ad8 18 ♕e1 c5 gave Black some initiative.

14 ♗f3 ♖b8 15 c4!? 0-0 16 ♗b2 ♖e8+ 17 ♔f1 ♘e4 18 ♗xe4 ♖xe4 19 ♘c3 ♖e6 *(D)*

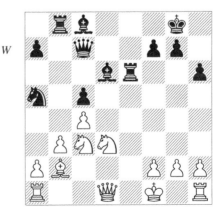

20 ♘b5?

Although this looks foolproof, 20 ♘d5! was the way to go.

20...♕d7 21 ♕c2 *(D)*

The alternative 21 ♕h5 ♗a6 might lead to 22 ♗c3 (22 ♘xd6?! ♕xd6 23 ♘e5 ♘xc4! 24 ♕xf7+ ♔h8 25 ♘xc4 ♗xc4+ 26 bxc4 ♖xb2 gives Black a meaningful advantage) 22...♗xb5 23 ♗xa5 ♗c6 with the idea ...♖g6. Black's unopposed light-squared bishop is a powerful attacking piece.

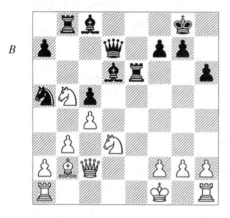

B

21...♖xb5!

This move changes the whole equation. Now White's interior weakness on d3 is exposed and Black's two bishops finally are freed for attack. 21...♗b7 isn't as effective after 22 ♖d1!, when Black's attack is petering out.

22 cxb5

If 22 ♕c3, then 22...♖g6 23 cxb5 ♕xb5 24 ♖d1 ♗b7 keeps the attack going.

22...♕xb5 *(D)*

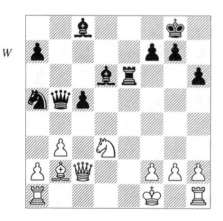

W

23 ♖d1

Black's two bishops and attack are more than enough compensation for the exchange. No better is 23 ♔g1 c4!, when 24 ♕c3!? is met by 24...♖g6.

23...♗a6 24 h4

Playing for ♖h3.

24...c4! 25 bxc4 ♘xc4

All of Black's pieces are participating in the attack now. White's h1-rook is a tempo short of getting into the action.

26 ♗c3 ♕f5 27 ♔g1 ♗b7 28 ♘b4 ♗e4

Or 28...♕g4 29 ♘d5 ♖g6.

29 ♕e2 ♖g6 30 ♕f1 0-1

A. Sokolov – Timmermans
Paris open Ch 1999

13 h3 *(D)*

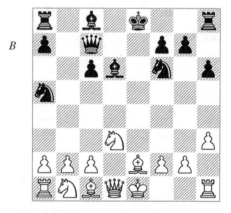

B

13...♗f5

Maybe Black should just castle and hold back on developing the bishop. It may want to go to b7.

14 ♘c3 0-0

14...0-0-0!? would be like Short-Van der Sterren in the notes to the last game.

15 0-0 ♖ad8 16 ♖e1 a6

Black wants to prevent ♘b5 in preparation for ...c5, but it's not necessary. Instead, 16...c5 17 ♘b5 ♗h2+ 18 ♔h1 ♕b8! *(D)* would keep the attack going.

Notice that after ...c5, Black can swing the knight back to c6 and perhaps d4. This plan, however you assess it, is the best try. From now on White gains control of the position and one is left wondering why anyone would sacrifice that pawn in the first place!

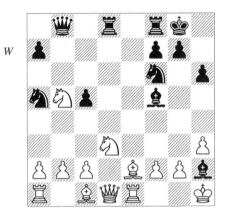

17 **♗f1 c5 18 ♕f3 ♘c6 19 ♗e3**

19 **♕xf5?? ♘d4** traps the queen. Trying to make something out of it by 20 **♕xf6 gxf6 21 ♗xh6 ♘xc2** is futile.

19...♗c8 20 ♘e4 ♘xe4 21 ♕xe4 ♘d4

Black tries to mix things up, since White is completing his development with no problems.

22 ♗xd4 ♗b7 23 ♕h4 cxd4 24 ♖e2! ♕a5?!

He may lack the firepower but it would be a good idea to try 24...f5 and see how White responds. After the text-move, Black is not only a pawn down but also has the worse position.

25 a3 ♕f5 26 ♖ae1 ♔h8 27 ♕g4 ♕f6 28 ♘e5 ♗b8 29 f4 g6 30 ♘d3 *(D)*

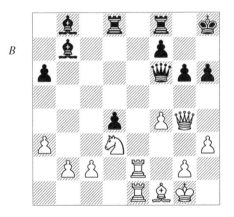

Protecting everything. Black tries to mark time.

30...h5 31 ♕g3 ♗c6 32 ♘e5 ♗b7 33 h4! ♔g7 34 ♕g5 ♗a7 35 ♘d3 ♕d6? 36 ♖e7 ♖d7 37 ♖1e6! ♕d5?

But 37...♕xe6 38 ♖xe6 fxe6 39 ♘e5 is hopeless for Black.

38 ♖xg6+ 1-0

Interposition with the Bishop

Another continuation that gains compensation for the pawn is 6...♗d7. Here's a sample encounter:

Bianchi – Escobar
corr. 1985

6...♗d7 *(D)*

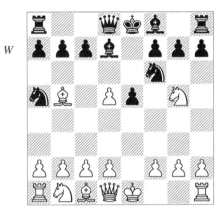

This continuation is less common than 6...c6, but has a very good theoretical reputation. What are the advantages of 6...♗d7? For one thing, it's a developing move, and developing quickly is one of Black's most important goals in this line. Moreover, 6...♗d7 doesn't necessarily lose a pawn (as 6...c6 does), because in some variations Black may recapture White's d-pawn. For the time being, White has an extra pawn, of course, and that provides consolation for his troubles. Furthermore, he has no weaknesses. These imbalances will almost always lead to interesting play.

7 ♕e2

7 ♗xd7+ ♕xd7 gives away any chances to gain an advantage because Black regains the d-pawn.

7...♗e7

Black also plays 7...♗d6 and defends his e5-pawn. Then his queen is more cut off from d5, so he probably won't recover his pawn (after White protects it with, for instance, 8 ♘c3). But when Black's kingside pawns get rolling his bishop will become more effective. It's a trade-off that in practice has worked rather well for Black.

8 ♘c3

White defends his most important asset, the d-pawn. Watch out for the trick 8 0-0? ♘xd5! 9 ♗xd7+ ♕xd7 10 d3 ♘c6. To assess this position, just look at Black's central control.

8...0-0 9 0-0 c6! *(D)*

Now it's a real gambit, one idea of which is to get that inactive knight off a5.

10 dxc6 ♘xc6 11 ♗xc6

White has to win time to get organized. Instead, multiple exchanges merely clarify Black's central superiority: 11 ♘f3 ♘d4! 12 ♘xd4 exd4 13 ♗xd7 ♕xd7 14 ♘e4 ♖ac8 15 ♘xf6+ ♗xf6 16 ♕d3 (16 d3 ♕c7 and Black wins the c-pawn) 16...♕c7 17 c3 ♖fd8!. This clamps down on White's development and leaves him struggling, Hendriks-Den Hamer, corr. 1985.

11...♗xc6 12 d3 ♘d5

Here Black's two bishops, control of d4 and mobile kingside pawns give him enough compensation for a pawn.

13 ♘xd5?!

Too cooperative. Maybe White should risk winning another pawn by 13 ♕xe5. Then Black has various dangerous moves such as 13...♘b4 and 13...♗f6, but White is two pawns ahead and will only have to give back one as he develops. Another possibility is 13 ♘ce4. You shouldn't get the impression that White has to sit back and get bowled over in this line.

13...♕xd5 *(D)*

Threatening checkmate. 13...♗xd5 should also be considered. In either case, Black plans to play ...f5 with a kingside attack.

14 ♘f3 ♗d6 15 ♗d2 ♖ae8 16 ♗c3 f5 17 ♖fd1 ♖e6 18 ♕f1 ♖g6

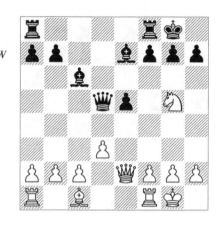

You can see the results of the opening. White is on the verge of getting massacred.

19 ♘e1 f4 20 f3 ♗c5+ 21 d4

A sample of Black's attack would be 21 ♔h1 ♖h6 22 h3 ♖f5 23 a3 ♖fh5 24 ♗b4 ♗b6 25 a4 ♗d7 and ...♗xh3! next.

21...exd4 22 ♔h1 ♖h6 23 h3 ♖e8 24 a4 a6 25 ♖d2 ♕g5 *(D)*

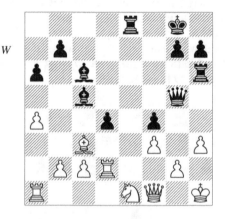

26 ♗xd4 ♗xd4 27 ♖xd4 ♕g3 0-1

The threat is ...♖xh3+ and ...♖xe1 followed by ...♗xf3+ and there's nothing good to do about it. White's best idea is 28 ♖ad1 ♖xe1 29 ♖xe1 ♖xh3+ 30 gxh3 ♗xf3+ 31 ♕xf3 ♕xf3+ 32 ♔g1 ♕g3+ 33 ♔f1 ♕xh3+ 34 ♔g1 f3, but White would be materially and positionally lost.

Central Play: 4 d4

4 d4 exd4 5 e5 *(D)*

It may seem odd to devote time to this continuation instead of its more famous alternative

5 0-0, yet the motivation for doing so is strong. Apart from its popularity among top contemporary players (it is called the 'Modern Line'), 5 e5 produces positions with notable positional features, at least before it degenerates into disarray like the rest of the Two Knights! All three of Black's replies are of interest.

An obvious alternative is 5 ♘g5 d5! (as usual, ...d5 frees Black's pieces if it doesn't fail tactically; see the main line) 6 exd5 ♕e7+ 7 ♔f1 ♘e5 8 ♕xd4 (8 ♗b5+ c6 9 dxc6 bxc6) 8...♘xc4 9 ♕xc4 ♕c5 with equality.

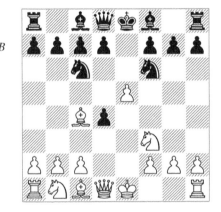

Now for a game:

Wendland – Groeber
corr. 1997

5...d5

As a rule, Black should make this move 'when he can' in the double e-pawn openings, and indeed, White has no way to avoid a loss of tempo without concessions. On the other hand, one can argue that e5 itself costs White a move, so barring a tactical disaster other responses may be playable. Indeed, White hasn't established an advantage against the following two rare replies, although he has a lot of leeway for improvements. At any rate, both moves contain useful positional ideas. I'll pick out a couple of characteristic lines:

a) 5...♘e4 *(D)*.

a1) 6 ♕e2 was originally thought to be the problem with 5...♘e4, since 6...d5 7 exd6 is no fun for Black. But after 6...♘c5, Black heads for the ideal blockading square on e6: 7 0-0 ♘e6 8 ♗xe6 (8 ♖d1 d5) 8...fxe6!? (a sharp

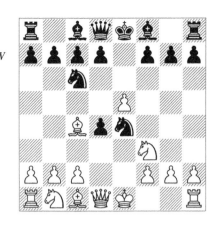

move that combines themes of using the open f-file in conjunction with an unopposed bishop at b7) 9 ♗g5 (9 ♖d1 d5 10 ♘xd4 ♘xd4 11 ♖xd4 c5 12 ♖d1 ♗e7 and here we have a good French Defence!) 9...♗e7 10 ♗xe7 ♕xe7 11 ♘bd2 0-0 12 ♘b3 ♖f4 13 ♖ad1 b6 14 ♘bxd4 ♗b7 and ...♖af8 is coming. This is based upon analysis by Renet.

a2) 6 0-0 d5 7 exd6 ♘xd6 8 ♗d5 ♗e7 9 ♗xc6+ bxc6 10 ♘xd4 ♕d7!? 11 ♕f3 (or 11 ♘b3 0-0 12 ♘c5 ♕f5) 11...♗b7 12 ♘b3 c5 with tactical complications in which the bishop-pair will hold its own.

b) 5...♘g4 also seems to work out well enough but needs to be tested a lot more before players will fully accept it. An obvious line is 6 ♕e2 ♕e7 7 ♗f4, when Black plays the surprising 7...d6! and White naturally replies with 8 exd6 *(D)*.

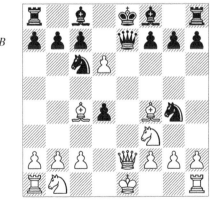

After the queens come off, White expects to recover his pawn on d4 and secure the better middle- and endgame by virtue of Black's remaining weak isolated d-pawn on an open file. But Black has a clever trick that neutralizes those plans: 8...♕xe2+ 9 ♗xe2 ♗xd6 10 ♗xd6 cxd6 11 ♘a3 ♘ge5 12 ♘b5 (12 0-0-0 d3! 13 cxd3 ♗e6 is equal) 12...d3! 13 ♘xe5 (13 cxd3 ♔e7 with symmetry and equality again) 13...dxe5 14 ♗xd3 ♔e7! with equality, Fernandez Garcia-Ivkov, Corunha 1990.

We return to 5...d5 *(D)*:

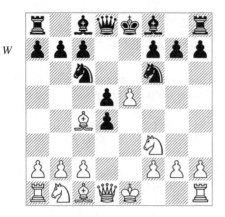

6 ♗b5

6 exf6?! dxc4 gives Black space, free development, the bishop-pair, and for the moment an extra pawn.

6...♘e4 7 ♘xd4 ♗d7

7...♗c5!? leads to complete anarchy in any number of lines, the most absurd-looking idea for White consisting of 8 ♘xc6 ♗xf2+ 9 ♔f1 ♕h4 10 ♘d4+ c6 11 ♘f3 ♘g3+ 12 ♔xf2 ♘e4++ 13 ♔e3 ♕f2+ 14 ♔d3 ♗f5 15 ♘d4 ♗g6 16 ♖f1 and deep analysis has revealed various forced draws. I'll refer you to specialists.

8 ♗xc6 bxc6 *(D)*

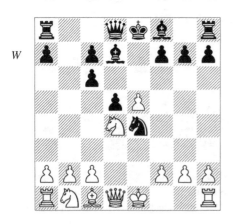

9 0-0

As always, there are move-order issues for both sides but that's more a matter of theory than understanding. As a case in point, delaying 0-0 at this juncture by 9 ♗e3 tips White's hand. Black can then do without the ...♗c5 idea; e.g., 9...♗e7 10 ♘d2 c5 11 ♘4b3 ♘xd2 12 ♕xd2 d4 13 ♗f4 ♗b5!?.

9...♗c5

It may be that 9...♗e7 is playable, but it allows a dangerous pawn-roller that represents Black's biggest nightmare in many double e-pawn openings. Look at this continuation: 10 f3 ♘g5 (10...♘c5 11 f4) 11 f4 ♘e4 12 f5 c5 (12...♗c5!? 13 ♘c3!?) 13 ♘e2 ♗b5 14 ♘a3 ♗c6 15 c4 d4 16 ♘f4 ♗g5 17 ♘d3!, Sveshnikov-Ferčec, Nova Gorica 1996. At first this seems all right for Black. Yet White's knight is the ideal blockader of the d-pawn and targets Black's weak doubled pawn on c5. This frees White's pieces to roam the board, in particular towards the kingside.

10 ♗e3!? *(D)*

White modestly protects his centre before advancing pawns and exposing his own position, but it may be too slow.

White also has the aforementioned f3-f4-f5, although with Black's bishop on c5 that may not be easy to implement. For example, White can trade off kingside expansion for reduced central control by 10 f3 ♘g5 11 ♗e3, when 11...♕e7 12 f4 ♘e4 13 ♘d2 or 11...0-0 12 ♘c3 is probably about equal.

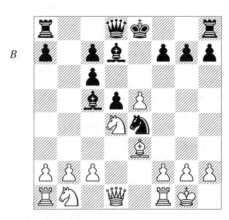

What is going on in this position? As usual, Black is counting upon his two bishops and activity to compensate for his positional problems.

He would like to move his bishop to b6 and then successfully achieve the advance ...c5. Given time, White would take advantage of the pawn-structure by a combination of moves such as (in some order) f3, ♕d2, ♘c3-a4 and/or ♘b3, dominating the board from c5 and rendering the bishops passive. That takes a few moves!

10...♕e7!

The side with the bishops often depends upon tactical niceties to avoid disadvantages. Now 11 f3 can be answered by 11...♘d6!, since the e3-bishop hangs. That would be followed up by ...♘f5 (or ...♘c4) with active counterplay.

11 ♖e1

Obviously ♕d2 isn't on the cards, so White prepares f3 another way. But there's quite a difference, in that f4-f5 won't be supported by a rook on the f-file.

11...0-0 12 f3 ♘g5 *(D)*

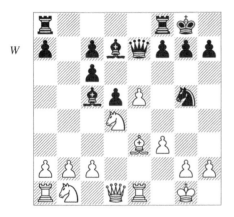

13 ♕d2

As a case in point, 13 f4 ♘e6! prevents f5 due to exchanges followed by ...♗xf5, and in the meantime Black plans to get his centre rolling by means of ...♗b6 and ...c5.

13...f6!

The last of Black's dynamic ideas: to break down the centre. The modest 13...♘e6 is also equal.

14 ♘c3

14 ♗xg5 fxg5 cedes Black the f-file, after which White can do little about ...♗b6 and ...c5.

14...♗b6!?

14...fxe5! 15 ♗xg5 ♕d6 was a tactical opportunity which, however, arose logically from Black's positional play. Then 16 ♘ce2 ♗b6!? 17 c3 exd4 18 cxd4 c5 keeps the initiative.

At any rate, after 14...♗b6, White stumbled:

15 ♘ce2? *(D)*

A serious oversight. 15 ♘a4 is much better.

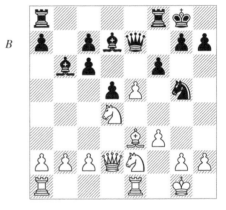

15...♘h3+!! 16 gxh3 fxe5 17 ♘b3 ♖xf3! 18 ♗xb6 cxb6 19 ♘g3 ♖af8 20 ♖f1 ♗xh3 21 ♖xf3 ♖xf3

Black's mass of pawns gives him a distinct advantage.

This opening is a good illustration of positional trade-offs; the static features were as important as the dynamic ones.

7 Philidor Defence

1 e4 e5 2 ♘f3 d6 (D)

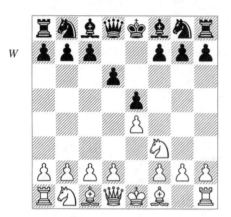

The Philidor Defence has one virtue that few 1 e4 e5 openings have: Black decides what opening is played! The underlying ideas of surrender of the centre in the Philidor were mentioned in Chapter 2; we'll explore them more thoroughly and even look at a wild counterattacking scheme. Then we'll turn to a version of the Philidor that uses a strongpoint approach in one of its purest forms. The characteristic ideas behind this not-so-old-fashioned opening are extremely instructive and applicable to many other openings. The Philidor is not a frequent visitor to master chess but has a remarkable following of contemporary players who have used the defence extensively through the years. These include quite a few grandmasters, and even Adams and Azmaiparashvili have dabbled in the Philidor. Reaching back a few generations, Tigran Petrosian was probably the last World Champion who tried it out.

It should be said, however, that most grandmasters who want to play the 'strongpoint' version of the Philidor Defence now use the order 1 e4 d6 2 d4 ♘f6 3 ♘c3 (thus far a Pirc Defence) 3...e5. The idea is that after 4 ♘f3 ♘bd7, Black has got into the main line of the Philidor while avoiding the problems associated with other move-orders that will be listed in this note

and the next one. They believe (and theory seems to verify) that the queenless middlegame after 4 dxe5 dxe5 5 ♕xd8+ ♔xd8 is perfectly fine for Black, who has the strategy ...♗e6 and ...♘bd7. White's main way to strive for an advantage is 6 ♗c4, when Black can accept doubled pawns in order to cover central squares: 6...♗e6!? 7 ♗xe6 fxe6 (D) with the idea ...♗d6 (or ...♗c5 first), ...♘bd7 and ...♔e7. The position is considered to be equal.

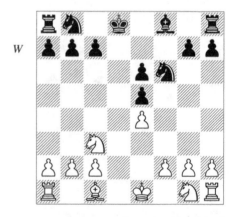

The reason that this move-order is considered to be superior to (or at least less difficult than) 1 e4 e5 2 ♘f3 d6 3 d4 is that in the latter case 3...♘f6 4 dxe5 ♘xe4 5 ♕d5 is awkward for Black. See the note to 3...♘d7 below (in the 'strongpoint' section). By playing 3...♘d7, Black can avoid this problem but runs into the possibility of 4 ♗c4!, as we see below, not to mention the move-order 3 ♗c4 examined in the next note. If all that is difficult to absorb, it will mean a lot more if you decide to take up the Philidor as Black or are faced with it as White.

The most interesting aspect of this overview is that some extremely highly-rated grandmasters have been willing to play the Philidor Defence via *any* move-order! After all, for many years the Philidor was considered to be an antiquated and inferior opening for Black. Let's see what ideas have reinvigorated it.

3 d4 *(D)*

3 &c4 is often overlooked with respect to move-order issues. Then 3...♘f6!? 4 &g5 d5 5 exd5 seems bothersome, although a serious examination reveals that Black has equality or stands only marginally worse after 5...h6 6 ♘f3 e4!; for example, 7 ♘e5 (7 ♕e2 can be met by 7...&e7 8 ♘e5 0-0 {e.g., 9 0-0?! &c5!} or 7...&b4!? 8 a3!? 0-0) 7...&d6 8 d4 exd3 9 ♘xd3 ♕e7+ with the idea 10 &e3 ♕e4!, equalizing.

Nevertheless, Black normally plays 3...&e7 4 d4 exd4 (4...♘d7? fails to 5 dxe5 ♘xe5 {5...dxe5 6 ♕d5!} 6 ♘xe5 dxe5 7 ♕h5 g6 8 ♕xe5) 5 ♘xd4 ♘f6 6 ♘c3 0-0. However, this transposes into a 3 d4 exd4 line, which means that White has successfully pre-empted Black's strongpoint approach, that is, one in which Black plays ...♘bd7 without ...exd4 (see the 'Strongpoint' section below). Thus Black may want to look into 3...♘f6. Otherwise, 3 &c4 makes another argument for the move-order 1 e4 d6 2 d4 ♘f6 3 ♘c3 e5.

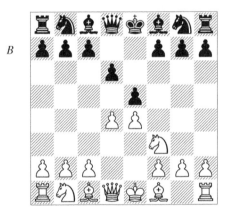

The first and obvious point is that Black has allowed White the greater share of the centre and blocked his own f8-bishop behind the d6-pawn, an unfortunate by-product of ...d6 but no terrible thing in itself. There are now two basic strategies that Black can pursue: surrender of the centre or making e5 a strongpoint.

Surrender of the Centre

3...exd4 4 ♘xd4

White has a reasonable alternative in 4 ♕xd4, although this hasn't scored as well as it did in the 19th century after 4...♘f6 (4...a6 intending to gain time by ...♘c6 without being pinned by &b5 has a respectable record; 4...♘c6?! 5 &b5 is the original continuation that made 4 ♕xd4 popular in the first place – after 5...&d7 6 &xc6 &xc6 7 &g5 with 0-0-0 soon to follow, White achieves considerable pressure) 5 ♘c3 &e7 6 &g5 0-0 7 &c4 ♘c6 with equality.

4...♘f6 5 ♘c3 *(D)*

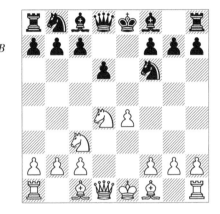

5...&e7 *(D)*

The alternate strategy of activity and potential attack begins with 5...g6, when White's most aggressive set-up is 6 f3 &g7 7 &e3 0-0 8 ♕d2, as in a Sicilian Dragon. There usually follows 8...♘c6 9 g4 &e6 10 0-0-0 ♘xd4 11 &xd4. This is a position from which White has won many games (and thus discouraged 5...g6). Black could certainly use an open c-file, as in the Dragon. He does succeed in throwing his queenside pawns forward after 11...c5 12 &e3 ♕a5 13 &h6 &xh6 14 ♕xh6 b5! 15 &xb5 ♖ab8 16 a4 a6, yet 17 ♖xd6! axb5 18 e5 gives a ferocious attack that has won several games for White. All this is difficult to improve upon. There have been scads of other attempts by Black but he still seems to be in search of a satisfactory solution. At any rate I shall concentrate upon lines with ...&e7.

With 5...&e7, Black introduces a strategy that was explicated by Nimzowitsch: ...0-0, ...♖e8, ...&f8 and ...♘bd7, both restraining and putting pressure on White's e-pawn. White has more space and can thwart a direct attack but still has to find a way to break down Black's defences without allowing his pieces to spring to life. This situation might remind you of similar positions in the King's Indian Defence, such as

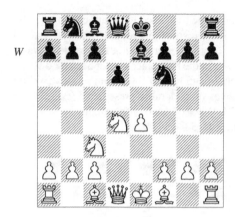

W

1 d4 ♘f6 2 c4 g6 3 ♘c3 ♗g7 4 e4 d6 5 ♘f3 0-0 6 ♗e2 e5 7 0-0 exd4 8 ♘xd4. In the case of the Philidor, White's c-pawn is on c2 (rather than c4, as in the King's Indian) and Black's bishop is on f8 (rather than g7). You could argue that in the King's Indian, White is more exposed in the centre (d4 is unsupported by pawns); but in the Philidor, Black's counterattacking chances are limited by his passively placed bishop on e7. Check out what happens in the second game below!

6 ♗e2

White decides to go for a safe space advantage. He has an active alternative in 6 ♗c4 0-0 7 0-0 leading to lines such as 7...♖e8 8 ♖e1 ♗f8 9 a3 ♘bd7 10 ♗a2 ♘c5 (10...a6!?) 11 f3. It takes a born defender (with an opportunistic streak) to embrace this kind of position for Black, yet it is relatively solid.

6...0-0 7 0-0 ♖e8 8 f4 (D)

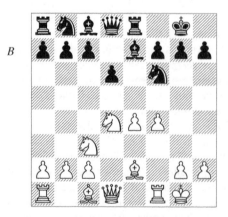

B

With this move White commits to a pawn-structure in which he restricts Black's pieces

and increases his space advantage, but fails to support the e-pawn (as f3 does). This position has arisen in many games; here's one in which Black takes the slow approach:

Restraint

Isanbaev – Sizykh
Novokuznetsk 1999

8...♗f8 9 ♗f3 ♘bd7 10 ♖e1 c6 (D)

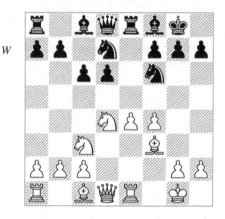

W

The strategies are set. Black has insufficient forces to attack and has to play with the backward d-pawn that we also see in the King's Indian Defence. But d6 is well-protected, which gives Black the leeway to turn his attention to the queenside; his main positive idea consists of attack on that wing based upon ...b5, with the idea that White's forces are tied to protecting against the freeing move ...d5.

For his part, White will develop, double on the d-file, and slowly increase the pressure. He may prepare a pawn-break via e5 or a general advance by g4.

11 ♗e3 ♘c5 12 ♗f2 ♘e6 13 ♕d2 ♘xd4 14 ♗xd4 ♗e6 15 ♖ad1 ♘d7

Directed against e5.

16 b3 f6 17 ♔h1 ♗f7

Black has a passive but playable position. White stands somewhat better but will need time to organize a breakthrough (perhaps the plan g4-g5 should be considered). In the event, the game was quickly drawn.

And now for something completely different:

Counterattack

Renet – Fressinet
Clichy (rapid) 2001

8...♗f8 9 ♗f3 c5!? *(D)*

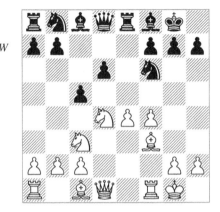

This bold move has been tried by at least two very strong grandmasters and in at least 20 games! Black doesn't feel like defending passively, so he aims at the central dark squares (with ...♘c6 next) and stays true to the basic idea of restraining White's centre. That by itself might not make up for his pawn-structure but Black also wants to advance his queenside pawns and attack White's pieces on that wing. To that end he will have support from a bishop on d7 and rook on b8. The obvious drawback is his backward d-pawn on an open file. But as we see in several variations of the Sicilian Defence, such a pawn isn't necessarily an issue.

There are lines like this in the Fianchetto Variation of the King's Indian Defence. In that opening White's bishop is on g2, which is obviously analogous to a bishop on f3 in the Philidor. In the position before us, however, Black is missing the powerful bishop on g7 that characterizes the KID, a condition that seems to be a serious drawback. Nevertheless, from f8 the bishop protects Black's only weakness on d6!

How should White react? Obviously he will have to restrain Black's expansion (presumably by a4). And he must eventually expand in the centre or on the kingside. The move g4 suggests itself, although it must be properly timed so as not to weaken his king position.

10 ♘de2

White's first decision is important: where to put the knight? From e2 it has prospects of assisting on the kingside but has no particular square to go to yet. 10 ♘de2 also allows one of Black's pieces to settle on g4.

The most common choice has been 10 ♘b3, which keeps White's pieces freer to move and the g4-square covered, but from b3 the knight doesn't have anywhere special to go to either. There result some fascinating ideas following 10...♘c6 *(D)*:

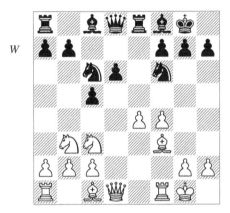

Here White has tried various moves to crack Black's strange-looking set-up:

a) 11 ♔h1 a5!? (11...♖b8 and 11...a6 appear more natural) 12 a4 ♗e6 13 ♘d5 ♖c8?! (13...♘b4! is equal) 14 ♗d2 gave White somewhat better pieces in Brodsky-G.Kuzmin, Pula ECC 1994.

b) 11 ♖e1 a5?! (this plan seems to appeal to players, but 11...♖b8 looks considerably better) 12 a4 d5? (12...♗e6) 13 e5 (or 13 ♘xd5!) 13...d4 14 ♘b5 ♘d7 15 c3! dxc3 16 bxc3, Yurtaev-Payen, Calcutta 2000. Black is at a loss for moves here.

c) 11 ♗e3 d5!? (the craziest move of all!) 12 exd5 ♖xe3 13 dxc6 ♕b6 14 ♕d2?! (14 ♘d2!?). Black's general strategy is a little hard to believe in, but at this point he uncorks 14...♖xf3! 15 ♖xf3 c4+ 16 ♘d4 ♗c5 17 ♔h1 (17 ♖d1 ♗g4) 17...♗xd4 18 ♖d1 ♗g4 19 ♕xd4 ♗xf3 20 ♕xb6 axb6 21 gxf3 bxc6 with equality, Smirin-G.Kuzmin, USSR Ch (Leningrad) 1990. Note that this was a high-level grandmaster game.

10...♘c6 *(D)*

Now the advance e5 is prohibited for some time, and placing a knight on d5 is harmless or

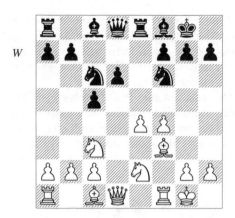

W

worse. You may recognize this kind of position from the Sicilian Defence.

11 h3

11 f5?! Rb8 (11...De5!) 12 Bg5 Be7 13 Bf4 b5! 14 Wd2 b4 15 Dd1 Ba6! 16 Rf2 Bf8 and White was totally disorganized in Scholl-Lutikov, Amsterdam 1968.

11...Bd7 12 g4!? h6! 13 Dg3 Dd4

Black's ideal square.

14 Bg2 b5!? 15 a3 Bc6

This uses up the best retreat-square for Black's d4-knight, but it does put pressure on e4. 15...Rb8 is safer and fully equal.

16 Be3 Wb6 17 b4!?

17 g5!? is interesting, now that Black's queen has abandoned the kingside.

17...a5! 18 bxc5?!

White aims for e5 but he activates Black's pieces instead of his own.

18...dxc5 19 e5 Bxg2 20 Kxg2 Wc6+ 21 Kh2 Rad8 22 Bxd4 Rxd4 23 Wf3?! (D)

23 We2 Red8 24 Rad1 De8 intending ...Dc7 is probably better for Black, but manageable.

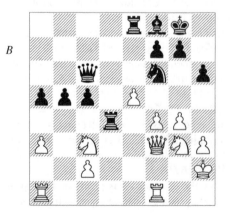

B

23...Rd2+ 24 Kh1 Wxf3+ 25 Rxf3 Dd5!

Now Black has the better ending.

26 Dxb5

26 Dge4 Rd4 27 Dxd5 Rxd5 28 Dc3 Rd2 29 Dxb5 Rxc2 30 Rc3 Rf2!. The active rook and bishop-versus-knight favour Black.

26...Rxc2 27 Rd1 Rb8! 28 a4 Db6 29 Da3 Rb2 30 Rc1 Dxa4 31 Dc4 (D)

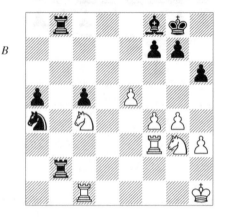

B

31...R2b3

31...Ra2! is better still.

32 Rxb3 Rxb3 33 Kg2 Rb4 34 f5? Db2! 35 Dxa5 Dd3

Here Black is clearly winning the endgame. Very instructive.

The e5 Strongpoint

3...Dd7 (D)

Although it doesn't overlap with the general themes that we're presenting, you should be aware that another move-order issue arises after 3...Df6 4 dxe5 (4 Dc3 Dbd7 is the main line) 4...Dxe4 5 Wd5 Dc5 6 Bg5 Wd7!? (after 6...Be7 7 exd6 Wxd6 8 Dc3 0-0, White is for choice) 7 exd6 Bxd6 8 Dc3; for example, 8...0-0 9 0-0-0 Dc6 10 Db5 Wf5 11 Dxd6 cxd6 12 Wxf5 Bxf5 13 Be3 Db4! 14 Dd4, Shur-Maliutin, Moscow 1997; now Black should play 14...Bg6, when White has some advantage, although the position is still complex.

4 Dc3

4 Bc4 causes its own set of problems for Black: 4...c6 (4...Be7? 5 dxe5 Dxe5 {5...dxe5?? 6 Wd5} 6 Dxe5 dxe5 7 Wh5 g6 8 Wxe5) 5 Dc3 Be7 6 dxe5 dxe5 7 Dg5! Bxg5 8 Wh5 with a two-bishop position for White. In this situation

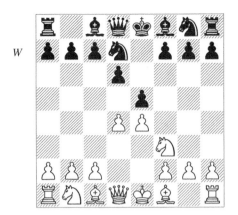

Black has decent counterplay if he moves quickly: 8...♕e7! 9 ♗xg5 ♘gf6 10 ♕h4 b5 11 ♗b3 ♘c5 and, for instance, 12 0-0-0 0-0 13 ♗xf6 ♕xf6 14 ♕xf6 gxf6 15 f3 a5. White must stand better in this variation as a whole, but not by much. Thus 3...♘d7 appears to hold together better than 3...♘f6. Again, the lines of the last two notes are a matter of practical play, not of understanding, but they are important if you decide to play the traditional Philidor move-order 1 e4 e5 2 ♘f3 d6 instead of 1 e4 d6 2 d4 ♘f6 3 ♘c3 e5.

4...♘gf6 5 ♗c4 ♗e7 6 0-0 0-0

This time we see Black fortifying e5 as he does in so many lines of the Ruy Lopez.

7 ♖e1 *(D)*

White frequently plays the set-up with 7 ♕e2 c6 8 a4 ♕c7 9 ♖d1, when Black can do as prescribed in the note to 8 a4.

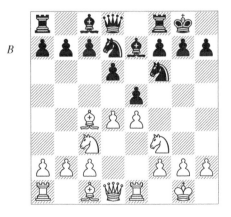

7...c6

A move necessary in order to get a little manoeuvring room, and also to continue with the

overprotection of the e5-pawn by means of ...♕c7.

8 a4 *(D)*

This move stops ...b5, which would win much-needed space with tempo. The only good way to do without it is to play d5, intending to meet ...b5 with dxc6, a theme described below. But in this position Black could merely work around the pawn by ...a5 and ...♘c5, since dxc6 is comfortably answered by ...bxc6, controlling d5.

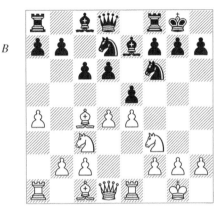

What are Black's goals now? He will generally follow up with ...♕c7 and/or ...♖e8, to bolster e5 while keeping a careful eye on the d6-pawn. Then we come to the point at which he needs to develop his queen's bishop. This may be prefaced by the safe moves ...h6, ...♖e8 and ...♗f8 (or even ...♘f8), or Black may commence immediately. If he is allowed to complete the following plan he will usually have solved his problems: Black places his pawns on b6 and a6, his bishop on b7, and then advances with ...b5. With completed development and queenside play, he should stand well, especially since his ideas of ...b4 and central attack are by no means trivial to defend against.

Then what is White to do? There are a number of answers depending upon one's style of play and the specifics of the position. He has the challenge of breaking down Black's defences, and this time there is no open file or backward pawn to focus upon. However, at the point that Black plays ...b6 (and before ...♗b7) he is vulnerable to the move d5, since capturing will leave White in possession of the key outpost on d5. If Black already has ...♗b7 in before White plays d5, then Black has better chances of making a favourable mass-exchange upon that square. The game will hang upon whether exchanges and simplification leave White anything at all, or whether he can stifle Black's counterplay by other means. There are three standard alternatives to d5:

a) b3 and ♗b2 or ♗a3;

b) a5, to hamper Black's queenside plans; and

c) ♘h4-f5.

Incidentally, this kind of analysis suggests that Black's plan would be even more effective were White's bishop on e2 or f1, where it is often placed.

We shall see these counter-strategies in the following sample game itself and in the note to White's 9th move.

Vehi Bach – Cifuentes
Platje d'Aro Barcino 1994

8...♕c7 *(D)*

A battle of heavyweights, Ivanchuk-Azmaiparashvili, Montecatini Terme 2000, illustrates Black's loss of the d5-square and his reaction to it: 8...♖e8 9 a5 (9 ♘g5 ♖f8 isn't helpful) 9...♗f8 10 d5 b5!? (10...♕c7 looks more natural but Black doesn't want to be squeezed to death) 11 ♗b3! (11 axb6 ♘xb6 12 ♗b3 cxd5 13 exd5 is a kind of position that we look at in several openings, where Black's potentially mobile kingside majority is theoretically superior to White's on the queenside; e.g., ...g6, ...♗g7, ...♘h5 and ...f5 might eventually follow; granted, the specifics of the position will outweigh that factor for some time, but I think that Black stands well) 11...cxd5 12 ♘xd5 h6 (versus ♗g5) 13 c3!? (13 ♕e2! a6 14 ♗e3 with a small but definite advantage), and here instead of 13...a6 14 ♗e3 with a grip on b6, Black should have played 13...♗b7 14 a6 ♗c6 when he has the backward d-pawn, but it is well-defended (as in the Sicilian Defence). Then White has only a formal superiority.

9 h3

White has other thematic continuations. Not all of them have been put into practice against challenging opposition.

a) White sometimes develops with 9 b3, having either ♗a3 or ♗b2 in mind. Then 9...b6!?

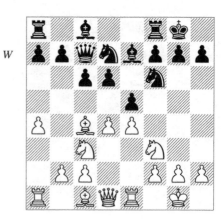

10 d5!? ♗b7 11 dxc6 ♗xc6 12 ♗b2 ♘c5 13 ♘d2 ♖ac8! provides piece-pressure to compensate for the d5-square and White's potential along the d-file.

b) One of White's main ideas is to try to get a knight to f5; for instance, 9 ♗g5 h6! (9...b6 10 ♕d2 ♗b7 11 ♘h4! {11 dxe5 ♘xe5} 11...exd4 12 ♘f5 gives White the better game; whenever something like this can't be stopped, the plan of ...♖e8 and ...♗f8 looks best) 10 ♗e3 ♖e8 *(D)*.

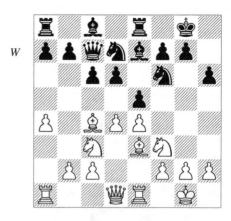

11 ♘h4!? (White should stand somewhat better in such positions, although it's not clear what he should play; maybe 11 a5) 11...exd4! (this is normally a good response to ♘h4, which weakens control over d4) 12 ♗xd4 ♘e5 13 ♗b3 ♗g4! 14 f3 ♘fd7 15 ♘f5 ♗xf5 16 exf5 d5. This position is difficult to assess, since both sides have advantages.

c) 9 a5 is a natural alternative to hamper Black's queenside plans. Then one standard idea for Black is to continue to batten down the hatches by 9...h6 (versus ♘g5) 10 b3 ♖e8 11

♗b2 and now 11...♗f8 or 11...♘f8!? 12 h3 ♗e6.

These are just sketches of various set-ups. In the majority of cases White will probably retain some advantage with proper play, but not enough to invalidate Black's opening. Incidentally, this kind of analysis again suggests that Black's strategy would be even more effective were White's bishop on e2 or f1, where it is often placed.

9...b6 10 ♗g5 a6!

Neutralizing the idea of a5 and at the same time contemplating expansion by ...b5.

11 ♕e2 ♗b7 *(D)*

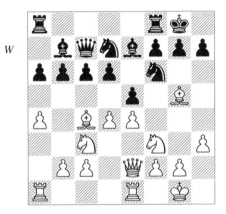

12 dxe5

12 ♖ad1 b5 13 ♗b3 yields a standard pawn-structure (also arising in the Old Indian and King's Indian Defences, and sometimes in the Ruy Lopez). Black has sufficient counterplay.

12...♘xe5

12...dxe5?! 13 ♘h4! and ♘f5.

13 ♘xe5 dxe5 14 ♖ad1 b5

Once this move is in, everything is OK. Notice how neither White's knight nor bishop have any forward square to go to.

15 ♗b3 h6 16 ♗h4 ♖ad8 17 axb5 axb5 18 ♖xd8 ♖xd8 19 ♖d1 *(D)*

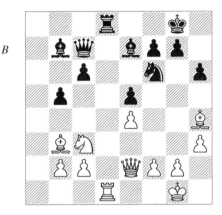

19...♗c8!?

A good idea, rerouting the bishop to a more active position. Since White's e4-pawn is still a concern and his bishop is away from the centre at h4, the move 19...♖d4! was probably even better. In general, Black has achieved excellent activity, creating some problems that White needn't have allowed in his rush to simplify.

20 ♖xd8+ ♕xd8

The opening is over and Black has at least equality and perhaps more, since White's h4-bishop isn't participating but the exchange ♗xf6 would cede the two bishops.

8 Ruy Lopez

1 e4 e5 2 ♘f3 ♞c6 3 ♗b5 *(D)*

These moves constitute the Ruy Lopez, aptly called the 'King of Openings'. It has dominated 1 e4 e5 chess for more than 100 years and is considered the best chance for White to gain the advantage in the play that follows 2...♞c6. Thereupon hangs the popularity of 1 e4 itself, no small burden for a single move to bear.

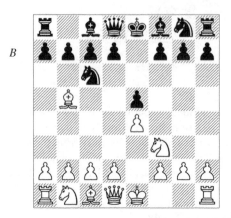

B

What's the point of 3 ♗b5? One's first instinct is that it threatens 4 ♗xc6 followed by 5 ♘xe5, but Black's most popular answer 3...a6 shows that not to be the case, at least not immediately. Then of course White wants to castle quickly. But then why do most players use 3 ♗b5 instead of the more aggressive-looking 3 ♗c4, which hits Black's weak f7-pawn? The answer is that 3 ♗b5 is a prophylactic move that works to squelch the opponent's opportunities. If you look at the main lines after 3 ♗c4, for instance, it turns out that Black's key defensive/counterattacking move in a majority of cases is ...d5 (as in most variations after 1 e4 e5), attacking the bishop and establishing himself in the centre. But putting a bishop on b5 either prevents or discourages that move. Let's see how this works in a few simple cases. Obviously, the immediate 3...d5? is bad due to 4 exd5 ♕xd5 5 ♘c3 with a terrible loss of time

for Black. But what if Black imitates his response to 3 ♗c4 by playing as follows?

3...a6 4 ♗a4 b5 5 ♗b3 *(D)*

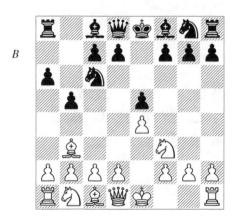

B

After all, White is on the same diagonal as after 3 ♗c4 and Black has a couple of extra moves in ...a6 and ...b5 that may help his position or at least not hurt it.

The answer is that the move ...d5 can no longer be played with tempo, which negatively impacts both of Black's normal defences after 3 ♗c4. That consideration overrides all others, as we can see from the following discussion (see Chapters 5 and 6 on 3 ♗c4 if you need to). First, compare the old line 3 ♗c4 ♞f6 4 d4 (notice that after 4 ♘c3, Black has the excellent response 4...♘xe4! 5 ♘xe4 d5, whereas this would be a blunder with White's bishop on b3) 4...exd4 5 e5, when 5...d5! gains a critical tempo. Not so with a bishop on b3 instead of c4. Then, look at other main-line defence to 3 ♗c4, i.e. 3...♗c5 4 c3 ♞f6 5 d4 exd4 6 cxd4 (6 e5 d5!) 6...♗b4+ 7 ♗d2 ♗xd2+ 8 ♘bxd2 d5! 9 exd5 ♞xd5 with equality; the Ruy Lopez prevents such solutions, as I'll show below for clarity's sake.

5...♗c5

The equivalent of the Two Knights Defence would go 5...♞f6 6 d4! *(D)* (6 ♘g5 is probably no improvement upon the main 3 ♗c4 ♞f6 lines, but this is strong):

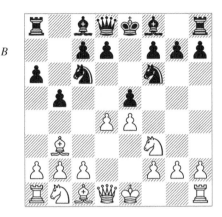

6...exd4 (after 6...♘xe4 7 dxe5 White threatens ♕d5 and ♗xf7+, so Black needs to play 7...♘c5, when 8 ♗d5 retains the bishop and establishes the superior position – the e5-pawn cramps Black's game) 7 e5 ♘g4 (there's no ...d5 response!) 8 0-0 and White threatens h3 and ♖e1. A sample line might be 8...♗b4 (preventing ♖e1; 8...♘gxe5?? loses to 9 ♘xe5 ♘xe5 10 ♖e1 d6 11 f4) 9 c3 (or 9 ♗d5 threatening h3) 9...dxc3 10 bxc3 ♗c5 11 ♕d5! ♕e7 12 ♗g5 ♕f8 13 h3 ♘xf2 14 ♖xf2 ♗xf2+ 15 ♔xf2 and White's pieces dominate the board. Notice how without the move ...d5 Black wasn't able to contest the centre.

6 c3 ♘f6 7 d4 exd4 8 e5!

Were White's bishop on c4, Black would have the resource ...d5! at this point. Instead the knight has to move and lose time. For instance:

8...♘e4

8...♘g4 9 cxd4 ♗b4+ 10 ♘c3 and White chases the knights with h3 followed in some cases by d5.

9 ♗d5! *(D)*

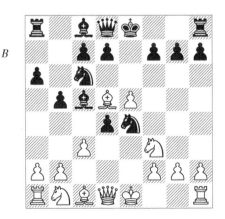

White's move serves not just to attack the almost-trapped e4-knight, but also to stop ...d5. That's the consistent theme involved in an early ♗b3.

9...f5

Black can try the somewhat cheap win of three pawns for a piece by 9...♘xf2?! 10 ♔xf2 dxc3+, but after 11 ♔g3! White connects rooks and threatens 12 ♗xf7+ ♔xf7 13 ♕d5+. Thus Black is stuck with 11...cxb2 12 ♗xb2 0-0 13 ♘c3! (or 13 h4) 13...♗b7 14 ♘e4 ♗e7 15 ♕d2 and White dominates the board. His king is untouchable, and in general three pawns aren't worth a minor piece this early in the game (unless two or three of them are passed and moderately advanced). When you factor in White's activity and far superior development, the assessment is clear.

10 cxd4 ♗b4+ 11 ♘bd2

Black can't even castle, but White will play 0-0 and gain a very large advantage.

For the record, Black can try to justify 1 e4 e5 2 ♘f3 ♘c6 3 ♗b5 a6 4 ♗a4 b5 5 ♗b3 with the odd move 5...♘a5!? (the 'Norwegian Variation'), based upon 6 ♘xe5 ♘xb3 7 axb3 ♕g5, etc. But simply 6 0-0 d6 7 d4 is thought to give White the advantage.

Returning to 3 ♗b5, we have seen one localized reason for preferring 3 ♗b5 over 3 ♗c4. But what characterizes the Ruy Lopez itself? Since each opening variation that begins on move 3 is so different in attributes, we cannot speak of the 'nature' of the Ruy Lopez without referring to specific systems. The most interesting way to approach the subject is to take a somewhat impressionistic historical look. In the early days of the Ruy Lopez we saw some understandable experimentation with moves such as 3...♘d4 and 3...f5, both still playable today but on the very margins of legitimacy. As positional concepts solidified, the great masters of the late 19th and early 20th centuries drifted towards 1 e4 e5 2 ♘f3 ♘c6 3 ♗b5 d6, which is featured in the games of Steinitz, Lasker, Capablanca and many others. Without taking the time to examine that variation (an exercise that is well worth it), I can't demonstrate its drawbacks; but the crucial thing to remember is that Black will immediately or eventually be forced to surrender the centre by means of ...exd4 in order to avoid complete passivity. Tarrasch is famous for helping to demonstrate this fact (and in fact he proposed the more dynamic Open Variation of the Ruy Lopez as an alternative to the ...d6 lines).

Then came the so-called 'Closed' variations. The majority of players ultimately grew discontent with having to live in the cramped situations that 3...d6 and ...exd4 usually imposed. Without dismissing options such as the recently-revived order 3...♘f6 (the Berlin Defence) 4 0-0 ♘xe4 5 d4 ♘d6 6 ♗xc6 dxc6 7 dxe5 ♘f5, we find that the preponderance of masters turned to the more subtle move-order 3...a6 4 ♗a4 ♘f6 followed by ...♗e7, ...b5 and ...d6. The resulting variations tended to prevent White from gaining the degree of space he commanded in the old ...exd4 lines. These formations, arguably the most consistently important in all of chess history, are collectively named the 'Closed Ruy Lopez'. They are characterized by well-defended pawns on d6 and e5 that form a bulwark against White's advances. Black generally achieves smooth development that targets each central square. To the extent that White prevents Black's freeing moves, so Black stops White from redeploying his pieces without risking the escape of his opponent's pieces from their cramped quarters. In particular, the moves ...d5 and ...exd4 carry with them the potential for dynamism that can take advantage of White's relatively defensive minor pieces. In the meantime, his strongpoint of e5 and pawn on d6 give him a 4th-rank anchor that is usually lacking in other e4 openings such as the Sicilian, Caro-Kann, Pirc, Alekhine, etc. Arguably only the French Defence routinely maintains a 4th-rank strongpoint, and that at the cost of a passive light-squared bishop. In the Ruy Lopez too, there is generally a passive piece in the form of the bishop behind the lines on e7. However, that bishop is always developed past the first rank and can theoretically influence both sides of the board.

Such was the broad story of the Ruy Lopez until the past two decades. After playing strongpoint positions for so long, Black began to look for more dynamic possibilities. First, without entirely jettisoning the idea of maintaining a pawn on e5 in the initial stages of the opening, top players increasingly used piece-play to target the centre. The Chigorin Defence and related lines were supplemented by systems which did without ...c5 entirely in order to attack e4 by means of ...♗b7 and ...♖e8, with the intention of pawn exchanges and even the freeing advance ...d5. Thus, for example, the development of the dynamic Zaitsev Variation and lively advances in the formerly stodgy Breyer Defence. Of late there have appeared new-found ways of opening lines in particular positions based upon White's mode of development. Within the ...e5/...c5 structures of the Chigorin Defence, for example, Black has skipped ...♕c7 in favour of immediately exchanging centre pawns, and in other cases the move ...exd4 alone has been used to establish a queenside majority accompanied by active piece deployments. Most interesting has been the complete liquidation of the centre by means of the two exchanges ...cxd4 and ...exd4. Finally, confrontation by ...d5 is on the increase.

What is White trying to do in the Closed variations? The first thing to realize is that there are very few variations in which he launches a mating attack or acts particularly aggressively within the first ten moves. In the main variations, his idea continues to be prophylactic, i.e. he tries to restrict Black's moves to those that are somewhat passive and fail to free his game. The idea is that his space advantage in the centre (by no means a substantial one) allows him to keep the game under control. When Black does get frisky and tries to go tactical, White has attempted to arrange it that he will come out on top in any melee. In the meantime White slowly builds up his position and puts pressure on at least one area of the board and often two. A queenside attack beginning with a4 is common because it is not so easy for Black to defend b5 without compromising his position. But over time White can also mount a kingside attack. In that regard, notice the direction in which White's bishops aim in the Ruy Lopez, and they can be reinforced by knights on f5 (after the exotic-looking but now routine ♘d2-f1-g3/e3) while the other knight can head towards g5 or, for example, to g4 via h2. If ♘f5 is prevented by ...g6 White sometimes plays ♗h6 (nudging the rook away from the sensitive f7-square), the move ♕f3, and so forth. Ideally (from White's point of view), Black will have to play defensively until he can't protect against every breakthrough on both wings. This game program is what's glibly referred to as the 'Spanish Torture'. We shall see how White's plans evolve when we inspect the individual Closed variations below. In its general contours, by the way, the above description also applies to the Open Ruy Lopez: White tries to keep Black's dynamism under control and then switches to a gradual augmentation of his positional advantages.

Let's look at the moves that introduce the Closed Ruy Lopez:

1 e4 e5 2 ♘f3 ♘c6 3 ♗b5 a6 4 ♗a4

We'll see the Exchange Variation with 4 ♗xc6 dxc6 later on. Note that after 5 ♘xe5 ♕d4 Black recovers his pawn. Thus if White's e-pawn becomes protected, the capture on e5 may become a threat.

4...♘f6 (D)

We saw the move 4...b5 above.

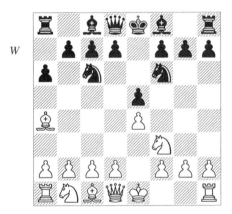

With this flexible continuation, Black threatens White's important e-pawn before deciding upon the development of his other pieces.

5 0-0

For example, the passive 5 d3 allows Black to become more aggressive without much risk: 5...b5 (notice that since e4 is covered, ♗xc6 and ♘xe5 has become a threat; however, 5...♗c5 is another legitimate move-order, since 6 ♗xc6 dxc6 7 ♘xe5? loses to 7...♕d4 – both f2 and the e5-knight hang) 6 ♗b3 ♗c5 7 0-0 (7 ♘xe5 ♘xe5 8 d4 ♗xd4 {8...♘xe4!? 9 dxc5 ♗b7 10 0-0 ♕f6 is also possible} 9 ♕xd4 d6 leaves Black a full tempo up on the Møller Variation;

we devote a section to that variation below) 7...d6. Black has his bishop outside his pawn-chain and stands solidly. Of course, there's much more that can be said about 5 d3, but in general White would rather wait a move or two until he sees what his opponent is up to.

5...♗e7

The first major decision about how Black will set his position up. After 5...b5 6 ♗b3, 6...♗c5 is the Møller Variation, examined in depth later; and 6...♗b7 is called the Arkhangelsk, a variation which I won't be investigating. The main alternative is 5...♘xe4, the important Open Variation, which reaches its standard position after 6 d4 b5 7 ♗b3 d5. This will be discussed in detail in its own section.

6 ♖e1

6 d4 is a sideline that might not be very interesting had we not seen something like it in the introduction to the Ruy Lopez above, but with the moves ♗b3 and ...b5 included. There White gained the advantage, but here the presence of the bishop on a4 makes equalizing relatively easy. Two brief examples after 6...exd4 (D):

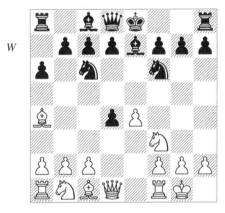

a) 7 e5 ♘e4 8 ♘xd4 (8 ♖e1 ♘c5 emphasizes the bishop's poor position on a4) 8...0-0 9 ♘f5 d5 10 exd6 (10 ♘xe7+ ♘xe7 11 c3 ♘c5 12 ♗c2 ♗f5 is equal) 10...♗xf5 11 dxe7 ♘xe7 12 ♗b3 ♘c5 13 ♘c3 ♘xb3 14 cxb3 ♕xd1 15 ♖xd1 ♖ad8 16 ♗f4 ½-½ Kramnik-Adams, Cap d'Agde (rapid) 2003. Neither side has any attack or structural weaknesses.

b) 7 ♖e1 b5 8 e5!? ♘xe5 9 ♖xe5 d6 10 ♖e1 (the initially attractive 10 ♖xe7+ ♕xe7 11 ♗b3 invites 11...c5!) 10...bxa4 11 ♘xd4 ♗d7 12 ♕f3 0-0 13 ♘c6 ♗xc6 14 ♕xc6 ♘d7!? 15

♘c3, Zapata-Anand, Manila OL 1992. The simplest is now 15...♗f6! intending ...a3.

6...b5 7 ♗b3 *(D)*

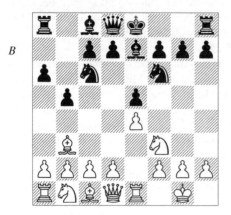

7...d6

This is actually a very important decision that is sometimes misunderstood. As always, it involves move-orders. If Black plays 7...0-0 at this point, he can answer 8 c3 with the famous Marshall Attack 8...d5, as discussed later. To avoid that White will often play the Anti-Marshall 8 a4 (as popularized by Kasparov) or 8 h3 with similar intent (in that case to allow White to capture the pawn safely after 8...d5 9 exd5 ♘xd5 10 ♘xe5). However, after 7...d6, the move 8 a4 is no longer very effective because e5 is defended and Black can develop smoothly by 8...♗d7, 8...b4, 8...♗b7, or even 8...♘a5!?; see the section on the Marshall Attack for details. After 8 h3, Black can play 8...0-0 (or 8...♗b7, or 8...♘a5!), when 9 c3 returns us to the main line.

To summarise: after 7...0-0, White can play the Anti-Marshall 8 a4 or allow the Marshall by 8 c3 d5. By choosing 7...d6 instead, Black foregoes the Marshall but takes the sting out of the Anti-Marshall's a4 move.

8 c3 0-0 9 h3 *(D)*

The immediate 9 d4 enjoys periodic popularity but you'll have to do the real work yourself to discover its secrets. Since the point of 9 h3 was to prevent the pin on his knight, Black will take immediate advantage of the chance to fight for d4 by 9...♗g4. This gives White the choice of 10 d5, when Black will try to break up White's pawn-chain by a timely ...c6; e.g., 10...♘a5 11 ♗c2 ♕c8!? (11...c6 12 dxc6 ♕c7

is the old variation, perhaps not as good; at any rate, Black wants to recapture with a bishop or queen on c6 to keep some control of d5) 12 h3 ♗d7! 13 ♘bd2 c6 with a complex battle ahead. The alternative 10 ♗e3 can lead almost anywhere; e.g., 10...exd4 11 cxd4 d5 (or 11...♘a5 and ...c5) 12 e5 ♘e4, but Black should avoid 10...♘xe4? 11 ♗d5 ♕d7 12 ♗xe4 d5 13 ♗c2! e4 14 h3 ♗h5 15 ♘e5!.

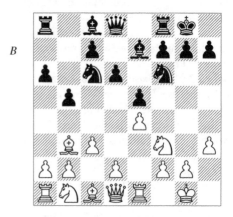

White prepares to play d4 next move. This is the starting-point of countless great battles, including games in the world championships between Kasparov and Karpov, Fischer and Spassky, and Smyslov versus Botvinnik. If you look at the games between leading grandmasters today, they continue to contest this same position and add new ideas.

We shall now discuss the Closed variations themselves.

Chigorin Defence

1 e4 e5 2 ♘f3 ♘c6 3 ♗b5 a6 4 ♗a4 ♘f6 5 0-0 ♗e7 6 ♖e1 b5 7 ♗b3 d6 8 c3 0-0 9 h3 ♘a5

Black makes the positional threat to exchange White's b3-bishop. This forces his response, since you cannot afford to cede the bishop-pair in such a position without considerable compensation.

10 ♗c2 c5 11 d4 ♕c7 *(D)*

This is the Classical Chigorin Defence to the Ruy Lopez, distinguished from the Modern Chigorin by the move 11...♕c7. So far Black's idea is clear: he has kicked the powerful Lopez bishop off its best diagonal, secured some space

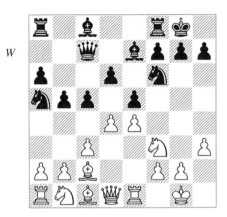

with ...c5, and then adopted a strongpoint policy by defending e5. He feels that an immediate exchange on d4 would amount to a surrender of the centre and puts that idea on hold with 11...♕c7. However, White must constantly watch over potential central exchanges, a situation that Black hopes will limit his opponent's free development. After 11...♕c7, Black will generally try to bring his pieces out slowly before taking any drastic action in the centre.

There are some drawbacks to this strategy. The first has to do with finding a useful, positive plan. Exerting pressure down the c-file is natural but generally White can defend the critical squares. Often Black will have to bring enough pieces to bear that a capture or two on d4 will make White's centre vulnerable. At that point White can implement his own ideas. He can exchange pawns on c5 and try to exploit the d5-square, or he can play d5 and then attack on the wings, sometimes by means of a4 and sometimes by piece-play on the kingside. In general White has the choice of developing his pieces or closing the centre.

Black's biggest problem tends to be his knight on a5. He can return it to c6, of course, but that consumes time and can provoke a timely d5. Furthermore, White's d5 advance in and of itself can keep the a5-knight out of play. At that point ...♘c4-b6 isn't bad, but it shows up an underlying problem with ...c5 combined with ...e5: a pawn on d5 can't be undermined by ...c6.

We shall come back to the idea of omitting ...♕c7. For the moment, here are two sample games which illustrate the classic Chigorin position:

Ivanchuk – Graf
Merida 2004

12 ♘bd2 *(D)*

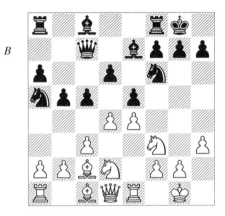

12...♖d8

This is a flexible move. It discourages White from playing dxe5 and leaves the bishop on the c8-h3 diagonal for now in anticipation of d5. We shall see 12...cxd4 in the next game, with a note on 12...♘c6.

13 b3!

Also flexible: White keeps Black's knight out of c4 and would like to make simple moves such as ♗b2 and ♖c1. Although it seems obscure at this point, b3 can also work with the moves a4 and ♗d3, which are designed to target b5 – watch for this theme in other games with the Closed Ruy Lopez.

13...♗d7

Black sometimes plays ...♗b7 instead of ...♗d7, but in the former case he should exchange in the centre first, because of 13...♗b7 14 d5! *(D)*.

This gives White almost everything that he could want from advancing his pawn, a committal decision that sometimes releases the pressure on Black's game. Let's consider this position. Black's bishop is badly placed on b7 because its scope is limited by White's pawn-chain and unfortunately the move ...f5 is nowhere in sight. Thus Black will play ...♗c8 and probably ...♗d7 with loss of time. What about that knight on a5? Right now it has no moves whatsoever because of White's pawns on b3 and d5; as a rule if Black permits White to play d5 it's a good idea to have the move ...♘c4 in

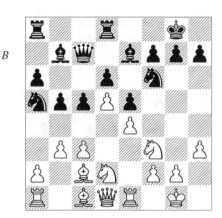

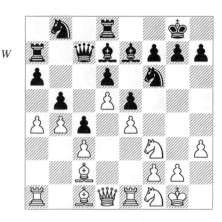

hand. Then even if the knight is driven away, b6 is a good place from which to keep an eye on White's a4 break, and Black reserves prospects of ...♘bd7. However, in the diagram (after 13...♗b7 14 d5), Black will have to move his bishop in order to reroute the knight to the uninspiring b7. From that square, alas, it is blocked from moving by the pawns on d6 and c5. Notice that if Black plays ...c4 and White plays b4, the situation is even worse. All right, it's a closed position and perhaps the knight can make just one more move from b7 to become useful, i.e. ...♘d8. But again, it is completely restricted, this time by White's d5-pawn! Even in a closed position, all this reorganization to little effect gives White plenty of time to prepare and launch an attack. The moral of the story is that with a bishop on b7, Black should almost always play ...cxd4 and perhaps even ...exd4 once the restrictive move b3 is in. Apart from that, both sides need to develop a feeling about whether to play/allow d5 if c4 is still available to the knight and/or Black's bishop is placed on d7 in support of the queenside. These decisions are terribly difficult and greatly assisted by playing experience with the opening.

14 ♘f1 ♘c6?!

Black gets into trouble after this. 14...cxd4 15 cxd4 ♖ac8 looks better.

15 d5 ♘b8 16 a4! ♖a7 17 b4!? c4? *(D)*

This kind of position is nearly always much better for White, who has more space and all the time in the world to build up. Black should have played 17...cxb4 18 cxb4 ♖c8 19 ♗e3 ♖b7 20 ♖c1 bxa4 21 ♗xa4 ♕d8, just to keep some lines open. Of course, he would still stand poorly.

18 ♗e3 ♖b7 19 axb5 axb5 20 g4!?

Sometimes White simply doubles or even triples on the a-file in this kind of position.

20...♖f8

Or 20...h5!? 21 g5 ♘h7 22 h4 f6 23 ♕d2.

21 ♘g3

White has come out of the opening with a large advantage. Black simply has to avoid these static positions unless he has already gained positional concessions.

21...♗c8 22 ♕d2 ♗d8 23 ♘f5 ♘e8 *(D)*

Or 23...♗xf5 24 gxf5 ♕e7 25 ♔h2 ♗b6 26 ♖g1.

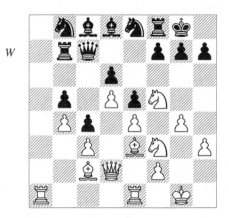

This position deserves a diagram. Notice Black's first rank. And the rook only recently left a8! Aesthetics aside, we shall become very used to one feature of the Closed Ruy Lopez: regardless of who stands better, there are uncommonly few exchanges. Here we are on move 23 and there have been no pieces exchanged, and only one pair of pawns.

24 ♔h1 ♘d7 25 ♘g5 ♘b6 26 f4! exf4 27 ♗xf4 ♗xf5 28 exf5 ♘f6 29 ♗g3!?

White could consolidate by means of 29 ♘e4! ♘xe4 30 ♗xe4 ♗h4 31 ♖e2.

29...h6 30 ♘f3?! *(D)*

Again, 30 ♘e4! was quite strong.

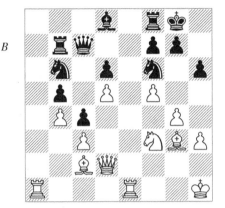

30...♗e7 31 ♖a5 ♘bxd5 32 h4 ♘xc3?!

32...♕c6 was Black's last chance to have a say in things.

33 ♕xc3 ♘xg4 34 ♖a6 ♕d7 35 ♕d4!

with a big advantage. White went on to win.

J. Polgar – Acs
Hoogeveen 2002

12 ♘bd2 cxd4

Black opens up the position to get some breathing room.

12...♘c6 is really asking for White to play dxc5, a Fischer favourite which intends ♘f1-e3-d5. If practice is any guide, this general plan causes little trouble for Black. Even in this favourable form for White (because the c6-knight is exposed to a recapture on d5), Black can apparently hold the balance: 13 dxc5 dxc5 14 ♘f1 ♗e6 (not a move that Black would like to make but he has to rush to cover d5) 15 ♘e3 ♖ad8 16 ♕e2 c4 17 ♘f5 (17 ♘g5 looks attractive but 17...h6! 18 ♘xe6 fxe6 gives equality – another case of the doubled e-pawns!) 17...♖fe8! 18 ♗g5 ♘d7 19 ♗xe7 ♘xe7 20 ♘g5 h6!? (or 20...♘f8!) 21 ♘xe6 fxe6 22 ♘e3 *(D)*, Fischer-O'Kelly, Buenos Aires 1970.

This is an interesting position of the type discussed in Chapter 3. Black's doubled pawns guard important squares and his knights have good prospects, so the apparent weaknesses are not meaningful.

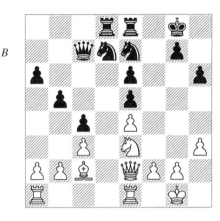

In the game Black should now have played 22...♘c5! 23 ♘g4 ♘c6 with at least equality.

13 cxd4 ♗d7 14 ♘f1 *(D)*

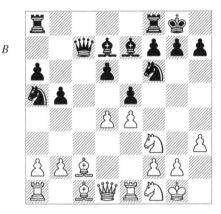

This is the standard Ruy Lopez manoeuvre that has been popular ever since Steinitz started playing it in variations with d3 instead of d4. White's knight will either go to e3, eyeing d5 and f5 (while protecting c2), or to g3 where it covers f5 and protects the e-pawn (this discourages ...exd4), while leaving the c1-bishop a good view of the kingside. Such meanderings are ordinarily only possible in a closed position or in one with a stable centre.

14...♖ac8 15 ♘e3 ♘c6 16 ♗b3!?

Other players have preferred 16 d5 ♘b4 17 ♗b1 a5 18 a3 ♘a6. Now 19 b4! should keep the advantage because after 19...axb4 20 axb4 ♘xb4? 21 ♗d2 White wins the knight. Black of course hopes that the new weakness of c4 may provide him compensation. Whether or not 16 d5 is good, White opts here for activating the light-squared bishop and keeping lines open.

This is a typical choice that the Lopez player faces, and sometimes depends upon the style of the player. Polgar is by any definition an attacker.

16...♘a5 17 ♘d5 ♘xd5 18 ♗xd5 ♘c4

18...♗e6 would eliminate the powerful d5-bishop; White maintains just a small edge with 19 a4.

19 ♗g5! ♗xg5

19...♘xb2? fails to 20 ♕e2 ♗xg5 21 ♘xg5 ♘c4 22 ♕h5, winning.

20 ♘xg5 h6?!

Not best, but White still has the advantage after 20...♗c6 21 b3! ♘b6 22 ♖c1.

21 ♘xf7! ♖xf7 (D)

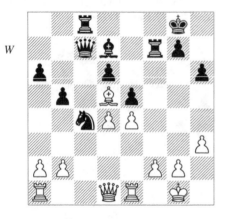

W

22 ♖c1?!

The right move-order to implement White's idea was 22 ♗xf7+! ♔xf7 23 ♖c1. Black fails to take advantage of this slip.

22...♕b8?!

Correct was 22...♗c6! 23 ♗xf7+ ♕xf7 24 b3 ♘b6.

23 b3 ♘b6 24 ♖xc8+ ♗xc8 25 ♗xf7+ ♔xf7 26 dxe5 ♔e7

26...dxe5 27 ♕d8 ♕b7 28 ♖c1 doesn't improve the situation.

27 exd6+

Still better is 27 ♕h5!, although that's not clear without lengthy and complicated analysis, so the text-move is the practical decision. White is winning in any case.

27...♕xd6 28 ♕c2 ♗b7 29 ♖d1 ♕c6 30 ♕d2 ♘d7 31 ♖c1 ♕f6 32 a4 ♗c6 33 ♕a5 bxa4 34 bxa4 ♘e5 35 ♕c7+ ♗d7 36 ♖d1 ♕e6 37 ♕c5+ ♔e8 38 ♖d6 ♕e7 39 ♕c7! a5 40 ♖a6 1-0

Modern Chigorin

Let's return to the position after 1 e4 e5 2 ♘f3 ♘c6 3 ♗b5 a6 4 ♗a4 ♘f6 5 0-0 ♗e7 6 ♖e1 b5 7 ♗b3 d6 8 c3 0-0 9 h3 ♘a5 10 ♗c2 c5 11 d4 (D):

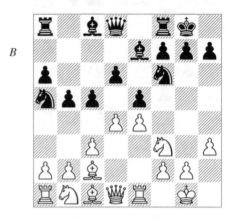

B

11...cxd4

Here we have what I call a Modern Chigorin Defence, in which Black skips ...♕c7.

12 cxd4 exd4!?

Rejection of the strongpoint approach! Black shamelessly liquidates (i.e., surrenders) the centre. With the recognition that the weakness on d6 isn't really serious (sometimes the pawn can even go to d5), this radical policy has become an accepted one in just a few years.

The alternative 12...♗b7!? (D) hits the centre immediately so as to save time by comparison.

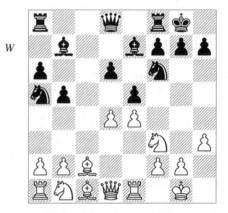

W

Then 13 ♘bd2 exd4 14 ♘xd4 transposes to the main line. However, White can also play 13 d5, which returns us to relatively normal channels and challenges Black to make something out of foregoing ...♕c7. Instead he found himself in a familiar pattern in Morozevich-Ponomariov, Moscow 2001: 13...♖c8? (Black should prefer 13...♘c4 14 b3 ♘b6 or 13...♗c8 14 ♘bd2 ♗d7) 14 b3! with problems similar to those seen in the note about 13...♗b7 in the Ivanchuk-Graf game above. Black's knight has no return path and even the b7-bishop can't yet get back to c8! Ponomariov understood these issues and went for tactics by 14...♕c7 15 ♗d3 ♘xe4!? 16 ♗xe4 f5, but they fell short following 17 ♗d3 e4 18 ♗g5! ♗f6 (18...♖fe8 19 ♗xe7 ♖xe7 20 b4 ♘c4 21 ♗xc4 ♕xc4 22 ♕d2!) 19 ♗xf6 ♖xf6 20 ♗e2 exf3 21 ♗xf3 b4 22 ♘d2 ♖ff8 23 a3! (threatening to win the knight) 23...♕b6 24 axb4 ♕xb4 25 ♖a4 ♕c3 26 ♖e3! ♕b2 27 ♘f1 ♖c5 28 ♕e1! and White won the knight that Black marooned so early on.

We now return to 12...exd4!? *(D)*:

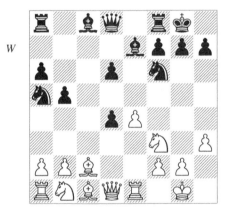

With 12...exd4, Black ignores his weakness on d6 for the sake of activity, in the style of modern openings from the Sicilian to the King's Indian. In the following game we have an example of good strategy by both players.

Sorokin – Ramesh
Sangli 2000

13 ♘xd4 ♗b7

The same idea is expressed by 13...♖e8 14 ♗g5!? (14 ♘d2 ♗b7 transposes to the main game) 14...h6 15 ♗h4 ♘d5!? 16 ♗xe7 ♘xe7 17 ♘d2 ♗b7 18 a4 ♕b6 19 ♘4b3 (19 ♘2f3

♘c4) 19...♘ac6 20 axb5 axb5 21 ♖xa8 ♖xa8 22 ♘f1 ♘e5 ½-½ Leko-Morozevich, Wijk aan Zee 2002.

14 ♘d2 ♖e8 15 b3 ♗f8 16 ♗b2 g6 *(D)*

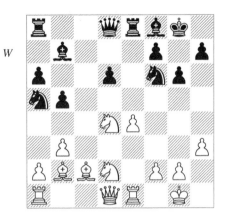

17 ♕f3

Black's dynamic possibilities were demonstrated by an inhuman following 17 ♖e2?! ♗g7 18 ♕e1 ♖c8 19 ♖d1 ♘h5! (knights on the rim!) 20 ♗b1 ♘f4 21 ♖e3 ♕f6 22 ♘2f3 ♘c6 23 ♔h2 ♘e5 24 g3?! ♘d5! 25 exd5 ♘xf3+ 26 ♘xf3 ♖xe3 27 ♗xf6 ♖xe1 28 ♘xe1 ♗xf6 and Black had the bishop-pair and a clear advantage in Leko-*Fritz 6*, Frankfurt (rapid) 1999.

17...♗g7 18 ♖ad1 ♖c8 19 ♗b1 *(D)*

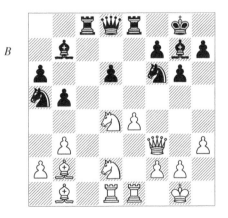

19...♘d7!?

Unveiling the g7-bishop and eyeing e5. Other moves have been played including 19...b4 and 19...♘c6! 20 ♘f1 ♘e5 21 ♘e3 ♘ed7 22 ♕f4 d5 23 ♘g3, when 23...♘xe4 (23...♕c7 24 e5!? was played in J.Polgar-Milos, Buenos Aires 2000, a marginally sound sacrifice but Polgar brought home the point) 24 ♘xe4 dxe4 25 ♗xe4 ♗xe4 26 ♖xe4 ♘c5 is equal.

20 ♘f1 (D)

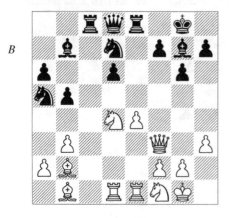

20...b4

20...f5! is also interesting and probably equal, because White cannot exploit the a2-g8 diagonal.

21 ♘e3

The game has proceeded logically to this point and instead of the ambitious 21...♕g5?! Black had 21...♘f6! with equality. This modern-style system seems to be fully playable. It represents a dynamic treatment of even this most staid of openings.

Keres Defence

Another way to bolster e5 has received renewed attention from some of the world's top players. It was first promoted by Paul Keres:

11...♘d7!? (D)

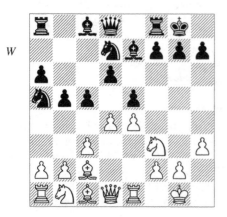

Moves like this make the Ruy Lopez one of the most fascinating openings in strategic terms. Black develops a piece backwards and cuts off his own c8-bishop, at the same time taking his eye off the vital d5-square! But he is intent upon forcing a resolution of the central dark squares, so 11...♘d7 serves the double purpose of protecting e5 and clearing a square for the bishop on f6 after pawn exchanges. Black also recognizes that his queen might go to b6 instead of c7 in some lines, and even ...f5 might come into play. Let's look at two games:

Damljanović – Ponomariov
Plovdiv Echt 2003

12 ♘bd2

12 d5?! releases the pressure just when Black's pieces are best situated to destroy the centre: 12...♘b6 13 g4?! (trying to anticipate the ...f5 break, which would probably lead to the loss of White's important d-pawn) 13...h5 14 ♘h2 hxg4 15 hxg4 ♗g5 and Black already had much the better game in Fischer-Keres, Curaçao Ct 1962.

12...exd4

12...cxd4 is the old continuation, and not necessarily worse. This move-order has something very specific in mind.

13 cxd4 ♘c6 14 d5 ♘ce5 (D)

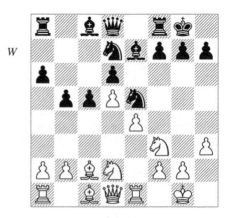

Black's idea is that he has achieved a Modern Benoni position with ...b5 already in! In fact, White's position is one that he might have arrived at via the Modern h3/♗d3 version of the Benoni. Black would be thrilled to complete the analogy by ...♗f6, so White has to act quickly:

15 ♘xe5! ♘xe5 16 f4 ♘g6 17 ♘f3 ♗h4!

The simple idea is to play ...♗g3 and force White into playing f5. Black is also ready to play ...f5 himself. There were several games with 17...f5 18 e5 dxe5 19 fxe5 ♗b7 before this one, but White finally got the better of the debate.

18 ♘xh4

18 ♖f1 ♗g3 19 f5 ♘e5 gives Black the dark squares that he needs.

18...♕xh4 19 f5?!

19 ♖f1! ♗xh3!? 20 gxh3 ♕g3+ draws, although Black might simply bring a rook to the e-file and see what develops.

19...♘e5

Black is at least equal, in part because White's c2-bishop is so bad.

20 ♖f1 ♗d7 21 ♗f4 ♕e7 22 ♕e1 f6 23 ♕g3 ♖fe8 24 b3 a5

Black has secured the key e5-square and begun to attack.

Petrović – N. Davies
corr. 2003

12 dxc5 dxc5 13 ♘bd2 (D)

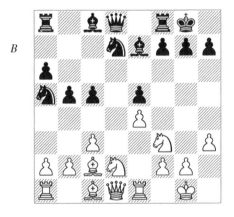

White intends to play the customary sequence ♘f1-e3-d5. These days, players aren't impressed by this single-minded attempt to get a knight to the outpost.

13...♗b7!

Black walked into it by playing 13...♕c7? 14 ♘f1 ♘b6 15 ♘e3 ♖d8 16 ♕e2 ♗e6 17 ♘d5! ♘xd5 18 exd5 ♗xd5 19 ♘xe5 in the famous game Fischer-Keres, Curaçao Ct 1962. White has a terrific attack and is probably already winning.

14 ♘f1 ♘c4 15 ♘3h2

15 b3 ♘d6 centralizes the knight and prevents ♘e3.

15...♘f6 16 ♕f3 ♕c7 17 ♘g3

White can get his pieces out by 17 ♘e3 ♘xe3 18 ♗xe3. Then 18...♖ad8 is at least equal for Black.

17...♘d6 18 ♘hf1 ♘d7 19 ♘e3 g6 (D)

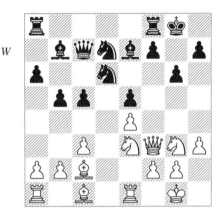

At first sight we have a typical Ruy Lopez situation in which White has a kingside attack and Black is trying to create queenside or central play. The problem for White is that Black's kingside position is almost impossible to get at. Thus Black has a significant advantage out of the opening, and wins quickly when White overreaches.

20 ♕e2 c4 21 ♘g4 h5 22 ♘h6+ ♔g7 23 ♘hf5+ gxf5 24 ♘xh5+ ♔h8 25 exf5 ♕c6 26 ♘f4 ♘f6 27 ♕xe5 ♖g8 28 f3 ♖xg2+ 0-1

Breyer Defence

1 e4 e5 2 ♘f3 ♘c6 3 ♗b5 a6 4 ♗a4 ♘f6 5 0-0 ♗e7 6 ♖e1 b5 7 ♗b3 d6 8 c3 0-0 9 h3 ♘b8!? (D)

As time went by, some players grew either tired of the Chigorin Defence and/or suspicious of its merits. Attention turned to this rather amazing retreat, the product of early 20th-century player Gyula Breyer's imagination.

10 d4

White sometimes holds off on this move, hoping to exploit some subtle issues relating to tempi, but it really hasn't helped his cause.

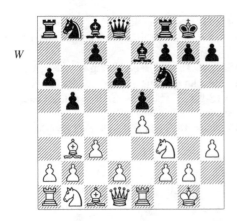

Indeed, the main alternative 10 d3 ♘bd7 11 ♘bd2 ♗b7 12 ♘f1 ♘c5 has been analysed to more than 20 moves with a verdict of equality.

10...♘bd7 11 ♘bd2 ♗b7 (D)

Note for the unwary: 11...♖e8?? allows 12 ♗xf7+! with the idea 12...♔xf7 13 ♘g5+ ♔g8 14 ♘e6.

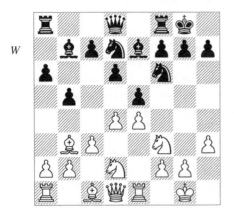

To reach the position in the diagram, Black has wasted two moves getting re-developed and his pawns do not fight for control of d4 as in the Chigorin and Keres variations (with ...c5). Nor has he chased White's bishop off the ideal a2-g8 diagonal. In fact, he has a position that resembles a Philidor Defence (as does the ♗xf7+ tactic). So what's the point? First of all, Black has no weakness on d5 and can expel any piece that lands there with ...c6. Then there's the elementary fact that White has to search for a plan. Consider his three main approaches against the Chigorin and Keres Defences. White sometimes played d5, a pawn that is now subject to undermining by ...c6 with the danger that White, if

compelled to play dxc6, will grant Black a central majority. The second idea of capturing Black's e-pawn and swinging a knight to d5 is not only fairly useless, as mentioned above, but hard to implement. And that leads to White's third normal plan and in this case the most promising: ♘f1-e3/g3. However, we see that 12 ♘f1? drops the e-pawn. How exactly will White get the reorganization he wants?

12 ♗c2

Remarkably, White abandons his favourite diagonal without being chased away! For the record, the move 10 d3 that we mentioned above had the point of ♘bd2-f1-e3 without needing to retreat by ♗c2. But in that variation Black could get ...♘c5 in, which in turn is the target of attack by d4, and so forth – this is all much too obscure for our purposes. After 12 ♗c2, the onus is on Black to make some sort of useful move as White pursues his knight tour. Hence:

12...♖e8 (D)

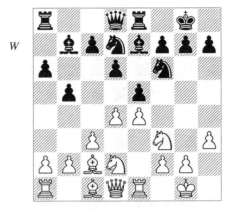

The basic plan now is ...♗f8, with ...g6, ...♗g7 and ...h6. This maximizes Black's minor-piece pressure upon e4 and d4 such that White needs to take into account the moves ...exd4 and even ...d5 at every turn. The move ...c6 is essential in many lines (again, compare the Philidor Defence), but given the opportunity, Black might even be able to sneak in our old Chigorin-style ...c5, when for starters his d7-knight sure beats a knight on a5! It's all extremely complicated and the stuff of high strategy rather than mating attacks (at least for the foreseeable future). I'll feature a first-class encounter.

Ponomariov – Gyimesi
Moscow 2005

13 ♘f1

At this juncture White has played some fundamentally different ideas such as 13 b4, 13 b3 and 13 a4. In the last case, for example, 13...♗f8 can be answered by 14 ♗d3 aiming at the queenside. In fact, White's main advantage in these lines is that if he can prevent any radical central action by Black, he can exert pressure on both wings. Generally White gains a limited edge if that happens, but nothing that allows him to exceed a normal percentage score; e.g., 14...c6 15 b3 g6 16 ♕c2 (often you'll see Black break out successfully; e.g., 16 ♗b2 ♗g7 17 ♗f1 ♕c7 18 ♖a2 d5! 19 axb5 cxb5 20 exd5 ♘xd5 with the initiative, Tseshkovsky-Dorfman, Erevan Z 1982) 16...♗g7 17 ♗b2 ♘h5 18 ♗f1 ♕b6 19 b4 ♘f4 20 dxe5 ♘xe5 21 ♘xe5 dxe5 22 c4 with the kind of typical slight pressure White often gets, Karpov-Beliavsky, Biel 1992.

But the absolute key for Black is not to allow an inflexible, passive structure, even if it is theoretically defensible. This happens in our main game, and in the following impressive contest in which White played 14 b4 (instead of 14 ♗d3) 14...♘b6 15 a5 ♘bd7 16 ♗b2 ♖b8 17 ♖b1 h6 18 ♗a1 ♗a8 19 ♖e3! g6 20 ♕e2 c6 21 c4 ♗g7? (never allow White a quasi-permanent bind unless forced to; now was the time to play the typical central counterattack with 21...exd4! 22 ♗xd4 bxc4! 23 ♘xc4 and then 23...d5 with equality, or Shirov's idea 23...c5!) 22 dxe5 dxe5 23 c5 ♘h5 24 g3 ♕c7 25 ♖d3 ♖bd8 26 ♖d1 ♘f8 27 ♘f1 *(D)*.

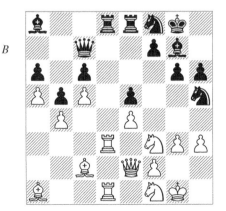

Here's the standard Breyer problem: Black has no obvious targets and no positive plan. This was illustrated by 27...♖xd3 28 ♕xd3 ♘f6 29 ♘e3 ♗b7 30 ♔g2 ♕b8 31 ♗b2 ♕c7 32 ♗b3! ♖e7 33 ♕d8 ♕xd8 34 ♖xd8 ♘6d7 35 ♘h4! ♔h7 36 ♘hf5! gxf5 37 ♘xf5 ♗f6 38 ♘xe7 ♗xe7 39 ♖e8 and White soon won in Shirov-Leko, Ljubljana 1995.

13...♗f8 14 ♘g3 g6 15 ♗g5!?

At this point White has done extremely well at the highest levels with 15 b3 intending c4, when 15...♗g7 16 d5 or 15...c6 16 ♗g5! has given Black fits. But Malcolm Pein and Andrew Martin have done a thorough analysis to show that 15...d5! works: 16 ♗g5 h6 17 ♗h4!? *(D)*.

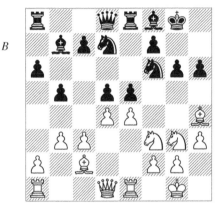

In this position Judit Polgar destroyed Boris Spassky in the 8th game of their Budapest match in 1993 following 17...dxe4 18 ♘xe4 g5 19 dxe5 ♘xe4 20 ♗xe4 ♗xe4 21 ♖xe4 gxh4 22 ♖d4 ♖e7 23 e6! fxe6 24 ♘e5. Pein and Martin tore into the line 17...g5! 18 ♘xg5 hxg5 19 ♗xg5 exd4! with huge complications ultimately favouring Black. Notice how the modern Breyer seems to do best when Black can successfully implement the 'blow it all to bits' strategy as opposed to the 'cleverly shift around' method of defence. That said, the latter can also be satisfactory with very accurate play.

15...h6 16 ♗d2 ♗g7 17 a4 c5!? *(D)*

We've switched back to Keres-style play! 17...c6 is the positional option which has in mind an eventual ...d5, and may be preferable. In spite of hundreds of games by the chess elite, you'll normally see the same set of basic structures and approaches. One wonders about a ...d5 break instead, as in the previous note.

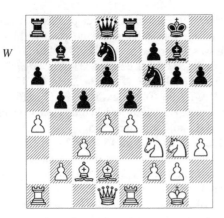

W

18 d5 c4

The point: Black gets a knight to c5. Otherwise shutting in his own bishop and not having the ...c6 option would be the worst of both worlds.

19 b4 cxb3

Black certainly doesn't want to get squeezed to death, although he made that huge misjudgement in a famous encounter: 19...♘h7? 20 ♗e3 h5 21 ♕d2 ♖f8 22 ♖a3! ♘df6 23 ♖ea1 ♕d7 24 ♖1a2! ♖fc8 25 ♕c1 ♗f8 26 ♕a1 ♕e8 (Black can only wait around and defend against White's threats on the a-file) 27 ♘f1 ♗e7 28 ♘1d2 ♔g7 29 ♘b1! *(D)*.

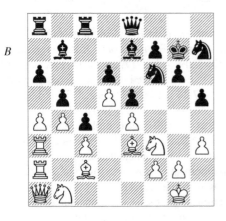

B

29...♘xe4!? (desperation because there was nothing to do about White's threat; for example, 29...♘d7 30 axb5 axb5 31 ♖xa8 ♖xa8 32 ♖xa8 ♕xa8 33 ♕xa8 ♗xa8 34 ♘a3; the rest of the game is pretty, so I'll give the moves) 30 ♗xe4 f5 31 ♗c2 ♗xd5 32 axb5 axb5 33 ♖a7 ♔f6 34 ♘bd2 ♖xa7 35 ♖xa7 ♖a8 36 g4 hxg4 37 hxg4 ♖xa7 38 ♕xa7 f4 39 ♗xf4 exf4 40 ♘h4

♗f7 41 ♕d4+ ♔e6 42 ♘f5! ♗f8 43 ♕xf4 ♔d7 44 ♘d4 ♕e1+ 45 ♔g2 ♗d5+ 46 ♗e4 ♗xe4+ 47 ♘xe4 ♗e7 48 ♘xb5 ♘f8 49 ♘bxd6 ♘e6 50 ♕e5 1-0 Fischer-Spassky, Sveti Stefan/Belgrade (1) 1992.

20 ♗xb3 ♘c5 21 c4

21 ♗c2 ♘fd7 is easy for Black.

21...bxc4?!

This gives up key squares. 21...♕d7! ended in a draw in another game. In fact, theory goes much further than this in some Breyer lines, which is pretty amazing considering that the play is so unforced.

22 ♗xc4 ♕c7 23 ♕e2 ♖eb8

Black has to get his rotten bishop back to a decent diagonal so he brings the rook into activity first. The one on g7 isn't looking so great either.

24 a5 ♗c8 25 ♗e3 ♘fd7 26 ♖ec1 ♔h7

You could argue that only now are we truly at the end of the opening. As so often Black stands very solidly but is at a loss for a plan.

27 ♘e1 ♗f6 28 ♘f3 ♕d8 29 ♕d2! ♗g7 *(D)*

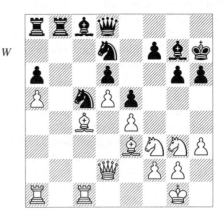

W

30 h4!

There you have it: once the opponent is tied down to passive defence, you open up another front. This is classic chess strategy.

30...h5?!

Maybe Black should make his stand on the g6-square instead by something like 30...♖a7 31 h5 ♖ab7. It's easier to defend third-rank pawns than to surrender outposts and try to survive.

31 ♘g5+ ♔g8 32 ♖a3!

The kingside beckons, and in any case this is a useful move.

32...♕e7 33 ♕d1

You can see the tactics coming now. All White needs is one more piece, and he doesn't fail to realize that.

33...♖a7 34 ♖ac3 ♖c7 35 ♗e2! ♖b4 36 ♘xh5! *(D)*

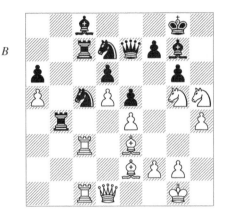

36...gxh5 37 ♗xh5 f6 38 ♗f7+ ♔f8 39 ♘e6+ ♔xf7

The attack continues successfully for White in lines like 39...♘xe6 40 ♖xc7 ♘xc7 41 ♖xc7 ♔xf7 42 ♖xc8 ♘f8 43 h5! ♖xe4 44 h6 and wins.

40 ♘xg7 ♔xg7 41 ♕h5 ♖xe4 42 ♗h6+ ♔h8 43 ♖g3 1-0

The rook got over there on the last move of the game!

If you look at a lot of games with the Breyer Defence you'll find that Black needs to fight for his own space (often by ...d5) and/or liquidate pawns; otherwise he can suffer through a long period of inactivity with little room to manoeuvre. Even in the latter case most of the positions are defensible with perfect play, but they are very difficult to handle in practice. Thus we can look forward to the fighting methods as holding the real key to the long-term success of the Breyer.

Zaitsev Variation

1 e4 e5 2 ♘f3 ♘c6 3 ♗b5 a6 4 ♗a4 ♘f6 5 0-0 ♗e7 6 ♖e1 b5 7 ♗b3 d6 8 c3 0-0 9 h3 ♗b7 10 d4 ♖e8 *(D)*

Zaitsev gets credit for developing this set-up with 9...♗b7 and 10...♖e8 into a complete

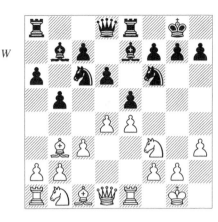

system. The game can easily turn extremely tactical and because it gives lively play is a great favourite among today's players on both sides of the board. Some of the attacking ideas associated with this variation have been among the most beautiful of modern chess. From a practical point of view, however, the fun and entertaining main lines cannot be worked out over the board and if your goal is opening mastery then they simply must be memorized. I have primarily tried to indicate the general contours of play, and for that purpose will present some dated but fantastic world championship games, along with a couple of more recent examples.

11 ♘bd2

From Black's point of view, the pure Zaitsev can only be used when a draw is acceptable, because 11 ♘g5 ♖f8 12 ♘f3 repeats the position. Some degree of bluff is involved. Of course Black can deviate at that point and play another defence to the Lopez, such as 12...h6 intending to enter a very similar but less immediately aggressive system by 13...♖e8 and 14...♗f8. That sequence is sometimes named after Smyslov.

As for White, he can play 11 ♘g5 ♖f8 12 f4, which originally was thought to deter Black from Zaitsev's move-order, but this is now considered fine for Black after 12...exf4, and enterprising players will most likely prefer 12...exd4 13 cxd4 d5 14 e5 ♘e4!, in view of 15 ♘xe4?! dxe4 16 ♖xe4 ♘a5, when Black will follow up by ...♘xb3 and ...c5 with two bishops and terrific pressure.

11...♗f8 *(D)*

White must now make an important decision between 12 a4, which keeps lines open, and 12

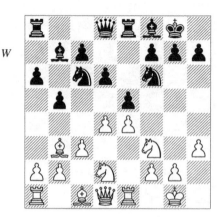

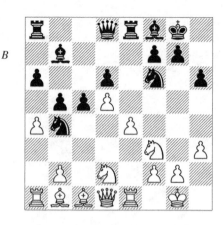

d5, a more restrained approach with which he hopes to cramp Black's game.

12 a3 stops Black's main ...②b4 idea, but it's slow. One interesting reply is 12...♕d7; e.g., 13 d5 ②e7 14 ②f1 ②g6!? 15 ♗c2 c6 (usually the sign of equality) 16 dxc6 ♗xc6 17 ♗g5 ②h5 18 ②h4 ②gf4 19 ♕g4 ♕xg4 20 hxg4 ②e6! with good counterplay, Bacrot-I.Sokolov, Reykjavik 2003.

Kasparov – Karpov
New York/Lyons Wch (22) 1990

12 a4

This simple move threatens to pile up on the b-pawn and practically compels Black to undertake something active.

12...h6 13 ♗c2

Again, as in the Breyer, White's knight can't continue its journey to f1 without this support for the e-pawn.

13...exd4 14 cxd4 ②b4! 15 ♗b1 c5

A dynamic plan with all kinds of consequences. We have a Benoni structure in which Black has already made considerable queenside progress, but after White's next move the b7-bishop will be shut off and White's pieces are aimed at Black's king.

16 d5 *(D)*

16...②d7

The whole point of ...②b4 resides in this move, which both prepares ...②e5 with ...c4 and ...②bd3 to follow, but also contemplates the risky ...f5 to destroy White's centre. Abandoning the protection of Black's king is not without danger, of course.

17 ♖a3!

White prepares to shift his pieces to the kingside, his only real area of strength. What follows is more a demonstration of attacking and defensive skill than understanding, but the latter is still important:

17...f5!?

When Karpov played this no one really understood how perilous it was. The idea is that a central takeover would tend to be of more value than a flank attack, but that has no real validity as a principle of play. Over the years more players have drifted towards 17...c4, although that is by no means easy either. Anand-Adams, San Luis Wch 2005 shows how White can target Black's king with a dangerous attack: 18 axb5 axb5 19 ②d4 ♕b6 20 ②f5 ②e5 21 ♖g3 g6 22 ②f3! ②ed3 *(D)*.

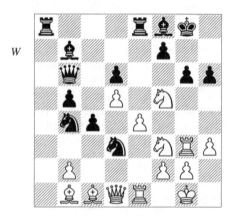

Now it looks as though Black will beat off the attack by eliminating White's bishops. First, he threatens ...♕xf2+. Unfortunately, all of this was theory, and Anand had prepared 23 ♕d2! ♗xd5? (very tempting, but Black had to be greedy and find his way through the 'only moves': 23...♘xe1! 24 ♘xe1 ♘xd5! 25 ♘xh6+ ♗xh6 26 ♕xh6 ♖a1! 27 ♖xg6+ fxg6 28 ♕xg6+ with a draw) 24 ♘xh6+! ♗xh6 25 ♕xh6 ♕xf2+ 26 ♔h2 ♘xe1 27 ♘h4! ♘ed3 (it's hopeless at this point) 28 ♘xg6 ♕xg3+ 29 ♔xg3 fxg6 30 ♕xg6+ ♔f8 31 ♕f6+ ♔g8 32 ♗h6 1-0.

It's now customary for Black to bring a knight to d3 and White to swing his rook to g3 in this line; what counts are the specific tactics and one's skill in carrying them out. Contrary to the impression given by this game, there's a fair amount of room for original play in even these critical Zaitsev lines, and the odds of the average player or even a master reaching something this theoretical are extremely low. Which is to say that the Zaitsev is still a fun system, both in the tactical variations and in the positional continuations given above.

18 exf5

A more famous and exciting contest from the same match went 18 ♖ae3 ♘f6 19 ♘h2!? ♔h8 20 b3! (White feels that the attack requires only one more piece and wants the bishop on the long diagonal) 20...bxa4 (20...fxe4 21 ♘xe4 ♘fxd5!? 22 ♖f3! ♘f6 23 ♖xf6 gxf6 24 ♘g4 is typically complicated) 21 bxa4 c4 22 ♗b2 fxe4 23 ♘xe4 ♘fxd5 24 ♖g3 ♖e6! 25 ♘g4! ♕e8? (a beautiful line is 25...♘f4? 26 ♘xh6! ♖xh6 27 ♘g5 ♕c7 28 ♘e6! ♘xe6 29 ♖xe6 ♖h4 30 ♖g4 ♖xg4 31 ♕xg4 ♘d3 32 ♖h6+ ♔g8 33 ♕e6+ ♕f7 34 ♖h8+!; best is 25...♘d3! 26 ♗xd3 cxd3 27 ♖xd3 ♕a5, which is unclear) 26 ♘xh6! c3 27 ♘f5! cxb2 28 ♕g4 ♗c8 (28...♘c3 loses to the pretty 29 ♘f6! ♖xe1+ 30 ♔h2; and 28...g6 29 ♔h2! is a similar theme, threatening ♕h4+ and ♘g5: 29...♕d7 30 ♘h4! ♗c8 31 ♘xg6+ ♖xg6 32 ♕xg6, winning) 29 ♕h4+ ♖h6 30 ♘xh6 gxh6 31 ♔h2! ♕e5 (31...♗g7 32 ♘xd6 ♕xe1 33 ♕xh6+!) 32 ♘g5 ♕f6 33 ♖e8 ♗f5 34 ♕xh6+! ♕xh6 35 ♘f7+ ♔h7 36 ♗xf5+ ♕g6 37 ♗xg6+ ♔g7 38 ♖xa8 ♗e7 39 ♖b8 a5 40 ♗e4+ ♔xf7 41 ♗xd5+ 1-0 Kasparov-Karpov, New York/Lyons Wch (20) 1990.

18...♗xd5!? 19 ♘e4 ♗f7!?

Still another game between these giants continued 19...♘f6 20 ♘xf6+ ♕xf6 21 ♗d2! ♕xb2 22 ♗xb4 ♗f7! 23 ♖e6! ♕xb4! 24 ♘b3! ♕xa4 25 ♗c2 with an unholy mess. That game, Kasparov-Karpov, New York/Lyons Wch (4) 1990, was eventually drawn.

20 axb5 d5 21 ♘c3 ♖xe1+ 22 ♘xe1 d4 23 ♘a2

Other involved lines begin with 23 ♘e4!? axb5 24 f6 ♖xa3 25 bxa3 ♘d5 26 fxg7 ♗xg7 and 23 ♗e4 dxc3 (23...♖a7 24 ♘e2 ♘f6 25 ♗f3 d3) 24 ♗xa8 ♕xa8 25 ♕xd7 ♕e4.

23...♘xa2 24 ♗xa2 c4! 25 ♖xa6 ♘c5! *(D)*

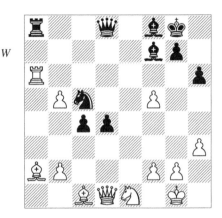

26 ♖xa8 ♕xa8 27 ♗b1 d3 28 ♗e3 ♕a5 29 b3! ♘xb3 30 ♘xd3! cxd3 31 ♗xd3 ♘c5 32 ♗f1 ♕c7 33 ♕g4 ♔h7

33...h5!? is answered by 34 ♕d4 with equality.

34 ♗c4 ♗xc4

The tempting continuation 34...♗e8? allows 35 ♗xh6! with the idea 35...♔xh6 36 ♕h4+ ♗h5 37 g4.

35 ♕xc4 ♕e5 36 ♕f7 ♗d6 37 g3 ♕e7 38 ♕g6+ ♔h8 39 ♗d4 ♗e5! 40 ♗xc5 ♕xc5 41 ♕e8+ ♔h7 42 ♕g6+ ♔h8 43 ♕e8+ ½-½

L. Dominguez – Morović
Havana 2002

12 d5 *(D)*

This changes the entire character of the game.

Notice how, as in the Breyer Defence, Black retains the option of playing ...c6 to break up White's centre. Speaking in general terms, White will usually answer by dxc6, after which he has been fairly successful in keeping Black from achieving ...d5. The problem is that he must devote all his resources to this effort and allow other equalizing methods. Here are a couple of ways in which this dilemma plays out:

12...♘e7

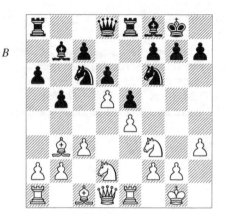

A more conventional approach is 12...♘b8 13 ♘f1 ♘bd7 14 ♘3h2 *(D)*.

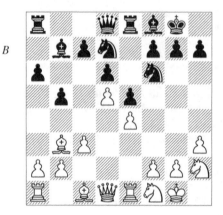

14...♘c5 15 ♗c2 c6 (Black is using a typical device from the Breyer Defence) 16 b4 ♘cd7 17 dxc6 ♗xc6 18 ♗g5 (the fight to stop ...d5 begins) 18...h6 19 ♗xf6 ♘xf6 20 ♘g4! ♘xg4 21 ♕xg4 ♗d7 22 ♕f3 ♖c8 23 ♗b3 ♗e6! 24 ♗xe6 (sadly, the moves thus far are all theory) 24...fxe6 25 a4 ♕d7 26 axb5 axb5 27 ♖ed1 ♕c6 28 ♖d3 ♖a8 29 ♖ad1 ♖a7 30 ♘g3 ♖f7 31 ♕g4 ♖f4 32 ♕g6 ♖f6 33 ♕g4 ♖f4 with equality, Pelletier-Bacrot, Biel 2004. A perfectly balanced game.

13 ♘f1 h6 14 ♘3h2!? c6 15 ♘g4 ♘xg4 16 hxg4 cxd5 17 exd5 ♕d7 18 ♘g3 a5 19 a3 a4 20 ♗a2 ♖ac8 21 ♘e4

Here Black uncorked a beautiful exchange sacrifice:

21...♖c4! *(D)*

22 ♗xc4 bxc4 23 ♗xh6! ♘xd5! 24 ♗d2 ♘c7 25 ♘g3 ♕c6 26 f3 ♘e6 27 ♕e2 ♘c5

½-½

Black has full compensation and, remarkably, 28 ♕xc4 fails to 28...d5 29 ♕e2 ♗a6 and ...♘d3 with ...♗c5+ to follow.

The Zaitsev is a wonderful opening whose results are determined by both positional and combinative skills. Much main-line theory (in the attacking lines) has been worked out and should be memorized if you're facing top-notch competition. On the other hand, both White and Black have alternatives at an early stage.

Møller Defence

1 e4 e5 2 ♘f3 ♘c6 3 ♗b5 a6 4 ♗a4 ♘f6 5 0-0

5 d3 is slow and there are several established solutions. But in our context it allows Black to get his bishop in front of the pawn-chain without punishment: 5...b5 6 ♗b3 ♗c5. As we said in the introduction to the Closed Ruy, there can follow 7 0-0 (7 ♘xe5 ♘xe5 8 d4 ♗xd4! 9 ♕xd4 d6 threatening ...c5 – compare 5...♗c5 6 ♘xe5 below) 7...d6 with equality. The following variation can be directly compared to our Møller analysis: 8 a4 ♖b8!? (8...♗b7) 9 axb5 axb5 10 c3 0-0. Now White can play 11 d4 ♗b6, but he's a tempo down on a note to our main game.

5...b5

5...♗c5 is also played at this juncture, normally transposing; for instance, 6 ♘xe5 ♘xe5 7 d4 b5 8 ♗b3 transposes to the note to White's 7th move below.

6 ♗b3 ♗c5 *(D)*

The Møller Variation. If you think about it, this is a real test of the entire Ruy Lopez concept:

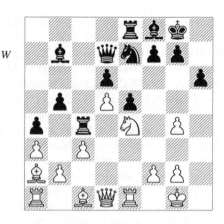

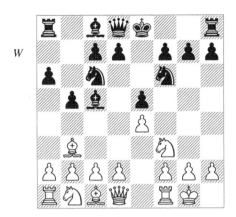

if Black manages to create a successful strong-point defence by ...d6 with his bishop *outside* the pawn-chain, then he has the best of both worlds. The Møller has enjoyed a great revival among the world's best players over the past ten years or so. You can imagine how liberating it feels to live for once without that passive bishop on e7! But along with his advantages, Black is presented with a few challenges. Concretely, White has the fork trick 7 ♘xe5 ♘xe5 8 d4. Then, on a positional level, White's ♗g5 can pin the f6-knight and it can't be unpinned by ...♗e7. It also turns out that Black's queen-side is difficult to protect, much as in the Closed variations but more awkwardly because the bishop gets in the way. Perhaps most importantly, Black has to be careful that, if his attacking ambitions are frustrated, he isn't left with a forlorn bishop cut off from the action on b6.

7 a4!

White can also play the critical variation 7 ♘xe5 ♘xe5 8 d4, forcing Black into 8...♗xd4 9 ♕xd4 d6 *(D)*.

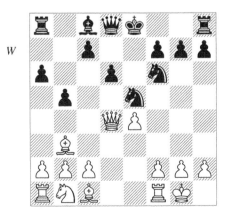

For years everyone assumed that this was a grave drawback to 6...♗c5. It gives White the two bishops and the greater share of the centre. It turns out, however, that Black's remaining pieces have great scope and are very well-placed to attack the key e4 point. First, ...c5-c4 is threatened, winning the bishop, and that threat gives Black time to develop his pieces aggressively. Here are just a couple of lines:

a) 10 c3 c5 (or 10...♗b7) 11 ♕e3 0-0 12 ♘d2 ♖e8 13 f3 ♗b7, as in Kholmov-Lomineishvili, Moscow 1997, illustrates how Black can use his active pieces to take the initiative. Among other things he threatens ...c4 and ...d5.

b) 10 f4 ♘c6 11 ♕c3 ♗b7 12 e5 (this position arose a few times at the top levels until White became satisfied that he had no advantage) 12...♘e4 13 ♕e3 ♘a5 14 ♘d2 ♘xb3 15 cxb3!? ♘xd2 16 ♗xd2 0-0 17 ♗c3 ♕h4 18 ♖ae1 ♖fe8 19 ♕f2 ♕xf2+ 20 ♖xf2 dxe5 ½-½ Anand-Topalov, Linares 1997.

7...♖b8 8 c3 d6 9 d4 ♗b6

We've arrived at the main line.

10 ♘a3!

10 axb5 axb5 11 ♘a3! usually transposes.

10...0-0!?

Black gambits a pawn for activity and pressure on the centre. In fact, there isn't a lot of choice. But the recommended order 10...exd4! might eliminate some later issues: 11 cxd4 (11 axb5 axb5 12 ♘xd4!? is another method that probably isn't any better but deserves attention) 11...0-0 12 axb5 axb5.

11 axb5 axb5 12 ♘xb5 *(D)*

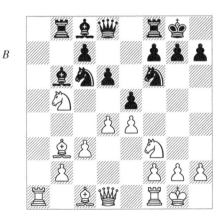

For his pawn Black has pressure on both the e4- and d4-pawns; in particular, ...♗g4 will be a bothersome move. Moreover, White's pieces on the b-file are loose.

12...exd4

This move-order bypasses one of White's options. The game Adams-Leko, Miskolc (rapid) (3) 2005 showed a clever new way for White to play following 12...♗g4 13 ♗c2 exd4 (13...d5!? is an ambitious way to mix it up; as so often in the Lopez, White is well-placed to meet early pawn-breaks and it seems he has some advantage after 14 h3 ♗xf3 15 ♕xf3 exd4 16 exd5 ♕xd5 17 ♕xd5 ♘xd5 18 ♗e4, as in L.Dominguez-Rodriguez, Buenos Aires 2005, but there may be improvements for Black) 14 ♘bxd4! (up to this game, 14 cxd4 was normally played) 14...♘xd4 15 cxd4 ♗xf3 16 gxf3 ♘h5 17 ♔h1. White has arranged a solid defence, and Black lacks the pieces to conduct a convincing kingside attack: 17...♕f6 18 ♗e3 ♘f4 19 ♖a4! ♖a8 20 ♖b4 (20 b3!? ♘e6 21 d5 yields a small advantage) 20...♘e6 (the crazy continuation 20...♖a1! 21 ♕xa1 ♘d5! 22 ♗d1! ♘xb4 23 ♕a4 ♘d3 24 ♕c2 ♘f4 25 ♕d2 ♘e6 26 d5 was suggested, with White keeping the edge) 21 ♖g1 ♖fb8 22 f4 and White keeps the pawn and the better game. 12...exd4 avoids all this confusion.

13 cxd4

13 ♘bxd4!? should again be considered, but it leads to a new set of complicated options that I'll have to leave to theory and practice.

13...♗g4 (D)

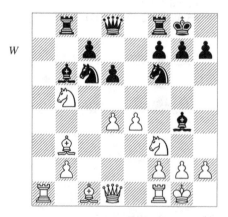

The basic position. You can see how White's centre is under pressure and his b5-knight is loose. But is it enough? We'll look at two contrasting games:

A. Ivanov – Zilberstein
USA Ch (San Diego) 2004

14 ♖a4

White plays one of the four or five moves that are available in this position. 14 ♖a4 has been used with success, but this game shows its risky side. Anand's 14 ♗e3 in the next game concedes the return of a pawn but to good effect.

14...♖e8 15 ♗c2!?

15 ♗g5 may well be better.

15...♕d7!

We begin to see what Black has for the pawn. This move indirectly attacks White's knight and, because White has to defend his centre, it's difficult to stop the queen from penetrating.

16 ♘c3 ♗xf3 17 gxf3

Naturally 17 ♕xf3 allows 17...♘xd4.

17...♕h3 (D)

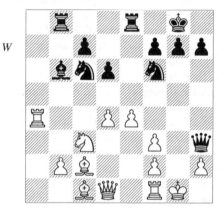

This is the logical result of this variation when Black's ideas have succeeded. He had just enough pressure on d4 to cripple White's f-pawns and at the same time keep enough pieces on the board to make threats. This leads to a nice tactical game, to which I shall give only a few notes:

18 ♗e3 ♖e5! 19 ♖e1?! ♖h5 20 ♗f4 ♖h4! 21 ♗g3 ♘h5!

With the idea 22 ♗xh4 ♘f4 and mate.

22 ♖e2 ♘e5! 23 ♖d2

23 dxe5 ♘xg3 and mate next move.

23...♘f4 24 ♗xf4

24 ♕f1 ♘xf3+ 25 ♔h1 ♕xh2+ 26 ♗xh2 ♖xh2#.

24...♘xf3+ 25 ♕xf3 ♕xf3

Black has a decisive material advantage.

Anand – Shirov

Groningen FIDE KO 1997

14 ♗e3 *(D)*

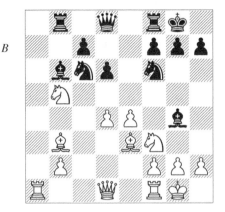

14...♕e8?!

This is Black's standard idea, to threaten ...♘xe4 without losing material after ♗d5, but it doesn't appear to work out. Also bad is 14...♕d7? 15 ♗a4! ♘xe4 16 ♘a3!. So the daring capture 14...♘xe4!? is probably best; for example, 15 ♕c2 (15 ♗d5 ♕e8) 15...♘a5! 16 ♗a4 d5.

15 h3!?

Not bad, but 15 ♗a4! is very strong, with the idea 15...♕xe4 16 ♘c3.

15...♗d7

Not 15...♗xf3? 16 ♕xf3 ♘xe4?? losing a piece after 17 ♗d5.

16 ♘c3!

White gives back material but ends up with the better pieces and a superior structure.

16...♘xe4 17 ♖e1 ♘xc3 18 bxc3 *(D)*

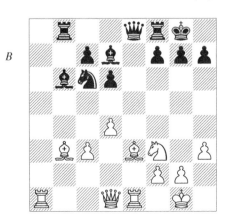

We are at the end of the opening stage, and Anand has won it. Black's b6-bishop is left with no good moves.

18...♕c8 19 c4!?

This is double-edged because it makes the light-squared bishop a bad one.

19...♗f5 20 ♖e2!

White threatens 21 c5, which if played immediately would have been answered by ...♗a5.

20...♘a5 21 ♗a2 c5! 22 d5?!

Now the a5-knight has no decent moves. On the other hand it exerts nice pressure on the queenside and White's a2-bishop is at least as bad. White should have preferred 22 ♗f4.

22...♗d8! 23 ♗d2 ♕a6?!

The nice idea 23...♗f6! 24 ♗xa5 ♕a6! provides equality, since 25 ♗d2? loses to 25...♗xa1 26 ♕xa1 ♖b1+.

24 ♕a4 ♖a8 25 ♗c3 ♘b7 26 ♕d1! ♗a5? 27 ♗b2 ♗b4?

The bishop should be back on the kingside for defence. The rest of the game demonstrates what happens when there are no pieces over there.

28 ♘h4! ♗g6 29 f4 ♕a4

29...f6 30 ♘xg6 hxg6 31 ♕d3 f5 32 ♕g3 is killing.

30 ♕xa4 ♖xa4 31 f5 ♖fa8 32 ♖e7! ♗h5

If 32...♘a5, 33 fxg6 wins.

33 g4! f6 34 gxh5 ♖xa2 35 ♖xa2 ♖xa2 36 h6! *(D)*

Attacks with reduced material are always fun to watch.

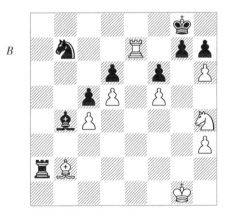

36...♖xb2

A pretty line is 36...gxh6 37 ♗xf6 ♘d8 38 ♘g6!.

37 ♖xg7+ ♔h8 38 ♖xb7 ♗c3 39 ♖d7 ♔g8 40 ♖d8+ ♔f7 41 ♖h8! ♗d4+ 42 ♔f1 1-0

Even with White's mistakes you can see how his strategy challenges Black to find sufficient counterplay. The Møller is a fascinating and unresolved variation.

Open Variation

1 e4 e5 2 ♘f3 ♘c6 3 ♗b5 a6 4 ♗a4 ♘f6 5 0-0 ♘xe4 (D)

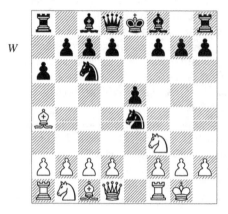

The starting position of the Open Variation of the Ruy Lopez. Now we're leaving the realm of Black's 1st-3rd rank manoeuvring in favour of staking a full claim to the centre. Perhaps because of this assertive posture, the Open Ruy has been the playground for some of the sharpest tacticians in history.

As always, you'll have to be careful about the move-orders, which we'll cover in the next few notes. For instance, the inverted moves 5...b5 6 ♗b3 ♘xe4?! can run into 7 a4! (D).

Instead, 7 d4 d5 transposes to the main line, and 7 ♖e1 d5 8 ♘c3 ♘xc3 9 dxc3 ♗e6 10 a4 b4 11 a5!? is a recurring tactical idea: White threatens ♗a4 and then ♘xe5. This is somewhat unclear but difficult for Black.

We've seen the power of a4 throughout the Ruy Lopez, and it especially applies to the Open Variation. After 7 a4, the play might go:

a) 7...b4 8 ♖e1 d5 9 d3 ♘f6 10 a5!.

b) 7...♗b7 8 ♖e1 ♘a5 9 ♗a2 and White has ideas of d3 or d4 and ♘g5.

c) 7...♖b8 8 axb5 axb5 9 ♖e1 d5 10 ♘c3!, and now, for example, 10...♘xc3 11 dxc3 ♗e6

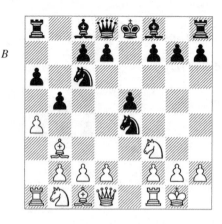

12 ♖a6 ♕d7 13 ♖xc6! ♕xc6 14 ♘xe5 ♕c5 (14...♕d6 15 ♗f4) 15 ♘xf7! ♔xf7 16 ♕f3+ ♔e7 17 ♗xd5 ♖b6 18 ♗g5+ ♔d7 19 ♗xe6+ ♖xe6 20 ♕f7+ and wins.

6 d4

6 ♖e1 provides another reason why delaying ...b5 until after ...♘xe4 is helpful: 6...♘c5 7 ♘c3 ♗e7 and the a4-bishop is attacked. However, Black should steer clear of 7...♘xa4 8 ♘xe5 ♘xe5?? 9 ♖xe5+ ♗e7 10 ♘d5.

6...b5 7 ♗b3 d5 8 dxe5 ♗e6 (D)

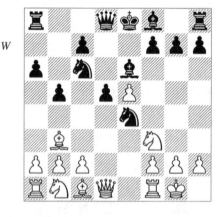

With these moves we have reached the principal variation of the Open Ruy Lopez. Black announces that he is playing dynamically and will steer clear of those protracted positional struggles that we have seen above (often with no exchanges in the first 20 moves). Nevertheless, the Open Ruy has a great number of consistent positional features, more so than the average attacking system. Already the fundamental question arises: tactics apart, what is each side playing for? In the positional phase, we have an answer that comes close to being universal: control of the d4-, e5- and c5-squares. Assuming that the e5-pawn isn't captured or liquidated, the real battle tends to be around d4 and c5. That may seem too broad a statement, yet if you study this opening you'll be surprised to see that games consistently come down to this theme, whether directly or in the background. If White can prevent Black from successfully playing the moves ...c5 and ...d4, he will generally have the upper hand. If Black gets one of those moves in without negative consequences, he'll usually equalize or better. The reasons are relatively simple. From White's point of view, securing an outpost on c5 can completely tie down his opponent and fix his backward pawn on c7 or c6. As for Black's prospects, you can imagine the effects of the move ...d4: freeing his e6-bishop, activating his c6-knight, and cramping White's pieces (or, in the case of cxd4, opening up the d-file). Since the opponents are usually very well aware how crucial these factors are, we'll often see one of them switch to an attacking or tactical mode if it appears they are losing the d4/c5 struggle.

From the diagrammed position on the previous page, I'll present game material with a series of different 9th moves. It will at least give you a start towards understanding how the Open Ruy should and should not be played by both sides.

Keres – Euwe
The Hague/Moscow Wch 1948

9 ♕e2 *(D)*

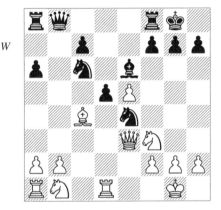

This queen move has always been hanging around in the margins. White's usual idea is ♖d1 followed by c4, although he may just play ♘bd2 depending upon Black's course of action.

9...♗e7

For example, 9...♗c5 is met by 10 ♘bd2.

10 ♖d1 0-0 11 c4! bxc4 12 ♗xc4

We have reached a well-known position. Black now enters a forcing sequence to salvage his d-pawn by means of a counterattack.

12...♗c5 13 ♗e3 ♗xe3 14 ♕xe3 ♕b8! *(D)*

Moving out of the pin and hitting b2. 14...f6!? is Black's normal source of counterplay when pressured in the centre. Theory doesn't like Black's chances in the tactics that follow, but they seem to work for him; e.g., 15 exf6 (15 ♕xe4?! dxe4 16 ♗xe6+ ♔h8 17 ♖xd8 ♖axd8 18 ♘fd2 ♘xe5) 15...♕xf6 16 ♖xd5?! ♕xb2 17 ♕xe4 ♗xd5 18 ♗xd5+ ♔h8 19 ♗xc6 ♖ad8!. Unfortunately, simply 15 ♘bd2! forces some kind of simplification with a small but definite edge for White.

W

15 ♗b3 ♘a5 16 ♘bd2 ♘xd2?!

A single piece deserts the fight for c5 and right away new problems appear. Later it was found that 16...♕a7! was the best way to fight for c5 and the dark squares, as shown by 17 ♘d4 ♘xd2 (now this is all right) 18 ♕xd2 ♕b6! 19 ♗c2 c5! 20 ♘f5 ♗xf5 21 ♗xf5 ♖ad8 22 b3 ♖fe8 23 ♖e1 c4 24 ♕g5 ♕c7! with equality, Kavalek-Karpov, Montreal 1979.

17 ♖xd2 ♘xb3 18 axb3 ♖c8?!

Black doesn't recognize how utterly decisive the control of c5 and d4 will prove. He should aim for both squares by 18...♕b6; e.g., 19 ♖c2!? (19 ♕xb6 cxb6 20 b4 is also interesting)

19...♕xe3 20 fxe3 ♖fc8 21 ♖ac1 ♖ab8 22 ♘d4. This looks good for White but his kingside pawns lack mobility and he may need a second theatre of action.

19 ♖c1

Here it is: White controls d4 and c5 and is ready to double rooks (or triple pieces) down the c-file. Euwe doesn't want to be squeezed to death, so he tries to rid himself of the backward pawn.

19...c5?!

Last chance for 19...♕b6, although this time it fails to free Black's game after 20 ♖c5.

20 ♖xc5 ♖xc5 21 ♕xc5 ♕xb3 22 ♘d4! (D)

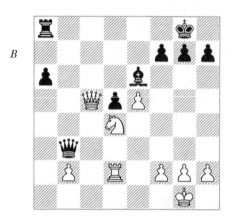

White has painted the ideal picture of dark-square control contrasting with Black's weaknesses. Note that Black's bad bishop has never moved from e6. In the broader sense the rest is 'just technique', but it turns out to be instructive indeed.

22...♕b7 23 h3 ♖d8 24 ♔h2

Preparing f4-f5.

24...g6 25 f4!

Even if you have wonderfully-placed pieces that are attacking weaknesses in the opponent's position, you usually need to have threats on both sides of the board to break down his defences.

25...h5

Versus g4.

26 ♖d3 ♕d7 27 ♕b6 ♖a8 28 ♖a3 ♕a7 29 ♕b4

29 ♕xa7 will ultimately win, of course, but White doesn't want any technical problems.

29...♕d7 30 ♕a5 ♗f5 31 ♖c3 ♖a7 32 ♖c5 ♗e4 33 ♕c3 ♕e7??

A blunder. It's worth showing how White wins anyway, due to his attack on two fronts: 33...♔h7 34 ♖c8 ♕b7 35 e6! f6 36 ♖d8 ♕g7 37 ♕c8! and the idea of ♖d7 closes things out.

34 ♘c6 1-0

Ponomariov – Korchnoi
Donetsk (3) 2001

9 ♗e3 (D)

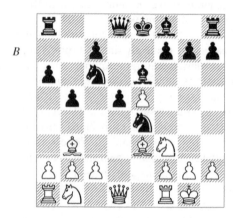

By this formerly-neglected but now popular move, White targets the key d4- and c5-squares right away. On the negative side he doesn't challenge the e4-knight (as 9 ♘bd2 does), and potentially the bishop interferes with the protection of White's e5-pawn by a rook on e1.

9...♘c5

Black can take up the gauntlet by 9...♗c5!?, daring White to win dark squares. A nice game, by no means decisive for theory, went 10 ♕e2 (10 ♗xc5!?) 10...♗xe3 11 ♕xe3 ♘a5 12 ♘c3! ♘xc3 13 ♕xc3 ♘c4 (the a5-knight was hanging and as usual the exchange 13...♘xb3? 14 cxb3! would prepare to double on the c-file, play ♘d4, and even indulge in f4-f5 in some cases) 14 ♗xc4 bxc4?! (14...dxc4 15 ♕e3 {15 ♖ad1 ♕e7 16 ♘d4 0-0 17 ♕f3} 15...0-0 16 ♕c5 ♕b8 17 ♘d4 is bothersome but not too bad) 15 b4! (it's coming down to d4 and c5 again) 15...0-0 (Black wisely keeps the files closed; 15...cxb3? allows White a big advantage for the usual reasons after 16 cxb3 or 16 axb3) 16 ♘d4 ♕d7 (16...♕e7) 17 a4 (D).

17...♖fe8 18 ♖fe1 ♖ab8 19 h3 (an escape-square, a second front, or both?) 19...♖b6? (using a valuable tempo, although it's not clear

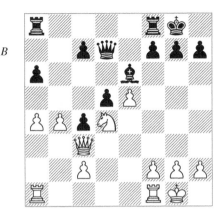

what was better) 20 a5 罝bb8 21 豐d2 罝ec8 22 罝a3! c5 23 bxc5 罝xc5 24 罝g3 (the point: because of the knight on d4, the attack will crash through) 24...奧f5?! (24...含h8 25 豐g5 罝g8 26 f4) 25 豐f4! 奧e6 (Motwani demonstrates a win after 25...奧g6 26 e6! 豐c7 27 exf7+ 奧xf7 28 罝xg7+! 含xg7 29 ❨f5+ – all these moves are found instantly by a computer) 26 豐h6 g6 27 ❨f3! 罝f8 28 ❨g5 f6 29 ❨xh7! 1-0 Korneev-Martinez Lizarraga, Madrid 2000.

10 ❨c3! ❨xb3 11 cxb3 奧e7 12 罝c1 豐d7

12...0-0 13 ❨xb5 axb5 14 罝xc6 罝xa2 15 豐c1! and the familiar ❨d4 is coming.

13 h3!? 0-0 14 ❨e2 f6 (D)

This looks effective and it is certainly a move with which Korchnoi has won many games, but it has to be followed up precisely. 14...罝fc8 may be better.

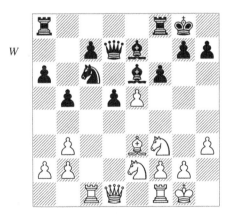

15 exf6 罝xf6?!

15...奧xf6 16 ❨ed4 奧xd4 17 ❨xd4 ❨xd4 18 奧xd4 would cement White's bind on the position. The influence of the opposite-coloured bishops is unclear; however, they help White to attack on the kingside. Compare the similar position in the Korneev game above.

16 ❨ed4 ❨xd4

Black's tactics are always dangerous in the Open Ruy, and White had to anticipate that 16...奧xh3?! fails to 17 罝xc6! 豐g4 18 ❨h4! 豐xh4 19 罝xf6 奧xf6 20 ❨f3 豐h5 21 gxh3.

17 奧xd4 罝f5 18 ❨e5 豐c8 19 ❨c6

Again White has command of the c-file and the d4-square, yet he must deal with Black's activity.

19...奧d6 20 奧c5! 豐d7 21 奧xd6 cxd6

To cover e5 and c5. Now White shifts gears to make progress.

22 ❨d4 罝e5 (D)

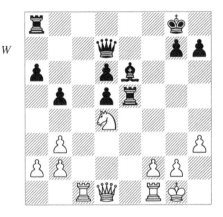

23 罝c3 b4 24 罝g3

As above, White needs both sides of the board to break through.

24...a5 25 含h2 奧f7 26 ❨f3 罝f5 27 豐d4! g6 28 豐d2! (D)

Black's bishop is awful.

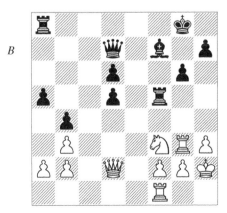

28...♖e8 29 ♘d4 ♖fe5 30 f4! ♖e4 31 f5 ♔h8 32 ♕h6! ♕e7 33 ♘f3! ♕f8 34 ♕g5 ♕g7 35 f6 ♕f8 36 ♖c1!

Once more to the queenside.

36...h6 37 ♕d2 g5 38 ♖c7 ♖e2 39 ♕c1 ♖2e6 40 h4! ♖xf6 41 hxg5 ♖g6 42 ♕f4 ♗e6

42...♖e7 43 ♘h4! ♖ge6 44 ♖xe7 ♕xe7 45 g6!.

43 ♘h4! ♖g7 44 ♕d4 ♔h7 45 ♕d3+ 1-0

A beautiful game, and another dream position for White.

It's time to see how Black can make his resources fully count. The themes in the notes complement the main game.

Naiditsch – Korchnoi
Zurich 2002

9 ♘bd2 ♘c5 10 c3 ♗g4

This standard move opens up the possibility of freeing Black's game by ...d4.

11 ♗c2 *(D)*

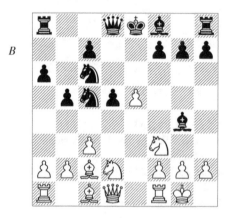

11...♗e7

A fascinating set-up is 11...♘e6!? 12 ♖e1 ♗c5, because Black has made two moves with his light-squared bishop and then four with his king's knight. Nevertheless, this is the ultimate and consistent attempt to control the d4-square – all of Black's minor pieces are devoted to it! A critical continuation was seen in Kariakin-Flear, Hastings 2002/3: 13 ♘f1 (13 ♘b3 ♗a7 is also important; it will be hard for White to hold off ...d4 and/or ...c5 forever) 13...♗h5 (13...d4 looks perfect until you see 14 ♗e4!, when the tempo and pin on Black's knight turn out to

give White a big advantage; both White and Black should be aware of this idea) 14 ♘g3 ♗g6 15 h4 d4! *(D)*.

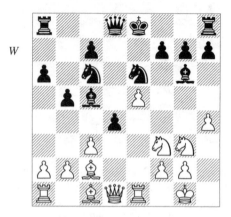

16 ♗g5 ♕d7 17 cxd4 ♘cxd4 18 ♘xd4 and here I think that 18...♗xd4! would have equalized or better. The point is that Black will get his cherished ...c5 in.

12 ♖e1 0-0

Korchnoi has also played 12...♕d7 with varying success. The idea is not just to overprotect the d-pawn by ...♖d8, but also to have the c6-knight protected in case White plays ♗e4 in reply to ...d4. Hübner-Korchnoi, Tilburg 1986 went 13 h3 ♗h5 14 ♘f1 ♖d8 15 ♘g3 ♗g6 (ready for ...d4) 16 ♘d4 0-0 17 ♗f5! ♘e6 (this knight is pinned but it's also a superb blockader) 18 ♗g4 ♘cxd4 19 cxd4 c5 *(D)*.

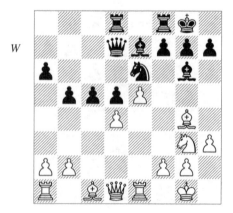

Here's the key break, not necessarily optimal because White will get an isolated pawn to work against and some weak squares on the queenside. Nevertheless, it's a good trade-off, because d4 is what counts in this position. The game continued 20 ᵂf5!? ᵂa7!? 21 ᵂxe7+?! ᵂxe7 22 ♗e3 cxd4 23 ♗xd4 ♖c8 (suddenly White has the bad bishop and Black has the queenside advantage) 24 ᵂd2 (24 ♖c1?? ♖xc1 25 ᵂxc1 ᵂxd4) 24...♖c2 25 ᵂe3 ᵂb4 26 ♗xe6 fxe6 27 f3 ♖fc8. Black's rooks are becoming dominant, and we again have opposite-coloured bishops. This time it's in Black's favour: 28 ♖ad1 h6 29 a3 ᵂe7 30 ♖c1 ᵂh4 31 ♖xc2 ♖xc2 32 ♖f1 ♗f5 33 ♖f2 ♖c4! 34 f4 (34 ♗b6 d4 35 ᵂd2 d3 – always the same theme: unleash the d-pawn if you can!) 34...ᵂh5 35 ♔h2 ᵂd1 36 ♖d2 ᵂb1 37 ♗c3 ♖e4 38 ᵂf2 ♖e1 39 ♖e2 ♖h1+ 40 ♔g3 ♗xh3! 41 gxh3 ᵂg6+ 42 ♔h4 ᵂf5! 0-1. A superb positional game.

13 ♘b3 ♘e6 *(D)*

This idea again: play ...d4 or bust! Or in any event threaten it. Black has also tried 13...♖e8 and 13...♘e4.

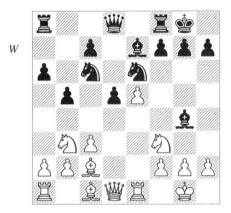

14 ♘bd4?!

Now Black gets what he wants: the ...c5 break. Better is 14 ᵂd3 g6 15 ♗h6 ♖e8 16 ♖ad1 ♗f5 17 ᵂd2 ♗xc2 18 ᵂxc2, Geller-Unzicker, Bad Wörishofen seniors Wch 1991.

14...♘cxd4 15 cxd4 g6!?

Versus ᵂd3. 15...c5 is also possible.

16 ♗e3

16 ♗h6 ♖e8 17 ♗e3 f5! is a typical idea, taking advantage of the fact that 18 exf6 ♗xf6 puts so much pressure on the d-pawn.

16...f5! *(D)*

17 ᵂd3!?

17 ♗b3 f4 and 17 h3 ♗xf3 18 gxf3 f4 19 ♗c1 c5! are as bad or worse. There's really no salvation.

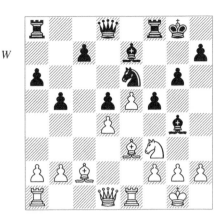

17...f4 18 ♗d2 c5! 19 ♗d1

19 dxc5? loses a piece to 19...♗f5 20 ᵂc3 b4.

19...c4 20 ᵂc3 b4 21 ᵂc1 ♗xf3 22 ♗xf3 ♘xd4 23 ♗xf4 ♘xf3+ 24 gxf3 ♖c8 25 e6 d4

The key move again. White could resign.

26 ♗e5 ♖f5 27 ᵂd2 d3 28 ♖ad1 c3 29 bxc3 ♖xe5 30 ♖xe5 bxc3 31 ᵂf4 c2 0-1

Svidler – Anand
Wijk aan Zee 2004

Here and in the game excerpts we see a more balanced fight with each side utilizing their advantages.

9 ♘bd2

We haven't seen a game yet in which the exchange of e-pawn for f-pawn on f6 gives Black compensation for White's greater command of central squares. Here's a short excerpt in which that's the case: 9 c3 ♗c5 10 ᵂd3 0-0 11 ♗e3 f5 12 exf6 ᵂxf6 13 ♘bd2 ♗xe3 14 ᵂxe3 ♘xd2 15 ᵂxd2 ♖ad8 16 ♖fe1 ♔h8 17 ♖e3 ♗g8 18 ♖d1 *(D)*.

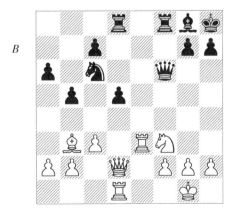

18...d4! 19 ♖ee1 (19 cxd4? ♘xd4) 19...dxc3 20 ♕xc3 ♕xc3 21 bxc3 ♘a5 22 ♗xg8 ♔xg8 23 ♘g5 ♘c4 with equality, Kamsky-Anand, Las Palmas PCA Ct (4) 1995.

9...♗e7

Perhaps the most disputed variation of the Open Ruy Lopez begins 9...♘c5 10 c3 *(D)*.

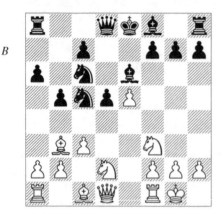

The first thing to note is that 10...♘d3 11 ♕e2 ♘xc1 is simply too slow and abandons the queenside; for instance, 12 ♖fxc1 ♗e7 13 a4! or 12 ♖axc1 ♗e7 13 ♘d4!. Here is an overview of Black's other options:

a) 10...d4 11 ♘g5! ♕xg5 12 ♕f3 0-0-0 13 ♗xe6+ fxe6 14 ♕xc6 is an ultra-ultra-theoretical variation that has been played and analysed for many years following Karpov's use of 11 ♘g5 versus Korchnoi in the 10th game of their 1978 World Championship match in Baguio City. Anyone wishing to study this has to hit the books. You also have to consider whether you want to go into 25-30 moves of tactical theory following things like 14...♕xe5 15 b4 ♕d5 16 ♕xd5 exd5 17 bxc5 dxc3 18 ♘b3 d4 19 ♗a3 g6 20 ♗b4 ♗g7 21 a4 d3, etc.

b) A more thematic yet unusual game went 10...♗g4 11 ♗c2 d4!? (it looks awfully early to advance in this manner, but Anand has played ...d4 on many early moves; we'll look at the game and just a fraction of the theory) 12 ♘b3 d3 13 ♗b1 ♕d5 14 ♘xc5 (14 h3?! ♗xf3 15 ♕xf3 ♕xf3 16 gxf3 0-0-0 looks pretty bad for White) 14...♗xc5 *(D)*.

15 ♕xd3 (a line given by Mikhalevski is typically dynamic: 15 ♗xd3 0-0-0! 16 ♗e2 ♕e4!? 17 ♕e1 ♘xe5 18 ♘xe5 ♗e2! 19 ♘xf7 ♖d1 20 ♕xd1 ♗xd1 21 ♘xh8 ♗c2! 22 ♗e3! ♗xe3 23

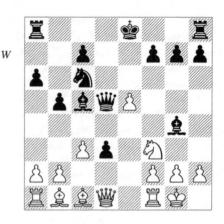

fxe3 ♕xe3+ 24 ♔h1 ♗d3, after which Black has the better of it) 15...♕xd3 16 ♗xd3 0-0-0 17 ♗e4 (17 ♗e2?! ♘xe5! 18 ♘xe5 ♗xe2) 17...♗xf3 18 gxf3 ♘xe5 19 a4?! (19 b4! ♗d6 20 a4 was suggested; watch out for the bishops!) 19...b4 20 ♗g5 f6 21 cxb4 ♗xb4 22 ♗e3 ♘c4?! (22...g6 and ...f5 would be strong) 23 ♗f4 ♗d2 24 b3 ♘d6 25 ♗xd6 ♖xd6 ½-½ Leko-Anand, Tilburg 1998.

10 c3 ♕d7 11 ♖e1!? ♘c5 12 ♗c2 ♗f5

Entering into a less complicated position than we're used to. The simplification seems to help White somewhat.

13 ♗xf5 ♕xf5 14 ♘b3 ♖d8 15 ♘xc5 ♗xc5 16 ♗e3 ♗e7 17 ♘d4 ♘xd4 18 cxd4 *(D)*

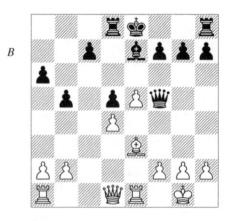

18...c5

This is a necessity before White plays ♖c1, and indeed it frees the d-pawn.

19 dxc5 d4 20 ♗xd4!

The problem is that White is now two pawns up!

20...0-0

20...&xc5 21 &xc5 &xd1 22 &axd1 puts Black in great danger; e.g., 22...h5! 23 &d5! &h6 24 &ed1 &c8 25 f4 with the idea f5.

21 c6! &d5! 22 &c1 &c8

Black will get one of his two pawns back. After that happens, bad bishop or not, White can still play for a win.

23 g3!?

23 f3 may be a tad more accurate in view of 23...&e6 24 &d3 &xc6 25 &e4! f5!? 26 exf6! &xe4 27 fxe4 &xc1 28 &xc1 &xd4 29 fxe7.

23...&e6 24 &d3 &xc6 *(D)*

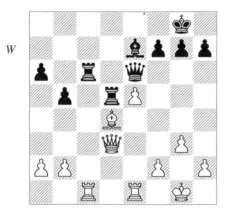

25 &xc6

25 &e4! is still good, but in that case 25...f5! 26 &e3 (26 exf6?? &xe4) 26...&xc1 27 &xc1 &d7 at least forms a fairly solid blockade.

25...&xc6 26 &e4

We'll stop here. White tried to press his advantage for many moves and after mutual inaccuracies the game was eventually drawn.

You can see that the Open Variation has a large number of variations to choose from. More significantly, both sides have options on so many moves that very little has been definitively worked out. This is an ideal system for the average player, both from a practical and educational point of view.

Exchange Variation

1 e4 e5 2 &f3 &c6 3 &b5 a6 4 &xc6 *(D)*

The Exchange Variation of the Ruy Lopez is probably best known for its use by World Champions Lasker and Fischer. Instead, 4 &a4 &f6 5

0-0 &e7 6 &xc6!? dxc6 is the 'Delayed Exchange Variation'. Oddly, White takes two moves to capture the knight on c6 when he could have taken it straightaway on move 4. In fact White gets a couple of options that he doesn't get in the Exchange Variation. For instance, 7 &e1!? gets out of the potential pin by ...&g4. After Black defends his e5-pawn by 7...&d7, White wants to develop by, for example, 8 b3 0-0 9 &b2 &d6 10 d3, when Plaskett-Davies, British League (4NCL) 2004/5 saw an effective set-up for Black by 10...&e8 11 &bd2 &f8! 12 &e3 c5 13 &c4 &g6 with no problems. There are other ways for Black to play, of course. Losing a tempo means something even in a positional opening.

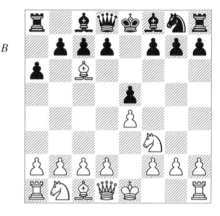

4...dxc6

Instead, 4...bxc6 captures towards the centre, but as in many openings the capture away from the centre is better. Instead of freeing Black's queen and queen's bishop, 4...bxc6 slows Black's development and puts no obstacles in the way of White's d4 (compare 5 d4 below). If Black could play an effective ...d5 at some point he might have some justification, but White will normally be able either to prevent that or to respond with e5 to good effect. Play can continue 5 0-0 (5 d4 is also good, forcing the surrender of the centre – remember that the side that surrenders the centre needs quick development in order to compensate for that by means of pieceplay) 5...d6 6 d4 exd4 7 &xd4 &d7 8 &c3 &f6 *(D)*.

Black is actually a tempo down on 1 e4 e5 2 &f3 &c6 3 &b5 d6 4 0-0 &f6 5 d4 exd4 6 &xd4 &d7 7 &xc6 bxc6, a position that is

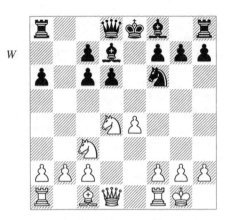

favourable to White anyway! Here's an example without variations: 9 ♗f4 ♗e7 10 e5 dxe5 11 ♗xe5 0-0 12 ♕f3 c5 13 ♘c6 ♗xc6 14 ♕xc6 (Black's c-pawns are a disaster, and White is about to establish a large lead in development) 14...♕d7 15 ♕xd7 ♘xd7 16 ♗xc7 ♗f6 17 ♗a5 ♖ab8 18 b3 ♖fe8 19 ♖ad1 ♘f8 20 ♘d5 ♗b2 21 ♖fe1 ♖xe1+ 22 ♖xe1 ♘e6 23 ♘c7 ♘xc7 24 ♗xc7 ♖c8 25 ♖d1 ♗f6 26 ♗f4 c4 27 g3 cxb3 28 cxb3 ♖c2 29 ♖c1! and White easily converted his extra pawn into victory in Illescas-Gueneau, French Cht 1991.

We now return to 4...dxc6 (D):

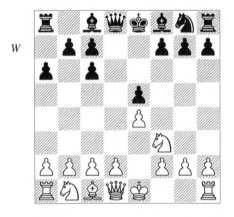

5 0-0

The first basic idea of the Exchange Variation is that White has the superior pawn-structure, and that he will sooner or later exchange his d-pawn for Black's e-pawn, establishing a 4:3 pawn-majority on the kingside. He hopes to win a simplified position by using that majority to create a passed pawn, whereas Black's 4:3 majority is 'crippled' and incapable of doing

the same thing. Consequently, White will tend to win the vast majority of pure king-and-pawn endings.

However, there's a lot more going on here. First of all, Black possesses the bishop-pair, which can be in and of itself compensation for a weakness. Then I think there's a rule of thumb in his favour: usually the earlier in the game that one side establishes an 'advantage in the long run' such as doubled, backward, or isolated pawns, the less likely it is to last into the endgame, or cause harm if it does persist that far. In large part this is due to the fact that the opponent has more time to adjust to the problem and solve it directly or find counterplay. With that in mind, one can imagine that having more pieces on the board favours the side with the weaknesses. And that's where a hypothetical problem arises: it may not seem vital at first, but White has a lead in development. This means that he can sometimes control the disposition of forces and arrive at the kind of position in which Black will be compelled to exchange pieces. If the pawn-structure isn't changed thereby, White comes closer to the sort of endgame that he would prefer. In my observation, however, the 4:3 endgame advantage very seldom arises in games between strong players. In reality it is just as likely that Black's bishops and active play will effect some structural change along the way. However, barring favourable exchanges (and it takes a lot of them before a true endgame will come into view), White may still be able to use his lead in development and in some cases his greater control of territory to build up his forces and break through in the centre before Black is ready for it. That seems to be the more common way in which White makes progress. Conversely, the variations in which Black successfully restrains White's central pawns or the ones in which he develops rapidly have proven the most effective in equalizing.

This brings us to the difference between White's more modern move 5 0-0 and the traditional 5 d4. The latter move has a certain logic, because White needs to disturb his opponent's game before Black can secure his position and find roles for his bishops. But after 5 d4 exd4 6 ♕xd4 (6 ♘xd4 c5 is easy for Black, because after the exchange of queens, the two bishops can develop quickly in coordination with harassing White's king) 6...♛xd4 7 ♘xd4 *(D)*, the situation has changed.

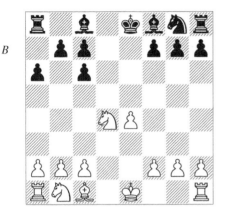

White's special advantage of having more pieces in play has disappeared. Given that circumstance, we're down to the effectiveness of the two bishops versus the potential advantages of White's pawn-structure. Let's see: 7...♗d7! (the idea is to get castled quickly, bringing the rook to the open d-file, and perhaps play ...c5 and ...♗c6; 7...c5 is a good alternative; on the other hand 7...♗d6!? commits Black to a particular development; then 8 ♘c3 ♘e7 9 0-0 0-0 10 f4 ♖e8 11 ♘b3 f6 12 f5!? b6 13 ♗f4 is the famous game Lasker-Capablanca, St Petersburg 1914, in which Black was probably not worse but he had to defend accurately and lost) 8 ♗e3 0-0-0 9 ♘d2 (9 ♘c3 ♗b4) 9...♘e7 (9...c5 10 ♘e2 b6 sets up a structure that Black normally likes, because it is sound and makes room on c6 for a bishop or knight; for instance, 11 0-0-0 ♘e7 12 ♘c4 ♘c6 with equality) 10 0-0-0 ♘g6 (10...f6 11 f3 ♘g6 12 h4 h5 13 ♘c4 c5 14 ♘f5 ♗e6 is solid and equal, if uninspiring, Miles-Karpov, Biel 1992) 11 h3 ♖e8 12 ♖he1 ♗d6 13 ♘e2 f5!? 14 exf5 ♘h4 15 ♘c4? (15 g4 ♘g2 16 ♖g1 ♘xe3 17 fxe3 ♖xe3 is to Black's advantage due to his bishops) 15...♘xg2 16 ♖g1 ♘xe3 17 fxe3 ♗c5 with a big advantage for Black, Peterson-Alekhine, Örebro 1935.

You can see how easy Black's play is after 5 d4 and why 5 0-0 *(D)*, to which we now return, is generally preferred.

After 5 0-0 Black can choose among a wide array of defences, but most of them offer White good prospects for advantage. We'll focus on

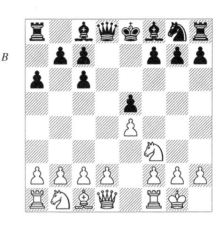

three that hold their own, and follow a few games (with a number of imbedded excerpts) in order to get a close feel for the ideas.

Milu – Vajda
Bucharest 1995

5...♗d6

This modest and logical development bolsters e5 and retains options for the knight and c8-bishop. It keeps the game interesting but is also non-forcing; thus it offers White more opportunities to create trouble for his opponent than the other two moves under consideration.

6 d4 *(D)*

White should develop as rapidly as possible, as explained above, and he also wants Black to play ...exd4 to establish his 4:3 kingside majority. Black's bishops would find the time to develop smoothly after 6 d3 ♘e7; for example, 7 ♗e3 0-0 8 ♘bd2 (8 c3!?) 8...f6 9 a3 (probably White would be better off with 9 c3 or 9 ♘c4, although in the latter case Black might cause the same kind of problems by 9...♗g4) 9...c5 10 ♘c4 ♗g4 11 b4? cxb4 12 ♘xd6 cxd6 13 h3 (13 axb4 f5! and the f3-knight is in trouble) 13...♗xf3 14 ♕xf3 bxa3 15 ♖fb1 b5, Ungureanu-Flear, Lenk 1992. Black is a clear pawn ahead.

6...exd4 7 ♕xd4!

7 ♘xd4 is slow: 7...♘e7 (7...♕h4!?) 8 ♗e3 0-0 intends ...f5, a double-edged move that is good in a position like this because it opens lines; e.g., 9 ♘c3 f5 10 exf5 ♘xf5 11 ♘xf5 ♗xf5 with free and easy development. You can see that White's kingside majority is no longer a relevant factor.

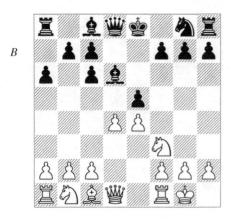

7...f6 *(D)*

An unfortunate necessity versus e5 which puts White even further ahead in development. However, if Black gets just a few moves to consolidate by ...♘e7-g6 and ...♗e6, he'll control e5 and stand well positionally.

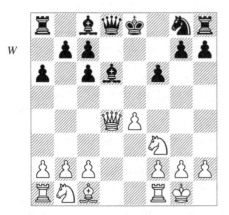

We looked briefly at this position in Chapter 2 when discussing the vanished centre. As explained there, static factors are temporarily more important than dynamic ones, although that might change at any moment. White would like to make inroads before Black can stabilize the position. Given time, the bishop-pair might begin to assert itself. White's other option is to eliminate one of the bishops, probably the one on d6; he can hardly stand worse in that case but the time it takes to achieve this will usually let Black equalize or come very close to doing so.

8 ♗e3

A flexible move that develops without committing the b1-knight. Alternatively:

a) 8 e5 fxe5 9 ♘xe5 lets Black catch up in development again: 9...♘f6 (or 9...♕f6 10 ♖e1 ♘e7 with equality) 10 ♖e1 0-0 11 ♗g5 (11 ♕c4+ ♘d5 12 ♘c3 ♕f6!) 11...♕e8 12 ♘d2 c5 13 ♕c4+ ♗e6 with full equality, Ungure-Lane, Cappelle la Grande 1995. Black's pawn-structure is the equal of White's. The moral for Black is to get on with his development and force the pace.

b) The most common move by quite a margin is 8 ♘bd2. Black has two sound options, both with a mind to watching over e5:

b1) 8...♘h6!? 9 ♘c4 ♘f7 is a relatively old but noteworthy idea: 10 b3? 0-0 11 h3 b5! 12 ♘xd6 cxd6 13 ♗f4 ♗b7! 14 ♖ad1 c5 15 ♕d3 ♖e8 16 ♖fe1 ♖e6 17 c4 ♕e7, Karaklajić-Gligorić, Manila 1975. Surrender of the centre for activity!

b2) 8...♗e6 9 b3 (not 9 ♘c4? losing a pawn after 9...♗xh2+! 10 ♔xh2 ♕xd4 11 ♘xd4 ♗xc4 – thus 8...♗e6 has a preventative function) 9...♘e7 10 ♗b2 (10 ♘c4 ♗b4! 11 ♘e3 c5 12 ♕xd8+ ♖xd8 13 ♗b2 0-0 and White hasn't achieved what he needed to in terms of either pawn-structure or neutralizing the black bishops, Schüssler-Westerinen, Copenhagen 1979) 10...0-0 11 ♖ad1 *(D)*

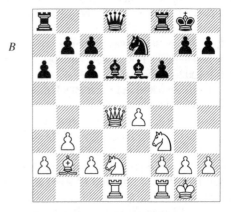

11...♕e8!? (a frequent theme: the queen will reinforce Black's bishops by ...♕f7 or run off to attack White's king; nevertheless, a good and probably superior alternative was 11...c5! followed by ...♕e8) 12 e5?! (White should try 12 ♘c4! with good prospects; Black is then under pressure to respond and e5 can wait until later) 12...fxe5 13 ♘xe5 c5 14 ♕e4 ♗d5. Here something has definitely gone wrong for White:

Black's bishop-pair is too effective. The game Lutikov-Westerinen, Jurmala 1978 continued 15 ♕g4 h5!? 16 ♕h3! ♘g6 17 ♘xg6 ♕xg6 18 c4 ♗c6 19 f3? (19 ♖fe1! improves considerably, although 19...♖ad8 would have the idea of ...♗f4 with continuing pressure) 19...♖ae8 20 ♘e4 ♗xe4 21 fxe4 ♖xf1+ 22 ♖xf1 ♖xe4 23 ♕f3 ♔h7, and Black was not only a pawn up but had the more active pieces.

8...♘e7 9 ♘bd2 ♗e6

Now Black intends ...♘g6, ...♕e7, ...c5 and ...0-0-0. In response, White finds a good plan to take advantage of his centralized pieces.

10 ♖fd1

A typical trick is 10 ♘c4? ♗xh2+ 11 ♔xh2 ♕xd4 12 ♘xd4 ♗xc4.

Apart from the text-move, 10 ♕c3! makes a lot of sense, preparing ♘c4 without allowing the ...♗xh2+ trick. Then Black can still play 10...♘g6 11 ♘c4 ♕e7, but in Webb-Hanley, British League (4NCL) 2005/6 he tried to get ...0-0-0 in faster by 10...♕d7!? 11 ♘d4 0-0-0 12 ♘xe6 ♕xe6 *(D)*.

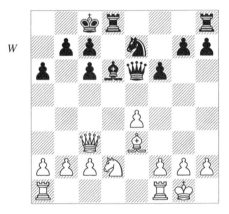

Only White can stand better here, although he will find it difficult to sustain a meaningful advantage. It's interesting that in this and similar positions, the same-coloured bishops help Black. Normally you'd think that it would be nice for Black to have the 'good' bishop on e6, but in practice you'll see that it's easier for White to implement his planned expansion on the kingside under those circumstances. The game continued 13 f4?! (a little impulsive; White can always delay this and keep an edge) 13...♖he8 (13...♘g6!? is tactically playable – 14 f5 ♕e5! or 14 e5 fxe5 15 f5 ♕e7! 16 fxg6

♗b4 – but then it would have been better to play the ...♘g6/...♕e7 plan earlier) 14 ♖f3?! f5! (the point; now White's bishop will look bad too!) 15 e5 ♘d5 16 ♕b3 ♗f8 17 ♘f1 g5! 18 fxg5 ♕xe5 19 ♗f2 f4 with the initiative.

10...0-0?!

Once again it's better to keep same-coloured bishops on by 10...♘g6 11 ♘c4 ♗xc4 12 ♕xc4 ♕e7. Now we'll see how White can exploit the structural advantage that he has so carefully maintained:

11 ♘c4 ♗b4 12 a3! ♕xd4 13 ♘xd4 ♗xc4 14 axb4

This pawn quashes potential queenside play by Black (not that the pawns were really going anywhere). Now that White has the position he wants, he's in no hurry.

14...♘g6 15 f3! ♖ad8 16 ♔f2 ♖d7 17 ♖d2 ♖fd8 18 ♖ad1 ♘e5 19 h4! *(D)*

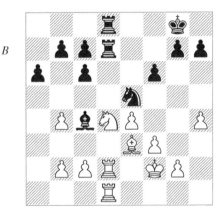

White begins to seize space; the f-pawn can wait for the right moment since its advance can weaken adjoining squares.

19...♗f7 20 b3 b6 21 ♘e2 ♖xd2 22 ♖xd2 ♖xd2 23 ♗xd2

Minor pieces are superior to rooks when you're trying to win these characteristic Exchange positions; knights are best of all.

23...♔f8 24 g4! c5?!

But White was eventually going to advance his pawns with a winning game.

25 bxc5 bxc5 26 ♗e3 c4 27 b4! ♘c6 28 f4 *(D)*

28...♔e8 29 c3 ♔d7 30 ♘g3 ♘d8 31 g5 ♘b7 32 ♗d4 fxg5 33 hxg5 g6 34 ♔e3 ♘d6 35 f5!

The advance is inexorable. ♔f4 is on the cards next.

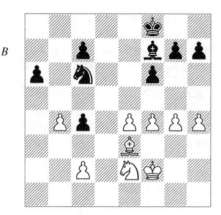

35...gxf5 36 exf5 ♗d5 37 ♗e5! ♗f7

Also hopeless are 37...♘b5 38 ♘e4 and 37...♘f7 38 ♔d4!.

38 ♔d4 ♔c6 39 ♗xd6 ♔xd6 40 ♘e4+ ♔e7 1-0

A beautiful display of White's 'ideal' goal when playing 4 ♗xc6. However, I think that this is the exception and not the rule, and that the most important lesson of these examples as a whole is that Black usually has the wherewithal either to change the pawn-structure or otherwise to create counterplay in return for his doubled c-pawns.

As indicated above, the way that White usually gets the edge in practice is by exploiting his development and space to create some *other* type of advantage, even if it means straightening out Black's pawns. White can often succeed in doing this and give himself real chances; whether he can achieve enough to win the game is another matter. Also, some of Black's early options deserve attention.

5...♗g4 (D)

This is the most radical move and the one that was originally thought to be the most serious problem with 5 0-0. Now 6 d4 loses a pawn, and slow moves allow, for example, ...♕f6 and ...0-0-0 and/or ...♗c5. Thus White prefers to attack the black bishop right away. It would take us too far afield to examine the many tactical lines following 5...♗g4 and it's another one of those moves that takes a lot of study and memorization. I'm only going to quote a few games to draw an outline of the play.

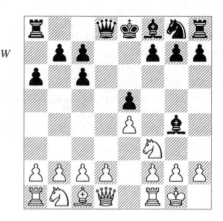

Volokitin – Akopian
Sochi 2004

6 h3 h5!

Really, this is forced if Black wants to equalize. He can't give up the bishop-pair for nothing.

7 d3

White needs to get some pieces out before he can contemplate capturing the bishop. You can easily work out the consequence of doing so; at the very least White will have to return the piece, since 7 hxg4? hxg4 8 ♘h2? ♕h4 is awful.

7...♕f6 (D)

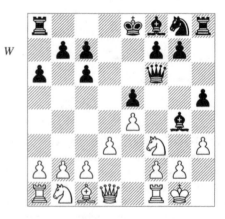

8 ♗e3

Somehow the games keep petering out in this line although there are plenty of ideas:

a) The first point is that, again, 8 hxg4? hxg4 wins Black's piece back with advantage, since the knight can't move without allowing ...♕h4.

b) 8 ♘bd2 has been the main line, but Black has done reasonably well. There are hundreds of games here; I'll just list a few excerpts after 8...♘e7:

b1) 9 hxg4 isn't played because of 9...hxg4 10 g3! gxf3 11 ♕xf3 ♕e6!? (or 11...♕h6 12 ♖e1, when 12...♕h3, 12...♘g6 and 12...c5 are all at least equal) 12 ♘c4 c5 13 ♗e3 ♘c6 14 ♕f5 ♕xf5 15 exf5 f6 with equality, Deviatkin-Fressinet, Internet 2004.

b2) Some big names have been involved in games after 9 ♖e1 ♘g6 10 d4 (10 hxg4? hxg4 11 ♘h2? ♗c5!) 10...♘f4 11 dxe5 (11 hxg4!? hxg4 12 g3 gxf3 13 ♕xf3 ♘e6 14 dxe5 ♕h6 15 ♘b3 g5! 16 ♗e3 ♕h3! 17 ♕g2 ♕h5 with equality, Macieja-Adams, Rethymnon ECC 2003; you see how crazy and specific this all is!) 11...♕g6 12 ♘h4 ♗xd1 13 ♘xg6 ♘xg6 14 ♖xd1 ♖d8 (14...0-0-0 is also equal) 15 ♖e1 ♘xe5 16 ♘f3 ♘xf3+ 17 gxf3 ♗b4 ½-½ Nisipeanu-Kasimdzhanov, Bundesliga 2005/6.

b3) 9 ♘c4 (this is positionally the most interesting move) 9...♗xf3 10 ♕xf3 ♕xf3 11 gxf3 ♘g6 12 ♗e3 ♗e7! (D).

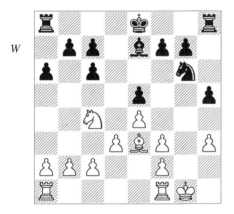

W

White has apparently lost his wished-for advantage in a possible pawn ending! But that's not very relevant, since the game won't get that far in most cases. Black can reorganize by ...f6 and ...♘f8-e6, or plunge ahead with ...0-0-0 followed by ...♖hf8 and ...f5, as suggested by Kindermann. White usually plays for either f4 or d4: 13 ♖fd1 (or 13 ♔h1 ♗f6 14 a4 0-0-0 15 a5 ♘h4 with equality, Hort-Spassky, Reykjavik Ct (16) 1977) 13...0-0-0 14 ♔f1 f6 (14...♖hf8!? intending ...f5 is Kindermann's idea) 15 ♔e2 ♘f8 16 f4 exf4 17 ♗xf4 ♘e6 and a draw was

agreed in Kindermann-Dorfman, Jenbach 2003. Kindermann analyses 18 ♗e3 g5 19 c3 ♖hf8 20 f3 f5 21 ♖g1 when 21...c5 looks equal. Plenty of ideas, but dubious results in terms of advantages for either side.

8...♗xf3 9 ♕xf3 ♕xf3 10 gxf3 ♗d6 11 ♘d2 ♘e7 (D)

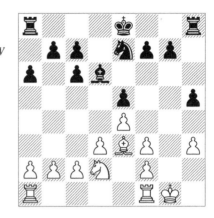

W

This time Black just wants to play ...c5 and ...♘c6. These kinds of positions are equal and don't say much for White's winning chances after 5...♗g4. On the other hand that can change with one new discovery or reassessment.

12 ♖fd1

Nothing much happened in this game either: 12 ♖fb1!? c5! 13 ♔f1 a5 14 a4 ♘c6 15 c3 f6 16 ♔e2 b6 17 ♖g1 ♔f7 18 ♘c4 ♖ad8 19 ♖g2 h4 20 ♖ag1 g5 with equality, de la Villa-Delchev, La Roda 2004.

12...c5 13 ♘c4 ♘c6 14 c3 ♔e7 15 ♔f1 f6 16 a3 a5 17 a4 g6 18 ♔e2 ♔e6 19 ♖g1 ♖hg8 20 ♖g2 ♖ad8 21 ♖ag1 ♔f7 ½-½

Thus 5...♗g4 gives every indication of being a complete solution for Black. Here's one more method of play that looks perfectly fine for him:

Hector – Beliavsky
Copenhagen 2004

5...♕f6 (D)

This is a simple way to defend e5. Black prepares an early ...0-0-0. Up to this point White hasn't found any way to gain the upper hand.

6 d4!

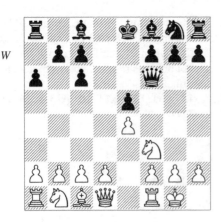

Versus the slow 6 d3, 6...♗g4 and 6...♗c5 are good aggressive moves.

6...exd4 7 ♗g5

Or:

a) 7 e5 ♕g6 gives Black nice scope for his bishops, as shown by 8 ♘xd4 ♗h3 9 ♕f3 ♗g4 10 ♕g3 0-0-0.

b) 7 ♕xd4 and now 7...♗g4!? puts White on the spot; e.g., 8 ♕e5+!? ♕xe5 9 ♘xe5 ♗e6 with equality. Black can also play 7...♕xd4 8 ♘xd4 ♗d7 or even 7...♗d7, yielding the standard type of equal position that we saw after 5 d4.

c) 7 ♘xd4?! ♗d7 8 ♗e3 0-0-0 gives Black everything he wants.

7...♕d6 *(D)*

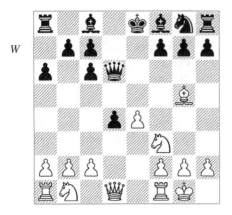

8 ♕xd4

8 ♘xd4 ♗d7 9 ♘c3 ♗e7 10 ♗xe7 ♘xe7 11 ♘b3 is Magem-Morozevich, Pamplona 1994/5. Easiest now is 11...♕xd1 12 ♖axd1 b6 intending ...c5, denying the b3-knight good squares, followed by ...0-0-0.

8...♗g4

Or 8...♕xd4 9 ♘xd4 ♗d7 and the idea ...f6 brings equality; or 8...♗d7.

9 ♕e5+ ♘e7 10 ♗xe7 ♕xe7 11 ♘bd2 0-0-0 12 ♕f4 h5 13 h3 ♗e6 14 ♘g5 g6 15 ♕e3? ♗h6 16 f4 ♔b8 17 ♘xe6? fxe6!

Black threatens ...e5.

18 e5 g5!

with a substantial advantage. At the time of writing, the ball's in White's court.

Marshall Attack

1 e4 e5 2 ♘f3 ♘c6 3 ♗b5 a6 4 ♗a4 ♘f6 5 0-0 ♗e7 6 ♖e1 b5 7 ♗b3 0-0

I'm going to emphasize and expand upon a point that I made in the Closed Lopez section about move-orders. 7...d6 is a way to circumvent the problems associated with White's 'Anti-Marshall' lines, which go 7...0-0 8 a4 and 7...0-0 8 h3 (see below). 7...d6 will usually lead to the normal Closed Lopez after 8 c3 0-0 9 h3, etc. After 7...d6, 8 a4 *(D)* is no longer very effective, in part because e5 is defended.

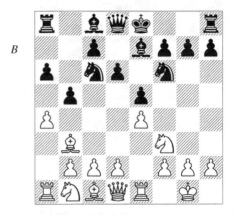

Here Black has equalized easily following each of the moves 8...♗d7, 8...b4 and 8...♗b7; compare 7...0-0 8 a4. For those with more immediate ambitions, there's 8...♘a5!? 9 ♗a2 (9 axb5 ♘xb3 10 cxb3 ♗b7 11 bxa6 ♗xa6 gives plenty of compensation: two bishops, activity, and those awful b-pawns) 9...b4 10 c3!? c5 11 d4 cxd4 12 cxd4 (12 cxb4 works out reasonably well for Black in the various complications following 12...♘c6 {12...♘b7!?} 13 b5 and now 13...♘b4 14 ♗xf7+ ♔xf7 15 ♕b3+ ♘bd5!? 16

exd5 axb5 or 13...axb5 14 axb5 ♗e6 15 bxc6 ♗xa2) 12...0-0! 13 ♘bd2 ♕c7, which is equal according to Ivanchuk.

We now return to 7...0-0 *(D)*:

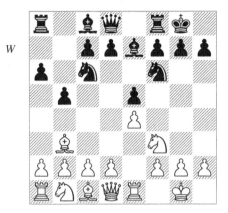

8 c3

At this juncture, White has got good mileage out of two of the 'Anti-Marshall' variations:

a) Kasparov has caused his opponents considerable difficulties with 8 a4, threatening simply 9 axb5. At the moment Black's remedies are holding up well, but this version of the Anti-Marshall is still a legitimate weapon and leaves plenty of play on the board. Here's a classic example between the former and current World Champions, with notes at critical junctures: 8...♗b7 (arguably the best defence) 9 d3 d6 10 ♘bd2 ♘d7 11 c3 ♘c5 12 axb5 axb5 13 ♖xa8 ♕xa8 14 ♗c2 b4 15 d4 bxc3 16 bxc3 ♘d7 17 ♘f1 ♗f6 18 d5 (the position looks like a main-line Closed Lopez and White faces a similar decision with respect to the centre; both this move and 18 ♘e3 have been played) 18...♘cb8! 19 h4 ♘c5 20 ♘g3 ♗c8 21 ♘g5!? h6 22 ♘h5! ♗e7 (22...hxg5? fails to 23 ♘xf6+ gxf6 24 hxg5 fxg5 25 ♕h5 f6 26 ♕g6+ ♔h8 27 ♔h2 followed by ♖h1; this is a position that illustrates perfectly Kasparov's technique of 'cutting the board in two' – Black has a numerical superiority in pieces, but four of them are sitting helplessly on the queenside, cut off from defence of their king) 23 ♘h3! ♕a2! (23...♗xh4? 24 ♘xg7! ♔xg7 25 ♕h5) 24 ♖e3 g6? (24...♗xh4! leads to balanced complications) 25 ♖g3 *(D)*.

Here 25...♗xh4? allows a beautiful combination: 26 ♕d2! g5 (26...♗xg3? 27 ♘f6+) 27

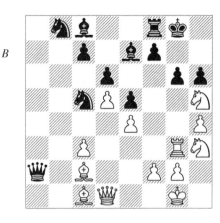

♘xg5! ♗xg3 28 ♘f6+ ♔h8 (or 28...♔g7 29 ♘e6+!) 29 ♘xf7+! ♔g7 30 ♕xh6+ ♔xf7 31 ♕h7+ ♔xf6 32 ♗g5+! ♔xg5 33 ♕g7+ ♔h5 34 ♗d1+ ♗g4 35 ♗xg4+ ♔h4 36 fxg3+ ♔xg3 37 ♗f5+ ♔f4 38 ♕h6+ ♔g3 39 ♕g5#. Instead, the game continued 25...♘bd7 26 ♗xh6 ♗xh4 27 ♖g4 ♗e7 28 ♗g5 ♗xg5 29 ♘xg5 f5 (29...♕b2 30 ♖g3 ♖e8 31 ♔h2!) 30 exf5 gxh5 31 ♖g3 ♘f6 32 ♘e6+? (Kasparov falters in time trouble – 32 ♘e4+! wins; for example, 32...♘g4 33 ♖xg4+ hxg4 34 ♕xg4+ ♔f7 35 ♕g6+ ♔e7 36 ♕g7+ ♖f7 37 f6+ ♔e8 38 ♘xd6+! cxd6 39 ♕g8+ ♖f8 40 ♗g6+ ♔d8 41 ♕xf8+ ♔c7 42 ♕e7+ ♘d7 43 f7) 32...♔f7 33 ♖g7+ ♔e8 34 ♘xc7+ ♔d8 35 ♘e6+ ♔e8 36 ♘c7+ ♔d8 37 ♘e6+ ♔e8 38 ♘c7+ ½-½ Kasparov-Topalov, Linares 2004.

b) The latest rage (and it again shows the respect that players have for the Marshall Attack) is 8 h3, a move that leading grandmasters have turned to with some (but not overwhelming) success. Then 8...d6 9 c3 transposes into the Closed Ruy Lopez. And 8...d5, the Marshall idea, comes up a little short after 9 exd5 ♘xd5 10 ♘xe5 ♘xe5 11 ♖xe5. This gives White a better grip on the kingside than he gets in the Marshall Attack. Furthermore, White will follow up with rapid development by ♘c3, surely an improvement over having a pawn on c3. For all that, White shouldn't feel overconfident: years ago, Blatny tried 11...♘b6 followed by ...c5 and ...♗d6; this deserves some attention. Of course, Black needn't gambit; he usually plays 8...♗b7 9 d3 *(D)*.

After this modest protection of the e-pawn, White has several methods of arranging his pieces. For example, he can divorce himself

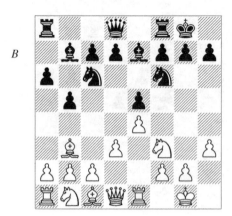

entirely from the Closed Ruy lines by ♘c3, perhaps to be followed by ♘d5. He can play c3, in more or less traditional fashion (♘d2-f1 might follow). Or he has ♗e3 followed by ♘d2, contemplating d4. What has become the main line goes 9...d6 (even the active 9...♗c5 has been played here, reacting to White's slow development, but Black's main alternative is 9...♖e8; e.g., 10 ♘c3 ♗b4!? 11 ♘g5 ♖f8 12 a3 ♗xc3 13 bxc3 ♘a5 14 ♗a2 c5 15 f4 exf4 16 e5 ♘d5 17 ♗xd5 ♕xg5 18 ♗xb7 ½-½ Kramnik-Leko, Brissago Wch (2) 2004) 10 a3 (D).

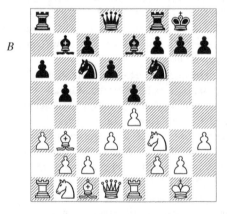

The minute that Black defends his e-pawn, he is free to play ...♘a5 and rid himself of White's active bishop. With 10 a3, White gives the bishop a square to drop back to. This contrasts with the customary set-up with c3 and ♗c2. Now Black has been playing 10...♘a5 (although world-class players are playing this way, I really wonder about the wisdom of setting up a Chigorin structure with ...c5 and ceding the d5-square; the logical 10...♖e8 is a good

option, with the idea of ...♗f8 and staying centralized; and there are a number of other sensible moves) 11 ♗a2 c5 12 ♘bd2 (12 ♘c3 ♘c6 13 ♘d5 ♘xd5 14 ♗xd5 ♕c7 15 c3 ♘b8 16 ♗xb7 ♕xb7 has also led to equality; this isn't written in stone, of course) 12...♘c6 13 ♘f1 ♗c8!? (Black plays the familiar rerouting move with his bishop even though there's no pawn on d5 – his idea is to play the also-familiar ...♗e6 and challenge White to exchange; early success often leads to repetition and I suspect that other moves will become more popular here) 14 c3 (14 ♘e3 ♗e6 15 ♗d5!, as in Sutovsky-Beliavsky, Gothenburg Echt 2005, is interesting and perhaps even favourable for White; for the moment these h3/d3 set-ups are still producing some original positions) 14...♗e6 15 ♗xe6 fxe6 (D).

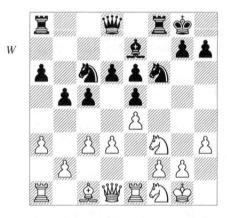

It's amusing that in a very similar position from this h3/d3 variation, the move ...♗e6 is almost never answered by ♗xe6, whereas here the world's best players have done so repeatedly. As explained in the introductory chapters, there is no rule about when to double Black's pawns. Sometimes the lack of central mobility after ...fxe6 is debilitating; and other times the extra squares that are covered by the e6-pawn make it worth it for Black. From this point the game Topalov-Kasimdzhanov, San Luis Wch 2005 continued 16 b4!? (previously Kasparov had achieved nothing from 16 ♘g3 ♘d7 17 ♗e3 d5 18 exd5 exd5 19 a4 ♖b8 20 axb5 axb5 21 b3 ♖a8 ½-½ Kasparov-Topalov, Linares 2005) 16...♕d7 (16...♘h5 17 ♘1h2 ♘f4 18 ♗xf4 ♖xf4 19 ♕b3 ♕d7 20 a4! favoured White in Adams-Kasimdzhanov, Linares 2005) 17

♕b3 ♖fb8 18 ♘1h2 with an unclear position. A terrifically complicated game ensued. It's hard to assess whether this relatively new approach will prove to be a durable weapon for White.

8...d5 *(D)*

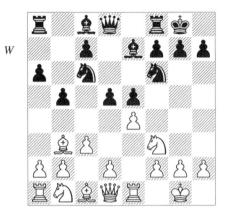

The Marshall Attack. In this horribly over-analysed (but highly instructive) variation, Black sacrifices a pawn in return for a kingside attack and active play.

9 exd5

Alternatives such as 9 d4 and 9 d3 are considered harmless, although the former makes good study material.

9...♘xd5

The attempt to complicate by 9...e4 *(D)* has been underestimated and might be a good alternative to the Marshall Attack proper.

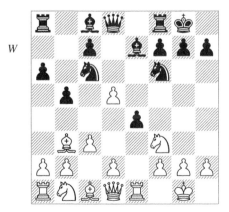

Not surprisingly, it is very risky. Analysis from diverse sources (see the article by Bücker in the Bibliography) includes these extremely abbreviated lines, with suggestions: 10 dxc6

(10 ♘g5 ♘a5 11 ♘xe4 ♘xe4 12 ♖xe4 ♗b7 13 d4 ♘xb3 14 axb3 ♕xd5 gives Black plenty of play for a pawn: two bishops, superior development, and attacking chances) 10...exf3 11 d4 (11 g3!?; 11 ♕xf3 ♗g4 12 ♕g3 ♖e8 13 f3 ♕d3!? 14 fxg4 ♗c5+ 15 ♖e3 ♖ad8 16 ♘a3?! – here's a good point to look for white improvements – 16...♘e4 17 ♕f3 ♘xd2 18 ♗xd2 ♕xd2 19 ♗xf7+ ♔h8 20 ♗xe8 ♗xe3+ 21 ♔h1 ♖xe8 with approximate equality) 11...fxg2 12 ♕f3 (12 ♗g5 a5!?) 12...a5 13 ♗g5 (13 a4!?) 13...a4 14 ♗c2 b4 15 ♕xg2 ♖a5! with an unclear attack. Who knows? 9...e4 is wide open to investigation.

10 ♘xe5 ♘xe5 11 ♖xe5 c6 *(D)*

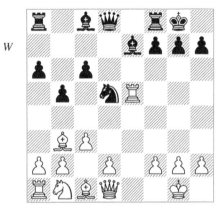

The starting position for the main lines of the Marshall Attack. Essentially, the idea for Black is to move pieces to the kingside and checkmate, whereas White wants to prevent that and remain a pawn ahead! It's not quite that simple, of course. For example, Black will usually gain some advantage in the centre as well, so that even if White beats back the attack and remains a pawn ahead, the game will often be drawn. Black's initial attack is based upon exploiting the light-square weaknesses that White will have to create in order to fend off mate. And White's defence will often consist of counterattacks that involve the sacrifice of material. At the very least he will try to open queenside lines with a4 and axb5, hoping for ♖a6 or ♖a7. Still, the action is mainly on the kingside.

When I opened a book on the Marshall Attack and looked at the first paragraph of the first chapter, I learned that for the 'old main line' (which is still extremely popular), "the real struggle begins around move 30"! And in fact, correspondence games sometimes take it a step further, with one side playing a new move as the endgame begins! Just to make it worse, the majority of these analyses end in drawn positions. In fact, this ultimate drawishness, in combination with the tiresome theory, has discouraged numerous players from trying the Marshall. However, on a practical level, such considerations may not be relevant. At any rate, even the very best players have discovered ways to create opportunities over the board, as in the game that follows.

Kramnik – Leko
Brissago Wch (8) 2004

12 d4

The main line. Although 12 ♗xd5 is sometimes played, by far the most important alternative is 12 d3, as in our final game.

12...♗d6 13 ♖e1

There is a good deal of theory on 13 ♖e2 ♕h4 14 g3 ♕h3, when a typical line is 15 ♘d2 ♗f5 (15...♗g4 16 f3 ♗f5 is also played, with good chances, although notice that the e2-rook participates in 2nd-rank defence, which was the main point of White's 13th move) 16 ♗c2 (16 a4 ♖ae8) 16...♗xc2 17 ♕xc2 f5 18 c4 ♕g4!.

13...♕h4 14 g3 ♕h3 *(D)*

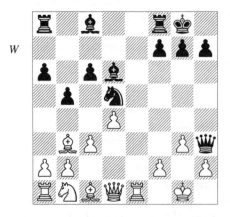

A few thousand master games have reached this position. Black has several attacking ideas, the main ones being ...♗g4, ...♖ae8 and ...f5-f4.

15 ♖e4

This is one of the more 'modern' moves (although it's very old). First, White prevents

...♗g4. He would also like to play ♖h4 and perhaps even begin his own attack.

Not to be contemplated is 15 ♘d2? ♗g4 16 f3? (16 ♘f3 ♕h5 17 ♔g2 f5 is scary, to say the least!) 16...♗xg3! and wins. The other important move is 15 ♗e3, to be seen in the next game.

15...g5!

Black stops 16 ♖h4. He is able to do so because of the tactic 16 ♗xg5? ♕f5!.

16 ♕f1!?

This move was discredited in the contest before you but was of course revived later.

An incredibly beautiful game followed 16 ♕e2 f5 17 ♗xd5+ (17 ♖e6!?) 17...cxd5 18 ♖e6 f4!! 19 ♖xd6 ♗g4 20 ♕f1 *(D)*.

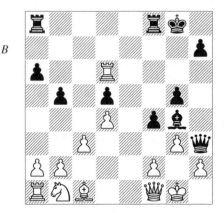

20...♕xf1+! 21 ♔xf1 ♖ae8 (does Black really have enough for a piece here?) 22 ♗d2 ♗h3+ 23 ♔g1 fxg3 24 hxg3 ♖e2 25 ♗e3 ♖xe3! 26 fxe3 ♖f1+ 27 ♔h2 g4! (a final twist! Black is threatening perpetual check and there's nothing to do about it) 28 ♖xd5 ½-½ Ponomariov-Anand, Linares 2002. Amazing. But (sigh) another draw.

16...♕h5

The position after 16 ♕f1 came up again in a different world championship encounter between Anand and Svidler. Who knows what either had in store for the other? The game continued 16...♕xf1+ 17 ♔xf1 ♗f5 18 f3 h6 19 ♘d2!? (a new move, at least among top players; in general I am probably slighting correspondence games, in which everything seems to have been played – at any rate, 19 ♖e1 is the older move) 19...♗xe4 20 fxe4 (for the exchange, White has a pawn, the bishop-pair, and a big centre) 20...♘c7! 21 ♔g2 c5 22 e5 ♗e7 23 ♘e4 cxd4 24 cxd4 a5 25 ♗e3 a4 26 ♗d1 ♘d5 27 ♗f2 ♖ac8 28 ♖b1 f6 29 exf6 ♗xf6 30 ♘d6 ♖c6?! 31 ♘xb5 ♖b6 32 ♗xa4 with a nice advantage, although naturally Black held on to draw in Anand-Svidler, San Luis Wch 2005.

17 ♘d2 ♗f5 18 f3! ♘f6!

18...♗xe4? 19 fxe4 ♘e3 20 ♕f3 ♘g4 21 ♘f1 and White is cleaning up.

19 ♖e1 ♖ae8 20 ♖xe8 ♖xe8 21 a4! ♕g6! *(D)*

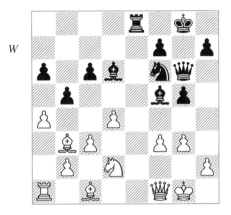

22 axb5

22 ♘e4 ♘xe4 23 fxe4 ♗xe4 24 ♗xg5! was suggested, and this is perhaps why Anand exchanged queens in the game above.

22...♗d3 23 ♕f2?

Falling for an insidious trap. 23 ♕d1 ♗e2! 24 ♕c2 ♗d3 25 ♕d1 draws.

23...♖e2 24 ♕xe2

This was Kramnik's point. At first it looks extremely promising for White.

24...♗xe2 25 bxa6 *(D)*

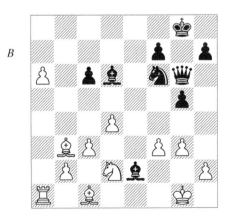

25...♕d3!!

White had probably calculated 25...♗b8 26 a7 ♗xa7 27 ♖xa7 with an excellent game. Or he missed the beautiful move in the next note.

26 ♔f2

26 a7 ♕e3+ 27 ♔g2 ♗xf3+! 28 ♘xf3 ♕e2+ 29 ♔g1 ♘g4!! 30 a8♕+ ♔g7 31 ♕xc6 ♕f2+ 32 ♔h1 ♕f1+ 33 ♘g1 ♘f2#.

26...♗xf3! 27 ♘xf3 ♘e4+ 28 ♔e1 ♘xc3!

This wins.

29 bxc3 ♕xc3+ 30 ♔f2 ♕xa1 31 a7 h6! 32 h4 g4 0-1

Leko – Kasimdzhanov
Linares 2005

12 d4 ♗d6 13 ♖e1 ♕h4 14 g3 ♕h3 15 ♗e3 *(D)*

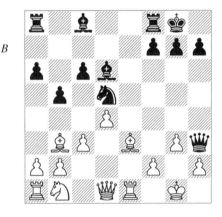

The position after 15 ♗e3 is still a point of controversy after decades of research. Again, Black wants to use those unsubtle ideas ...♗g4, ...♖ae8-e6, and ...f5-f4. Here is some utterly incomplete study material, finishing with some up-to-date happenings.

15...♗g4 16 ♕d3 ♖ae8

16...f5 intends to blast open White's kingside; it can transpose to other lines, although Black skips the move in our main game. In fact, I'm jumping over all kinds of move-order issues as I go along. Here's one of hundreds of games: 17 f4! ♔h8!? (considered best by most analysts) 18 ♗xd5 cxd5 19 ♘d2 g5?! (consistent, but the brute-force method comes up short, so other moves have to be looked at here) 20 ♕f1 ♕h5 21 a4 bxa4 22 fxg5 f4 23 ♗xf4 ♖xf4 24 gxf4 ♖f8 25 ♖e5! ♗xe5 26 dxe5 h6 27 ♕xa6 and White is winning because Black's position is so loose, Sax-Ehlvest, Skellefteå 1989.

17 ♘d2 ♖e6 *(D)*

17...f5 18 f4! g5!? is the so-called 'Pawn Push' variation, analysed by H.de Jongh in ungodly detail. I interpret him as concluding that Black is a bit worse in some endgame but should draw!

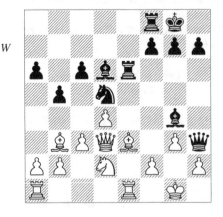

W

18 a4

The standard counterattack in this and most Marshall Attack systems. A bizarre tactic is 18 c4? ♗f4!! of G.Kuzmin-Malinin, Sudak 2002, threatening ...♖h6.

18...♕h5

This time 18...♗f4?? loses to 19 ♗xd5!.

19 axb5 axb5 20 ♕f1 *(D)*

A famous game Tal-Spassky, Tbilisi Ct (1) 1965 went 20 c4 bxc4 21 ♘xc4 ♗b4 22 ♖ec1 ♗e2 23 ♗d1 ♕xh2+!? 24 ♔xh2 ♗xd3 25 ♘e5 ♗b5 26 ♗b3 ♖d8 27 ♖a7 f6 28 ♘xc6! ♗xc6 29 ♖a6 ♔f8 30 ♖axc6 ♖xc6 31 ♖xc6 ♘xe3 32 fxe3 ♗d2 with equality.

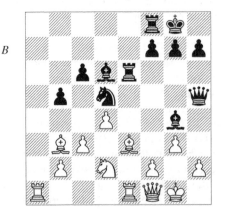

B

20...♖fe8

We're getting to something more contemporary. Another recent test was 20...♗h3 21 ♗d1 ♕f5 22 ♕e2 g6?! (22...c5) 23 ♕f3 ♕d3 24 ♗b3 ♖xe3 (the usual exchange sacrifice, although sometimes White makes his first!) 25 ♖xe3 ♕xd2 26 ♗xd5 cxd5 27 g4 ♕xb2 28 ♖ae1 b4, Ivanchuk-Grishchuk, Sochi 2005, and now 29 cxb4! ♕xd4 30 ♕xh3 ♕xb4 31 ♖d1 is strong. Is White getting the better of things in this line? It's too early to tell.

21 ♗xd5 ♕xd5 22 h3 ♗f5 23 ♕g2 ♕xg2+ 24 ♔xg2

With an extra pawn, even facing the bishop-pair, White has chances to win this position. He came very close but only drew.

J. Polgar – Svidler
Wijk aan Zee 2005

12 ♖e1 ♗d6 13 d3

Here we have the other main system, superficially more modest for White but also full of poison.

13...♕h4 14 g3 ♕h3 15 ♖e4 *(D)*

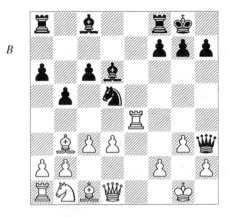

B

15...♘f6

15...g5? 16 ♗xg5 ♕f5 was the trick in the last game, but here the rook is protected.

16 ♖h4 ♕f5 17 ♘d2! ♖e8

17...♕xd3?? 18 ♖d4.

18 ♘e4 ♘xe4 19 ♖xe4 ♖xe4 20 dxe4 ♕xe4 21 ♗c2

This doesn't look like much, but White has a certain initiative and Black's weak pawn on c6 is a bother.

21...♕e7 22 ♗g5! f6!?

22...♕c7! 23 ♕d3 g6 24 ♖d1 ♗f8 also favours White, but not by much.

23 ♗e3 ♗e6 24 ♕f3! *(D)*

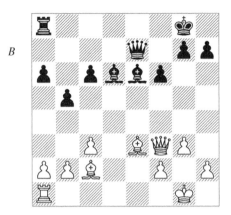

24...♕d7?

24...♖c8! is an improvement. Nevertheless, White would maintain her advantage after 25 ♖e1 (or 25 ♗e4 ♕d7! 26 ♖d1 ♗g4 27 ♖xd6 ♗xf3 28 ♗xh7+ ♔xh7 29 ♖xd7 ♖e8, but Black still has to fight for a draw) 25...♗e5! (avoiding the trappy 25...♕f7!? 26 ♗c5! ♗e5 {26...♗xc5 27 ♖xe6!} 27 ♕e4 g6 28 f4 ♗f5 29 ♕xf5 gxf5 30 ♗b3 ♗b8 31 ♖e7! ♕xb3 32 axb3, when Black is terribly tied down) 26 ♗d4 ♕f7 27 ♕e4 g6 28 ♗xe5 fxe5 29 ♕xe5 ♗xa2 30 h4 with initiative to White, according to Polgar.

25 ♖d1 ♖d8 26 ♗e4!? *(D)*

Even better is 26 ♗b6! ♗g4 27 ♕d3 ♗xd1 28 ♕xh7+ ♔f8 29 ♗xd1 ♗c7 30 ♗c5+ ♗d6 31 ♗e3! c5 (to cut off ♗b3+) 32 ♕h8+ ♔f7 33 ♗h5+ ♔e6 34 ♕h7, when Black can hardly defend.

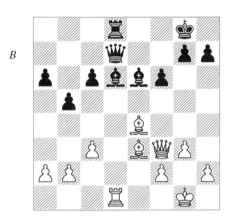

26...♗xa2?

But it's already pretty bad in view of the lines 26...♗g4? 27 ♖xd6 and 26...♖c8!? 27 ♕e2 ♖d8 28 ♗b6 ♖e8 29 ♕d3, etc.

27 ♗b6 ♗b3 28 ♖d4! c5 29 ♗xc5 ♕e6 30 c4! 1-0

The forced finish would be 30...♗xc4 31 ♗b6! (31 ♖xc4?! ♗xg3 32 ♖d4 ♗xh2+) 31...f5 (31...♖c8 32 ♖xc4!) 32 ♖xc4 fxe4 33 ♖xe4 ♕d7 34 ♗xd8 ♕xd8 35 ♖d4.

9 King's Gambit

1 e4 e5 2 f4 *(D)*

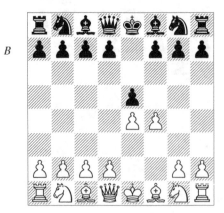

B

With the move 2 f4 we come to the King's Gambit, opening of the great romantics of the 19th century. It is associated with wild attacks and sacrifices of pieces, with each side focused firmly upon their opponent's king. In modern times, however, it has become commonplace to describe the King's Gambit as an opening that has taken on a simplifying character and leans towards the endgame. Neither of these descriptions is very relevant to today's play, because most if not all of the great attacking lines have been neutralized and the early transition into endgames is a relatively unusual occurrence, given publicity by just a few older games involving well-known players. Although the King's Gambit has no fixed disposition, modern players interpret it primarily in a positional manner, with sudden outbreaks of irrationality.

Why would White play 2 f4? For a few fundamental reasons:

a) It tries to exchange a flank pawn for a central pawn, thereby giving White a central majority. This is no small achievement, as we see in numerous openings ranging from the Queen's Gambit to the Sicilian Defence.

b) After either one of the moves ...exf4 or fxe5, White gains the open f-file. This dovetails

nicely with quick development by means of the moves ♘f3, ♗c4 and 0-0. In the best of worlds, White might even get d4 and ♗xf4 in, establishing the elementary picture of ideal piece placement.

c) The traditionally weak f7-square (which is guarded only by the king) is a target both from a bishop on c4 and the rook on the newly-opened f-file.

Of course, Black has something to say about these grandiose plans. In the King's Gambit Declined with 2...♗c5 we see that the a7-g1 diagonal has been ceded, making castling difficult. We shall look at that in detail, because it expresses some common ideas and illustrates the dynamic imbalance that the King's Gambit can still give rise to.

Varied problems occur after the most frequently played move 2...exf4, called the King's Gambit Accepted. It's interesting that when he accepts the pawn, Black's defences all seem to involve one or both of two moves:

a) The advance ...g5. This protects the f4-pawn and claims a material advantage, with the additional benefit of blocking off the aforementioned f-file. The g-pawn can also advance further to g4 (or be forced to advance), when it may win time by attacking a knight on f3 and has other possibilities including the common idea of ...f3, disturbing White's pawn-structure and introducing some tactical ideas if White opens lines by gxf3 and exposes his king.

b) As might be expected, ...d5 is an ideal freeing move (as in almost all double e-pawn openings). In particular, after White plays exd5, this allows Black to place his knight on f6 without being harassed by e5. It also frees the c8-bishop, gives the queen room, opens the often useful e-file, and gives Black a comfortable square for his king's bishop on d6, protecting the gambit pawn. That's quite a bit for one move, but naturally things don't go as smoothly as Black would have it either.

Now we'll look at two illustrative variations out of the many that have been thought up by both sides over the years. One is the main line of the King's Gambit Declined, the other the 'Modern Defence' to the King's Gambit Accepted.

King's Gambit Declined

1 e4 e5 2 f4 ♗c5 *(D)*

If one wants to decline the King's Gambit, 2...♗c5 has to be the most logical way, taking over the critical g1-a7 diagonal and preventing White from castling. It certainly leads to complicated and challenging play.

A couple of other ways to forego acceptance are 2...♘c6 3 ♘f3 f5!? and 2...♕h4+ 3 g3 ♕e7, both plausible and requiring some preparation. Note that 2...♘f6?! 3 fxe5 ♘xe4 4 ♘f3 leaves Black's knight stranded in the middle of the board, as well as securing a central majority. In one game Black made the best of a bad situation by 4...♘g5! 5 d4 (5 c3 ♘xf3+ 6 ♕xf3; 5 ♗c4?? ♘xf3+ 6 ♕xf3 ♕h4+ and ...♕xc4) 5...♘xf3+ 6 ♕xf3 ♕h4+ 7 ♕f2 (to protect d4) 7...♕xf2+ 8 ♔xf2 d6, when 9 exd6! ♗xd6 10 ♘c3 c6 (versus ♘b5) 11 ♘e4 ♗c7 12 ♗d3 would have secured White a small but persistent edge.

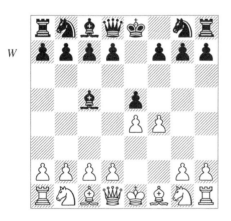

3 ♘f3

Almost always played. For one thing, Black was threatening 3...♗xg1 4 ♖xg1 ♕h4+ 5 g3 ♕xh2, and 3 fxe5?? ♕h4+ is a blunder of major proportions.

3...d6

This time White was threatening ♘xe5, but 3...♘c6? doesn't protect the pawn due to 4 fxe5

♘xe5?? 5 ♘xe5 ♕h4+ 6 g3 ♕xe4+ 7 ♕e2 ♕xh1 8 ♘g6+ ♘e7 9 ♘xh8 and White will win.

After 3...d6, White has two basic options, 4 ♘c3 and 4 c3:

Piece-Play

4 ♘c3 ♘f6

4...♘c6?! is an inaccurate move-order as it allows 5 ♗b5!, when Black's centre is under pressure.

5 ♗c4

White doesn't get mated after 5 fxe5 dxe5 6 ♘xe5?! ♕d4! 7 ♘d3 ♗b6, but Black has a bind and very quick development for the pawn; e.g., 8 ♕f3 ♘c6 9 ♗e2 ♗g4 10 ♕e3 ♕d7 11 ♕g3 ♗xe2 12 ♔xe2 0-0.

5...♘c6 6 d3 ♗g4 *(D)*

White still can't castle! But Black has to watch out too. For instance, an unfavourable pawn-structure follows 6...0-0? 7 f5! with the idea ♗g5 or in some cases g4-g5.

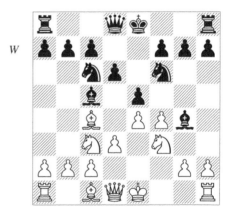

However, after the main continuation 6...♗g4, 7 f5?! is a mistake because 7...♘h5! threatens ...♘d4, and there is hardly a good way to respond. White has at least two other candidates. I'll try to present the main ideas without even dreaming of covering the complicated theory associated with this position.

Chigorin – Pillsbury
Hastings 1895

7 h3

A note on 7 ♘a4 follows the game.

7...♗xf3 8 ♕xf3 ♘d4

Actually, 8...exf4 9 ♗xf4 ♘d4 seems fine, but I'm not trying to rewrite theory.

9 ♕g3 *(D)*

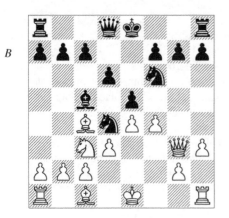

This is an infamous sacrifice. Pillsbury had previously declared the move unsound! Since this classic game has been critiqued many times, I'll just add a note or two relevant to the opening:

9...♘xc2+!?

The alternative 9...0-0!? is totally unclear: 10 fxe5 (10 ♔d1 exf4 11 ♗xf4 ♘h5 12 ♕g5 ♘xf4 13 ♕xf4 c6, and with White's king in the centre one would rather play Black) 10...dxe5 11 ♔d1 (11 ♗b3 ♕d6 12 ♖f1 c6 13 ♗g5 ♘d7 14 0-0-0 a5 gives Black the attack, according to Renet) 11...♕d6 12 ♖f1 c6 13 a4; perhaps dynamic equality is the fairest assessment in this situation.

10 ♔d1 ♘xa1

It seems to me that 10...♘h5 11 ♕f3 ♘xa1 12 ♕xh5 ♕d7 intending ...0-0-0, or simply 12...0-0 may cast doubt upon the whole idea. It probably isn't so easy.

11 ♕xg7 *(D)*

11...♔d7!

11...♖f8 12 fxe5 dxe5 13 ♗g5 ♗e7 14 ♖f1 looks like a winning attack in view of the long line 14...♕d4 15 ♗xf6 0-0-0 16 ♕g4+ (16 ♗xe7? ♕xc4) 16...♔b8 17 ♗xe7 ♕xc4 18 ♔c1!, which I'll truncate at this point.

12 fxe5 dxe5 13 ♖f1! ♗e7 14 ♕xf7?!

According to the analysts, 14 ♗g5! was winning. That's enough for the opening, so I'll just let you enjoy the rest of this titanic struggle unperturbed:

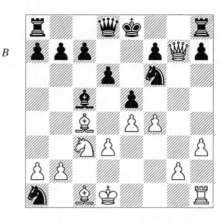

14...♔c8 15 ♗g5 ♖f8 16 ♕e6+ ♔b8 17 ♗h6 ♖e8 18 ♕xe5 ♘d7 19 ♕h5 ♘b6 20 ♗d5 a6 21 ♔d2 ♘xd5 22 ♘xd5 ♖g8 23 g4 ♗b4+ 24 ♘xb4 ♕d4 25 ♘c2 ♘xc2 26 ♔xc2 ♖g6 27 ♗d2 ♖d6 28 ♖f3 ♕a4+ 29 ♔c1 ♕xa2 30 ♗c3 ♖c6 31 ♕xh7 b5 32 ♕e7 ♕b3 33 ♔d2 a5 34 ♖f5 ♔b7 35 ♖c5 ♖aa6 36 g5 ♖xc5 37 ♕xc5 ♖c6 38 ♕d5 ♕a4 39 g6 b4 40 g7 bxc3+ 41 bxc3 ♕a1 42 g8♕ ♕xc3+ 43 ♔e2 ♕c2+ 44 ♔f3 ♕d1+ 45 ♔g3 ♕g1+ 46 ♔h4 ♕f2+ 47 ♔h5 ♕f3+ 48 ♕g4 ♕f6 49 ♕gf5 ♕h6+ 50 ♔g4 ♕g7+ 51 ♕g5 1-0

Eliminating the bishop by 7 ♘a4 is also very complicated. Generally Black retreats his bishop to b6 but there seems to be another possible formation: 7...0-0 8 ♘xc5 dxc5 *(D)*.

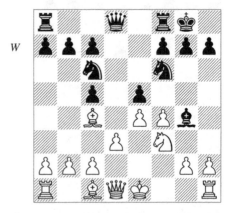

Here's a structure that you'll see in the Giuoco Piano and the Vienna Game as well. Black has good control of the centre; his doubled c-pawns secure d4 and open up the d-file. Black can even get rid of White's c4-bishop in most cases if he needs to. In return, White temporarily has the two bishops, a good pawn-structure and prospects of a kingside attack. It's probably about even, but certainly worth a look by both sides. Renet offers the following line, full of many options: 9 0-0 ♘h5 10 h3 ♗xf3 11 ♕xf3 ♘xf4 12 ♗xf4 ♘d4!? 13 ♕h5!? (13 ♕d1 exf4 14 ♖xf4 b5 15 ♗b3 ♘xb3 16 axb3 ♕d4+ 17 ♔h1 ♕xb2; the pawn is real) 13...exf4 14 ♖xf4 g6 15 ♖g4!? b5 16 ♖xg6+ hxg6 17 ♕xg6+ with perpetual check. This could be a fascinating variation to look into.

Central Expansion

4 c3

White simply goes for d4. This is instructive, as it illustrates themes of the ideal centre.

4...♘f6

The whole game revolves around whether White's centre can be compromised. Because of this the alternative 4...♗b6!? would be intriguing. The idea is to make a sort of prophylactic semi-waiting move, because d4 won't come with a tempo on the bishop: 5 d4 (White still has to get castled, so this is necessary; 5 ♗c4 ♘c6 doesn't help) 5...exd4 6 cxd4 ♗g4! *(D)*.

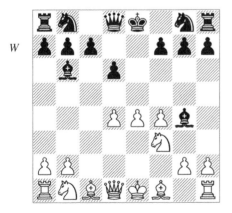

Black's scheme reminds one of the Modern Defence in which the bishops precede the knights in attacking the same e4/d4/f4 centre (1 e4 g6 2 d4 ♗g7 3 ♘c3 d6 4 f4 c6 5 ♘f3 ♗g4, etc.). 7 ♗e3 ♘c6 (or 7...d5!? 8 e5 ♘e7 intending ...♘f5, a fascinating position with double-edged chances; Black's pieces will be well-placed but the b6-bishop could end up

stuck) 8 ♗b5 ♘ge7 9 ♘c3 f5 10 h3 (10 e5? dxe5 11 fxe5 0-0 and the e5-pawn hangs) 10...♗xf3 11 ♕xf3 fxe4 12 ♕xe4 d5. Black has achieved the central dissolution that he was aiming for and the fight is just starting. This is all analysis.

5 fxe5

5 d4 exd4 6 cxd4 ♗b6 7 e5 (7 ♗d3 ♗g4; Black has to work fast to compromise White's centre or it will dominate the position) 7...dxe5 8 fxe5 ♘d5 9 ♗c4 ♗e6 (or 9...♘c6!?) with equality; White's space is balanced by Black's outpost.

5...dxe5 *(D)*

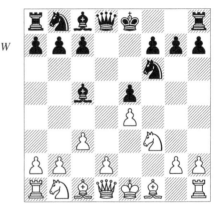

6 d4

6 ♘xe5 ♕e7!? 7 d4 ♗d6 recovers the pawn and allows Black to work against an isolated e-pawn in return for the bishop-pair: 8 ♗c4 ♗xe5 9 dxe5 ♕xe5 10 0-0 ♘c6 is equal (Black threatens ...♕c5+).

6...exd4 7 cxd4 ♗b4+ 8 ♗d2 ♗xd2+ 9 ♘bxd2 0-0 10 ♗d3

White has maintained his centre up to this point, but it gets attacked right away:

10...♘c6 11 d5 ♘b4 12 ♗b1

12 ♗e2 ♖e8 13 a3 ♘a6 leaves e4 weak, and Black can be happy with his position.

12...c6 13 a3 ♘bxd5!? 14 exd5 ♖e8+ 15 ♔f1 ♘xd5

with an exciting and unclear attack.

King's Gambit Accepted

1 e4 e5 2 f4 exf4

Black takes up the challenge and plays a move that has been studied for over 150 years.

At this point we have an important alternative, as well as our usual move-order discussion. It begins with the move 2...d5! (or '?' if, as Black, you would like to get to the Kieseritzky Gambit below) 3 exd5, and now 3...e4 *(D)* is the Falkbeer Counter-Gambit.

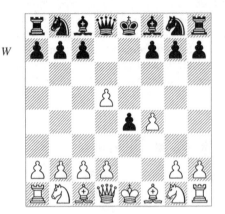

Black's idea in the Falkbeer is to cramp White's development. White's extra pawn on d5 is not impressively-placed anyway. The problem is that the powerful pawn on e4 has trouble staying there after 4 d3 ♘f6 5 dxe4 ♘xe4 6 ♘f3, the old main line going 6...♗c5 7 ♕e2 ♗f5 8 ♘c3 ♕e7 9 ♗e3!, when Black has never found a route to complete equality. The main idea is 9...♗xe3 10 ♕xe3 ♘xc3 11 ♕xe7+ ♔xe7 12 bxc3 ♗xc2 13 ♔d2. This position has been analysed for some years and seems to favour White.

But after 3 exd5, Black can also play 3...exf4! 4 ♘f3 ♘f6, when we have transposed into the Modern Line that Black may be hoping for (it is the variation analysed in this section). So 2...d5 might be reasonable after all. Notice that this order avoids 1 e4 e5 2 f4 exf4 3 ♗c4 in the next note.

3 ♘f3

There must be at least a thousand master games with 3 ♗c4 *(D)*, the Bishop's Gambit.

It has been subject to lengthy analyses for well over a century. The old main line was 3...♕h4+ 4 ♔f1, which offers White intriguing attacking chances beginning with 5 ♘f3, and Black also enjoyed some brilliant attacks on White's vulnerable king. But 3...♘f6 is a big problem for White:

a) 4 e5 d5! is our familiar device in e-pawn openings. Then 5 ♗b5+ ♗d7! 6 exf6 ♗xb5 7

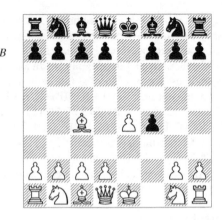

♘c3 ♗a6 keeps White from castling and employs the two bishops effectively; for example, 8 d3 ♕xf6 9 ♘xd5 ♕e6+ 10 ♕e2 ♔d7! and everything is covered: 11 ♘xf4 ♕xe2+ 12 ♘gxe2 ♘c6. Black has some advantage because for one thing he can reorganize by ...b6 and ...♗b7 with powerful bishops.

b) 4 ♘c3 c6!. In this position White has tried nearly every move, but after ...d5, he loses a key tempo. Later, when White plays d4 and captures with a piece on f4, he is left with a serious internal weakness on e3. You can check the theory (critically, please!), but I don't believe that White ever gets full equality.

3...d5

The 'modern' way of treating the King's Gambit. But in fact, most contemporary players use 3...g5 *(D)*, the venerable Kieseritzky Defence, to try to refute the King's Gambit.

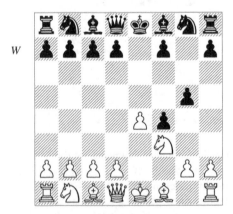

Everything gets very tactical and we'll primarily concern ourselves with 3...d5, but I'll mention two noteworthy continuations after

3...g5 (again, a variation with thousands of games to its credit):

a) 4 ♗c4 g4 5 0-0 gxf3 6 ♕xf3 is the time-honoured Muzio Gambit, in which White sacrifices a whole piece for a dangerous attack against Black's exposed king. A line subject to much analysis goes 6...♕f6 7 e5 ♕xe5 8 ♗xf7+ ♔xf7 9 d4 with the idea 9...♕xd4+ 10 ♗e3 (D).

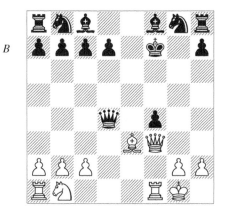

I show this merely to indicate how the old-style King's Gambit was played. In a book purporting to promote general understanding of openings, this picture of anarchy has to be referred to the specialists!

b) A fairly important line seems to be 4 h4 g4 5 ♘e5 ♘f6 6 d4 d6 7 ♘d3 ♘xe4 8 ♗xf4 ♕e7 9 ♗e2 ♘c6 10 c3 ♗f5 which hovers between equal and somewhat better for Black.

4 exd5 ♘f6 (D)

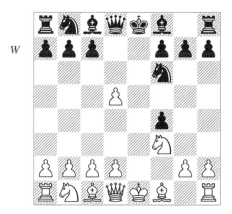

One of the main lines of the King's Gambit. Structurally it looks good for White, at least at first glance. He has a majority in the centre and queenside (even after the forward d-pawn disappears). What's more, White's move 5 ♗b5+ could further weaken Black's pawns while ridding himself of his only weak pawn. His natural plan will be to plunge forward with d4 and c4, securing free development. At the same time Black's majority on the kingside is crippled, and his f4-pawn is subject to attack along an open file. He has no prospects of creating a passed pawn on that side of the board.

But Black has one major advantage. White will have to (and want to) move his d-pawn at some point, but this creates an internal weakness on e3. If Black manages to keep his f-pawn, he can use that square to threaten White's position by, for example, ...♖e8 and ...♘g4. Even if White manages to win the f-pawn by ♗xf4, the exchange of that bishop only worsens the situation with respect to e3. Furthermore, White's only real chance for advantage (or even equality) is to advance his pawn to d4, since d3 renders his game too passive. The problem then is that the e4-square also becomes a weakness, making moves like ...♗f5 and ...♘e4 particularly attractive. It's anybody's guess which side's advantages will be more important than the other's. Let's look at a game with sample lines in the notes:

M. Ginzburg – Zarnicki
Villa Martelli 2002

5 ♗b5+

This is the only continuation that really tests both sides. The others show why White should be in a bit of a hurry:

a) 5 ♗c4 ♘xd5 6 ♗xd5 (or 6 0-0 ♗e6) 6...♕xd5 7 ♘c3 ♕e6+ 8 ♔f2 ♕b6+ 9 d4 ♗e6 is probably already better for Black, Fedorov-Godena, Batumi Ech 2002. For years, Fedorov was the leading King's Gambit player among grandmasters.

b) 5 c4?! leads to typical developmental and positional problems after 5...c6! 6 dxc6 (6 d4 cxd5 7 ♗xf4 ♗b4+ and White's interior central squares are vulnerable; e.g., 8 ♘bd2 0-0 9 ♗e2 dxc4 10 0-0 b5 11 ♗g5 {versus ...♘d5-e3} 11...♗b7 and Black can be happy) 6...♘xc6 (D).

We see this sort of position in several openings. With Black's development and control of

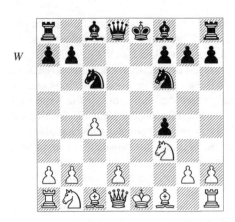

d4, he must be better. Moves like ...♗c5, ...0-0, ...♖e8 and ...♗g4 are too strong, but if White fights for the centre by 7 d4 (7 ♘c3 ♗c5), he runs into 7...♗b4+ 8 ♘c3 ♗g4 9 ♗xf4 ♗xf3 10 ♕xf3 ♘xd4 11 ♕e3+ ♘e6 with a substantial edge.

c) 5 ♘c3 ♘xd5 6 ♘xd5 ♕xd5 7 d4 ♗e7 is very easy for Black. Notice White's troubles with his interior weaknesses: 8 c4 (probably not best) 8...♕e4+ 9 ♗e2 ♘c6 10 0-0 ♗g4 11 ♗d3 ♗xf3 12 ♗xe4 ♗xd1 13 ♖xd1 g5, remaining a pawn ahead.

5...c6 6 dxc6 ♘xc6 7 d4 ♗d6 *(D)*

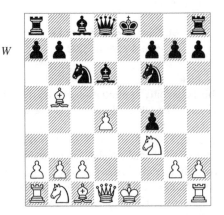

It's even material at the moment. White is banking upon his potentially powerful central pawns (the one on d4 is passed). Black has thwarted the development of White's c1-bishop and has weaknesses on e4 and e3 to exploit.

8 0-0

8 ♕e2+ ♗e6! 9 ♘g5 0-0!. Black sacrifices a pawn, but look at his terrific development after 10 ♘xe6 fxe6 11 ♗xc6 bxc6 12 0-0 (12 ♕xe6+ ♔h8 13 0-0 ♖e8 14 ♕h3 ♕b6 with an attack) 12...♗c7!? 13 c3 ♘d5 with a great game. Kaufman offers 14 ♕xe6+ ♔h8 15 ♕xc6 ♖f6! 16 ♕c5 f3! and Black's attack is almost decisive already.

8...0-0 9 ♘bd2 ♗g4! 10 c3 ♖e8 *(D)*

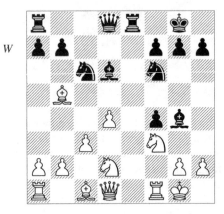

11 ♘c4 ♗c7 12 ♗d2

If White is reduced to this, he's in trouble.

12...♕d5 13 ♘a3 ♘e4

Black stands better. The weaknesses on the e-file are hurting White.

The 'Modern Defence' to the King's Gambit looks appealing for Black. Of course, there's always more to the story. It would be nice if White could figure out a way to bypass such technicalities and return to gambit play in the romantic spirit.

10 Introduction to the Semi-Open Games

The Semi-Open Games are a disparate group of openings with few characteristics in common except that they immediately unbalance the play. Another unifying factor is that they all prepare to counter in some manner White's plan to create a classic pawn-centre with 2 d4. It has been said that each of the openings under the 'Semi-Open Games' rubric has to 'give something up' in order to fulfil its mission. The French Defence (1 e4 e6 2 d4 d5), for example, blocks in the c8-bishop. The Caro-Kann Defence (1 e4 c6 2 d4 d5) takes c6 away from Black's knight. The Alekhine Defence (1 e4 ♘f6) loses a tempo to 2 e5 and fails to contest the centre. The Pirc Defence (1 e4 d6 2 d4 ♘f6) gives White an ideal centre, and the Sicilian Defence (1 e4 c5) doesn't open lines along which Black's pieces can develop.

None of this applies to 1...e5, so one could argue that in some sense that is the 'best' defence to 1 e4. But 1...e5 makes its own concession in that Black's e-pawn becomes an unprotected target of attack. Furthermore, if we look at the other Semi-Open Games listed above, all of them except one attack White's centre pawn at e4, as can be seen from 1 e4 e6 2 d4 d5, 1 e4 c6 2 d4 d5, 1 e4 ♘f6, 1 e4 d5 and 1 e4 d6 2 d4 ♘f6. In the case of the Alekhine (1 e4 ♘f6) and the Scandinavian (1 e4 d5), the fact that White will effectively gain a tempo by 2 e5 and 2 exd5, respectively, gives the counterattack an ambiguous character, but Black nevertheless creates an imbalance that he fails to bring about by playing 1...e5. The Sicilian Defence goes its own way, as usual, neither developing nor attacking. What an irony that it's the favourite move of the best players in the world!

Since the chapter introductions cover the basics strategies (and the games much more so), I won't repeat what's said there. Still, it might be interesting to make a few general comparisons between apparently similar openings before turning to the practical material. First, it should be clear that the Caro-Kann would be a better defence than the French if the disadvantages mentioned above were their only problem. After all, bringing a bishop out freely as Black does in the Caro-Kann contrasts dramatically with Black's imprisoned bishop on c8 in the French. It overshadows any other developmental problem. In the Caro-Kann, limiting the options of the b8-knight (i.e., preventing it from occupying c6) doesn't seem that severe a penalty. In the abstract, a hypothetical knight might be best off on c6; but in this particular opening that piece will generally be happy on d7, controlling e5 and defending f6 in key situations. And in the main line with ...♗f5 the knight doesn't even temporarily block Black's light-squared bishop from developing. Of course, the availability of c6 for a knight in the French Defence shouldn't be underestimated, not only because a knight there attacks d4 and e5, but because d7 is left free for a bishop or for a knight retreating to d7 after White plays e5 (a major sequence in the French). So the trade-offs between the two openings aren't completely one-sided, but if forced to compare, you feel that Black gets the better bargain by playing the Caro-Kann. However, what evens the scales is the respective central situations of the two openings. Regardless of whether you play ...dxe4 (as in the main lines of the Caro-Kann) or maintain your pawn on d5 (as is the case in most variations of the French), it's unlikely that you'll be able to attack White's d4-pawn by means of ...e5; White can put a knight on f3, a bishop on f4, a queen or rook on the e-file, etc. So the remaining way to attack the centre and free one's pieces is ...c5. Black plays that move in most variations of the French Defence, truly threatening to liquidate White's centre. But in the

Caro-Kann Defence, playing ...c5 would cost Black a full tempo (i.e. ...c6-c5). For that reason, the Caro-Kann defender will generally delay or forego ...c5 and count upon the restraining influence of his pawn on c6. That is the right decision (...c5 on an early move is usually impractical anyway); nevertheless, it's almost always better to break up the opponent's centre than to surrender the centre yourself. In the Caro-Kann, Black does gain counterplay against White's centre along the open d-file, but that is relatively easy to fend off. So both openings have their appealing and unappealing sides.

The Alekhine Defence makes a funny contrast with the Pirc Defence. In the Pirc, Black plays ...d6 first, to restrain White's centre, and then ...♘f6 to attack it. In the Alekhine, Black reverses this order, playing ...♘f6 first, losing a tempo, and then within a few moves after e5 he plays ...d6. It's as though Black had allowed White to play e5 successfully against the Pirc, an advance that is Black's top priority to prevent! Thus one's first instinct is that the Pirc is a superior opening. It may or may not be, but the flaw in this argument can be stated more or less as follows: in the Pirc, White often *shouldn't* play e5 because Black will either capture once and then retreat the knight, or retreat without capture, in both cases undermining the centre by ...c5 or if appropriate ...f6. In the case of the Alekhine, Black has got White to commit his pawn to e5 from where he is already in a position to undermine it. So in a way, he has achieved the

Pirc player's dream! Well, of course it's not at all clear whether Black can undermine White's e-pawn Pirc-style. But the point is that he has an extended centre to attack whereas in the Pirc Black is waiting for that opportunity. Again, there are advantages and disadvantages to each approach. Most strong players would probably worry more about their space disadvantage were they to play one of these openings.

Black's side of the Scandinavian variation 1 e4 d5 2 exd5 ♕xd5 with 3 ♘c3 ♕a5 might be compared with the Centre Game for White after 1 e4 e5 2 d4 exd4 3 ♕xd4 ♘c6 4 ♕a4. White has the extra move e4 in, but as with most reversed openings you have to decide whether that move is good or bad. The e4-pawn can be a target down an open file, following, for instance, ...♘f6, ...♗c5 (or ...g6 and ...♗g7), ...0-0 and ...♖e8. On the other hand, the e4-pawn does guard d5 in classical fashion. Perhaps this one's a toss-up as well.

One can make this kind of comparison between any number of positions in opening theory, and it's a useful exercise to do so. The reader might want to think about other fundamental properties of Semi-Open Games and how they offer advantages or disadvantages. You will find that every defence has a balance between negatives and positives whose sum can't be too different from that of other openings. Otherwise, some defences wouldn't be played at all, and others would find no willing opponents!

11 Sicilian Defence

1 e4 c5 *(D)*

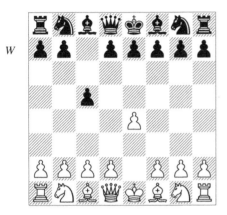

The Sicilian Defence has been the most popular opening in top-level chess for the past several decades and continues to be so today, accounting for about 17% of all contests between grandmasters, and an astonishing 25% of the games in a database of Informators. Since young players and aspiring masters show such enthusiasm for the Sicilian, it's hard to see those figures diminishing much.

What's so special about this opening? First of all, 1...c5 effectively prevents 2 d4, the primary goal of a defence to 1 e4. To be more specific, 2 d4 cxd4 3 ♕xd4 loses a tempo and already risks disadvantage after 3...♘c6. If, instead, White plays 3 c3 and sacrifices a pawn (the Morra Gambit), we have many years of experience and analysis to show that Black at the very least should have no problems equalizing and almost certainly should gain an advantage with accurate play. Of course other openings also discourage d4 or prepare to meet it effectively, so we have to look for more reasons to choose specifically the Sicilian Defence. Since the vast majority of games are contested in the Open Sicilian, i.e. 2 ♘f3 and 3 d4, let's see what we can learn from the resulting positions. We need a concrete example to think about, so let's start with the most popular

Sicilian Defence played by masters, the Najdorf Variation:

2 ♘f3 d6 3 d4 cxd4 4 ♘xd4 ♘f6 5 ♘c3 a6 *(D)*

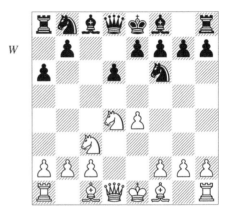

What's going on? Can Black really get away with this 4th pawn move, when it's not even a centre pawn? Let's make some more sample moves:

6 ♗g5 e6 7 f4 ♗e7 8 ♕f3 ♕c7 9 0-0-0 ♘bd7 10 ♗d3 b5 11 ♖he1 *(D)*

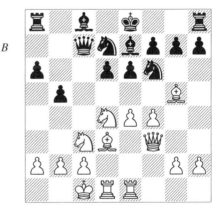

White has all seven pieces developed, Black just four, having made six pawn moves thus far. Furthermore, Black has only one piece beyond the second rank; White has five. And of course

White commands more space. Before commenting upon all this, let's compare it with the Sozin Variation of the Najdorf. After 1 e4 c5 2 ②f3 d6 3 d4 cxd4 4 ②xd4 ②f6 5 ②c3 a6, White continues 6 ②c4 e6 7 ②b3 ②e7 8 0-0 b5 9 ②e3. In that case, White has five pieces out to Black's two.

A traditional Scheveningen/Najdorf line goes 6 ②e3 e6 7 ②e2 ②e7 8 0-0 *(D)*. In this case, White has five pieces out to Black's two, and out of seven moves Black has played five with pawns.

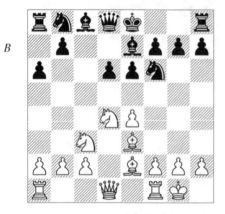

B

Just to drive the point home, Black sometimes plays an even more extreme version of these ideas, namely, 1 e4 c5 2 ②f3 e6 3 d4 cxd4 4 ②xd4 a6 5 ②c3 d6 6 ②e3 b5, which adds up to six straight pawn moves and not even a piece out! You should notice another negative aspect of every one of these lines, as if they need it: Black's centre pawns on e6 and d6 are in passive positions blocking his own pieces, as third-rank pawns are known to do. Thus his pieces have few prospects of being as active as White's. As we shall see, the same thing is true of most other Sicilian systems.

Back to our question: why then would anyone, much less the world's elite, play the Sicilian Defence? Well, Black has an open c-file. But wait! White has an open d-file attacking a weak pawn on d6. That should be even more effective. How about Black's minority attack with the pawn advance ...b5? OK, at least that's a real plus (unfortunately at the cost of more time taken away from development); but if he wants to, White has the time to stop that move by playing a4. In many cases this reduces Black

to developing by ...b6 and ...②b7, thereby putting another pawn on the third rank.

Any experienced player knows that Black stands reasonably well in these positions. Again, can we say why? The real key to the Open Sicilian is that Black has a central majority. A central majority is a basic positional advantage that should never be underestimated and can compensate for other problems in the position. If we consider the centre with ...d6 and ...e6, Black's d- and e-pawns protect against incursions by white pieces, thus giving Black time to catch up in development. Next, every central majority threatens to advance and this one is no different: once Black's pieces begin to get developed, the move ...d5 will expand the scope of some of them (for example, a bishop on e7, queen on c7 and a rook on d8 or e8), and create good posts for others (e.g., a knight on e4 or d5). Because White has to be constantly on the lookout for this move (as well as ...e5 followed by ...d5 on the next move) he has to devote forces to its prevention. That brings us to another important advantage for Black in almost all Open Sicilians: White's e-pawn is a target. It can be attacked by a knight on f6, a bishop on b7, and perhaps another knight on c5. White can defend his e-pawn with his light-squared bishop, but where should he put it? If the bishop goes to d3, it is blocked by its own pawn, and if it goes to g2 or f3, then the bishop will also be passively defending. In fact, in both of these positions Black may at some point be able to play ...e5 and fix the e-pawn, preventing that bishop from getting out. What does this all translate to? White's light-squared bishop is by definition a bad bishop, because his centre pawn is on a light square. I once heard the great Larsen say that after 3 d4 cxd4 White was positionally lost! Tongue-in-cheek or not, he was undoubtedly referring to Black's central majority, and the diversion of White's resources to the defence of his e-pawn.

What can White do in the face of these problems? He generally doesn't want to wait around for an ending without changing the pawn-structure, lest Black's central majority and queenside minority attack become too influential in that stage of play. In order to make progress, White has to exploit his space advantage (he almost always controls four ranks to Black's three, with the other disputed). Hence you will see that many encounters feature White's advance e5, activating his bishop and other pieces to gain serious and sometimes unstoppable attacking chances. A potential problem in that case is that the e5-pawn will become weak, so this decision has to be undertaken cautiously. He can also turn to the advance f4-f5, hoping to force ...e5; sometimes, however, that cedes the e5-square to Black's pieces – as always, proper timing is the key. Another attacking option at White's disposal is g4-g5, perhaps in conjunction with h4, risking kingside exposure in order to drive back Black's pieces. That has been an increasingly popular and successful strategy over the last decade. Finally, in addition to all those ideas, White can try to take direct advantage of Black's slow development and refined pawn-play to sacrifice material and blow open the enemy position. His knights on c3 and d4 may be restricted by Black's pawns, but those same knights are habitually sacrificed on the squares d5, f5, b5 and e6.

A completely different structure arises when Black has a pawn on d6 and one on e5. That would seem worse than the ...d6/...e6 systems, because he gives up the d5-square to White's pieces (and the f5-square can be handy for a knight). Let's see the best-known early version of this structure: 1 e4 c5 2 ♘f3 d6 3 d4 cxd4 4 ♘xd4 ♘f6 5 ♘c3 a6 6 ♗e2 (6 ♗e3 can also be answered by 6...e5, but that's another story) 6...e5 7 ♘b3 ♗e7 8 0-0 0-0 9 ♗e3. Both sides have played natural-looking moves and now Black illustrates a basic idea: 9...♗e6 *(D)*.

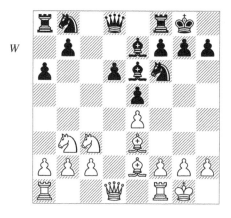

This standard move contains the notion of playing ...d5 soon, totally freeing Black's game.

White has plenty of options, but one is to occupy that square immediately. Then after 10 ♘d5 ♗xd5!? (10...♘xe4? 11 ♗b6 and 12 ♘c7) 11 exd5, White has two bishops but has lost his outpost. More importantly, Black now has a mobile central pawn-mass. One encounter proceeded 11...♘bd7 12 c4 a5 13 ♘d2 ♘e8 14 f3 ♗g5 15 ♗f2 f5 and Black's 4:3 kingside majority (a variant of the one we see in so many openings) establishes itself. Black appears to have achieved a game with equal chances. Note that White's bishop on e2 is still bad. Obviously one of the most complicated openings in chess can't be boiled down to a couple of generalities, but such themes will appear along with a multitude of others that directly or indirectly stem from the basic properties of the opening.

Before moving on to concrete variations, let me refer again to the very abbreviated description that I gave in the introductory chapters regarding the evolution of the Sicilian Defence. I'll expand upon it in certain particulars, but the point is the same. In the second half of the 19th century, players met the Sicilian with 2 ♘c3 more than any individual variation (2 f4 was also a big favourite). When White played a line of the Open Sicilian (i.e., 2 ♘f3 and 3 d4), Black responded primarily with the Pin Variation (2 ♘f3 e6 3 d4 cxd4 4 ♘xd4 ♘f6 5 ♘c3 ♗b4) or the similar Four Knights Variation (2 ♘f3 e6 3 d4 cxd4 4 ♘xd4 ♘f6 5 ♘c3 ♘c6), assuming that White let him get that far. Notice that both of those variations have the primary goal of rapid development, and bear little resemblance to the modern set-ups ...d6/...e6/...a6 or ...d6/...e5, with pieces generally constrained to the second and third ranks. A few players experimented with such systems, such as Louis Paulsen. Among top players, he had to be the most devoted Sicilian player of his time and his games included everything from the Scheveningen to ... the Paulsen! The latter variation is truly hypermodern: 1 e4 c5 2 ♘f3 e6 3 d4 cxd4 4 ♘xd4 a6.

In the first part of the 20th century, leading players began to investigate more Sicilian Defences with limited success, and in particular we see more Open Sicilians, including the Dragon Variation and to a limited extent the Scheveningen Variation. But the Sicilian only began to be truly accepted as a leading defence in the

1930s, and it took off in the 1940s. The popularity of 1...c5 hasn't stopped growing since, turning ever more modern as it evolved. Variations featuring fast development for Black are now proportionally rare.

1 e4 c5 2 ♘f3 *(D)*

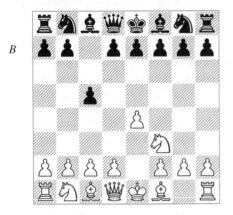

By bringing out his knight White contests d4, but he also prevents ...e5, a move that might come in handy for Black. 2 ♘f3 introduces White's Open Sicilian variations, those in which he plays 3 d4, and after Black's response 3...cxd4, recaptures with 4 ♘xd4. These variations constitute about 90% of master games with 1...c5. I shall group them according to Black's second move in so far as it is useful to do so.

Introduction to Systems with 2...d6

1 e4 c5 2 ♘f3 d6 3 d4

As so often, the less frequently played variations say something about the main lines, i.e. why they *are* the main lines. Here are some alternatives to 3 d4 and a few move-order issues to think about.

a) 3 ♗b5+ *(D)* is called the Moscow Variation. It has its followers, in part because some players don't want to enter into all the complications that arise from the Dragon, Najdorf and Classical Variations that we shall be looking at.

If one simply judges by appearances, there doesn't seem to be anything wrong with 3

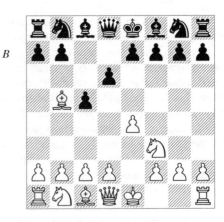

♗b5+. It gets the bishop out of the way to speed up White's development, especially castling. If the bishop is exchanged, that may be of benefit to White because, as we have seen, his light-squared bishop can be a problem in the Sicilian Defence; formally speaking, it's a bad bishop whether or not White follows up with c4 (a common Moscow Variation theme). This is all true and indeed 3 ♗b5+ can hardly be a bad move. Certain specialists have done well with it at the highest levels. Yet the large majority of players prefer to use the Open variations with 3 d4. The achievement of positive prospects is the main reason behind their decision. In the Open variations of the Sicilian Defence, White tends to get a healthy lead in development and space. But after 3 ♗b5+, an exchange of this bishop on d7 will bring out another of Black's pieces and let him begin to catch up in development. If Black plays 3...♘c6, White's only threat is to cede his bishop-pair. That said, a number of Black's set-ups offer White good chances for advantage, so the defender should know his theory and/or be a good intuitive player. We won't analyse the Moscow in depth because there is so much to explore elsewhere. In the broadest possible terms, and glossing over many options, the most frequently-played lines and ideas are as follows:

a1) 3...♗d7 4 ♗xd7+ ♕xd7 (after 4...♘xd7, 5 d4 gives White some useful space, or he can play 5 c4, although neither course guarantees an advantage) 5 c4 *(D)*.

The idea is to set up a Maroczy Bind without White's light-squared bishop, which in the original Maroczy Bind (see the Accelerated Fianchetto Sicilian) tends to be a bad piece

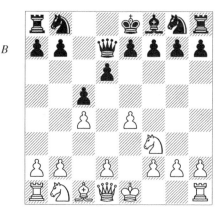

B

imprisoned behind its own centre pawns. Castling kingside, d4 and b3 are all in the mix with a number of tricky move-orders. Needless to say, Black can generate counterplay in the centre either by targeting d4 with ...g6 and ...♗g7, or by playing ...♘c6, ...♘f6 and ...e6. He can also play ...a6 and aim for ...b5, much as in the Accelerated Fianchetto lines. The very absence of White's light-squared bishop will make this easier to achieve.

a2) 3...♘d7 4 d4 cxd4 5 ♕xd4 leaves White better developed and well centralized. The moves ♘c3 and ♗g5 can follow. Black has difficulty getting developed without allowing a favourable e5 at some point, so he usually plays ...e5 and brings his pieces out via ...♘f6 and ...♗e7, probably followed by ...♘c5. This is very 'Najdorf-like', absolutely legitimate, and not easy to talk about without specific examples.

a3) 3...♘c6 4 0-0 (4 d4 cxd4 5 ♕xd4 transposes to 2...d6 3 d4 cxd4 4 ♕xd4 ♘c6 5 ♗b5, thus giving that intriguing system added significance; we'll look at it immediately below via the latter order) 4...♗d7 5 ♖e1 ♘f6 6 c3 a6 7 ♗f1 ♗g4 8 d3 and White plans ♘bd2 and h3. In general Black is equal as long as he is able to respond to d4 aggressively.

b) White can always play a move such as 3 ♗c4. Ordinarily anything of this nature can be met by ...♘c6, ...g6 and ...♗g7. Then, because of the bishop's position, ...e6, ...♘ge7 with ...d5 in short order will gain space and time; ...a6 is also a useful move. However, Black may not like that structure and can set up by 3...♘f6 4 d3 (4 e5 dxe5 5 ♘xe5 is the sort of thing that worries less experienced players but after 5...e6 it

transpires that Black controls the d4-square, and without being able to play d4 White has little chance of making progress; Black simply castles and exchanges off the forward knight) 4...e6 with the idea of ...♗e7, ...0-0, ...♘c6 and perhaps ...d5 at a later stage. From White's point of view the idea is to go for plain development by d3, 0-0 and perhaps a3 to hide the bishop away on a2. Other ideas are a combination of ♘c3 and ♗g5, fighting for control of d5. As a whole, White will have difficulty making progress.

c) A tricky alternative is 3 c3 ♘f6! (now that White's knight cannot go to c3 to protect the e-pawn) 4 ♗e2!? (or 4 ♗d3) 4...g6 (4...♘xe4?? 5 ♕a4+) 5 0-0 ♗g7 and with accurate play Black will find himself free from trouble.

All of these lines have their own theory that can be researched in books and databases.

3...cxd4 4 ♘xd4

A fascinating and inviting variation is 4 ♕xd4 ♘c6 (this knight will be pinned, minimizing White's loss of time; alternatively, Black can guarantee the win of a tempo against White's queen by playing 4...a6, when White also 'gains' a move to play 5 c4 if he wants to – this is a sort of Maróczy Bind position that we shall be discussing in various contexts) 5 ♗b5 ♗d7 (to renew the threat on the queen; after 5...♕a5+ 6 ♘c3 ♕xb5 7 ♘xb5 ♘xd4 8 ♘fxd4 ♔d8 9 c4 or 9 ♗e3, White has space and some development edge, whereas Black has no weaknesses and the bishop-pair – theory assesses this position favourably for White, perhaps optimistically so) 6 ♗xc6 ♗xc6 (6...bxc6 7 c4 is interesting) 7 ♘c3 ♘f6 8 ♗g5 e6 9 0-0-0 ♗e7 10 ♖he1 0-0 (D).

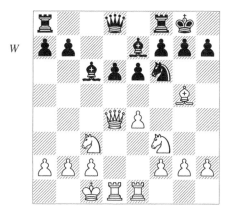

W

A thought-provoking situation has arisen, pitting White's knights, space, and superior development against Black's bishop-pair and central majority. The general rule with knights is that their owner needs to hurry to achieve an attack or gain outposts before his opponent consolidates. Otherwise there will come a counterattack on the queenside (in this situation by ...b5) and/or in the centre (by ...d5 or ...e5). Theory isn't particularly extensive on these lines and they afford a lot of scope for creativity. One example that panned out well for Black was 11 ♔b1 h6 12 ♗h4 ♖e8 (Black must always be wary of some variant of the trick 12...♕a5 13 ♕d2 ♖ac8?! 14 ♘d5! ♕d8 15 ♘xe7+ ♕xe7 16 ♘d4 with space and a simple advantage, because 16...g5? 17 ♗xg5 hxg5 18 ♕xg5+ is killing) 13 ♗g3 (this is probably attempting to avoid the standard idea 13 ♕d2 ♘xe4 14 ♘xe4 ♗xh4 15 ♘xd6 when Black can play 15...♖f8 or 15...♗xf3 16 gxf3 ♖f8; but here we have a good example of the unexplored nature of this variation; White could just play 13 ♕d3!?, when, for instance, 13...d5 14 ♗xf6 ♗xf6 15 e5 ♗e7 16 ♘d4 ♖c8 17 f4 is promising; also possible is 13 h3!? with the idea g4, as was actually played in one game) 13...d5! 14 e5 (compare the last note – here White's bishop on g3 is just bad) 14...♘e4 15 ♘xe4 dxe4 16 ♕xd8 ♖exd8 17 ♘d4 (D).

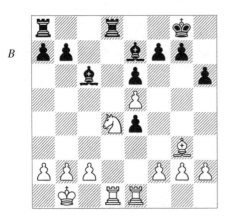

17...♗e8! (two bishops will be worth more than a pawn, even in this relatively simplified position) 18 c3 (18 ♖xe4 ♗c6 19 ♖ee1 ♗xg2) 18...♖ac8 19 ♔c2 b5! 20 ♖xe4 b4 21 ♖e3 a5 22 ♘e2 ♗c6 23 f3 ♖xd1 24 ♔xd1 ♗c5 25 ♖d3 ♗b5 26 ♖d2 ♗e3 27 ♖d6 bxc3 28 ♘xc3 (28 bxc3 ♗c4 29 a4 ♖b8) 28...♗f1 and Black wins

his pawn back with his bishops still on a rampage, Svidler-Kasparov, Linares 1999.

4...♘f6 (D)

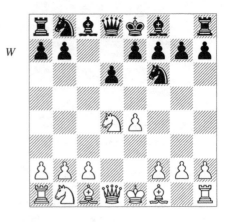

5 ♘c3

Notice that now the move 5 ♗b5+ simply helps Black to bring his pieces out by 5...♗d7, especially since White has forfeited the idea of c4. The alternative 5 f3!? has been played infrequently and yet without disappearing over the years. White's idea is to avoid blocking his c-pawn by 5 ♘c3 and thus be able to play c4, before or after ♗b5+. Black's principled response to this plan is 5...e5! (D).

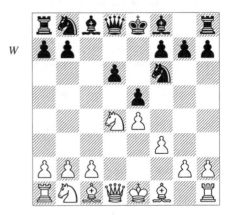

This is our first example of the ...d6/...e5 structure. If Black makes conventional developing moves he can be tied down by c4 again; that's not the end of the world but not what most players want. Here are two instructive variations:

a) 6 ♘b3 (not 6 ♘f5?! d5!) 6...♗e6 (aiming for ...d5) 7 c4 a5 8 ♗e3 a4 9 ♘3d2 ♕a5 10 ♗e2

♗e7 11 0-0 ♘c6 12 ♘a3 0-0, Rublevsky-Ki.Georgiev, Yugoslav Cht (Budva) 1996. Both sides have plenty of things to do.

b) 6 ♗b5+ ♘bd7 7 ♘f5 d5! 8 exd5 a6! 9 ♗xd7+ ♕xd7 (9...♗xd7 10 ♘e3 ♗c5 11 ♘c3 0-0 12 0-0 ♗f5 with active play, Malakhov-Nisipeanu, Holon jr Ech 1995) 10 ♘e3 b5 11 ♘c3 ♗b7 12 0-0 b4 13 ♘e4 ♘xd5 and Black has more than his share of the centre.

We now return to 5 ♘c3 (D):

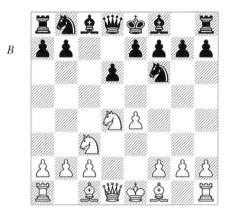

After 5 ♘c3, we have finally arrived at a great dividing point in Sicilian Defence theory, and will proceed to the main variations with 2...d6.

Dragon Variation

1 e4 c5 2 ♘f3 d6 3 d4 cxd4 4 ♘xd4 ♘f6 5 ♘c3 g6 (D)

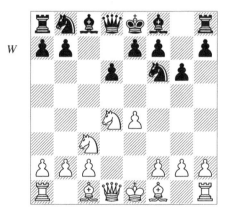

The Sicilian Dragon is one of the oldest forms of the Open Sicilian. Black gets his pieces out, especially the long-ranging bishop on g7, and can castle early without creating any pawn weaknesses. His next moves are traditionally ...♗g7, ...0-0, ...♘c6 and perhaps ...♗d7 (or ...♗e6) with ...♖c8 next. Thus Black activates his pieces rather quickly, especially by comparison with most other Sicilian Defences. He can attack on the queenside by, say, ...a5-a4, or ...a6/...b5, in part because the g7-bishop exerts so much pressure in that direction.

What are the problems in Black's position? Perhaps pawn-structure should be the first topic of discussion. It's true that Black's important central pawn on d6 is well defended by its neighbour on e7, unlike the queen's pawn in the ...d6/...e6 structures which distinguish so many Sicilian systems. We might also compare variations beginning with 1 e4 c5 2 ♘f3 e6 3 d4 cxd4 4 ♘xd4, when there is an immediate weakness down the open file on d6, whether or not it is occupied by a pawn. At least at first sight that difference favours the Dragon, and should be worth something. But as in so many openings, every advantage carries with it some disadvantage. In this situation a white knight can land on d5 at the right moment and disturb Black's game. For instance, if White is attacking Black's king on g8, the move ♘d5 might eliminate the king's best defender. Or in a more positional setting, White's ♘d5 might force an exchange on that square that results in open lines for White's pieces. Then there's the question of what Black can do with his central majority, normally his biggest asset in the Sicilian Defence. Obviously ...e6 is risky, because the d6-pawn could be very weak, in contrast to the normal Sicilian lines where Black's bishop defends it from e7. And ...e5, the other typical Sicilian advance, will block the g7-bishop if Black isn't careful. Naturally both of those pawn advances can be played under the right circumstances, but they certainly aren't major themes. This means that Black's main central break is ...d5, which White will do his utmost to prevent. Assuming that White is successful in doing so, Black will be using pieces more than pawns to achieve his goals. Indeed, once we see the typical positions from either the Classical or Yugoslav Dragon we shall focus on piece-play on the queenside such as ...♖c8, ...♗e6-c4, ...♘e5-c4, ...♕a5, ...♘d7-c5, ...♖xc3, etc. In the most frequently played system, the Yugoslav Attack, the players castle on opposite sides of the board and it's interesting to see the priority that White's pawns take in the attack (g4, h4-h5, f4-f5, etc.). This can be compared to Black's queenside pawns, which often stay at home until his attack is complete. Finally, before leaving the subject of pawn-structure, there's the simplest factor of all: the g6-pawn offers a target for attack, in particular by h4-h5. In other Sicilian Defence variations, White may achieve an attacking advance such as g4-g5 (or a positional one like a4-a5) but there's no specific pawn target. As usual, these various structural issues tend to balance out; if they didn't, no one would play the Dragon! I won't indulge in any more generalities, considering that the Dragon quickly breaks up into numerous variations that superficially have little in common with each other. It's better to glean the ideas from the play itself.

Classical Dragon

1 e4 c5 2 ♘f3 d6 3 d4 cxd4 4 ♘xd4 ♘f6 5 ♘c3 g6 6 ♗e2 (D)

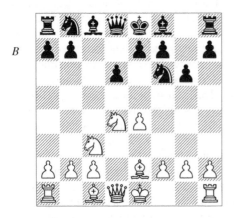

White develops and announces the likelihood of his castling kingside.

6...♗g7 7 0-0

7 ♗e3 ♘c6 8 0-0 0-0 is probably the most common alternative. A famous contest that is often cited with this move-order was Daniliuk-Malakhov, Russian Ch (Elista) 1995: 9 ♘b3 (this position can also arise if White plays 9 ♗e3 in the main line) 9...♗e6 10 f4 ♖c8 11 f5!? (winning a tempo but ceding e5) 11...♗d7 12

g4?! (too loosening; White needs to develop his pieces first by, for example, 12 ♕d2) 12...♘e5 13 ♘d2!? (White wants to prevent the exchange sacrifice on c3, but in vain; unfortunately, the attacking move ....♗c6 was coming regardless, and 13 g5 would be met by 13...♖xc3! 14 bxc3 {14 gxf6 ♖xe3 15 fxg7 ♔xg7} 14...♘xe4 with a dominant position for Black; compare the game) 13...♖xc3! 14 bxc3 ♗c6 (D).

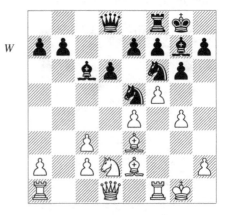

Although the e4-pawn is protected, White's weaknesses (pawns on e4 and c3, and the internal weakness on e3) make it impossible to keep things under control: 15 ♗f3 ♘xf3+ 16 ♕xf3 d5! (White's kingside is exposed and Black has an active bishop-pair) 17 ♗d4 (17 e5 d4 18 ♕e2 dxe3 19 exf6 ♗xf6 20 ♕xe3 ♕d5!) 17...dxe4 18 ♕h3 ♘xg4! 19 ♗xg7 (White is paying the price for f4-f5 and g4; 19 ♕xg4 ♗xd4+ 20 cxd4 ♕xd4+ leaves no defence) 19...♔xg7 20 ♘xe4 (20 ♘b3 ♘e5!) 20...♕b6+ 21 ♘f2 gxf5. Black is not just threatening ...♖g8 with a mating attack; he has regained his material. This kind of thing has happened to White a lot, and perhaps explains why the Yugoslav with 0-0-0 is so popular: White can push all of his kingside pawns without his king being exposed.

7...0-0 (D)

8 ♘b3

This strange-looking move is almost always played in the Classical Dragon, in part out of necessity. First and foremost it prevents ...d5 (Black's most important freeing advance), which is difficult to stop otherwise. It also covers the a5-square (often used by Black's queen or knight) and supports the advance a4-a5.

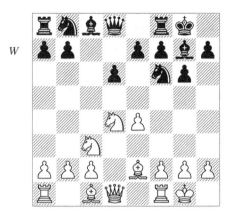

W

Furthermore, 8 ♘b3 protects the knight from tricky ideas involving ...♘g4 or ...♕b6. Naturally, there are also drawbacks to this retreat. The main one by far is that on d4 the knight reaches more squares and is more effective for positive purposes. In fact, after securing his position against ...d5, White will often return the knight to d4. Beyond that consideration, on b3 the knight is vulnerable to ...a5-a4 and if White blocks this advance by a4, the move ...♗xb3 can be productive in some (but certainly not all) positions.

Note that after 8 ♗e3 ♘c6, 9 ♘b3 will generally transpose, but 9 f4?! allows the tricky 9...♕b6!, when Black's threats of ...♘xe4 and ...♕xb2 turn out to be difficult to meet. Always watch out for ...♕b6 in Dragon positions whether you're playing White or Black.

8...♘c6 *(D)*

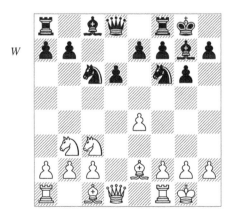

W

We'll spend a lot of time from this position because it shows so many ideas fundamental to any Sicilian Defence in which White castles

kingside. This position appears with opposite colours in the ultra-popular 'Reversed Dragon' variation of the English Opening. The latter is used more by grandmasters as a reply to the English than any other single system! That adds weight to our coverage of the ideas and strategies here.

9 ♗g5

It seems that most Dragon experts consider this the most interesting system. It brings the bishop to the most active square and prepares f4-f5, often followed by g4-g5 or a well-timed e5. This carries with it two problems: Black may get pressure along the a8-h1 diagonal (using the exchange sacrifice ...♖xc3 and ...♗c6, for example, as we saw above), and White's advance f5 gives away the critical e5-square. Both sides have chances. White can also play more safely with ♔h1 and f4, perhaps with ♗f3, or ♗d3, or ♖e1 and ♗f1, to protect the vulnerable e4-pawn.

These instructive options and equally popular alternatives to 9 ♗g5 show a plethora of standard Sicilian themes:

a) 9 ♔h1 ♗e6 10 f4 and then:

a1) 10...♖c8 (this is a fundamental position) 11 ♗f3 ♗c4!? *(D)*.

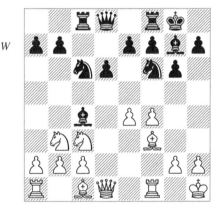

W

12 ♖f2 (the best idea in almost all these positions because the rook stays on the f-file and can also swing over to the d-file if desired; Black's centre would be unleashed after 12 ♖e1? e5! 13 f5 gxf5! 14 exf5 d5) 12...e5! 13 ♗e3 b5 14 fxe5 ♘xe5 15 a3 ♕e7, Čabrilo-Chatalbashev, Čačak 1991. The trade-offs are visible: White has the d5-outpost and possibilities of putting pressure on the d6-pawn with all three

major pieces; Black has control of e5, pressure on the queenside, and the pleasure of watching White's horrible Sicilian bishop on f3. It's probably about equal.

a2) Black can also play for the key c4-square by 10...♘a5 11 f5 ♗c4 12 ♘xa5 ♗xe2 13 ♕xe2 ♕xa5 14 g4?! ♘d7 (heading for e5, the key to Black's defence) 15 ♖f3 e6 (16 ♘d5 was becoming a problem) 16 ♗d2 ♕d8?! (anticipating White's idea of ♕h4, for one thing, but 16...♖ac8 must be better) 17 ♖h3 ♖e8 18 ♖f1 a6 19 ♕f2 (D).

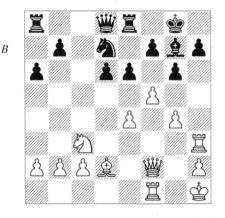

B

We have a primitive yet powerful attack, since all of White's pieces can be directed towards the king. This is a picture of what Black shouldn't allow. Bednorz-Selig, Porz 1989 continued 19...♖f8? (19...♕e7 had to be tried; Black must remember to defend along the second rank) 20 g5 ♗xc3 21 ♗xc3 exf5 22 ♖xh7! f6 23 ♕h4 ♕e8 24 exf5 gxf5 25 ♖h8+, winning.

b) 9 ♖e1!? is a calm move, giving extra support to the e-pawn if the e2-bishop decides to move. Although it's not obvious, a lot of Black's counterplay will have to do with putting pressure on White's e-pawn, so this is a sensible precaution.

We now return to the position after 9 ♗g5 (D):

9...♗e6

Black develops simply, with an eye on c4 but not abandoning the idea of ...d5.

a) Another idea is 9...b6 10 f4 ♗b7 11 ♗f3 ♘a5!. This illustrates a common and important idea: if White doubles Black's a-pawns via ♘xa5, Black will exert unpleasant pressure down the b-file. Remember that, as discussed in

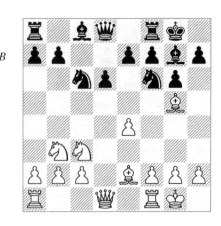

B

the introductory chapters, doubled rook's pawns are usually not a problem until the endgame.

b) 9...a6 is a popular choice; for instance, 10 f4 b5 11 ♗f3 b4 12 ♘d5 (12 ♘a4! has ideas of e5 that are hard to stop; then access to c5 and b6 could prove critical) 12...♘xd5 13 exd5 ♘a5. This position has done well for Black. One example is 14 ♖b1?! ♘c4 15 ♕e2 ♕c7! 16 ♔h1 ♗f5 17 g4 ♗d7 18 f5? ♘e5! 19 ♕e4 ♗b5 20 ♗e2 ♗xe2 21 ♕xe2 ♖fc8 22 ♖f2 a5! with the idea of ...a4, Zapata-Miles, Thessaloniki OL 1984. Compare Black's pieces with White's.

10 ♔h1 (D)

White makes a somewhat slow move, but a major tactical and positional theme is that White's immediate 10 f4 opens up his king to attack along the g1-a7 diagonal and allows 10...b5! 11 ♗xb5?! (11 a3 a5!; 11 ♕d3 ♗c4 is equal) 11...♘xe4 12 ♗xc6 (12 ♘xe4 ♕b6+ 13 ♔h1 ♕xb5) 12...♕b6+ 13 ♔h1 ♕xc6 14 ♘a5 ♘xc3 15 ♘xc6 ♘xd1 16 ♘xe7+ ♔h8 17 ♖axd1 ♗xb2 and White's queenside weaknesses will cause him some trouble, although it's close to equal.

10...♘a5

Another established plan is 10...♕c8 11 f4 ♖d8, hoping for ...d5: 12 ♗f3 ♗c4 (12...a5 13 ♘d5!) 13 ♖f2! e6?! 14 ♖d2! ♕c7 15 ♕e1 h6 16 ♗h4 ♖d7 17 ♖ad1 e5 18 ♗xf6! ♗xf6 19 ♗g4! exf4?! (but Black saw the alternative 19...♖dd8 20 ♗e2!, when White wins the d5-square and has the upper hand) 20 ♗xd7! ♕xd7 21 ♖xd6 ♕e7 22 ♖d7 ♕e5 23 ♘d2! ♗e6 24 ♘f3, consolidating his material, Karpov-Miles, Bad Lauterberg 1977. When Karpov was an e-pawn player, he was one of the greatest interpreters of ♗e2 systems against the Sicilian.

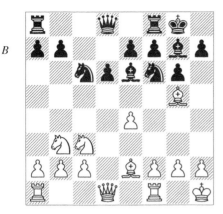

11 f4 ♖c8!? *(D)*

Another typical tactical idea is 11...♘c4! 12 f5!? ♘xb2 13 ♕c1 ♗c4 14 ♕xb2 ♗xe2 15 ♘xe2 ♘xe4 16 f6 ♘xf6 with three pawns for the piece and prospects against White's weakened queenside.

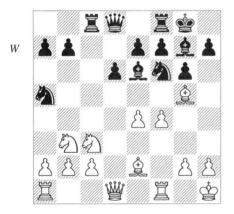

12 f5

The surprising thrust 12 e5! is a tactical theme to watch out for when a knight is on a5. Since 12...dxe5?? loses a piece after 13 ♕xd8 and ♘xa5, Black has to calculate in advance whether he can afford to play 12...♘xb3 (not 12...♘e8? 13 ♘xa5 ♕xa5 14 ♗xe7 dxe5 15 ♗xf8 ♗xf8, when Black has some compensation for the exchange but not enough) 13 axb3 (13 exf6 exf6; this kind of position isn't always satisfactory for Black, although here it is) 13...dxe5 14 fxe5 ♘d5 (14...♘d7 15 ♖xa7 ♕b6 16 ♖a4) 15 ♖xa7 ♘xc3 16 ♕xd8 ♖fxd8 17 bxc3 ♗xe5 18 c4 with ♗f3 to come and a small advantage.

12...♗c4 13 ♗d3 b5 *(D)*

Here we have a picture of both sides consistently following their plans in what seems like an idealized form.

14 ♕d2 b4

At this point 15 ♘e2 leads to a balanced position with intriguing opportunities. Instead White blundered with 15 ♘d1?? ♘xe4! 16 ♗xe4 in Onoprienko-Karr, Paris 1996, and now 16...♗xf1! would have given White almost nothing for the exchange.

Yugoslav Attack

1 e4 c5 2 ♘f3 d6 3 d4 cxd4 4 ♘xd4 ♘f6 5 ♘c3 g6 6 ♗e3

This is the usual move-order to introduce the Yugoslav Attack.

6...♗g7 *(D)*

Not 6...♘g4?? 7 ♗b5+, when White wins material since 7...♗d7 loses a piece after 8 ♕xg4.

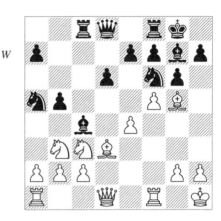

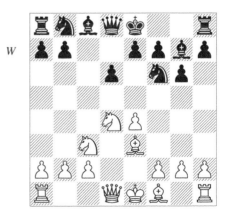

7 f3 *(D)*

Here is the Yugoslav pawn-structure. At this point 7 ♕d2 can be met by 7...♘g4, when 8 ♗b5+ ♗d7 achieves little, and 8 ♗g5 h6 9 ♗h4 ♘c6 10 ♘xc6 bxc6 11 f3 ♕b6 12 ♘d1 g5 13 ♗g3 ♘e5 is obscure. This idea becomes more relevant after 7 ♗c4 ♘g4 8 ♗b5+!? (8 0-0 ♘xe3 9 fxe3 is bad, as might be expected; Black has a permanent outpost on e5 that White simply won't be able to get around; e.g., 9...0-0 10 ♕f3 e6 11 ♖ad1 ♘d7 12 ♘db5 ♘e5 13 ♕e2 ♘xc4 14 ♕xc4 ♗e5, etc.) 8...♔f8 9 0-0 (9 ♗g5 h6 10 ♗h4 g5 11 ♗g3 ♕b6!) 9...♗e5! 10 h3 ♘xe3 11 fxe3 ♔g7 12 ♕f3 ♖f8 and Black's control of the e5-square gives him the better position. Hence those wishing to play a system with h3 and ♗c4 should do it by the move-order 7 h3 ♘c6 8 ♗c4.

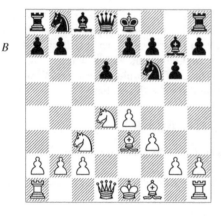

B

7...0-0

7...♘c6 generally won't make much difference (unless you're a 'Dragdorf' player who puts his knight on d7; this odd hybrid system has been moderately popular of late). If White prefers to play 8 ♗c4 at this point (delaying ♕d2), then 8...♕b6 should be answered by 9 ♗b5 threatening ♘f5, which probably gives White a small edge. More fun is 9 ♘f5 ♕xb2 10 ♘xg7+ ♔f8 11 ♘d5 ♘xd5 12 ♗xd5 with the dark squares and the bishop-pair in return for a pawn.

8 ♕d2 ♘c6 (D)

Since the freeing move ...d5 is so vital, it's instructive to see what White might do if it is played right away, something that most players don't even consider. After 8...d5?! it seems necessary for White to respond aggressively if he is to gain the advantage, beginning with 9 e5 ♘e8

10 f4 f6. Then everything is fine for Black unless White plays the critical 11 h4!?, leading to an atypical attack: 11...fxe5 12 fxe5 ♗xe5 13 0-0-0! ♘f6 14 ♘f3 ♗xc3 15 ♕xc3 ♘c6 16 ♗h6 ♖e8 (16...♖f7 17 ♘g5) 17 h5! ♗f5 18 hxg6 ♗xg6 19 ♖xd5 ♘b4 20 ♕xb4 ♘xd5 21 ♕d4 ♘f6 22 ♗c4+ ♔h8 23 ♕f4 intending ♘e5 and Black's not in very good shape.

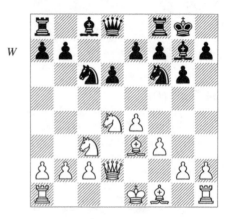

W

After 8...♘c6, we have formally arrived at the Yugoslav Attack. Since 9...d5 is a huge positional threat, White has only three major moves. I'll focus on the traditional main-line move:

9 ♗c4

a) 9 0-0-0 has less theory than 9 ♗c4, which means only a few books' worth! Castling doesn't stop 9...d5 (indeed, it's the main line), even though that move allows White, after 10 exd5 ♘xd5 11 ♘xc6 bxc6, to win a pawn by 12 ♘xd5 cxd5 13 ♕xd5. Fortunately, Black can then play the clever 13...♕c7! with good compensation, the first point being that after 14 ♕xa8 ♗f5 (threatening the queen and checkmate on c2) 15 ♕xf8+ ♔xf8 Black recovers most of the material with an ongoing attack. Thus White usually plays 12 ♗d4, when the most combative continuation is 12...e5 13 ♗c5 (D).

Now 13...♗e6! 14 ♘e4! ♖e8 15 h4! h6 16 g4 leads to all kinds of complications. Notice that White didn't take the rook by 14 ♗xf8; it turns out that 14...♕xf8 (threatening ...♗h6) gives Black wonderful play for the exchange due to his dark-square control and attack via ...♖b8 and ...f5, sometimes mixed with ...♕b4 or ...♘b4. This is a typical case of a bishop being worth as much as or more than a rook until the players

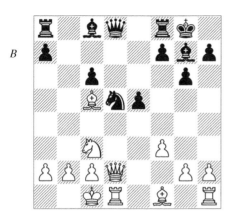

reach a simplified position, assuming that White makes it that far.

This is just the very briefest of introductions to 9 0-0-0. It's up to you to plunge into that territory if you get the inclination.

b) 9 g4 is played much less frequently. The idea is 9...d5? 10 g5, winning a pawn. Few Dragon aficionados use this line as White, however, primarily because of 9...♘xd4 10 ♗xd4 ♗e6 or the immediate 9...♗e6 *(D)*.

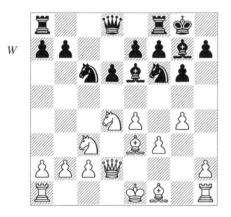

The point of the latter move is that 10 ♘xe6 fxe6 covers the key d5-square and opens the f-file against the weak f-pawn. Black's basic ideas of attack along the c-file in conjunction with the g7-bishop are essentially the same, and in some cases it's convenient to have an escape-square on f7. After the natural 11 ♗c4, Black can play either 11...♕c8 followed by ...♘e5 or 11...d5!? 12 exd5 ♘e5 13 ♗e2 ♘xd5 14 ♘xd5 exd5 15 0-0-0 e6. This is a line you might want to look into as White and should definitely be aware of if you're playing Black.

We now return to 9 ♗c4 *(D)*:

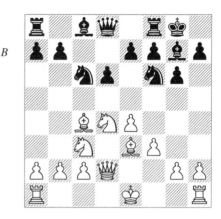

We have arrived at the starting-point of one of the most analysed opening variations in chess, and quite possibly the most analysed. In 1975 many of us believed that the Yugoslav Dragon was beginning to get 'analysed out', but decades later theory is continuing to expand, with perhaps 200 times as much serious material having been played and analysed. Since the main variations are so tactical and so critical, you simply need to study in detail those that you have chosen. Authors of the many Dragon books and CDs are fond of saying that you can play even the main lines of this opening armed only with a firm grasp on the general ideas. In fact that would only be possible on a low level of play where you are more or less guaranteed that whomsoever you play will not know much theory. The simple fact is that the player who is familiar with a Dragon variation and knows it by heart will almost always beat the opponent who doesn't. For one thing, it took untold hours of home study and computer analysis to work out most of the Dragon positions that are now part of theory, so the knowledgeable player will benefit from the specific results of that work. On top of that, many of the best Dragon moves are counterintuitive and not the choice that you would make under time constraints. Consequently the most practical solution for those who want to play the Dragon as Black or use the Yugoslav Attack as White is to find lines in which to specialize and/or require less work. At any rate, this book is not intended as a theoretical tome so I'll just present games that show a number of themes for both sides.

In many ways the Dragon has simpler basic ideas than most other Sicilian Defences, which contributes to its appeal. The Classical variations feature standard kingside set-ups for White and a limited group of queenside attacking schemes for Black. I have devoted space to it partly as a matter of practicality for the average player. In the Yugoslav Attack we find a set of fairly straightforward themes to become familiar with. For White, one such motif is the primitive h4-h5 to open the h-file, followed by ♗h6, exchanging the bishop that defends the vulnerable dark squares around the king. Then White proceeds to checkmate or otherwise overwhelm Black by hook or by crook, using thematic moves such as ♘d5 and ♘xf6, g4-g5 or whatever is at hand. Such is the barbaric stuff of tens of thousands of games. On a much less frequent but arguably more sophisticated level, White plays centralizing and prophylactic moves such as ♔b1 and ♖he1, perhaps in conjunction with ♘b3, ♗d4 and either e5 or ♘d5. Alternatively, playing ♔b1 and ♘b3 by themselves is a way to batten down the hatches against Black's queenside attack. That may come in conjunction with the simplifying ♘d5. ♗g5 is a common move in many variations, increasingly popular as the years have gone by, and particularly against the ...h5 lines. This serves the purpose of threatening ♗xf6 and ♘d5 at some point, but also has the idea that strategies involving f4 and e5 have more chance of success. The bishop move can be beneficial in that if Black plays his standard ...♘e5-c4 manoeuvre, White may be able to slide the queen away, perhaps to e2, because capture by ...♘xe3 is no longer possible. As a general rule, neither side can lose their dark-squared bishop without putting their position in peril, unless of course that happens via sacrifice or other forcing sequence.

Obviously you have to play this variation for quite a while to understand or be helped by that characterization. What about Black? He has no natural pawn-breaks to open lines, but has two major ideas in the form of ...♘e5-c4, to rid White of one of his bishops, and ...♖xc3. The latter exchange sacrifice can be played as part of a mating attack, or to set the stage for an all-out assault, or simply to weaken White's structure such that if the right endgame or queenless middlegame comes along, Black will be happy

to enter into it. He can use his queenside attack by ...b5-b4 to chase White's pieces from defence, and it is quite common to sacrifice that b-pawn in order to open queenside lines for the attack. There are numerous other ideas – too many, in fact, to explore here.

Returning to 9 ♗c4, what specifically does it do? It puts the bishop on an aggressive diagonal, yes, but also stops ...d5. For this purpose White subjects himself to a time-consuming retreat in the face of c-file pressure and ...♘e5 or ...♘a5, hoping that the bishop's defensive role on b3 (guarding a2, protecting the king from b-file attack) will justify its exposure, even to the longer-term idea ...a5-a4. There is no way to explore all of the intricate theory of the entire attack, of course, so I'll show a few games and game excerpts.

Stefansson – Ward
Reykjavik 1998

9...♗d7
Black simply develops. His idea is to put a rook on c8 and play ...♘e5, sometimes directly by ...♖ac8 but often with the order ...♕a5, ...♖fc8 and then ...♘e5, as in this contest.

10 0-0-0
The immediate 10 h4 will often transpose after 10...♕a5 and 11...♖fc8, but this order is said to discourage the 'Chinese Dragon' which uses the scheme ...♖b8 and ...b5; I won't go into any details of that still-controversial notion, but it's worth considering. A variation with a long and independent history is 10...♖c8 11 ♗b3 ♘e5 12 0-0-0 (12 g4 can now run into 12...a5!? 13 a4 h5 when one can argue that the weakening of White's queenside favours Black by comparison with other ...h5 lines) 12...♘c4 (12...h5 transposes into a form of the Soltis Defence, which we shall see later on) 13 ♗xc4 ♖xc4 14 h5!? (14 g4 b5!? 15 h5 has also been analysed in depth) 14...♘xh5 *(D)*.

15 g4 (seemingly small variations in move-order can make all the difference in the Dragon; e.g., 15 ♘de2 ♕a5 16 ♗h6?! {a typically crazy continuation is 16 g4! ♘g3!? 17 ♘xg3 ♗xc3 18 bxc3 ♕a3+ 19 ♔b1 ♗e6 20 ♕h2! h5 21 ♘f5!! ♖b4+ 22 cxb4 ♗xa2+ 23 ♔a1 ♗b3+ 24 ♔b1 ♗a2+ with a draw} 16...♗xc3! 17 ♘xc3

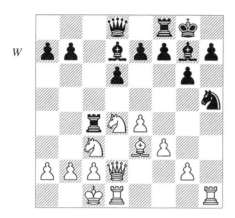

Ξfc8 and it's hard to stop ...Ξxc3 without compromising White's position) 15...$\textcircled{4}$f6 16 $\textcircled{4}$de2! (the classic game that follows shocked the chess world for its simplicity: instead of launching all his pawns and pieces into the kingside attack, White guards the c3-knight with both the other knight and a rook, and then proceeds to attack undisturbed) 16...$\textcircled{1}$a5 (16...Ξe8! has been played since this time with decent chances, salvaging the bishop in the case of 17 $\textcircled{2}$h6 $\textcircled{2}$h8!; in the meantime bold ideas such as 17 e5 $\textcircled{4}$xg4! 18 fxg4 $\textcircled{2}$xg4 with dynamic compensation became commonplace) 17 $\textcircled{2}$h6 $\textcircled{2}$xh6? (offering the exchange with the retreat 17...$\textcircled{2}$h8!? is a better try) 18 $\textcircled{1}$xh6 Ξfc8 19 Ξd3! (now White's e2-knight will come to the aid of the attack) 19...Ξ4c5 (D).

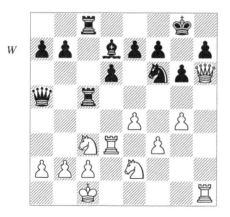

20 g5! Ξxg5 (20...$\textcircled{4}$h5 21 $\textcircled{4}$f4!) 21 Ξd5! Ξxd5 22 $\textcircled{4}$xd5 Ξe8 23 $\textcircled{4}$ef4! (23 $\textcircled{4}$xf6+? exf6 24 $\textcircled{1}$xh7+ $\textcircled{8}$f8 and there is no mate) 23...$\textcircled{2}$c6 24 e5! (these are wonderful tactics in what was effectively a world championship

match) 24...$\textcircled{2}$xd5 (24...dxe5 25 $\textcircled{4}$xf6+ exf6 26 $\textcircled{4}$h5 and mates) 25 exf6 exf6 26 $\textcircled{1}$xh7+ $\textcircled{8}$f8 27 $\textcircled{1}$h8+ 1-0 Karpov-Korchnoi, Moscow Ct (2) 1974.

10...$\textcircled{1}$a5

After 10...$\textcircled{4}$e5 11 $\textcircled{2}$b3 Ξc8 12 $\textcircled{8}$b1, the modern move 12...Ξe8!? (D) has been surprisingly successful:

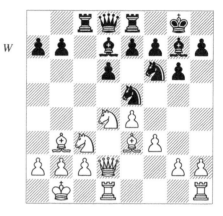

The idea is that ...Ξe8 gives the critically important g7-bishop a chance to save itself from exchange (13 $\textcircled{2}$h6 $\textcircled{2}$h8), and it also guards the e-pawn in some lines with $\textcircled{4}$d5 (thus preparing ...$\textcircled{1}$a5). Finally, ...Ξe8 is a key element in many of the variations in which Black defends by ...h5, so it also serves a purpose against a kingside pawn avalanche. An amazing amount of good from such a nondescript move! White can proceed 13 $\textcircled{2}$h6 $\textcircled{2}$h8 14 h4 $\textcircled{4}$c4 15 $\textcircled{2}$xc4 Ξxc4 16 $\textcircled{4}$de2 b5 17 h5 b4! 18 $\textcircled{4}$d5 $\textcircled{4}$xd5 19 hxg6 hxg6 20 $\textcircled{1}$xd5 $\textcircled{2}$e6 21 $\textcircled{1}$d3? (21 $\textcircled{1}$b5) 21...$\textcircled{1}$a5 (Black is already on the verge of winning) 22 b3 Ξec8! 23 $\textcircled{2}$c1 (23 bxc4 $\textcircled{2}$xc4 24 $\textcircled{1}$e3 $\textcircled{1}$xa2+ 25 $\textcircled{8}$c1 $\textcircled{2}$xe2! 26 $\textcircled{1}$xe2 $\textcircled{2}$c3 and mate next move) 23...$\textcircled{2}$g7 24 Ξd2 $\textcircled{1}$e5 (this is one way to win, just lining up along the powerful diagonal; although 24...Ξ8c5 threatening 25...$\textcircled{1}$xa2+! would have ended things quickly) 25 c3 bxc3 26 Ξc2 Ξb4 27 $\textcircled{2}$h6 $\textcircled{2}$xb3! 28 axb3 Ξxb3+ 29 $\textcircled{8}$c1 $\textcircled{2}$xh6+ 30 Ξxh6 $\textcircled{1}$g5+ 0-1 R.Perez-Y.Gonzalez, Holguin City 2002.

We now return to the position after 10...$\textcircled{1}$a5 (D):

11 h4

This is the most principled move for the attacker: waste no time and go for the kill! These days h4-h5 is normally played without the

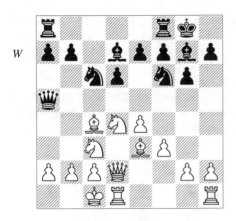

support of g4 if ...h5 hasn't been played, since the g-pawn advance costs a crucial tempo and weakens f3. But against 10...Rc8 instead of 10...Wa5 there is a great body of theory about both approaches. White has other related options after 10...Wa5, notably 11 Kb1, but also 11 Bb3 with 12 Bg5 and Rhe1 in mind.

11...Ne5 12 Bb3 Rfc8 13 Kb1

This patient move introduces a plan combining defence with attack. The more aggressive 13 h5 Nxh5 gives Black a free view down the long diagonal. Then we have more standard themes, such as in this encounter from the old days: 14 Kb1 (this looks similar to 13 Kb1, but falls into the usual exchange sacrifice) 14...Rxc3!? 15 Wxc3 (15 bxc3 Rc8 16 Bh6 Nc4 17 Bxc4 Rxc4 with a positionally winning game for Black) 15...Wxc3 16 bxc3 Rc8 17 Kb2 (17 Bg5!?; 17 Ne2 Bb5) 17...a5 18 a3 Nf6 19 Bf4 Ne8!? (19...b5) 20 Bg5 a4 21 Ba2 Nc6 with equality, Spassky-Stein, Russia-Ukraine (Uzhgorod) 1967.

13...Nc4 14 Bxc4 Rxc4 15 Nb3 Wc7 *(D)*

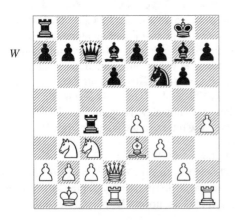

16 Bd4

Here is the kind of centralized defence that we haven't seen yet: Kb1, Nb3 and Bd4; these moves secure White's king and prevent all those ...Rxc3 sacrifices, at least for now. 16 h5 allows the predictable 16...Rxc3! 17 Wxc3 Wxc3 18 bxc3 Nxh5 and even with the queens off Black has more than enough play, with moves like ...a5-a4, ...Be6 and ...Rc8 to come.

16...Be6 17 h5 a5

Black in response charges forward with his pawns, also not the main strategy that we have seen him employ.

18 a4 b5!! *(D)*

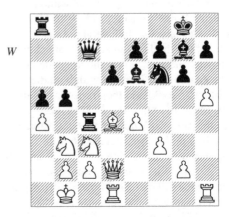

Apparently first used in over-the-board GM practice in this game. Black insists upon opening lines with the maximum speed.

19 Nxb5 Wb8 20 Nc3

Ward analyses 20 h6 Bh8 21 e5?! dxe5 22 Bxe5? Wxe5 23 Wd8+ Ne8! and Black wins.

20...Rb4! 21 hxg6 hxg6 22 Bxf6?!

Trying to exchange some pieces. 22 Rh4! was played in several other contests, when the play is dynamic and unclear; for example, 22...Rxb3 (or 22...Wb7) 23 cxb3 Rxb3 24 Nb5 Rb4 25 Rdh1 (25 Wc2 Wb7) 25...Rxa4 26 Nc3 Rxd4! 27 Wxd4 Nh5 28 Wd2 a4 threatening ...a3, and Black has a real attack, Mallee-Mikhailov, corr. Wch 1977-83.

22...Bxf6 23 Nd5 Bxd5 24 Wxd5 Ra6!

Preparing to triple the rooks and queen on the b-file, and also to play ...e6.

25 f4 e6 26 Wd3 Rab6 27 Rh3 Rxa4

Intending ...Rab4 and ...a4.

28 f5 d5! 29 fxe6 We5

The point: White's queenside is collapsing.

30 exf7+ ⌷f8 31 c3

Best but depressing is 31 ♕c3 ♕xc3 32 bxc3 ♖xe4 33 ♔a2 ♖e2.

31...♖xb3 32 exd5 ♖ab4! 33 ♖d2 ♕e1+ 34 ♔a2 ♕c1 0-1

A cute finish would be 35 ♕e2 ♖a3+!.

Soltis Variation

1 e4 c5 2 ♘f3 d6 3 d4 cxd4 4 ♘xd4 ♘f6 5 ♘c3 g6 6 ♗e3 ♗g7 7 f3 0-0 8 ♕d2 ♘c6 9 ♗c4 ♗d7 10 0-0-0 ♖c8 11 ♗b3 ♘e5 12 h4 h5 *(D)*

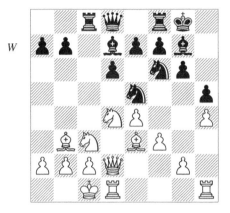

This is the Soltis Variation, the most frequently played line of the Yugoslav Attack. Black simply stops White's pawn advance and dares him to break down Black's own defences before getting overrun on the queenside. The typical Dragon themes that we showed in the first game still apply, so we'll discuss a few additional ideas as we go along. Remember that this is a non-technical inquiry that undertakes to instruct by example.

Anand – Kasparov
New York Wch (11) 1995

13 ⌷b1

A rather slow move, although White prepares to meet 13...♕a5 by 14 ♘d5!.

Instead, 13 g4?! lets Black break up White's centre way before his king feels any danger: 13...hxg4 14 h5 ♘xh5 15 ♗h6 e6 (cutting off White's bishop and opening up a diagonal for Black's queen) 16 ♖dg1 ♕f6 17 ♗xg7 (17 fxg4? ♗xh6 18 ♕xh6 ♕f4+ 19 ♕xf4 ♘xf4 20 ♖f1 g5 is positionally killing) 17...♕xg7 18

fxg4 ♘f6 19 ♖h4 ♖fd8! 20 ♖gh1 ♘exg4 and Black has extra material and all the key squares, Valeriani-Raty, corr. 1985.

13...♘c4 14 ♗xc4 ♖xc4 *(D)*

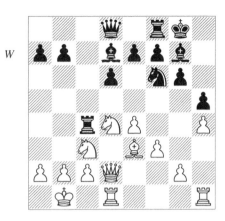

15 ♘de2

The best attribute of ...h5 is that White has to prepare so long to play an effective g4; for instance, 15 g4?! hxg4 16 h5 ♘xh5 17 ♖dg1 ♕c8! 18 fxg4 ♗xg4 19 ♘d5 ♖e8 20 ♖h4 e6! 21 ♘c3 f5! 22 ♘db5 ♕c6 and Black had a clear material and positional advantage in Hardicsay-Herndl, Oberwart 1984.

Another option for White is 15 ♘b3 ♕c7 16 ♗d4 *(D)*, the plan that we saw in the last section, with Black a 'tempo' ahead due to playing ...♕c7 in one move rather than two (...♕a5-c7).

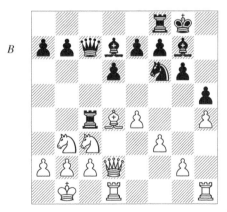

Play is fairly balanced; e.g., 16...♗c6 17 g4!? (17 ♕e3 ♘d7!? 18 ♗xg7 ♔xg7 19 g4! hxg4 20 h5 ♘f6 21 ♘d4 ♗d7 22 hxg6 fxg6 23 ♕h6+ is a little scary but probably all right for Black) 17...e5! 18 ♗e3 hxg4 19 h5 gxf3! 20 h6

♘xe4! 21 ♘xe4! ♗xe4 22 hxg7 ♖xc2! 23 gxf8♕+ ♔xf8 24 ♔a1 ♖xd2 25 ♘xd2 ♗d5 26 ♘b1 ♗e6, Pieretti-Perilli, corr. 1985. Probably Black's pawns should outweigh all those pieces!

15...b5 16 ♗h6

Short but tension-filled was 16 e5!? dxe5 17 ♗g5 ♖c7 18 ♗xf6 exf6 19 g4 ♕e8 20 gxh5 ♗e6 21 ♖dg1 b4 22 ♘e4 f5 23 h6 fxe4 24 hxg7 ♔xg7 25 h5 ♗xa2+! 26 ♔xa2 ♕a4+ 27 ♔b1 ♖d8 28 ♕xd8 ♖xc2+ 29 ♔a1 ♕a4+ ½-½ Liberzon-Miles, Haifa OL 1976.

16...♕a5 17 ♗xg7 ♔xg7 18 ♘f4 ♖fc8 19 ♘cd5 ♕xd2 20 ♖xd2 ♘xd5 21 ♘xd5 ♔f8

The game is equal.

To wrap up the Dragon section, we'll explore two games, each one featuring a move by White's dark-squared bishop.

Short – Fleck
Bundesliga 1986/7

13 ♗h6 *(D)*

For years this natural continuation was considered the real test of 12...h5, and it arguably did more for the Soltis Variation than anything else because of the great games it produced. The conventional wisdom is that Black, if well prepared, has nothing to fear.

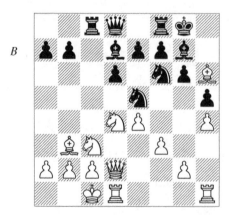

13...♘c4

The popular alternative 13...♗xh6 14 ♕xh6 ♖xc3 15 bxc3 features your customary exchange sacrifice again, which is risky but has a respectable standing. For example, 15...♕c7 (15...♕a5 and 15...♕c8 are also possible – refer to the books for pages of games and analysis on

this stuff) 16 ♔b1 ♖c8 (or 16...b5) 17 ♘e2 a5 18 ♖d4 (18 ♘f4! is an excellent alternative). Now in Cabanas Bravo-Semprun, 2004, Black found the nice idea 18...a4! 19 ♗xa4 ♗xa4 20 ♖xa4 ♕b6+ 21 ♖b4 ♕f2 with complications generally in his favour. I'll just give the raw moves: 22 ♘f4 ♖xc3 23 ♖c1 ♖xc2 24 ♘h3? (24 ♖xb7) 24...♖xc1+ 25 ♕xc1 ♕xg2 26 ♘g5, and now Black had 26...♘d3! 27 ♕c8+ ♔g7 28 ♕xb7 ♘xb4 29 ♕xb4 ♕h1+ 30 ♔c2 ♕xh4, winning.

14 ♗xc4 ♖xc4 15 ♗xg7 ♔xg7 16 ♔b1

16 ♘d5 e5! *(D)* is strangely logical, in spite of giving up d5 as a permanent outpost and exposing the d6-pawn to attack!

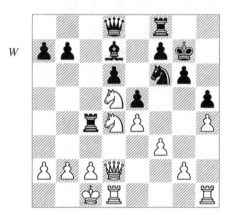

Since Black has traded off his g7-bishop, he can place his central pawns on dark squares. Ridding himself of the well-placed knight on d4 hurts White's queenside defensive prospects and is worth a pawn if necessary; for instance, 17 ♘e2 ♘xd5 18 ♕xd5 ♗e6! 19 ♕xd6 ♕a5 20 a3 ♖fc8 21 c3 ♖4c6 22 ♕b4 ♕a6 23 ♖d2 ♖b6 with a powerful attack, Westerinen-H.Müller, Germany tt 1989/90.

16...♕a5 17 ♘b3 ♕c7

17...♕e5! is probably better.

18 g4!? hxg4 19 h5 gxf3 20 ♖dg1! ♖g8! 21 hxg6 fxg6 22 ♘d5 ♕d8 23 ♘d4 e6 24 ♘f4

and White has a dangerous attack.

Ivanchuk – Topalov
Belgrade 1995

13 ♗g5 *(D)*

We already discussed the virtues of this continuation in the introductory remarks to the

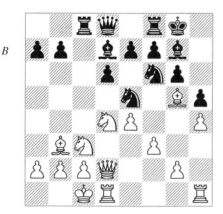

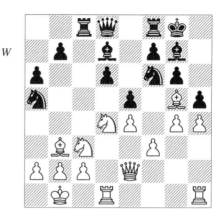

Yugoslav Attack. I should note that, along with the idea of being able to sidestep ♗xc4 after ...♘c4, there is a similar idea connected with the move ...♘g4. As a response to f4 (or even as the second move of the sacrificial device ...♗xg4), ...♘g4 will not gain a crucial tempo on the dark-squared bishop because it has gone to g5.

At present 13 ♗g5 is considered the main line of the Soltis 12 h4 h5 variation and the themes are useful to study.

13...♖c5!

The move that salvaged Black's cause in the Soltis Variation. It is useful in several ways:

a) It protects the 4th rank against advances by f4 and e5.

b) It opens up the possibility of a sacrifice on g5 to eliminate the crucially-important bishop.

c) The rook helps to defend b5, sometimes as a preliminary to ...b5.

d) Black prepares to double rooks on the c-file.

White has several options and there are countless games from this position connected with intricate analysis by many strong masters. At this point if Black plays 13...♘c4, White can take advantage of the absence of his bishop from e3 to play 14 ♕e2. Then 14...♘a5 15 ♔b1 a6? illustrates how one slight error in these lines can land you in terrible trouble: 16 g4! e5 *(D)*.

17 gxh5!! exd4 18 ♘d5 ♘xb3 19 h6!! ♗b5 20 ♕h2 d3 21 cxb3 ♘xd5 22 hxg7 ♖c2 23 ♗xd8 ♖xd8 24 ♖d2 1-0 Nunn-Mestel, London 1986. I like these old games; they seem so innocent and refreshing!

14 g4 hxg4 15 f4!

15 h5 appears to let Black get through on the queenside before White can do the same on the other wing, but it's a close call and could change with one new move. The play can degenerate into a primitive slugfest; for example: 15...♘xh5 16 ♘d5 ♖e8 (16...♖xd5! 17 ♗xd5 ♕b6 is another course) 17 f4 ♘c4 18 ♕f2!? b5 19 f5 a5 20 ♕h4 ♖xd5! 21 exd5 ♘xb2! 22 fxg6 fxg6 23 ♘c6 ♕b6 24 ♖de1 a4 25 ♗e3? ♕c7 26 ♕g5 axb3 27 axb3 ♘d3+! 28 cxd3 ♗xc6 29 ♔d1 ♖a8 30 ♗f4 e5! 31 ♕xg6 ♗xd5 32 ♖xh5 ♗f3+ 33 ♔d2 ♖a2+ 34 ♔e3 exf4+ 35 ♔xf4 ♕f7+ 36 ♕xf7+ ♔xf7 37 ♖f5+ ♗f6 38 ♖c1 ♔g6 0-1 Kravtsov-Soloviov, St Petersburg 1999. Fun stuff.

15...♘c4 16 ♕e2 *(D)*

A popular move at the time of writing, but 16 ♕d3 has hundreds of games and truckloads of analysis to its credit.

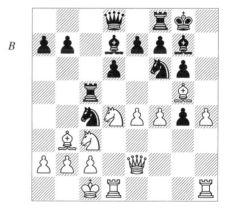

16...♕c8

16...♘a5!? 17 e5 ♘xb3+ 18 ♘xb3 ♖xc3 19 bxc3 ♗c6! is a wild line that appears to be dynamically equal, the high-level stem game going 20 ♖hf1 ♘e4 21 ♕c4 d5 22 ♕xe4!? dxe4 23 ♖xd8 ♖xd8 24 ♗xe7 ♖d7 25 ♗g5 ♗f8 26 ♘d4 ♗c5 27 f5 ♖xd4 28 cxd4 gxf5 29 ♖xf5 ♖xd4 30 ♗e3 ♖a4 31 ♖g5+ ♔h7 32 ♖h5+ ♔g8 33 ♖g5+ ½-½ Smirin-Ivanchuk, Paris 1994.

17 ♗xf6

Typical tactics arise from 17 f5 ♘xb2! 18 ♔xb2 ♖xc3! 19 fxg6! ♖xb3+! 20 axb3 fxg6 21 ♖he1 ♕c5 and things are still unclear, Fogarasi-Palkovi, Budapest 1996.

17...♗xf6 18 ♘d5 ♖xd5!?

Another exchange sacrifice! This one eliminates White's best piece and allows Black's mighty bishop to survive. There are also games with 18...b5!?, allowing 19 ♘xf6+ (paradoxically, letting the bishop live by 19 h5 g5! 20 ♗xc4 bxc4 21 ♕e3 ♖xd5 22 exd5 is White's best try) 19...exf6 20 h5 g5 *(D)*.

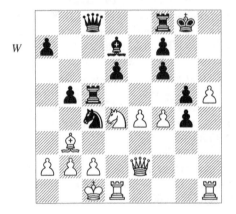

In modern chess you basically play what works! You'd think that giving up your most important piece in the middle of getting attacked would be suicidal, but the specifics of the resulting odd-looking pawn-structure actually hold up. White can't seem to make progress; e.g., 21 ♕f2 ♕d8! 22 h6 ♕e7 23 ♖de1 gxf4 24 ♕xf4 ♕e5 25 ♕f2 g3! 26 ♕g1 ♕f4+ 27 ♔b1 ♘d2+ 28 ♔a1 ♘xe4 and Black has a winning game, Kasarova-Krasilnikova, Ekaterinburg 1997.

19 exd5 b5 20 h5? *(D)*

Even though Black's had plenty of options in the notes, White could show that he's still on the right track by playing 20 ♗xc4! bxc4 21 c3!, when he stays material up and may well be able to consolidate and/or keep up the attack.

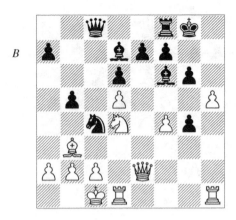

20...g5! 21 fxg5 ♗xg5+ 22 ♔b1 f5! 23 ♖d3 f4 24 ♗xc4 ♕xc4 0-1

Ivanchuk is known for resigning early. Nevertheless, in the hands of a player like Topalov the pawns and bishops will definitely win in the end. This is another relatively old game between world-class players that shows how paradoxical and counterintuitive the best play in the Dragon can be. Don't think that you can depend upon this section as reliably up-to-date theory, because that is always changing. Instead, it is intended to be a set of noteworthy schemes and tactics.

Najdorf Variation

1 e4 c5 2 ♘f3 d6 3 d4 cxd4 4 ♘xd4 ♘f6 5 ♘c3 a6 *(D)*

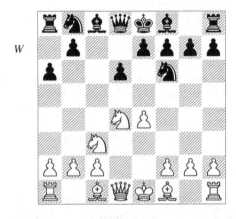

Whereas the Dragon Variation may have the most appeal to the average player, the Najdorf Sicilian has been the favourite opening of top-level players for many years now. Part of this was certainly the influence of World Champions Fischer and Kasparov, consistent devotees of the variation. There is also the inherent complexity and diversity of the Najdorf concepts and themes, to some extent in contrast to the *relatively* straightforward ideas of the Sicilian Dragon. White has a large variety of absolutely independent systems available for choosing, and Black can respond with varying basic structures. The Najdorf has an especially fluid character: again in contrast to the Dragon, we see more central breaks to go along with flank attacks, and in most variations the centre ultimately plays as large a role as the attacking formations on either side of the board.

What is that magical little move 5...a6 all about? First of all, flexibility, which is perhaps the most valuable asset in modern openings. As the move 4...a6 does in the Paulsen Sicilian (1 e4 c5 2 ♘f3 e6 3 d4 cxd4 4 ♘xd4 a6), so Black's 5...a6 in the Najdorf makes an implicit challenge to his opponent. White has played five unexceptionable moves (e4, ♘f3, d4, ♘xd4 and ♘c3), which essentially tell Black nothing about what he is up to. But now it is time for White to commit one of his bishops, which by defining the play will allow Black to respond accordingly. The development of White's light-squared bishop is particularly meaningful in that regard. If it goes to e2, then Black might play ...e5, which would not be highly recommended in the Dragon or Taimanov Sicilians, for instance. If White's bishop ends up on c4, Black can block the bishop by ...e6, and so forth. Similarly, a dark-squared bishop on e3 or g5 will require different strategies from Black.

For all that, 5...a6 is fundamentally slow and simply invites White to go on an offensive. Thus the Najdorf is a risky system in which the slightest inaccuracy can spell disaster. But as Kasparov says, 'High risks mean high rewards', adding that with the Najdorf, Black will usually get a chance to seize the initiative at some point. But he cautions that any generalizations about strategy need to be supported by thorough homework.

We shall investigate 6 ♗g5, 6 ♗c4, 6 ♗e2 and 6 ♗e3.

The continuation 6 f4 is rare these days. One idea that demonstrates a basic Sicilian theme is

6...e5 7 ♘f3 ♘bd7 8 a4 (versus ...b5) 8...♗e7 9 ♗d3 0-0 10 0-0 (*D*).

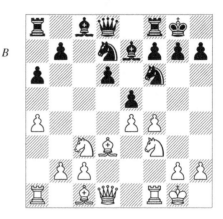

Now with 10...exf4!? Black strives to control the e5-square in return for d5. This is the quintessential Sicilian strategy, since it provides an outpost on e5 at the same time that it opens up the e-file and the h8-a1 diagonal in support of that square. But White gets something from the deal too: he gains the key d4-square (usually for a knight), gets an open f-file, and may be able to put pressure on d6 more effectively because of a bishop that occupies f4. These trade-offs have to be constantly evaluated when Black considers whether to play – and White considers whether to allow – the capture ...exf4. Of course Black has other moves which we won't elaborate upon here, notably 10...♕c7 and 10...♘c5. After 10...exf4, White plays 11 ♔h1! (after 11 ♗xf4 Black takes the pawn and lives to tell the tale: 11...♕b6+ 12 ♔h1 ♕xb2) 11...♘e5 12 ♗xf4 ♕c7 13 ♕d2 ♗e6 14 ♘d4 ♖fe8!? and now:

a) 15 ♘f5!? could be answered by 15...♗xf5 16 exf5 d5! with active play in return for the bishop-pair; nevertheless, this line is unclear. 15...♗f8 16 ♗g5 ♘fd7 is also possible, but then 17 a5! (to keep a knight out of b6) 17...f6 18 ♗f4 ♖ac8 19 ♘e3! gets a knight to d5 with some advantage. The odyssey of the knight from f3 to d5 in four moves brings to mind ♘bd2-f1-e3-d5 in the Closed Ruy Lopez. It also shows that giving up d4 to a centralized piece can have more than the obvious consequences.

b) 15 ♗xe5 dxe5 16 ♘xe6 fxe6 (*D*).

We see this structure in several Sicilian lines, and also in other openings where the move

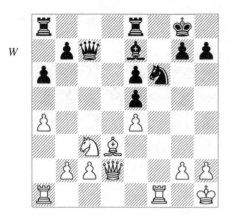

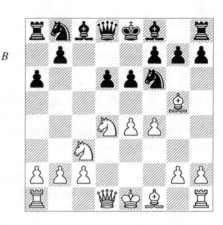

&xe6 or ...&xe3 occurs, or even ♘g5 and ♘xe6. Black's pawns protect the key central squares d5 and d4, as well as f5 and f4. In such positions the key questions are whether the pawns can be attacked (they are unsupported by other pawns) and who has the better pieces. Mainly because of the relative strengths of the bishops, I prefer Black. Of course this is just one example, not a verdict!

The ♗g5 Attack

6 ♗g5

White's predominant choice for years was this direct attacking line, and it is still the choice of many experts. White wants to play f4 followed by pawn-breaks like e5 or f5 if allowed. Since Black usually prevents those, White's main set-up begins with ♕f3 and 0-0-0. We shall see the associated themes as we go along. In the meantime Black plays ...e6 followed by what are the most typical Najdorf moves ...♘bd7, ...♕c7, ...b5 and ...♗b7, usually but not always with an early ...♗e7. Again, the standard set-ups will appear with examples.

6...e6 7 f4 (D)

This is the most direct attacking scheme that you will see in the Najdorf and has led to crazy sacrificial brilliancies for both sides for years. Three games will follow, and since the variations are so tactical and diverse, I shall lean towards recent examples and stay at least within shooting distance of current theory. Again, only specific study of concrete variations will let you truly master 6 ♗g5, whether White or Black. It should be said, however, that if you can pick up some of the ideas that

repeat themselves you will have a good headstart.

There are of course many ways in which the play can develop. Most of them have White either attacking on the kingside or in the centre. In both cases he will resort to piece sacrifices whenever they are useful or necessary, because the pawns alone won't generally be enough to break down Black's position. Black has some interesting counterattacking ideas on the kingside, but will usually proceed with a basic plan of development followed by central and queenside attacks. Or he can leap into action by playing the so-called Poisoned Pawn Variation and grabbing material. I'll outline these possibilities in a few games.

Sulskis – Pelletier
Warsaw Ech 2005

7...♗e7 8 ♕f3 ♕c7 9 0-0-0 ♘bd7 10 g4
Or:

a) After 10 ♕g3 Black has a key defensive manoeuvre that comes up again and again: 10...h6 11 ♗h4 g5! *(D)*.

12 fxg5 ♘h5 (12...♖g8 has also equalized, quickly recovering the pawn) 13 ♕e3 ♕c5! (this attacks g5 for the third time) 14 ♔b1 (14 ♕d2 ♗xg5 15 ♗xg5 ♕xg5 16 ♗e2 ♘hf6 17 ♘f3 ♕xd2+ 18 ♖xd2 ♔e7 is equal) 14...hxg5 15 ♗f2 ♘e5. Here is the main point of ...g5: Black counts upon this knight to hold everything together. Kengis-Vitolinš, Jurmala 1983 continued 16 ♕d2 ♕c7 17 ♘f3 b5! 18 ♗e3 (18 ♘xg5 gives Black good queenside play after 18...b4 19 ♘a4 ♗b7 20 ♘b6 ♖b8) 18...g4 19 ♘xe5 dxe5 20 ♗d3 ♘f4 21 ♕f2 ♗b7 with equality.

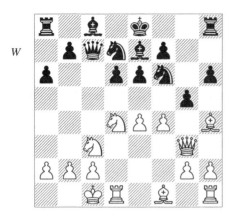

W

b) The same idea can be introduced by 10 ♗d3 h6 11 ♗h4 g5 12 fxg5 ♘e5 13 ♕e2 ♘fg4. This time the queen is better placed on f3 than on g3, so the play is less clear: 14 ♘f3! hxg5 15 ♗g3 ♗d7 16 h3!? (16 ♖df1 would be more like a real test, because Black has to protect his f7-pawn before he can castle; e.g., 16...♘xd3+ 17 ♕xd3 0-0-0!? 18 h3 ♘e5? 19 ♘xe5 dxe5 20 ♖xf7 ♗e8 21 ♖xe7!) 16...♘xf3 17 gxf3 ♘e5 18 f4 gxf4 19 ♗xf4 0-0-0. This pawn-structure is fine for Black, who can now become active with ...♗c6 and perhaps ...f5.

10...b5 11 ♗xf6 ♘xf6 12 g5 ♘d7 *(D)*

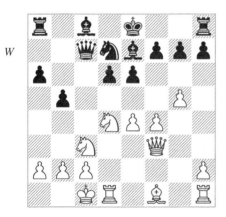

W

A line contested in untold numbers of games throughout the years. We'll outline a few ideas while we follow the main game.

13 ♘f5!?

Hardly the main move; I'll promote it because it's refreshing, and also so that we have something current to mull over. In the Sicilian Defence we see knight sacrifices on b5, d5, e6 and f5, all hoping to break down Black's defences.

The idea is that occupation of d5 is worth a piece if you add to it an attack along an open e-file and dangerous kingside pawns.

For decades 13 f5!? has been the principal continuation (13 a3 is supposed to be met by 13...♖b8 and ...b4). I'll give some illustrative lines (and not necessarily best play): 13...♘c5 (13...♗xg5+ has also been tested for years and it seems that White has more than enough for his temporary pawn loss; to emphasize the degree of specific study surrounding these lines, I'll note John Emms's reference to the case of one grandmaster losing to another because of a novelty on move 28 that produced a brilliant defence on move 31!) and here are two moves:

a) 14 g6!? is a thematic break that is featured all over the Sicilian landscape: 14...hxg6 15 fxg6 fxg6 16 b4!? ♘a4 17 ♘xa4 bxa4 18 e5!? (aggressive, but that doesn't necessarily mean good!) 18...dxe5? *(D)* (18...d5 feels right; Black may even get time for ...♗xb4).

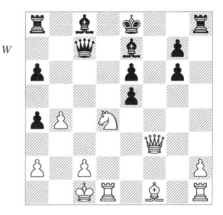

W

19 ♗d3! (19 ♕xa8 exd4 20 ♗xa6 0-0 was Black's idea, after which 21 ♖hf1 is unclear) 19...♗g5+ 20 ♔b1 ♗f4! 21 ♕xa8 exd4 22 ♗xg6+ (White should play 22 ♗xa6!, and this time 22...0-0 23 ♖xd4 doesn't seem to cut it for Black) 22...♔e7 23 ♖hf1!? e5 24 ♕e4 ♕c4 25 ♖xf4! ♕xb4+ ½-½ Markzon-de Firmian, New York Open 1991.

b) 14 f6 gxf6 15 gxf6 ♗f8 16 ♖g1 ♗d7 (16...h5!? 17 ♖g7 b4 18 ♘d5! exd5 19 exd5 is a typical tactic; White has cleared out the e-file and captured the c6-square – whether that's sufficient for a piece has to be decided upon a case-by-case basis) 17 ♖g7 b4 18 ♘d5! exd5 19 exd5 *(D)*.

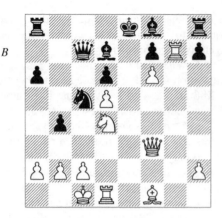

B

The same idea. This time Black can escape the e-file checks by castling, but he's still under attack; for example, 19...0-0-0 20 ♖xf7 ♗h6+ 21 ♔b1 ♖df8 22 ♖xf8+ ♖xf8 23 ♘e6! 1-0 Shmuter-Kaspi, Tel Aviv 1996; Black could play on, but 23...♘xe6 24 dxe6 ♗xe6 25 ♗h3! ♗xh3 (25...♕d7 26 ♕a8+) 26 ♕xh3+ ♕d7 27 ♕xh6 is pretty hopeless.

13...exf5

13...b4!? may be better but this is more illuminating.

14 ♘d5 ♕b7!?

A typical line given by Kosten is 14...♕c5 15 exf5 ♗b7 16 f6! gxf6 17 ♘xf6+! ♗xf6 18 ♕xb7 ♖c8 19 ♗d3 ♗g7 20 ♖he1+ with an unclear attack.

15 ♕c3!

15 exf5? ♘b6 exchanges White's key piece.

15...♘b6 16 ♘xe7!?

Or 16 ♕xg7! ♖f8 17 ♘xe7 ♕xe7 18 ♕d4 ♖b8 19 ♗g2.

16...♔xe7!? 17 ♕xg7 ♗e6 18 exf5 ♗d5 19 ♗h3! *(D)*

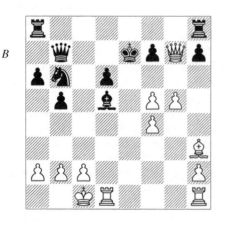

B

Offering a rook.

19...♖ae8!

After 19...♗xh1? 20 f6+ ♔d8 21 ♕xh8+ ♔c7 22 ♕xh7 White wins three pawns and has an ongoing attack for the knight.

20 ♖d3! ♔d8 21 ♖hd1 ♖hg8 22 ♕c3?!

22 ♕f6+! is better.

22...♖e2 23 ♗g4! ♖f2 24 ♕f6+ ♔c8 25 ♕xd6 ♕c7 26 ♖c3 ♗c4 27 b3 ♖xf4 28 h3 ♕xd6 29 ♖xd6 ♔c7 30 ♖f6 ♖xg5

The game is equal and was eventually drawn.

When Black delays ...♗e7, another set of tactics can arise. A couple of these are represented in the course of examining another slugfest:

Kosten – Kr. Georgiev
Saint Affrique 2005

7...♘bd7 8 ♕f3 ♕c7 9 0-0-0 b5 *(D)*

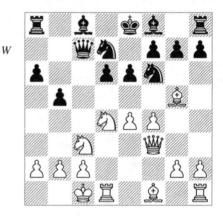

W

10 ♗d3

Here we see the centralization strategy: White ignores the idea of kingside attack by g4 in favour of ♖he1 and potential advances and/or sacrifices in the middle of the board.

10...♗b7

After 10...b4?, we get that sacrifice 11 ♘d5! again, but this time White is simply better after 11...exd5 12 ♖he1! ♗b7 13 exd5+ ♔d8 14 ♘c6+ ♗xc6 15 dxc6.

11 ♖he1 ♕b6!?

The older move 11...♗e7 runs into another ♘d5 idea: 12 ♕g3! b4 13 ♘d5 exd5 14 exd5 (threatening ♘f5) 14...♔d8 (14...g6 15 ♕h4!) 15 ♘c6+! ♗xc6 16 dxc6. This position has been played and analysed extensively by Thomas Luther. I'll just follow a recent game: 16...♘c5 17 ♗h4! ♖g8 18 ♗xh7! ♖h8 19 ♕xg7 ♖xh7 (D).

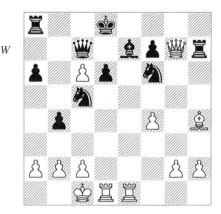

20 ♕xf6! ♖xh4 21 ♕xf7 ♖h8 22 ♖e5! ♖f8!? 23 ♕g7 ♖a7? (23...b3!? is better) 24 ♖xc5 ♕b6 (24...♖xf4 25 ♖c4! ♖xc4? 26 ♕g8+) 25 ♕e5! and White had enough attack to convert to a winning position in B.Vučković-Tadić, Herceg Novi 2005. Of course you needn't study specifics to play the Najdorf, just rely upon general ideas. Right.

12 ♘d5!? (D)

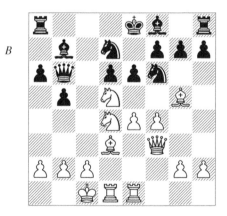

Again! There have been a lot of games between leading grandmasters with other moves, but this move is the scariest for Black.

12...♕xd4!

Or:

a) One simple but very pretty variation is 12...♘xd5? 13 exd5 ♕xd4 14 ♖xe6+! fxe6 15 ♕h5+ g6 16 ♕xg6+ hxg6 17 ♗xg6#.

b) Even nicer is 12...exd5? 13 ♘c6!! (look for this in similar positions!) 13...♗xc6 14 exd5+ ♗e7 15 dxc6 ♘c5 16 ♗xf6 gxf6 17 ♗f5 ♕c7 18 b4! ♘e6 19 ♕h5 ♘g7 20 ♗d7+ ♔f8 21 ♕h6, Chiburdanidze-Dvoirys, Tallinn 1980.

13 ♗xf6 gxf6 14 ♗xb5! ♕c5 15 ♘xf6+ ♔d8 16 ♘d7 ♕xb5 17 ♘xf8 ♖xf8 18 ♕a3 ♖c8! 19 ♕xd6+ ♔e8 20 ♖e3 ♖g8?

A fatal mistake. Nevertheless, 20...♕c6 21 ♕d2 leaves White with three pawns and a nice attack for the bishop.

21 ♖c3 ♗c6 22 f5! ♖xg2 23 fxe6 ♖f2? 24 ♖c5

White is winning.

Poisoned Pawn Variation

1 e4 c5 2 ♘f3 d6 3 d4 cxd4 4 ♘xd4 ♘f6 5 ♘c3 a6 6 ♗g5 e6 7 f4 ♕b6 (D)

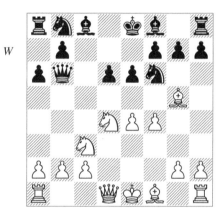

This is an astonishing move that those raised with classical chess principles would simply reject as a typical beginner's mistake. Black goes running after a pawn when he is undeveloped and already under attack. What's worse, he does so with the queen, which you're not supposed to bring out too early because it will lose time.

8 ♕d2 ♕xb2 9 ♖b1

Sometimes White plays 9 ♘b3 instead, but we'll stick with the overwhelming favourite.

9...♕a3 (D)

Now it's White's move and he has perfect attacking squares for his pieces; in addition, after White castles he will very likely put his rook on an open f-file after the normal advances e5 or

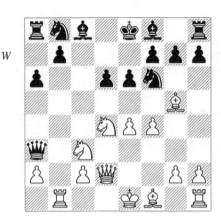

W

f5. His other rook is already on an open file and after ♖b3 (with tempo!) it can swing along the third rank and attack where needed – this is a standard theme in many openings, by the way. Thus every white piece will be participating in an attack against an opponent with almost no pieces out and no safe place for his king. For Black, this is a sure recipe for disaster.

Or is it? In fact, the Poisoned Pawn Variation has been taken seriously for well over four decades now and has survived countless attempts to refute it. In the meantime, Black's outrageous pawn theft has played a considerable role in revolutionizing chess theory and practice. Under the leadership of World Champions Fischer and Kasparov, players began to realize that Black could play this and similar positions with every expectation of success. Why? There are several general answers, but three stand out:

a) The queen on a3, although subject to further attack, is also an attacking piece, able to tie White down to protecting his own position and prevent him from straying at will. Older theory would say (at least when the queen sortie is being contemplated) that most pawn raids with the queen would have to be accompanied by other retreating moves by her to get back to safety. But now there are plenty of situations in openings where a queen retains her position in the enemy camp, saves time, serves a useful function, and says 'Show me'. Computer analysis has assisted in finding new examples.

b) Black has no weaknesses! White, on the other hand, has a problem that we often refer to in this book: internal weaknesses, especially those on the third rank. The main one here is on the c3-square, adjacent to the centre

and unprotected by a pawn, and the central square e3 also qualifies. In addition, the fourth-rank squares c4 and e4 turn out to be vulnerable, especially significant since a white bishop on c4 would be loose. Even d4, although potentially able to be protected by a pawn on c3, can be shaky in practice. In this variation, weaknesses tend to mean loose pieces and potential outposts for the enemy.

c) Central pawn-majority. It cannot be overstressed what Black's strongest weapon is in the Sicilian Defence: his extra central pawn, which in the main line of the Poisoned Pawn Variation sometimes becomes a central pawn-mass capable of giving exceptional protection to Black's king and pieces.

Having said that, the most important point to remember is something that Kasparov eternally stresses: this variation depends upon specific tricks and tactics for both sides, and there is no overriding reason that White's attack *shouldn't* win, nor that Black's defence shouldn't prevail; to a large extent the result is just the way things work out.

We'll examine one game and a bundle of notes from the key position after 9...♕a3.

Thinius – Kersten
Bad Zwesten 2006

10 f5!

The modern continuation. White doesn't fully burn his bridges as he does in the old and extremely natural line 10 e5 dxe5 11 fxe5 ♘fd7 12 ♗c4 *(D)*, in which White is blasting open so many lines and developing so quickly that it's amazing Black can survive. But Fischer and others demonstrated that he does so and then some.

Now 12...♘xe5? goes too far after 13 ♘xe6, but Black has no fewer than three satisfactory moves, at least two apparently leading to an advantage for Black in a position that at first was considered close to a forced win for White!

a) Fischer and others used 12...♕a5 with success; its theory has advanced considerably and the verdict seems to be dynamic equality.

b) One classic line goes 12...♗b4 13 ♖b3 ♕a5 14 0-0 0-0 15 ♗f6!? (15 ♘xe6?! fxe6 16 ♗xe6+ ♔h8 17 ♖xf8+ ♗xf8 18 ♕f4 ♘c6! 19 ♕f7 ♕c5+ 20 ♔h1 ♘f6! 21 ♗xc8 ♘xe5 22

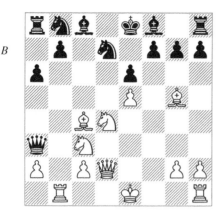

B

♕e6 ♘eg4 0-1 Tringov-Fischer, Havana 1965) 15...♘xf6 16 exf6 (formerly considered a draw) 16...♖d8! 17 ♖xb4 ♕xb4 18 ♕g5 g6 19 ♘xe6 (19 ♕h6 ♕f8) 19...♗xe6 20 ♗xe6 ♕xc3! 21 ♗xf7+ ♔xf7 22 ♕h6 ♘c6 23 ♕xh7+ ♔e6 24 ♕xg6 ♕d4+ 25 ♔h1 ♖f8! 26 ♖e1+ ♔d6 27 ♕g3+ ♔c5 28 c3 ♕xf6 0-1 Ballester-Monteau, French Cht 2002.

c) According to modern theory, 12...♕c5! is probably best of all, attacking those weaknesses that we discussed and pretty much forcing 13 ♗xe6 fxe6 14 ♘xe6 ♕xe5+ 15 ♕e3 ♗d6!, when White is coming up short.

10...♘c6 11 fxe6 fxe6 12 ♘xc6 bxc6 13 e5!

White had better strike fast in order to open lines and weaken Black's effective central defenders.

13...dxe5

The most popular line, establishing a central pawn-mass with which to defend the king. That said, there is a long history behind 13...♘d5. One line out of hundreds goes 14 ♘xd5 cxd5 15 ♗e2 dxe5 16 0-0 *(D)*.

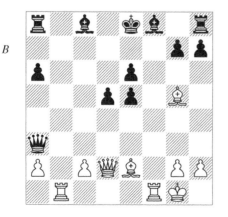

B

Now:

a) 16...♗c5+?! 17 ♔h1 ♖f8 18 c4 ♖xf1+ 19 ♖xf1 ♗b7 20 ♕c2! (not 20 ♗g4? dxc4 and Black defended by ...♕d3 and won easily in Fischer-Geller, Monte Carlo 1967) 20...e4 21 ♗g4 ♗e7 22 ♕f2 winning for White, Tal-Bogdanović, Budva 1967.

b) 16...♖a7! 17 c4 ♕c5+ 18 ♔h1 d4 19 ♗h5+ g6 20 ♗d1! with a powerful attack that keeps Black's king running around in the centre; e.g., 20...♗e7 21 ♗a4+ ♔d8 22 ♗f7 (22 ♗xe7+ ♖xe7 23 ♕g5 ♔c7 24 ♖fe1 is unclear) 22...h6 23 ♗xh6 e4 24 ♗e3 e5 25 ♗g5 e3 26 ♗xe3 and Black is struggling, Grijalva-B.Gonzalez, Internet ICC 2000.

14 ♗xf6 gxf6 15 ♘e4 ♗e7

Maybe 15...♕xa2 16 ♖d1 ♗e7 17 ♗e2 0-0 is also adequate. After some 15 more moves of analysis and game tests, it apparently draws no matter which of several attacking methods White uses!

16 ♗e2 *(D)*

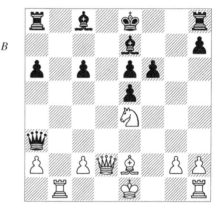

B

16...h5

This stops ♗h5+. Gipslis-Korchnoi, USSR Ch (Leningrad) 1963 shows how delicate Black's situation is: 16...0-0? 17 ♖b3 ♕a4 18 c4 ♔h8 19 0-0 ♖a7 20 ♕h6 f5 21 ♖g3 ♗b4 22 ♘f6 1-0. Mate is unstoppable.

17 ♖f1!?

17 ♖b3 has its own lengthy theory, as does 17 0-0 f5 and now 18 ♖f3 or 18 ♗f3. In both cases Black seems to survive, with draws being the customary result.

17...f5 *(D)*

17...♕xa2 is risky: 18 ♖d1 ♕d5 19 ♕e3 with a strong attack, Radjabov-Ye Jiangchuan, Calvia

OL 2004. The new generation is still finding new ideas in this mess!

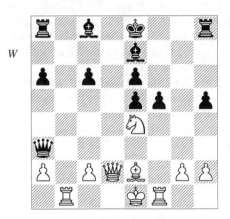

W

18 ℤf3! ♕xa2 19 ℤfb3 ♕a4!

The variations are almost infinite; for example, 19...fxe4 20 ♕c3 (intending ℤa1) 20...♗d8! may hold on, although that is shaky.

20 ♘d6+ ♗xd6 21 ♕xd6

Threatening ℤb7.

21...♕a5+

This position had already been played! In Fernandez Siles-Gamundi Salamanca, Albacete 2004, Black misplaced his queen and lost quickly by 21...♕e4? 22 ℤb7 ♕h4+ 23 g3 ♕d8 24 ♕xe5 ℤh6 25 ♕g7 1-0.

22 ♔f1 ♔f7?!

This attempt to evacuate the king loses. 22...ℤa7! is Kosten's suggestion, using second-rank defence. This move is the key to many lines.

23 ℤb7+! ♔g6 24 ♕e7!

Improving upon yet another game, where the inferior 24 ℤc7? had been played.

24...♗xb7 25 ♕xe6+ ♔g5 26 ♕e7+ ♔g6 27 ♕d6+ ♔g5 28 h4+ ♔f4 29 ♔f2! 1-0

Black is helpless in the face of 30 g3+ or 30 ℤb4+.

I'm sure that all this back-and-forth activity will persist for years to come. The theoretical result is probably a draw, but the practical outcome depends heavily upon one's preparation.

Najdorf Sozin Attack

1 e4 c5 2 ♘f3 d6 3 d4 cxd4 4 ♘xd4 ♘f6 5 ♘c3 a6 6 ♗c4 *(D)*

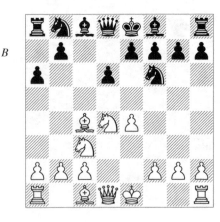

B

The name 'Sozin' is connected with ♗c4 in both the Najdorf and the Classical lines, so I'll designate 6 ♗c4 as the Najdorf Sozin. Although this direct bishop development has never been as popular as 6 ♗g5, and in these days not as popular as 6 ♗e3, it is still used successfully by loyal adherents. The play after 6 ♗c4 divides into a set of positional and primarily tactical lines, so I'll treat it that way. It's probably fair to say that the slower lines tend to end up in equality or even in Black's favour because of his long-term advantages, but the more numerous dynamic lines are much harder to assess, with beautiful tactics seemingly the rule rather than the exception.

Black almost always plays ...e6 (usually 6...e6) in order to restrict the scope of the c4-bishop. After that White has to be careful about the move ...d5 or ...♘xe4 followed by a ...d5 fork, so he will retreat his bishop to b3. That's the basic position from which strategies are formed, as we shall see.

6...e6

6...♘xe4? walks into 7 ♕h5! with multiple threats, when the best that Black can do is 7...d5! 8 ♗xd5 ♘d6. Then, however, White plays 9 0-0 and Black has trouble getting his pieces out, since ...e6 is met by a capture on that square and ...g6 by ♕e5.

Players often wonder why Black doesn't simply attack the bishop right away with the useful move 6...b5. One problem is that the b-pawn advance is committal; since ...e6 will doubtless be played anyway, Black may not want White to know on what basis he will set up his attack. Velimirović-Mrdja, Yugoslavia 1984 went 7 ♗b3 (7 ♗d5!? is also very interesting because 7...♘xd5 8 exd5 yields a structure that is almost always favourable to White, so Black might try 7...♖a7!?, and if 8 ♗e3, then 8...♖c7!?) 7...♗b7 (7...e6 transposes to a main line) 8 ♗e3!? (or 8 ♕e2; or 8 0-0 b4 9 ♘d5 ♘xe4? 10 ♖e1 ♘c5 11 ♗g5! – White has too many pieces out) 8...♘bd7 9 f4 ♘c5 10 0-0! (10 e5 dxe5 11 fxe5 ♘xb3 12 axb3 ♗xg2!). White's 10th move introduces a type of e-pawn sacrifice that has dozens of variants and forms. Sometimes it works and sometimes it doesn't. The positional basis consists of a lead in development, the opening of White's e-file, and Black's difficulties in proceeding with his own development. This particular game continued 10...♘fxe4 11 ♘xe4 ♗xe4 (11...♘xe4 12 f5) 12 f5! (stopping both ...e6 and ...g6) 12...♘xb3 13 axb3 ♕d7 14 ♕g4! ♗d5 (14...d5 15 c4) 15 ♖f2 g6 16 c4! (it seems that in almost every game with this kind of attack White needs to open up another front) 16...bxc4 17 bxc4 gxf5 18 ♘xf5 ♗b7 19 ♗d4 e5 20 ♗b6 f6 21 ♖d1 d5 22 cxd5 ♕f7 23 ♖c2 ♕g6 24 ♕a4+ ♔f7 25 ♕d7+ ♔g8 26 ♖d3 1-0.

7 ♗b3 *(D)*

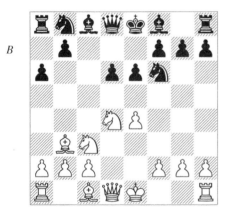

The starting position for most variations. If White plays f4-f5 and Black responds with ...e5, the argument revolves around occupation of the d5-square. Should White succeed in exploiting it as a pure outpost, he will probably stand better. When Black can prevent a piece from establishing itself there or gain compensating advantages, his natural Sicilian attack on the queenside will usually come into play. The variations that top players such as Fischer entered into (he played both sides of 6 ♗c4) were primarily positional and revolved around these factors.

As in many Najdorf variations, if White plays f4 and e5 (instead of f5) the game will often turn very tactical, and White may have to shift his strategy to piece sacrifices before his advanced central pawn falls. Those lines are very position-specific and exciting. Alternatively, White sometimes foregoes f4 altogether and simply brings his pieces out. This has become a very popular strategy, although it contradicts what for years was the conventional wisdom, i.e. that the b3-bishop ran into a brick wall at e6 and that it took pawn advances to remedy that.

We'll follow various games from this position. I'll show a lot of tactical ideas which are fairly universal in their character and apply elsewhere, but there will also be some purely unique and creative combining for your enjoyment. Dynamic attacking play is what has always drawn the average player to the Najdorf Sozin.

Morozevich – Agrest
St Petersburg Z 1993

7...♗e7 8 f4

Other common continuations are 8 0-0 and 8 ♗e3.

8...b5!?

This natural move allows a typical tactical sequence although Black is used to such things in the Najdorf. His main alternative is 8...0-0, when 9 0-0 is usual; a fairly obscure continuation is 9 f5!? exf5 (9...e5 10 ♘de2 and White will have an easier time of controlling d5 with Black having castled and he not having done so) 10 exf5 d5 11 0-0 ♘c6 12 ♔h1! with a quite interesting isolated d-pawn position. White doesn't have the usual restraint on Black's centre, but his advanced pawn interferes with Black's customary IQP activity.

9 e5! dxe5 10 fxe5 ♘fd7 11 ♗xe6!? *(D)*

This thematic sacrifice pervades the 6 ♗c4 lines, and also occurs in the Classical Sicilian and even in the English Attack (usually via g4-g5, ♗h3 and ♗xe6). When it works, it is the ultimate triumph of the bishop over its nemesis on e6. In this situation, objectively, maybe White should prefer 11 ♕g4 with the idea 11...♕c7 12

♕xg7 ♕xe5+ 13 ♕xe5 ♘xe5 14 ♗f4 and White enjoys a pleasant advantage.

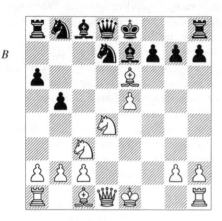

11...♘xe5!

We get to see two of the major themes of the ♗c4 Najdorf: destruction of Black's centre by ♗xe6 and of White's by ...♘xe5. White obtains an overwhelming attack after 11...fxe6?? 12 ♘xe6 ♕a5 (12...♕b6 13 ♘d5!) 13 ♘xg7+ ♔f8 (13...♔d8 14 ♘e6+ ♔e8 15 ♕h5#) 14 0-0+ ♘f6 (14...♔xg7 15 ♕g4+) 15 exf6 ♗c5+ 16 ♔h1, and Black is getting slaughtered.

12 ♗xc8

12 ♗d5!? is another idea.

12...♕xc8 13 ♘d5 ♗c5!

Black gets busy defending his dark-square weaknesses. White was threatening ♘b6 and ♕e2, with secondary ideas of ♗f4 and 0-0.

14 b4!? ♗a7

After 14...♗xd4 15 ♕xd4 ♘bc6 16 ♕c5, Black is tied up and White can develop by ♗f4 or ♗b2 with ideas of castling on either side of the board.

15 ♗f4 ♕d7

15...♕c4 16 ♘f5! ♕e4+ 17 ♕e2 is nicely symmetric. If Black plays 17...♕xd5, 18 ♖d1 wins, but 17...♕xf5 18 g4! drives the queen away from protecting e5.

16 ♗xe5 ♕xd5 17 ♗xg7 ♕xg2 18 ♕e2+ ♕xe2+ 19 ♔xe2 ♗xd4

Probably 19...♖g8 20 ♘f5 ♘c6 improves for Black.

20 ♗xd4 ♖g8 21 a4 ♘c6 22 ♗c5

Although this position is probably within Black's drawing range, White's bishop proved decisively superior to Black's knight in the long run.

Reutsky – Shtyrenkov
Noiabrsk 2003

7...♘bd7

This development has been popular for some years, especially after Kasparov used it versus Short in their world championship match. The knight temporarily prevents e5, but generally it goes to c5 next, from which post it can protect e6 against f4-f5 and eliminate the b3-bishop when Black chooses to do so. White is challenged to find a way to attack Black's solid structure.

8 f4 ♘c5 *(D)*

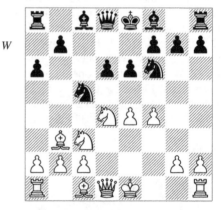

9 ♕f3

White can return to traditional positional play by 9 f5 ♗e7 10 ♕f3! (10 fxe6 was played in many games following Short's example, but then White turned to this developing move, which reserves the idea of exchange on e6, and also prepares g4-g5) 10...0-0 11 ♗e3 (otherwise it's hard to develop) 11...e5 12 ♘de2 ♘xb3 13 axb3 b5 14 g4 (we see the difference between the early days of ♗c4 with f4-f5 and today's version! The advance of the g-pawn changes the entire dynamic of the position) 14...b4 (Black certainly can't wait around for g5 and ♘d5) 15 ♘a4 ♗b7 16 ♘g3 ♕c7!? (the aggressive 16...d5 has also been played, when the battle begins between White's rapid development and Black's central play) 17 0-0-0 ♖ac8 18 ♖d2 d5! (White was again ready for g5 followed by f6 and a kingside attack) 19 g5 d4?! (19...♘xe4! 20 ♘xe4 dxe4 21 ♕g2! f6 22 ♖hd1 is difficult to assess but White has notions of ♘b6-d5) 20 gxf6 dxe3 21 ♕xe3 ♗xf6 22 ♘h5 *(D)*.

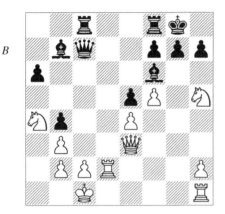

22...♕e7 23 ♖g1 (23 ♖d7 ♗g5!) 23...♖c7 (everything seems to be holding together, but now comes the overloading move) 24 ♘c5! with a nice attack based upon either ♘d7 or ♘xb7 and ♖d5, Vega-Lopez Gomez, corr. 1995.

9...♗e7 10 0-0 0-0 11 ♗e3 ♕c7 12 ♖ae1 ♖e8 13 g4 b5 14 g5 ♘fd7 15 f5

No subtlety here: White goes for the kill but Black gets the wonder square e5. Again positional factors determine the tactical possibilities.

15...♘e5 16 ♕h5 g6 17 ♕h4 ♗f8

Or 17...♘xb3 18 cxb3 b4. Now White can try 18 fxe6!? and ♘d5.

18 fxg6 hxg6 19 ♗d5!? ♗b7 20 ♗xb7 ♕xb7 21 b4 ♘cd7 22 ♖f2 ♖ac8 23 ♘ce2 *(D)*

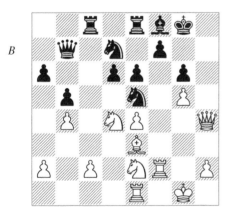

23...♘c4?

Black will get punished for moving this key defender; it's almost impossible to break down such an ideally-placed piece when it's supported by a bishop and another knight. He would stand very well with either 23...♗g7 or 23...♘b6.

24 ♖xf7! ♗g7

Black had probably missed 24...♔xf7 25 ♕h7+ ♔g7 26 ♖f1+ ♔e7 27 ♘xe6!! (instead of 27 ♕xg7+? ♔d8) 27...♔xe6 28 ♕xg7 with mating threats and a quick win.

25 ♖xg7+! ♔xg7 26 ♕h6+ ♔g8 27 ♕xg6+ ♔h8 28 ♘xe6 ♘de5 29 ♗d4 ♕h7 30 ♕f6+ ♔g8 31 ♗xe5 ♘xe5 32 ♘2d4 ♕f7 33 ♖f1 1-0

Resignation seems premature but there follows 33...♕xf6 34 ♖xf6! threatening g6-g7 and Black can't do much about it.

Finally, we get to Black's main move:
7...b5 *(D)*

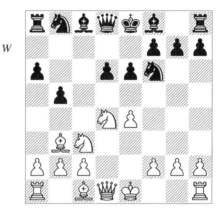

Here are three games with two fundamentally different strategies.

Kristjansson – Tukmakov
Reykjavik 1972

8 f4

This is the traditional pawn attack. White wants to play for f5 and force a response that gives him control of d5. Options that emphasize piece attack are given in the next game.

8...♗b7 9 f5 e5 10 ♘de2 ♗e7

Playing 10...♘bd7 first may be the most precise order; for instance, 11 ♗g5 ♗e7 12 ♘g3 ♖c8! (Black tries to counter White's appropriation of d5 with queenside action) 13 0-0 (13 ♗xf6!? ♘xf6 14 0-0 {14 ♘h5} 14...h5! threatens to win the e-pawn after ...h4) 13...h5! *(D)*.

A fantastic move that directly stops White's only real threat, which was to bring the knight to h5 in order to eliminate another defender of d5. Now White went rapidly downhill: 14 h4? b4 15 ♗xf6 ♗xf6 (15...♘xf6 is also good) 16

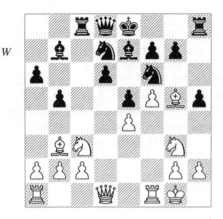

W

♘d5 ♗xh4 17 ♘xh5 ♕g5 (the contest is already over!) 18 f6 g6?! (18...♖xh5! 19 ♖f5 ♗f2+! wins right away due to 20 ♖xf2 ♕h6) 19 ♘g7+ ♔d8 20 ♖f3 ♗g3 21 ♕d3 ♗h2+ 22 ♔f1 ♘c5 23 ♖h3 ♖h4 24 ♕f3 ♘xb3 25 axb3 ♖xh3 26 ♕xh3 ♗xd5 27 exd5 ♕xf6+ 28 ♔e1 ♕f4 0-1 R.Byrne-Fischer, Sousse IZ 1967. A game that went a long way toward discrediting 8 f4.

11 ♘g3!

This move improves upon 11 ♗g5, which as we just saw only assists Black's attack.

11...h5!?

The same idea, but without ♗g5 in, maybe Black is asking for too much. Instead, 11...♘bd7 is natural and probably best.

12 ♕f3?!

White could take over d5 directly by 12 ♗d5! ♘xd5 13 ♘xd5 h4 14 ♘h5.

12...♘bd7 13 ♗g5?

Losing the thread. He should have developed by 13 0-0.

13...h4 14 ♗xf6 ♘xf6 15 ♘ge2 b4 16 ♘d5 ♘xd5 17 exd5 (D)

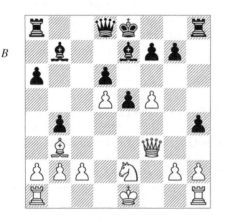

B

In general White won't get much advantage if he has to capture on d5 with a pawn instead of a piece. Here he stands considerably worse.

17...♕b6 18 a3 a5 19 axb4 axb4 20 ♖xa8+ ♗xa8 21 ♕f2 ♕a5! 22 0-0 ♗xd5 23 c4 ♗c6 24 ♖e1 h3 25 g3 ♖h5 26 ♘d4?

Better, but still depressing, would be 26 ♗d1 ♖g5 27 ♘c1 ♗d7!.

26...exd4 0-1

Christiansen – Wojtkiewicz
USA Ch (San Diego) 2006

8 ♕f3 (D)

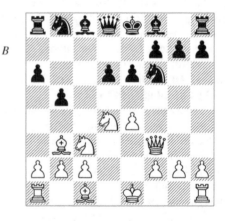

B

Originally no one liked this idea but over the years it has assumed the mantel of 'Main Line'. 8 ♕f3 is less weakening and develops the pieces more quickly than 8 f4.

8...♕c7

8...♕b6 9 ♗e3 ♕b7 is the other conventional defence, slow but perhaps playable.

9 ♗g5 ♘bd7 10 0-0-0

White's moves are very natural but rarely used until recently. This was probably due to Fischer's example; he consistently employed the idea of f4-f5 to break down Black's e6/f7 structure. The logic was that the e6-pawn rendered White's b3-bishop ineffectual, so it had to be eliminated. However, that strategy simply didn't succeed versus accurate play, so White finally turned to a different concept. Pieces can precede pawns in an attack as long as the two ultimately cooperate. The great Tal always seemed to bring his pieces out to active squares before organizing pawn-breaks, if indeed his opponent survived up to that point.

10...♗e7 11 e5! *(D)*

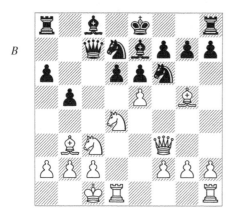

The introduction to a fantastic pawn sacrifice. Before White's idea had always been ♕g3.

11...♗b7 12 ♕g3! ♘xe5

12...dxe5 13 ♗xe6 fxe6 14 ♘xe6 ♕c6 15 ♘xg7+ ♔f7 has also been tried.

13 ♗xe6! fxe6

13...0-0 would bail out. As always, it's very hard to assess things. One line might be 14 ♗xf6 ♗xf6 15 ♘d5 ♕d8 16 ♘xf6+ ♕xf6 17 ♗f5.

14 f4!

The attack peters out after 14 ♘xe6 ♕d7! 15 ♘xg7+ ♔f7.

14...♘g6?!

14...♘c4 is the main test, when 15 ♘xe6 ♕a5!? 16 ♘xg7+ ♔f7 17 ♖he1 needs help from a combination of computers and imagination.

15 ♘xe6 ♕d7 16 ♖he1! ♔f7 17 f5! *(D)*

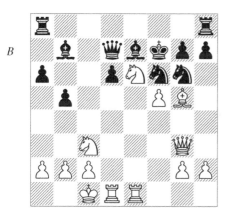

White has just a pawn for his piece, but Black can only watch as his position collapses.

17...♘f8 18 ♗xf6! ♗xf6 19 ♖xd6 ♕c8

Or 19...♕e8 20 ♘xf8 ♕xf8 21 ♖d7+ ♔g8 and one nice win is 22 ♘e4! h6 (22...♗xe4 23 ♕b3+) 23 ♘xf6+ ♕xf6 24 ♖ee7! ♕g5+ 25 ♕xg5 hxg5 26 ♖xg7+ ♔f8 27 ♖df7+ ♔e8 28 ♖xb7, etc.

20 ♘g5+! ♔g8 *(D)*

20...♗xg5+ 21 ♕xg5 is resignable.

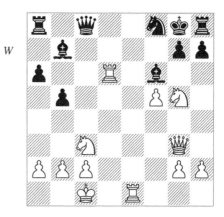

21 ♖xf6 gxf6 22 ♘ge4+

Or 22 ♖e7! ♘g6 23 ♘e6 and ♖g7# follows.

22...♘g6 23 fxg6 1-0

A similar and wild example of putting development first is seen in the following game:

Michalek – Fedorchuk
Plzen 2003

8 ♗g5 ♗e7 9 ♕f3 ♕c7 10 0-0-0

Now we have the same position as in the Christiansen game, but with a bishop on e7 instead of a knight on d7.

10...b4!? 11 e5! *(D)*

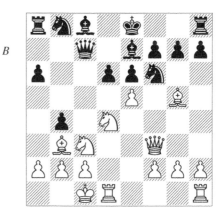

11...♗b7?!

a) Typical tactics follow 11...bxc3? 12 exf6! ♗b7 13 ♘xe6! fxe6 14 ♕h5+ g6 15 ♕h3! cxb2+ 16 ♔xb2 and Black is getting killed.

b) But sacrificing an exchange by 11...dxe5! is also typical. For instance, 12 ♕xa8 (12 ♗xf6 might improve) 12...exd4 13 ♖xd4! bxc3 14 ♖c4 cxb2+ 15 ♔b1 ♗c5 16 ♗f4 e5 17 ♖e1 (17 ♗a4+ may be better) 17...0-0 18 ♖xe5 ♗b7 19 ♖exc5 ♕xf4! 20 ♖xf4 ♗xa8 21 f3 ♘bd7 22 ♖c7 ♘b6 and White has only a minimal advantage.

12 exd6 ♗xd6 13 ♕h3 0-0

13...bxc3 14 ♘xe6 fxe6?! 15 ♕xe6+ ♕e7 16 ♖xd6!.

14 ♗xf6 bxc3 15 ♕g4 *(D)*

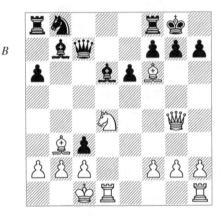

15...♗f4+

Or 15...g6 16 ♘xe6.

16 ♔b1 ♗h6 17 ♘xe6!

Unleashing a devastating series of tactics.

17...fxe6 18 ♕xe6+ ♔h8 19 ♗e5 ♕a5 20 ♗xc3 ♕c5 21 ♗d4 ♕c6 22 ♕e7 ♖e8

Just as bad are 22...♖c8 23 ♗xg7+ ♗xg7 24 ♖d8+ and 22...♘d7 23 ♖he1!.

23 ♗xg7+! ♗xg7 24 ♖d8 ♘d7 25 ♕xe8+ ♘f8 26 ♕f7! 1-0

Classical 6 ♗e2 System

1 e4 c5 2 ♘f3 d6 3 d4 cxd4 4 ♘xd4 ♘f6 5 ♘c3 a6 6 ♗e2 *(D)*

As various systems have come in and out of fashion, this solid and unpretentious development has always been there as a sensible alternative to the heavily theoretical attacking systems. The last world-class player to play it

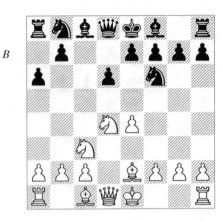

consistently with great success was Karpov, yet practically every major player has been on one or both sides of it. Kasparov played it at least four times versus major players with an idea that will be seen below. White's concept is simple, at least at first sight. He wants to develop and get castled without exposing his pieces to the tempo-gaining attacks that 6 ♗g5, 6 ♗c4 and 6 ♗e3 are often hit with. 6 ♗e2 also covers the g4-square against an invading knight and thus prepares to put a bishop on e3. While 6 ♗e2 is almost always associated with f4, the advance g4 has increasingly been used in conjunction with it in order to drive away the f6-knight and prevent ...d5 before undertaking more aggressive action.

The negative side of ♗e2 is fairly obvious: it is passive and creates no threats. Nor does the bishop protect the critical e-pawn, which indicates that it will most likely end up on f3 or d3 at some point. Consequently, White's bishop will often take two moves to get to a relatively passive square.

6...e5 *(D)*

Although Black can play 6...e6 and transpose into another variation, this is the original 'point' of 5...a6. On the move before, 5...e5 would have been met by 6 ♗b5+, creating some awkwardness on the light squares; for example, 6...♗d7 7 ♗xd7+ ♕xd7 8 ♘f5, after which the knight will head for e3 in many situations, already with a complete grip on d5. None of this can occur once ...a6 is in. The move 6...e5 sets up one of the archetypal Sicilian structures. Black's idea will be to threaten ...d5 as soon as possible and force White to react in a way that is otherwise unfavourable. The analogous idea is Boleslavsky's innovative 6...e5 after 5...♘c6 6 ♗e2 e5, a move that at first shocked the chess world because it gave up an outpost on the crucial d5-square and also created a backward pawn on d6. Boleslavsky's move is analysed in the section 'Sozin Attack (and the Classical Sicilian)' below. Note, by the way, that after 6 ♗g5, 6...e5? would be a self-pin; and after 6 ♗c4, 6...e5 fails to block off White's dangerous bishop. On the other hand 6 ♗e3 e5 is very common.

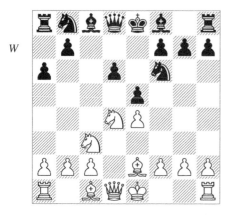

I'll fit the variation 6 ♗e2 e5 into one game; please forgive the dense notes, which attempt to encompass the major ideas of the variation.

Geller – Fischer
Curaçao Ct 1962

7 ♘b3

Although knights on b3 are often poorly-placed in the Sicilian, this retreat leaves the move f4 available to attack Black's centre and kingside. It also supports the idea a4-a5, and has a defensive function by keeping an eye on c5 and potentially exchanging a knight on that square. We shall see that White's action in the 6 ♗e2 Najdorf is very often on the queenside, in contrast to his main 6th-move alternatives.

a) 7 ♘f5 d5! exploits the white knight's hanging position to achieve Black's favourite freeing move. White can develop quickly and control d5 by 8 ♗g5, but 8...d4 9 ♗xf6 ♕xf6 10 ♘d5 ♕d8 gives Black a space advantage with easy development for Black's bishop-pair. He also has a handy break with ...g6 and ...f5 in store.

b) 7 ♘f3 is played reasonably often. White sometimes follows with the sequence of moves a4, 0-0 and ♘d2-c4-e3, to reinforce control of d5, but that is obviously very slow. An exciting if speculative game continued 7...h6 (a good solution is 7...♗e7! 8 ♗g5 ♘bd7 9 a4 0-0 10 0-0 h6 11 ♗xf6 ♘xf6 12 ♗c4 ♗e6, Van der Wiel-Beliavsky, Wijk aan Zee 1985) 8 ♗c4!? *(D)*.

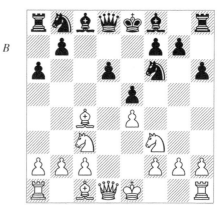

Now:

b1) The natural 8...b5?! 9 ♗d5 ♘xd5 10 ♘xd5 ♗b7 runs into 11 a4!. One of the first things to know about the ♗e2 system is that Black must be careful about ...b5, which can be a weakening move. Obviously that doesn't apply to other Najdorf systems in which White castles queenside.

b2) 8...♗e6!? 9 ♗xe6 fxe6 (we've arrived at that central doubled-pawn structure again – it covers all the central squares but generally lacks mobility; this would be equal except for White's tactical ideas) 10 ♘h4! (10 0-0 ♘c6) 10...♘c6?! (10...♔f7) 11 ♘g6 (11 f4! was an opportunity missed) 11...♖g8 12 0-0 ♔f7 13 ♘xf8 ♖xf8 14 f4 ♔g8 15 ♗e3 (15 f5 d5!) 15...exf4 16 ♖xf4 ♕c7 17 ♕e2 ♘e5 (all at once Black has the piece placement he wants: e5 for his knight and no outpost on d5 for White's) 18 ♗d4 ♖f7 19 ♖d1 ♖af8 20 ♔h1 ♕c4! 21 ♕d2 b5 22 a3 ♕c6! 23 ♗xe5 dxe5 24 ♖f3 ♘xe4 25 ♘xe4 ♕xe4 and in Van der Wiel-Portisch, Tilburg 1984, the passed extra pawn was enough to win.

7...♗e7

Black will sometimes aim for an immediate ...d5 by means of 7...♗e6, but that is asking for f4-f5; e.g., 8 f4 ♕c7 (the difference between this and normal lines is that White is able to answer 8...exf4 with 9 ♗xf4 in one move, as opposed to having to play ♗e3 first) and now:

a) It's increasingly popular to push the g-pawn in all Sicilian variations but here's an older example: 9 g4!? h6 (9...exf4 10 g5! ♘fd7 11 ♗xf4 ♘c6 12 ♕d2 ♗e7 13 0-0-0 ♘ce5 14 ♘d4 with a big advantage; White is already set up for ♘f5) 10 g5 hxg5 11 fxg5 ♘fd7 *(D)*.

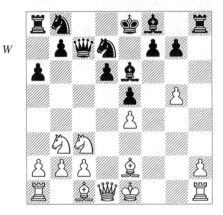

12 ♗g4! ♖h4 13 ♗xe6 fxe6 14 ♗e3 ♗e7 15 ♕f3 ♘c6 16 ♕g3 ♖h8 17 ♕g4. Black is tied down, and h4-h5 can follow, D.Gurevich-Balashov, USSR 1974.

b) 9 0-0 ♘bd7 10 f5 ♗c4 11 a4! (preventing ...b5, and planning a5 in order to restrict Black's queenside) 11...♗e7 12 ♗e3 0-0 13 a5 b5 14 axb6 ♘xb6 (fine, but now Black has an isolated a-pawn in one of those exceptional positions where he has insufficient counterplay down the b-file) 15 ♔h1 ♖fc8 16 ♗xb6! ♕xb6 17 ♗xc4 ♖xc4 18 ♕e2 ♖b4 19 ♖a2 (White's manoeuvre has given him control of d5 and a useful open a-file; note that this rook protects b2) 19...h6 (19...♕b7 20 ♖e1) 20 ♖fa1 ♗f8 21 ♖a4! (21 ♖xa6?! ♖xa6 22 ♖xa6 ♕b7 {hitting e4} 23 ♘a5 ♕c7 is equal) 21...♖c8 22 ♖xb4 ♕xb4 23 ♕xa6. White is a clear pawn ahead, Karpov-Bronstein, Moscow 1971. A model treatment.

We now return to 7...♗e7 *(D)*:

8 0-0

Again 8 g4 has been played, as well as 8 ♗e3 ♗e6 9 ♘d5. But Black will have plenty of counterplay if White rushes to exchange his dark-squared bishop for the sake of controlling d5: 8 ♗g5 ♗e6 9 ♗xf6!? ♗xf6 10 ♕d3 ♘c6 11

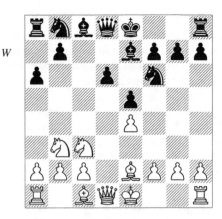

♘d5 ♗g5 12 0-0 ♘e7!, when the pieces are coming off while Black retains his two bishops and an advantage, Arnason-Kasparov, Dortmund jr Wch 1980.

8...0-0

8...♗e6 9 f4 ♕c7 10 a4 (10 f5!?) 10...♘bd7 11 ♗e3 0-0 12 ♔h1 exf4 13 ♖xf4 (White tries a different idea; he's not too worried about ...♘e5 and would rather aim the e3-bishop at the queenside, where a5 and ♘d5 may be influential) 13...♘e5 (now we'll get a particularly instructive game, especially with regard to piece placement in typical pawn-structures) 14 ♘d5 ♗xd5 15 exd5 ♘fd7 16 ♖b4 ♖fe8! 17 a5 ♗f6 *(D)*.

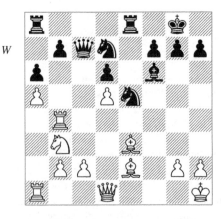

It's very hard to break down a structure like Black's when there's a pawn on d5 and when Black is able to use his strongpoint on e5 as a stepping stone. In this game, White drifts and Black takes over the initiative: 18 ♗g1 ♗g5 19 ♘d2 ♘f6 20 ♘f1 g6 21 ♖d4?! ♗e7 22 c4 ♖ae8 23 b4, Hulak-Portisch, Indonesia 1983, and now the thematic 23...♘ed7! controls all the key squares.

9 ♗e3

9 ♔h1 has been played by Kasparov on occasion. It's a move that White will want to make anyway, and then wait to see how Black is committing his pieces, but that may not be too helpful:

a) 9...b6!? (this is the accepted solution, avoiding 9...b5 10 a4!) 10 ♗e3 ♗b7 11 f3 b5! 12 a4 b4 13 ♘d5 ♘xd5 14 exd5 ♘d7 15 c3 bxc3 16 bxc3 ♗g5! 17 ♗g1 ♕c7 18 c4 a5 19 ♘d2 f5 ½-½ Anand-Gelfand, Dos Hermanas 1997. Black has secured the c5 outpost and he already has his kingside majority.

b) 9...♘c6 10 f3 ♗e6 is also fine; for example, 11 ♘d5 a5 12 ♗e3 a4 13 ♘c1 ♗xd5!? 14 exd5 ♘d4! (D).

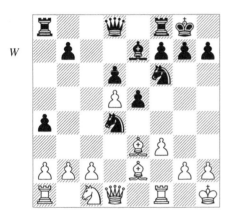

This pawn sacrifice turns Black's f6-bishop into a powerful piece while White's on e2 remains passive: 15 ♗xd4 exd4 16 ♕xd4 ♕a5 17 ♖d1 ♘d7 18 ♖b1 ♖fe8 with plenty of play for the pawn, which may very well have to be returned anyway, Adams-Kariakin, Wijk aan Zee 2006.

9...♕c7

9...♗e6 10 ♕d2 ♘bd7 11 a4 ♖c8 (11...♘b6 generated active play following 12 a5 ♘c4 13 ♗xc4 ♗xc4 14 ♖fd1 ♖c8 15 ♘c1 d5! 16 ♗b6 {16 exd5 ♗b4!} 16...♕e8 17 exd5 ♗b4 18 d6 ♕d7 19 ♘d3 ♕xd6 20 ♘xb4 ♕xb4 21 ♘e4 ♕xd2 22 ♘xf6+ gxf6 23 ♖xd2 ♗e6, with equality, in Leko-Shirov, Dortmund (2) 2002) 12 a5 ♕c7 13 ♖fd1 ♖fd8 14 ♕e1 ♕c6 15 ♗f3 ♗c4 16 ♘c1! (heading for b4; Karpov typically concentrates his pieces on the weak point) 16...h6

17 ♘1a2 ♘c5 18 ♘b4 ♕e8 19 g3! ♖c7 20 ♗g2 ♖dc8 21 b3 ♗e6 22 ♘cd5 ♘xd5 23 ♘xd5 ♗xd5 24 ♖xd5. White has control of d5 and the two bishops, Karpov-Nunn, Amsterdam 1985.

10 a4 ♗e6 11 a5 ♘bd7 12 ♘d5 ♘xd5!?

Black is trying to save the bishop-pair.

13 exd5 ♗f5 14 c4 ♗g6 15 ♖c1 ♘c5?!

White has the advantage in any case, but 15...f5 16 c5!? (or 16 f4) 16...f4 17 cxd6 ♕xd6 18 ♗c5 ♘xc5 19 ♘xc5 ♗f7! 20 ♗f3 ♖fb8! and ...b5 doesn't look too bad.

16 ♘xc5 dxc5 17 b4! *(D)*

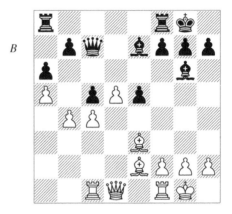

Geller's opening strategy has resulted in a textbook position.

17...♖ac8

The idea is 17...cxb4 18 ♗b6 with c5 next.

18 ♕b3 ♗d6 19 ♖fd1

White can also secure two passed pawns by 19 bxc5 ♗xc5 20 ♗xc5 ♕xc5 21 ♕xb7 ♕xa5 22 ♕b2!.

19...♕e7 20 bxc5 ♗xc5 21 ♗xc5 ♖xc5 22 ♖a1! ♖d8 23 ♖a4 ♗f5 24 ♖b4 ♗c8 *(D)*

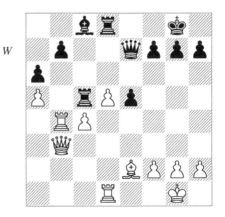

25 ♖b6! ♖d6

25...♖xa5 26 d6 ♕d7 27 ♗f3 leaves Black short of reasonable moves.

26 ♕b4 ♕c7 27 ♖xd6 ♕xd6 28 ♖b1 ♕c7 29 ♕a4! ♗d7 30 ♕a3 ♖xa5 31 ♖xb7! ♕xb7 32 ♕xa5 g6 33 h3

White is getting ready to push the passed pawns.

33...♕b1+ 34 ♔h2 ♗f5 35 ♕c3 ♕e4 36 ♗f3 ♕d4 37 ♕xd4 exd4 38 g4 ♗c8 39 c5 a5 40 c6 ♔f8 41 d6 1-0

The game might finish with 41...♔e8 42 ♗d1 ♗a6 43 g5 ♗b5 44 c7 ♗d7 45 ♗a4, etc. Geller was one of the great 6 ♗e2 players, and of course Fischer was the premier Najdorf player of his time.

English Attack

1 e4 c5 2 ♘f3 d6 3 d4 cxd4 4 ♘xd4 ♘f6 5 ♘c3 a6 6 ♗e3 *(D)*

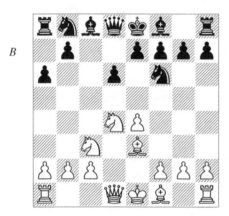

B

This move in conjunction with 7 f3 is known as the English Attack, which can be used against systems with or without ...♘c6. Here we look at Najdorf variations, primarily those that use ...e6 and skip ...♘c6 in favour of moves like ...b5, ...♗b7, ...♗e7 and ...♕c7. This is a hot line in contemporary chess and full of analysis going 20 moves or more, so my coverage will be limited. Nevertheless, the English Attack lines are full of interesting and original positional ideas that express a new way of playing the Sicilian Defence for both sides. These positional considerations make it a good topic of study.

The move-order 6 f3 with 7 ♗e3 is a way of transposing to the main English Attack without

allowing ...♘g4. However, Black does have the move 6...♕b6!? preventing 7 ♗e3 due to 7...♕xb2. This has the same idea as ...♕b6 in the Classical Sicilian, namely, to force the knight back to b3 even at the cost of a tempo (...♕b6-c7). Then if the knight returns to its 'best' square d4, it's Black who has gained the tempo. But with the knight remaining on b3 it's not so easy for Black; e.g., 7 ♘b3 e6 8 g4!? (8 ♕e2 intending ♗e3 is also played; perhaps 8 a4 is also good, since a5 can't be prevented) 8...♘c6 (Judit Polgar has played both 8...♕c7 9 ♗e3 b5 and 8...♘fd7; these both look like better ways to go) 9 ♕e2 ♕c7 10 ♗e3 b5 11 0-0-0 with advantage. In view of White's many options against 6...♕b6, it looks as though 6 f3 is safe enough and avoids the ...♘g4 lines mentioned in the next note.

6...e6

Or:

a) 6...♘g4 7 ♗g5 h6 8 ♗h4 g5 9 ♗g3 ♗g7 *(D)* has been the subject of many grandmaster games, notably Kasparov's.

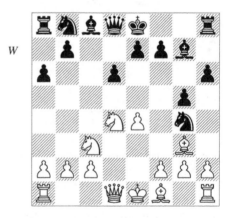

W

The idea is to take White's dark-squared bishop away from its most effective diagonal and use the e5-square productively. Still, Black has weakened his kingside and the variation seems to have fallen out of favour, so we won't be looking into it here.

b) 6...e5 is the typical Najdorf solution that we saw under 6 ♗e2 e5. A unique idea is 7 ♘f3!? ♗e7 8 ♗c4, which resembles 6 ♗e2 e5 except for three things:

1) White generally would like to play ♗g5 in lines with ♘f3, so as to weaken Black's control of d5. But here White has already moved

the bishop to e3, so it would be a loss of tempo to bring it to g5.

2) White has gained a move by playing ♗c4 in one jump (instead of ♗e2-c4). Of course White may not want the bishop to be exposed so early to ...b5, but that doesn't seem to be much of a problem.

3) On a less important note, White's some-times-useful manoeuvre of ♘d2-c4-e3 (after a4) is no longer possible because both c4 and e3 are occupied.

At any rate, after 8 ♗c4 play can continue 8...0-0 9 0-0 ♗e6!? 10 ♗b3 ♘c6 11 ♗g5 *(D)*.

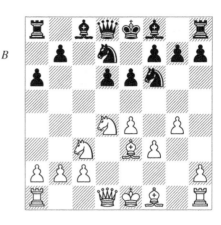

B

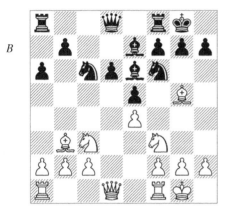

B

White has excellent control of d5 now, but having that one square at your disposal isn't sufficient for a significant advantage in the Sicilian Defence. Anand-Leko, Wijk aan Zee 2006 continued 11...♘d7! (Black gets rid of his bad bishop) 12 ♗xe7 ♕xe7 13 ♘d5 ♕d8 14 c3 ♘a5! 15 ♖e1 ♖c8 16 h3 (this prepares ♖e2-d2 without allowing ...♗g4) 16...♘b6 17 ♘xb6 ♕xb6 18 ♗xe6 fxe6 19 ♖e2! ♖c6 20 ♕d3 ♕c7 21 ♖d1. White has some pressure, but Black isn't yet in serious trouble.

7 f3 b5

Little-played alternatives are usually revealing, and here we have a couple of ideas to consider:

a) 7...♘bd7?! is the most natural continuation for Najdorf players but they should understand that it gets in the way when White pursues his normal English Attack: 8 g4! *(D)*.

Black would have liked to play ...b5 and ...♘fd7-b6 (compare the main line below for an 'explanation' of this bizarre idea). Unfortunately, 7...♘bd7 means that he doesn't have

time to get all three moves in, that is, ...b5, ...♘fd7 and ...♘b6. Now 8...♘b6 9 g5 ♘fd7 blocks ...b5, when both 10 a4 ♘e5 11 f4 ♘ec4 12 ♗c1 and 10 f4 (preventing ...♘e5) yield considerable advantages. After 8 g4, therefore, Black may as well play 8...h6 9 h4 (9 ♕d2 b5! gives Black the extra time he needs for a productive transfer to the queenside and in fact transposes into the 'Main Line' of the English Attack, but 9 ♕e2!? and 0-0-0 is definitely worth looking into) 9...b5 10 ♖g1 (10 a4! is strong, with the idea 10...b4 11 ♘c6 ♕c7 12 ♘xb4 d5 13 ♘d3) 10...♘b6 (so Black has gained his tempo but at the cost of loosening his position on both wings) 11 g5 ♘fd7 (Wedberg-Åkesson, Örebro 2000) and again 12 a4! looks strong, intending 12...♘c4 13 ♗c1!, when Black has to do something about axb5, and White can respond to 13...♕a5 with 14 g6! ♘de5 15 gxf7+ ♘xf7 16 axb5! ♕xa1 17 ♗xc4. In this entire subvariation we see the problems with playing ...♘bd7 and blocking Black's retreat ...♘fd7.

b) 7...h5!? *(D)* is a positional theme to remember, since it prevents g4, which is White's main idea in the English Attack.

Of course this comes at a cost, both in terms of weakening the kingside and time, but in some Sicilian positions that's worth it (notably the Classical lines with ...♘f6 and ...♘c6). Here it's rather unclear: 8 ♕d2 ♘bd7 9 ♗c4 ♘e5!? (not 9...b5? 10 ♗xe6; but a plausible move is 9...♘c5!?, intending ...b5 or even ...d5) 10 ♗b3 b5 11 0-0-0 ♗b7 12 ♗g5! (taking advantage of ...h5) 12...♕a5!? (12...♗e7 may be better) 13 ♔b1 (Khalifman-Van Wely, Wijk aan Zee 2002), and Fedorowicz suggests 13...♖c8,

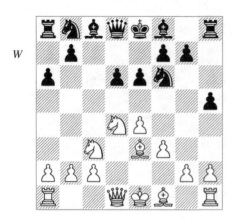

W

limiting White to a moderate advantage. Even if ...h5 doesn't appeal to you in this exact position, you should be aware of it (as both Black and White) when playing or confronted with the many different versions of the f3/g4 attack.

8 g4

Although it's a complicated issue, it's probably better to toss in g4 first, before ♕d2, because after 8 ♕d2 ♘bd7 Black has more options, whereas 8 g4 ♘bd7?! 9 g5 drives the knight away.

8...h6

For the reason given in the last note, this is needed if Black wants to play ...♘bd7. But 8...♘fd7!? 9 ♕d2 ♘b6 *(D)* is an important and still viable alternative.

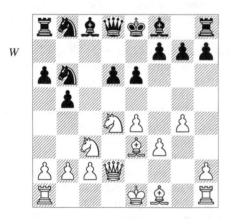

W

As with so many Sicilian ideas, this is initially hard to believe: Black has made nine moves to get one piece out! And yet 8...♘fd7 and 9...♘b6 has been played by many of the world's leading players including Kasparov. How can Black ignore the classical rules of

development in this manner? The answers are several. Consider that Black saves the move ...h6 (played in the main line), thereby 'gaining' a tempo and, crucially, keeping his kingside without weaknesses. Thus White will have to play a lot more moves (such as g5, h4, h5 and g6) in order to make contact with the enemy king (which normally castles kingside). Secondly, if attacked by ...b4, White will not be able to play ♘a4 as he does in many lines. This can speed up Black's attack, especially since ♘ce2 can be met by ...♘c4. So White is reduced to ♘b1 in most cases. To be fair, ♘b1 is a good enough answer in most cases but it's not White's first choice. Finally, the ...♘fd7-b6 manoeuvre allows for a very harmonious development by Black involving ...♗b7, ...♘bd7 and ...♖c8. This is also one of the few lines in which an early ...d5 is feasible, because the usual problems of g5 and e5 (with tempo) are not present.

On the flip side, White has five aggressively placed pieces and a large space advantage, both in the centre and on the kingside. His e4-pawn, usually a target of attack in the Sicilian, is doubly supported and not yet threatened. Imagine being unhappy with that!

Anyway, from the diagram, we have:

a) 10 ♕f2 and 10 f4!? are both feasible.

b) 10 a4 bxa4 11 ♘xa4 ♘xa4 12 ♖xa4 *(D)* is an important yet funny line.

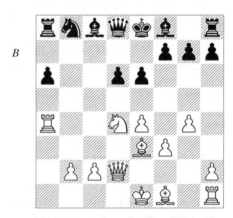

B

Now Black has no space, *no* pieces out after 12 moves, and his a-pawn is isolated! This position is a tribute to the central pawn-majority and the ...d6/...e6 structure. It also provides evidence for a recurrent idea: that an isolated a-pawn on an open file normally isn't a serious problem until the ending. 12...♗e7 and now:

b1) 13 ♗e2 0-0 14 0-0 ♗b7 15 ♖fa1 ♘d7 16 ♘b3 (really stacking up on the queenside in order to win that a-pawn; White finally wins it but all his forces are so diverted by that task that he leaves the rest of the board open) 16...♖b8!? 17 ♗a7 ♖c8 18 ♘a5 ♗a8 19 ♗xa6 ♘e5! 20 ♗e2 f5! with obvious compensation for Black, Anand-Kasparov, Kopavogur (rapid) 2000.

b2) Anand tried to improve with 13 g5 versus Topalov in Wijk aan Zee 2004, when Dearing suggests 13...♗b7 (13...0-0 14 h4! was played, when h5 followed by g6 is a problem) 14 ♗e2 d5 15 e5 ♘d7 16 f4 ♘b6 17 ♖a2 ♘c4. Black appears to stand reasonably well.

c) 10 0-0-0 ♘8d7 11 ♕f2 (11 ♘cxb5!? axb5 12 ♘xb5 is a wild sacrifice that is currently under a cloud) 11...♗b7 12 ♗d3 ♖c8 13 ♔b1?! (13 ♘ce2 is the main line, when Black can delay castling to get something going in the centre by 13...d5, 13...♕c7 14 ♔b1 d5, or Kasparov's 13...♘c5) 13...♖xc3! (another instance of the positional exchange sacrifice ...♖xc3; it is played in other Sicilians, notably the Dragon) 14 bxc3 (D).

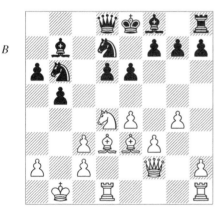

Black's compensation is obvious with moves like ...♘a4, ...♕a5 or ...♕c7, ...♘e5, etc., in the air. What's worse, White can't undertake anything useful, since as so often his rooks will be fairly useless until an ending, which probably isn't going to happen! 14...♕c7 (or 14...♘a4!) 15 ♘e2 ♗e7 16 g5 0-0 17 h4 ♘a4 and Black's attack was too powerful (even ...d5 followed) in Movsesian-Kasparov, Sarajevo 2000.

9 ♕d2 (D)

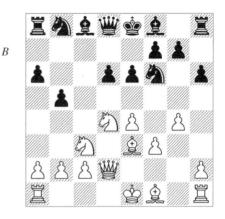

From this point we'll follow a relatively recent game.

Anand – Kasimdzhanov
Leon (rapid) 2005

9...♘bd7 10 0-0-0 ♗b7 11 h4 b4 12 ♘a4 ♕a5 (D)

After this comes a long sequence of theoretical moves. 12...d5!? is a fascinating but very risky alternative.

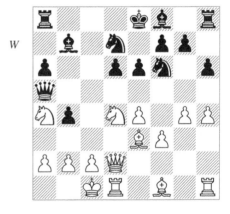

13 b3 ♘c5 14 a3 ♖c8 15 ♕xb4

15 axb4 ♘xb3+ 16 ♘xb3 ♕xa4 is the Main, Main Line! The games and analysis are fascinating, but extend beyond 30 moves at points and are decided by details that don't have much to do with chess understanding. So I'll go with something cleaner:

15...♕c7 16 ♔b1 ♘fd7 17 ♘b2 d5 18 ♕d2 dxe4

18...♘e5!? has also been played.

19 f4 ♘f6 (D)

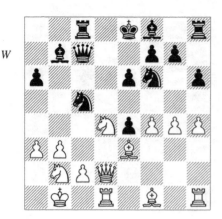

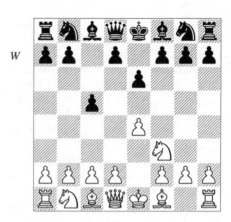

20 ♗e2!

Credit this '!' to Anand. He also mentions 20 ♖g1. Dearing has analysed 20 ♗h3 ♘d5 21 b4! out to a wonderful position, although my analytical engines produce absurd-looking things like 21...♗d6!? 22 bxc5 ♕xc5 with the idea 23 c4 ♕xa3 24 ♘c2 ♕b3 25 ♘a1 ♘c3+, leading to a repetition.

20...♘d5 21 ♘c4 ♘d7?!

Anand claims a small advantage for White after 21...♗e7 22 g5, and leaves 21...♖d8 without comment. The opening is well past, so let's just visually enjoy the rest.

22 g5! ♘xe3 23 ♕xe3 ♗d5 24 ♖hf1 ♗c5 25 ♕c3! hxg5 26 ♘f5! ♗xc4? 27 ♘xg7+ ♔e7 28 ♗xc4 ♖hg8 29 hxg5 e3 30 f5 ♘e5 31 fxe6 ♖xg7 32 ♖d7+! ♘xd7 33 ♕xg7 1-0

Introduction to Systems with 2...e6

1 e4 c5 2 ♘f3 e6 *(D)*

This advance of the e-pawn caught the attention of many early practitioners of the Sicilian Defence. Black threatens to challenge, if not take over, the centre by playing ...d5 next or within a few moves. The game as a whole takes on a different character with 2...e6 as opposed to 2...d6 or 2...♘c6. Naturally, it can transpose to the same lines and structures if an early ...d6 follows; but if not, Black has new options with respect to his development and overall strategy.

One noteworthy difference with 2...e6 is that White has no ♗b5 option, as he does after 2...♘c6 and 2...d6. A few years back that might

not have meant much, but ♗b5 systems are increasingly popular, and 2 ♘f3 ♘c6 3 ♗b5 has even driven top-level grandmasters to change their preferred variations or at least their move-orders. Another benefit has to do with the f8-bishop, which after 3 d4 cxd4 4 ♘xd4 is now free to go to various positions such as c5 and b4; both carry the prospect of more confrontational chess than, say, 2...d6 offers. We also see a lot of early queen moves; for example, to c7 and b6 without first playing ...d6.

Needless to say, 2...e6 comes with some negatives. On a smaller scale, Black has less flexibility in meeting the moves 3 c3 and 3 d3. It should be added that these moves pose no serious threat; however, Black may not get to choose the variation with which he is most comfortable (see below). And ...e6 does weaken the d6-square, which is a drawback in a number of lines, especially those in which Black delays ...d6. Moves such as ♘b5 and ♗f4 can be problems, and in general White's move e5 can have more force in many positions since it can't be captured by a pawn.

Oddly enough, the fact that 2...e6 cuts off the path of the c8-bishop isn't of great consequence. Normally that bishop will attempt to go to b7 or if necessary take its place on d7, and these are the usual squares in other Sicilian variations as well. Taken as a whole, 2...e6 is neither better nor worse than the alternatives, as can be seen from its percentage scores in various lines.

3 d4

The alternatives are not threatening but both sides might want to look into 3 c3 and 3 d3. These moves are good study material in any case because the positions are of a standard nature:

a) After 3 c3, Black has to decide which anti-c3 method to choose. It's important to know something about the move-orders, especially when compared to 1 e4 c5 2 c3, which is covered in the Alapin section of this chapter. A big difference is that after 2 c3, Black can play 2...d5 3 exd5 ♛xd5 4 d4 ♘f6 5 ♘f3 ♗g4, a move that is no longer available when he plays 2 ♘f3 e6 3 c3 d5 4 exd5 ♛xd5 5 d4. Furthermore, in the main lines after 2 c3 ♘f6 3 e5 ♘d5 4 d4 cxd4 5 cxd4, Black retains the option of ...d6 without ...e6. That isn't true after 2 ♘f3 e6 3 c3 ♘f6 4 e5 ♘d5. Thus Black needs to operate within a narrower range of systems, which have to be studied if one is to gain real understanding. I'll pursue just a few themes out of many:

a1) Several basic structures can arise from 3...♘f6 4 e5 ♘d5 5 d4 cxd4 6 cxd4 d6, which Black has played with adequate results for many years. One idea is that he can forego the development of his queen's knight until White's formation is clear; e.g., 7 ♗c4 ♘b6 and now 8 ♗d3!? dxe5 9 dxe5 ♘a6!? 10 0-0 ♘c5 11 ♗c2 ♛xd1 12 ♖xd1 ♗d7 13 ♘c3 ♖c8 with comfortable development, Shaw-Short, Catalan Bay 2003. If White plays 8 ♗b3 instead, Black has 8...dxe5 9 ♘xe5 (9 dxe5 ♛xd1+ 10 ♔xd1 ♘a6! and ...♘c5 or ...♘b4, another case in which delaying the development of the queen's knight is beneficial) 9...♘c6 10 ♘xc6 bxc6 (D).

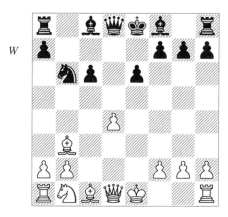

Here we have a standard position from several openings, with the backward c-pawn versus the isolated queen's pawn. Even if White were better developed than he is here, Black would have enough play by combining pressure down the b- and d-files. In this position he can also liquidate the weaknesses and gain activity; for example, 11 0-0 ♗e7 12 ♘c3 0-0 13 ♗c2 ♗a6 14 ♖e1 c5 15 dxc5 ♛xd1 16 ♖xd1 ♗xc5, Blatny-Shaked, Kona 1998.

a2) The other obvious response to 3 c3 is 3...d5, when 4 exd5 can lead to two unrelated set-ups:

a21) Upon 4...♛xd5, we might get 5 d4 ♘f6 6 ♗d3 (6 ♗e2 ♘c6 7 ♗e3 cxd4 8 cxd4 ♗e7 9 ♘c3 ♛d6 transposes to one of the lines stemming from 2 c3; it is considered harmless) 6...♘c6 7 ♗e3 cxd4 8 cxd4 ♗e7 9 ♘c3 ♛d6 with analogous ideas to lines versus 2 c3; again, refer to the Alapin section. Of course there are options on every move.

a22) Black can also play 4...exd5 5 d4 ♘c6, when an isolated queen's pawn position can easily follow:

a221) 6 ♗b5 ♗d6 7 dxc5 ♗xc5 8 0-0 ♘ge7 9 ♘bd2 0-0 10 ♘b3 ♗d6 (D).

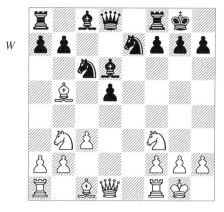

We've transposed to the French Defence variation 1 e4 e6 2 d4 d5 3 ♘d2 c5 4 exd5 exd5 5 ♗b5+ ♘c6 6 ♘gf3 ♗d6 7 dxc5 ♗xc5 8 ♘b3 ♗d6 9 0-0 ♘e7, except that White might not want to play 10 c3 in that case; that is, in the Sicilian 2...e6 3 c3 version he has committed to making that move before he might want to. This is a rather sophisticated thing to worry about for all but very experienced players; nevertheless, it makes the position easier for Black to play than it usually would be, and might give less-advanced players a feel for the considerations that go into top-level opening play. At any rate, all the themes of isolated queen's pawns apply to the diagrammed position; for instance, White blockades the d-pawn and seeks appropriate simplification while Black uses his active pieces and freedom of movement to compromise White's position. Typical moves for White are ♖e1, ♗g5-h4-g3, ♘bd4, ♕c2 and ♗d3. Typical moves for Black are ...♗g4, ...♘f5, ...♖e8, and ...♕b6 or ...♕f6. Whether you want to play this position for either colour is a matter of taste.

a222) You sometimes see the line 6 ♗e3, when apart from 6...cxd4 7 ♗xd4, Black has the interesting move 6...c4. This is particularly appropriate so as not to allow dxc5 and justify the passive position of White's bishop on e3. White can't yet bring his bishop into active play on d3, and Black can develop effortlessly by ...♗d6 and ...♘ge7 unless White does something right away. So there usually follows 7 b3! cxb3 8 axb3 ♗d6 9 ♗d3 ♘ge7 (D).

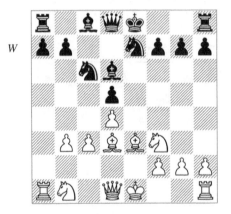

Since the procedure c4 and ♘c3 won't really break down Black's centre (...♗e6 or even ...♘b4 should do well to protect the d5-pawn), Black can be happy with both his pawn-structure and development. After 10 ♕c2 (10 0-0 ♗f5), Adams-Nunn, Hastings 1996/7 continued 10...h6 11 0-0 0-0 with equality. Nunn suggests the more interesting sequence 10...♗g4 11 ♘bd2 ♖c8 12 ♕b1 ♗h5 intending ...♗g6 to exchange White's good bishop on d3.

b) Some players believe that 3 d3 with a King's Indian Attack set-up (g3, ♗g2 and 0-0) is more appropriate against 2 ♘f3 e6 than against either 2 ♘f3 ♘c6 or 2 ♘f3 d6. There are at least two ideas behind this assertion:

1) Black's queen's bishop can't get out to an aggressive square.

2) Black will need to use an extra tempo if he wants to play ...e5. The implication is that Black would find ...e5 a desirable move to make, which can be the case in lines with ...g6, ...♗g7, ...♘ge7 and ...0-0. This ...d6/...e5 formation (called the Botvinnik structure) discourages some practitioners of the King's Indian Attack.

In more specific terms, most players would rather face the 'French Defence' set-up of ...e6, ...d5, ...♘c6, ...♘f6 and ...♗e7 than others which do not involve the move ...e6. However, the issues that I raise regarding reversed openings apply here. Those who are familiar with the King's Indian Defence (which is the King's Indian Attack with colours reversed) know that some of the moves that Black might play in a King's Indian Defence don't work out as well in the King's Indian Attack, because Black hasn't committed to the position which makes those moves effective. Here's an example: 3...♘c6 4 g3 g6 5 ♗g2 (in a paradoxical turnabout that characterizes the flexibility of chess positions, White can seek a radical change in the course of the game by 5 d4!?, moving his pawn a second time but hoping to exploit of the weaknesses created by ...e6 and ...g6; it turns out that there are several good answers, including 5...d5!? and 5...cxd4 6 ♘xd4 ♗g7 7 ♘b5 d5!?, a productive pawn sacrifice) 5...♗g7 6 0-0 ♘ge7 7 ♘bd2 (the typical King's Indian Attack move) 7...0-0 8 ♖e1 d6 (or 8...e5!? 9 ♘c4 d6) 9 c3 e5! (D).

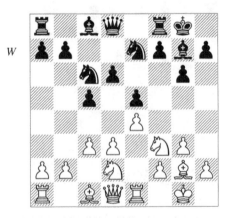

In some ways White's rook is misplaced on e1 because it doesn't support the pawn-break f4 and is generally not useful against the Botvinnik structure, which consists of ...c5, ...d6 and

...e5. Of course if the rook returns to f1, White is actually a tempo *down* on a King's Indian Defence position! Therefore White may well turn to the idea of queenside attack by a3 and b4 with an interesting struggle ahead.

Let's return to 2 ♘f3 e6 3 d4:

3...cxd4 4 ♘xd4 *(D)*

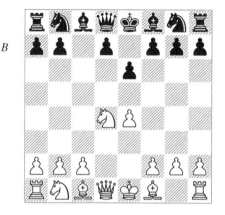

After 4 ♘xd4, Black has a number of options, from which I shall choose two basic strategies: the Sicilian Four Knights Variation, and the Paulsen/Taimanov complex.

Sicilian Four Knights

4...♘f6 5 ♘c3

Not 5 e5? ♕a5+ and 6...♕xe5.

5...♘c6 *(D)*

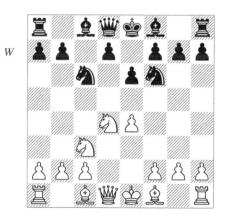

The Four Knights is a perfect example of a Sicilian line that emphasizes development over structure. That is true of only a couple of Sicilian

variations, mostly old-fashioned and out of favour, so it is instructive to see how the players' considerations differ from those in the conventional lines. The Four Knights itself is still playable but I should warn you that it probably falls short of equality after 6 ♘xc6 bxc6 7 e5 ♘d5 8 ♘e4, a highly tactical line that has been thoroughly tested in recent years. It makes sense that a variation that targets the weak d6-square would be a good weapon against this opening. However, we'll follow another variation that produces games with fundamental conflicts between positional and tactical ideas.

Buchenthal – Rosen
German Cht 1978/9

6 ♘db5 ♗b4 *(D)*

At this point 6...d6 7 ♗f4 e5 8 ♗g5 transposes into the Sveshnikov Variation, which is more commonly arrived at via 1 e4 c5 2 ♘f3 ♘c6 3 d4 cxd4 4 ♘xd4 ♘f6 5 ♘c3 e5 6 ♘db5 d6 7 ♗g5. With the first move-order, both sides have made an extra move due to ...e6-e5 and ♗f4-g5. The Sveshnikov contains all kinds of positional and tactical themes, but I felt it less instructive over a broad range of strengths than other variations of the Sicilian, so have not discussed it in depth in this book.

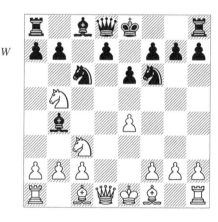

7 ♘d6+

7 ♗f4 leads to crazy tactics and lengthy theory after 7...♘xe4 8 ♕f3! d5 9 ♘c7+ ♔f8 10 0-0-0 ♗xc3 11 bxc3 g5, which ultimately yields equal play according to the books and computers. By contrast, a notoriously dull line for both sides is 7 a3 ♗xc3+ 8 ♘xc3 d5 9 exd5 exd5 10

♗d3 0-0 11 0-0. In spite of White's two bishops, Black is supposed to be able to reach equality. Unfortunately, he may have to play some thankless defence in order to demonstrate that.

7...♔e7

The king may be subject to some attack here, but it would definitely be a mistake to give up the dark squares by 7...♗xd6?. As it is, Black ends up with a significant lead in development.

8 ♘xc8+ ♖xc8 9 ♗d3 *(D)*

A case in point of how Black's development can outweigh other factors is 9 ♗d2 d5! (or even 9...♗xc3 10 ♗xc3 ♘xe4 11 ♗xg7 ♖g8) 10 exd5 ♘xd5 11 ♘xd5+?! (11 ♕g4 ♗xc3 12 bxc3 ♕d6) 11...♕xd5 12 ♗xb4+? (12 c3 ♗c5 favours Black) 12...♘xb4 13 ♕xd5 ♘xc2+ 14 ♔d2 exd5 15 ♖c1 ♘b4 and Black was a pawn ahead in Sanz Calzada-Jordan Garcia, Catalunya Club 1999.

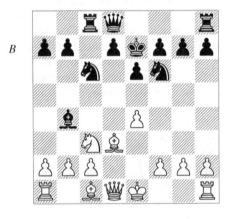

A common decision in chess now arises: does Black double the c-pawns and then protect his position by ...d6, slowly exploiting the weaknesses, as in the Nimzo-Indian Defence? Or does he emphasize space and rapid development, using his lead in those departments to force concessions from his opponent?

9...d5!

Here the open-lines approach is more striking. Nevertheless, 9...♗xc3+ 10 bxc3 ♖e8 11 ♗a3+ d6 is also legitimate: 12 0-0?! (12 ♖b1! ♕c7 13 0-0 ♖ed8 14 f4 is better; e.g., 14...e5 15 fxe5 ♘xe5 16 ♖f5 ♕xc3 with complications) 12...♔f8!? (or 12...♕a5! 13 ♗b4 ♕c7) 13 ♕e2 ♔g8 14 ♖ab1 ♕c7 15 ♖fd1 d5, Major-Binder,

Budapest 1995. Black has equality and perhaps more.

10 exd5 ♕xd5 11 0-0 ♗xc3

11...♕h5?! 12 ♕xh5 ♘xh5 was played in several old games, with activity and quick development pitted against the bishops. Maybe White is a bit better, but not necessarily so, because he still has to neutralize Black's positional threats; e.g., 13 ♗d2 ♘f6 (or 13...♖hd8; the king is useful on e7) 14 a3 ♗d6 15 ♘e4 ♘xe4 16 ♗xe4 f5! 17 ♗d3 ♘e5 with equality, Keres-Trifunović, Moscow 1947.

12 bxc3 *(D)*

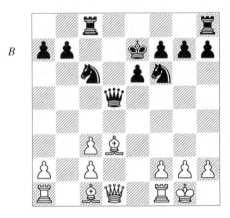

A stark picture of knights versus bishops in which it seems as though Black is swarming all over his opponent's position. But White can catch up quickly with the moves ♖b1, c4, and ♗a3+ or ♗b2, so there is some urgency to act.

12...♖hd8

12...♕a5! looks more accurate, preventing ♗a3+ and attacking c3.

13 ♖b1

13 c4!? ♕a5 might lead to 14 ♗b2 ♔f8! 15 ♗xf6 gxf6, when White's weaknesses are more important than Black's; for instance, 16 ♕g4 ♘e5 17 ♕h5 ♘xc4 18 ♕xh7 ♔e7 and Black's king is completely safe. White might do best to activate his pieces by the slightly odd manoeuvre 13 ♗a3+ ♔e8 14 ♕b1!.

13...♖d7

Also possible is simply 13...b6, with equality.

14 ♗a3+ ♔e8 15 ♕c1 a6!? 16 c4 ♕h5 17 f4?!

17 ♕f4 looks better, with a highly unclear situation.

17...♘a5 18 c5 ♕d5 19 f5 ♘c4 20 fxe6 fxe6 21 ♖d1 *(D)*

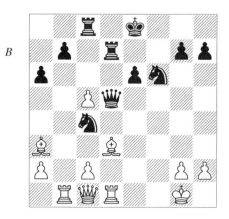

In this position Raetsky points out that 21...♕d4+! 22 ♔h1 ♘e4 (perhaps 22...♕h4! is even better) is fine. At any rate, this example of Black's unusually rapid development in the Sicilian shows that he can achieve equal chances in this traditional variation.

Apart from the Sicilian Four Knights, Black has various means of setting up a structure that includes ...a6 within the next few moves, but delays ...d6. The immediate 4...a6 (without a very early ...♘c6 or ...d6) is the Paulsen System, also called the Kan Variation, whereas 4...♘c6 followed by ...a6 on one of the next two moves is usually referred to as the Taimanov Variation. Some of Black's ideas in these lines are typical of the other Sicilian systems but many are unique to the ...e6/...a6 structure.

Paulsen System

4...a6 *(D)*
It's curious that this was one of the first Sicilian Defence lines that was taken seriously by Louis Paulsen, and therefore by many of his successors. For example, Alekhine felt that when facing the Sicilian, one of the most important set-ups to solve was that of ...e6 and ...a6. The reason that this strikes us oddly is that the Paulsen is so modern in spirit: Black fails to develop a piece and creates dark-square weaknesses on b6 and d6. His play is extremely flexible, and that is one of its points. Having

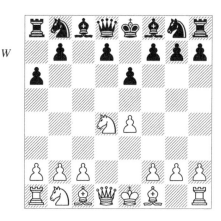

prevented ♘b5, ♘f5 and ♘c3-d5, he can wait to see how White develops and then react accordingly. Among other plans are expansion on the queenside by ...b5 and ...♗b7, queen development to b6 or c7 (again awaiting events), active piece-play by ...♗b4 and/or ...♘ge7-g6, and return to a conventional formation with ...d6 and ...♘f6. His king's bishop in particular can go to e7, d6, c5 or b4; it even finds its way to g7 in some lines, with the move ...g6 creating the travesty of four dark-square holes on Black's third rank.

What about White? Let's think about those Sicilian knights in their customary positions on c3 and d4. This is as good a place as any to talk about their positive role in positional as well as attacking terms. Granted, these white knights are ideally restricted by Black's pawns on a6 and e6 (the one on e6 being rock solid versus direct fire by f4-f5). And if there were a knight on b3 it would merely aim at the well-protected squares c5 and a5. But the knight is generally preferable on d4 in working together with the one on c3 because their effect is prophylactic, i.e. they prevent Black from making desired freeing moves. Thus if Black plays ...e5, the knights are well-placed to land on d5 and f5. And if Black plays ...d5, then the c3-knight plays a role by attacking the pawn. Moreover, if White responds to ...d5 by exd5, then after ...exd5 the knight on d4 becomes an ideal blockader. In the same situation, if White is able to respond to ...d5 with e5, the d4-knight will be powerfully placed and can support f4-f5 as well. Thus White's knights are restricted, but so are Black's centre pawns, so we might call this a situation of mutual prophylaxis. Notice

that this state of affairs also applies to the Taimanov Variation and to a lesser extent, every
Sicilian line with pawns on a6 and e6. The
modest difference in the case with ...d6 and
...e6 in is that the e6-pawn is easier to attack.

After 4...a6, White's first decision is whether
to:

a) put a pawn on c4 and emulate the Maroczy Bind;

b) play for normal development by 5 ♘c3;
or

c) wait to decide by playing 5 ♗d3.

Playing Maroczy-Style

5 c4 ♘f6 6 ♘c3 ♗b4!? *(D)*

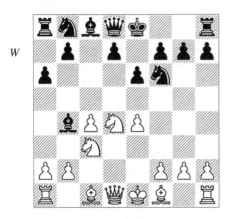

What are the ideas here? With the move 5 c4,
White is doing his best to prevent Black from
even thinking about ...d5 and ...b5, his traditional freeing moves. And Black's development
is rather strange. At this point he appears to
have lost a tempo on the analogous Taimanov
line, which (as shown in the next section) goes
1 e4 c5 2 ♘f3 e6 3 d4 cxd4 4 ♘xd4 ♘c6 5 c4
♘f6 6 ♘c3 ♗b4. After all, in the Paulsen line,
Black's a6-pawn is pretty irrelevant compared
to having a knight on c6 (as he would have in
the Taimanov Variation – see also below). That
may on balance be true but there is also the
typical paradox of modern Sicilian lines that
being a move behind will sometimes result in
the better position! In the Taimanov version
above, White's best move is probably 7 ♘xc6,
whereas in the Paulsen White doesn't have that
option because there's no knight on c6 to capture.

This is a specialized instance of what can be
a beneficial thinking tool. It's often useful to
imagine yourself having an extra move when
you're playing an opening variation. What
would you do? Can you use the move productively? This is a very good exercise that will
sometimes give you greater understanding of
an opening than detailed and time-consuming
study might.

7 ♗d3

Black does well after 7 e5!? ♘e4 8 ♕g4
♘xc3 9 a3 ♗f8! 10 bxc3 ♕a5 11 ♕g3 d6!, a
book line that has remained unchallenged for
years.

7...♘c6 8 ♘xc6 dxc6! *(D)*

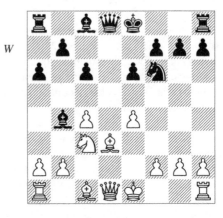

Another 'tempo-loss' paradox: if you compare the equivalent Taimanov line again, White
has gained the move ♗d3 in return for the ineffectual move ...a6. Surely that must improve
White's prospects? But without ♗d3 having
been played, the sequence 7 ♘xc6 dxc6!? in the
Taimanov allows 8 ♕xd8+, as we shall discuss
in that section. This is probably playable for
Black, but leaves him with a different set of
problems. As it stands in the Paulsen after
8...dxc6, 9 ♕xd8+ isn't possible. So White has
gained in development but lost in opportunity.

9 e5

9 0-0 e5! frees the c8-bishop and wins an
outpost on d4. In that situation as well, it's good
for Black to have queens on the board.

9...♕a5

Now the play gets forced:

**10 exf6 ♗xc3+ 11 bxc3 ♕xc3+ 12 ♗d2
♕xd3 13 fxg7 ♖g8 14 ♗h6 ♕c3+ 15 ♔f1 ♕f6
16 ♕c1 e5 17 c5**

17 ♖b1?! ♗e6! 18 ♖xb7 0-0-0 with ...♖d4 next.

17...♗e6

Up to here we have theory. If Black is happy with this position then 5 c4 doesn't pose a problem for him. Otherwise Black should consider a positional approach, such as 6...♕c7. The point is that you have to be ready for concrete lines but also understand positions like the one after 9 0-0 e5.

Conventional Development

5 ♘c3 ♕c7 (D)

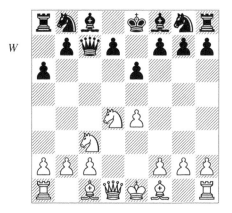

6 ♗d3

The most popular of several continuations, at least in club-level chess.

a) I'll present just one example of 6 g3. Black could then transpose into a Taimanov or other Sicilian by 6...♘c6 or 6...d6, but he has a unique and effective move in 6...♗b4!: 7 ♘e2 ♘f6 8 ♗g2 ♗e7 (it's as if Black played ...♗e7 and White had his knight transferred to e2 without using any time) 9 0-0 0-0 10 h3 d6 (D).

This position should be equal, since Black has his normal queenside expansion themes and White can't do much on the long diagonal. Generally White will turn his attention kingside: 11 ♗e3 ♘c6 12 g4 (the beginning of an ambitious advance) 12...b5 13 f4 ♘d7 14 ♘g3 ♖e8 15 ♕d2 ♗b7 16 ♘ce2 (this is a sign that White doesn't know how to continue with his kingside attack and indeed there doesn't seem to be a good plan in that area of the board) 16...♖ad8 17 ♘d4 ♘xd4 18 ♗xd4 e5! (the standard manoeuvre) and now:

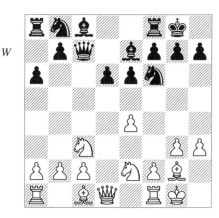

a1) Take a look at 19 ♗e3 exf4 20 ♗xf4 ♘e5 21 ♘f5 ♗f6. We've seen this ideal set-up for Black before; ...♘c4 or ...♘g6 will come next. If White had any chance of equalling the effect of Black's domination of e5 and his threats to the e-pawn, he would have to have some pieces ready to come to d5, which is not realistic at the moment.

a2) 19 ♗c3 d5! (the standard freeing move; White's position is falling apart) 20 ♔h1 (20 ♗a5 ♗c5+ 21 ♔h2 ♗b6 22 ♗xb6 ♘xb6) 20...dxe4 21 ♗a5 (21 fxe5 b4 with the idea 22 ♗xb4 e3) 21...♘b6! 22 ♕c3 ♕xc3 23 bxc3 exf4 24 ♘xe4 ♗xe4 25 ♗xe4 ♗c5 26 ♗d3 g5 27 ♖ae1 ♖c8 and Black is winning, Fontaine-Svidler, French Cht 2003.

b) 6 f4 b5 (the early fianchetto is a trademark of the Paulsen; 6...♘c6 is another option in Taimanov-style) 7 ♗d3 ♗b7 8 ♕e2 ♘c6 9 ♘xc6 ♕xc6 10 ♗d2 (the beginning of a mediocre plan; more interesting is 10 a3 ♗c5 11 ♗e3 or 10 0-0 ♗c5+ 11 ♔h1 ♘e7 12 e5!?) 10...♗c5 (D).

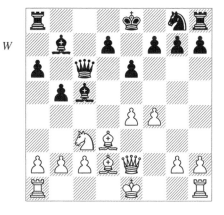

11 0-0-0!? (when Black's only action is on the queenside, this seems strange, especially since White has no real prospect of attacking on the kingside, where Black stands so solidly; still, White isn't in any trouble at this point) 11...♘e7 (whether you are White or Black, be aware of 11...b4 12 ♘d5!) 12 ♕h5! ♖c8 13 ♔b1 b4 14 ♘e2 a5 15 f5 ♗a6!? 16 ♖hf1 ♗xd3 17 cxd3 exf5 18 exf5 ♘d5 19 ♖c1 0-0! and the position is unclear, Meister-Poluliakhov, Krasnodar 2001. 20 d4?! would be answered by 20...♘f6.

c) There are of course countless games with 6 ♗e2, when one can return to a Taimanov with 6...♘c6 followed by ...♘f6 or to a Scheveningen set-up with 6...♘f6 and 7...d6. But the Paulsen faithful like to play 6...b5 7 0-0 ♗b7 in every position. Here it looks wrong after 8 ♖e1!. That's a useful move in any case but in quite a few variations of the Sicilian it prepares some form of the sacrifice 8...b4?! 9 ♘d5! *(D)*.

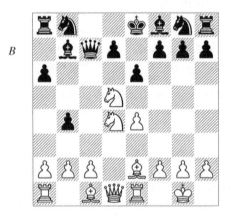

9...exd5 10 exd5 ♔d8. Now White has various ways to pursue the attack, and chooses a good one: 11 ♗f3! d6 (this begs for a check on c6, but it's not easy to get one's pieces out in the face of ideas such as ♕e2 and ♘f5, with ♗e3, c3 and ♖c1 if needed) 12 ♗f4 ♘d7 13 ♘c6+ ♗xc6 14 dxc6 ♘c5 15 ♕d5! ♘f6 16 ♕xc5! dxc5 17 ♖ad1+ ♔c8 18 ♗g4+ ♔b8 19 ♖d8+ ♔a7 20 ♖xa8+ ♔xa8 21 ♗xc7 ♘xg4 22 ♖e8+ ♔a7 and my database game gives 23 ♖b8 1-0 Yang Xian-Ramos, Moscow OL 1994. I suspect that this is a typo for 23 ♗b8+! ♔b6 24 c7 with an instant win. Otherwise 23 ♖b8? ♘f6 would definitely be worth playing on.

6...♘c6

This is a solid choice which results in fixing White's pawns. Naturally, 6...♘f6 is playable. Instead, a nice attack followed 6...b5!? (risky) 7 0-0 ♗b7 8 ♖e1 d6 9 ♗g5 (creating the same problem for Black as he had in the last note: White prepares his sacrifice by cutting off escape-squares from Black's king) 9...♘d7?! (9...♘f6) 10 a4! b4 11 ♘d5! exd5 12 exd5+ ♗e7 13 ♘f5 ♘e5 14 ♘xe7 ♘xe7 15 ♗xe7 ♔xe7 16 f4 ♕c5+ 17 ♔h1 ♕xd5 18 ♕g4 h5 19 ♕h3 ♕d4 20 fxe5 ♕g4 21 exd6+ ♔xd6 22 ♕xg4 hxg4 23 ♖ad1! and White should win, Ghinda-Kirov, Timisoara 1987.

7 ♘xc6 dxc6 8 0-0 ♘f6 9 f4 e5! *(D)*

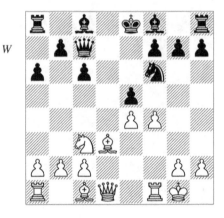

Reaching a type of position that we see in other Sicilian variations. Black has two excellent bishops and active pieces so it's up to White to use his superior development quickly.

We'll follow a game with all the customary ideas:

Lanka – Santo-Roman
Prague 2000

10 f5!

Other moves:

a) 10 fxe5?! ♗c5+ 11 ♔h1 ♘g4 12 ♕f3 0-0!? (12...♗e6 13 ♗f4 ♘xe5 14 ♕g3 f6 15 ♗xe5 fxe5 gives Black the two bishops; or 12...♘xe5 with equality) 13 ♗f4 ♘xe5 14 ♕g3 ♗d6! 15 ♖ad1 f6. Black has his outpost on e5 in front of an isolated pawn again, and this time he doesn't have to worry about ♘d5 ideas or a weak pawn on d6.

b) 10 ♔h1 and now 10...♗c5 intends ...h5, while queenside castling via 10...♗d7 is another option (10...h5!? could also be played immediately).

10...♗c5+ 11 ♔h1 h5! *(D)*

A characteristic move of this system. Now the game is double-edged. Another encounter went 11...h6!? 12 a4 ♖b8 13 ♕f3 b5 14 ♕g3 ♔f8 15 ♕f3 ♗b7 and Black did well in Qin Kanying-Ye Jiangchuan, Shanghai 2000; his king doesn't seem comfortable on the kingside, however.

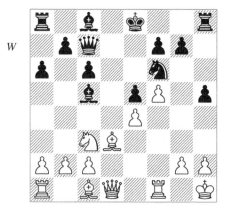

12 ♕f3

The main alternative is 12 ♗g5!?; for example, 12...♘g4 13 ♕e2 ♗e7!? (13...b5!?) 14 ♗d2 (14 ♗xe7 ♕xe7 15 ♕f3) 14...♗c5 15 h3 (15 ♘d1) 15...♕e7 16 ♘a4 ♗a7 17 b4 (17 ♗a5 ♕h4) 17...b5 18 ♘c5?! ♗xc5 19 bxc5 ♕xc5 20 a4 ♗b7 21 ♖ab1 ♖d8, Tiviakov-Cacho Reigadas, Arco 1998. White went on to win, but Black's position looks quite healthy.

12...b5 *(D)*

Black plays to prevent ♘a4; an alternative is 12...♘g4 13 ♕g3 ♗d7!? 14 ♗e2 0-0-0! 15 ♗xg4 hxg4 16 ♕xg4 g6!.

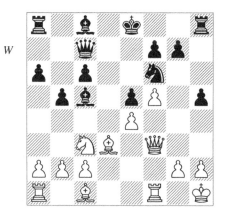

13 a4 ♗b7 14 ♗g5 ♘g4 15 ♘d1!

White covers his weak squares; the knight wasn't getting to d5 anyway.

15...♗e7 16 ♗xe7

Or 16 ♗d2!? with equality.

16...♕xe7 17 ♘f2

Black is well off with 17 ♘e3 ♕h4 18 h3 ♘f6!.

17...♕h4 18 h3

Although Black went on to win after 18...0-0, he should prefer either 18...♘xf2+ or 18...♖d8, with equality in either case.

The Non-Committal Line

5 ♗d3 *(D)*

By comparison with the analogous Taimanov Variation (4...♘c6) White is glad to be able to post his bishop on d3 without first having to defend, retreat, or exchange his d4-knight. Importantly, he retains the option of playing c4.

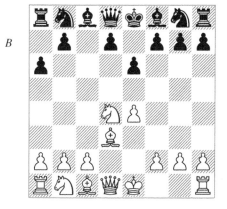

5...♘f6

Black's position is ultra-flexible, with seemingly infinite room for creativity. At this point he has moves such as 5...♘e7, 5...♕c7, 5...♗c5 (6 ♘b3 ♗a7 or 6...♗e7), 5...♕b6 (with the idea of misplacing the knight and then playing ...♕c7; we discuss that ploy elsewhere in this chapter), or 5...g6 *(D)*, which deserves a diagram.

All of Black's pieces are on the back rank and his position is the definition of holes! Too bad there isn't a pawn left over to put on c6. Yet plenty of grandmasters have played 5...g6 and at least one of them, a leading Paulsen theoretician, thinks that Black can equalize from this position with two different set-ups. To me, the most

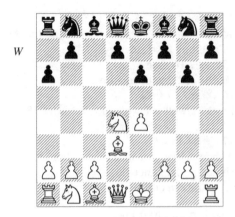

plausible idea is ...♗g7, ...♘e7 and ...d5; but if he can't get ...d5 in, Black can settle for ...d6, ...♘bc6, etc., when he has done reasonably well.

That's not all. Are you ready for the outrageous 5...d5? In the few tests of this move thus far, no one seems to have come close to refuting it. Most games have gone 6 exd5 ♕xd5 7 0-0 ♘f6 (7...♗d7!? in some sense gains a tempo, because now 8 ♘c3?? allows 8...♕xd4 and there's no check; of course you may not want your bishop on d7) 8 ♘c3 and now 8...♕d8, but Black could also play 8...♕d6 (D):

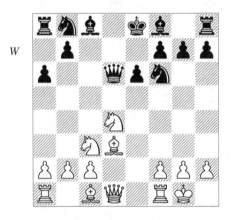

Then Black has another of those 4:3 kingside pawn-majorities that we talk about in so many openings, including the French Defence Tarrasch line that this resembles so strongly. Compare that variation: 1 e4 e6 2 d4 d5 3 ♘d2 c5 4 exd5 ♕xd5 5 ♘gf3 cxd4 6 ♗c4 ♕d6 7 0-0 ♘f6 8 ♘b3 ♘c6 9 ♘bxd4 ♘xd4 10 ♘xd4. It would be a confirmation of the Paulsen's remarkable flexibility if Black could actually get away with (and equalize following) 5...d5.

My feeling is that one of these many 5th-move alternatives might be more rewarding than 5...♘f6, which allows White to set up a common and generally effective formation.

6 0-0 d6

6...♕c7 7 ♕e2 d5!? (uh-oh, this again!) 8 exd5 ♘xd5 9 ♗c4 ♘f6 10 ♗g5 ♗e7 11 ♘c3 0-0 12 ♖ad1 b5 13 ♗d3 ♗b7 14 ♕e3 ♘bd7 15 ♘e4 ♖fe8 16 ♘xf6+ ½-½ Akopian-Svidler, Moscow 2004. Average rating of the players? Over 2700.

7 c4! b6 8 ♘c3

8 b3 ♗b7 9 ♕e2 ♘bd7 10 ♘c3 g6! (duelling fianchettoes are common in this line, and the one on g7 hits the loose d4-square; perhaps White is a little better but that has to be demonstrated) 11 ♗b2 ♗g7 12 ♖ad1 0-0 13 f4 e5! 14 fxe5 ♘xe5 15 ♗b1 ♖e8 and Black won his e5-square in Seitaj-Gheorghiu, Thessaloniki OL 1984. For his part, White's got a wonderful d-file to use, so he might claim equality. Then again, there's that awful bishop on b1 which needs attention, so maybe Black has the better of it after all.

8...♗b7 (D)

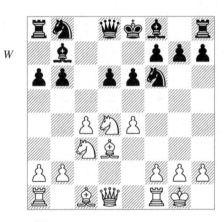

This is a normal position, from which we'll follow a model game.

P. Popović – Pikula
Banja Koviljaca 2002

9 f4 ♗e7 10 ♕e2

This set-up introduces a strategy with which White has won many games.

10...0-0 11 ♗d2 ♘bd7?

A fundamental mistake. 11...♘c6 is much better, although still not problem-free.

12 ♖ae1 *(D)*

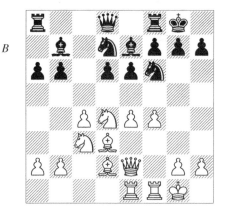

This is a great piece-formation for White. It's not that the attack is so powerful yet, but that Black hasn't a shred of queenside or central counterplay.

12...g6

Played to prevent a breakthrough by e5; it looks necessary.

13 f5!

Now you can see why that knight was better off going to c6.

13...e5

13...gxf5 14 exf5 e5 15 ♘c2 ♖e8 16 ♘b4! b5 17 ♘bd5 doesn't look so bad at first, but after inevitable exchanges on d5 Black will be positionally lost. A good position to study; White will subsequently get space and two bishops, a deadly combination.

14 ♘b3 ♔h8 15 fxg6 hxg6? *(D)*

But 15...fxg6 16 ♗h6 is pretty bad.

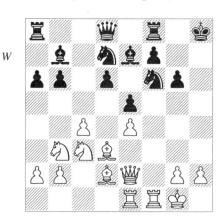

16 ♖f3!

White doubles, triples, occupies the outpost, and wins.

16...♔g7 17 ♖ef1 ♘h7 18 ♕f2 ♕e8 19 ♘d5! ♗xd5 20 cxd5 ♗g5 21 ♗c3 ♗d8 22 ♕e2! b5

Otherwise White simply takes the a-pawn and attacks on the queenside too.

23 ♘a5 ♘g5 24 ♖g3 ♖h8 25 ♘c6 ♗b6+ 26 ♔h1 ♖h5?

But Black won't like 26...f6 27 ♗d2! or 26...♘h7 27 ♗d2 ♘b8 28 ♘xb8 ♖xb8 29 ♖h3.

27 ♕xh5! gxh5 28 ♖xg5+ ♔f8 29 ♖xh5 ♔g8 30 ♖g5+ ♔f8 31 ♗d2 f6 32 ♖g3 ♔f7 33 ♗e2! ♕h8 34 ♖h3 ♕g7 35 ♗h6 ♕h7 36 ♗h5+ ♔g8 37 ♗g4 ♘f8 38 ♗xf8 ♕xe4 39 ♗e6+ ♔xf8 40 ♖xf6+ ♔g7 41 ♖f7+ ♔g6 42 ♘e7+ ♔g5 1-0

White stood much better all the way. This is a good piece-formation to remember.

Taimanov Variation

1 e4 c5 2 ♘f3 e6 3 d4 cxd4 4 ♘xd4 ♘c6 *(D)*

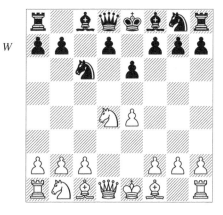

By deploying the knight to c6, Black breaks with the noncommittal Paulsen approach. He decides early upon the position of the queen's knight rather than keeping open the option of ...♘d7. He also allows White to play ♘b5. In return, he has developed a piece, and his c6-knight limits White's options (for instance, the anti-Paulsen move 5 ♗d3 simply loses a piece here). We'll briefly examine White's three major lines: 5 c4, 5 ♘b5 and 5 ♘c3.

5 g3 allows the freeing advance 5...d5. Then 6 ♗g2 can be met by 6...♗c5! 7 ♘b3 ♗b6 8 exd5 exd5, a convincing pawn sacrifice for Black; for

example, 9 ♗xd5 (9 ♘c3 ♘ge7 10 ♘xd5 ♘xd5 11 ♕xd5 ♕xd5 12 ♗xd5 ♘b4) 9...♕e7+ 10 ♕e2 ♕xe2+ 11 ♔xe2 ♘b4. Instead, the somewhat dull 6...dxe4!? has been used in practice, achieving equality.

'Maroczy Lite'

5 c4 *(D)*

This advance is somewhat rare but leads to material that is potentially useful. White tries to set up a sort of Maroczy Bind. This is slow in the face of the rapid development that 2...e6 and 4...♘c6 makes possible, yet both sides must play accurately.

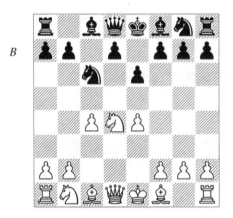

5...♘f6

5...♕h4!? 6 ♘b5!? (6 ♘c3 ♗b4) 6...♕xe4+ 7 ♗e2 ♕e5 could get wild and woolly; if Black can get away with an extravagant move like 5...♕h4, it shows that the loss of time involved with 5 c4 is meaningful.

6 ♘c3 ♗b4 7 ♘xc6

White exchanges so as to play ♗d3 and protect the e-pawn (we discussed this in the Paulsen section). It's important to see that Black is not committed to setting up a prepared formation with, say, ...♕c7 and ...a6. The Taimanov move ...♘c6 goes well with quick development. For instance, White can't simply make Maroczy Bind moves such as 7 f3?! 0-0 8 ♗e3, because 8...d5! *(D)* is precisely the type of pawn-break that Black wants to make, and White needs to prevent, in any Sicilian Defence.

Sometimes students are so intent upon setting up some restricted Sicilian position with ...d6 and ...e6 that they forget about the basics.

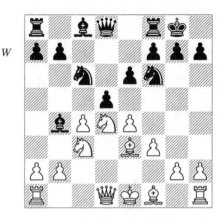

You don't see this kind of freeing move very often in the Sicilian because, behind the scenes, White makes his moves so that there is a specific drawback to ...d5, such as a multiple capture or e5. He is normally successful in doing this, and that's why you seldom see an effective early ...d5 in any well-played Sicilian, including the Najdorf, Rauzer, Scheveningen, Dragon or for that matter Taimanov. This is obvious to a player accustomed to the Sicilian, but perhaps not to a newcomer who sees many games with ...d6 and ...e6 and assumes that Black just prefers to play with less active pieces. In the diagrammed position White can't even maintain equality, as a short analysis will show you.

Returning to 7 ♘xc6 *(D)*, Black has two recaptures.

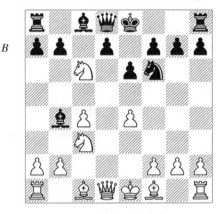

Muzychuk – Gershon
Dresden 2003

7...bxc6

This is the usual move, strengthening Black's centre. He can also play 7...dxc6!? 8 ♕xd8+ ♔xd8, which is awkward but probably OK so long as Black is able to achieve ...e5, the ideal move that he needs, in order both to get his light-squared bishop out and to secure an outpost on d4. For example, 9 f3!? (9 e5! is probably better, interfering with Black's plans; then 9...♘e4 10 a3!? ♗xc3+ 11 bxc3 b6 should be looked at – White has no worries, but on the other hand it's hard to see how he will make progress) 9...e5 10 ♗e3 ♔c7 (D).

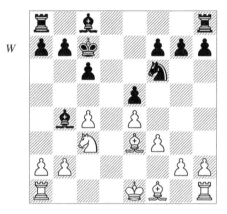

11 ♖c1 ♘d7! 12 ♔f2!? ♗c5 (removing a defender of d4 while getting rid of White's good bishop) 13 ♘a4! (preventing ...♘c5 and ...a5 after the exchange of bishops) 13...♗xe3+ 14 ♔xe3 ♘f8!, intending ...♘e6 and ...♘d4, Lautier-Ivanchuk, Tilburg 1992. Now White has 15 c5!, to get his bishop to c4 (thus the reasoning behind ♖c1 and ♘a4). But Black can still play 15...♗e6 16 b3 ♘g6! 17 ♗c4 ♗xc4 18 ♖xc4 ♘f4! 19 g3 ♘e6 20 ♖d1 ♖hd8, etc., with the same advantageous outpost on d4.

For those who are familiar with the King's Indian Defence, notice that we have here the same central pawn-structure, same weakness, and same manoeuvres by Black as appear in the Exchange Variation of that opening! Of course White didn't put up much resistance to this plan.

We now return to 7...bxc6 (D):

8 ♗d3

After 8 e5 comes 8...♘e4 9 ♕d4 ♕a5!.

8...e5

Or 8...0-0, or 8...d5!?, but in the latter case watch out for 9 cxd5 cxd5?? 10 ♕a4+.

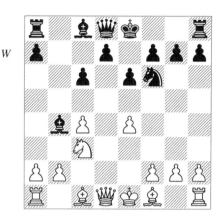

9 0-0 ♗c5

It can be advantageous to delay castling for reasons that will be seen, and it won't hurt to increase Black's control of d4. But 9...♗xc3 10 bxc3 d6 has also been played.

10 ♗g5?! (D)

This looks natural enough but turns out badly. White has the interesting option of 10 ♕f3!, flirting with ♕g3 but also preparing ♗g5 if it makes positional sense.

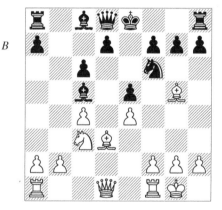

10...h6 11 ♗h4 d6 12 ♖b1 g5 13 ♗g3 h5! 14 h3 h4 15 ♗h2 g4!

A tactical ploy to remember.

16 hxg4 ♘xg4 17 b4 ♗d4 18 ♘e2 ♗b6 19 c5

Otherwise 19...h3 or 19...♕f6 comes.

19...h3! 20 ♗g3 dxc5 21 bxc5 ♗xc5 22 ♕c2 ♕d6 23 ♖bc1

In this position, the easiest path to advantage lay in 23...hxg2 24 ♔xg2 ♗b6 25 ♖xc6+ ♕xc6 26 ♖xc6 ♗b7 27 ♖c2 f5, when White's position is declining.

Hedgehog

5 ♘b5 d6 6 c4

With this move White sets up another sort of Maroczy Bind and Black generally plays in what is called 'Hedgehog' fashion: pieces and pawns curled up on the first three ranks waiting for the chance to burst out into activity. This particular form of the Hedgehog has done reasonably well over the years, although at the very top levels Black still seems to run into problems from time to time.

Before entering into that discussion, a variation with a colourful history begins 6 ♗f4 e5 7 ♗e3. Now Black can play 7...a6, but the main line goes 7...♘f6 8 ♗g5!? (the bishop moves for the third time in a row! This move protects e4, of course, and also strengthens White's control over d5) 8...♗e6 (D).

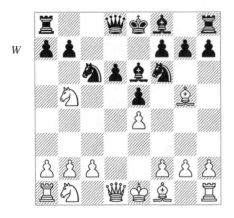

Without going into too much detail, Black's development has again been quite rapid, and White can't keep a grip on the position. There are two options here:

a) The old main line 9 ♘1c3 a6 10 ♗xf6 gxf6 11 ♘a3 (threatening ♘c4-e3, or ♘d5, or in some cases ♕h5) was solved in style by 11...d5! 12 exd5 ♗xa3 13 bxa3 ♕a5 14 ♕d2 0-0-0. It becomes clear that White won't win the piece, and his development is slow while his extra pawn on the a-file is hardly useful: 15 ♗c4 ♖hg8 16 ♖d1, and various analysts have looked at 16...♖xg2! (16...♗f5!? 17 ♗d3 ♗xd3 18 ♕xd3 ♘d4 19 0-0 ♔b8 yielded equality in the famous game Fischer-Petrosian, Buenos Aires Ct (1) 1971) 17 ♕e3 (17 ♘e4 ♕b6) 17...♘d4 18 ♔f1! ♘xc2!? (or 18...♕c7) 19

♕d3 (19 ♕f3 ♖xf2+! 20 ♔xf2 ♕c5+) 19...♖g4 with the upper hand. The variations are much more complicated than that, but the verdict remains the same.

b) 9 ♘d2! (D) improves, albeit not enough for White to get excited about:

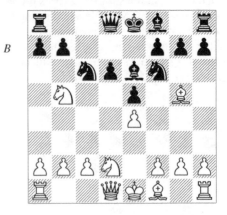

9...♗e7 10 ♗xf6 ♗xf6 11 ♘c4 0-0! 12 ♕xd6 ♕c8!. White has invested a lot of time and the bishop-pair to win one pawn. There have been quite a few games from this position demonstrating full compensation for the pawn. Black has very active pieces and White's are subject to attack. Also, Black may play ...a6 followed by ...♘d4 and dominate the board from that square. One illustration: 13 c3 ♖d8 14 ♕c7 ♗e7 15 ♕xc8 ♖axc8 (Black's initiative persists even without queens) 16 ♘ba3 ♘d4! 17 cxd4 ♗b4+ 18 ♔e2 ♗xc4+ 19 ♘xc4 ♖xc4 20 ♔f3 ♖cxd4 21 ♗e2 ♖8d6! and Black eventually won an opposite-coloured bishop ending in Borisek-Navara, Balatonlelle 2003.

6...♘f6 7 ♘1c3 a6 8 ♘a3 (D)

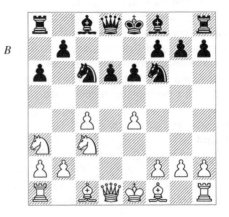

At this juncture we look at two games. The first will illustrate White's set-up with the aggressive f4. The second serves to represent the overall main line with f3.

Before that I should mention Kasparov's famous gambit in the 1985 world championship match against Karpov, which went 8...d5!? 9 exd5 exd5 10 cxd5 ♘b4 (D). Contrary to the general opinion, this is still unresolved.

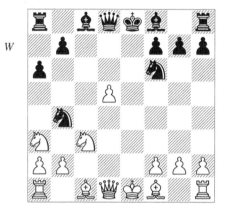

In the critical encounter Karpov played 11 ♗e2 ♗c5?! 12 0-0? ♗f5 and got into great difficulties, losing a brilliant game. Later Karpov played 12 ♗e3! with advantage, the point being 12...♗xe3 13 ♕a4+ and 14 ♕xb4. The best move after 11 ♗e2 is 11...♘fxd5, which has been heavily analysed down to a promising piece sacrifice for White, as has 11 ♗c4 ♗g4 (11...b5 12 0-0! bxc4 13 ♖e1+ ♗e7 14 d6) 12 ♕d4 b5 13 ♘cxb5! with a big mess. The point of mentioning all this is twofold:

a) If you play moves such as 8...d5 you simply have to memorize a lot of material.

b) If the move 8...d5 works it invalidates 5 ♘b5, because if White can't prevent ...d5 in the Sicilian by direct means it is extremely unlikely that there will be any way to gain a positional advantage thereafter.

White Plays f4

Nunn – P. Cramling
Zurich 1984

I'll use this game without much analysis to demonstrate an ambitious plan with f4 that affords White attacking chances but at the cost of

loosening his position. Although strong masters have had success neutralizing this strategy, it is still a valid approach and in any case quite instructive.

8...♗e7 9 ♗e2 0-0 10 0-0 b6 11 ♗e3 ♘e5

11...♗b7 is a more accurate choice if Black wants to prevent f4 from being effective, because his knight has not used up time on ...♘e5-d7. Then the immediate 12 f4 gives Black some easy ways to counteract White's structure, including 12...♖c8 13 ♖c1 ♖e8. Development of the rook to e8 supports ...d5, because the exchange of White's e-pawn will bring the rook into a position facing the vulnerable e3-bishop. Nevertheless, White can play 12 ♖c1, hoping for 12...♘e5 13 f4.

12 f4 *(D)*

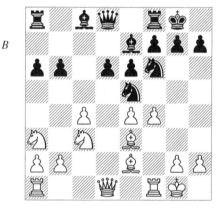

The majority of masters have used a formation with f3 in this variation, as in the next main game below. Those positions are very well-known and fairly easy to play because of the limited set of piece placements that they logically allow for. Although his chances of gaining an advantage are slim if Black plays accurately, White has more opportunities for original play after f4.

12...♘ed7 13 ♗f3 ♗b7 14 ♕e2

Black implemented a positionally effective plan with ...h6 in Brüggemann-Lutz, Erfurt 2004: 14 ♔h1 h6 *(D)*.

Black's point is to answer 15 g4?! with 15...♘h7! and ...g5 next. Then Black has essentially made White's f3-bishop a bad one, since e5 can't be played and he has neutralized any pawn advances at the same time. The game proceeded 15 ♖c1 ♕c7 16 ♘ab1 ♖ac8 17 b4 ♖fe8

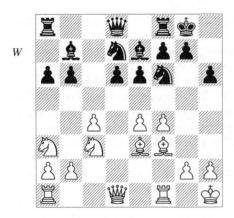

18 a3 ♕b8 19 ♘d2 (a standard reorganization, but over the years it's become clear that a knight on d2 versus the Hedgehog is primarily defensive and limits positive operations; traditionally the knight belongs on d4) 19...♗f8 20 ♕e1 ♗a8 21 ♕f2 ♗c6 22 ♖fe1 ♗e7 and neither side was doing much.

We now return to 14 ♕e2 (D):

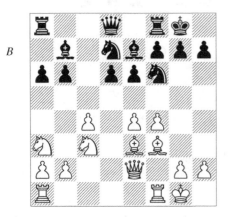

14...♖e8

The very young Kasparov played 14...♕c7 15 ♖ac1 ♖ac8 16 g4 ♘c5 and the game demonstrates that Black needn't play ...h6 if he has other central prospects: 17 ♕g2 d5! 18 e5 ♘fe4 19 cxd5 exd5 20 b4 (20 ♖fd1) 20...♘xc3 21 ♖xc3 d4! (a typically tactical solution) 22 ♗xd4 ♕d7 23 ♘c2 ♗xf3 24 ♖cxf3! (24 ♖fxf3? ♘e6! and White's pawns and pieces are loose; 24 ♕xf3 ♘a4 25 ♖xc8 ♖xc8 also costs White material) 24...♘e6 25 ♗e3! (25 ♗xb6 ♕c6 hits two pieces, so 26 ♗c5 ♘xc5 27 bxc5 ♗xc5+ could follow; Black's activity provides plenty of compensation) 25...f5!? 26 exf6 ♗xf6 27

♔h1 ♕d5 28 a3 ♕c4 29 f5!? ♕xc2 (29...♘g5!? might be worth a try) 30 ♕xc2 ♖xc2 31 fxe6 ♖c6 32 a4 ½-½ Tseshkovsky-Kasparov, USSR Ch (Minsk) 1979.

15 ♖fd1 ♕c7 16 ♖ac1 ♖ac8

This was the time for 16...h6!, to answer 17 g4 with 17...♘h7!; compare what happens next.

17 g4! h6

Kasparov's idea 17...♘c5 18 ♕g2 d5? fails now that White's rook is on d1: 19 cxd5 exd5 20 e5 ♘fe4 21 ♘xd5.

18 h4!

This is a different story, because ...g5 is prevented.

18...♘h7 19 ♕h2

A good move, and the natural 19 g5 also looks promising; e.g., 19...hxg5 20 hxg5 e5 21 ♘d5 ♗xd5 22 cxd5 ♕b7 23 ♖xc8 ♖xc8 24 ♗g4.

19...♘c5 (D)

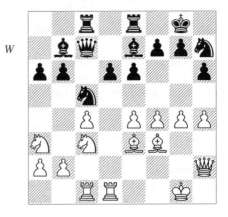

20 ♕h3!

Now 20 g5 can be answered by 20...f5!? 21 ♗h5 ♘xe4 22 ♘xe4 ♗xe4 23 ♗xe8 ♖xe8 and Black possesses the terrible a8-h1 diagonal. The text-move prevents ...f5.

20...♗f6

20...g5?! is met by 21 hxg5 hxg5 22 ♖c2! and ♖h2.

21 ♘ab1 g6 22 ♖c2 ♗g7 23 ♖cd2 ♗f8 24 g5 h5 25 ♗f2 ♗c6 26 ♘a3! (D)

Terrific! The knight heads towards its rightful square on d4. White has shown admirable patience throughout this manoeuvring stage.

26...♘d7 27 ♘c2 ♘c5 28 ♘d4 ♗b7 29 f5!

Finally! White transforms his space advantage into concrete gains.

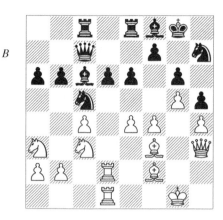

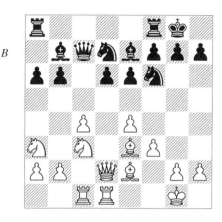

29...exf5 30 exf5 ♘e4 31 fxg6 fxg6 32 ♘xe4 ♗xe4 33 ♘e6 ♕b7 34 ♗xe4 ♕xe4 35 ♘xf8 ♘xf8 36 ♖xd6

White has a considerable advantage now, although the mutually exposed kings make the position difficult for both sides. We are past the opening stage and I'll let the moves speak for themselves. Towards the end White's king looks exposed but according to my chess engine Black never had any kind of perpetual check.

36...♖xc4 37 ♖e1 ♕a8 38 ♖xe8 ♕xe8 39 ♕b3 ♕f7 40 ♖f6 ♕d5 41 ♖xb6 ♔h8 42 ♖f6 ♖c1+ 43 ♔h2 ♖h1+ 44 ♔g3 ♕e5+ 45 ♔g2 ♕h2+ 46 ♔f3 ♕h3+ 47 ♔e4 ♕g4+ 48 ♖f4 ♕e2+ 49 ♕e3 ♕c2+ 50 ♕d3 ♕c6+ 51 ♕d5 ♕c2+ 52 ♔f3 ♘e6 53 ♗d4+ ♘g7 54 ♖f8+ 1-0

White Plays f3

Anand – Illescas
Linares 1992

8...b6 9 ♗e2 ♗b7 10 0-0 ♘b8!?

An old move-order that ends up transposing to the main line. This knight normally travels to e5 and then back to d7. I should also mention that the moves ...♗e7, ...b6, ...♗b7, ...0-0, ...♕c7 and ...♖ac8 have been played in almost every sequence. For once I'm going to ignore move-order issues and concentrate upon the basic position.

11 f3 ♗e7 12 ♗e3 ♘bd7 13 ♕d2 0-0 14 ♖fd1 ♕c7 15 ♖ac1 *(D)*

15...♖ac8

We're roughly at what might be considered the main line; at any rate, several high-level games have gone this way. Black should be

doing reasonably well if you compare this with a 'normal' Hedgehog arising from the English Opening. The knight on a3 can't possibly be superior to that on d4 and it has used four moves to get to the edge of the board! On the other hand Black can't even think about ...b5. So what's going on here? From Black's point of view it would be nice to do something positive before White catches up by rerouting his knight and pushing his queenside pawns. But in this sort of Hedgehog formation Black famously waits until the opportunity comes for ...b5 or ...d5. What to do? There are two main strategies. One is to play moves like ...♖e8, ...♕b8 and ...♗f8, and then get serious about ...d5. The other is to embark upon the now-famous plan of ...♗d8-c7 (with minor threats on the kingside) followed by ...♔h8, ...♖g8 and ...g5-g4, generally with more serious threats. This is an important strategy for both sides to know, if only because White has been blown away by the attack in so many games. There's another rather silly-looking attack by ...h5-h4 (and, if allowed, ...h3 to enhance the power of the b7-bishop). This has been tried several times in recent master practice without White having found a convincing counterplan. Of these three ideas, the easiest for White to stop should be the first (a ...d5 break) but he has to be careful, as shown by 15...♖ad8 (instead of 15...♖ac8, which is probably objectively better) 16 ♗f1 ♕b8 17 ♘c2?! ♖fe8 18 ♔h1? d5! 19 cxd5 exd5 20 exd5 ♗d6 21 g3 b5 22 a3 ♕a8 23 ♗g2 ♘e5!? (23...♘c5 wins back the d-pawn) 24 ♖b1?! ½-½ Morović-Leitão, São Paulo 2002. Probably 24...♘c4 favours Black; at any rate he can be satisfied if he achieves ...d5 safely.

How about White? Taking the ...♗d8-c7, ...♖g8, ...g5 idea first, White will first play ♔h1 and ♗g1 to guard h2, and then ♗f1 for potential second-rank defence by the queen. With that formation you can see that in our main game those first moves of the plan, ...♗d8-c7, can be difficult to implement. Furthermore, White's knight on a3 may not be badly placed to meet Black's strategy. With the queen on b8, for instance, the moves ♖b1 and b4 will discourage ...d5, when Black has to watch out for the move c5, followed in some cases by ♘c4. Alternatively, White can run his queenside pawns at Black by ♘c2 and b4, a4 and a5. Right in the middle of that process Black has to be able to strike in the centre based upon the looseness of White's queenside; whether he is able to do so resolves the question of who stands better.

16 ♗f1 (D)

As explained, this clears the second rank, and the bishop might have been a target along the e-file anyway.

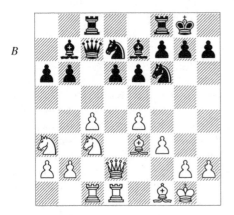

16...♖fe8

Fun with move-orders: 16...♕b8 is right if Black's plan is to play ...♗d8-c7, but it's very unclear and involves a pawn sacrifice: 17 ♔h1 (17 ♘c2 ♗d8!? 18 ♕xd6? ♗c7; there are plenty of options here) 17...♗d8!? (or 17...♖fe8) 18 ♗f4 (18 ♕xd6!? ♗c7 19 ♕d2 ♗xh2 20 g4 ♕g3!) 18...♘e5 19 ♕xd6!? ♗c7 20 ♕d2 ♘h5 21 ♗e3, and now 21...♘g6 22 g3!? f5! is scary. Needless to say, this just scratches the surface.

17 ♔h1 ♕b8 18 ♘c2 ♘e5

This time 18...♗d8? 19 ♕xd6 ♗c7 20 ♕d2 ♗xh2?? 21 g4 ♗e5 22 g5 costs Black a piece.

19 b3 ♗a8 20 ♗g1 ♖ed8?! 21 ♘d4 ♗f8?!

Black makes it difficult to protect b6.

22 ♖e1 ♘ed7 23 a3 ♗b7 24 b4 ♖c7 25 ♘b3 ♗a8 26 ♘a4! ♗c6 27 ♘b2!

Very original! c4 needs protection in a lot of lines and ♘d3 could be useful at the right time.

27...♗a8 28 ♗d4 ♖dc8 29 ♖ed1 ♗e7 30 ♕f2 ♕b7?

But 30...b5 31 ♘a5! is good for White.

31 ♘a4 ♖b8 32 ♘xb6! ♘xb6 33 ♘a5 ♕a7 (D)

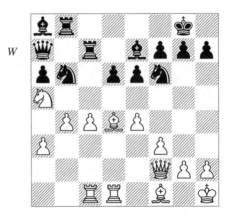

34 c5

A nice combination. White wins his piece back with more to come.

34...dxc5 35 bxc5 ♘c8

After 35...♗xc5 36 ♗xc5 ♘fd7 37 ♖xd7 ♖xd7 38 ♗xb6 White wins due to the back rank.

36 c6 ♖b6 37 ♖b1 ♖xb1 38 ♖xb1 1-0

Conventional Development

Lukin – Taimanov
St Petersburg 1995

1 e4 c5 2 ♘f3 e6 3 d4 cxd4 4 ♘xd4 ♘c6 5 ♘c3

White chooses the simple path. If Black plays 5...♘f6 in this position, we return to the Sicilian Four Knights. In spite of many fascinating struggles resulting from the most frequent continuation 5...♕c7, I'm going to forego that and explore only one set-up within the Taimanov Sicilian proper.

5...a6 (D)

This sequence can sometimes transpose into the ...♕c7 lines. But Black often uses this move-order because he wants to play 6...♘ge7 next, the system that Taimanov himself loved

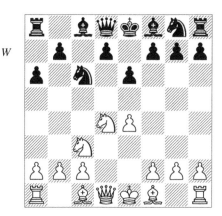

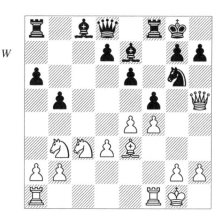

and promoted. That move prepares ...♘xd4 followed by ...♘c6, or ...♘g6 with dark-square control over e5. Black's strategy provides yet another demonstration of the flexibility associated with ...e6 and ...a6.

6 ♗e2

There is also independent theory on 6th-move deviations after 5...a6 showing ideas that do not also apply to the Paulsen:

a) After 6 ♘xc6 bxc6, White can play 7 e5!? (not considered too dangerous for Black after 7...♕c7 8 f4 d6) or 7 ♗d3. In the latter case White has an aggressive posture but his knight might be better-placed on d2, from where it has the squares c4 and f3 within reach. In both cases the move ...a6 tends to be wasted; on the other hand these may not be the best plans for White versus a Paulsen/Taimanov structure.

b) Here's a really exotic opening idea for those who've never seen it: 6 g3 ♘ge7 7 ♘b3 d6 8 ♗g2 ♗d7 9 0-0 ♘c8!? (Black prepares to transfer his knight to the queenside and in the meantime lends extra support to d6) 10 f4 ♗e7 11 ♗e3 0-0 12 ♕e2 b5 with the idea ...♘b6-c4. This can apply to several positions.

6...♘ge7 7 0-0

7 ♘b3 b5 8 0-0 ♘g6 9 f4 ♗e7 10 ♗e3 0-0 11 ♗d3?! (this doesn't seem to work out; possibly 11 ♕d2 is better) 11...♘b4 12 ♕h5 ♘xd3 13 cxd3 (often this pawn-structure is a pleasant one for White, and his queen on h5 looks particularly well situated) 13...f5! (D).

One move turns everything around: White's advance f5 is no longer a factor, his e3-bishop has been restricted, and Black's b7-bishop will have assistance with attacking the centre. White even has to keep a watch on his f4-pawn because

of the possibility of ...fxe4. Arnason-Romanishin, Lone Pine 1981 continued 14 ♘d4 (14 ♘d5! ♗b7! {the idea was 14...exd5 15 exf5 ♘h8 16 f6!} 15 ♘xe7+ ♘xe7 16 ♘c5 ♗c6 17 ♗d4 ♕e8! with equality, Orlov-Taimanov, St Petersburg 1995) 14...♗c5 15 exf5 ♗xd4 16 ♗xd4 ♖xf5 17 ♕g4 ♗b7 with advantage for Black. Compare the bishops and rooks!

7...♘xd4 8 ♕xd4 ♘c6 9 ♕d3 ♕c7

This is a normal Taimanov/Paulsen move which incidentally renders ♕g3 useless.

10 ♗g5

White interferes with Black's development, and his bishop strengthens the effect of a potential knight sacrifice on d5.

10...♗d6! (D)

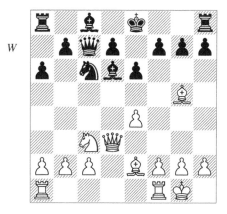

It's not unusual for the dark-squared bishop to go to this square in the Paulsen and Taimanov. In general (i.e., in a broader context than this specific line), ...♗d6 has several points:

a) It sometimes develops a piece with tempo by threatening ...♗xh2+. Then if White replies h3, he has weakened his kingside and failed to contest the f4-square. But upon g3, Black's advance ...h5-h4 can be extremely annoying. Furthermore, the bishop can switch to the g1-a7 diagonal when called upon to do so. If White plays f4, a bishop on c5 may be very strong.

b) Black's bishop controls important dark squares from d6; in some lines it goes to e5 in advance of moving the d-pawn, or it may go to f4 and trade bishops. As this can leave d6 weak, Black will often keep his king in the centre, ready to go to e7 if necessary.

c) Black may also be able to delay f4, which is key to White's strategy. One theme in this regard is ...♘e5-g6, perhaps in conjunction with ...f6. Along those lines, it's worth noting that if White had avoided the exchange of knights on d4, then the same idea could be expressed by ...♘ge7-g6. By the time f4 *is* played (probably supported by the preparatory move g3), then Black will normally have ...b5 and ...♗b7 in, so that White has some weakness on the long diagonal which will discourage him from playing e5. All this is rather exotic and clearly won't be achieved in one game, but it demonstrates the same sort of flexibility that we saw in the Paulsen Variation.

11 ♔h1 *(D)*

Here's another typical set-up for Black: 11 ♕h3 0-0 12 ♖ad1 f6! 13 ♗c1 b5!? (13...b6 would prevent the next move). White now has a common tactic that must always be weighed by both sides: 14 ♗xb5!? axb5 15 ♘xb5 ♗xh2+ 16 ♕xh2 ♕xh2+ 17 ♔xh2 ♖xa2 18 ♖fe1 g5! 19 f3 ♘e5 (a pseudo-outpost) 20 ♔g1 ♗b7 21 ♘c3 ♖aa8 22 ♔f2 ♗c6 23 ♖h1 ½-½ V.Mäki-Øst Hansen, Gjøvik 1985.

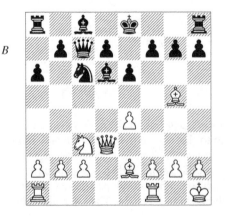

11...♘e5

Not 11...♗xh2? 12 g3. However, 11...f6 12 ♗e3 b5 13 f4 ♗e7 14 e5 is perfectly good, Nijboer-Van Mil, Dutch Ch (Eindhoven) 1993. Sommerbauer then suggests that Black snatch the centre pawn and hold on to it by 14...fxe5 15 fxe5 ♘xe5 16 ♕d4 ♗b7 17 ♖ad1 ♖f8, a continuation admitting of some risk, of course.

12 ♕d2 f6 13 ♗h4 ♘g6 14 ♗g3 ♗xg3

It might be more Taimanov-like for Taimanov to have continued 14...♘f4 looking for a dark-square grip following ...g5, with ...b6, ...♗b7 and a kingside attack to follow; for example, 15 ♗h5+ ♔e7 16 ♖ad1 ♗e5 17 ♗f3 g5, etc.

15 hxg3 b5 16 f4 ♗b7 17 ♗d3 0-0

The position is equal.

Sozin Attack (and the Classical Sicilian)

1 e4 c5 2 ♘f3

The Sozin Variations are characterized by the move ♗c4, and can arise from either 2...e6 or 2...d6. The following variation is known as the 'Classical Sicilian':

2...d6 3 d4 cxd4 4 ♘xd4 ♘f6 5 ♘c3 ♘c6 *(D)*

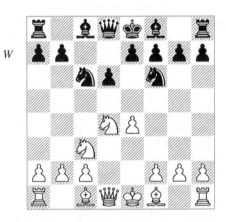

This can include a variety of lines but the most important ones are the Richter-Rauzer Attack (6 ♗g5), and the Sozin Attack (6 ♗c4), which is the subject of this section. These moves both strongly discourage Black from playing ...e5.

Instead, 6 ♗e2 e5 *(D)* is the Boleslavsky Variation, one of the original ...e5 Sicilians that still discourages players from 6 ♗e2.

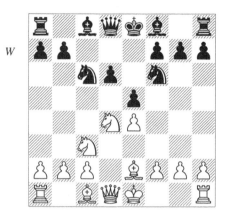

When compared to the Najdorf with 5...a6 6 ♗e2 e5, it turns out that ...♘c6 is usually more useful than ...a6. An example with typical central themes:

Apicella – Kramnik
Moscow OL 1994

1 e4 c5 2 ♘f3 ♘c6 3 d4 cxd4 4 ♘xd4 ♘f6 5 ♘c3 d6 6 ♗e2 e5 7 ♘f3 h6

This is played to prevent 8 ♗g5, which would strengthen White's control of d5, although Black has done well enough with 7...♗e7 too.

8 h3 ♗e6 9 0-0 ♗e7 10 ♖e1 ♖c8 11 ♗f1 ♘b8!? *(D)*

Delaying castling has certain positive effects.

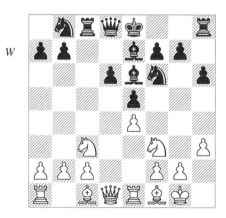

12 ♘d5 ♘xd5

For one thing, this capture no longer loses a piece and Black retains his bishops.

13 exd5 ♗f5 14 c4 0-0 15 ♕a4!? a5

And here the moves ...♖c8 and ...♘b8 help to set up a blockade on c5.

16 a3 ♗d7 17 ♕d1 a4 18 b4 axb3 19 ♕xb3 ♘a6 20 ♗e3 ♕c7 21 a4 ♘c5! 22 ♗xc5 ♕xc5 23 ♕xb7 ♖c7 *(D)*

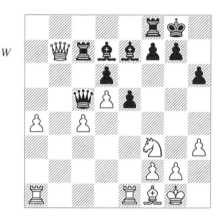

Black has the benefit of the bishop-pair, controls the dark squares, and can play against the weaknesses on a4 and c4. Meanwhile White's f1-bishop is pathetically bad. All for a pawn.

24 ♕b3 ♖a8 25 ♘d2 f5

The central majority is a weapon in any line where a knight capture on d5 has been met by exd5.

26 ♘b1 ♗h4 27 g3 ♗f6 28 ♘c3 e4 29 ♖a2 ♕a5

29...♗xc3 30 ♕xc3 ♖xa4 is already better for Black but Kramnik wants more.

30 ♖c1 ♗e5 31 ♖cc2 ♖c5 32 ♘b5 ♔h8

Now even a pawn-storm by ...g5 and ...f4 becomes a possibility.

33 ♕e3 ♕b4 34 ♘d4 ♖cc8 35 ♘e6 ♖xa4 36 ♖xa4 ♕xa4 37 ♖d2 ♕a1! 38 ♔g2 ♖b8 39 ♘f4 ♖b1 40 ♕e2 ♖e1 41 ♖a2 ♖xe2 42 ♖xa1 ♖xf2+ 43 ♔xf2 ♗xa1 44 ♔e3 ♔g8 45 ♘e6 g6 46 c5 ♗e5 47 g4 ♗xe6! 48 dxe6 d5

And so forth – Black has three passed pawns!

Another significant difference between 2...e6 and the Classical order (with 2...d6, 4...♘f6 and 5...♘c6, for example) is that after 6 ♗c4 in the latter instance, Black has the option of 6...♕b6 (the 'Benko Variation') rather than transposing to a Sozin by 6...e6. His idea is to disturb the d4-knight. White can respond in a number of ways, but by far the most common one is 7 ♘b3, in order to protect the b-pawn and play ♗e3; for example, 7...e6 8 0-0 ♗e7 9 ♗e3 ♕c7. As I describe elsewhere, this creates a situation in which Black seems to have wasted an important tempo by ...♕b6-c7, but White may make up for that by playing ♘b3-d4. Lines with ...♕b6 have become more popular over time for this reason.

1 e4 c5 2 ♘f3 e6 3 d4 cxd4 4 ♘xd4 ♘f6

Here both 4...♘c6 5 ♘c3 d6 and the Najdorf move-order 2...d6 3 d4 cxd4 4 ♘xd4 ♘f6 5 ♘c3 a6 circumvent the Keres Attack described in the next note, but of course they have their own peculiarities.

5 ♘c3 d6 (D)

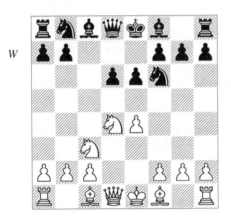

6 ♗e3

6 g4 is the Keres Attack, which has a high reputation among players, and accounts for the fact that the Scheveningen with ...e6, ...d6 and ...♘f6 (before other moves) is not played as much these days – Scheveningen lines more often arise by transposition from the lines mentioned in the previous note.

However, I am using this sequence of moves in order to lay out some move-order issues and transpositions. Instead of 6 ♗e3, for instance, 6 ♗c4 a6 transposes to the 6 ♗c4 Najdorf.

The traditional 6 ♗e2 can also transpose into other variations such as the Najdorf with ...♘bd7; but if ...♘c6 is played soon the variations take on their own character. One line is 6...a6 7 0-0 ♗e7 8 f4 ♘c6 9 ♗e3 0-0 10 a4 ♕c7 11 ♔h1 ♖e8 12 ♗f3 ♗f8 13 ♕d2 ♘a5!?

(13...♗d7 develops simply and sensibly) 14 b3! (to stop ...♘c4) 14...♖b8 15 ♖ad1 (a positional mistake is 15 f5? ♘c6! 16 fxe6 fxe6 17 ♗g5 ♗e7 18 ♖ad1 ♘e5, Hossain-Goloshchapov, Dhaka 2003; in this position a major plus for Black is that d5 and f5 are unavailable to White's pieces) 15...♘c6 (or 15...♗d7 with equality) 16 ♗f2 (heading for g3 or h4) 16...♘d7?! 17 ♗g3 ♘xd4 18 ♕xd4 b5 19 axb5 axb5 20 b4 g6 21 e5! d5 22 f5! gxf5 23 ♘xd5! ♕c4 (23...exd5? 24 e6) 24 ♕d2 h6 25 h3 exd5 26 ♗xd5 ♕xb4 27 c3 ♕c5 28 ♖xf5 ♖e6 29 ♖xf7! ♘b6 (29...♔xf7 30 ♕f4+ ♔e8 31 ♗xe6 is decisive) 30 ♖df1 ♘xd5 31 ♖xf8+ ♕xf8 32 ♖xf8+ ♔xf8 33 ♕xd5 and White went on to win easily in Adams-Topalov, Wijk aan Zee 2006.

6...♘c6 7 ♗c4 (D)

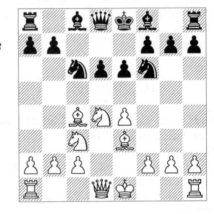

We have arrived at the Sozin Attack. It is similar to the Najdorf 6 ♗c4 variation but Black's knight is on c6. That implies the possibility of earlier simplification by ...♘xd4, which renders White's idea f4-f5 less effective. Black is also unlikely to have to worry about the sacrifice ♗xe6 that was a hallmark of the Najdorf line. And even the possibility of f4 followed by e5 can lose force because Black has a natural retreating and counterattacking square for his attacked knight on d7.

White has ample resources, the nature of which are completely dependent upon his choice of piece deployments, especially that of the queen. If she goes to f3, for example, Black will struggle to achieve ...b5 unless he exchanges on d4. But ...♘xd4 brings another piece to the centre, normally White's bishop, which then aims at Black's king. In the absence of that exchange, the move f5 can still be effective. If White castles kingside he will almost certainly play f4 and aim for e5. But the most compelling variations arise when White castles queenside and plays his remaining attacking weapon, namely g4-g5. It is no coincidence that the g-pawn advance established itself in this variation some years back and presaged the flood of g4 attacks in the Sicilian and other openings. Somehow modern theory keeps settling upon that move as the most effective one in long-disputed attacking variations.

7...♗e7

Here we'll show three games illustrating the ...e6/...♘c6 positions: one in which White castles kingside, another in which his king stays in the middle of the board, and a modern one in which he plays 0-0-0.

Sozin with Kingside Castling

Fischer – Spassky
Reykjavik Wch (4) 1972

8 0-0

This introduces a traditional and still important line.

8...0-0 9 ♗b3

White has to watch out for 9...d5, and also for the trick 9...♘xe4! 10 ♘xe4 d5, opening up the centre and freeing Black's game.

9...a6 *(D)*

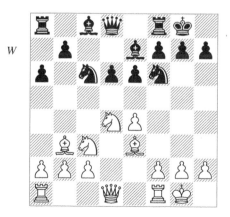

This position could also have come from 2...d6 via the Najdorf 6 ♗c4 Variation, as it did in the main game that we are looking at.

10 f4 ♘xd4 11 ♗xd4

11 ♕xd4 runs into 11...♘g4!.

11...b5! 12 a3

This is the slow approach. The main line for years, and indeed what still may be the main line of the entire Classical Sozin, goes 12 e5 dxe5 13 fxe5 ♘d7 14 ♘e4 (there's not enough force behind 14 ♕g4 ♘c5 15 ♖ad1 ♗b7 16 ♔h1 ♕c7, when the game is equal) 14...♗b7 *(D)*.

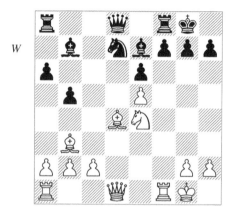

Here we have a quintessential old-style Sicilian scenario: White's forces aim at the kingside, including his knight, queen, both of his bishops, and his rook on the open file. He would like to play ♕g4 and ♘f6 (even as a sacrifice), and ♖ad1, whereas the sacrifice ♖xf7 might easily enter into the picture.

For his part, Black will be sure to target White's unsupported weakness on e5. Black's kingside is generally solid and his e6-pawn negates the pressure from White's b3-bishop. He would also like to simplify, beginning by exchanging off the bothersome knight on e4, before White can cause him tactical difficulties. In the meantime Black has his usual control of the c-file, supporting desirable moves such as ...♘c5 at the right moment. Play usually continues 15 ♘d6 (15 ♕g4 ♗xe4 16 ♕xe4 ♘c5 is equal) 15...♗xd6 16 exd6 ♕g5 17 ♖f2! (this protects the 2nd rank and prepares ♕d2; after any exchange of queens the two bishops will be a major advantage; 17 ♕e2 e5 18 ♗c3 ♕g6 has been analysed thoroughly following the Short-Kasparov world championship match, leading to equality with best play) 17...a5! 18 ♕e2 ♖a6! (White was threatening ♗xe6) 19 ♗c3 (or 19

♗xe6 ♖xd6 with equality) with unclear play; perhaps 19...b4 20 ♗d2 ♕c5 21 ♗f4 is best. A great study line!

12...♗b7 13 ♕d3

13 ♕e1 a5! with ...b4 next; then 14 ♘xb5?! ♘xe4 (or 14...a4 and then ...♘xe4) conquers the centre and eliminates White's attacking chances.

13...a5! *(D)*

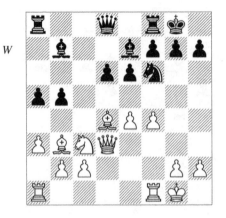

This pawn sacrifice diverts White from the centre by threatening ...b4.

14 e5?!

The right spirit, but weakening. A better try is the aggressive 14 f5!?, but then Black can counter by 14...b4 15 axb4 axb4 with approximate equality after 16 ♕b5.

14...dxe5 15 fxe5 ♘d7 16 ♘xb5

16 ♘e4 ♗xe4! 17 ♕xe4 ♘c5 18 ♗xc5 ♗xc5+ 19 ♔h1 ♕d4; that pawn on e5 is a structural problem, so White has to be wary of too much simplification.

16...♘c5 17 ♗xc5 ♗xc5+ 18 ♔h1 ♕g5 *(D)*

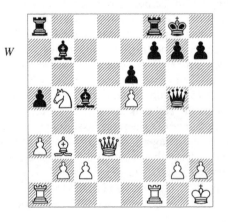

In return for a pawn, Black's bishop-pair rakes the kingside and White's e5-pawn is weak. The opening has ended successfully for Spassky. I'll skimp on the notes as we proceed through the middlegame:

19 ♕e2

Here 19 ♕g3! ♕xg3 20 hxg3 improves. Then 20...♗a6 21 a4 ♗xb5 22 axb5 ♗d4 is only nominally better for Black.

19...♖ad8 20 ♖ad1 ♖xd1 21 ♖xd1 h5!?

21...♗e3! 22 ♘d6 ♗c6 is better, when a cute line is 23 ♖f1 ♗f4 24 ♕f2 ♕g4! with the idea of ...♕h3!.

22 ♘d6?! ♗a8 23 ♘c4

Not 23 ♖f1?! h4 24 ♘xf7? h3! 25 ♘xg5 hxg2+ 26 ♕xg2 ♖xf1#.

23...h4 24 h3 ♗e3 25 ♕g4 ♕xe5

As the centre pawn falls, so does White's ability to control the enemy pieces and keep his own out of trouble.

26 ♕xh4 g5! 27 ♕g4 ♗c5! 28 ♘b5 ♔g7

Now ...♖h8-h4 looms.

29 ♘d4 *(D)*

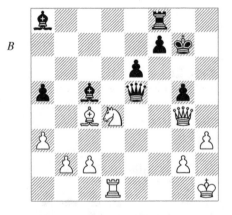

29...♖h8?!

But now 29...♖d8! 30 c3 ♕e3! was terribly strong. Spassky's model use of the bishop-pair falls short only for tactical reasons.

30 ♘f3 ♗xf3 31 ♕xf3 ♗d6?

31...♖h4! may still have been winning, one line being 32 ♖f1 ♖f4 33 ♕e2 ♖xf1+ 34 ♕xf1 ♗d6 (34...♗xb2) 35 ♔g1 ♕h2+ 36 ♔f2 ♗c5+ 37 ♔e1 ♕e5+ 38 ♕e2 ♕xb2 and the opposite-coloured bishops are still helping Black.

32 ♕c3! ♕xc3 33 bxc3 ♗e5 34 ♖d7 ♔f6 35 ♔g1

and the game was drawn shortly thereafter.

Short – Kasparov

London PCA Wch (12) 1993

8 ♗b3 0-0 9 f4 a6 10 ♕f3

This attacking move used to be popular, understandably, since it gets ready to castle queenside and blow the opponent off the board. But the queen on f3 is subject to harassment on the long diagonal, especially in the game line.

10...♘xd4 11 ♗xd4 b5 *(D)*

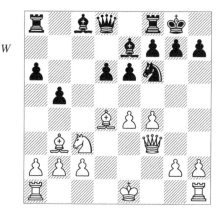

12 ♗xf6!

12 e5 dxe5 hits the d4-bishop, almost forcing 13 ♗xe5 (13 ♕xa8 ♕xd4 14 ♕f3 exf4 already gives Black two pawns, the bishop-pair and a load of weaknesses to work on, all for an exchange) 13...♖a7! 14 ♖d1 ♖d7 15 0-0 ♗b7 with the better pawn-structure and position.

12...♗xf6! 13 e5 ♗h4+ 14 g3 ♖b8! *(D)*

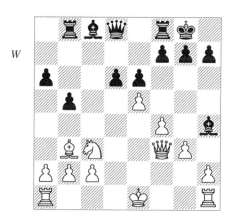

15 gxh4

The superiority of Black's pawn-structure shows in lines like 15 ♖f1 ♗e7 16 0-0-0 b4! (or

16...♗b7) 17 exd6 bxc3 18 dxe7 cxb2+ 19 ♔xb2 ♕xe7 with the idea of ...a5, ...♗b7 and ...♖fc8.

15...♗b7 16 ♘e4 dxe5!

Threatening ...♕d4 among other moves.

17 ♖g1 g6 18 ♖d1 ♗xe4 19 ♕xe4 ♕xh4+

With an attack. At the very least Black can get three pawns for the piece, but White has some activity, so an assessment of 'equal' seems fair. Many similar tactical themes appear in the positions with ...e6 and ...b5.

Velimirović Attack

Boto – Buntić

Bosnia 2001

8 ♕e2 *(D)*

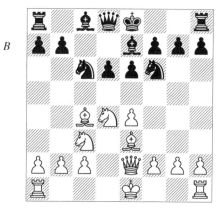

This move, together with queenside castling, characterizes the Velimirović Attack. Within hundreds of brilliancies that have been played by both sides of this opening, we find certain themes that are fundamental to attacking in the Sicilian Defence. Many of them were first played in games with this variation, or at least brought to prominence by their use in them. I'll try to show a few of these essential building blocks of Sicilian attacks.

Looking over the older games by Velimirović himself, you see the tactical philosophy expressed by Kasparov, who stresses 'cutting the board in two', resulting in attractive-looking pieces uselessly stranded from defence of the king.

8...a6

8...0-0 9 0-0-0 ♕a5 was played in the famous encounter Fischer-Geller, Skopje/Krusevo/Ohrid

1967. It isn't too stunning by Velimirović Attack standards, but since most of the fun in this section will be White's, I'll show how Black fights back when apparently lost: 10 ♗b3 ♘xd4 11 ♗xd4 ♗d7 12 ♔b1 ♗c6 13 f4 ♖ad8 14 ♖hf1 b5 15 f5 b4 16 fxe6 bxc3 17 exf7+ ♔h8 18 ♖f5 ♕b4 19 ♕f1 ♘xe4 20 a3? (20 ♕f4!) 20...♕b7 21 ♕f4 ♗a4!! (a brilliant move that turns the tide) 22 ♕g4 ♗f6 23 ♖xf6 ♗xb3 0-1.

9 0-0-0 *(D)*

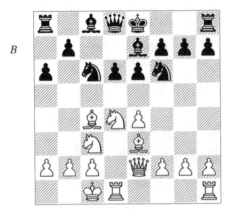

In this position Velimirović's first idea was the uninhibited g4-g5 followed by whatever was necessary to get at Black's king. Then attention focused mainly upon g4 and ♖hg1, with precisely the same strategy but differently executed. Sometimes White has also succeeded after f4 and either f5 or e5, but that hasn't established itself as well as the other two.

9...0-0

Here is one of Velimirović's games in the first days of the Attack. The thing that shocked people about this and games in the next notes was not that sacrifices like ♘f5 and ♘d5 were being made but how slow they seemed to be and how little material was needed to make the attacks work: 9...♕c7 10 ♗b3 ♘a5 11 g4 b5 12 g5 ♘xb3+ 13 axb3 ♘d7 14 ♘f5!! *(D)*.

The '!!' comes from annotators at the time of the game, deservedly so for the attack's originality; these days the idea is second nature, but the specific tactics and White's sustained attack are still mind-boggling. 14...exf5 15 ♘d5 ♕d8 16 exf5 ♗b7 17 f6 gxf6 18 ♖he1 ♗xd5 (Black's exchanging all the pieces off – this must be right) 19 ♖xd5 ♖g8 20 gxf6 ♘xf6 21 ♖f5 (still a full piece down) 21...♖b8 22 ♗a7 ♖b7 23

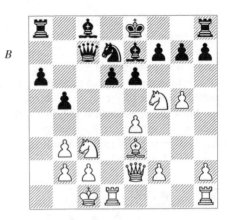

♗d4 ♘g4 24 ♕f3 ♖d7 25 ♕h3! (wonderful geometry) 25...♘e5 26 f4 ♗h4 27 ♖e2 ♖e7 28 fxe5 (finally recovering his material) 28...dxe5 29 ♗c5! ♗g5+ 30 ♔b1 f6 31 ♕h5+ ♖g6 32 h4 ♕c8 33 ♗xe7 ♕xf5 34 ♗b4 ♕f4 35 ♕xh7 ♖h6? 36 ♕e7# (1-0) Velimirović-Popović, Novi Sad 1976.

10 ♗b3 ♕c7 11 ♖hg1

Let's look at another Velimirović *tour de force* and representative of the themes that he brought to the fore: 11 g4 ♘d7 12 ♘f5! exf5 13 ♘d5 ♕d8 14 gxf5 ♘a5 15 ♘xe7+ ♕xe7 16 ♗d5 ♔h8 17 ♖hg1 ♘f6 *(D)*.

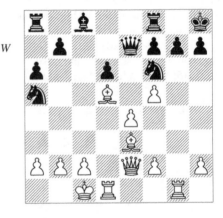

18 ♕f3! (these relatively slow moves characterize the Attack to this day) 18...♘xd5 19 ♖xd5 ♘c4 20 f6!! ♕xf6 21 ♕xf6 gxf6 22 ♗d4 ♘e5 23 f4 ♘d7 24 ♖xd6 ♖g8 25 ♖d1 ♖e8 26 f5 ♖xe4 27 ♖g1 h5 28 ♖g5! ♖g4 29 ♖xf6! ♖g1+ (29...♔h7 30 ♖xh5+ ♔g8 31 ♖h8+!) 30 ♔d2 ♖g2+ 31 ♔e3 1-0 Velimirović-Bukal, Yugoslavia 1971.

11...♘d7

Now we're getting around to some real fireworks. Try this out: 11...b5 12 g4 b4 13 ♘xc6 ♕xc6 14 ♘d5 exd5 15 g5 dxe4 16 gxf6 ♗xf6 17 ♗d5 ♕a4 18 ♕h5! ♗e6 *(D)*.

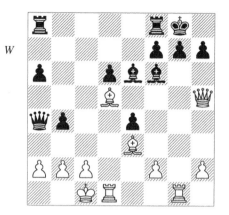

19 ♖xg7+!! ♔xg7 20 ♖g1 ♖fc8 (20...♖ac8 21 ♖xg7+ ♔xg7 22 ♗d4+ f6 23 ♕g5+ ♔f7 24 ♕xf6+ ♔e8 25 ♕xe6+, etc.) 21 ♖xg7+ ♔xg7 (21...♔f8 22 ♖xf7+!) 22 ♕h6+ ♔g8 23 ♗e4 b3 (23...♖c4 24 ♗xh7+ ♔h8 25 ♗g5 ♖f4 26 ♗f5+) 24 ♗xh7+ ♔h8 25 ♗f5+ ♔g8 26 ♕h7+ ♔f8 27 ♗h6+ ♔e8 28 ♕g8+ ♔e7 29 ♗g5+ ♔d7 30 ♕xf7+ ♔c6 31 ♗xe6 ♔b6 32 ♗e3+ ♔a5 33 ♗xc8 ♖xc8 34 ♕f5+ ♖c5 35 ♗xc5 ♕b5 (35...bxa2 36 b4+ ♔b5 37 ♕d7+) 36 ♗b4+ ♔xb4 37 a3+ ♔c4 38 ♕xb5+ axb5 39 cxb3+ ♔d3 40 ♔d1 1-0 Ostapenko-Yartsev, USSR 1969.

But let's enjoy another of those classic games by the master: 11...♘a5 12 g4 b5 13 g5 ♘xb3+ 14 axb3 ♘d7 15 f4 b4 *(D)*.

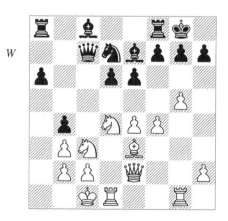

16 ♘f5! exf5 17 ♘d5 ♕d8 18 exf5 ♖e8 19 g6! fxg6 20 fxg6 h6 21 ♕c4 ♔h8 22 ♗d4 ♗f8

23 ♘c7 ♘c5 24 ♘xa8 ♗e6 25 ♕e2 ♕xa8 26 ♕h5 ♔g8 27 ♖xc5 dxc5 28 f5 ♗d5 29 f6 (a gorgeous attack, begun 15 moves before!) 29...♖d8 30 f7+ ♔h8 31 ♕h4 a5 32 ♖ge1 a4 33 ♕xd8 ♕xd8 34 ♖e8 ♕g5+ 35 ♔b1 ♕xg6 36 ♖xf8+ ♔h7 37 ♖h8+ ♔xh8 38 f8♕+ ♗g8 39 ♖d8 1-0 Velimirović-B.Ivanović, Nikšić 1978.

Ultimately you could say that it's White's positional advantages (space, occupation of d5, harmonious piece placement, and so on) that allow these attacks to succeed, as indicated by their duration and the absence of direct tactics for so many moves after the sacrifice.

12 g4 ♘xd4

Now let's allow Shirov to show his amazing talent from the black side of the board: 12...♘c5 13 ♘f5 b5! 14 ♗d5 *(D)*.

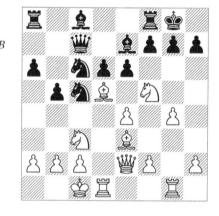

14...♗b7! (he'll just continue to leave everything hanging!) 15 g5 ♖fc8 16 ♖g3 ♗f8! 17 ♕h5 g6 18 ♘h6+ ♔h8 19 ♕h4 b4 20 ♗xc6 bxc3 21 ♗xc5 (I'm ignoring the mistakes; obviously any game like this can't be flawless) 21...cxb2+ 22 ♔b1 ♗xc6 23 ♖xd6! ♗a4!! 24 ♖c3 ♗xd6! 25 ♗d4+ e5 26 ♖xc7 ♖xc7 27 ♗xb2 ♖b8! 28 ♔a1 ♖xb2! 29 ♘xf7+ ♖xf7 30 ♔xb2 ♖f3 31 ♕g4! ♗a3+ 32 ♔a1! ♖xf2 33 ♕h3! (it goes on and on!) 33...♗e7 34 ♕c8+ ♖f8 35 ♕xa6 ♗xc2 36 h4 ♗c5 37 ♔b2 ♖xe4 38 ♕e6 ♖b8+ 39 ♔c3 ♗d4+ 40 ♔c4 ♗f5 41 ♕f7 ♖c8+ 42 ♔d5 ♗h3 43 h5 gxh5 44 ♕f3! ♗g4 45 ♕f6+ ♔g8 46 g6 hxg6 47 ♕xg6+ ♔f8 48 ♕f6+ ♔e8 49 ♕g6+ ♔e7 50 ♕g7+ ♔d8 51 ♕f6+ ♔c7 52 ♕c6+ ♔b8 53 ♕b5+ ♔a7 54 ♕a4+ ♔b7 55 ♕b4+ ♗b6 56 ♔xe5 ♖c5+ and Black won in Onishchuk-Shirov, Bundesliga

1996/7. Any and all of these games will give you some of the best possible lessons in Sicilian tactics and combinations.

13 ♗xd4 b5 14 g5 b4 15 ♕h5 ♘e5 (D)

After 15...bxc3, there's nothing fancy: 16 ♖d3! and wins.

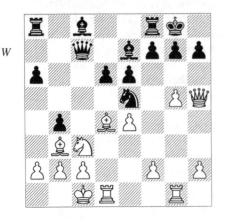

16 f4 ♘g6 17 f5! ♘f4

A wonderful variation that you shouldn't miss: 17...bxc3 18 ♖df1! cxb2+ 19 ♔b1 ♘e5 20 ♖f4 f6? 21 ♖h4 ♘c4 22 ♗xc4 ♕xc4 23 ♕xh7+ ♔f7 24 ♕g6+ ♔g8 25 ♕xg7+! ♔xg7 26 gxf6++ ♔f7 27 ♖g7+ ♔e8 28 ♖xe7+ ♔d8 29 ♗b6+ ♕c7 30 ♗xc7#.

18 ♕f3 e5 19 g6!! (D)

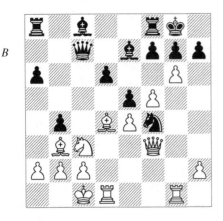

19...bxc3

The variations are amazing: 19...hxg6 20 ♕xf4! exf4 21 ♖xg6 and Black is helpless; 19...♗f6 20 ♕xf4! exf4 (20...exd4 21 ♕h6!!) 21 ♗xf6 ♔h8 22 ♗xg7+ ♔xg7 23 gxf7+ ♔h6 24 ♖d3.

20 ♕xf4! ♔h8

After all those ideas, 20...exd4 21 ♕h6! looks pedestrian.

21 gxf7 ♗f6 22 ♖xg7! ♗xg7

Or: 22...♗xf5 23 ♖xh7+!; 22...♗e6 23 ♗xe6 ♗xg7 24 f6 ♖xf7 25 ♗xf7 ♕xf7 26 fxg7+ ♕xg7 27 ♗xc3.

23 f6 ♕d8 24 ♖g1 1-0

The above presentation may have been self-indulgent, but those attacks *are* the Velimirović Attack, and to understand them is to understand the variation. More significantly, the same attacking themes quickly spread to the practice of the Sicilian Defence in general and appear in multitudinous variations today.

Accelerated Fianchetto

1 e4 c5 2 ♘f3 ♘c6 3 d4 cxd4 4 ♘xd4 g6 (D)

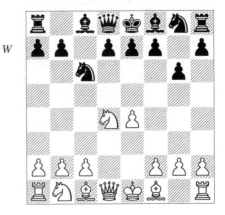

This system is similar to the Dragon (into which it often transposes), so my treatment will mainly concern White's most important challenge to Black's move-order, one that is not available in the Dragon:

5 c4

This variation is known as the 'Maroczy Bind', and indeed the same name is often applied to White's pawn-structure when it arises in other openings.

Before moving on to it, let me point out a few unique features in the Accelerated Fianchetto after the normal-looking 5 ♘c3 ♗g7, which is loaded with tricks and positional traps:

a) After 6 ♘b3, 6...♘f6 7 ♗e2 0-0 8 0-0 d6 leads us back to a Classical Dragon. Instead, the Accelerated Fianchetto move-order gives Black another option in 6...♗xc3+!? 7 bxc3 ♘f6, trying to exploit White's doubled c-pawns at the cost of losing the important dark-squared bishop; see the section of Chapter 3 devoted to doubled c-pawns for a short discussion of precisely this position.

b) 6 ♗e3 ♘f6 *(D)* and then:

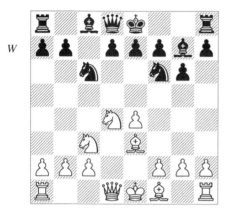

b1) 7 f3?! 0-0 8 ♕d2, in order to get into a Yugoslav Dragon, allows Black to free his game immediately in the classic fashion: 8...d5! and White should probably simplify by 9 exd5 ♘xd5 10 ♘xc6 bxc6 11 ♘xd5, with rough equality, before he stands worse due to the weaknesses that f3 has created; see how Black has saved a tempo by playing ...d5 rather than ...d6 and ...d5.

b2) Likewise, the Classical moves 7 ♗e2 0-0 8 0-0 can be answered by 8...d5!.

b3) Therefore White might want to play in the style of the Reversed Dragon by 7 ♘b3 0-0 8 ♗e2, if slower play is his inclination.

b4) 7 ♗c4 *(D)* and then:

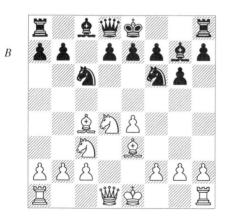

b41) At this point the move 7...♕a5 has some other tricks associated with it. For example, 8 ♕d2? ♘xe4! 9 ♘xc6 ♕xc3!!, or 8 f3? ♕b4! 9 ♗b3 ♘xe4!. White should simply play 8 0-0 0-0 9 ♘b3 ♕c7 10 f4 d6 11 ♗e2 with a sort of Classical Dragon in which the queen is arguably a little misplaced on c7. This line has proven a disincentive for those who are considering playing 7...♕a5.

b42) Black usually plays 7...0-0 8 ♗b3! (another trick is 8 f3 ♕b6! with the ideas of ...♘xe4 and ...♘g4 as well as the direct ...♕xb2) 8...d6 (Black has speculative options such as 8...a5!?, an extremely complicated line; however, top masters who have specialized in that move have usually abandoned it) 9 f3 ♗d7 10 ♕d2. This gives Black one extra opportunity to steer clear of the main lines: 10...♘xd4!? 11 ♗xd4 b5 with a complicated game that seems to favour White slightly. On the flip side, many players and theoreticians feel that 10...♖c8 11 h4! saves a critical tempo over 11 0-0-0 and leads to an advantage for White. This is all in the books (or at least most of it is), and will certainly repay study.

We now return to 5 c4 *(D)*:

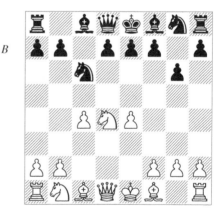

After 5 c4, White has a large space advantage that will usually dominate the centre for as long as White maintains the c4/e4 structure. On the negative side, he has a weakness on d4 (much as in a queen's pawn opening where White plays d4, c4 and e4). White's plan is to use his superiority in space to expand and throttle Black's position. All three areas of the board are available, but he will normally use the centre and queenside. Many endgames favour White, and in particular Black has to be sure that with his queen on a5 and White's on d2, the move ♘d5 won't be effective.

Black would like to achieve the break ...b5 in order to chip away at White's centre; obviously this usually involves ...a6. Sometimes he can play ...f5 for the same purpose, but that is uncommon until later in the game. Finally, he would like to work on the dark squares, especially in view of the unprotected state of d4.

Some specifics follow:

Bareev – Pavlović
Plovdiv Echt 2003

5...♗g7

This is the traditional main line of the Maroczy Bind.

5...♘f6 6 ♘c3 d6 (6...♘xd4 7 ♕xd4 d6 is another well-known idea, when White has various ways to proceed, including 8 ♗g5 ♗g7 9 ♕d2) 7 ♗e2 ♘xd4 8 ♕xd4 ♗g7 9 ♗e3 0-0 10 ♕d2 ♗e6 11 0-0 ♕a5 12 ♖ac1 (12 ♖fc1 puts both rooks on the queenside, which seems a good idea; White would like to play f3 and in some cases ♖ab1 and/or ♘d5; for instance, 12...♖fc8 13 f3! with the idea 13...♗xc4? 14 ♘d5) 12...♖fc8 *(D)*.

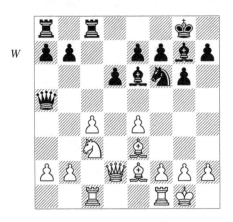

We have reached a standard position. Here's an example of a successful anti-Maroczy Bind idea for Black: 13 b3 a6 14 f3 (14 f4 b5 15 f5 is a highly-charged line with plenty of theory to study) 14...b5! 15 ♘d5 (after 15 cxb5 axb5 16 ♘xb5 {16 ♗xb5 ♖xc3 17 ♕xc3 ♕xb5 and Black has won material} 16...♕xd2 17 ♖xc8+ ♗xc8 18 ♗xd2 ♖xa2 Black has the more active

position) 15...♕xd2 16 ♗xd2 ♘xd5 17 exd5 (17 cxd5 ♗d4+ 18 ♔h1 ♗d7 with equality) 17...♗d4+ 18 ♔h1 ♗d7 and Black has no problems, Uribe-Perelshteyn, Oropesa del Mar U-18 Wch 1998.

6 ♗e3

6 ♘c2!? ♘f6 7 ♘c3 can be a very irritating sequence for Black because it prevents exchanges and increases White's control over d5. The succeeding play is rather technical, but White will continue ♗e2, 0-0, and aim to gain more space by b4, while Black will play ...0-0, ...d6, perhaps with ...a5 and ...♗e6 depending upon what White does. The analogous Rubinstein Variation of the English Opening goes 1 c4 c5 2 ♘c3 ♘f6 3 g3 d5 4 cxd5 ♘xd5 5 ♗g2 ♘c7 6 ♘f3 ♘c6 7 0-0 e5. Even a tempo down, Black has reasonably good prospects.

Incidentally, if Black likes one of the options with an early ...♘xd4, that exchange will prevent the ♘c2 variation.

6...♘f6 7 ♘c3 0-0 8 ♗e2 d6 9 0-0 ♗d7

9...♘xd4 10 ♗xd4 ♗e6 is a long-studied line which has lost some of its popularity. Needless to say, that may be only a temporary situation.

10 ♕d2 ♘xd4 11 ♗xd4 ♗c6 12 f3 *(D)*

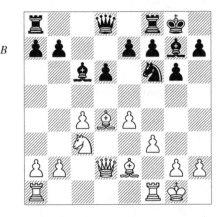

White's development has been natural and normal. He still controls more space and is ready to attack in the centre and on the queenside.

12...a5

Preparing to take over the dark squares.

13 b3 ♘d7!

This is the point of Black's system: he wants to end up with a wonderful knight on c5 opposing a restricted light-squared bishop.

14 ♗e3!

14 ♗xg7 ♔xg7 used to be played, but White wants to keep his good bishop in order to support his queenside play. Otherwise he has nothing to challenge the c5-knight with.

14...♘c5 *(D)*

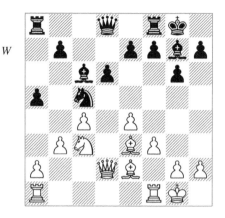

15 ♖ab1

The basic idea is simple: ♖fc1, a3 and b4. The execution turns out to be more complicated.

15...♕b6

More dark-square control. He wants to restrain b4, and also to connect rooks.

16 ♖fc1 ♖fc8 17 ♖c2!

17 a3? ♘xb3! 18 ♗xb6 ♘xd2 19 ♖b2 ♘xc4! 20 ♗xc4 ♗d7 turns out to be good for Black. Now White is ready for a3.

17...♕d8! 18 ♗f1

After Black's last move, 18 a3 a4! 19 b4 ♘b3 is unclear.

18...h5!?

A wild idea: Black isn't doing anything serious on the kingside, as we shall see. He just wants to redeploy.

19 a3

Another game proved the strength of White's queenside pressure: 19 ♕e1 ♗e5 20 ♖d1 ♕b6? 21 ♘b5! ♗xb5 22 cxb5 ♕a7 23 ♗c4! (now that all of Black's pieces are on the other wing, White turns to the kingside) 23...♕b8 24 f4 ♗f6 25 e5! dxe5 26 ♗xc5 ♖xc5 27 ♗xf7+! ♔xf7 28 ♖xc5 and White was winning in Agrest-Brynell, Nordic Ch (Bergen) 2001.

19...♔h7 20 ♘e2!?

White is heading for d4 or f4. The knight was also a target in some lines in which White played b4.

20...♕h8 *(D)*

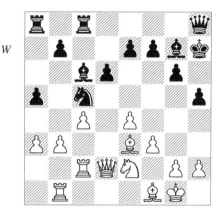

The purpose behind ...♕b6, ...♖fc8, ...h5, ...♕d8 and ...h5! Black tries to maximize his pressure on the long diagonal. But White still has more space and central control, so he can't be too worried. The opening is finally over and both sides have followed their plans. Bareev proceeded to win the battle of ideas, at least this time:

21 ♘f4 b6 22 ♔h1

22 ♘d5 also leads to some advantage after 22...♗xd5 23 exd5 and b4 to follow after due preparation. White's bishops are aiming the right way.

22...♔g8?! 23 b4 axb4 24 axb4 ♘d7 25 ♘d5 ♗xd5 26 cxd5 ♖xc2 27 ♕xc2 ♗d4 28 ♕c6!

White has a large advantage that he converted in good order.

Clearly, one of the key questions surrounding the Accelerated Fianchetto is whether Black can actually gain anything significant from the 'Accelerated' aspect of it, by comparison with the standard Dragon. If not, then why allow White the extra option of the Maroczy Bind, which at the very least reduces Black's chances of playing for a win? After 1 e4 c5 2 ♘f3 ♘c6 3 d4 cxd4 4 ♘xd4 g6 5 ♘c3 ♗g7 6 ♗e3, etc., you will see that even in this best of worlds, Black may not achieve all that he wants. That is, Black uses a bag of tricks in order to lure White away from the Yugoslav Attack, but a moderately knowledgeable opponent will know how to avoid the pitfalls and return play to the main-line Yugoslav channels. Black indeed gains in some respects by limiting White's options: specifically, White has to commit his bishop to c4 and has lost the opportunity to play the popular antidote to the Dragon involving 9 0-0-0. But Black needs to be clear that he can only avoid the 9 ♗c4 version of the Yugoslav Attack by playing sidelines such as 8...a5, which are unlikely to equalize fully.

None of this should discourage a player who is below master level, of course. There will always be plenty of winning chances against average competition, even with the Maroczy Bind. I do think, however, that you probably won't want to play this system for life.

Alapin Variation

1 e4 c5 2 c3 *(D)*

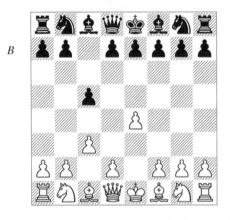

Known as the 'Alapin Variation', 2 c3 particularly appeals to those turned off by the massive theory associated with the Open Sicilian. On the positive side, White tries to build up a centre with minimal risk. Generally, however, 2 c3 lacks punch and might not appeal to the attacking player.

My stated philosophy in this book is to examine the most 'important' openings, especially older and established ones that have played a leading role for many years. For the purposes of presenting a Sicilian variation that isn't in that mould, I've chosen the Alapin Variation instead of, for instance, the Closed Sicilian, because it has some universal ideas that are applicable to other lines in this book and opening study in general.

The main responses are 2...d5 and 2...♘f6. We'll have only a partial look at those but with relevant details. Other fairly respectable continuations include 2...b6, 2...d6 (and perhaps even 2...♕a5!?), but I'll skip those and talk briefly about some alternatives that are better known:

a) 2...e6 is discussed under the order 2 ♘f3 e6 3 c3 in the 'Introduction to 2...e6', except for the line 3 d4 d5 4 exd5 (4 e5 is the Advance French, an important transposition to bear in mind) 4...exd5 (4...♕xd5 will usually transpose) 5 ♗e3 when 5...cxd4 6 ♗xd4 ♘c6 7 ♗b5 a6 is considered equal. The plan discussed via the 2 ♘f3 move-order of 5...c4 still has the effect of making ♗e3 look like an unnecessarily passive move and with care to bring his pieces out quickly Black should stand satisfactorily.

b) 2...g6 3 d4 cxd4 4 cxd4 d5 will often transpose to the variation 1 e4 c5 2 ♘f3 g6 3 c3 ♗g7 4 d4 cxd4 5 cxd4 d5. The main lines are 5 exd5 (5 e5 ♗g7 is similar to the transposition mentioned; then 6 ♘f3 ♗g4 7 ♗b5+ ♘d7 has been played, among others) 5...♘f6 6 ♘c3 (6 ♘f3 ♘xd5 7 ♘c3 ♗g7 comes directly from that line) 6...♗g7 7 ♗c4, when Black chooses his method of regaining the pawn: ...a6, or ...♘bd7 and ...♘b6. According to current knowledge, he is able to get a quite playable game and come close to achieving full equality.

Counterattack with ...d5

2...d5 3 exd5 ♕xd5 4 d4 ♘f6

4...♘c6 5 ♘f3 ♗g4 is also played, when one ambitious line for White is 6 ♗e2 cxd4 7 cxd4 e6 8 ♘c3 ♕a5 9 h3 ♗h5 10 d5!? but 10...exd5 11 ♘d4 ♘xd4 (11...♗xe2) 12 ♗xh5 ♘c6 was easy enough (and equal) for Black in Nayer-Lautier, Khanty-Mansiisk FIDE WCup 2005.

5 ♘f3 *(D)*

5...♗g4

5...♘c6 is an important alternative for those who are unhappy with some aspect of 5...♗g4, perhaps 6 dxc5 in the next note. Play usually continues 6 ♗e2 cxd4 (or 6...e6 7 0-0 cxd4) 7 cxd4 e6 8 ♘c3 ♕d6 9 0-0 ♗e7. Black wants to play ...0-0, ...b6 and ...♗b7, with ...♖fd8 in some cases. White can build up by ♗e3, ♕d2 and ♖fd1, but his position would contain little dynamic potential. Therefore White sometimes

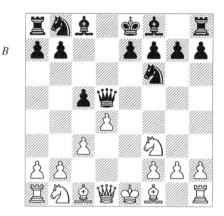

tries to force the pace: 10 ♘b5 ♕d8 (10...♕b8!? 11 g3 ♘d5 12 ♗c4 a6 13 ♗xd5 axb5 14 ♗e4 favours White's active pieces) 11 ♘e5!? (11 ♗f4 ♘d5 12 ♗g3 0-0 {or 12...a6} 13 ♗c4 a6 14 ♗xd5 exd5 15 ♘c7 ♖b8 with equality) 11...0-0 (11...♗d7 12 ♘xd7 ♕xd7 13 ♗e3 0-0 is also fine: d5 is permanently blockaded) 12 ♘xc6 bxc6 13 ♘c3 ♖b8 *(D)*.

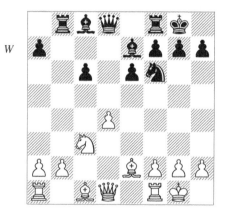

We see this kind of position in several openings. As long as Black can develop quickly and use the b-file, his isolated c-pawn is not a problem. White's d-pawn is just as exposed and is obviously not going anywhere if Black doesn't exchange it. Neither side can claim much, if any, advantage, but either side can play for a win.

6 ♗e2

6 dxc5 was brought to the forefront about a decade ago and has enjoyed a steady popularity. That may say less about the move's merits than it does about White's difficulties in getting an advantage with 2 c3. In any case, the main

line goes 6...♕xc5 (6...♕xd1+ 7 ♔xd1 e5 8 b4 e4 9 h3 has been tested and argued about for some years now; most players seem to shun it as Black) 7 ♘a3 (7 ♗e3 ♕c7 8 h3 ♗h5 9 ♘bd2 ♘bd7) 7...♘bd7 8 h3 ♗h5 9 ♗e3 ♕c8! and Black should have a satisfactory position. That assessment is not shared by everyone, however.

6...e6 7 ♗e3

7 c4 ♕d7 only serves to expose White's centre.

7...cxd4

Now that 8 dxc5 is a threat (in some cases c4 is as well), Black exchanges. But by delaying he has committed White's bishop to the rather passive post on e3.

8 cxd4 ♘c6 9 ♘c3 ♕d6 *(D)*

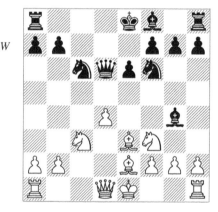

This retreat is better than another (for example, 9...♕d8) for two reasons: it stops the active move ♗f4 and allows Black to increase the pressure on White's d-pawn after ...♖d8 at some point. The dark-squared bishop belongs on e7 anyway.

10 0-0 ♗e7

We've reached a standard isolated pawn position in which White will pit his activity against Black's more static advantages, primarily pressure on the isolated queen's pawn and well-placed pieces. White may nudge Black's bishop to h5 by h3 and reserve the move g4 for later. He sometimes builds up by means of ♕b3 followed by bringing a rook to d1. We saw many examples of this type of position in the introductory chapters. This particular one appears unpromising for White, since his pieces are less active than in those positions and d5 will be extremely hard to achieve.

The 2...♘f6 Variation

2...♘f6 3 e5 ♘d5 *(D)*

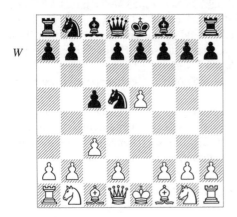

This set-up resembles an Alekhine Defence, and Black would very much like to have ...c5 in if he were playing that opening! But it's not so simple, because White is not intending to kick the d5-knight around with pawns when he can develop his pieces instead. The Alapin with 2...♘f6 can lead to rather theory-heavy play. Here's an outline of some of the wide range of continuations:

4 d4

4 ♘f3 ♘c6 5 ♗c4 ♘b6 6 ♗b3 c4 7 ♗c2 g5!? is another eccentric line; current theory has it as equal, whatever that means in such an unbalanced position.

4...cxd4

The usual starting-point. Only a 2 c3 specialist would know if White has any way to squeeze something from the position.

5 ♘f3

White can also play the direct 5 cxd4 d6 (5...e6 6 ♘c3 ♘xc3 7 bxc3 ♕c7 8 ♗d2 b6 has been a popular system in the past) 6 ♘f3 ♘c6, when a traditional line is 7 ♗c4 (or 7 ♘c3 ♘xc3 8 bxc3 e6) 7...♘b6 (7...e6) 8 ♗b5 dxe5 9 ♘xe5 ♗d7 10 ♗xc6 ♗xc6 11 ♘xc6 bxc6, giving us the standard structure discussed above in the 2...d5 line. The game is equal.

5...♘c6 *(D)*

5...d6 6 cxd4 e6 leads to a line discussed in the introduction to the 2 ♘f3 e6 section.

6 ♗c4

6 cxd4 d6 7 ♘c3 can be met by 7...e6 8 ♘xd5 exd5 with equality.

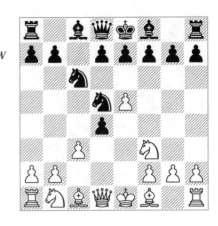

6...♘b6

If Black plays 6...e6 7 cxd4 d6, we again have the line referred to in the note to 5...♘c6.

7 ♗b3 d5

Capturing the offered pawn by 7...dxc3 8 ♘xc3 is risky.

8 exd6 ♕xd6 *(D)*

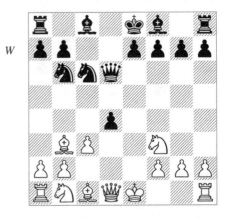

Black is generally thought to have equality here, although as usual there are lengthy analyses of variations which, fortunately, your average opponent will never have heard of.

9 0-0

Among many other established lines is 9 ♘a3 a6 10 0-0 ♗e6 11 ♗xe6 ♕xe6 with equality.

9...♗e6 10 ♗xe6 ♕xe6 11 ♘xd4 ♘xd4 12 ♕xd4 ♖d8 13 ♕h4 ♕e2 14 ♘d2

Now Black can play 14...h5!? or 14...g6, both of which have been satisfactory for him. Nevertheless, White may be interested in playing such a position because it's double-edged enough to be interesting.

12 Caro-Kann Defence

1 e4 c6 *(D)*

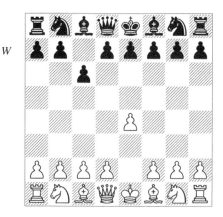

This is the official starting-point for the Caro-Kann. Now 2 d4 is played in a clear majority of games, though naturally White can try to react to the idea of 2...d5 in other ways. As always, these early deviations can be very educational, and one of them sets up a respectable structure that is played on a regular basis:

Caro-Kann Two Knights

2 ♘f3

2 c4 is another important alternative to the main lines: 2...d5 (2...e5 3 ♘f3 d6 4 d4 is some sort of Old Indian Defence that most Caro-Kann players won't be comfortable with) 3 exd5 cxd5 usually transposes to the Panov Attack by means of 4 d4 – see later in this chapter. White can also try 4 cxd5, when 4...♕xd5 loses a tempo after 5 ♘c3. However serious that may or may not be, White will follow up with d4 and some advantage; e.g., 5...♕a5 6 d4 ♘f6 7 ♘f3 *(D)*.

This compares well for White with a Scandinavian Defence (1 e4 d5 2 exd5 ♕xd5 3 ♘c3 ♕a5 4 d4 ♘f6 5 ♘f3), because Black cannot restrain White's centre by the useful ...c6. In return, White has no pawn on c2. But in the Scandinavian, the c2-pawn can be a disadvantage

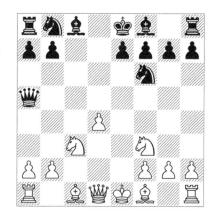

for White for a couple of reasons. For one thing it's a target of a bishop on f5 and sometimes a knight on b4; but more significantly it's not up on c4 to make the centre more mobile, nor on c3 where it would protect White's d4-pawn. Furthermore, you should note that without a c-pawn, White has the handy move ♕b3 if Black's c8-bishop strays from the queenside.

Thus, instead of 4...♕xd5, Black almost always plays 4...♘f6 5 ♘c3 (5 ♗b5+ will eventually lead to White losing back his d-pawn after either 5...♗d7 or 5...♘bd7; in the latter case, ...a6 and either ...b5 or ...♘b6 can follow) 5...♘xd5 6 d4 and we're back to the isolated queen's pawn position that characterizes the Panov Attack.

The text-move (2 ♘f3) is easily White's most promising independent try and deserves a look for those who want a somewhat less-travelled path.

2...d5 3 ♘c3 *(D)*

This sequence tries to use piece-play and quick development to cause Black discomfort. For instance, line 'a' in the next note is a good example of this.

3...♗g4

This is most players' choice. Otherwise:

a) If Black plays 3...dxe4 4 ♘xe4 ♗f5?!, White shows the benefit of his quick development by harassing the bishop with 5 ♘g3 ♗g6

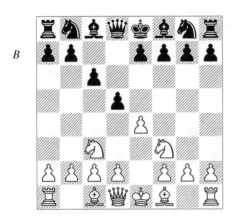

6 h4 threatening h5. Compare this with the standard line 2 d4 d5 3 ♘c3 dxe4 4 ♘xe4 ♗f5 5 ♘g3 ♗g6. In our current position with 2 ♘f3 d5 3 ♘c3, the f3-knight is ready to spring to e5. White will at the very least win the two bishops and remain with good development (keep in mind that winning the bishop-pair often comes at the *cost* of development). After 6 h4, play goes 6...h6 (6...♘f6 7 h5 ♗e4 8 ♘xe4 ♘xe4 9 d4 e6 10 ♗d3 gives White two bishops and good development) 7 ♘e5 ♕d6 (7...♗h7??, to preserve the bishop, loses to 8 ♕f3! ♘f6 9 ♕b3 with a double attack on f7 and b7) 8 ♘xg6 ♕xg6 9 d4 and White will soon play ♗d3 forcing the queen to move again.

b) 3...♘f6?! 4 e5 ♘fd7 5 e6! fxe6 6 d4 favours White, who would like to play ♗d3 with ♘g5 or, if Black plays ...♘f6, then ♘e5 paralyses him.

c) The move ...c6 doesn't go very well with 3...d4 4 ♘e2; for instance, 4...c5 5 c3 and Black's centre can't be held after 5...♘c6 6 cxd4 cxd4 7 ♕a4 d3.

4 h3 ♗xf3

This is the standard choice. Instead, 4...♗h5 is very risky in view of 5 exd5 cxd5 6 ♗b5+ ♘c6 7 g4 ♗g6 8 ♘e5. This position is supposed to be playable for Black, although it is dangerous for him in view of h4-h5 or simply d4 and ♗f4. Several books touch upon it, perhaps not thoroughly enough; if I were White I would look at (and as Black I would worry about) 8...♖c8 9 h4!, intending 9...d4 (Black is suffering after 9...f6 10 ♘xg6 hxg6 11 d4) 10 h5 ♗xc2 11 ♕xc2 dxc3 12 ♖h3! (or 12 ♕b3 e6 13 dxc3) 12...e6 13 ♘xc6 bxc6 14 ♖xc3, etc.

5 ♕xf3

Many readers are aware that chess-players all over the world fell in love with World Champion Mikhail Tal's brilliant and romantic attacks, which have influenced all of us since. What they may not know is that Tal also delighted chess fans with his astonishing originality and piquant humour. One of the most wonderful moves in his career reflected both of these qualities: 5 gxf3!!? *(D)*.

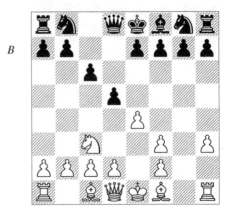

To play such an absurd move in a casual game is one thing; in an international tournament, another. But in the refined atmosphere of the World Championship one doesn't do such things! Nevertheless, in Tal-Botvinnik, Moscow Wch (3) 1960, White shocked everyone (and, I hope, made them laugh) by recapturing with the g-pawn. I think that only recently have we begun to see a growth in players' receptivity towards apparently unprincipled moves in the opening. Tal would have been pleased by this. At any rate, he promptly got an inferior game but recovered and fought his way to a draw. In spite of the condemnation that 5 gxf3 received, Tal's mistaken follow-up is easily improved upon (by his own suggestions, for starters), and it's a little disappointing that so few players have risked their precious ratings just once to give the move a try. Kudos to Chris Depasquale, who has two games out of the 28 with 5 gxf3 in Megabase 2006.

We now return to 5 ♕xf3 *(D)*.

This move, on the other hand, is represented by about 2100 Megabase games, still somewhat less than 2% of all Caro-Kanns.

White has gained the two bishops in return for somewhat reduced central control. Black is

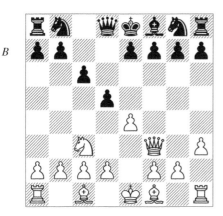

happy to have exchanged his light-squared bishop, since he will be setting up his pawns on light squares. Play can develop along several lines.

5...e6

Another set-up begins with 5...♘f6 6 d3 e6. White's bishops don't have any exceptionally good squares, and while White gets reorganized Black will get all his pieces out and play ...e5, trading space and active pieces for the two bishops. A good piece organization for Black to achieve that is ...♘d7, ...g6 and ...♗g7.

6 d4 *(D)*

White can also play 6 d3 ♘d7 7 ♗e2 (7 ♗d2 ♗d6 8 d4 a6 9 0-0-0 b5 10 ♗d3 ♘e7 11 h4 ♕b6 is also equal, Planinc-Petrosian, Yugoslavia-USSR (Ohrid) 1972) 7...g6 8 0-0 ♗g7 9 ♕g3 ♕b6 10 ♔h1 ♘e7 with equality, Anand-Karpov, Brussels Ct (3) 1991.

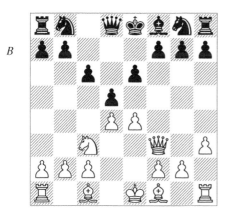

6...♘f6

6...dxe4 is also possible.

7 ♗d3 dxe4

Black intentionally surrenders the centre.

8 ♘xe4 ♘xe4

8...♕xd4 9 c3 ♕d8 10 0-0 is risky because White's pieces come out so quickly, but it's hardly clear.

9 ♕xe4 ♘d7 10 c3 ♘f6 11 ♕e2 ♗d6 *(D)*

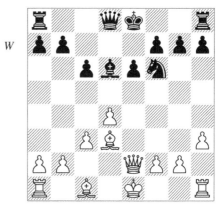

Black sets up the kind of restraint structure that is seen in the Slav, Scandinavian and other defences: pawns on light squares to complement the dark-squared bishop while restraining White's centre. As in those openings, one idea is to get developed quickly and play either ...c5 or ...e5. See Chapter 3 on structures for some examples.

Let's now turn to the main lines.

1 e4 c6 2 d4 d5 *(D)*

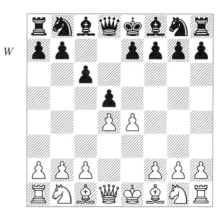

The Caro-Kann resembles the French Defence in that Black places a pawn on d5 on the second move and forces White to decide what to do with his e4-pawn: advance, exchange, defend or gambit. Some of the resulting positions are quite similar. It has also been said that the Caro-Kann resembles the Slav because 1...c6 takes away the 'best' square c6 from the knight, but keeps an open view for his light-squared bishop. Not surprisingly, however, the characters of the positions arising from 1 e4 and 1 d4 turn out to be radically different: there isn't a Slav Advance Variation, and e4 by White is a rarity in the Slav.

In any event, 2...d5 compels a response. I'll be looking at 3 exd5 (both the Exchange Variation and Panov Attack) and 3 e5, the Advance Variation. I think that those variations are the most useful and consistent in terms of this book's organization. I won't be dealing with the 3 ♘c3 main lines, although naturally they're full of wonderful ideas. I'm also leaving out the 'Fantasy Variation' 3 f3, although it has its points of interest. A curious positional comparison arises after 3 f3 e6!? 4 ♘c3 ♗b4 (these are not the only moves, of course), when 5 e5(?) c5 is actually a good version of the French Defence because White's 'extra' tempo due to ...c6-c5 has been used for the awful move f3, which not only loosens White's kingside but takes away f3 for the knight and cuts off White's queen from the kingside.

Exchange Variation

3 exd5 cxd5 *(D)*

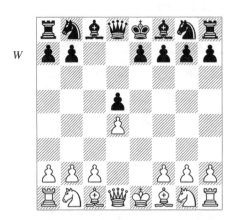

An enormously instructive variation, the study of which will benefit all chess-players. We'll look at White's slow build-up with c3, and then turn to the more aggressive Panov Attack with c4.

The c3 Systems

4 ♗d3 ♘c6 5 c3

This more conservative development isn't supposed to promise White much, but it has some sting and the pawn-structure is particularly thought-provoking.

5...♘f6 *(D)*

Now we'll run into some familiar ideas.

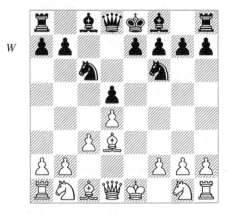

6 ♗f4

This is the customary approach, and most likely to achieve something tangible.

However, let's say that White plays 6 ♘f3, Black answers with the natural 6...♗g4, and there follows 7 0-0 e6 8 ♘bd2 ♗d6 9 ♖e1 0-0. All very logical. Then White might want to respond to the presence of Black's bishop on g4: 10 ♘f1 ♕c7 11 ♗g5 ♘d7 12 ♘g3 *(D)*.

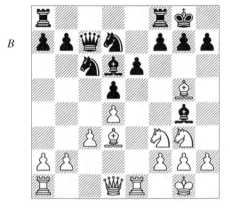

What do we have here? A classical Queen's Gambit Declined Exchange Variation (Carlsbad) with colours reversed! In this position, especially since one of the standard QGD plans ...♘e4 is not available (that's ♘e5 in our Caro-Kann case), Black might want to play the minority attack 12...♖ab8 13 h3 ♗xf3 14 ♕xf3. Then it's as though White has played four of Black's common Queen's Gambit moves (...♗e7, the recapture ...♗xf6 and the repositioning ...♗e7-d6) in one move! Of course neither side has played according to a conventional Caro-Kann plan, but it's interesting to see how the same pawn-structure in both an e-pawn opening and a d-pawn opening leads to the theme of minority attack vs kingside attack. Naturally we could have obtained an exactly reversed position by 4 ♘f3 ♘c6 5 c3 ♗g4 6 ♗e2 e6 7 0-0 ♗d6 8 ♘bd2 ♘f6 (or 8...♘ge7!?), etc., but those are not the most pointed moves, especially for White.

Let's return to the Caro-Kann line after 6 ♗f4. We'll follow the young Kasparov.

Lanka – Kasparov
Leningrad jr 1977

6...♗g4 *(D)*

Black gets out in front of his pawn-chain, an advantage in both the Caro-Kann and the Queen's Gambit Exchange Variation.

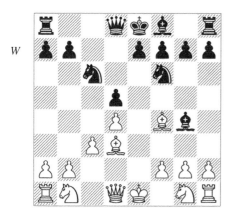

7 ♕b3

7 f3 ♗h5 has the idea of ...♗g6 with the exchange of White's good bishop. This is a common theme even with a knight on f3; in that case, after ♘e5 and ...♗g6, Black isn't afraid of ♘xg6 because knights are strong in these positions and he gets a useful h-file. Moreover, the light-squared bishop *is* still Black's bad bishop

(see the pawns on d5 and e6). Of course, 7 ♘e2 is also possible.

7...♕d7 8 ♘d2 e6 9 ♘gf3 ♗d6!

This discovery hurt the popularity of the set-up with c3, ♗d3 and ♗f4.

10 ♗xd6 ♕xd6 11 0-0

After 11 ♕xb7 ♖b8 12 ♕a6 0-0! (and not 12...♖xb2? 13 ♗b5), Black is considered to have at least enough play for his pawn; e.g., 13 b3? (to protect b2) 13...♖b6 14 ♕a4 e5! 15 dxe5 ♘xe5 with the e-file and threats against White's king. Then Black stands considerably better.

11...♗xf3 12 ♘xf3 0-0 13 ♖ae1 ♖ab8 14 ♘e5 b5 15 a3 a5 *(D)*

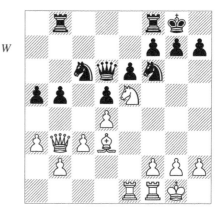

The minority attack in pure form.

16 ♖e3 ♖fc8 17 ♕d1 b4 18 axb4 axb4 19 ♖fe1

19 f4 bxc3 20 bxc3 gives White some attack and may well be better.

19...bxc3 20 bxc3 ♕d8 21 ♖h3?!

Passive. The most interesting move is 21 ♘g4!.

21...g6 22 ♕d2 ♘xe5 23 dxe5 ♘d7 24 ♕h6 ♘f8 25 ♗f1 ♖b3 26 ♖c1 ♕a5 27 ♕e3 *(D)*

Kasparov has achieved the isolation of the c-pawn but his f8-knight is much worse than the f1-bishop, so he needs to make concrete progress.

27...♕a3 28 ♖f3!? ♖c7 29 ♕f4 ♕b2

Black has had chances for a while to play ...d4; e.g., 29...d4! 30 c4 ♖xf3 31 gxf3 ♘d7 32 ♖b1 ♕c3 33 ♖d1 ♖c5.

30 h4 h5 31 ♔h2 d4

This is still good.

32 ♗d3!? dxc3!

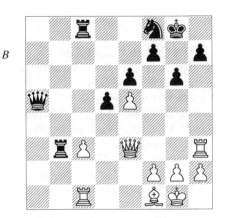

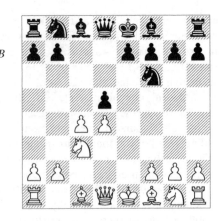

On 32...℞bxc3, 33 ℞d1 stops Black in his tracks.

33 ℞c2 ♕a3?

Perhaps missing White's next move. Instead 33...℞b4! was very strong and would probably produce an eventual win. Now White will gain the advantage.

34 ♗c4 ℞b4 35 ℞fxc3 ♕a4 36 ♕c1 ♕a7 37 f4!?

This is loosening. 37 ♕d2! ♕a4 38 ♕e2 would retain White's superior position, although making progress will be difficult.

37...♕d4! 38 g3 ♔g7 39 ♔h3 ♘d7 40 ♗f1 ℞xc3 41 ℞xc3 ♘b6 42 ♕e3 ♕d1 43 ♕f3 ♕a1 44 ♗g2 ♘d5

The game is equal.

45 ℞d3 ℞b2 46 f5!? gxf5 47 ♕xh5 ♕c1 48 ℞d1 ♕c2 49 ♕g5+ ½-½

Panov Attack

4 c4

This introduces one of the classic variations of the Semi-Open Games, one that has attracted many great players through the years. The attack on d5 poses some problems for Black, because if he captures on c4, White's bishop gets out to an active square in one jump, whereas in many isolated queen's pawn positions like the one soon to occur, White has to play two moves (usually ♗d3 and then ♗xc4) to get there, or he has to play a less desirable extra 'waiting' move such as a3, ℞c1 or ♗g5. Compare isolated queen's pawn positions in the Queen's Gambit Declined or Nimzo-Indian, for instance, and see the further comments below.

4...♘f6 5 ♘c3 (D)

This is the starting position of the Panov Attack, also known as the 'Panov-Botvinnik Attack' because of the former World Champion's contributions to it.

5...e6

5...g6 gives a Grünfeld-like position in which Black usually lets White temporarily win the d-pawn and then tries to win it back via ...♘bd7-b6 or ...a6/...b5. I'll forego that line here.

The main alternative is 5...♘c6, which introduces a different set of problems and structures that I shall try to outline in broad-brush fashion. The presentation will most likely be inaccurate from an advanced theoretical point of view but should be helpful for the student:

a) 6 ♗g5 (D) threatens 7 ♗xf6 followed by 8 cxd5.

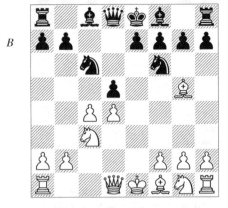

Black can respond by 6...e6, or by various refreshing set-ups that begin with 6...♕a5 and 6...♗e6!?, the popularity of the latter illustrating the flexibility and pragmatism of chess ideas. Although I won't be looking into those, I should mention that 6...e6 7 ♘f3 ♗e7 leads to one of those positions that we were talking about in which White may not want to lose a tempo after 8 ♗d3 dxc4 9 ♗xc4, and thus considers moves such as 8 ♖c1 and 8 a3. The independent idea of 8 c5 is also possible. These positions will repay study, and in fact you might want to sit down and try to work out the details without recourse to books or other sources.

b) 6 ♘f3 *(D)* is the main move.

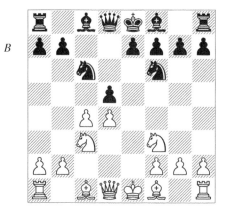

Then:

b1) Sometimes 6...♗e6 is played to threaten ...dxc4 and protect the centre at the same time. Anand-Miles, Wijk aan Zee 1989 shows one way to convert the pawn-structure (pretty much by force) and then build up a superior position: 7 c5 g6 8 ♗b5 ♗g7 9 ♘e5 ♗d7 10 ♗xc6! bxc6 11 0-0 0-0 12 ♖e1 ♗e8 13 h3 (or 13 ♕e2) 13...♔h8 14 ♗f4 ♘g8 15 b4 f6 16 ♘f3 ♕d7 17 a4. White has a moderate but certain advantage. It's difficult for Black to find anything positive to do, and Anand won rather easily.

b2) The most important reply is 6...♗g4, because it carries with it the positional threat of 7...♗xf3 and gives White few serious options. The most common and well-analysed one is 7 cxd5 ♘xd5 8 ♕b3 ♗xf3 9 gxf3 *(D)*.

White has implemented the mini-rule that when one side brings their queen's bishop out early, the opponent should strongly consider bringing his queen to the queenside, in this case to b3, because the bishop has abandoned defence of that wing. Here White has carried out that idea at the cost of doubled f-pawns. Now 9...♘xd4?? loses to 10 ♗b5+, and 9...♘xc3 10 bxc3 is considered good for White because of

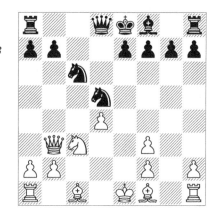

his bishops, queenside pressure, and the move d5.

But 9...♘b6 is not fully worked out. It allows White attacking sequences beginning with 10 d5! (or 10 ♗e3 e6 11 0-0-0, which may be best defended by 11...♗e7 12 d5 exd5 13 ♗xb6 ♕xb6 14 ♕xb6 axb6 15 ♘xd5 ♖xa2 16 ♔b1 ♖a5 with equality) 10...♘d4 11 ♗b5+ ♘d7 12 ♕a4 ♘xb5 (12...e5? 13 dxe6 ♘xe6 14 ♗g5! with the idea 14...♘xg5 15 0-0-0) 13 ♕xb5 g6 14 0-0 *(D)*.

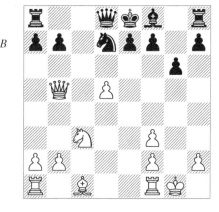

White intends ♖e1 and/or ♗g5. This is all theory, one nice idea being 14...♗g7 15 ♗g5 (15 ♖e1 0-0 16 ♗g5 is supposed to be somewhat better for White) 15...h6? 16 ♗xe7! ♔xe7 17 ♕b4+ ♔e8 18 ♖ae1+ ♗e5 19 f4 ♕h4 20 ♕e4! and White is virtually winning with extra material and terribly strong pawns. Such tactics stem from open lines and rapid development.

Returning to 9 gxf3, the main continuation is 9...e6, when 10 ♕xb7 leads to the line 10...♘xd4 11 ♗b5+ ♘xb5 12 ♕c6+ ♔e7 13 ♕xb5 ♕d7

14 ♘xd5+ ♛xd5 15 ♗g5+ f6 16 ♛xd5 exd5 17 ♗e3 (D).

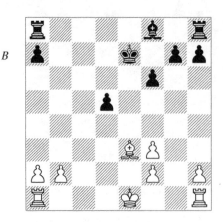

Again, we have bookloads of theory on this fascinating and educational ending. White's horrible doubled f-pawns are compensated for or outweighed by his open files (providing some bothersome threats against the king), his more effective bishop, and Black's own two weak pawns. Probably the result with perfect play is a draw, but Black has to play more accurately than White does, which probably explains a lot of players' inclination towards the more common move 5...e6 (D), to which we return now.

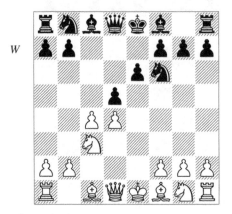

6 ♘f3

Here we'll look at a few of the thousands of games that have been played from this position. Fortunately there's quite a bit of material on isolated queen's pawns throughout this book (for a lengthy introduction to the subject, see Chapter 3), so this lesson will not stand on its own. We'll see three different 6th moves for Black.

Velimirović – Benko
Vrnjačka Banja 1973

6...♗e7 7 cxd5 exd5 (D)

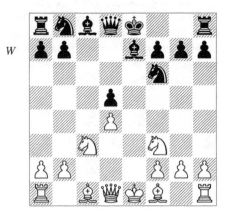

I think it's important to understand that this recapture, while safe-looking, can give White some real prospects.

8 ♗b5+ ♘c6

8...♗d7 9 ♗xd7+ ♘bxd7 10 0-0 0-0 11 ♛b3 ♘b6 12 ♖e1 ♖e8 13 ♗g5 with a definite advantage, Petronijević-Nikolić, Belgrade 1997. Here we see one danger in the pawn-structure after 7 cxd5 exd5, which is that the d-pawns are isolated. Normally when such a pawn is masked by another (and thus not on an open file), it poses no problems. But the fact that 11 ♛b3 targeted the d5-pawn caused Black's knight to go to a miserable position on b6, which became the reason for White's advantage.

9 ♘e5 ♗d7 10 0-0 0-0 11 ♖e1 ♖c8 12 ♗g5 ♗e6 13 ♗xc6 bxc6 14 ♘a4 h6 15 ♗xf6 ♗xf6 16 ♘c5 (D)

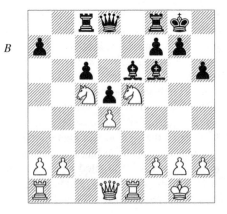

White stands well, although 16 ♖c1 was possibly more accurate.

6...♗e7 7 cxd5 ♘xd5 is a main-line IQP position and is similar to 6...♗b4 below. If this were a book on theory I'd have to be more specific, but this really *is* one of those instances in which it's fair to say that the ideas are much more important than the details. Therefore I'll limit myself to one main game, although another very attractive contest is embedded in the note to White's 8th move.

Matveeva – Anand
Frunze 1987

6...♗e7 7 cxd5 ♘xd5

This transposes to a Queen's Gambit Accepted (since ♗c4 is played next), but just as often it arises from a Panov move-order. The themes are like those after 6...♗b4 below, and they can in fact transpose if White plays ♗d2-g5 while Black plays ...♗b4-e7.

8 ♗c4

8 ♗d3 0-0 9 0-0 (9 h4!? has also been tried) and we're in another standard IQP position. Watch out if you're trying to transpose into a formation with ...b6, ...♗b7 and ...♘bd7, which is standard in isolated queen's pawn positions. That plan often doesn't fit if you don't have a knight on f6; for example, 9...b6?! 10 ♘xd5! exd5 (10...♕xd5? 11 ♗c2! hits h7 and threatens ♗e4) 11 ♘e5 ♗a6?! 12 ♗xa6! ♘xa6 13 ♕a4 (D).

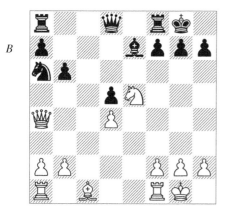

Look at those wonderful light-square targets. Just as importantly, the attack on the a6-knight makes it almost certain that a white rook will reach the c-file before Black's: 13...♕c8 14 ♗f4 ♕b7 15 ♕c6! ♖ab8 16 ♖fc1 ♘b4 17 ♕d7! ♘a6 18 ♖c3 ♗f6 19 ♕f5! ♖fe8 (19...♗xe5 20 ♗xe5 ♖bc8 21 ♕f6! would be a pretty finish) 20 ♖h3 h6 21 ♗xh6! ♕c8 (21...♗xe5 22 ♗g5!) 22 ♘d7 ♖e6 23 ♗xg7! 1-0 Larsen-Pomar, Spanish Cht (Centelles) 1978.

8...♘c6 9 0-0 0-0 10 ♖e1 (D)

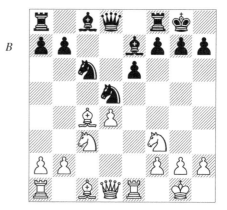

We have reached a standard position. Although the theory of the line was to change later, the game shows a beautiful defensive effort and a model for Black:

10...a6 11 ♗b3 ♘xc3 12 bxc3 b5 13 ♕d3

Black can hold White off after the thematic 13 d5: 13...♘a5! 14 dxe6 ♗xe6 15 ♗xe6 ♕xd1 16 ♗xf7+ ♖xf7 17 ♖xd1 ♗f6.

13...♗b7 14 ♗c2 g6 15 ♗h6 ♖e8 (D)

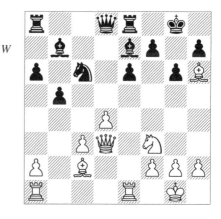

16 ♖ad1

Here was a chance for 16 a4! b4 17 c4 with a small advantage, according to G.Kuzmin.

16...♖c8 17 h4!? ♕d5!

A beautiful trap is 17...♗xh4? 18 d5! ♘a5 19 d6! ♗xf3 20 d7!! ♗xd1 21 dxe8♕+ ♕xe8 22 ♕d4 f6 23 ♗xd1!, winning.

18 ♗b3 ♕h5! *(D)*

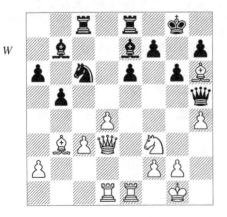

19 ♕e3 ♘a5! 20 ♗g5 ♘xb3 21 axb3 ♗xg5 22 hxg5 ♗xf3! 23 gxf3 ♖ed8

White's position has been shredded, and it's hard to see what actually went wrong.

24 d5 ♖xd5 25 ♖xd5 exd5 26 ♔g2! h6! 27 gxh6 ♔h7 28 ♕e7?! ♕f5 29 ♕e3 ♕f6! 30 ♖c1

At this point, although 30...a5? kept some advantage and Anand eventually won, the strongest way was 30...b4! 31 c4 (31 cxb4 d4 32 ♕d2 ♖c3!) 31...dxc4 32 ♖xc4 ♖xc4 33 bxc4 a5. Then the connected pawns would have been too strong.

Kasparov – Anand
Amsterdam 1996

6...♘c6

This gives White the chance to play a scheme that isn't available (or effective) in most other positions:

7 ♗g5 ♗e7 8 c5!? *(D)*

There are a couple of ideas behind this move. One is to launch a queenside attack by b4-b5 and drive Black's pieces back. The other is to control e5 by whatever means possible without White having to attend to his d-pawn after ...dxc4. White's key moves in this process are ♗b5, 0-0, ♗f4 and ♖e1, followed by ♘e5 itself. This most famous game with 8 c5 illustrates both a good solution for Black and White's attacking possibilities.

8...h6! 9 ♗f4

After 9 ♗xf6 ♗xf6 10 ♗b5 0-0 11 0-0, 11...♘e7! 12 b4 b6 illustrates a way to stop White's queenside roller: 13 ♕d2 bxc5 14 bxc5 ♗d7 with equality, Timman-Kramnik, Amsterdam 1996.

9...♘e4 10 ♗b5

Perhaps 10 ♖c1!?.

10...♘xc3 11 bxc3 ♗d7 12 0-0 0-0 13 ♖c1! ♖e8!

13...b6 runs into 14 c4!, which was the point of 13 ♖c1.

14 ♖e1 ♗f6 *(D)*

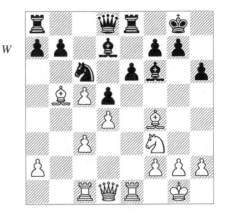

15 ♖b1

Kasparov mentions 15 ♗d3!? b6 16 cxb6 axb6 17 ♗b1 with a small edge. The opening is over and White has the initiative.

15...b6 16 ♗a6 ♗c8

16...bxc5 17 ♗b7.

17 ♗b5 ♗d7 18 ♗a6 ♗c8 19 ♗d3!? bxc5

19...♗d7! is best, when White still has to demonstrate how to get through.

20 ♘e5 ♗d7

20...♘xe5!? 21 dxe5 ♗g5 22 ♗xg5 ♕xg5 23 ♗b5! ♖d8 24 ♗c6.

21 ♖b7

Now things go downhill for Black. White's opening strategy has been a major success.

21...♗xe5 22 dxe5 ♖b8

Or 22...♗c8 23 ♕g4!. Kasparov doesn't let up in what follows.

23 ♖xb8 ♕xb8 24 ♕g4 ♔f8 25 ♖e3 ♕d8 26 h4! ♕a5 27 ♖g3 ♔e7 28 ♕xg7 ♔d8 29 ♕xf7 ♕xc3 30 ♗b5 ♕a5 31 ♖g7 ♘e7 32 ♗xd7 ♔xd7 33 ♕f6 d4 34 ♗xh6 c4 35 ♗g5 ♕c5 36 ♖xe7+ 1-0

The finish would be 36...♖xe7 37 ♕xe7+ ♕xe7 38 ♗xe7 ♔xe7 39 ♔f1.

Fedorowicz – Enkhbat
USA Ch (Seattle) 2003

6...♗b4 (D)

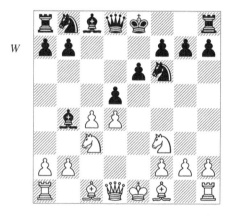

7 cxd5 ♘xd5

For those of you wondering, 7...exd5 is a respectable alternative, although seldom played. Black may have the most problems with 8 ♗b5+ again; compare 6...♗e7 7 cxd5 exd5 above.

8 ♕c2

More often 8 ♗d2 is played here. A game in which White wasn't ambitious enough went 8...♘c6 9 ♗d3 ♘f6 10 0-0 0-0 11 ♗g5 h6!? 12 ♗e3 (12 ♗h4!?) 12...♗d6 13 ♖c1!? (13 ♖e1) 13...e5! 14 h3 (14 ♘xe5 ♘xe5 15 dxe5 ♗xe5 is equal) 14...♗e6 15 ♕d2 ♕a5 16 ♗xh6 exd4! 17 ♘b5 ♕xd2 18 ♗xd2 ♗b8 with equality, J.Polgar-Karpov, Dos Hermanas 1999. Instead, 8...0-0 9 ♗d3 ♗e7 10 0-0 ♘c6 11 a3 ♘f6 12

♗g5 would have transposed to a normal IQP position.

8...♘c6 9 a3 ♗e7

9...♗a5 10 ♗d3!? ♘xc3 11 bxc3 ♘xd4 12 ♘xd4 ♕xd4 13 ♗b5+ ♗d7 14 0-0 is an unclear gambit.

10 ♗d3 ♘f6?!

This just doesn't seem to work out. 10...♘f6 is a normal isolated queen's pawn position, when White has a lead in development and could gambit a pawn but probably just plays 11 ♗e3.

11 0-0 ♘xc3

Not 11...♘xd4?? 12 ♘xd4 ♗xd4 13 ♕a4+; nor 11...♗xd4? 12 ♘xd5 exd5 13 ♗b5.

12 bxc3 (D)

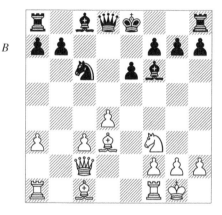

12...h6

In order to get castled.

13 ♕e2! ♕d5

He still can't castle due to 13...0-0 14 ♕e4. Something has already gone wrong.

14 ♖b1 a6 15 c4 ♕h5 16 ♕e4 ♔f8

A terrible concession.

17 ♖e1 ♘e7 18 ♗d2 ♕f5 19 ♕e3 ♕h5 20 ♕f4! ♘g6 21 ♕c7 ♔g8 22 ♗e4 ♔h7 23 ♕xf7

Now it's really over. Black only lasted a few more moves.

23...♖d8 24 ♗e3 ♖d7 25 ♕e8 ♖e7 26 ♕a4 ♗d7 27 ♕d1! ♗e8?

But 27...♔g8 28 ♖xb7 is awful.

28 ♘g5+ 1-0

Advance Variation

1 e4 c6 2 d4 d5 3 e5 (D)

This extremely popular move has led to remarkably exciting, creative play. There have

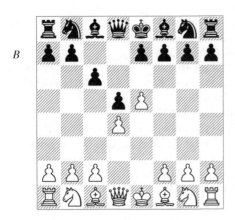

been more discoveries here than in any other variation of the Caro-Kann, and indeed more than most openings.

3...♗f5

Strong players over the years have tried to attack White's pawn-chain at the base by 3...c5, the idea being that 4 c3 might allow Black's c8-bishop to develop outside Black's own pawns; e.g., 4...♘c6 5 ♘f3 cxd4 6 cxd4 ♗g4 or some such. But this takes Black two moves with his c-pawn, and 4 dxc5 changes the structure dramatically. After 4...e6 *(D)*, you may recognize the similarity to the French Defence Advance Variation, i.e. 1 e4 e6 2 d4 d5 3 e5 c5 4 dxc5, but then it's Black's move!

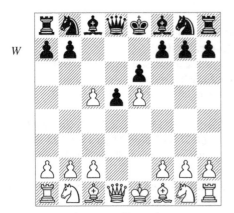

That's because of the tempo loss ...c6-c5. In the French Defence move-order, 4 dxc5 is harmless or worse because it weakens e5 and brings Black's pieces out quickly. The first question, then, is whether having lost a whole tempo, this position can still be played for Black. That is at least possible, since it is generally favourable

for Black in the French. The flip side of the question is whether this basic white pawn-structure, advocated by Nimzowitsch, really can be played for an advantage. According to conventional theory, White is supposed to over-protect the e5-pawn against assault by ...f6, such that any capture with ...fxe5 will leave him with a permanent outpost on e5 from which his pieces can't be driven away. That is not so easily done. Alternatively, White can use his extra tempo simply to hold on to the c5-pawn and remain a pawn up! It's worth examining these two strategies, which can be introduced in a few ways:

a) 5 ♗d3 ♘c6 (5...♗xc5? 6 ♕g4 forces Black into an awkward defence of his g-pawn; he either has to move his king or make the very weakening move ...g6) 6 ♘f3 (this is the same as 5 ♘f3 ♗xc5 6 ♗d3) 6...♗xc5 7 0-0 ♘ge7! (7...f6 8 ♕e2! – strongpoint – 8...fxe5 9 ♘xe5 ♘f6 10 ♗f4 0-0 11 ♘d2 ♘xe5 12 ♗xe5 ♕b6 13 ♘b3 ♗d6 14 ♗xd6 ♕xd6 15 ♖ae1) 8 ♕e2 ♘g6 9 c3 0-0. Black appears to be doing fine in these positions.

b) Also by analogy with the French Defence, the apparently untried 5 ♕g4! would be very interesting, tying Black's bishop to f8 and preparing ♘f3, ♗d3, etc. The queen is ready to overprotect e5 from g3, as shown by 5...♘c6 6 ♘f3 f5 (6...♕c7 7 ♗b5) 7 ♕g3 ♕c7 8 ♘c3 (or 8 ♗e3) 8...♗xc5 9 ♘b5 ♕d7 10 ♗e3!? ♗xe3 11 ♘d6+ ♔f8 12 fxe3 *(D)*.

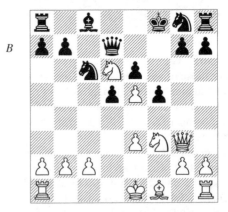

The strong point lives, and before d6 can be challenged White will have played 0-0-0 and c4.

c) Black has yet another difficulty if White uses his extra tempo to hang on to the c5-pawn:

5 ♗e3 (which is the preference in practice)
5...♘h6 6 c3 ♘f5 7 ♗d4 ♘c6 8 ♘f3 ♕c7 9
♗b5 with a solid advantage. Probably Black
can play better but he looks short of equality in
any event.

Although playable, it appears that after 3...c5
4 dxc5, White's extra tempo somewhat out-
weighs Black's pleasant pawn-structure. The
move 5 ♕g4! is particularly worrisome.

Thus the normal move 3...♗f5 *(D)*, to which
we now return, is critical:

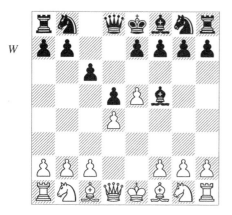

W

White has an amazing number of valid options in the position after 3...♗f5, expressing
diverse and creative approaches. I've chosen to
look at two modern variations (4 ♘f3 and in
particular 4 ♗e3) in most detail because they
represent a mix of approaches, from the purely
positional to tactical.

However, some of the alternatives are themselves main lines and hence deserve close attention:

a) 4 ♘c3 e6 5 g4 ♗g6 6 ♘ge2 has led to
great attacking chess and been a favourite for
over a decade now. Unfortunately, there isn't
much to say about the line in a short space except that it generally leads to random-looking
chaos! The resulting melees are completely dependent upon the precise tactics of individual
positions (and the preparation put into them).
While there are naturally consistent themes and
even buried positional indicators, I can't begin
to clarify what goes on. Consider, for example,
making sense of this: 6...c5 7 h4 h6 8 f4!? ♗e7
9 ♗g2! ♗xh4+ 10 ♔f1 ♗e7! 11 f5! ♗h7 12
♘f4 ♕d7 13 ♘h5!? ♗f8 14 dxc5 ♘c6 15 ♘b5!
♗xc5 16 c4!! *(D)*.

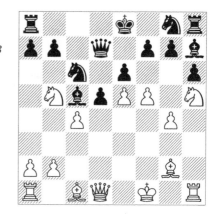

B

16...♘xe5! 17 ♕e2 ♘xc4 18 ♗xd5! ♕xb5!?
19 ♗xc4 ♕b6 20 fxe6?! 0-0-0! 21 exf7 ♘e7
22 ♕e6+ ♔b8 23 ♗f4+!? ♔a8 24 ♕xb6 axb6
25 ♗e5 ♖hf8! and so forth, Shirov-Nisipeanu,
Las Vegas FIDE KO 1999, a game in which
half of the moves are worth a page of analysis
each.

Or, more recently, 6...f6 7 h4! fxe5 8 h5 ♗f7
9 dxe5 ♘d7 10 f4 ♕b6 11 ♘d4! 0-0-0 12 ♗h3!
♘e7 13 a4! c5? 14 a5 ♕a6 15 ♗f1 c4 16 b4! b6
17 ♗e3 bxa5 18 ♖xa5 ♕b6 19 ♘f5 ♘xf5 20
♗xb6 ♘xb6 21 gxf5 ♗xb4 22 ♕d4 1-0 Nai-
ditsch-Dautov, French Cht 2005.

The 4 ♘c3 and 5 g4 variation is rich in ideas
and recommended to the tactically inclined, but
not explicable in organized fashion. We have
more useful ground to cover in the sense of understanding chess in general.

b) 4 h4 is the sort of exotic move provoked
by the bishop's placement on f5, i.e. g4 would
now drive it off the h7-b1 diagonal. Again, the
play will be based upon specifics, but there's a
wonderful line from older days that goes 4...h6
(4...e6?? loses a piece to 5 g4, but, among others, 4...h5 and 4...♕b6 5 g4 ♗d7 are played) 5
g4 ♗d7 (5...♗h7 6 e6! fxe6 7 ♗d3 has ideas
like ♗xh7, ♕d3 and ♘f3-e5 in mind; this is a
standard idea in several openings) 6 h5 e6 7 f4
c5 8 c3 ♘c6 *(D)*.

This is a classic picture of space advantage
versus rapid development and undermining
blows. White hasn't moved a piece yet but he
threatens to squeeze Black to death. The latter
must develop as fast as possible and open lines
to counteract that. 9 ♘f3 ♕b6 and now:

b1) Tal-Pachman, Bled 1961 continued 10
♘a3 cxd4 11 cxd4 0-0-0 12 ♘c2 ♔b8 13 ♗d3

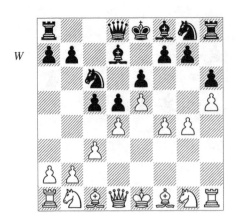

2ge7 14 罝b1 and White was ready to play b4-b5. In keeping with his open-lines approach, Black should play 14...f5!, when the positional threat of ...fxg4 encourages 15 g5 g6! and White has failed to close the kingside so Black will have an attack there.

b2) 10 ⟂f2!? (White continues with the anti-development theme) 10...f6 11 ⟂g3 0-0-0 12 a3 (now b4 is the idea) 12...c4 13 ②bd2 (D).

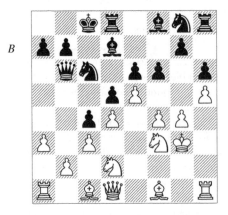

After 13...⟂b8 14 b3! White launched a successful assault on the queenside in Malaniuk-Psakhis, USSR 1979: 14...cxb3 15 ②xb3 豐c7 16 ⟂d3 ⟂c8 17 a4 ②a5 18 ②xa5 豐xa5 19 豐b3 ②e7 20 ⟂d2 豐c7 21 罝hc1 f5 22 c4!, breaking through. Instead, Black could have opened lines by 13...f5! 14 gxf5 (14 g5 g6! 15 hxg6 ②ge7 16 ⟂xc4 ②xg6 17 ⟂d3 ⟂g7) 14...②ge7!, when the fight switches to control of the kingside light squares, as illustrated by the sequence 15 fxe6 ⟂xe6 (15...②f5+!?) 16 ⟂h3 ⟂xh3 17 ⟂xh3 ②f5 18 b3 g5 19 hxg6

②ce7 and who knows what's happening! But this example only emphasizes both the potential of cramping pawns to shut down counterplay completely and the consequent necessity of immediate action by the other side.

c) 4 ②e2 is another variation that can easily become tactical, sometimes right off the blocks. One line that resembles 4 ②c3 e6 5 g4 is 4...e6 5 ②f4 c5 6 g4!? ⟂e4 7 f3 豐h4+ 8 ⟂e2 and so forth – you can imagine how important home analysis is in such a line!

d) 4 ⟂d3 was eliminated from general use by the manoeuvre ...⟂xd3 and ...豐a5+ and ...豐a6; e.g., 4...⟂xd3 5 豐xd3 e6 (or 5...豐a5+ 6 ⟂d2 豐a6) 6 f4 (6 ②c3 豐b6 7 ②ge2 豐a6 8 豐h3 ②d7, Sax-Arlandi, Baden 1999) 6...豐a5+! 7 c3 豐a6! 8 豐d1? (this costs a tempo and gives Black the light squares and better piece placement; although 8 豐xa6 ②xa6 leaves a good bishop versus a bad one, White has space as a compensating factor) 8...c5 9 ②e2 ②c6 10 ⟂e3 cxd4 11 cxd4 ②ge7 12 0-0 ②f5 13 ⟂f2 h5 14 ②bc3 ⟂e7 15 a3 罝c8 16 ⟂h1 ②a5 17 豐a4+ 罝c6 18 b4 ②c4 (D).

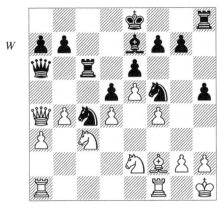

In the introductory chapters we talked about colour complexes. Here everything goes to the light squares. 19 b5 豐xa4 20 ②xa4 罝c8 21 罝fc1 0-0 22 罝c3 ⟂d8 23 h3? h4 24 g4 hxg3 25 ②xg3 ②xg3+ 26 ⟂xg3 ⟂a5 27 罝d3 ②d2 28 ②c5 b6 (or 28...②e4! 29 ②xe4 dxe4 30 罝e3 罝c3) 29 ②b3? (29 ②b7) 29...②xb3 30 罝xb3 罝c2 31 罝d3 罝fc8 32 ⟂e1 ⟂xe1 33 罝xe1 罝f2 34 a4 罝cc2 35 罝a1 g6 36 a5 罝b2 37 axb6 axb6 38 ⟂g1 罝xf4 39 罝a8+ ⟂g7 0-1 Wachweger-Schmitzer, Bergen Enkheim seniors 1997. White had an off-day but the point should be clear enough.

The Short Variation

4 ♘f3 *(D)*

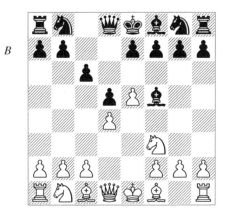

This move revolutionized the Advance Variation by showing that White could opt for slow and simple development with protection of the pawn-chain, usually by c3. This is in spite of the fact that Black has a 'good' French Defence due to the development of his bishop outside the pawn-chain. As it turns out, such an abstract theoretical view doesn't mean much in practice and there are cases when the bishop would be better-placed on d7. Short and others won various nice games until theory caught up and roughly evened things up. Today the same structure is widely seen, and the Short Variation itself has evolved, often involving ♗e3 instead of c3. Here's one of Short's original wins. It illustrates some of the underlying ideas and some that have more to do with pawn-chains as a whole.

Short – Seirawan
Manila IZ 1990

4...e6 5 c3 c5 6 ♗e2 ♘c6 7 0-0 h6 8 ♗e3!
With the idea dxc5.
8...cxd4 9 cxd4 ♘ge7 10 ♘c3 ♘c8 11 ♖c1
White has active development and the c-file.
11...a6 12 ♘a4 ♘b6 13 ♘c5 ♗xc5 14 ♖xc5
Now Short has gained the two bishops. His opening has been a success. Let's see how it plays out:
14...0-0 15 ♕b3! ♘d7 16 ♖c3 ♕b6 17 ♖fc1 ♕xb3 18 ♖xb3

White has queenside pressure and the f5-bishop is cut out of the action.
18...♖fb8 19 ♘d2 ♔f8 *(D)*

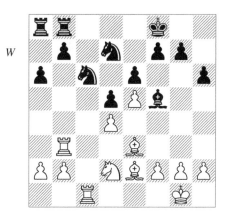

20 h4! ♔e8 21 g4 ♗h7 22 h5
Short wins space on a second front that is to be opened later – a classic chess technique. Often you simply have to have more than one area of attack to break down a well-fortified position.
22...♘d8 23 ♖bc3 ♘b6 24 ♘b3! ♘a4 25 ♖c7 ♘xb2 26 ♘c5
He concludes by switching to that second front and conducting a direct attack on the king.
26...b5 27 g5! *(D)*

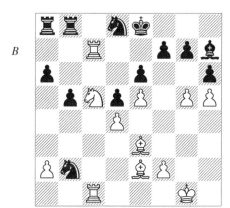

27...♘c4
Or 27...hxg5 28 ♗xg5 ♗f5 29 ♖e7+ ♔f8 30 ♘d7+ ♔g8 31 ♖e8+.
28 gxh6 gxh6 29 ♘d7 ♘xe3 30 fxe3 ♗f5 31 ♔f2 ♖b7 32 ♘f6+ ♔f8 33 ♖g1! 1-0
There would follow 33...♖xc7 34 ♖g8+ ♔e7 35 ♖e8#.

The Zviagintsev Variation

4 ♗e3 *(D)*

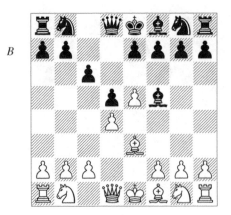

This modern move (a typical case of bishop-before-knight development) has several points. First, it helps to stop ...c5, which after all is Black's goal once he has played ...♗f5, and all the more so after ...e6. It also directly protects d4, the main target of Black's attack. Moreover, a piece gets out that normally has difficulty doing so in the Advance Variation. Now the queen's knight can follow by moving to d2 and not interfere with that bishop, leaving the pawn moves c3 and c4 free to be played.

Here you might compare 4 ♘c3 above; one of the reasons that White must strike out with the early tactical move g4 in that line is that he is no longer able to play c3 and protect d4, so his centre is faced with demolition by ...c5 and ...cxd4. After 4 ♗e3, however, the option of c3 exists, or White can defend with pieces following ♘d2-b3 or he can counterattack by c4. On the kingside we have a somewhat similar situation, in that delaying ♘f3 retains the option of f4, while the g4/h4 ideas that we see after 4 ♘c3 are not ruled out. Eventually White will probably play ♗e2 and 0-0, but he doesn't want to waste a precious tempo on those moves until it is necessary. As in so many openings today, White's underlying philosophy is one of flexibility.

There are of course drawbacks to all this, first and foremost that White is not granted two moves for every one of Black's, and can only implement these strategies one at a time! Furthermore, there is the concrete problem that ...♛b6 has to be answered should Black choose to play it within the next few moves. Let's recall again our idea about the early development of White's dark-squared bishop: whenever that happens, Black should always consider targeting the queenside dark squares. That normally applies to ♗f4 or ♗g5, but there's no particular reason to reject the same thought after ♗e3 (although at least White needn't worry as much about d4). The queen sortie to b6 also assists with ...c5. So it is probably best played right away or early on, because given a little time White can play ♘b3 or c3 and b4.

Black, having been informed that a bishop is on e3, can also aim to put a knight on f5 or g4 and look for a favourable way to obtain the two bishops. One might want to compare all this to the Kupreichik line in the Advance French: 1 e4 e6 2 d4 d5 3 e5 c5 4 c3 ♘c6 5 ♗e3. In that case, too, Black will often play ...♘ge7, aiming for ...♘f5, or even more often ...♘h6 with the dual ideas ...♘f5 and ...♘g4. Of course there's much more in terms of strategy in this wonderfully complex line. The players' positional understanding will usually be put to the test, and therein lies the chance for a challenging and competitive game.

We look at two games after 4 ♗e3:

Shirov – Dreev
Poikovsky 2006

4...e6 *(D)*

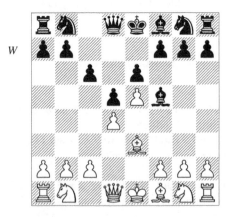

5 ♘d2

5 c3 can be slow and is perhaps out of touch with White's philosophy of flexibility: maybe

the pawn wants to go to c4, so don't decide yet. In Haba-Dautov, Bundesliga 2002/3 Black played 5...♘d7 6 ♘d2 f6. Now 7 f4?! looked a little loose after 7...♕b6! – compare the Advance French. The b2-pawn is attacked, but if White doesn't protect e5 again he can run into ...fxe5 or even the risky ...g5!?. In fact, the game continued 8 ♕b3 g5 9 exf6 g4! 10 f7+ ♔xf7 and Black already had a pleasant advantage.

5...♘d7 6 ♗e2!? *(D)*

Utterly noncommittal! There have been all kinds of moves played here, especially 6 f4, strengthening the centre and meeting 6...c5 with 7 ♘gf3. Again this seems loose after 7...♕b6, when White went 8 ♗e2!? in Morozevich-Bareev, Russian Cht (Sochi) 2004, sacrificing the b-pawn based upon development and open lines. The game went 8...♘h6 9 h3 ♕xb2 10 c4 ♗c2! (to exchange queens and clear f5 for a knight) 11 ♕c1 ♕c3!? (11...♕xc1+! 12 ♖xc1 ♗e4 should be fine) 12 ♔f2 ♘f5 13 ♘f1 and Black had to deal with White's centralized pieces and some tactics based upon the c2-bishop. Nevertheless, he stood well in the opening. Maybe f4 isn't such a great idea. The simplest option is 6 ♘gf3, as in the Short Variation.

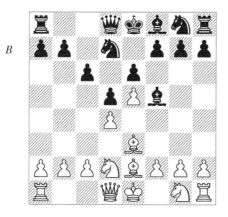

6...♕b6 7 ♘b3 ♗g6

A natural alternative is 7...f6. White's centre is hard to assail, as shown by 8 ♘f3 ♘e7 9 0-0 ♗g6 10 c4!? (pretty good, but the simple 10 ♗f4! keeps a nice advantage) 10...a5 11 ♘c5!? ♘xc5 12 dxc5 ♕xb2 13 ♘d4!? (13 ♗d4! ♕c2 14 ♕xc2 ♗xc2 15 exf6 is very strong, but Shirov is known for taking a few chances for fun) 13...fxe5? (13...♔f7!) 14 ♘xe6 ♖c8 15

♗g4 with an obvious advantage, Shirov-Erenburg, Caleta 2005.

8 h4

An innovation. 8 f4 had been played previously.

8...f6 9 h5 ♗f7 10 ♘f3 ♘h6!?

10...♘e7 11 g4! covers f5 and is typical of the unrestrained expansion in this variation.

11 ♗xh6!? gxh6 12 exf6 a5 13 a4 ♗b4+ 14 ♔f1!

14 c3 ♗d6 destabilizes the b3-knight, tying down White's queen.

14...♕d8 *(D)*

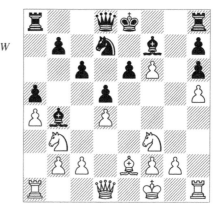

15 ♕c1 ♕xf6 16 ♘h2!

Aiming at the h6-pawn. Shirov has also played this move in the French Defence.

16...♖g8 17 ♘g4 ♕g5 18 g3!? ♗f8 19 ♔g2 ♕xc1 20 ♖axc1

This position illustrates the two-sided nature of 4 ♗e3: it can lead to tactics or positional play. Here White controls e5 and can add f4 and c4 into the mix.

20...♖g5?!

This sacrifices the exchange for insufficient compensation (perhaps Black thought that he could retain the two bishops), but 20...♗g7 21 f4! was pretty bad.

21 f4 ♖xh5 22 ♖he1! ♗e7

22...♖f5 23 ♗d3 ♗g6 24 ♖xe6+ wins for White.

23 ♘e3 ♘f6 24 ♗xh5 ♗xh5 25 f5!

Now it's a matter of technique, although when you hear that phrase, remember that some players' technique is better than others.

25...♗d6 26 c4 ♗b4 27 ♖f1 ♗e2 28 ♖f2 ♗xc4 29 ♘xc4 dxc4 30 ♖xc4 ♘e4 31 ♖e2 exf5

32 ♘c5 0-0-0 33 ♘xe4 fxe4 34 ♖xe4 ♔d7 35 ♖h4 ♗f8 36 ♖h5 ♖a8 37 d5! ♗g7 38 b3 ♔d6 39 ♖g4 ♗f8 40 dxc6 bxc6 41 ♖g8 ♔e6 42 ♖xh6+ ♔f7 43 ♖h8 ♖a6 44 ♖6xh7+ ♔g7 45 ♖c8 ♔g6 46 ♖h4 ♖b6 47 ♖g4+ ♔h6 48 ♖c4 1-0

Grishchuk – Anand
Mainz (rapid) (8) 2005

This closely-fought encounter is full of positional niceties in the opening and early middle-game.

4...♕b6 5 ♕c1! *(D)*

Avoiding dark-square weaknesses, and assisting White's forthcoming plan in this game.

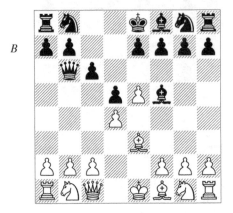

5...e6

5...♘h6!? is frequently played. It has the idea we mentioned above, aiming at g4. In one game White played simply 6 h3 and 7 ♘f3, asking where the knight is going, but that is rather slow. A more provocative course is 6 ♘f3 e6 (6...♘g4 7 ♗f4 e6 8 h3) 7 c4! (7 ♘bd2 c5 8 ♘b3!?) 7...dxc4?! 8 ♘bd2!? (or 8 ♗xc4 with a small but definite advantage) 8...♗d3 and now:

a) 9 ♗xd3!? (a little too fancy) 9...cxd3 10 ♗xh6 gxh6 11 0-0 ♘d7?! (11...♘a6!) 12 ♖d1 ♕a6 13 ♘e4 ♖g8 14 ♘e1 0-0-0 15 ♘xd3 with a pleasant position, Anand-Khenkin, Bundesliga 2002/3.

b) White should simply win the pawn back with tempo by 9 ♗xh6! gxh6 10 ♘xc4! ♗b4+ (10...♕b4+?! 11 ♘fd2 ♗xf1 12 ♖xf1 with a3 and ♘e4 to come) 11 ♔d1 ♗xc4 12 ♗xc4. Then White is in the pleasant position of being able to claim the advantage after ♔e2 and ♖d1,

while also targeting Black's weakened king-side.

6 c4!? *(D)*

The strategy of opening queenside lines is common with 4 ♗e3, and all the more so with a queen on c1. There are many options in these positions; for instance, 6 ♘f3 c5 7 ♗d3!? might be a refreshing idea.

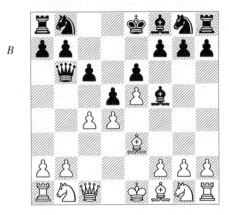

6...dxc4!

Black has had some difficulty with the loss of territory after these alternatives:

a) 6...♘e7?! 7 c5! ♕a5+ 8 ♗d2 ♕c7 9 ♘c3 ♘d7 10 ♗e2 h6?! (after 10...f6, White's flexible strategy pays off with 11 f4!; Kasparov suggested 10...♗g6!? 11 ♘f3 ♗h5) 11 b4 g5? 12 g4! ♗g6 13 h4 and White will win at least a pawn, Kasparov-Shirov, Moscow (Russia-RoW rapid) 2002.

b) 6...♗xb1?! 7 ♖xb1 ♗b4+ 8 ♗d2 ♗xd2+ 9 ♕xd2 and White had space and smooth development in Gelfand-Dreev, Moscow 2002.

7 ♘d2!?

Simply 7 ♗xc4 ♘e7 8 ♘e2 ♕d8 9 0-0 led to some advantage in Shirov-Anand, Monaco (blindfold) 2005. In that manner White keeps his space advantage, which is the key to the Short Variation and to 4 ♗e3 (its derivative).

7...♕a5!

To stop ♘xc4.

8 ♗xc4 ♘e7 9 ♘e2 ♘d7 10 0-0 ♘d5 11 ♘g3 ♗g6 12 h4! h6 13 h5

White's whole idea here, rightly or wrongly, is to acquire space. Black has found a perfect reorganization, however, and has equal play.

13...♗h7 14 a3 ♕d8 15 ♘f3 ♗e7 16 ♖d1 ♖c8

16...♘7b6 17 ♗e2 ♕d7 would emphasize the light squares, although I see no special plan for Black.

17 ♗d3!? *(D)*

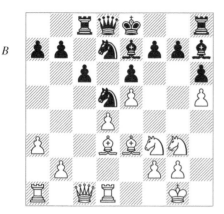

What a decision! Once again White opts to exchange his good bishop and retain his bad one. However, there is a compensating factor here. When one has space, a bad bishop can be used to protect your weakest central point (d4) while you advance on the wings.

At any rate, Anand chooses to turn the game down tactical channels, spoiling White's fun:

17...c5 18 dxc5 ♗xc5

18...♘xc5? 19 ♗xh7 ♘b3 20 ♕b1 ♘xa1 21 ♗e4 ♘b3 22 ♗xd5 exd5 23 ♘f5! ♔f8 24 ♕a2! followed by ♖xd5 is devastating.

19 ♗xh7!? ♗xe3 20 ♕b1 ♗f4! 21 ♘e2 ♘xe5

Black is obviously better now.

22 ♘xf4?

Slightly crazy: White wants to confuse matters. Black would have an easy advantage following 22 ♗e4 ♘xf3+ 23 ♗xf3 ♗e5, although in theory this is the better of evils.

22...♘xf3+ 23 ♔f1 ♘h2+! 24 ♔e1

Or 24 ♔g1 ♘g4 25 ♗f5! ♕h4!.

24...♕e7 25 ♕e4 ♘f6?

Anand falters. 25...♖xh7! 26 ♕xh7 ♘xf4 27 ♕xg7? ♕c5! is winning due to the idea of ...♕b5.

26 ♕a4+ ♔f8 27 ♖ac1 *(D)*

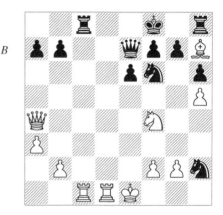

27...♖a8

Avoiding Grishchuk's clever idea 27...♖xc1 28 ♖xc1 ♖xh7 29 ♖c8+ ♘e8 30 ♘g6+! fxg6 31 hxg6 ♖h8 32 ♕f4+ ♕f6 (32...♔g8 33 ♕b8) 33 ♕d6+ ♕e7 34 ♕f4+ with a draw. What follows is unclear:

28 ♗b1! ♘hg4 29 ♕b4!? ♕xb4+ 30 axb4

By this means White wins the seventh rank.

30...e5 31 ♘d5 ♘xh5 32 ♖c7 g6 33 ♘e3!? ♘xe3 34 fxe3 ♔g7 35 ♖dd7 ♖hf8 36 ♗a2 ♖ac8?

Much better and unclear is 36...♔f6! 37 ♖xf7+ ♖xf7 38 ♖xf7+ ♔g5.

37 ♖xb7 ♖c1+ 38 ♔d2 ♖f1 39 ♖xa7 ♘g3 40 ♗d5! ♖f2+ 41 ♔c3 ♘f1 42 ♔d3 ♖d2+ 43 ♔e4 ♖f2 44 b5 h5 45 ♖xf7+ 1-0

The b-pawn queens.

13 French Defence

1 e4 e6

Strictly speaking, this move defines the French Defence. However, I shall pass over White's second-move options, and get straight to the position that most players think of as the starting-off point.

2 d4 d5 *(D)*

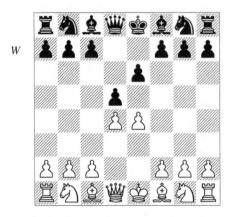

The French Defence ranks behind only the Sicilian Defence and 1...e5 as a reply to 1 e4. It is hard to characterize in general terms since it combines highly tactical and ultra-positional types of play. But the French has one quality that few other openings have, and perhaps none to this extent: a persistence of central structure. In the main lines (mostly characterized by White's move e5), the fundamental formation of ...e6 and ...d5 has a tendency to last for many moves into the middlegame and fairly often into an endgame. The exceptions consist of variations with ...dxe4, which are proportionately infrequent, and lines in which Black achieves the freeing move ...e5, something that White usually denies his opponent until the middlegame.

This brings us right away to the main disadvantage of the French Defence, Black's light-squared bishop. Whether that piece assumes a useful role can determine the success of the opening. We run into a similar phenomenon in

the Queen's Gambit Declined (1 d4 d5 2 c4 e6), where in most of the traditional lines the move ...e5 is needed to bring the c8-bishop into play. A significant exception in the Queen's Gambit occurs when the bishop is freed by White's voluntary exchange on d5. The situation with the Semi-Slav (1 d4 d5 2 c4 c6 3 ♘f3 ♘f6 4 ♘c3 e6) is obviously worse still. In any event, returning to the matter of the French Defence, we find that if White advances his pawn to e5, the freeing move ...e5 becomes unlikely in the short term, so Black may try to develop his light-squared bishop via ...b6 and ...♗a6. More often it stays on c8 or d7 for a while, perhaps awaiting the move ...f6, after which it plays a useful defensive role guarding e6. The bishop may later transfer to the kingside (g6 or h5) via e8. It's interesting that the Sicilian Defence variations which include the moves ...d6 and ...e5 are a mirror image of certain Tarrasch French main lines, right down to the role of the bad bishop as protector of a backward d-pawn (in the Sicilian) or a backward e-pawn (in the French); see the section on 3 ♘d2 ♘f6 for more about that remarkable comparison. Finally, Black's light-squared bishop may go in the other direction to c6, b5 or a4. Where it ends up will reflect the pawn-structure and thus indicate the nature of the play.

What else is going on in the initial position? On the most basic level, Black's second move of the French Defence attacks the e-pawn! According to the Hypermodern theorists, White's e4-pawn is too much of a target for 1 e4 to be a good move, and in fact Black puts the question to White, who has to choose between exchanging the pawn, advancing it, protecting it, and gambiting it. We discuss this in the Introduction to the Semi-Open Games (Chapter 10).

Looking over White's options against the French, we find:

a) There is no realistic method of gambiting White's e4-pawn that doesn't leave him struggling for equality.

b) Exchanging the e-pawns by 3 exd5 exd5 (D) immediately frees Black's queen's bishop and dissipates White's advantage. This is called the Exchange Variation.

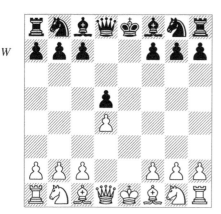

In spite of the symmetrical result of this exchange, a player on either side of the board who seeks a double-edged game will find it easy to do so. Not only are all the pieces on the board still present, but the only file down which rooks can penetrate is the e-file. However, the 5th, 6th and 7th ranks are thoroughly covered. This negates the need to put the rooks on an open file at all and allows them to support pawn advances on either wing. See theoretical books and master practice to confirm this.

c) The two most popular lines against the French Defence protect the e-pawn: 3 ♘d2 and 3 ♘c3. Those are what I'll be concentrating upon. Both moves are exceptionally rich in strategic concepts. Black's responses to the Tarrasch Variation (3 ♘d2), for example, are diverse enough to cover in depth major subjects such as the isolated queen's pawn, the central majority, and pawn-chains. And 3 ♘c3 leads to some of the most complex play amongst the 1 e4 openings.

d) The Advance Variation (3 e5) has somewhat narrower strategic scope, concentrated mainly around pawn-chains. I talked about 3 e5 at some length in Chapter 3. Since pawn-chains are also part of the Tarrasch, Classical and Winawer Variations, I've not dealt with the Advance Variation in this chapter. As always, it's better to study some variations in depth rather than all of them superficially, and I think the selected variations have the most to offer in terms of chess understanding.

Tarrasch Variation

1 e4 e6 2 d4 d5 3 ♘d2 *(D)*

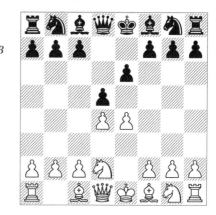

This move defines the Tarrasch Variation, for many years considered White's safest choice and a good way to get a small advantage without taking many chances. Most contemporary players have abandoned that point of view; it's now become obvious that White will have to risk something to gain something. However, as with all openings, White's rewards in these riskier variations are greater than in the old days, when he would end up in the superior position but in some drawish ending with his opponent having one weak pawn or a bad bishop.

What's the basic idea for White? First of all, convenience. White protects his e-pawn but avoids the annoying pin that occurs after 3 ♘c3 ♗b4. Then there's flexibility. White can still play either e5 or exd5 (or sometimes dxc5) and doesn't commit himself until he sees what Black is doing. In that sense he gains the advantage of setting the agenda, at least in some main lines. If Black plays 3...♘f6, for example, it's pretty much compulsory to play 4 e5 if one wants an advantage, but after 4...♘fd7, there's already a choice between 5 f4 and 5 ♗d3, and in the latter case White has another choice after 5...c5 6 c3 ♘c6, between 7 ♘e2 and 7 ♘gf3. Naturally Black has a few options too, but if he commits to 3...♘f6 they're not so bothersome during the first few moves. On the other hand, 3...c5 4 exd5 gives Black two main options, 4...exd5 and 4...♛xd5. If he so desires, White can play 4 ♘gf3 and avoid the ...♛xd5 lines by answering

4...cxd4 with 5 ♘xd4. On the other hand, this gives Black new options such as 4...♘f6 and 4...♘c6 – there are always trade-offs.

We'll consider the most popular responses to 3 ♘d2: the central counterattack 3...c5, and the provocative 3...♘f6, a variation featuring pawn-chains. I'll try to provide just enough detail to communicate the primary ideas in each branch. Those two moves are still the main variations because they challenge the centre in a way that forces White to concede something and fix the structure. I'll concentrate on them for that reason. Nevertheless, I should say that 3...♗e7 has established itself as a main-line anti-Tarrasch weapon, and at this point of time 3...♘c6 gives every indication of becoming an alternative of equal worth to the others. Today, in fact, for the first time since the Tarrasch was introduced, strong players with Black are *consistently* playing the moves 3...♘c6 (the Guimard Variation) and 3...♗e7 (D), whereas even 3...h6!? has been used with success by grandmasters (although much less often).

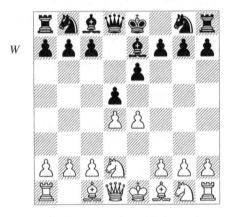

I think that there's a common idea here, namely, that the knight isn't that well-placed on d2! Can it really justify its position, blocking off the c1-bishop and queen? Clearly it will have to move again, and to a useful position. Which leads to the question: why bail it out? Why give it a useful role? Black's traditional 3rd moves do just that; for example, 3...c5 leads to lines such as 4 exd5 exd5 5 ♘gf3 ♘c6 6 ♗b5 ♗d6 7 dxc5 ♗xc5 8 0-0 ♘ge7 9 ♘b3; in that variation the knight on d2 has become a superb one, gaining a tempo on Black's bishop and covering the d4-square, right in front of the

isolani. Or consider 4...♕xd5 5 ♘gf3 cxd4 6 ♗c4 ♕d6 7 0-0 ♘f6 8 ♘b3, when the knight will capture on d4 with a centralized position.

The old main line of 3...♘f6 4 e5 ♘fd7 also justifies the knight's placement on d2; for example, 5 ♗d3 c5 6 c3 ♘c6 7 ♘e2 cxd4 8 cxd4 f6 9 exf6 ♘xf6 10 ♘f3 and White's pieces are coordinated, centralized, and aiming at the kingside. Similarly, 5 f4 c5 6 c3 ♘c6 7 ♘df3 shows the knight in a favourable light.

If Black's newly-popular moves 3...♗e7 and 3...♘c6 have less positive effect on the game in terms of forcing the play, they also make it difficult for the d2-knight to do as much. Moreover, 3...♗e7 and 3...h6 (along with the mildly revived 3...a6) are the kind of useful waiting moves that we talk about in Chapter 2. Accordingly, in spite of their own serious drawbacks (mainly the fact that they don't attack the centre as effectively in various situations), such third-move alternatives deserve attention. I shall make a comparison between 3...♘f6 4 e5 ♘fd7 and the Guimard line 3...♘c6 4 ♘gf3 ♘f6 5 e5 ♘d7 below.

Tarrasch with 3...c5

3...c5 (D)

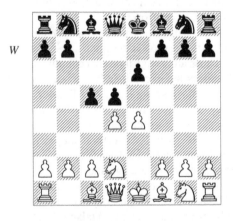

Black challenges the centre immediately. The idea is twofold, depending upon what kind of position he wants and what White does. After 4 exd5 by White, Black can accept an isolated pawn by 4...exd5, or undertake to work with a central/kingside majority by means of 4...♕xd5. I'll illustrate those options using games.

4 exd5

a) One idea after 4 c3 is 4...cxd4 (4...♞f6 5 e5 ♞fd7 is a transposition to 3...♞f6) 5 cxd4 dxe4 6 ♞xe4 ♝b4+ 7 ♞c3 ♞f6 8 ♞f3 0-0, when Black is a tempo up on some well-known isolated queen's pawn positions from the Caro-Kann and Nimzo-Indian.

b) 4 ♞gf3 *(D)* is a main option that I won't go into except to point out three unique, non-transpositional lines:

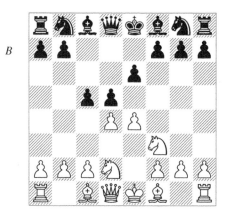

b1) 4...♞f6 5 exd5 ♞xd5!? and, for example, 6 ♞b3 ♞d7 7 g3 ♝e7.

b2) 4...♞c6 5 ♝b5 (for 5 exd5 exd5 see below) 5...dxe4 (5...cxd4) 6 ♞xe4 ♝d7 7 0-0 ♞xd4 8 ♝g5 f6 9 ♞xd4 cxd4 10 ♝h4 ♝e7 11 c3 ♝xb5 12 ♕h5+ ♚f8 13 ♕xb5 ♕d5 with an excellent game.

b3) 4...cxd4 is a third choice. You can refer to theory for the details.

Recapture with the Pawn

4...exd5 *(D)*

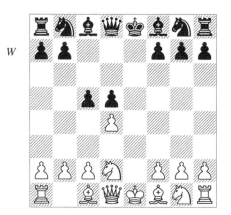

4...exd5 is a classic, well-respected system that directly tests an isolated queen's pawn position. White's next few moves have historically been the choice of most grandmasters.

5 ♝b5+ *(D)*

The more common move-order is 5 ♞gf3 ♞c6 (in spite of appearances, 5...c4!? seems to be holding its own theoretically, but White is generally not put off by it) 6 ♝b5. This transposes, and is the usual route, to the main line. Here an easy answer to 6 ♝e2 is 6...♞f6 (or 6...cxd4 7 0-0 ♝d6) 7 0-0 ♝d6 8 dxc5 ♝xc5 9 ♞b3 ♝b6!; compare the main lines below.

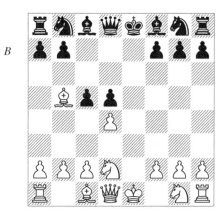

5...♞c6

5...♝d7 6 ♕e2+!? ♝e7 7 dxc5 ♞f6 8 ♞b3 0-0 intending ...♜e8 has always offered enough play to equalize. The more interesting challenge to ...♝d7 systems begins with 5 ♞gf3 and goes 5...♞f6!? 6 ♝b5+ ♝d7!? 7 ♝xd7+ ♞bxd7 8 0-0 ♝e7 9 dxc5 ♞xc5. Some top players use this for Black with the idea of getting rid of his bad bishop for White's good one. The trade-off is that it is much easier for White to maintain a d4 blockade after simplification. The line may well be equal for Black with great care, but it's very hard to get winning chances.

6 ♞gf3 ♝d6 7 dxc5

7 0-0!? cxd4 at best gets to the same position but gives Black more options, as in these samples from the 1974 Karpov-Korchnoi Candidates match after 8 ♞b3 ♞e7 9 ♞bxd4 0-0 10 c3 ♝g4 11 ♕a4 *(D)*:

a) 11...♝h5 12 ♝e3 ♕c7 13 h3 (...♞xd4 was threatened) 13...♞a5! 14 ♝d3 ♞c4! 15 ♞b5 ♕d7! 16 ♝xc4 dxc4 17 ♜fd1 ♞f5! (it doesn't take much to get in trouble: 17...a6? 18

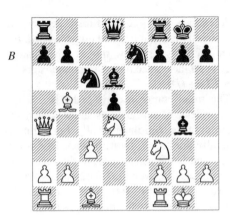

Ξxd6 ♕xb5 19 ♕xb5 axb5 20 ♘d4 and White's pieces dominate) 18 ♕xc4 ♗xf3 19 gxf3 ♘xe3 20 fxe3 ♕xh3 21 ♘xd6 ♕g3+ 22 ♔f1 ♕xf3+ 23 ♔e1 ♕g3+ ½-½ Karpov-Korchnoi, Moscow Ct (12) 1974.

b) 11...♕d7 12 ♗e3 a6 13 ♗e2 ♘xd4 14 ♕xd4 ♘c6 15 ♕d2 Ξfe8 16 Ξad1 Ξad8 17 ♗b6 ♗c7 (it's OK to simplify because every piece of Black's is active and White has to watch out for ...d4) 18 ♗xc7 ♕xc7 19 Ξfe1 h6 20 h3 ♗f5 21 ♗f1 Ξxe1! 22 ♕xe1 ♕b6 (always a good square for the queen, eyeing d4 and b2) 23 Ξd2 ♗e4! 24 ♕e2 ♘a5 25 ♕d1 ♕f6 with equality, Karpov-Korchnoi, Moscow Ct (16) 1974.

7...♗xc5 8 0-0 ♘e7 9 ♘b3 ♗d6 *(D)*

9...♗b6!? 10 Ξe1 and ♗e3 has always been judged to be in White's favour and it probably is; nevertheless, White doesn't have much after the gambit 10...0-0 11 ♗e3 ♗g4 12 ♗xb6 ♕xb6! 13 ♗xc6 ♘xc6 14 ♕xd5 ♘b4.

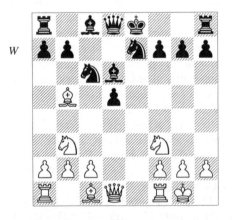

We'll follow three main games from the point after 9...♗d6:

Karpov – Uhlmann
Madrid 1973

10 ♗g5 0-0 11 ♗h4

This is straightforward positional chess: White wants to exchange pieces via ♗g3, because simplification helps to secure the static disadvantages of the isolated pawn. But it's not just any piece that White wants off the board: it's Black's good bishop that might, for instance, have supported a freeing pawn-push to d4.

11...♗g4 *(D)*

The right move, neutralizing a defender of d4. If he later captures on f3 and White recaptures with the queen, two fewer pieces will protect that crucially important square. In the meantime the pin is awkward to meet.

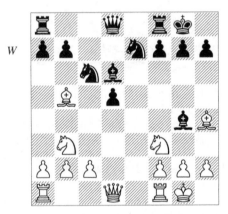

12 ♗e2 ♗h5

This is a funny-looking retreat, but it makes sense to be able to avoid more exchanges by putting the bishop on g6. But these are difficult positions, and later Uhlmann found a better way to play it. See the next game.

13 Ξe1 ♕b6

Again Black eyes d4. But Karpov will be very careful not to let the isolated queen's pawn advance.

14 ♘fd4 ♗g6 15 c3 Ξfe8 16 ♗f1 ♗e4 17 ♗g3 ♗xg3 18 hxg3 *(D)*

Finally White rids himself of Black's good bishop. It's amazing how he handles this position, since Black looks actively placed. The next idea is exactly what Black usually does, but it seems to land him in more trouble:

18...a5

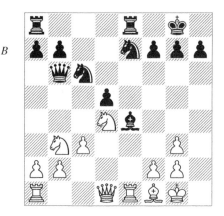

Perhaps 18...罩ad8!? should be tried, although White still has the better game.

19 a4 ②xd4 20 ②xd4!

Not 20 cxd4 ②c6 with equality.

20...②c6

After 20...豐xb2? 21 ②b5 White threatens 罩e2 and ②c7.

21 盒b5 罩ed8 22 g4! (D)

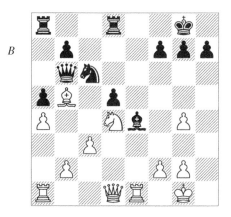

The move of the game! And the timing is perfect. White allows Black to rid himself of his isolani; at first sight he seems to have only the slightest of advantages. The point is that Black's bishop will never get back for defence. How this happens is worth seeing:

22...②xd4 23 豐xd4 豐xd4 24 cxd4 罩ac8 25 f3 盒g6 26 罩e7 b6 27 罩ae1 h6

No better is 27...f6 (to get the bishop back to f7) 28 罩1e6! 罩c1+ 29 含h2 罩b8 30 罩d6 and 罩dd7.

28 罩b7 罩d6 29 罩ee7 h5 30 gxh5 盒xh5 31 g4! 盒g6 32 f4

So simple.

32...罩c1+ 33 含f2 罩c2+ 34 含e3 盒e4

Or 34...罩e6+ 35 罩xe6 fxe6 36 罩xb6.

35 罩xf7 罩g6 36 g5 含h7 37 罩fe7 罩xb2 38 盒e8 罩b3+ 39 含e2 罩b2+ 40 含e1 罩d6 41 罩xg7+ 含h8 42 罩ge7 1-0

There could follow 42...罩b1+ 43 含d2 罩b2+ 44 含c3 罩c2+ 45 含b3 罩c8 46 盒d7 罩f8 47 f5!, etc. An unassuming masterpiece.

The next game shows the good points of having an isolated queen's pawn, namely, increased activity.

Vogt – Uhlmann
East German Ch (Potsdam) 1974

10 盒g5 0-0 11 盒h4 盒g4 12 盒e2 (D)

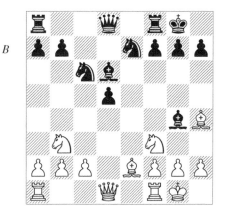

12...罩e8!

Uhlmann's improvement over the Karpov game; it essentially gains a tempo for central action. It seems that ...盒h5 was too slow.

13 罩e1 豐b6!

This covers d4 and peeks at b2, because ...a5-a4 will expose that square.

14 ②fd4

14 盒xe7?! 罩xe7! leaves Black terribly active, with the idea of 15 豐xd5?! ②b4!.

14...②g6! (D)

Suddenly White is in trouble because his pieces are too loose. Black threatens ...②xh4.

15 ②xc6

White strengthens Black's centre, but it's the only move. 15 盒xg4? 罩xe1+ 16 豐xe1 ②xd4 threatens both c2 and h4, and there's no defence because after 17 ②xd4 豐xd4 Black wins a piece.

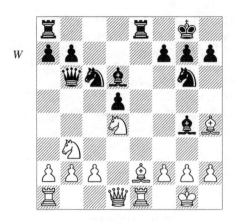

15...Rxe2! 16 Rxe2 bxc6

There's no hurry to take the rook on e2 because the f-pawn is pinned.

17 Bg3 Be7!

Black surprisingly avoids the exchange of bishops, seeing that his bishop will become strong and White's subject to harassment. But to lose time like this takes some courage. Actually, 17...Bxg3!? 18 hxg3 Nf8! wasn't bad either because Black's knight would cover all the good squares from e6. This is more or less the end of the opening but it's worth seeing more because the moves are wonderfully instructive.

18 h3 Bxe2 19 Qxe2 a5!

Threatening ...a4 and ...Qxb2.

20 c3 h5! (D)

A great stratagem: Black puts White's bishop into temporary oblivion. Perhaps even more significant is Black's aggrandisement of space. This by itself is a good thing, as long as you don't give the opponent targets to attack by doing so.

21 Nd4

One point of 20...h5 is 21 Qxh5 a4 22 Nd4 Qxb2.

21...h4 22 Bh2 Bf6 23 Rd1 a4!

More space!

24 Qc2 Qc5 25 Qd3 Re8 26 b4! axb3 27 axb3 Qb6 28 b4 (D)

White fights back, securing the c5-square as a potential outpost for his knight.

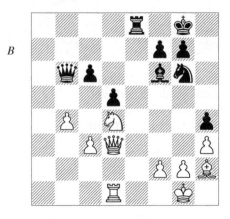

28...Re4 29 Bd6

The logical 29 Nb3 is frustrated by 29...Rc4! 30 Rc1 Qb5!, preventing 31 Nc5?? due to 31...Rxc5!.

29...Bxd4 30 cxd4 Qd8! 31 Bc5 Nf4

Now ...h5-h4 is looking especially foresighted because White's kingside is vulnerable.

32 Qf3 Qg5 33 Ra1

Trying to get the bishop back for defence loses the d4-pawn: 33 Bd6 Ne2+.

33...Kh7 34 Kh2 Re6! 35 Qg4 Qxg4! 36 hxg4 Re2! (D)

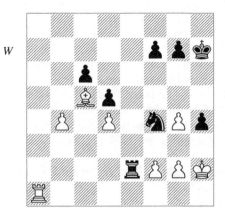

Well anticipated. White can't hang on to everything. And White's officially 'bad' bishop (because of the dark-squared centre pawn) really *is* bad!

37 ☖f1

White loses material anyway after 37 ☗g1 ♞d3.

37...♞d3 38 f4 ♞f2! 39 ☖a1 ♞xg4+!?

Instead, 39...♔g6!! would have been a brilliant move to make just before the time-control, based upon 40 ♝f8 ♞xg4+ 41 ♔h3 ♔h5 42 ☖g1 ☖e3+ 43 g3 ♞f2+ 44 ♔h2 h3! 45 ♝xg7 ♔g4! and Black will actually checkmate after ...☖e2. The rest of the game is also enjoyable:

40 ♔h3 ♞e3 41 ☖a6 ☖xg2 42 ♔xh4 *(D)*

42 ☖xc6? ☖g3+ 43 ♔h2 ♞g4+ 44 ♔h1 h3 45 b5 ♞f2+ 46 ♔h2 ☖g2#.

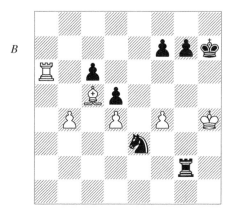

B

42...☖g4+! 43 ♔h3 ☖xf4 44 ☖xc6 g5! 45 b5 g4+ 46 ♔h4

46 ♔h2 ☖f2+ 47 ♔g3 ☖f3+ 48 ♔h4 f6! with ...☖h3# next.

46...f6! 47 ♝d6 ☖f3 48 ♝g3 ♔g6 0-1

Adams – Yusupov
Port Barcares 2005

10 ☖e1 0-0 11 ♝d3 *(D)*

This position has been considered the main line for some time now. 11 ♝d3 doesn't cover d4, but prevents 11...♝g4? due to 12 ♝xh7+ ♔xh7 13 ♞g5+. The d4-square never seemed to be quite enough for White to win with anyway.

11...h6 12 h3

From what we've seen, stopping ...♝g4 is a good idea.

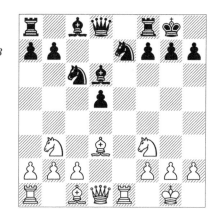

B

12...♞f5

Black concentrates upon d4 as usual. He can also think about a move like ...♞h4. Or, after his dark-squared bishop vacates d6, the knight can go there to great effect.

13 c3 ♛f6 14 ♝c2 ☖d8 15 ♛d3 g6 *(D)*

16 g4 was threatened.

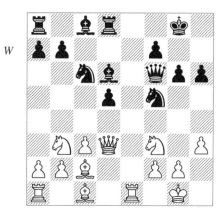

W

16 ♛d2

Rublevsky-Dolmatov, St Petersburg 1998 went 16 ♝d2 a5! (with the idea ...b6 and ...♝a6; this also gains space, a key consideration for both sides) 17 a4 b6 18 ♝e3 ♝a6 19 ♛d2 ♞xe3 20 ♛xe3 ♝g7 21 ♝d3 ☖e8 22 ♛d2 ♝c4! 23 ♞bd4 ♞xd4 24 ♞xd4 ♝c5 with equality.

16...♝f8 17 ♛f4 ♝g7

17...♝d6 18 ♛a4 ♝d7 doesn't look so bad, but White could repeat by 18 ♛d2.

18 ♝d2

Adams-Lputian, Armenia-RoW (Moscow) 2004 pitted a super-grandmaster against one of the world's leading French Defence experts: 18 h4 ♛d6 (with so much pressure on d4, Black

can afford an ending) 19 ♗d2 ♗e6 20 ♖ad1
♕xf4 21 ♗xf4 d4! *(D)*.

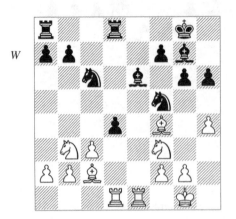

W

As always, the thematic break. Normally if it
works (as it does here) Black will equalize because he liquidates his potentially weak IQP.
However, the main idea is to free Black's pieces,
in this case the rook and e6-bishop. The next
few moves were 22 ♗xf5 ♗xb3 23 axb3 gxf5
24 ♘xd4 ♘xd4 25 cxd4 ♗xd4 26 ♗xh6 ♗xb2,
with equality.

18...g5 19 ♕h2 b6?!

There have been two other suggestions here,
both reasonable-looking, but perhaps not fully
equal. Maybe 17...♗d6 was the real solution.

a) McDonald offers 19...♗f8! 20 ♖ad1 ♗d6
21 ♕h1.

b) 19...♘d6!? 20 ♖ad1 ♘c4 21 ♗c1 ♗f8 22
♘bd4 ♗d6 is given by Pedersen.

**20 ♖ad1 ♗a6?! 21 ♗xf5! ♕xf5 22 ♗e3
♗c4!? 23 ♘bd4!** *(D)*

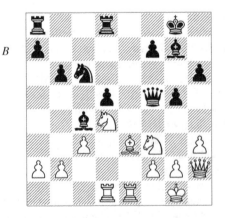

B

23...♗xd4?

It's very risky at best to leave only the opposite-coloured bishops on the board. Generally
bishops of opposite colour favour the attacker,
and only in a simplified ending do they become
drawish.

24 ♘xd4 ♘xd4 25 ♗xd4 *(D)*

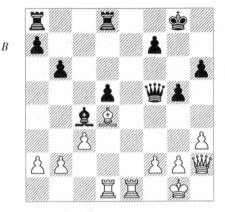

B

Now we have opposite-coloured bishops with
Black's king a little weak. Generally this is
enough to make the attack work.

25...♖e8 26 ♕c7! ♗xa2? 27 ♕c6!

Ouch. This hits a8, e8 and h6.

**27...♖f8 28 ♕xh6 f6 29 ♖e7 ♖f7 30 ♖de1
♖af8 31 ♖xf7 ♔xf7 32 g4! 1-0**

If the queen goes to f4 or f3 in order to keep
f6 guarded, it's mate on h7. If 32...♕g6, then 33
♖e7+ wins the queen.

Recapture with the Queen

4...♕xd5

This recapture represents a very different approach from that of 4...exd5, as we'll see.

5 ♘gf3 cxd4 6 ♗c4 ♕d6 *(D)*

6...♕d8 is also played from time to time. The
only unique variation of note in that case arises
when Black follows up with ...a6, ...♕c7 and
...♗d6. That is quite rare but interesting. In any
event, we'll concentrate upon 6...♕d6.

We see that with 4...♕xd5, Black is willing
to lose quite a lot of time to get to a Sicilian-like
structure with an extra central pawn (the one on
d4 is usually recovered by White) and a kingside majority (4:3). In doing so he braves many
attacking tries by White, whose lead in development and tactical tricks were probably the
reason that French Defence players were put

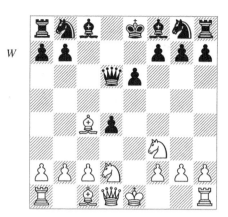

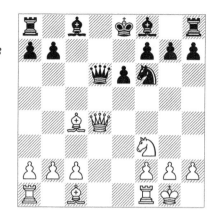

off this line for so many years. With more and more willingness to defend difficult positions in openings, players who recognized the very real advantages in Black's pawn-structure and his smooth development began to try out the line. A standard plan goes ...♘c6, ...♘f6, ...a6, ...♕c7 and ...b5 with ...♗b7, depending upon how much is permitted him. These are typical Sicilian ideas and, as in the Sicilian, players realized that the pawn on e6 in particular makes Black's position hard to crack. White in turn uses his lead in development to restrict Black's own pieces from getting out by posting pieces on support-points like e5, still looking for and often finding attacking chances. For Black, it's all about structure: White doesn't have a centre pawn to attack with, and his c- and f-pawns tend to take a long time to enter the fray. About 15 years ago this turned into the most popular line of the Tarrasch at the very top levels and it is still leading to great wins for both sides. We'll explore three games from this position.

Lastin – Bareev
Russian Cht (Sochi) 2004

7 0-0 ♘f6 8 ♘b3 ♘c6 9 ♘bxd4 ♘xd4 10 ♘xd4

White has recovered his pawn. In the early days of the variation, quite a few players tried 10 ♕xd4 *(D)*.

In spite of White's lead in development, Black has a solid position. If the game actually reached a simplified ending with no structural changes, Black's central majority would give him the advantage. In any case, Black's most popular continuation is 10...♗d7 (10...♕xd4 11

♘xd4 ♗c5! is also reasonable: 12 ♘b3 ♗e7 13 ♗f4 ♗d7 14 ♗e2 {White intends to exert pressure from f3; this is the standard plan} 14...♘d5 15 ♗g3 h5! 16 h3 h4 17 ♗h2 0-0-0, Akopian-Shirov, Merida 2000) 11 ♗f4 ♕xd4 12 ♘xd4 ♖c8 (or 12...♗c5) 13 ♗e2 ♘d5 14 ♗g3 h5! *(D)*.

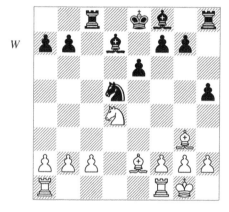

Black even has some initiative! Acs-Shaked, Budapest 1997 continued 15 h4 ♗c5 16 ♘b3 ♗b6 17 c4 ♘e7 18 ♗d3 f6!.

10...a6 11 ♗b3 ♕c7 12 ♕f3

A renowned line that has been analysed to death is 12 ♖e1 ♗d6 13 ♘f5 ♗xh2+ 14 ♔h1 0-0 15 ♘xg7 ♖d8, eventually leading to a draw.

12...♗d6 13 ♔h1

White uses this defensive technique a lot; he refuses to weaken himself by h3 or g3.

Another line runs 13 h3 0-0 14 ♗g5 ♘d7 15 c3 b5!? *(D)*.

This standard 'sacrifice' usually works because Black gets active play regardless of the material: 16 ♗c2 (too greedy is 16 ♕xa8 ♗b7

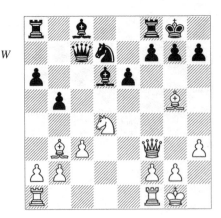

W

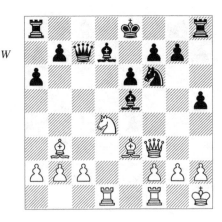

W

17 ♕xf8+ {not 17 ♕a7? ♗c5} 17...♘xf8; although White has two rooks for a queen, Black's bishops rake the kingside and ...♕c5 together with ...♘g6-h4 can follow) 16...♗b7 17 ♕h5 g6 18 ♕h4 and now:

a) In one game Black got careless and fell for a nice sacrificial piece attack: 18...e5? 19 ♘f5! f6 (19...gxf5 20 ♗xf5) 20 ♘xd6 ♕xd6 21 ♗h6 ♖fe8 22 ♖ad1 ♕e7? 23 ♗b3+ ♔h8 24 ♖xd7! 1-0 Azarov-Wiedenkeller, Saint Vincent ECC 2005.

b) 18...♖fe8! 19 ♖fe1 ♘b6 20 ♖e2 ♗e7 (20...e5? 21 ♘f5! gxf5 22 ♗f6) 21 ♖ae1 ♗xg5 22 ♕xg5 ♘d5 23 ♖e4 f6! 24 ♕h4 e5 25 ♗b3 ♔g7 26 ♗xd5 ♗xd5 with complicated play in which Black seems to have the better of it, Tiviakov-Lalić, Port Erin 2005.

13...♗e5

Another characteristic move to know about. Black anticipates ♗g5 (attacking his f6-knight), and also forces White to commit to a method of defending his knight.

14 ♗e3

Logically developing and covering d4. Instead, 14 c3 ♗d7 15 ♗g5 ♗xd4!? (15...0-0 is solid) 16 cxd4 ♗c6 17 ♕e3 ♘d5 is one of the ideas that originally made the ...♗e5 idea popular. Black blockades the IQP and equalizes.

14...♗d7 15 ♖ad1 h5! (D)

Yet another standard procedure! From now on White has to be careful about ...♘g4 ideas.

16 ♕e2!

Not 16 h3?? ♘g4 (threatening ...♗xd4 and ...♕h2#) 17 ♖fe1 ♗xd4 18 ♗f4 ♕b6 and wins.

16...♗xh2 17 g3

This is the idea behind ♔h1; White wants to win the bishop, although it is obviously risky to do so. This type of position has arisen repeatedly. Who prevails is a question of specifics.

17...e5! 18 ♔xh2!?

Perhaps better is 18 ♘f3 ♗g4 19 ♗g5 (19 ♔xh2? 0-0) 19...h4 20 ♗xf6 gxf6 21 ♔xh2 hxg3++ 22 ♔g1.

18...h4 19 ♔g1 (D)

This time 19 ♔g2!? is worth looking into. All these moves are hard to assess.

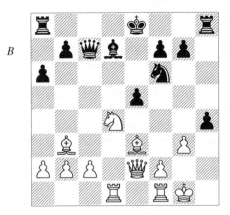

B

19...0-0-0?

Bareev gave the improvement 19...♔f8! 20 ♘f3 ♗g4 21 ♗g5 e4 22 ♗f4 exf3 23 ♕xa6! bxa6 24 ♗xc7 h3 25 ♔h2 ♗f5 26 ♗b6, and the situation is still uncertain.

20 ♘f3 hxg3 21 fxg3?

21 ♕c4! was practically winning, according to Bareev. White is keeping the extra piece: 21...gxf2+ 22 ♗xf2 ♗c6 23 ♖xd8+ ♔xd8 24 ♕d3+ with ♗g3 to follow.

21...e4 22 ♗f4

Perhaps 22 ♕c4!? was still the move.

22...exf3 23 ♕f2 ♕c6! 24 ♖d6? (D)

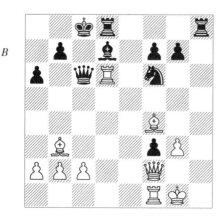

24...♘g4!

Bareev had presumably seen this blow long before.

25 ♖xc6+ ♗xc6 26 ♗xf7

The queen can't move because ...f2+ forces mate.

26...♘xf2 27 ♗e6+ ♗d7 28 ♗xd7+ ♖xd7 29 ♔xf2 ♖h2+ 30 ♔xf3 ♖xc2 31 ♖e1 ♖f7 0-1

Another important variation is:
7 ♕e2 *(D)*

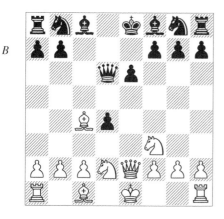

This is a line that goes directly for the kill. White forgets about recovering his pawn on d4 for the moment and concentrates on quick development, normally including 0-0-0. The current main line continues:

7...♘f6 8 ♘b3 ♘c6

Black has to catch up in development and anyway, the harder he can make it for White to recover his pawn on d4, the better. But White isn't going to slow down.

9 ♗g5! a6

What's this move about? In some positions we get from 4...♕xd5, it helps Black rearrange by ...♕c7 and ...♗d6. But in this case he wants to strike out with ...b5 before anything else happens. If White's bishop retreats, he will have fewer worries about a sacrifice on e6, a problem that is always present when White has rooks on the open central files and a knight on d4. To some extent the game is becoming a race.

10 0-0-0 b5 11 ♗d3 ♗b7 *(D)*

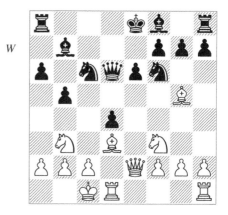

I'll show two games from this position.

Oral – Khuzman
Batumi Echt 1999

12 ♘bxd4 ♘xd4 13 ♘xd4 ♕d5! *(D)*

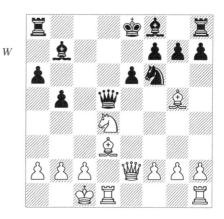

Black attacks g5 and a2 (and g2!).

14 ♗xf6 gxf6 15 ♘xb5!?

15 ♔b1! is solid. Then 15...0-0-0 16 ♘f3 could be followed by c4 or ♗e4 depending upon Black's response.

15...♕xa2 16 ♘c7+ ♔e7 17 ♕h5 *(D)*

Not 17 ♘xa8?? ♗h6+ and White has to give up his queen on e3.

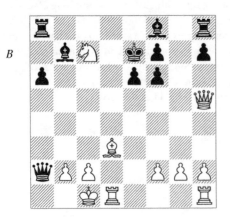

17...♗h6+!

A shot! The obvious 17...♖d8? 18 ♕c5+ ♖d6 fails to 19 ♕xd6+! ♔xd6 20 ♗c4+ ♔xc7 21 ♗xa2.

18 ♕xh6 ♕a1+

The point was to distract White's queen from a5.

19 ♔d2 ♕a5+ 20 ♔c1 ♕xc7

Black wants to keep playing instead of accepting 20...♕a1+ 21 ♔d2 ♕a5+.

21 ♖he1!? ♗d5 22 ♗e4 ♗xe4 23 ♖xe4 ♕a5 ½-½

Typical of the back-and-forth nature of this variation.

Rozentalis – Luther
Panormo ECC 2001

12 ♔b1

This looks slow but is interesting to compare with Oral-Khuzman. There the key move ...♕d5 hit a2 as well as the kingside, while here Rozentalis protects his a-pawn, at the cost of time.

12...♗e7 13 ♘bxd4 ♘xd4 14 ♘xd4 ♕c5 *(D)*

Black has also played simply 14...0-0 here, but that's risky. The text-move gets the queen off the d-file and gains a tempo by attacking White's g5-bishop.

15 h4!

Or maybe he hasn't gained a tempo, since the h-pawn will be handy in an attack!

15...0-0

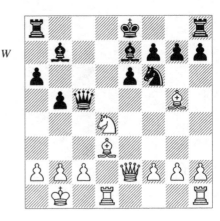

15...0-0-0!? is obviously risky. White might try 16 ♘f3 ♔b8 17 ♘e5 ♖hf8 18 ♗e3!?.

16 ♖he1

White piles up on e6. This is one of those openings where Black knows what's coming but can't always stop it.

16...♖fe8

A typical tactic follows 16...♖fd8!? 17 ♘f5!? (this move seems to appear in every line! But in this case it's probably not that great) 17...exf5 18 ♕xe7 ♕xe7 19 ♖xe7 ♗xg2 20 ♖g1 ♔f8 (forced) 21 ♗xf6 gxf6 22 ♖ee1 ♗e4 and Black should come out OK.

17 ♘f3 h6

Better seems 17...♖ac8 18 ♘e5 ♖c7. The text-move is weakening and Black probably overlooked the reply.

18 ♘e5! hxg5?! 19 hxg5 g6 20 gxf6 ♗xf6 21 f4! *(D)*

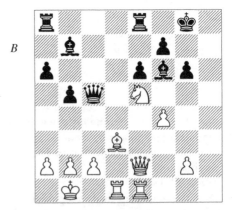

Now how can Black get any play going? ...♗xe5 will leave the dark squares unbearably weak.

21...♖ad8 22 ♕g4 ♗g7?

He had to try something like 22...♕f8.

23 ♘xf7! ♔xf7

Black was probably counting upon 23...♖xd3 24 ♖xd3, but it's not even close. Rozentalis gives 24...♕f2 25 ♘h6+! ♔f8 26 ♖xe6 ♖xe6 27 ♖d8+ ♔e7 28 ♖e8+ ♔xe8 29 ♕xe6+ ♔d8 30 ♘f7+ ♔c7 31 ♕d6+.

24 ♗xg6+ ♔f8 25 ♖xd8 1-0

There follows 25...♖xd8 26 ♕xe6 with mates threatened on both f7 and e8.

Tarrasch with 3...♘f6

1 e4 e6 2 d4 d5 3 ♘d2 ♘f6

With this move Black challenges White to set up a pawn-chain and the game enters typical French territory. White's e-pawn is threatened, so he has little choice but to advance.

4 e5

4 exd5?! exd5 already favours Black because the knight on d2 is poorly placed for an Exchange Variation.

4...♘fd7 *(D)*

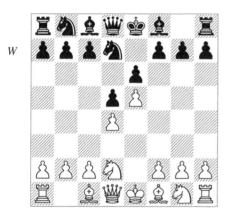

Now we have a position characterized by pawn-chains. The traditional choices here are 5 ♗d3 and 5 f4.

Development by 5 ♗d3

5 ♗d3

5 c3 c5 6 ♗d3 is another move-order, and avoids the loss of time in the next note.

5...c5

5...b6 is possible, when if 6 c3 ♗a6 7 ♗xa6 ♘xa6, White has 'lost' a tempo by ♗d3 and

♗xa6; however, this is not so clear, as Black's knight can be misplaced on a6. White can also choose 6 ♘gf3 or 6 ♘e2 ♗a6 7 ♗xa6 ♘xa6 8 0-0, reserving the move c4 for later use.

6 c3 ♘c6

Now 6...b6 allows White options such as 7 f4 ♗a6 8 ♗b1!?, intending ♘df3, ♘e2 and 0-0.

Now I'll examine the two main moves, 7 ♘e2 and 7 ♘gf3.

The Traditional 7 ♘e2

7 ♘e2

This continuation has dominated the practice of 3...♘f6 since time immemorial, but recently it's been sharing the spotlight with 7 ♘gf3.

7...cxd4 8 cxd4 f6 *(D)*

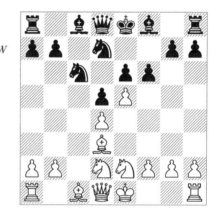

9 exf6

Don't fall for 9 f4?! fxe5 10 fxe5 ♘xd4! 11 ♘xd4 ♕h4+ 12 g3 ♕xd4.

A big-time alternative whose consequences have never quite been solved is the tactical and less common 9 ♘f4. It's a real mess, and unfortunately very theoretical, in the sense that many logical moves are losing and the forced nature of the play doesn't admit of time-consuming over-the-board reflection. I'll give a few important moves, skipping most of the options: 9...♘xd4 (9...♕e7 10 ♘f3 fxe5 11 dxe5 ♘dxe5 12 ♘xe5 ♘xe5 13 ♕h5+ ♘f7 14 0-0 g6 15 ♕e2 makes it hard for Black to develop) 10 ♕h5+ ♔e7 *(D)*.

11 exf6+! (11 ♘g6+ hxg6 12 exf6+ ♔xf6!? 13 ♕xh8 ♔f7 is a very old line, but at the least Black can also transpose by 12...♘xf6, so why give him an additional option?) 11...♘xf6 (now

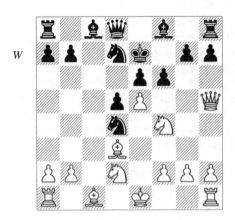

W

11...♔xf6? 12 ♕h4+ g5 13 ♘h5+ ♔f7 14 ♕xd4 is killing) 12 ♘g6+ hxg6 13 ♕xh8 ♔f7 14 ♕h4 (notice the trap 14 ♘f3?? ♗b4+, winning the queen; people have lost this way!) 14...e5 15 ♘f3 e4!? (15...♘xf3+ 16 gxf3 ♗f5 17 ♗xf5 gxf5 18 ♗g5 also leads to deep analysis) 16 ♘xd4 ♗b4+ 17 ♗d2 ♗xd2+ 18 ♔xd2 ♕a5+ 19 ♔d1 exd3. These are mad positions; I refer you to the books and databases.

9...♘xf6

It's a shame that this venerable line, which has generated such great games and so many attractive and thought-provoking ideas, has become laden with theory in so many byways. Nevertheless, we'll take a look at the basic complex of variations, so that you can get a start in understanding what's going on.

9...♕xf6, keeping an eye upon the critical e5-square, is another idea that is moderately alive after some years of experimentation. The essential idea can be seen after 10 ♘f3 h6 (D) (to stop ♗g5-h4; e.g., 10...♗d6 11 ♗g5 ♕f7 12 ♗h4 0-0? 13 ♗xh7+).

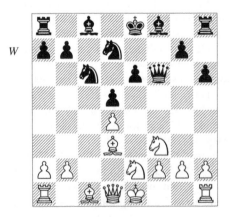

W

Now if White plays conventionally by 11 0-0 (11 ♗b1! ♗d6 12 ♕d3 is much harder to meet; compare what follows) 11...♗d6 12 ♗b1 0-0! 13 ♕d3 Black replies 13...♖d8! 14 ♕h7+ ♔f7 and plays ...♘f8 next. Although gaining a tempo with 11 ♗b1 poses Black a problem, it may be amenable to solution.

10 ♘f3 ♗d6 11 0-0 (D)

11 ♗f4 ♕a5+ confuses White's pieces: 12 ♕d2 (12 ♔f1 ♕c7 13 ♗xd6 ♕xd6 is equal) 12...♗b4! 13 ♘c3 0-0 14 0-0 ♘e4.

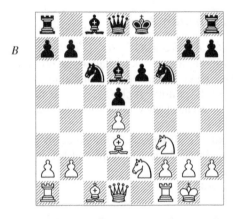

B

11...♕c7

Black aims at White's kingside, but even more significantly, he stops ♗f4, which effectively exchanges Black's good bishop. This comes at the cost of committing the queen early on, which could be considered a relative loss of time.

I'd guess that at least a thousand pages of analysis (adding up all sources and annotations) have been devoted to the lines beginning with 11...0-0 (D).

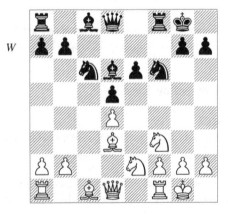

W

I'm going to stick with the queen development instead. But I do think that it's intriguing to compare this position with the Sicilian line 1 e4 c5 2 ♘f3 d6 3 d4 cxd4 4 ♘xd4 ♘f6 5 ♘c3 ♘c6 6 ♗e2 e5 7 ♘b3 ♗e7 8 0-0 0-0 9 ♗e3 ♗e6 (D).

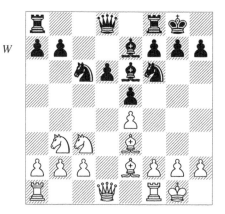

It's a mirror image! Notice especially the roles of the bad bishops protecting backward pawns. The biggest difference in structure is Black's open f-file in the French Defence. He also has the opportunity to attack White's vulnerable d-pawn. Both of these are comparative advantages. But in the Sicilian Defence position, Black has an important minority attack with ...a6 and ...b5, by which he gains space, attacks the queenside, and helps with control of d5. In the French, Black has nothing of the sort; as such, his strategy is more piece-based, with moves like ...♕c7 (supporting the idea of ...e5), ...♘h5 (or ...♘g4), intending to attack on the kingside.

And as long as we're digressing, a thought-provoking comparison also arises between this sort of position and that of the Guimard Defence, 3 ♘d2 ♘c6. It turns out that the lack of a c-pawn in our 3 ♘d2 ♘f6 French Defence can be a disadvantage in comparison with the Guimard! Let's look at a fairly normal example:

Rašik – Cernousek
Ostrava 2005

1 e4 e6 2 d4 d5 3 ♘d2 ♘c6 4 ♘gf3 ♘f6 5 e5 ♘d7 6 ♗d3 f6 7 exf6 ♕xf6

7...♘xf6 is also played in this kind of position. The same ideas apply.

8 0-0 ♗d6 9 c4 0-0 10 c5 ♗e7 11 ♘b3 h6 12 ♗e3 e5! 13 dxe5 ♘dxe5 14 ♘xe5 ♘xe5 15 ♗e2 c6 *(D)*

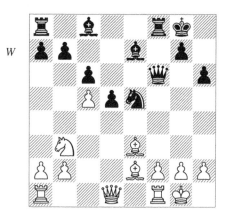

This is the relevant position. Black has made his ...e5 break and retains a healthy centre because his d5-pawn is fully protected. Contrast this with the case of the 3...♘f6 main lines: because of the insertion of the moves ...c5 and ...cxd4, Black almost always ends up with a weak isolated queen's pawn if he plays ...e5.

16 ♖c1 ♕g6 17 ♗h5 ♕h7!?

Or 17...♕f5 with the idea ...♘g4. Black may stand slightly better.

18 ♖c3 ♗f5 19 ♘d4 ♗g6 20 ♗e2 ♖ae8 21 ♘e6 ♖f7 22 ♘f4 ♗e4 23 ♗h5 g6 24 ♗e2 ♗f6 25 ♗d4 ♕h8! *(D)*

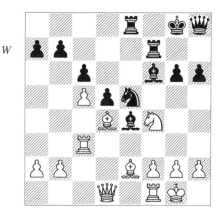

26 ♖g3 ♔h7 27 ♗c3 ♕f8!

Threatening both 28...♕xc5 and 28...♗h4. Suddenly Black is winning.

28 ♘d3 ♘xd3 29 ♗xd3 ♕xc5 30 ♕g4? ♗xd3 0-1

There would follow 31 ♖xd3 ♗xc3 32 ♖xc3 ♕xf2+ 33 ♖xf2 ♖e1+.

Now let's return to the 3...♘f6 variation with 11...0-0. As I said, I'm going to be following 11...♕c7, but here are a few notes on 11...0-0, partly for the sake of showing some typical themes but mainly to demonstrate how crazy and specific these lines have become! After 11...0-0, White usually takes the opportunity to exchange bishops by 12 ♗f4 (which is why 11...♕c7 is played) 12...♗xf4 13 ♘xf4 ♘e4. The main line goes 14 ♘e2 ♖xf3 15 gxf3 ♘g5 *(D)*.

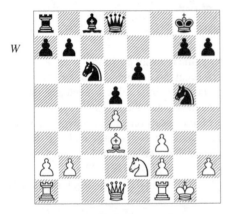

Now:

a) One serious option is 16 ♔h1 e5! 17 dxe5 ♘xe5 (right at this moment in time this seems better than 17...♘xf3 18 ♗xh7+! ♔h8 19 ♘g1 ♘cd4! 20 ♗d3!) 18 ♘g1 ♕f6 19 ♗e2 ♗d7!? (this has ideas of both ...♗c6 and the powerful ...♘e6-f4! – always remember the power of a knight on f5/f4 in front of doubled pawns; Black could try 19...♘e6!? 20 ♕xd5 ♔h8 21 ♖fd1 ♗d7) 20 ♕xd5+ ♔h8 21 ♗b5. White may have a small edge in the whole line; this is just to get you started!

b) 16 f4 ♘f3+ 17 ♔g2 *(D)*.

Now look at the deranged things some players do: 17...♕h4!? 18 ♔xf3 ♕h3+ 19 ♘g3 e5 20 ♔e3! exf4+ 21 ♔d2 fxg3 22 hxg3 ♕h6+ 23 f4 ♘xd4!? (23...♕f6) 24 ♖h1 ♕b6 25 ♗xh7+?! ('obviously' better is 25 ♔c1 ... perhaps!) 25...♔f8 26 ♔c1 ♕c6+ 27 ♔d2 ♕b6 with a draw! Unless you adore theory (and making improvements on moves 20-35 of an opening variation), you might want to play something else.

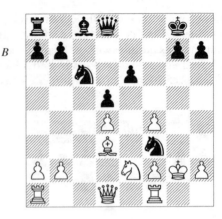

We now return to the position after 11...♕c7 *(D)*:

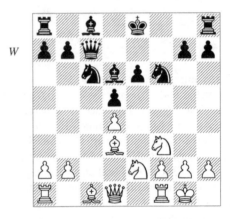

Let's look at a real game:

Biti – Gleizerov
Zadar 2005

12 ♗g5

The main line, which has the logical idea of ♗h4-g3 to exchange off that good bishop of Black's. Then White can start thinking about occupying the juicy outpost on e5 by means of ♖e1. If Black plays ...e5 first, he gets saddled with an isolated queen's pawn and remember that they tend to be weaker after simplification, especially the exchange of the better bishop. That's White's general strategy, but of course it takes time. As explained after 11...0-0, Black tends to rely on piece-play, so he'll start putting everything close to the king, provoke weaknesses and then strongly consider ...e5 in order to bring the last pieces into the attack. 12 ♘c3,

12 g3 and 12 h3 are all interesting alternatives which we won't go into.

12...0-0 13 ♗h4 ♘h5 14 ♕c2

Since Black's doing all right here (I guess), White might want to try 14 ♘c3 a6 15 ♖c1 g6 16 ♘a4. Then best seems 16...♗d7! 17 ♗g3 (17 ♖e1 ♖xf3!) of Mamedov-Hanley, Nakhchivan jr Wch 2003, when McDonald likes 17...♘xg3 18 hxg3 ♕a5!?.

14...h6 15 ♗g6

McDonald also analyses 15 ♖ac1 g5! (D).

It's typical of the French Defence that such a move can be good – it also works in several lines of both the Advance and the Winawer Variations. Aside from snatching space and launching an attack on the king, it gives Black's pieces more room to move about safely and not get too cramped on the queenside. Black's possible follow-ups include ...♗d7-e8-g6 and ...♕g7. Black's knight is also better protected after ...♘f4. Specifically, this version of the ...g5 plan combines ideas of ...g4 with ...♘f4, threatening to exchange White's good bishop on d3.

The analysis continues 16 ♗g6 (trying to disrupt Black's build-up; Pedersen analyses 16 ♗g3 ♘xg3 17 ♘xg3 {17 hxg3 ♕g7} 17...♕g7 18 ♘h5 ♕e7! intending 19...g4, 19...♘b4 or 19...♗d7) 16...♘f4 17 ♘xf4 ♗xf4 (17...gxf4!?) 18 ♗g3 ♗xg3 19 hxg3 (19 fxg3!?) 19...♕g7 with pressure on d4 after, e.g., ...g4.

15...♖xf3!

Alas, we now enter into high theory again. I'll reduce things to an outline, with few details. The standard exchange sacrifice on f3 is hardly surprising in the French, of course, but it's hard to determine if it's good. It seems to

be in this case, although theory hasn't yet settled down.

16 gxf3 ♗xh2+ 17 ♔h1 ♘f4! (D)

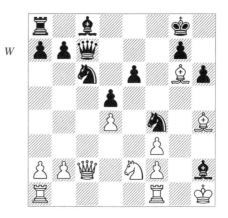

18 ♘g3 e5!?

Typical tactics for this variation. As usual, I'm not going to go into much detail about such a precise tactical variation. 18...♕d6 used to be considered brilliant, but maybe not so much these days. Check the books. 18...♕b6, however, is at the moment theoretically satisfactory after 19 ♖ad1 ♘xd4 20 ♕a4 ♘xg6.

19 ♖fe1

Or 19 ♔xh2 ♕d6 20 ♗h7+ ♔h8 21 dxe5?! ♘xe5 22 ♗f5 ♗xf5 23 ♘xf5 ♕e6! with a great attack, Ulybin-E.Berg, Santa Cruz de la Palma 2005.

It looks like 19 ♗h7+? ♔h8 20 ♔xh2 g5! 21 ♗f5 gxh4 22 ♗xc8 ♕xc8 23 ♘f5 ♕d7!! is winning for Black, Can-E.Berg, Kusadasi 2006. It's enough to make your brain explode. On the other hand, these tactics *are* kind of amazing!

19...♗h3! (D)

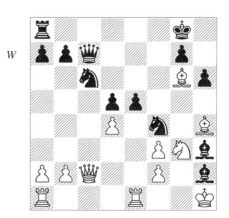

20 ♖ad1

A simple but beautiful idea is 20 ♔xh2? ♘xd4! 21 ♕xc7 (21 ♕d1 ♘xg6 22 ♔xh3 ♕d7+ 23 ♔h2 ♘f4!) 21...♘xf3+ 22 ♔h1 ♗g2#.

20...♗xg3?

Much better is 20...♘xd4 21 ♖xd4 (a different version of the last note is 21 ♕xc7? ♗g2+ 22 ♔xh2 ♘xf3#) 21...♕xc2 22 ♗xc2 exd4 23 ♔xh2 d3 24 ♗b1 g5.

21 ♗xg3?

He should play 21 fxg3!.

21...♗g2+ 22 ♔h2 ♗xf3 23 ♖d2 e4 *(D)*

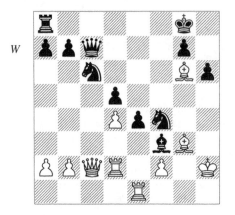

24 ♗xe4!?

And here another brilliant line is 24 ♕b3 ♕d7! 25 ♗xf4 ♘a5!! 26 ♕b4 ♕g4 27 ♗g3 ♕xg6 28 ♕e7 ♘c4! 29 ♖c2 ♘d6! 30 ♔g1 (30 ♕xd6 ♕h5+) 30...♘f5! 31 ♕xb7 ♕h5! 32 ♕xa8+ ♔h7, as given by McDonald.

24...dxe4 25 ♖xe4 ♗xe4 26 ♕xe4 ♖f8 27 d5 ♕e5 0-1

The Fashionable 7 ♘gf3 Variation

1 e4 e6 2 d4 d5 3 ♘d2 ♘f6

There are two ways to transpose into the main line here: 3...c5 4 ♘gf3 ♘f6 5 e5 ♘fd7 6 c3 ♘c6 7 ♗d3 and 3...♗e7 4 ♘gf3 ♘f6 5 e5 ♘fd7 6 ♗d3 c5 7 c3 ♘c6. The latter is a variation that could also arrive by the game's order but with 7...♗e7. There is a lot of theory on that position.

4 e5 ♘fd7 5 ♗d3 c5 6 c3 ♘c6 7 ♘gf3 *(D)*

Developing the knight in this way was always regarded as second-best, because now the d2-knight has nowhere good to go. Then players began to feel that the tempo White 'gained'

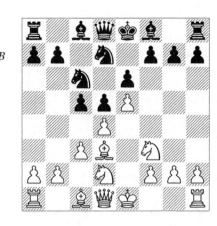

(instead of ♘d2-f3, White plays ♘gf3 directly) was worth something, and that he might have a clearer path for his queen to the kingside than with having two knights to jump over (on e2 and f3).

Still, in some respects Black calls the shots. As long as Black doesn't commit to a radical move right away, White needs a positive plan. He can't play ♘b3 due to ...c4, and dxc5 gives up the centre. That means that a slow move by Black at this point could be the most effective course, as in the following game.

Zhang Pengxiang – M. Gurevich
Hoogeveen 2004

7...g6!?

Black has the strange-looking idea of playing ...♗g7 and ...f6, breaking up White's centre. It's hard to stop!

At this juncture an especially noteworthy alternative is 7...♗e7, preparing the now-routine attack with ...g5. Then the critical continuation is 8 0-0 and Black has two main tries:

a) 8...g5 9 dxc5! *(D)* has done fantastically well and is an instructive positional device for White.

By surrendering the centre he gives his king's knight the d4-square, which ruins Black's attacking plan, and he can blast away at the suddenly poor-looking g-pawn by f4; for example, 9...♘dxe5 (9...g4 10 ♘d4 ♘dxe5 11 ♗b5 ♗d7 12 ♘2b3 gives White the advantage, Smirin-Akobian, Minneapolis 2005) 10 ♘xe5 ♘xe5 11 ♘b3 ♗d7 12 f4!, Hráček-Stellwagen, Solingen 2005. White is ripping open the f-file and Black's king will have trouble getting away.

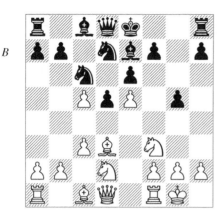

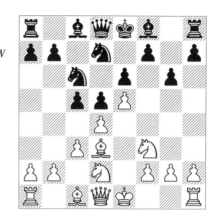

b) 8...a5 is a sort of prophylactic move, discouraging ♘b3 at any point due to ...a4. One game went 9 ♖e1 (9 dxc5 ♘dxe5 doesn't make much sense without the g-pawn as a target) 9...cxd4 10 cxd4 g5!? *(D)* (now that there's no dxc5, Black can go ahead).

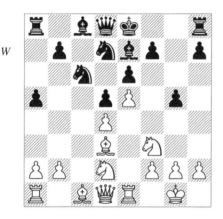

11 g4!? (this radically prevents ...g4; unfortunately, it exposes White's king; so does 11 h3! h5 12 ♘f1 g4 13 hxg4 hxg4 14 ♘3h2, but at least then White wins the g-pawn! Black has to break up White's centre while he still can: 14...♘xd4! 15 ♕xg4 ♗c5, and we reach another position that is hard to assess; it looks about equal) 11...h5 12 h3 hxg4 13 hxg4 ♕b6 14 ♕a4 (Gormally-McDonald, London 2001) and McDonald suggests 14...♘f8 (14...f6!? 15 ♘f1!) 15 ♘f1 ♗d7, when White has to respond to the discovered threat: 16 ♗e3 (16 ♗b5 ♘xe5! – remember that tactic; it's seen all over the place) 16...♕xb2 17 ♖ab1 ♘b4. Black has some advantage.

Let's return to 7...g6 *(D)*:

8 h4!

The critical move. 8 0-0 ♗g7 9 ♖e1 0-0 10 ♘f1 has been played a lot but Black comes out well after 10...cxd4 11 cxd4 ♕b6! (White controls the critical squares after 11...f6 12 exf6 ♘xf6 13 ♗b5!) 12 ♗c2 f6 13 exf6 ♘xf6 14 ♗a4 ♘e4 15 ♗xc6 bxc6 16 ♘g3 e5! (if Black can play this in the French he's usually in good shape) 17 ♗e3 exd4 18 ♗xd4 (18 ♘xd4 ♘xf2 19 ♘xc6 ♕xc6 20 ♗xf2 ♖xf2 21 ♔xf2 ♕c5+ 22 ♖e3 ♗a6 is winning for Black) 18...♗xd4 19 ♕xd4 ♘g5!, with clearly the better position for Black.

8...h6!?

A strange-looking move, yet consistent with the waiting policy. Now 9 0-0 looks inconsistent with h4, so White must try to make something happen. 8...♗e7 9 ♔f1!? *(D)* is another odd idea, but White wants to 'castle' while leaving the rook on h1!

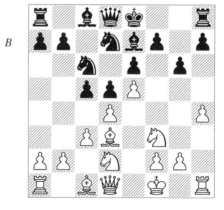

For example, 9...0-0 (if 9...♕b6, then 10 ♔g1! cxd4 11 cxd4 ♘xd4 12 ♘xd4 ♕xd4 13

♘f3 is a typical gambit in this line; Black has a lot of weak squares) 10 ♔g1 f6 11 exf6 ♗xf6 12 ♘g5!? ♗xg5? (12...♕e7 has the idea of playing ...e5) 13 hxg5 ♕e7 14 ♘f1! e5 15 ♘e3 ♕f7 16 ♘g4 ♔g7 17 dxc5 ♘xc5 18 ♘f6 and White had a winning game in Sebag-V.Popov, Cappelle la Grande 2006.

9 0-0

Another game with typical themes continued 9 a3!? ♕b6 10 0-0 g5! 11 hxg5 hxg5 12 ♘xg5 cxd4 13 cxd4 ♕xd4! 14 ♘df3 ♕g4 15 ♘xf7! ♖g8! 16 ♘7g5 ♘dxe5 17 ♗e2 ♘xf3+ 18 ♗xf3 ♕h4, Perunović-E.Berg, Gothenburg Echt 2005; here 19 ♗h5+ ♔d8 20 ♕f3 is best, with mutual chances after 20...♗e7.

9...g5

You'd think that White had gained a tempo, but now his king is committed and ...g4 is a real threat.

10 h5!?

After 10 hxg5 hxg5 11 g4 ♗e7 12 ♖e1, Black might try 12...♘f8!? with the idea ...♘g6 and ...♘f4 or ...♘h4. The position is closed enough to justify these elaborate knight manoeuvres, and White can do the same by 13 ♘f1! cxd4 14 cxd4 ♗d7 15 ♘g3! (D).

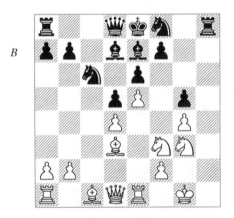

I'll leave you to contemplate this picture.

10...♕b6 11 c4!? cxd4 12 cxd5 exd5 13 ♘b3 ♗g7 14 ♘fxd4!

A pseudo-sacrifice. White has to move rapidly or his centre will fall as Black's king scurries to safety. White now threatens 15 ♘f5.

14...♘xd4 15 ♗e3 ♗xe5 16 ♖e1! (D)

White (assisted by ♗f1 if needed) recovers the piece with a strange position. Black's extra pawn and some weakness are pitted against

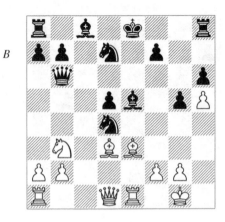

White's somewhat better pieces. The opening has come out about even, as the game continuation shows.

16...0-0 17 ♘xd4 ♕f6!? 18 ♖c1 ♖d8 19 ♕d2 ♘f8!?

Black is attempting to combine kingside defence with challenging d4 via ...♘e6. Instead, 19...♘b6! is solid, protecting the d-pawn.

20 ♘f3! ♗f4 21 ♗xf4 gxf4 22 ♕b4

22 ♗e2!? ♗g4.

22...♗g4 23 ♘e5 ♗xh5 24 ♕xb7 f3 25 ♘c6 fxg2! 26 ♖e3!?

Or 26 ♘xd8 ♕h4 (26...♖xd8 27 ♖e3) 27 ♔xg2 ♕g4+ 28 ♔f1 ♕f3 (28...♕h3+ 29 ♔g1 ♖xd8? 30 ♗f1) 29 ♔g1 ♕g4+ with a draw.

26...♖e8 27 ♘e7+ ♔h8 28 ♕xd5 (D)

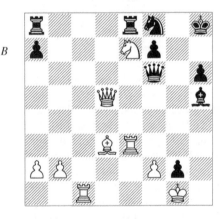

28...♗g4?!

28...♘e6 29 ♕xh5 ♖xe7 30 ♖f3 ♕g5 31 ♕xg5 hxg5 32 ♔xg2 ♘f4+ 33 ♔g3 ♖d8 is roughly equal.

29 ♖g3 ♖ad8 30 ♖xg4! ♖xe7 31 ♕xd8 ♖e1+ 32 ♖xe1 ♕xd8 33 ♗c4

Now it looks as though White stands better but Black works his way out.

33...♘g6 34 ♗xf7!? ♘e5 35 ♖g8+ ♕xg8 36 ♗xg8 ♘f3+ 37 ♔xg2 ♘xe1+ 38 ♔f1 ♘d3 39 ♗b3 ♔g7 40 ♗c2 ♘xb2 41 ♔g2 ♔f6 42 ♗b3 ½-½

A fantastic back-and-forth battle!

Seizing Space by 5 f4

1 e4 e6 2 d4 d5 3 ♘d2 ♘f6 4 e5 ♘fd7 5 f4 *(D)*

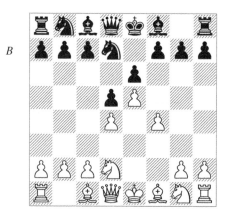

White constructs a big centre, with the pawns forming a wedge that extends into Black's position. The advantage is obvious: it's now extremely hard to break down the front of the pawn-chain, which is always the essence of Black's strategy in the ♗d3 lines. The moves ...f6 and ...fxe5 can be answered by fxe5 (or in fewer cases by dxe5, which cedes the c5-square to Black's pieces). I'll concentrate on this d4/e5/f4 pawn-chain structure here and in the Classical French because it's different from most other pawn-chains in this book. The only other major opening with similar properties is the King's Indian Defence with pawns on e4, d5 and c4, and Black's treatment in that opening is radically different from what we shall see in the French Defence.

White's strategy has one major drawback: he has to make so many pawn moves, not only these first four but also c3 and usually g3 and/or h4. Even a3 and b4 are part of a typical formation. Because of this it turns out that Black can almost inevitably sacrifice something in the centre to open up attacking lines for his better-developed pieces. The result is often a confused disarray of pieces and threats, with White trying to defend an exposed king against Black's open lines and advanced centre. Of course, there are two possible outcomes in White's favour. Either the sacrifice isn't possible, when White will almost always enjoy a large, cramping space advantage and potential attacks on both wings. Or Black's sacrifice may prove insufficient for equality. Ensuring such a result takes a lot of accuracy on White's part, however, and many players seem to have grown tired of being on the receiving end of brilliancies.

The normal and logical response to 5 f4 is to attack the d-pawn with 5...c5. As a mini-rule, we can generalize that attacking the front of a *double-winged* pawn-chain like this with ...f6 is best delayed until some of your other pieces are out. You might compare the King's Indian c4/d5/e4 double-wing, in which ...c6 can be very useful, but doesn't usually occur until Black has castled. Nevertheless, you will see that eventually ...f6 will be essential to open counterattacking lines.

5...c5 6 c3

I should mention that 5 c3 c5 6 f4 is another move-order that reaches this position.

6...♘c6 7 ♘df3

This is played in the great majority of games. Otherwise the knight on d2 is only getting in the way.

7...♕b6

Here Black has the option of a 'closed' system with 7...cxd4 8 cxd4 f5 *(D)* that is quite playable.

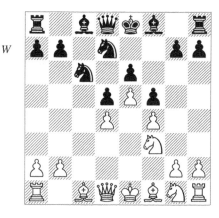

The idea is ...♗e7, ...0-0 (this may be delayed), ...♘b6, ...a5-a4(-a3), ...♗d7 and attack on the queenside. White can never fully neutralize this attack if Black is careful. His problem is that White plays for ♖g1 and g4 and Black's king must be defended. The manoeuvre ...♗d7-e8-g6 can be useful in that respect. It's an interesting system for positional players. One example after 9 ♗d3, by transposition: 9...♗e7! 10 ♘e2 ♘b6 11 h3 0-0 12 g4?! (12 a3! a5 13 b3 a4 14 b4 ♘a7 15 ♖g1 ♗d7 and now 16 ♘c3 ♕e8!? 17 g4 ♘b5 or 16 g4 ♗b5) 12...a5! 13 a4?! ♘b4 14 ♗b1 ♗d7 15 ♔f2?! ♖c8 16 ♖g1 ♔h8 17 ♔g2 ♗e8! 18 ♔h2? (18 ♔h1!?) 18...♗g6 19 ♘c3 ♕e8 20 ♘e1 ♕f7 21 ♖g2 fxg4 22 ♗xg6 ♕xg6 23 hxg4 ♕h6+ 24 ♔g1 g5! and Black stood much better in Ye Jiangchuan-Short, Lucerne Wcht 1989.

We now return to 7...♕b6 (D):

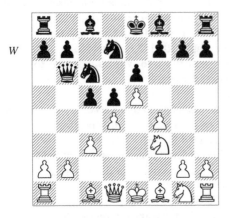

We'll look at three games with characteristic tactical motifs that you should know.

Saltaev – M. Gurevich
Cappelle la Grande 2001

8 h4 cxd4 9 cxd4 ♗b4+ 10 ♔f2 f6 11 ♗e3 fxe5!?

Or 11...0-0, denying White squares such as f4.

12 fxe5 0-0 13 ♗d3?

This move tends to interfere with White's control over d4 and in general exposes the bishop to later attack by Black's centre. 13 a3 ♗e7 14 b4 is one course, and 13 ♘e2! tries to take advantage of Black's 11th: 13...♘dxe5!? (McDonald's recommendation) 14 dxe5 d4 15 ♘exd4 (15 ♗xd4! ♘xd4 16 ♘exd4 ♗c5 17 ♔e3 looks solid enough; Black should probably

play 17...♕xb2 18 ♗e2 ♕c3+ 19 ♕d3 ♖xf3+! – somehow Black always has tactics in these lines – 20 ♔xf3 ♕xd3+ 21 ♗xd3 ♗xd4 22 ♖ae1, and probably White still has a tenuous advantage) 15...♗c5 (or 15...♘xe5!?) 16 ♘c2 ♘xe5 with a strong attack.

13...♘xd4! (D)

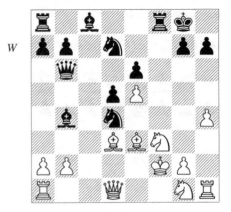

A theme that occurs again and again; you need to know it whether you're playing White or Black.

14 ♘e2! ♘xe5

This is good, but a creative suggestion by Kalinichenko is more fun: 14...♘xf3! 15 ♗xb6 ♘fxe5+ 16 ♔g3 ♘xb6. This looks overwhelming. Black has only two pieces for the queen but his minor pieces will slaughter White.

15 ♗xd4 ♘g4+ 16 ♔g3?!

Better is 16 ♔g1 ♗c5 17 ♗xh7+!? ♔h8! 18 ♗xc5 ♕xc5+ 19 ♘ed4 e5, but it's obviously good for Black.

16...♕d6+ 17 ♔xg4 e5+ 18 ♔g3 exd4+ 19 ♔f2 ♗g4 20 ♖c1 (D)

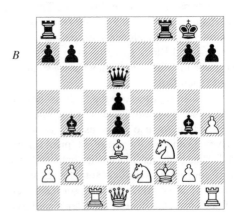

20...Rae8!?

20...We5! is decisive, since ...We3+ can't be stopped except by 21 Bxh7+ Kxh7 22 Nexd4 Rae8, etc.

21 Nexd4?!

21 Wb3 Bd2!.

21...Ba5!

Threatening ...Bb6.

22 b4 Wxb4 23 Kg3 h5 24 Rb1 Bc7+ 0-1

Gufeld – Hummel
Las Vegas 2000

8 g3 cxd4 9 cxd4 Bb4+ 10 Kf2 g5!?

This is a theoretical line that should ultimately be equal. Neither of the games I'm giving is best play, but show how each colour can quickly get into trouble.

11 Be3?!

A win for White with a great finish went 11 fxg5 Ndxe5 12 Nxe5 Bxe5 13 Be3 Nc6 14 Nf3 Bf8 15 Wd2 Bg7 16 Bd3! Bd7 17 Rac1 Nxd4 18 Wc3 e5 19 Bxd4 exd4 20 Rhe1+ Kd8 21 Wa3?! Bf8 22 Ne5! Be8 23 Wa4! h6?? 24 Wd7+! 1-0 Šolak-Kozamernik, Ljubljana 2003 (24...Bxd7 25 Nxf7#).

11...g4! 12 Nd2 f6! *(D)*

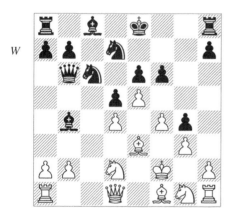

13 Wxg4?

White should have played 13 Nb3! fxe5 14 dxe5 Bc5 15 Nxc5 Nxc5, which is equal or perhaps slightly better for Black.

13...Bxd2 14 Bxd2 Wxd4+ 15 Ke1 We4+ 16 Kf2 Ndxe5! 17 Wg7 Rf8! 18 Be2 Wxh1 19 Nf3 Ng4+! 20 Wxg4 Wxa1 21 f5 exf5 22 Wf4 Bd7 23 Wd6 Wxb2 24 Bf4 Rf7 25 Wxd5 Kf8 0-1

Krupkova – Gleizerov
Mariehamn/Österaker 1997

8 g3 cxd4 9 cxd4 Be7 10 Bh3

White follows a traditional plan in which he tries to force Black to defend his e-pawn. That's simply too slow, so Black will be forced to sacrifice a piece instead:

10...0-0 11 Ne2 f6! 12 Rf1?

White has to be consistent and take the pawns: 12 Bxe6+! Kh8 13 Bxd5 fxe5 14 fxe5 Ndxe5! 15 dxe5 Nxe5 and Black has a powerful attack, but with White a piece up it's hardly clear.

12...Kh8 13 Nc3!? fxe5 14 fxe5 *(D)*

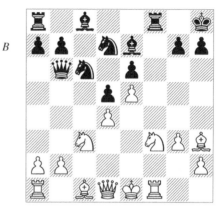

14...Rxf3!

A sacrifice that's almost as old as the French Defence itself. It's a little more difficult in this situation to summon up the courage to do it, because Black has to reorganize before he can bring all his pieces into the attack. Generally, however, ...Rxf3 should become your first instinct as Black in these f4 positions, and Public Enemy Number One for White!

15 Wxf3 Nxd4 16 Wh5! Wd8!

White's back-rank threats are prevented and Black's pieces get out to aggressive positions.

17 Wd1?

17 Kd1! is the best try, even if it is no fun to defend: 17...Nc6! 18 Bf4 (18 Bxe6?! Ndxe5 and Black is well on top) 18...Nc5 intending ...Bd7. With the king on d1, these positions are awfully hard to play for White. Black even has a pawn for the exchange.

17...Nc6 18 Bxe6 d4! *(D)*

19 Nd5

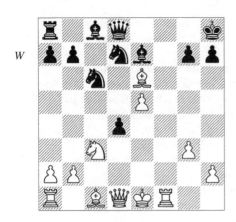

Or 19 ♘e2 ♘dxe5 20 ♗xc8 ♖xc8 with moves such as ...d3, ...♘c4 and ...♘g4 to come. Black is practically winning already.

19...♘dxe5 20 ♗xc8?

A blunder. But 20 ♘xe7 ♗xe6 21 ♘xc6 ♘xc6 is terrific for Black because of his tremendous unopposed bishop and White's king position.

20...♕xd5 (D)

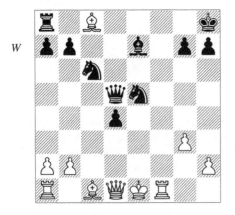

Everything is falling apart for White.

21 ♗xb7

Or 21 ♗f5 ♖f8!, which threatens ...♖xf5 and there's no defence.

21...♗b4+

21...d3! 22 ♗xc6 ♕xc6 23 ♗e3 ♕e4 wins for Black.

22 ♔f2

Now 22...♕f7+ 23 ♔g1 ♕xb7 wins.

After the inconsistent 12 ♖f1? the opening was a disaster for White, but the objective assessment of the g3/♗h3 manoeuvre is anyone's guess.

Classical Variation

1 e4 e6 2 d4 d5 3 ♘c3 ♘f6 (D)

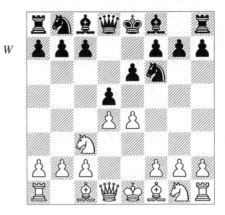

The Classical lines of the French begin here. To continue our discussion of the d4/e5/f4 centre, we're going to examine the main line with that set-up.

4 e5

I won't be discussing the important alternative 4 ♗g5, when the MacCutcheon, 4...♗b4, can resemble the Winawer Variation.

4...♘fd7 (D)

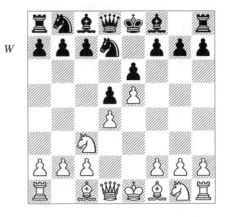

5 ♘ce2

This odd-looking move is designed to avoid a number of Black's options. For example, White could play 5 f4 c5 6 ♘f3 ♘c6 7 ♘e2 (7 ♗e3 is one of the main lines of the Classical French, not covered in this book) 7...♕b6 8 c3, transposing to the variation that we are examining. But Black would have the choice of capturing the pawn on d4 on moves 6 and 7, or of playing a move other than ...♕b6 on move 7.

5...c5 6 c3

6 f4 leads to its own move-order deviations like 6...♗e7 7 ♘f3 0-0 8 c3 f6!? or 6...♕b6 7 ♘f3 ♗e7; or even 6...♕a5+!? 7 c3 b5!?. All of these deserve more trials, as they are seldom seen in master play.

6...♘c6 7 f4 *(D)*

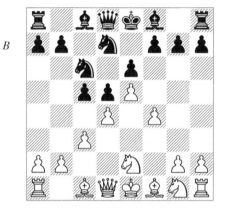

These pawn-chain lines look like the Tarrasch lines with 5 f4 and sometimes transpose into them, but in some ways White has a better grip on the centre. For example, there are no lines in which ...cxd4 followed by ...♗b4+ bothers him. We'll look at two games from this position, one in which White tries to maintain his entire pawn-chain and another in which White plants a piece on d4 and establishes himself there:

Anand – Shirov
Teheran FIDE Wch (4) 2000

7...♕b6 8 ♘f3 f6 *(D)*

The lines are formed for a classic battle: White wants to batten down the hatches, avoid making any weaknesses in his own position, secure and increase his space advantage, and finally, drive back Black's pieces. For his part, Black wants to blast open the centre, sacrificially if necessary.

9 a3 ♗e7 10 h4 0-0 11 ♖h3! a5 12 b3

All these pawn moves can be a little slow. White's got a lot of space on the kingside and might want to use a move to secure it. With that in mind, he could simply allow Black to get

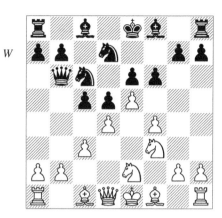

...a4 in and let him try to infiltrate on the queenside; even if he gets a piece to b3 it doesn't look as though Black would get anything useful out of it. In the meantime, that's a big and dangerous pawn-mass that White would have at his disposal on the kingside.

12...♕c7 13 ♘eg1!? *(D)*

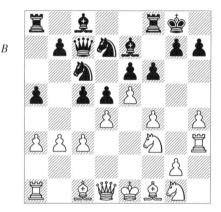

A surprising and clever retreat: White undevelops his pieces only in order to hold the centre together and anticipate all of Black's threats. On the other hand, although Anand's last few moves are ingenious and were praised by one and all, they're also slow. That's Black's cue to throw everything he's got at the white centre.

13...a4!

This loosens things up a bit before launching into the complications. You'll see later how useful this interpolation is. Anand recommends 13...b6, but is exchanging bishops useful? See my comments in the next game.

14 b4 fxe5 15 fxe5 ♘dxe5! *(D)*

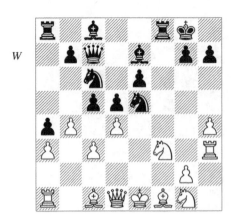

It's now or never. That's about all you need to know about these lines when playing Black: if you don't sacrifice at an early stage, you'll probably never be able to sacrifice later! White will just have too many pieces covering all the key squares and then you'll die slowly, waiting around as he slowly advances on your cramped position.

If you're handling the white pieces, the sacrifices are also about all that *you* need to know! If you can prevent those, the rest won't be difficult. So try to set up your pieces for maximum post-sacrifice defence, as Anand has tried to do here by playing ♖h3 and ♘eg1, both designed to overprotect the f3-square, which is generally the most vulnerable target. It pays off for him in this game.

16 dxe5 ♘xe5 17 ♘xe5 ♕xe5+ *(D)*

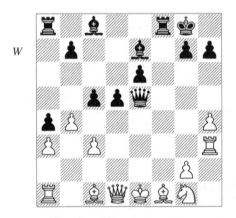

18 ♕e2 ♗xh4+!?
Shirov pours more gasoline on the fire. He could also say to himself, "I've got two mobile centre pawns and tremendously active pieces,

so I'll just take it easy and retreat by 18...♕c7 *(D)*. Then I'll play ...e5 (hitting h3) and ...♗f6." That's probably a good plan:

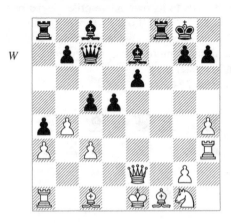

If you want to see Black's reward for sacrificing his piece, try to defend the diagrammed position for White. It may or may not be that he can succeed in repulsing the attack, but few players could do so in practice. One line would be 19 ♗g5! (19 ♕h5, to get out of the way of the bishop and play ♗d3 next, can be answered by 19...cxb4 20 axb4 g6 21 ♕h6 e5; for instance, 22 ♖g3 ♖xf1+! 23 ♔xf1 ♕c4+ 24 ♘e2 ♗g4! 25 ♖xg4 ♕xg4 with a big attack) 19...♗xg5 20 hxg5 e5 21 ♖f3 ♗f5 22 ♕f2!? cxb4 23 cxb4 e4 24 ♕g3 ♖ac8! 25 ♕xc7 ♖xc7 26 ♖f2 d4 and the pawns and open files make life pretty tough for White. Objectively it's hard to assess this as favourable for either side.

19 ♔d1 *(D)*
Not 19 ♖xh4? ♕g3+.

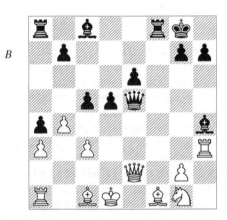

19...♕f6?!

After this White gets his pieces out too fast. There was nothing wrong with 19...♕xe2+! 20 ♗xe2 (D).

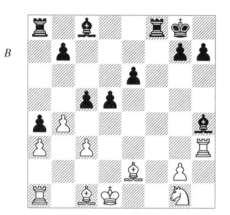

B

Don't forget how valuable centre pawns are! It's instructive how they remain so after simplification. Of course White has his chances too. A sample line would be 20...♗f2 (20...♗f6! also has some good points; e.g., 21 bxc5 ♖a5 22 ♗e3 ♗xc3 23 ♖b1 d4 or 23...e5) 21 ♗e3! e5 22 ♗xf2 ♖xf2 23 ♖g3 b6 24 ♔e1 ♖f6 25 ♖e3 ♖e6 and it's not clear who's better. Maybe the whole ending is about equal. At least it's not boring!

20 ♘f3!

Finally White's pieces are active. Now Anand isn't worried about the centre any more. The rest is pretty easy.

20...♕xc3!? 21 ♗b2 ♕b3+ 22 ♔c1 e5

22...♗f6 23 ♗xf6 ♖xf6 24 ♘e5 and the queen is trapped.

23 ♖xh4 ♗f5 24 ♕d1 e4 25 ♕xb3 axb3 26 ♘d2 e3 27 ♘f3 ♖ae8 28 ♔d1 c4 29 ♗e2 ♗e4 30 ♔c1 ♖e6 31 ♗c3

White is two pieces ahead for the blockaded pawns. Anand went on to win easily.

Macieja – Ivanchuk
Moscow FIDE KO 2001

7...♗e7 8 ♘f3 0-0 9 a3 a5

Once again Black is not thrilled with allowing b4, although White needs to spend extra time doing so, and maybe 9...f6 is good; for example, 10 b4!? cxd4 11 cxd4 fxe5 12 fxe5 ♘b6 would be an interesting positional solution. Even the bad c8-bishop would get out.

10 h4

10 ♘g3 was suggested, although then 10...f6 keeps the pressure up. The move 10 b3!?, as in the Anand game, also looks slow because Black's queen doesn't have to go to b6. On the other hand, a rook on the second rank is one of the best defensive pieces in almost any position (don't forget that!), and one on a2 might come in very handy later.

10...f6 11 ♘eg1?!

White plays like Anand in the Shirov game, but without Black's queen on b6. Probably 11 ♖h3! is best. After that move Anand's idea of ...b6 and ...♗a6 has been suggested. The problem I have with this positional device is that if White's good bishop is exchanged for Black's bad one, all that does is give White a few precious extra tempi to defend his massive centre. Then he can begin an advance with his f-pawn that will free his other bishop. It seems much better to pursue the usual sacrificial ideas in the centre.

11...cxd4 12 cxd4 ♕b6 13 ♗d3?! fxe5 14 fxe5 ♘dxe5! (D)

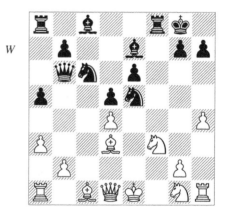

W

There it is again! You can see why these positions are so difficult for White to defend, regardless of whether he's in satisfactory condition according to theory.

15 dxe5 ♘xe5 16 ♗c2

16 ♘xe5?? ♕f2#.

16...♗d7!

When you've got this kind of attack and there are no immediate sacrifices, you can always bring up the reserves. The centre is your long-term compensation. Besides, ...♗b5 could be strong at some point. If you're White, the best thing to do is to try to simplify, and if that's impossible, obscure the issue as much as you can.

17 ♕e2 *(D)*

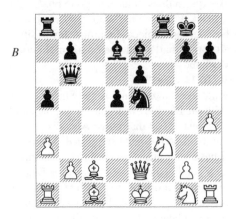

17...♖ac8!!

Now every piece is in the act. Of course Ivanchuk has a few of them hanging, but he's got it all worked out. Instead, 17...♘xf3+?! 18 ♘xf3 ♗b5 looks attractive except for 19 ♗e3!.

18 ♗xh7+!

Tough defence! The variations after 18 ♘xe5 ♗xh4+! *(D)* are fantastic:

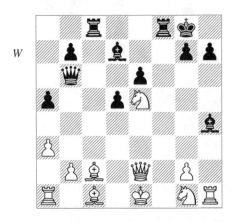

a) 19 ♖xh4 ♖xc2! (Black must avoid the tempting 19...♕xg1+? 20 ♔d2 ♖f2 because 21 ♗xh7+ ♔f8 22 ♖f4+! ♖xf4 23 ♘g6+ ♔e8 24 ♘xf4 refutes the attack; White's got a lot of pieces, and sometimes they simply do the job) 20 ♕xc2 (20 ♕e3 ♖xc1+ 21 ♕xc1 ♕xg1+) 20...♕xg1+ 21 ♔d2 ♖f2+ 22 ♔c3 d4+ 23 ♔b3 a4+! and the queen goes.

b) 19 ♔d2 ♕d4+ 20 ♕d3 ♖f2+ 21 ♘e2 ♖xe2+! 22 ♔d1 (22 ♔xe2 ♗b5 23 ♕xb5 ♖xc2+)

22...♕xe5 23 ♕xh7+ ♔f8 24 ♕xh4 ♖exc2 and Black wins.

c) In response to 19 ♔d1 there is a simple but hard-to-see piece of geometry: 19...♗a4!! 20 ♗xa4 ♕d4+ 21 ♘d3 ♕xa4+, mating in a few moves.

18...♔xh7 19 ♕xe5 ♗d6 20 ♗e3 ♕b3 21 ♘d2 *(D)*

21 ♕xd6 ♕xe3+ 22 ♘e2 ♖c2 wins at once. Now Ivanchuk finishes it off prettily:

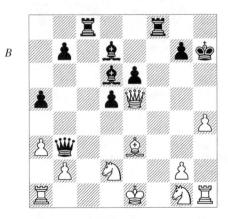

21...♖f1+! 22 ♔xf1 ♕d3+ 23 ♔f2 ♗xe5 24 ♘gf3 ♗xb2 25 ♖ab1 ♖c2 26 ♖hd1 e5 27 g3 ♗g4 0-1

Winawer Variation

1 e4 e6 2 d4 d5 3 ♘c3 ♗b4 *(D)*

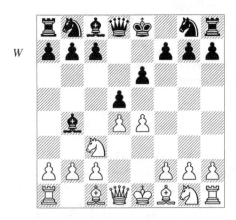

This is the Winawer Variation. Black pins the c3-knight and, in the same way that he does when he plays 2...d5, puts the question to White:

exchange, gambit, protect, or advance? We are going to concentrate upon the main line, which is marked by the advance.

4 e5

Easily the most ambitious move, restricting Black's development and staking out territory on the side of the board that Black's dark-squared bishop has just abandoned.

Various other lines may be found in the books, several of them involving the sacrifice of White's e-pawn with subsequent recovery. For example:

a) 4 a3 ♗xc3+ 5 bxc3 dxe4 6 ♕g4 ♘f6 7 ♕xg7 ♖g8.

b) 4 ♗d2 dxe4 5 ♕g4 ♘f6 6 ♕xg7 ♖g8.

c) 4 ♘e2 dxe4 5 a3 ♗e7 6 ♘xe4.

And so forth. There are numerous options on every move of these lines, with theory tending towards a verdict of equality with best play. As always, the reader may want to consult specialized books to learn more.

4...c5 *(D)*

Black decides to attack the base of the pawn-chain first. He will almost inevitably attack the front of it later.

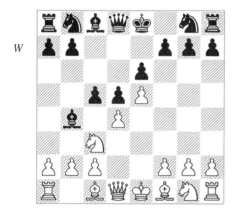

5 a3

White wants to force a decision by Black's bishop; you'll have to check theoretical works and databases in order to find out about the alternatives. Of these, 5 dxc5 and 5 ♗d2 are perhaps the most interesting. If you are not inclined to play the main lines presented below, this may be a good place to investigate potential weapons for use. The defender, of course, should be aware of and prepared for White's various 4th-and 5th-move alternatives.

5...♗xc3+

Black cedes the bishop-pair to White in order to gain a tempo and inflict doubled pawns on his opponent. 5...♗a5 is a respectable option played by some specialists, but isn't nearly as popular; we'll pass that by.

6 bxc3 ♘e7 *(D)*

6...♕c7 is also played, posing a different set of problems. Those who enjoy play upon colour complexes may be attracted to lines such as 7 ♕g4 f5 8 ♕g3 cxd4 9 cxd4 ♘e7 10 ♗d2 0-0 11 ♗d3 b6 12 ♘e2 ♗a6, when White's concentration upon dark squares (h4-h5-h6, ♘f4-h5 and ♗b4 are typical ideas) contrasts with Black's on the light squares (by ...♖c8 and ...♘b8-c6-a5, for example).

It is my belief that the most instructive and engrossing lines follow from the positions after 6...♘e7.

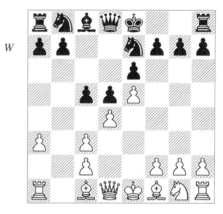

At this juncture, White chooses between the Positional variations, involving the moves ♘f3, a4 and/or h4 in various orders, and the 'French Poisoned Pawn Variation' 7 ♕g4.

Positional Variations

In this section we'll look at lines in which White bypasses tactics for a while and tries to establish a positional edge. In spite of initial appearances, both players will use both sides of the board to generate play. We'll look at a series of games beginning with 7 h4 and 7 ♘f3.

7 h4 *(D)*

With this move White charges forward to assault Black's position, not caring about piece development. He has several ideas, beginning

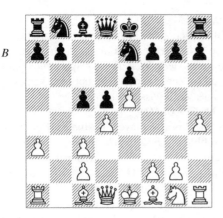

with h5-h6 to compromise Black's kingside. Black's kingside dark squares are already weakened due to the loss of his f8-bishop, so if White can establish holes on f6 and h6 it will not only give him good squares for his pieces, but also discourage Black from attacking on the kingside. White's advantage in space is on the kingside, and h4 only enhances that advantage.

Other matters of note, many of which apply to the Winawer in general:

a) White has the two bishops;

b) The pawn advance h4-h5 makes kingside castling very difficult for Black, and almost compels ...0-0-0;

c) The rook's pawn advance doesn't block off White's queen as lines with ♘f3 do, so ♕g4 is always an issue;

d) White has a potentially strong resource in ♖h3-g3/f3 or ♖h4-g4/f4, the latter rook move also introducing the possibility of dxc5 and ♖hb4 for attack.

Black's main advantage is less subtle: a growing lead in development. It's quite possible that he'll have every piece except one of his rooks in action when White still only has one piece out! White also has weak doubled pawns on his c-file, with the usual problem that if Black exchanges pawns on d4 White gets rid of his doubled pawns only to find that his remaining backward c-pawn on an open file can be as least as much a problem as the doubled pawns. In general, Black would like to exploit White's queenside light-square weaknesses on c4 and a4. Finally, Black can usually open files on the kingside, after which his rooks directly face White's king. There are many other positional

and tactical issues and I shall discuss as many as possible in context.

7...♘bc6 8 h5 ♕a5

Black attacks White's c-pawn and, incidentally, threatens ...♘xd4.

9 ♗d2 *(D)*

9 ♕d2? cxd4 10 cxd4 ♕xd2+ and 11...♘xd4 wins the d-pawn.

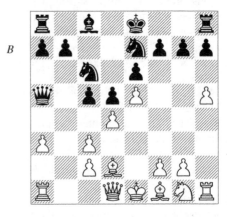

There follow two games that stem from this strategically rich position.

Hector – Hillarp Persson
York 1999

9...♗d7

Developing as quickly as possible; Black announces his intention to castle queenside.

10 h6 gxh6 *(D)*

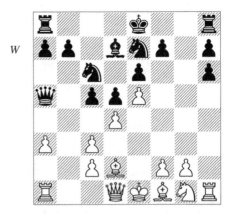

A funny position because Black's doubled h-pawns are so weak on an open file and White apparently controls the kingside. But Black finds a remarkable idea after which both players have the opportunity to play on both sides of the board! In fact that's often the case in the Winawer. Although White has space on the kingside, Black can counter with ...f6 and open lines for his pieces there. And Black's attack on White's weak queenside squares can boomerang when White uses the b-file and dynamic pawn moves on that side of the board including c4, a4-a5, and sometimes dxc5.

11 ♘f3 0-0-0 12 ♗d3 c4

Black closes the side of the board on which he appears the strongest!

13 ♗e2 ♘g8!! *(D)*

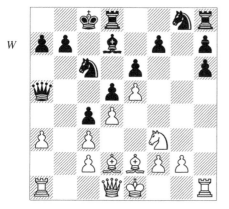

This retreat is Black's salvation, a move invented by Uhlmann, the Hercules of the French Defence. Instead of going to the obvious f5, the knight deters ♗xh6 (which would mean giving up White's dark-squared bishop) and prepares the key move ...f6. After that, Black's two files on the kingside can cause trouble.

14 a4!?

Both sides' ideas begin to become clear after 14 ♔f1 f6!? 15 ♕e1 fxe5 16 ♘xe5?! (16 dxe5! ♖f8 17 g3 ♕c7! 18 ♗f4 ♘ce7 intending ...♘g6 is very complicated; when White maintains a pawn on e5 he improves his defensive prospects) 16...♘xe5 17 dxe5 ♘e7! 18 ♗xh6 ♖hg8 19 ♗f3 (19 ♕d2 ♘f5 20 ♗g5 ♖xg5 21 ♕xg5 ♕xc3) 19...♗e8! and Black has the superior game, Short-Psakhis, Isle of Man 1999. Black will play ...♗g6 and has a solid advantage. But these lines always have play for both sides and White eventually won the game. In view of White's improvement on his 16th move I think a verdict of dynamic equality is fair, an assessment which also applies to the opening in general.

14...♖f8! 15 ♕c1! *(D)*

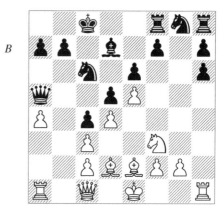

15...f6 16 ♕a3

This is White's point: to activate his queen on the precious dark squares, thereby freeing his dark-squared bishop to help on the kingside. This would be positionally winning except that time is an element that can't be discounted.

16...♖f7 17 ♗f4 ♘ge7 18 exf6 ♖xf6 19 ♗xh6 ♖g8 20 ♔f1

20 g3 ♘f5 21 ♗d2 ♖fg6 transposes.

20...♘f5 21 ♗d2 ♖fg6 22 g3

Now White would like to secure his entire position with ♗f4, but it's Black's move:

22...e5! *(D)*

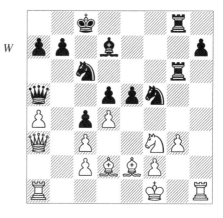

23 ♖xh7

A torrent of tactics follows 23 ♘xe5!? ♘xe5 24 dxe5 ♖xg3!; for example, 25 ♕b4 ♕xb4 26 cxb4 ♖3g7 and it's hard for White to unravel and counter ...d4; e.g., 27 c3? ♘d4!! 28 cxd4 ♗h3+ 29 ♔e1 ♖g1+ 30 ♗f1 ♖xh1.

The other try is 23 dxe5, but 23...♖xg3! 24 fxg3 ♘xg3+ 25 ♔f2 ♕b6+! is also strong for Black, a rook down, because his key move ...♘e4+ will ruin any normal defence like 26 ♘d4 ♘xd4 27 cxd4 ♕xd4+ 28 ♕e3? (28 ♗e3 ♕xe5 with a huge attack and material to come) 28...♘e4+.

23...e4! 24 ♘e5?

A resourceful try is 24 ♘h4! ♘xh4 (not 24...♘xg3+? 25 fxg3 ♖xg3 26 ♖xd7! ♔xd7 27 ♗f4) 25 ♖xh4 ♘xd4! 26 cxd4 ♕xd2 and Black stands better but it's messy.

24...♘xe5 25 dxe5 *(D)*

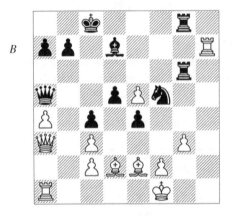

25...e3!

Black maintains a constant initiative before his king can get into trouble.

26 ♗xe3 ♘xe3+ 27 fxe3 ♖xg3 28 ♔f2

28 ♕e7 ♗c6 defends everything.

28...♕b6 29 ♖f1 ♖xe3! *(D)*

Accurate to the end.

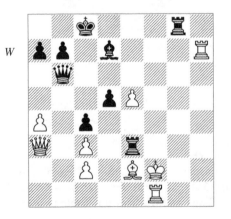

30 a5

30 ♕d6 ♖xc3+ 31 ♕xb6 axb6 is hopeless; Black will end up with four passed pawns.

30...♖g2+! 31 ♔xg2 ♕g6+ 0-1

A typical game, of the kind that White can also win (and sometimes does) if he penetrates to the king before Black can drum up a sound attack.

Hellers – Gulko
Biel IZ 1993

9...cxd4 10 cxd4 ♕a4

Here we have an innocent-looking position in which White had originally played 11 c3 or 11 ♗c3 with equality. Then, playing against Anand in Linares 1992, Kasparov found an ingenious sacrifice to get his usual initiative for a pawn.

11 ♘f3!? ♘xd4 12 ♗d3 ♘ec6 13 ♔f1 *(D)*

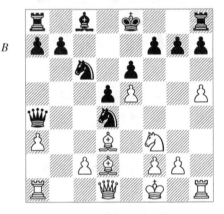

White's idea is to use his two bishops on newly-opened lines. In addition, his move h6 can potentially weaken Black's kingside dark squares. Indeed, the game Kasparov-Anand went 13...♘xf3!? 14 ♕xf3 b6? 15 h6! with a powerful initiative. Later an instructive solution was found that uses Black's pieces to maximum efficiency:

13...♘f5 14 ♗xf5 exf5 15 h6 ♖g8! 16 ♗g5! ♗e6 17 ♖h4!?

The obvious 17 hxg7 ♖xg7 18 ♗f6 runs into 18...♕c4+ 19 ♔g1 ♗g4 20 ♖xh7 ♔d7 *(D)*, when Black has some advantage.

Every piece on light squares!

17...♕a6+ 18 ♔g1 gxh6 19 ♗f6 ♖g4!

With opposite-coloured bishops, both sides have rushed to exploit their respective strengths.

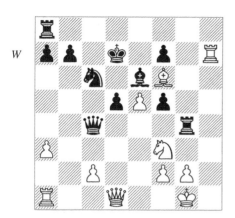

20 ♖b1

Better, but still good for Black, is 20 ♖xh6!? ♔d7 21 ♖xh7 ♖ag8 22 ♖h2.

20...♖xh4 21 ♗xh4?!

Perhaps 21 ♘xh4 would improve.

21...♖c8 22 c4 ♕xc4?!

Not a terrible move, but Black could play 22...dxc4 23 ♕d6 (23 ♘d4 ♘xe5 24 ♘b5 ♘d3 is even better for Black) 23...c3 24 ♘d4 ♕d3! (D).

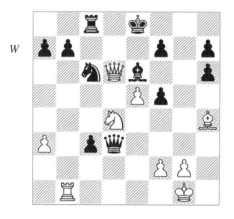

Notice again the colour-complex motif for both sides. Now Black simplifies into a winning position: 25 ♘xe6 ♕xd6 26 ♘g7+ ♔f8 27 exd6 ♔xg7 28 d7 ♖c7! 29 d8♕ ♘xd8 30 ♗xd8 ♖d7.

23 ♖xb7 ♘xe5 24 ♘xe5 ♕xh4 25 ♖xa7 ♕f4 26 ♘d3 ♕d4 27 ♖a4 ♖c4! 28 ♖a8+ ♔e7 29 ♕b1 ♖a4?

29...♔f6 would still keep a considerable advantage.

30 ♕b7+ ♔f6 31 ♖xa4 ♕xa4 32 ♕b2+ d4 33 ♕d2 ♔g7 ½-½

White is not short of opportunities for creative play in these lines. We turn to 7 ♘f3:

Short – Ivanchuk
Horgen 1995

7 ♘f3 *(D)*

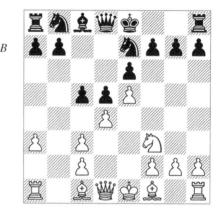

White develops and guards the centre. Not surprisingly, this is his traditional move in the Positional lines.

7...♕c7 8 h4 ♗d7 9 h5 h6

This time Black wants to hold the kingside while he works on White's queenside weaknesses.

10 ♗d3 ♗a4 11 dxc5! *(D)*

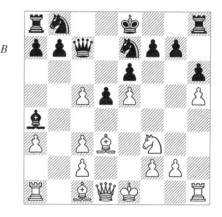

Tripling pawns may seem odd, especially since White gives up protection of the e5-pawn as well. Indeed, all of White's pawns will be vulnerable, but Black can only take one at a time! In compensation, White gains d4 as a transfer point for his pieces and the rooks can spring into action along the 4th rank; for example, by ♖h4 and ♖b1-b4. The bishop-pair can also become more effective with more room to manoeuvre in. Here and in other Winawer positions the move dxc5 is an important part of White's bag of tricks.

11...♘d7 12 ♖h4 ♕a5?!

A mistake; Black's queen belongs on c7 in these lines. Note that 12...♘xc5? is a blunder due to 13 ♖xa4, but 12...♗c6! is double-edged, when White has to attend to his pawns and a complex battle will result.

13 ♗e3! ♖c8

Logically bringing another piece into play along the open file, but 13...♗c6 was still correct. Not 13...♕xc3+?! 14 ♔f1 and the queen is in trouble.

14 ♖b1 ♗c6 15 ♕d2 ♕xa3 16 ♖g4 ♔f8 (D)

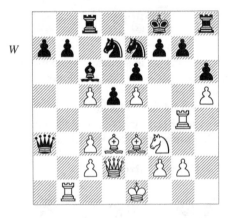

17 ♖bb4

Not a bad move, preparing to swing the rook into action along the fourth rank. Perhaps even better was Short's line 17 ♔f1!? ♘xc5 18 ♗xc5 ♕xc5 19 ♘d4 with the idea ♕f4 and a strong attack. This illustrates White's use of the tripled pawns to secure a support-point for his knight.

17...♘f5

Practically a necessity in order to defend key squares. The knight is Black's best piece, so White will get rid of it. In the meantime, White gets a situation with opposite-coloured bishops that will aid his attack.

18 ♗xf5 exf5 19 ♖gf4! ♕a1+ 20 ♕d1!

The advantage is also clear in a queenless middlegame.

20...♕xd1+?!

20...♕xc3+! should have been tried, when the trick 21 ♗d2 ♕xc5 22 ♖xb7! (with the idea ♗b4) can be answered by 22...a5.

21 ♔xd1 ♖e8 22 ♖xf5 ♔g8 23 ♖g4 ♖e7 24 ♖g3 ♔h7 25 ♗d4 ♖he8 26 ♖f4 ♘f8 27 ♖fg4 (D)

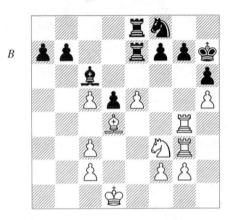

27...g5

Instead, occupying the natural blockading square on e6 only lets White's knight in on the ideal attacking square f5: 27...♘e6 28 ♘h4 ♖g8 29 ♘f5 ♖d7 30 ♘d6 and the f-pawn rolls forward.

28 hxg6+ ♘xg6

28...fxg6 is met by 29 ♖f4 or 29 ♖h4.

29 ♖h3 ♗d7 30 ♘g5+ ♔g8 31 e6! (D)

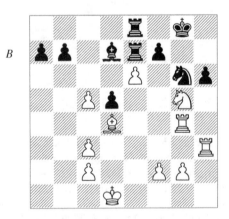

Finally this key breakthrough, opening the fatal diagonal for White's unopposed bishop on d4. From now on White has a clearly winning advantage.

31...♗xe6 32 ♘xe6 ♖xe6 33 ♖xh6 ♖e1+ 34 ♔d2 ♖8e2+ 35 ♔d3 ♔f8 36 ♖h5! ♖e4

White wins the ending after 36...♘e5+ 37 ♗xe5 ♖xe5 38 ♖xe5 ♖xe5 39 ♖b4.

37 ♖xe4 dxe4+ 38 ♔d2 ♖b1 39 c6

Or 39 g3!.

39...bxc6 40 ♗xa7 ♔e7 41 ♗d4 ♖b5 42 ♖xb5 cxb5 43 c4!

The finishing blow. Bishop vs knight with an extra passed pawn will win.

43...bxc4 44 ♔c3 ♘f4 45 g3 ♘e6 46 ♔xc4 ♔d6 47 ♗f6 ♔c6 48 g4 ♔d6 49 c3 ♔c6 50 ♗e5 ♘c5 51 ♔d4 ♘d3 52 ♗g3 ♘c5 53 ♗f4 1-0

White manoeuvres his bishop to the centre: 53...♘d3 54 ♗e3 ♘c5 55 ♔e5 ♘a4 56 ♗d4.

French Poisoned Pawn

1 e4 e6 2 d4 d5 3 ♘c3 ♗b4 4 e5 ♘e7 5 a3 ♗xc3+ 6 bxc3 c5 7 ♕g4 *(D)*

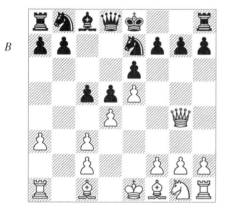

The grand old flagship of the Winawer Variation. White wants to exploit Black's lack of the dark-squared bishop by direct means. He will try to get Black to weaken himself or castle into a potential attack. It makes sense to work on the side of the board where he has space and towards which his bishops aim. In addition, the e5-pawn cramps Black in that part of the board. As is true in the positional lines, White would love to get rid of the g-pawn so that his unopposed dark-squared bishop can have a field day on squares like h6 and f6.

For his part Black's first goal is to attack White's centre and queenside, where White already has serious weaknesses. Ironically, however, he usually ends up playing on the kingside too, whether or not he castles in that direction.

The key move is ...f6, which helps defensively but also gives him central threats and a very useful f-file. In any case, Black's first decision is whether to gambit the pawn by 7...♕c7, or play 7...0-0 and hang on to his material for a while. The latter is the preferred choice these days but it's not clear that the former won't come back into fashion.

As in so many lines of the French Defence, one notices the persistence of the central pawn-structure. This gives both the positional and tactical themes a certain logical consistency, although it doesn't seem to limit their variety.

The Gambit

7...♕c7 8 ♕xg7 ♖g8 9 ♕xh7

Now in addition to the other advantages listed above, White has a passed h-pawn. It is worth remembering, however, that the advance of a passed rook's pawn very seldom poses a threat until far into the middlegame. Their real strength appears in simplified positions and, of course, as outside passed pawns in an ending.

9...cxd4 10 ♘e2 *(D)*

Other moves like 10 ♔d1 are possible, yet this is how they've played it for 50 years in the vast majority of games.

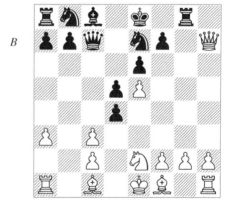

We'll examine two of those encounters from this position, with general considerations discussed therein.

Karpov – Agdestein
Oslo 1984

10...♘bc6 11 f4

11 cxd4? ♘xd4! (threatening c2) 12 ♘xd4? is bad in view of 12...♕c3+.

11...♗d7 12 ♕d3 dxc3 13 ♕xc3 *(D)*

Simply recapturing the c3-pawn is very popular, since it has both a cramping effect and attacking strengths. On the other hand, the c-file is open for Black's rooks. There are many other moves here such as 13 ♖b1, 13 ♖g1 and 13 ♘xc3.

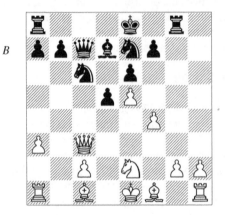

Let's take stock. White's advantages are pretty obvious: he has cleared out the kingside, which for one thing means that the move ...f6 (to undermine his centre) would be unsupported by a pawn. His bishop-pair can be usefully placed on d3 and e3 for both attack and defence, although the dark-squared bishop can be a target in that case. A bishop on a3 would be wonderful but generally it's just too hard to achieve. In view of this his most potent positional threat is to expand on the kingside by means of g4 (preceded by either h3 or ♖g1). That would deny Black's knight the powerful f5-square. Alternatively, White can try to play g3, ♗g2 and 0-0; that arrangement of pieces is another trade-off because when the bishop moves off its original diagonal White tends to be subject to central and queenside attack. Finally, we shouldn't forget that h-pawn. If White can get bishops to d3 and f6, then Black will at the very least have to devote several pieces in an attempt to stop it from marching up the board and promoting.

What is Black doing in the meantime? He has sacrificed a pawn, apparently in order to get at White's queenside and gain development. That lead in development is absolutely critical

because if he waits too long for White to get his position organized (and especially to get his bishops out!) he will have little to counter White's space, extra pawn, and bishop-pair. Fortunately, his knights at the moment are very well-placed and influential. It's a kind of semi-closed position in which for now the knights are superior to bishops. He also has play down the c-, g- and h-files, whereas right now White isn't using his king's bishop or rook at all. Is that enough to make up for White's own advantages? Probably not, except that White also has isolated c- and a-pawns, and hasn't castled. Note too that there is an important interior weaknesses on e3, a square that can be anchored by ...d4 and is particularly vulnerable to a knight on f5 and a queen on b6. Generally speaking, White's advantages, if he can keep them, are probably the better ones in the long term, so you will usually find Black trying to upset the equilibrium in the near term.

All in all one can see why players would be willing to take both sides of this position.

13...♘f5

A multipurpose move that holds off ♘d4 and controls e3. This introduces the idea of ...♕b6 at some point, which White promptly forestalls.

14 ♖b1 *(D)*

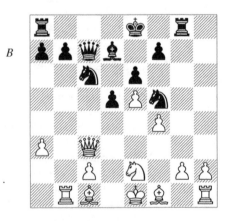

14...♖c8!?

14...0-0-0 connects rooks and is considered better. Then ...♔b8 clears the way for ...♖c8, and also for the intriguing manoeuvre ...b6, ...♗c8 and ...♗a6 or ...♗b7. For all the time that takes, White cannot easily find his way into Black's position.

15 ♗d2

White protects against 15...♘cd4, which was otherwise a strong move.

15...d4 16 ♕d3 ♘ce7 17 ♘xd4! ♘xd4 18 ♕xd4 ♘f5 19 ♕xa7 ♕xc2 (D)

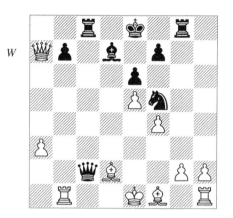

This sort of position is not easy in spite of White's extra pawns, because Black has all the light squares and a superb piece placement if he gets ...♗c6 in.

20 ♕xb7!

A good example of what we saw in the introductory chapters: a pawn-raiding queen, as long as it can't be trapped, often does better to stay close to the enemy camp to bother his pieces instead of retreating to hypothetical safety.

20...♖c7 (D)

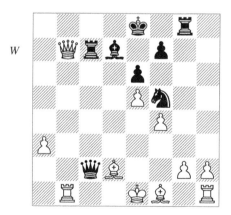

21 ♕b8+

Karpov gives the remarkable variation 21 ♕a8+ ♖c8 22 ♖b8 ♔e7!? 23 ♗b4+? (23 ♕b7!) 23...♖c5! 24 ♗xc5+ ♕xc5 25 ♖xg8 ♕c1+ 26 ♔e2 ♗b5+ 27 ♔f3, which should be a draw after 27...♕d1+ 28 ♔f2, because 27...♗c6+? 28

♔g4! ♗xa8 loses to the double attack 29 ♗b5!, threatening the queen and mate! Amazing.

21...♖c8 22 ♕b4

Now the situation looks bad for Black, in spite of a few tactical details.

22...♘d4! 23 ♔f2 ♖g4?

23...♕e4! 24 ♖e1 ♕d5 was suggested, but 25 ♖c1 ♘c2 26 ♕d6! should do.

24 ♕xd4! ♕xb1 25 ♖g1! ♕a2 26 ♗e2 ♖c2 27 ♖d1! (D)

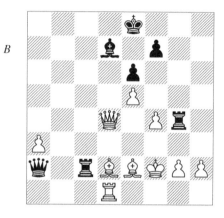

Having given up the exchange, Karpov's bishops and three extra pawns reign. Notice how the central structure has remained basically the same throughout the entire game. That is typical not only of the Winawer but of the French Defence in general.

27...♖g8 28 g3 ♗c6 29 ♕d3 ♗d5 30 ♕b5+ ♔f8 31 f5! exf5 32 ♕xd5! ♕xd5 33 ♗h6+ ♔e7 34 ♖xd5 ♔e6 35 ♖d6+ ♔xe5 36 ♗f4+ ♔e4 37 ♖d7 ♖a8 38 ♖e7+ 1-0

Fichtl – Golz
Dresden 1959

10...dxc3 11 f4 ♘bc6 12 ♗e3

A slightly odd move-order by both sides. 12 ♕d3 ♗d7 13 ♗e3 ♘f5 would transpose. White is playing this way in order to keep the c-file closed and develop quickly.

12...♗d7 13 ♕d3 ♘f5 (D)

14 ♗d4!?

One of White's ideas with ♗e3 was to discourage ...d4 and this move flat-out prevents it. Nevertheless, the bishop can't be maintained on d4 without allowing exchanges that at least equalize for Black. Other games have seen 14

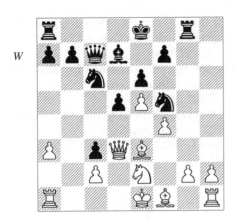

W

♗f2; e.g., 14...0-0-0 15 ♖b1!? (15 ♕xc3 returns us to a more modern look) 15...d4 (anyway) 16 ♘g3 (headed for e4 if possible) 16...f6! (a useful resource to remember) 17 ♘xf5 exf5 18 exf6 ♕xf4 with a nice advantage, Fuchs-Uhlmann, Dresden 1959. White can't afford to give up the centre in this line without compensation.

14...0-0-0 15 ♗xc3?!

White wants to win material before Black exchanges on d4. After 15 ♖b1?! f6 16 exf6 ♘fxd4 17 ♘xd4 ♕xf4, Black's advancing centre will dominate the board. Perhaps the best move was 15 g3; for example, 15...♔b8 16 ♖b1?! (16 ♗g2 ♘fxd4 17 ♘xd4 ♘a5 followed by ...♕c5 is a commonly-occurring piece disposition that gives Black at least equality) 16...♘fxd4 17 ♘xd4 ♘xd4 18 ♕xd4 f6! 19 exf6 e5! with the idea 20 fxe5 ♖g4! and ...♖e4+.

15...d4 16 ♗d2

16 ♘xd4? loses to 16...♘cxd4 17 ♗xd4 ♗b5! 18 ♕xb5 ♘xd4.

16...f6! 17 exf6 e5! *(D)*

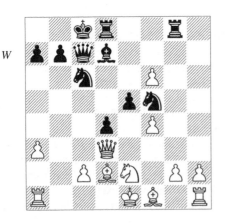

W

This is a standard device for Black, intended to destroy White's central structure at all costs.

18 0-0-0 ♖ge8!

Now the idea is ...e4.

19 g4 e4 20 ♕h3?! ♘d6 21 ♗e1

White has four passed pawns but is getting crushed in the centre.

21...d3 22 ♘c3 ♘c4! *(D)*

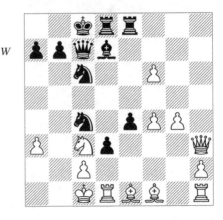

W

Introducing the ideas of ...♕a5 and ...♕b6.

23 cxd3 ♕xf4+ 24 ♗d2 ♘xd2 25 ♖xd2 ♘d4 26 ♕g2

White can't stop ...♘b3+.

26...♘b3+ 27 ♔c2 ♘xd2 28 ♕xd2 e3!

and Black won in short order.

The Contemporary 7...0-0

1 e4 e6 2 d4 d5 3 ♘c3 ♗b4 4 e5 c5 5 a3 ♗xc3+ 6 bxc3 ♘e7 7 ♕g4 0-0 *(D)*

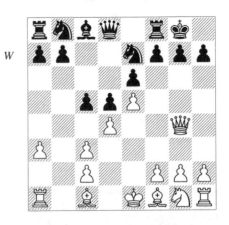

W

Instead of sacrificing the g-pawn, Black defends it and intends to confront White on the kingside, almost always by means of ...f6 or ...f5. He retains the option of ...c4 (keeping White's bishop away from d3) or ...cxd4 (attacking the centre).

The drawback of 7...0-0 is that it subjects Black to a dangerous attack by White's pieces, in particular the queen on g4, knight on f3, and one or both bishops. The attack can be supplemented by h4-h5 and ℤh3, or by f4, assuming that White's knight has moved.

Now 8 ♗d3, bringing the bishop to d3 before deciding upon anything else, is the overwhelming favourite. 8 ♘f3 is the most natural move, but was put under a cloud by several games, including the following:

Roth – Kindermann
Vienna 1996

8 ♘f3 ♘bc6 9 ♗d3 f5 10 exf6 ℤxf6 11 ♗g5 e5!

This is the characteristic pawn-break in the 7...0-0 line. If Black gets ...e5 in, he'll usually be in control of events. Of course, White will sometimes prevail for tactical reasons.

12 ♕g3 *(D)*

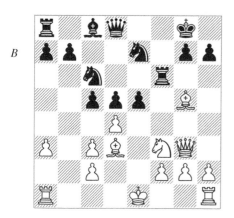

12...ℤxf3!

Here is another instance of the eternal exchange sacrifice on f3 in the French Defence; it is only rivalled in frequency by the ...ℤxc3 sacrifice in the Sicilian Dragon.

13 gxf3

13 ♕xf3 e4.

13...c4 14 ♗e2 ♕a5!

Black attacks the c3-pawn, but also unpins his knight.

15 ♗d2 ♘f5 16 ♕g5 exd4 17 cxd4 c3 18 ♗e3 ♘cxd4 19 ♗xd4 ♘xd4 20 ℤg1

Most of these moves are forced. Now White seems to have an attack but everything is covered.

20...g6 21 ♕e5 ♕c5 22 ♕e8+ ♕f8 23 ♕xf8+ ♔xf8 *(D)*

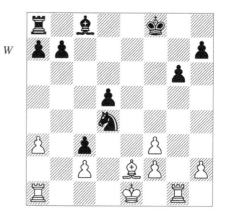

Black is an exchange for a pawn down, yet he's winning easily; look at White's five isolated pawns and his rooks.

24 ♔d1 ♗f5 25 ℤc1 ℤe8 26 ℤe1 b5! 27 ♗d3 ♗xd3 28 ℤxe8+ ♔xe8 29 cxd3 c2+ 30 ♔e1 a5

A pleasant finish. Kindermann will just march his pawns homeward.

31 f4 b4 32 axb4 axb4 33 ♔d2 ♘b3+ 34 ♔xc2 ♘xc1 35 ♔xc1 ♔d7 0-1

We'll look at a few games after 8 ♗d3, beginning with two very nice ones for White.

J. Polgar – Uhlmann
Amsterdam 1990

8 ♗d3 *(D)*
8...f5 9 exf6 ℤxf6 10 ♗g5 ℤf7 11 ♕h5

White's unsophisticated strategy comes down to checkmate.

11...h6

11...g6 is also played. We won't cite theory here but follow the game instead.

12 ♗g6 ℤf8 13 ♘f3 ♘bc6 14 0-0 ♕c7!?

14...♗d7! is probably the best move (and certainly the most practical one), leading to complicated play.

15 ♗xe7 ♕xe7

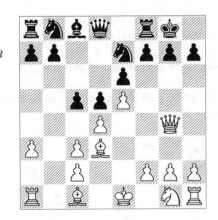

15...♘xe7 16 ♘e5 (D) is the very picture of a dominant knight versus a bad bishop:

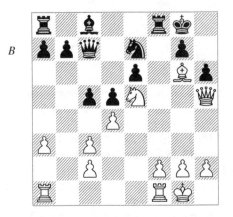

Black can try to get rid of the knight by 16...♘c6 17 f4 cxd4, but 18 ♗d3! threatens ♕g6 with a mating attack, and 18...♘xe5 19 fxe5 doesn't help because it opens the f-file.

16 ♖ae1 ♕f6!?

Maybe 16...♗d7 is better, but then 17 c4 is tough to meet.

17 ♘e5! cxd4?! 18 f4! dxc3

A cute line is 18...♘xe5 19 fxe5 ♕g5 20 ♖xf8+ ♔xf8 21 ♕f3+ ♔e7 22 ♕f7+ ♔d8 23 ♕f8+ ♔c7 24 ♕d6#.

19 g4! (D)

White plays inventively, combining f4 with g4. Polgar is devastating in such positions.

19...♕e7 20 ♗d3!

20 g5 ♘xe5 isn't clear.

20...♕e8 21 ♘g6 ♗d7

On 21...♖f7 comes 22 g5.

22 g5! ♖f7 23 gxh6 gxh6 24 ♔h1! ♘e7 25 ♖g1 ♘f5

and here the easiest of several wins was 26 ♗xf5 ♖xf5 27 ♕xh6 ♔f7 28 ♕h7+ ♔f6 29 ♘e5.

Polzin – Giemsa
Bad Wiessee 2004

8 ♗d3 ♕a5 9 ♗d2 ♘bc6 (D)

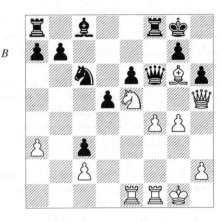

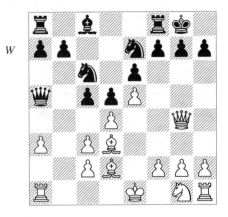

Black tries to tie White down to defending his queenside.

10 ♘f3

By the way: whether White or Black, always watch out for ♗xh7+.

10...f5 11 exf6 ♖xf6 12 ♕h5 ♘f5 13 c4!

13 g4 is also promising. Then 13...c4 leads to a heavily-analysed sequence that shows pure attack vs defence at its best and is probably somewhat in White's favour, one line being 14 gxf5 cxd3 15 ♖g1 ♗d7 16 c4 ♕c7 17 ♗h6 ♗e8 18 ♕h4 ♖xh6 19 ♕xh6 dxc4 20 cxd3 cxd3 21 f6 ♗g6, Shirov-Khalifman, Dos Hermanas 2003; now 22 ♖xg6!? hxg6 23 ♕xg6 looks

promising: 23...♕f7 24 ♕xf7+ ♚xf7 25 fxg7 ♚xg7 (25...♖d8 26 ♖b1) 26 ♚d2. As this is a variation involving high theory, you'd do well to check recent developments.

13...♕a4 14 g4 dxc4 15 ♗e4 ♘cxd4 (D)

15...♘ce7 16 ♗g5 ♕a5+ 17 ♔f1 g6 18 ♕h3 ♖f8 19 gxf5 exf5 20 ♗d3! cxd3 21 ♗xe7 and White was on the verge of winning in Stellwagen-Kim, Iraklion 2004.

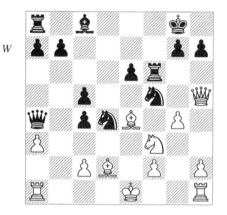

16 gxf5! ♘xc2+ 17 ♔f1! ♘xa1 18 ♗c3 ♕d1+

18...e5 19 ♘xe5 ♗xf5 20 ♗xf5 ♖xf5 21 ♕xf5 ♕d1+ 22 ♗e1 ♕d5 23 ♖g1 and there's no counterattack. Now it's just a slaughter:

19 ♔g2 ♕d8 20 ♘g5 h6 21 ♖d1 ♗d7 22 fxe6 ♕e8 23 exd7! ♕xh5 24 d8♕+ ♖f8 25 ♕d5+ ♔h8 26 ♗xg7+ 1-0

For something more attractive from Black's point of view, we'll look at a game in the same variation with another result. Remember that these are meant to be edifying games, not theoretical ones, as shown by the date.

Aseev – Vladimirov
USSR Army Cht (Leningrad) 1989

8 ♗d3 f5 9 exf6 ♖xf6 (D)
10 ♕h5!? h6 11 g4 ♘bc6! 12 g5 g6! 13 ♕h4

White cedes the initiative entirely after 13 ♕xh6 ♖f7 14 ♗xg6 ♖g7 15 ♗d3 e5!?, when it is difficult for White to keep a balance (or Black could even force a draw by 15...c4 16 ♗e2 ♖h7 17 ♕f6 ♖f7, etc.).

13...♘f5 14 ♕h3

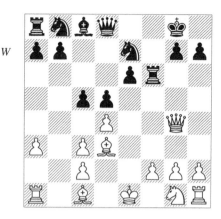

14 ♗xf5!? ♖xf5 15 ♕xh6 ♘e7 works out nicely for Black because of his outpost on f5, the potential for ...e5 or ...♕c7, and the specific idea of ...♖f7-h7.

14...♖f8 15 gxh6 e5 16 ♕g2 ♕e8!

16...♔h7 17 ♘f3 e4 18 ♘g5+ ♔h8 may also favour Black, although White would have more active pieces than in the game.

17 dxc5

Even worse is 17 ♕xd5+? ♗e6 18 ♕g2 exd4.

17...e4 18 ♗b5 ♗d7 19 ♘e2 ♘e5 20 ♗xd7 ♕xd7 (D)

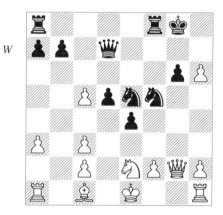

21 ♘d4!?

White wants Black to have to earn his attack by straightening out White's centre pawns. After the sequence 21 0-0? ♘f3+ 22 ♔h1 ♘5h4 23 ♕g3, 23...♕b5! is a nice shot. Probably 21 ♔d1! is best, although naturally Black also has the upper hand after 21...♔h7.

21...♘xd4 22 cxd4 ♘f3+ 23 ♔d1 ♔h7 24 ♖b1 ♖ac8 25 h4 b6! 26 ♖h3?

Although hardly desirable, 26 h5 ♖g8! 27 ♕h3! is best.

26...♘xd4! (D)

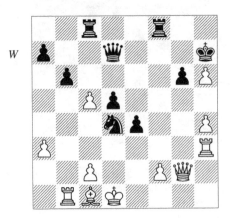

27 ♖g3?

Last chance for 27 ♗e3.

27...♕a4 28 ♖c3 ♕a6! 29 ♗e3 ♕e2+ 30 ♔c1 ♘f5 31 ♕g5 d4 32 ♗xd4 ♘xd4 0-1

Due to 33 ♕e7+ ♔xh6 34 ♕g5+ ♔h7 35 ♕e7+ ♔g8.

Finally, a short demonstration of primitive attacking power:

Guseinov – Riazantsev
Moscow 1997

8 ♗d3 ♘bc6 (D)

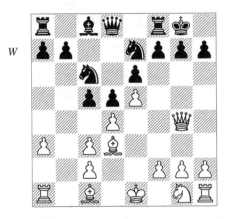

9 ♕h5 ♘g6 10 ♘f3 ♕c7 11 h4!? cxd4 12 ♔d1! dxc3 13 ♘g5

Black is fine after 13 ♖h3 f6! 14 exf6 e5 15 fxg7 ♖f6!.

13...h6 14 f4 (D)

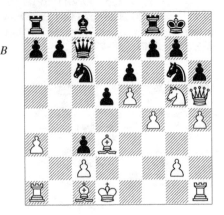

14...hxg5??

You really can't afford to make a mistake in these lines! The way to play it was 14...♘ce7! 15 ♖h3 ♘f5 with the idea 16 g4?? ♘xf4 17 ♗xf4 g6.

15 hxg5 ♖d8 16 a4!

Probably what Black missed. ♗a3 becomes the decisive factor.

16...a5 17 ♕h7+ ♔f8 18 ♗a3+ ♘ce7? 19 ♕h8+ 1-0

There are hundreds and hundreds of wild attacking and counterattacking games in the variations after 7 ♕g4 and I highly recommend that you take some time to study and enjoy them. But the most interesting feature of these games is that there are dozens of consistently recurring tactical themes that stem from the nature of the underlying position, that is, from the pawn-structure. Thus the term 'characteristic tactics' applies to these and other Winawer lines as much as to any other in chess. The wonderful part is that so many basic types of tactics mixed with creative thinking can generate a near-infinite number of combinative possibilities.

14 Pirc Defence

1 e4 d6 2 d4 ♞f6 (D)

This is the Pirc Defence, an opening plentiful in useful strategic ideas. With 1...d6 Black restrains White's e-pawn in preparation for 2...♞f6, 3...g6 and 4...♝g7, much as in the traditional King's Indian Defence (1 d4 ♞f6 2 c4 g6 3 ♞c3 ♝g7 4 e4 d6). The immediate difference is that White doesn't have time for c4 in the Pirc.

Before we move on to alternatives and move-orders, let's examine some characteristics of the opening. In the great majority of cases, the first moves are 1 e4 d6 2 d4 (setting up the ideal centre) 2...♞f6 3 ♞c3 (see alternatives below) 3...g6 (D), when we have arrived at the basic position.

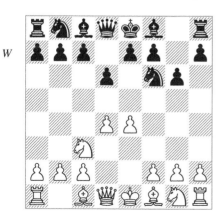

By way of comparison with the King's Indian Defence, White has omitted the move c4 in favour of ♞c3. How does this influence the play? First of all, the d4-square is theoretically stronger than in the King's Indian, because it can be supported by c3. In reality, defending d4 still turns out to be a problem for White after moves like ...e5 and/or ...♞c6 (in some cases supported by ...♝g4), because it's not so easy to redirect the c3-knight without losing too much time. Furthermore, if White plays d5 (say, in response to ...e5 or ...c5), that pawn lacks the support of White's c-pawn. Black also has some queenside attacking ideas that may not be as effective in the King's Indian; for example, ...c6 and ...a6, both intending ...b5.

Let's continue with the comparison by looking at the positive side of White's position. First, 3 ♞c3 is a developing move, unlike c4 in the King's Indian. Traditionally, development of knights to c3 and f3 is the best way of arranging your pieces when you have an ideal centre. By playing 3 ♞c3, White also gives himself leeway to try more ambitious moves after 3...g6 such as 4 f4. In the King's Indian Defence this advance is playable and more menacing (4 e4 d6 5 f4 is the Four Pawns Attack), but it is also riskier because White has made so many pawn moves and he has a broader centre to defend. In the Pirc Defence, the main line with 4 ♞f3 yields a solid, classically centralized position. White has aggressive piece deployments available such as ♝c4 or ♝e3 in combination with ♛d2. Direct moves such as these are generally easier to implement than in the King's Indian because the Pirc centre is not quite as vulnerable to ...c5 and ...e5 moves (which is not to say that those moves won't be played).

Notice that the move-order 1 d4 d6 2 e4 ♞f6 also lands us in a Pirc Defence. White of course has some good alternatives in that case, such as 2 c4 and 2 ♞f3, but 2...♞f6 is perfectly viable against those moves as well, possibly leading into a version of the King's Indian Defence.

Black can go his own way with things like 1 d4 d6 2 c4 e5 or 1 d4 d6 2 ♘f3 ♗g4!?. A great deal of theory now exists on these and related positions. We've come a long way from the days of a near-compulsory 1 e4 e5 and 1 d4 d5.

3 ♘c3

White plays the most natural and important move, defending the attacked pawn. The Pirc is one of those openings in which the early options are instructive, so we'll look at a couple over the next few moves. Here 3 ♗d3 is sometimes played, intending to enter into a system with c3 and perhaps ♘e2. There's nothing wrong with that, of course, but apart from the normal and good 3...g6 it allows Black to strike out in the centre immediately by 3...e5. Then 4 c3 allows the cute idea 4...d5!. It's a case of "If you don't want to take the centre, I shall!" I've discussed this position briefly in Chapter 3 (under 'Cross-Pollination'). Let me repeat and expand upon that exposition. After 3 ♗d3 e5 4 c3 d5, we find that it's a great asset to know about a wide variety of chess positions and themes. Chernin did a fascinating analysis of 4...d5, which I've abbreviated and modestly revised. The play will usually continue 5 dxe5 ♘xe4 *(D)*.

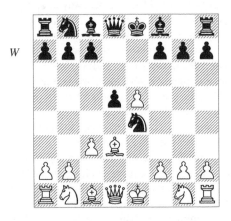

In Chapter 3, we already looked at White's option 6 ♗xe4 dxe4 7 ♕a4+ (7 ♕xd8+ ♔xd8 gives Black the two bishops and active play; e.g., 8 ♗f4 ♘d7 9 ♘d2 ♘c5) 7...♗d7 8 ♕xe4 ♗c6. The position is similar to pawn sacrifices made in various openings. Here 9 ♕g4 is forced, when 9...♕d7! is very strong: 10 ♕g3 (10 ♕xd7+ ♘xd7 11 ♘f3 ♗xf3 12 gxf3 ♘xe5 13 ♔e2 0-0-0) 10...♘a6!; for example, 11 ♘e2 ♗b5! 12

a4 ♘c5! 13 axb5 ♘d3+ 14 ♔f1 ♘xc1, etc. Chernin's 9...h5 is also good.

But let's continue with a better and more realistic way for White to develop: 6 ♘f3 ♘c6 7 0-0 (7 ♕e2 ♘c5 8 ♗c2 ♗g4!; a high-level encounter Yusupov-Adams, Hastings 1989/90 went 7 ♘bd2 ♘c5 8 ♘b3 ♗g4 {or 8...♘xd3+} 9 0-0 ♕d7 10 ♖e1 0-0-0 with equality) 7...♘c5 8 ♗c2 ♗g4! 9 ♖e1 (9 ♘bd2 ♗e7 or even 9...d4!?) 9...♗e7 *(D)*, shown in the diagram.

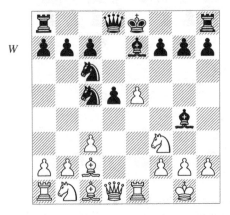

This position is remarkably like a main line of the Open Variation of the Ruy Lopez, namely, 1 e4 e5 2 ♘f3 ♘c6 3 ♗b5 a6 4 ♗a4 ♘f6 5 0-0 ♘xe4 6 d4 b5 7 ♗b3 d5 8 dxe5 ♗e6 9 c3 ♘c5 10 ♗c2, and now (for example) 10...♗e7 11 ♖e1 (or 11 ♕e2 ♗g4) 11...♗g4! *(D)*, which helps to control d4 and in many cases is followed by ...d4 or even ...♘e6 and ...d4.

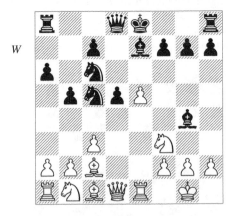

In fact, the only difference between the two lines is Black's insertion of ...a6 and ...b5 in the Ruy Lopez version. Without entering into yet another digression, I'll just say that this has both positive and negative features.

3...g6

Here there's an important transposition 3...e5 4 ♘f3 ♘bd7, when we're in a Philidor Defence! What's more, this is arguably the only safe way to get to this version of the Philidor because 1 e4 e5 2 ♘f3 d6 3 d4 ♘f6 allows 4 dxe5 ♘xe4 5 ♕d5, which is not to everyone's taste. Details about this and associated move-order issues can be found in Chapter 7.

We shall now move on to a discussion of the main lines of the Pirc.

Austrian Attack

4 f4 *(D)*

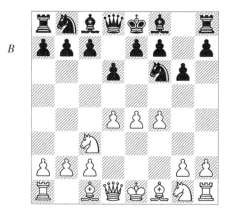

As I've pointed out with many examples at the very beginning of Chapter 3 on pawn-structures, the first reaction to 'unusual' defences that cede the centre is generally to throw as many pawns forward as possible and push the opponent off the board. The Pirc was infrequently played and generally held in low regard until the mid-1960s, and indeed this response dominated early theory.

4...♗g7

Before moving on to the main line 5 ♘f3, played in thousands of games, let's see if we can understand what the relation between this structure and pawn advances might be.

Austrian Attack with 5 e5

5 e5 *(D)*

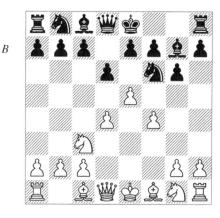

What about advancing right away? You won't find much in the books about this, and it's easy to say that 5 e5 is too ambitious, especially since it resembles other openings in which rash pawn attacks are insufficiently supported and expose the centre. But it's another thing to show that. Let's do our own analysis and perhaps pick something up about how to study an opening while we're at it. As we know, variations that are not highly respected are often the most instructive. Let's look at two answers to 5 e5 as representative of typical ideas in the Austrian Attack:

A: 5...♘fd7
B: 5...dxe5

A)

5...♘fd7

This is a dynamic move in the spirit of the Pirc, avoiding simplification and accepting the challenge. The positions that result are little-explored and instructive to investigate.

6 ♘f3 c5!

The recommended continuation for Black. It's consistent to destroy White's centre before he consolidates; of course, that depends upon the outcome! This line transposes into 5 ♘f3 c5 6 e5 ♘fd7. By the 5 e5 move-order, White has avoided a few of Black's options along the way.

7 ♘g5!?

This odd sortie may well be the best move, although 7 ♗c4 could use more investigation. Positions with a knight on d7 and the possibility of the move e6 are notoriously tactical, so the move 7 ♘g5 is likely to occur to you if you've run across such positions before.

Black's hope was to see something along the lines of 7 exd6 0-0 8 dxc5 (8 dxe7 ♕xe7+ 9 ♕e2 ♕xe2+ 10 ♘xe2 ♖e8 11 ♔f2 ♘c6 12 c3 ♘f6 with an initiative for the pawn) 8...♗a5! 9 ♗e2 ♗xc3+! 10 bxc3 ♕xc3+ 11 ♗d2 ♕xc5 12 dxe7 ♖e8! 13 ♖b1 ♘c6 (D).

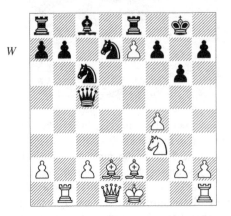

This is the game B.Ivanović-M.Gurevich, Lucerne Wcht 1989. White can't easily reorganize, and look at those exposed internal weaknesses on e3 and e4! This way of destroying White's centre is relatively common, especially the device of allowing White's capture dxe7 and responding with ...♖e8.

7...cxd4

Worse is 7...h6?! 8 ♘xf7! ♔xf7 9 e6+ ♔g8 10 exd7 ♘xd7 11 ♗e3.

8 e6! (D)

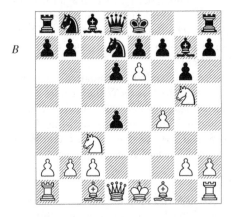

8...♕a5!?

Not 8...dxc3?? 9 exf7+ ♔f8 10 ♘e6+. But a good move to counter White's attack might be 8...♘c5 9 exf7+ ♔f8, when Black's mass of

central pawns makes up for his poor king position.

9 exf7+ ♔f8

And above all, not 9...♔d8?? 10 ♘e6#.

10 ♘e6+ ♔xf7 11 ♘xd4 ♘c5!?

Now Black gets good piece activity. Play might continue as follows:

12 ♗c4+ ♗e6 13 ♘xe6! ♗xc3+ 14 ♔f2 ♘xe6 15 bxc3 ♕c5+!? 16 ♕d4 ♖c8 17 ♗b3 (D)

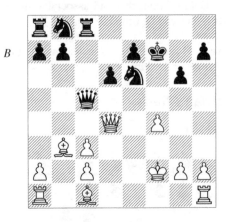

17...♘d7!?

Black still has difficulty freeing his king, and he isn't out of the woods after 17...♕f5 18 ♖e1 ♘c6 19 ♕d5 either.

18 ♖e1 ♘df8 19 g4!

Here White still has threats. Naturally both sides have a lot of other options along the way, and it's unlikely that White can actually force an advantage in this line. But the characteristics of the position are what count here, and they can only be indicated by analysis (which in this case is a lot of fun). Mainly, I wanted to show that it's easy to dismiss 'premature' attacks on principle without testing whether the principle in question applies to a specific position (or even whether it is valid at all).

B)

5...dxe5 6 fxe5!? ♘d5 7 ♘f3 (D)

White retains his centre. Then we have Black's bishop looking rather restricted on g7. An apparently logical move is:

7...f6?

However, this tends to be dubious before Black has castled and developed, and is extremely poor in this exact position. We shall look at a better option after the end of this line.

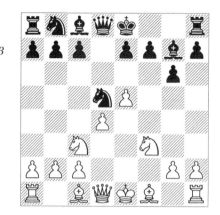

8 exf6

White makes his usual response to ...f6. The recapture 8...♗xf6 would leave Black with a weak isolated e-pawn on an open file; then 9 ♘e4, 9 ♗c4 and 9 ♗h6 are all good moves. Therefore Black in principle would prefer:

8...exf6?! *(D)*

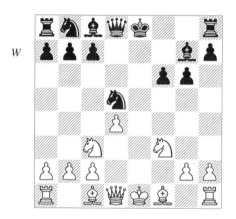

Recapturing with the pawn might be OK in some positions but here it is much too early because Black's king is stuck in the centre and he also suffers from a weakness on e6 and a bishop on g7 that is blocked off.

9 ♗c4 ♕e7+

Against 9...♗e6, 10 ♕e2 simply wins. The only apparent try is 10...♔f7, but after 11 0-0 there's no defence to both ♘g5+ and ♘e5+. Moreover, the supporting move 9...c6 fails to 10 ♕e2+! ♔f7 11 0-0 ♖e8 12 ♘g5+ ♔f8 13 ♕f3!.

10 ♔f2!

Threatening ♖e1.

10...♘xc3 11 bxc3 ♕d6 12 ♖e1+ ♔d8 13 a4 ♗f5 14 ♗a3

White has a massive advantage. This is a poorly-played example, but it serves as a warning as to the consequences of neglected development.

Obviously, Black is much better off accepting the limited problems that stem from 7...0-0 8 ♗c4 *(D)*.

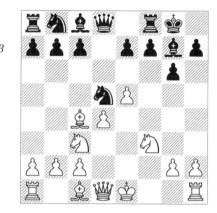

In this position the defence that has actually been played by grandmasters is 8...♗e6, when 9 ♗xd5 ♗xd5 10 ♘xd5 ♕xd5 11 ♕e2 is a modest line with an excellent record. Black normally plays 11...b5 (to stop c4) 12 0-0; for example, 12...♘d7 13 c3 (13 b3!, intending 13...b4 14 a3!) 13...♘b6 (13...a6) 14 b3! a5 15 ♗a3 ♕d7 16 ♗c5 with the better game for White, Unzicker-Chandler, Buenos Aires OL 1978. At the end White is enjoying more space, while Black's bishop is still hemmed in on g7. Possibly Black should opt for 8...♘xc3 9 bxc3 c5 10 0-0, or 8...♘b6 9 ♗b3 ♗g4 10 0-0 ♘c6 11 ♗e3 ♘a5 12 ♕d3!? and White's centre and space may count for somewhat more than the bishop-pair, but that's open to argument.

After all that, I should add that after 5...dxe5, 6 dxe5 *(D)* is less instructive but may be even a better move (or at least an easier one to handle in practice).

Theory gives White a slight advantage after 6...♕xd1+ 7 ♔xd1 ♘g4 (7...♘h5 resembles the main line 5 ♘f3 0-0 6 e5 dxe5 7 dxe5 ♘h5, but in our case you won't get the pin on g4 that happens there – see below; one of several ways for White to proceed is the calm 8 ♗e2! ♗h6 9 ♘d5 ♔d8 10 g3 c6 11 ♘c3 ♔c7 12 ♗e3 with better-placed pieces) 8 ♘d5! ♔d8 9 ♔e1 c6 10 ♘c3 f6!? 11 h3 ♘h6 12 ♘f3.

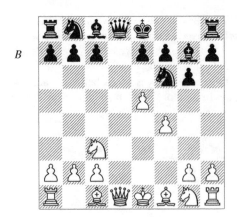

In general, 5...dxe5 may leave something to be desired; it illustrates the dangers of early simplification when the opponent commands more space.

What have we learned by this exercise? For one thing, White seems to have more positive chances after 5 e5 than indicated by what little existing theory is devoted to it. More significantly, we see how one might go about investigating a position on one's own, and how helpful it is to have general knowledge about structures and their characteristic properties.

The Austrian Attack Main Line: 5 ♘f3

5 ♘f3 *(D)*
With this natural move we return to normal theory.

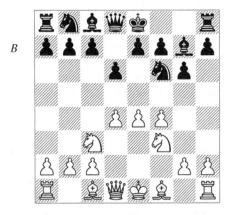

Now in the face of 6 e5 (or 6 ♗d3 and 7 e5), Black has two logical reactions, the natural developing move 5...0-0 and the central counter-attack 5...c5. We'll try to understand each.

Austrian with Conventional Development

5...0-0
From this basic position we'll look at some games:

Ljubojević – Timman
Bugojno 1980

6 e5
Again White attempts to run the opponent over.

6...dxe5
6...♘fd7 aims for ...c5. Since after 7 ♗c4 ♘b6 8 ♗b3, 8...♘c6, 8...c5 and 8...♘a6 all give Black fairly easy equality, I'll mention 7 h4!?. White is intent upon checkmate. This leads to very long and supposedly worked-out variations that you are invited to study in depth with whatever resources are available. One main line is 7...c5 8 h5 cxd4 *(D)*.

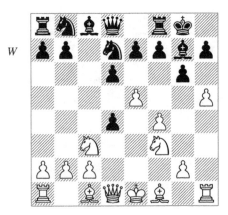

9 ♕xd4 (9 hxg6 dxc3 10 gxf7+ ♖xf7 11 ♗c4 e6 12 ♘g5 ♘xe5 13 ♕h5 h6!) 9...dxe5 10 ♕f2! e4! 11 ♘xe4 ♘f6 12 ♘xf6+ exf6 13 hxg6 ♖e8+ 14 ♗e3 hxg6 15 ♗d3 ♕b6! (15...♕a5+ 16 c3 with an edge for White, Banas-Kindermann, Trnava 1987) 16 ♔d2 ♕a5+ 17 ♔c1 (17 c3 ♗f5) 17...♘c6 18 ♗d2 ♕d5 (18...♘b4! 19 ♗c4 ♗f5) 19 ♕h4? (19 ♕h4 ♗f5 20 ♗c3 ♖e6 is equal) 19...♗g4 20 ♕f1 ♘d4 21 ♗c4 ♕c6 and Black was winning in Varadi-V.Ivanov, Nyiregyhaza 2002. You get the idea: this is a line demanding preparation from both sides. It would be fun to look for an improvement in the middle of the confusion from move 9 on.

7 dxe5!?

If White wants to keep the pieces on, 7 fxe5 ♘d5 8 ♗c4 will generally transpose to the 5 e5 line; that's a position that's a little irritating for Black and makes you wonder about 6...dxe5.

7...♕xd1+ 8 ♔xd1 ♘h5! *(D)*

Black sees a third option (other than 8...♘fd7 or 8...♘g4). With a knight on the rim Black can try to force weaknesses. Instead, 8...♖d8+ 9 ♗d3 ♘d5 10 ♘xd5 ♖xd5 11 ♔e2 is probably better for White, at least in practice.

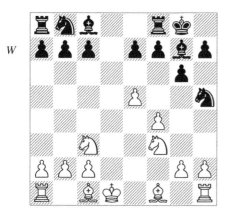

9 ♗c4!?

Allowing doubled pawns but gaining the bishop-pair in return.

9...♗g4!

As mentioned above, this pin wasn't available in the line 5 e5 dxe5 6 dxe5 ♕xd1+ 7 ♔xd1. White has to be very careful now.

10 ♘e2! *(D)*

Odd, but perhaps best. The natural 10 ♔e2 ♘c6 11 ♗e3 runs into 11...♗xf3+ 12 ♔xf3? ♗xe5!; and 10 ♗e3 ♗h6! shows another point of ...♘h5.

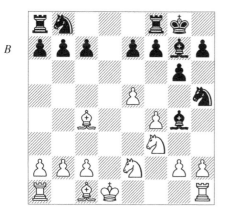

10...♗xf3 11 gxf3 ♘c6 12 c3 ♖ad8+ 13 ♔c2

Remember this handy square for the king; you'll want to go there in queenless middlegames that arise from numerous openings.

13...♗h6 14 b4 e6

The game is equal.

Beliavsky – Anand
Munich 1991

6 ♗e3 *(D)*

This has been a successful move in many games; White not only develops, but also discourages ...c5, which is Black's main source of counterplay. Anand finds a way to challenge White's centre that draws upon several of the main ideas that the Pirc has to offer. Then he applies a touch of ingenuity.

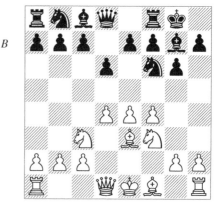

6...b6

Black prepares to play ...c5 anyway, and he hopes that the move ...♗b7 will come in handy at some point. Notice that 6...♘g4 is met by 7 ♗g1 followed by h3. That's why White didn't castle first before playing ♗e3.

7 e5 ♘g4 8 ♗g1 c5

This is the standard picture of an undermining process by Black.

9 h3 ♘h6

A standard Pirc manoeuvre: from here the knight can go to f5 hitting g3 and d4. But while this happens, White will form a huge centre.

10 d5! ♗b7 11 ♕d2

11 g4 keeps the knight trapped and unable to move (another Pirc theme that has won White

many a game), but Black has anticipated that: 11...dxe5 12 fxe5 e6! (there are no obvious threats but suddenly all of Black's pieces will be aimed at the centre) 13 ♗c4 ♘d7! 14 ♗h2 ♖e8! (D).

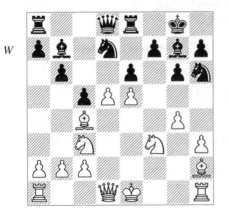

'The threat is stronger than its execution'! 15 0-0 exd5 16 ♗xd5 ♗xd5 17 ♘xd5 ♘xe5 18 ♘xe5 ♗xe5 19 ♗xe5 ♖xe5 20 ♘f6+ ♔g7 and Black is a pawn ahead.

11...♘f5 12 ♗h2 dxe5 13 fxe5 e6! 14 0-0-0

14 g4? ♘h4 takes away another central defender; 14 d6 is met by 14...♘d7 and the long diagonal adds to White's worries.

14...exd5 15 ♘xd5 ♘c6

If Black gets a knight to d4 everything will fall apart for White, so:

16 c3 ♘cd4!

Black plays it anyway!

17 ♘f6+!

17 cxd4 ♕xd5 18 ♔b1 ♖ad8 and ...♘xd4 will follow, picking up material.

17...♗xf6 18 cxd4 ♗g7 19 d5 (D)

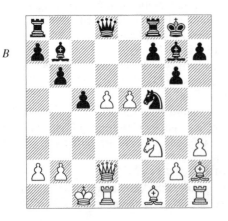

Look at White's wonderful centre pawns! Surely Black has gone wrong?

19...c4!

The star move, which of course Anand has anticipated. First, he stops ♗c4 in the most radical manner, and at the same time he prepares the line-opening ...c3!. It's amazing that he can do all this against White's well-protected advanced pawns, but White is also slightly behind in development.

20 ♗e2!? ♖c8 21 ♔b1!?

Probably 21 ♗f4 was better, but 21...♘e7! 22 d6 ♘d5 has the idea of ...c3 and also the sneaky ...♕d7-a4.

21...♗h6! 22 ♗f4 ♗xf4 23 ♕xf4 ♗xd5 24 h4 (D)

On 24 g4 ♘g7!, the knight will get to the ideal blockading square e6.

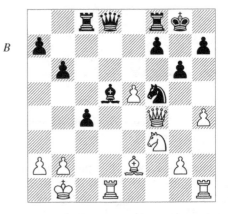

24...c3 25 bxc3 ♖xc3 26 h5 ♘e3! 27 ♘g5 ♕c7 28 ♘xh7 ♖b3+! 0-1

The end would be 29 axb3 ♕c2+ 30 ♔a1 ♕c3+ 31 ♔b1 ♕xb3+ 32 ♔a1 ♘c2#.

The Main Line with 6 ♗d3

6 ♗d3 (D)

Here White takes a breather from immediate attacking mode. The initial idea is pretty obvious: he wants to castle and decide later upon which attack to pursue. Apart from e5 again, a likely candidate for attack consists of the transfer of the queen to the kingside by ♕e1-h4 followed by f5 and ♗h6. White can also build up patiently by means of ♔h1 and ♗e3.

We'll follow two games with 6...♘a6 and 6...♘c6. A natural question arises: why not

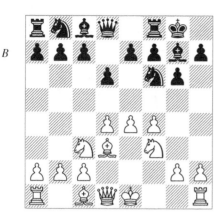

play 6...♗g4 directly? A plausible answer is that, without the possibility of ...♘g4, White can play 7 ♗e3, but then 7...e5!? is rather complicated. Better is 7 h3 ♗xf3 8 ♕xf3; for example, 8...e5 9 dxe5! dxe5 10 f5! with a straightforward advantage, intending 10...♘c6 11 g4 ♘d4 12 ♕f2.

J. Polgar – Svidler
Tilburg 1996

6...♘a6 (D)

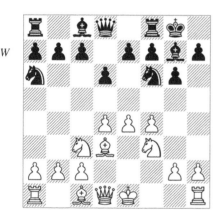

By developing his knight to the rim, Black prepares ...c5, keeps a diagonal open for his c8-bishop and, non-trivially, stays out of the way of pawn attacks by White. The move's main drawback, obviously, is that the knight is far from the centre and cannot be fully effective in that area of the board. As an instructive lesson in positional themes you couldn't do better than to study this variation.

7 0-0 c5 8 d5

Since 8...cxd4 was a positional threat, and since 8 dxc5 ♘xc5 brings the knight into the centre with an easy game, White tries to take the c5-square away from the knight and cramp Black's position at the same time. If he gets the chance he will simply forge ahead with his central pawns by e5 and drive Black back, or he might play for f5 in conjunction with moves like ♕e1-h4. This is all quite dangerous.

For the moment, however, it is premature for White to play 8 e5? ♘g4! 9 h3 cxd4 10 ♘e2 ♘e3!. See how the centre keeps collapsing in these extended-centre lines? White should also avoid 8 ♗xa6?! cxd4! 9 ♘xd4 bxa6 (D).

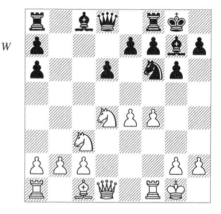

We talk about doubled a-pawns at several points in this book. Generally speaking, the surrender of one's light-squared bishop and ceding of the b-file is a poor deal. Here White's sound position should balance out those advantages; e.g., 10 ♕d3 with the idea of ♔h1 and ♗e3, or perhaps ♗d2. But L.Barczay-Sandor, Hungary 1968 showed how easily the active black pieces can create threats: 10 ♘b3? a5! 11 ♕f3 ♗b7 12 a4? (but 12 ♗e3 a4 13 ♘d2 a3!) 12...♕b6+! 13 ♗e3 ♕b4 (suddenly the e-pawn is falling) 14 ♖ae1 (14 ♗d4 ♘xe4!) 14...♗xe4 15 ♘xe4 ♕xe4 16 ♕xe4 ♘xe4 17 ♗d4 ♗xd4+ 18 ♘xd4 f5! 19 ♘c6 ♔f7 20 ♘xa5 ♖fc8 (White has regained his pawn – the a-pawn – but Black's e4-knight is a rock and he has two open queenside files) 21 ♖e2 ♖ab8 22 ♘b3 ♖c4 23 a5 a6 24 ♖d1 ♘c5! 25 ♖de1 ♖b7 26 ♘xc5 ♖xc5. White loses a pawn, and Black stands to win.

8...♗g4 (D)

A position with some curious features has arisen. It's often the case that if Black tries to

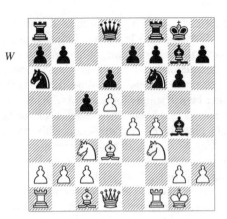

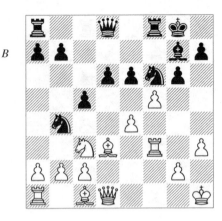

play a Benoni structure when White has a knight on c3 and no pawn on c4, he can't drum up much play on either side of the board. The key move ...b5 is hard to get in before White's centre starts rolling. But in this case the elimination of White's f3-knight not only takes the pressure off e5, but gets rid of the c8-bishop, which is often in the way (for example, it interferes with the connection of Black's rooks). Now Black's plan will be ...♘c7, ...a6, ...♖b8 and ...b5, supported by ...♕d7 or ...♘e8-c7 if necessary. Barring that, the move ...e6 may undermine White's centre. Of course, White will have the considerable advantage of the bishop-pair to compensate him for these troubles.

9 a3

A few other instructive excerpts:

a) 9 ♔h1 e6!? (not the only move, of course) 10 dxe6 fxe6 11 f5! (this is an excellent move that does several things at once: it activates the c1-bishop, short-circuits Black's planned ...d5 due to e5, and attacks the e6 point which, if it falls, will give White the chance to control d5) 11...♘b4 (Black has to forget the ...b5 plan and concentrate upon the centre) 12 h3 (also dangerous is 12 fxg6 hxg6 13 e5 dxe5 14 ♗g5!) 12...♗xf3 13 ♖xf3 *(D)*.

13...♘d7! (try not to forget this move! A knight on the e5 outpost is the best defender and attacker in most Sicilians, King's Indians, and Benonis, as well as in a variety of other openings) 14 fxe6 ♘e5!? (14...♖xf3! is a better and more adventurous idea, because 15 ♕xf3 ♘e5 keeps White's pieces under check, and the positionally superior 15 gxf3 ♘xd3 16 ♕xd3 ♕h4 17 ♔g2 ♗d4 18 ♗e3 ♘e5 and ...♖f8 gives Black attacking chances) 15 ♘d5?! (15 ♖xf8+!

♕xf8 16 ♗e2 ♕f2 17 ♘d5! and Black has no attack) 15...♖xf3 16 gxf3 ♘exd3 17 cxd3 ♘xd5! 18 exd5 ♕h4 (ouch; the dark squares are falling) 19 ♔g2 ♕h5 20 ♗f4 ♕xd5 21 ♕b3 ♕xb3 22 axb3 ♗xb2 23 ♖a2 (23 ♖e1 d5!?) 23...♗e5 24 ♗xe5 dxe5 25 ♖e2 ♔f8 and Black eventually won in Korneev-Marin, Spanish Cht (Lanzarote) 2003.

b) Two younger giants played very accurately in Grishchuk-Ponomariov, Lausanne 2000: 9 ♗c4 ♘c7 10 h3 ♗xf3 11 ♕xf3 a6 12 a4 b6 13 ♕d3 (13 f5!? ♘d7) 13...♕b8! 14 ♗e3 ♕b7 15 ♖ab1 *(D)*.

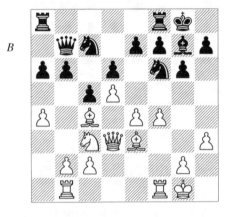

15...e6! (perfectly timed; Black is stuck on one front and takes the chance to hit the centre, based upon tactics) 16 b4! (16 dxe6 fxe6 17 ♕xd6 ♖fd8! 18 ♗xe6+ ♔h8 19 ♕e7 ♖e8) 16...exd5 17 exd5 cxb4 18 ♖xb4 b5! 19 axb5 axb5 20 ♗b3 (White doesn't want to lose his d-pawn but now Black utilizes the a-file to equalize) 20...♖a5 21 f5 ♕a6 22 fxg6 hxg6 23 ♘e4 ♖a1 24 ♘xf6+ ♗xf6 25 ♖bf4 ♗e5 (that square again!) 26 ♖4f3 ♖xf1+ 27 ♖xf1 ♘e8 28 ♗d4 ½-½. White's remaining bishop is bad, so he doesn't have the forces to do any damage.

9...♘d7 10 h3 ♗xf3 11 ♕xf3 ♖c8! (D)

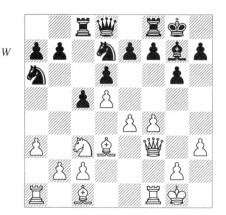

Simple but also insightful. White will stop ...b5 and use his bishop-pair if given half a chance, so Svidler decides to make room for his pieces in a more aggressive way, based upon some good calculation.

12 ♗e3

12 ♕e2 would prevent c4 temporarily but 12...♕a5 13 ♘d1 (not 13 ♗d2?? c4! 14 ♗xc4 ♕c5+) 13...♘c7! (threatening ...b5) 14 ♗d2 ♕b6 15 c4 e6! breaks up the centre just in time.

12...♕a5 13 ♕f2 c4 14 ♗e2 ♘ac5

Now that the knights have access to c5 they're roughly as good as the bishops. Giving up the dark squares by 14...♗xc3? 15 bxc3 ♕xc3 is not recommended in any case, but White even has 16 ♗g4! (protecting c2) 16...♖c7 17 ♗d4 ♕a5 18 ♕h4 with a terrific initiative.

15 ♗f3 ♘a4 16 ♘xa4 ♕xa4 (D)

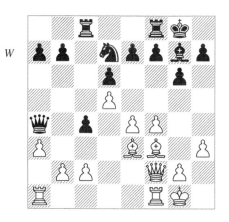

17 c3

The b2-pawn needs protection, and neither 17 ♗d4? ♗xd4 18 ♕xd4 ♕xc2 nor 17 ♖ab1 b6 is very inspiring.

17...♘c5 18 ♗xc5 ♖xc5 19 ♖ae1 ♕a5 20 ♕g3 ♕b6 21 ♖f2 e6 22 dxe6 fxe6 23 ♗g4 ♖f6 24 ♕e3 h5 25 ♗d1 ♖c8 26 ♕xb6 ½-½

The opposite-coloured bishops ensure equality. A fair result from a well-played game.

Hellers – Ftačnik
Haninge 1989

6...♘c6 (D)

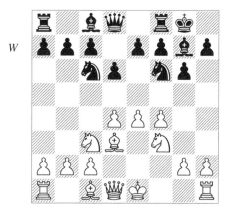

This is the most conventional move. It strikes at the slightly shaky d4 point (...♗g4 can follow) and Black contemplates ...e5. Having given 6...♘a6 so much attention, I'm going to pick out only a few points of interest here.

7 0-0

White has one very dangerous alternative:

a) 7 ♗e3 ♘g4 8 ♗g1 e5 9 fxe5 dxe5 10 d5 ♘d4 is not clear, but probably Black stands satisfactorily.

b) 7 d5 ♘b4 8 ♗c4 (8 ♗e2 c5!?) 8...c6! changes the central equation and should be OK after 9 a3 cxd5 10 exd5 ♘a6 or 10...♕a5!?. These ideas also show up in the main line with 4 ♘f3.

c) 7 e5 is not so easy to equalize against, since Black has neither ...c5 nor ...e5 at his disposal; for example, 7...dxe5 8 fxe5 ♘d7!? (D) (with the idea of ...♘b4 and ...c5, although that may not achieve much; Black has the moves 8...♘g4 and 8...♘h5 to look at, and the same moves before exchanging – a key move against every one of them is ♗e4, strengthening White's control over the centre; both sides should check theory for details).

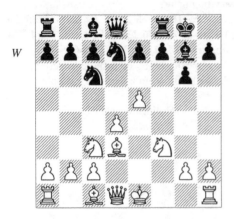

W

Now:

c1) 9 ♗e4!? is very interesting, because Black needs a plan, and White does well after 9...♘b6 10 0-0 ♗g4 11 ♗e3! with the idea 11...♘c4 12 ♗f2 ♘xb2? 13 ♕b1 ♘c4 14 ♕xb7 ♘4a5 15 ♕b5 ♗d7 16 ♖ab1 ♖b8 17 ♕c5, when Black's pieces are uncoordinated, especially that knight on a5.

c2) 9 ♗e4 ♘b4 10 ♗c4 c5 11 c3 ♘c6 12 0-0 cxd4 13 cxd4 ♘b6 14 ♗b3. Here is the key point. Since ...f6 isn't possible, Black needs to put pressure on the d-pawn or eliminate some of White's pieces: 14...♗g4 (14...♘a5 15 ♗c2 ♗e6!? looks initially promising, but 16 ♕e1 ♘c6 17 ♕h4 threatens various attacks with ♗h6, ♘fg5, ♖f3-h3, ♘c5, etc., in whatever order works!) 15 ♘eg5 e6 16 h3 ♗xf3 17 ♘xf3 ♕d7 18 ♗g5 with a small but definite advantage because of the dark squares and Black's hemmed-in g7-bishop, Wang Zili-D.Gurevich, Lucerne Wcht 1989.

7...♗g4 8 e5 *(D)*

It makes a lot of sense to make this move when ...c5 is a long way off.

8...dxe5!

There are two other possibilities that should give you an idea of the strength of White's centre:

a) 8...♘d7 9 ♗e3 dxe5 (9...♘b4 10 ♗e4!) 10 dxe5 f6 (10...♘b6) 11 exf6 exf6 (as so often, this turns out to leave Black's position a little airy) 12 h3 ♗e6 13 ♗b5 ♘b6 14 ♕e2 ♖e8 15 ♖ad1 ♕e7 16 ♖fe1 ♕b4 17 ♘d4 ♗c4 18 ♕f3

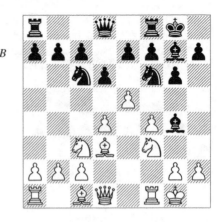

B

with a distinct edge, Hector-Ftačnik, Haninge 1990.

b) 8...♘h5? 9 ♗e3 dxe5 10 dxe5 f6 11 exf6 ♗xf6 12 h3 and Black's got that awful e-pawn and e6-square to deal with.

9 dxe5 ♘d5 10 h3?!

Better is 10 ♘xd5 ♕xd5 11 ♕e1!.

10...♘xc3 11 bxc3 ♗f5 12 ♗e3

The g7-bishop is suffering, but we've already seen that ...f6 would come with problems and isn't worth it yet.

12...♕d7

It's about equal. White should play 13 ♖b1 and ♘d4.

Austrian with 5...c5

1 e4 d6 2 d4 ♘f6 3 ♘c3 g6 4 f4 ♗g7 5 ♘f3 c5 *(D)*

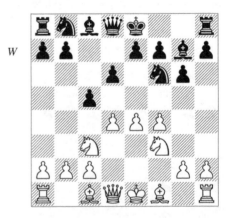

W

Black plays to free his game immediately and avoid the cramped games that can arise after 5...0-0. The problem is that many lines here are simply tactical sequences of 'only' moves, so I'll try to limit the quantity of material. Note that 6 e5 ♘fd7!? (not the only move) transposes to the 5 e5 line.

Hermlin – Chipashvili
USSR 1976

6 ♗b5+

This is still the critical line. Black has held his own for years after 6 dxc5 ♕a5 7 ♗d3 ♕xc5, but this is the variation that most resembles other openings in its positional themes, and deserves a look. We'll follow Kindermann-M.Gurevich, Haifa Echt 1989: 8 ♕e2 0-0 (if Black wants to be sure of getting ...♗g4 in, he can play it now) 9 ♗e3 ♕a5 10 0-0 *(D)*.

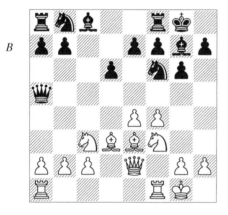

10...♘c6 (10...♘bd7!? is a Sicilianesque move that has been tried out, but most players don't want to be so cramped) 11 a3 ♗g4 (the move-order has been a bit strange; normally 10...♗g4 comes first) 12 h3 ♗xf3 13 ♕xf3 ♘d7 (Black is essentially playing a Sicilian Defence, where his knights are harmoniously placed and he should have equality; for the moment, ...♗xc3 is threatened) 14 ♗d2 ♕b6+ 15 ♔h1 ♘c5 16 ♖ab1 ♘xd3 17 cxd3 f5!. An excellent move. It creates a few weaknesses, but blocks off the f1-rook and especially the d2-bishop from entering the game; the move f5 would have freed them both. The game continued 18 ♘d5 (18 g4 e6 19 gxf5 exf5 20 ♘d5 ♕b3 21 ♗c3 ♖ae8 22 ♕g2 ♘e7, Glek-Lobron, Bundesliga 1990/1; Black should have no problems) 18...♕b3 19 ♗c3 (the same position but without g4; the difference should favour Black

somewhat, as ...e6 remains in the air) 19...♖f7 20 ♗xg7 ♔xg7 21 ♕e3 e6 22 ♘c3 d5! *(D)*.

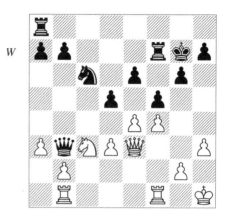

Black has dissolved his weakness and taken over the initiative. He was never in trouble in the opening. We'll follow the game with minimal notes: 23 ♕f3 fxe4 24 dxe4 d4!? (24...♖af8! 25 exd5 ♖xf4 26 ♕xf4 ♖xf4 27 ♖xf4 exd5 and ...d4 follows) 25 ♘e2 ♕xf3 26 ♖xf3 e5 27 fxe5? ♖xf3 28 gxf3 d3! 29 ♘c3 (29 ♘f4 ♘xe5 30 ♖d1 g5!) 29...♖f8 30 ♔g2 ♘xe5 31 ♖f1 g5 32 ♖f2 ♘g6 33 ♖f1 ♘f4+ 34 ♔g3 ♔f6 35 h4 ♔e5!? 36 hxg5 ♖g8 37 ♔h4 h6!? 38 gxh6 ♖g6 39 ♘d1 (39 h7! ♖h6+ 40 ♔g3 ♖xh7 41 ♔f2 ♖h2+ 42 ♔e3 ♖xb2 43 ♖b1!) 39...♖xh6+ 40 ♔g3 ♖g6+ 41 ♔h4 ♔d4 0-1.

6...♗d7 7 e5

This is the main move, leading to complications that any player of 5...c5 must know. 7 ♗xd7+ is a more interesting move from a positional point of view: 7...♘fxd7 (7...♘bxd7 8 d5 isn't as easy for Black, in part because 8...b5 can now run into 9 e5 and 8...0-0 9 ♕e2 isn't comfortable) 8 d5 b5!? 9 ♕e2! b4 10 ♘d1 ♘b6!? (to prevent e5 by hitting the d-pawn) 11 0-0 0-0 (or 11...♕c8!?), and now:

a) 12 c4 bxc3 13 ♘xc3 ♕c8! intending ...♕a6, Martinović-Jansa, Lingen 1988. Endings should be fine for Black: the combination of ...c4 and the b-file grant active play.

b) 12 ♘f2 ♕c8 13 ♖e1?! a5 ½-½ Shirov-Beliavsky, Madrid 1997. Once again ...♕a6 is coming.

c) 12 f5! has been suggested, because the knight can't get to e5 yet. Then 12...gxf5 13 c4 yields surprising compensation. As usual, f5 frees the c1-bishop and f1-rook.

7...♘g4 *(D)*

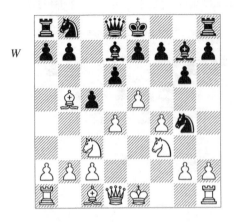

8 h3!?

a) 8 e6 is White's most famous continuation: 8...fxe6 (8...♗xb5?! leads to well-analysed complications beginning 9 exf7+ ♔d7 {forced} 10 ♘xb5 ♕a5+ 11 ♘c3 cxd4 12 ♘xd4 ♗xd4 13 ♕xd4 ♘c6 14 ♕c4 ♕b6 15 ♕e2 h5 16 ♗d2 ♘d4 17 ♕d3 ♘f5 18 ♘e4 ♖ac8 19 0-0-0 and White comes out with somewhat the better game) 9 ♘g5 ♗xb5 *(D)*, and now we have more theory:

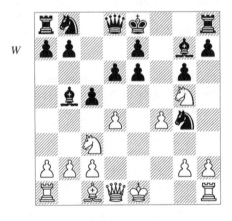

a1) 10 ♘xb5 ♕a5+ 11 c3 ♕xb5 12 ♕xg4 cxd4 13 ♘xe6 ♕c4! 14 ♘xg7+ ♔f7 with mind-boggling complications – you'll need to consult the books and databases for this one.

a2) 10 ♕xg4 ♗c4 11 b3 ♗xd4 12 ♗d2 ♗d5 is another line that will require study.

a3) 10 ♘xe6 and now Black has the famous resource 10...♗xd4!, with the point that 11 ♘xd8 ♗f2+ 12 ♔d2 ♗e3+, etc., is a draw. There are further well-worked-out tactics after

11 ♘xb5 ♕a5+ 12 c3 (12 ♕d2 ♗f2+ 13 ♔d1 ♘e3+ 14 ♔e2 ♕xb5+ 15 ♔xf2 ♘g4+ 16 ♔g3 ♘a6! turns out well) 12...♗f2+ 13 ♔d2 ♗e3+ 14 ♔c2 ♕a4+, etc., which is apparently equal.

b) 8 ♗xd7+ ♕xd7 9 d5 dxe5 10 h3 e4! 11 ♘xe4 ♘f6 is a trick worth remembering that comes up again and again. Now 12 ♘xf6+ ♗xf6 gives Black equality thanks to his powerful bishop on f6, and the pawn-grab 12 ♘xc5 can be met by 12...♕d6! 13 ♕d4 (13 ♘xb7?? ♕b4+) 13...0-0 14 ♘e4 ♘xe4 15 ♕xe4 ♘d7 with compensation. There may be a way for White to do better in this less-investigated line.

8...cxd4

Convoluted theory focuses upon 8...♗xb5 9 ♘xb5 dxe5! 10 hxg4 ♕a5+ 11 ♗d2 (11 c3 e4; 11 ♘c3 exd4) 11...♕xb5 12 dxe5 ♕xb2! 13 ♖b1 ♕xa2 14 ♖xb7 ♕d5 15 ♕b1 with an unclear situation.

9 ♕xd4 ♘h6 *(D)*

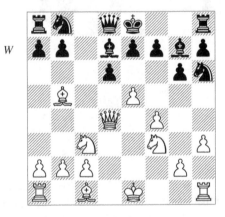

10 g4

White shuts out the knight from re-entering the game. 10 ♗xd7+ ♕xd7 11 g4 ♘c6 12 ♕e4 0-0 is a standard position in which neither side has made much progress, even though there's plenty of play; e.g., 13 ♗d2 dxe5 14 fxe5 ♕e6?! (14...f5! 15 exf6 exf6 is equal) 15 0-0-0 f5 16 exf6 ♕xe4 17 ♘xe4 exf6 18 ♘c5 (18 ♗c3) 18...♖ae8 19 ♖he1 (19 ♘xb7) 19...♖xe1 20 ♖xe1 f5 21 g5 ♘f7 22 ♗f4 b6 23 ♘d3 ♖c8 24 ♔d2 with equality, Thorhallsson-Gretarsson, Hafnarfirdi 1992.

10...♗xb5 11 ♘xb5 ♕a5+ 12 ♘c3 ♘c6 13 ♕e4 0-0-0 14 ♗d2 dxe5 15 fxe5 f5!? 16 ♕c4?

Best is 16 exf6 exf6 17 ♕e6+ ♔b8 18 0-0-0.

16...fxg4 17 hxg4 ♖hf8

White's e-pawn is weak. Most of the lines in this whole variation (excluding 6 dxc5) have a positional basis but are also forcing. They should probably be learned by heart.

The ♗c4 Variation

1 e4 d6 2 d4 ♘f6 3 ♘c3 g6 4 ♘f3

4 ♗c4 could be the right move-order if you want to play this system, depending upon what you think of 4...♘xe4 5 ♗xf7+ (or 5 ♘xe4 d5 6 ♕e2!? dxe4 {6...dxc4?? 7 ♘f6#} 7 ♕xe4) 5...♔xf7 6 ♘xe4 ♗g7, when a sample line is 7 ♘f3 ♖f8 8 c3.

4...♗g7 5 ♗c4 *(D)*

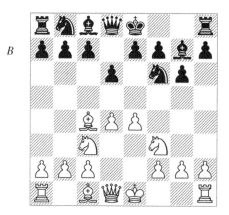

We'll take a quick look to see how both sides handle this potentially tactical line.

Rublevsky – Khalifman
St Petersburg 1999

5...0-0

Now 5...♘xe4!? 6 ♗xf7+ (6 ♘xe4!? is also possible) 6...♔xf7 7 ♘xe4 ♖f8 8 0-0 ♔g8 might be worth trying. Black has the bishop-pair and a central majority with a nice f-file. On the other hand, White has a space advantage and Black's squares down the e-file are vulnerable, while at the same time White's knights are nicely centralized. Probably it's one of those many chess positions in which, if the owner of the two bishops (Black) can stabilize the position and avoid serious weaknesses, his centre and bishop-pair will assert themselves in the long run. But White looks ready to use his knights and major pieces along the open e-file to prevent that.

6 ♕e2 c6

Black can't stop e5, but this stabilizes the centre.

7 e5 dxe5 8 dxe5 ♘d5 9 ♗d2 ♗g4!

This gets rid of some pieces and puts real pressure on White's e-pawn at the same time.

10 h3

Not 10 0-0-0?! e6 11 h3 ♗xf3 12 gxf3 ♘d7 13 f4 ♕h4. Then Black has real pressure on the f4-pawn and White's pawn-structure is bad.

10...♗xf3 11 gxf3 *(D)*

11 ♕xf3 e6 12 ♕e2 ♘d7 13 f4 ♕h4+ 14 ♕f2 ♕xf2+ 15 ♔xf2 f6 16 exf6 ♗xf6 and Black has some attack even with the queens off, Sermek-Nogueiras, Moscow OL 1994.

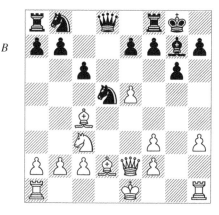

11...e6

Or 11...♘xc3 12 ♗xc3 e6. Notice that we're now in another of those ...e6/...c6 restraint structures and White has no d-pawn. White lacks a good plan.

12 f4 ♘d7

Very solid. Black has at least equalized. 12...♕h4 13 ♕g4! would gain a tempo because Black doesn't want to straighten out White's pawns when he also has the advantage of two bishops.

13 h4!?

Trying to break things open a bit for his bishops.

13...♘xc3 14 ♗xc3 ♘b6 15 ♗b3 h5 16 ♗d2 a5 17 a3 ♘d5! 18 c4 ♘e7

Black heads for the perfect outpost on f5.

19 0-0-0 ♘f5 20 ♗c3 ♕e7 21 ♗c2 ♖fd8 22 ♖xd8+ ♕xd8 23 ♗xf5 exf5 24 ♕e3 ♕e7 25 ♖d1 ♗f8 26 ♕b6 ♖e8! *(D)*

27 e6!?

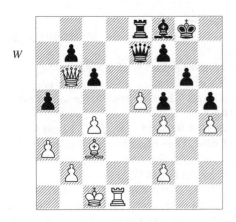

White wants to attack. Instead, 27 ♗xa5 ♗h6 28 ♗d2 ♕xh4 29 ♕xb7 ♗xf4 30 ♕xc6 ♖xe5 is a mess – look at all those passed pawns! But White's king isn't safe.

27...fxe6

Not 27...♕xe6? 28 ♕d4.

28 ♕xa5 ♗g7 29 ♖g1 ♗xc3 30 ♕xc3 ♔f7 31 ♕g3 ♕f6 32 ♖d1 ♖d8 ½-½

A double-edged variation, but Black was positionally better out of the opening.

Classical Variation

1 e4 d6 2 d4 ♞f6 3 ♞c3 g6 4 ♞f3 ♝g7 5 ♝e2 0-0 6 0-0 *(D)*

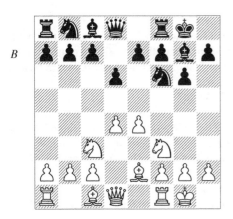

6...♝g4

This is Black's most logical and classically-motivated development. With this move he prepares to put pressure on d4 by ...♝xf3 and a combination of ...♞c6 and ...e5, when his knights may well be a match for White's bishops. 6...♝g4 also helps to clear his back rank (if

Black waits for h3, his bishop often has nowhere useful to go), and discourages White from pressing too hard in the centre.

You can get a feel for White's space advantage after 6...♞c6?!, which allows 7 d5. A funny line is 7...♞e5 8 ♞d4!? (8 ♞xe5! dxe5 9 ♝e3 leaves Black looking for a plan) 8...c5! 9 dxc6 ♞xc6 10 ♝e3 with an exact transposition to a Sicilian Dragon. White can meet 7...♞b8 with 8 h3, preventing ...♝g4, when Black is pressed for space. Another good approach is 8 ♖e1 e5!? (8...♝g4 9 ♝f4) 9 dxe6! ♝xe6 10 ♝f4 with a simple central advantage: 10...h6 11 ♞d4 ♝d7 12 ♕d2 ♔h7 13 e5! dxe5 14 ♝xe5 *(D)*.

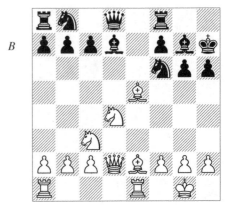

White has a substantial advantage in this game between two ex-World Champions, and it surprisingly turned into a miniature following 14...♞e4? 15 ♞xe4 ♝xe5 16 ♞f3 ♝g7 17 ♖ad1 ♕c8 18 ♝c4 ♝e8 19 ♞eg5+! hxg5 (19...♔g8 20 ♞e6 wins for White) 20 ♞xg5+ ♔g8 21 ♕f4 ♞d7 22 ♖xd7! ♝xd7 23 ♝xf7+ 1-0 Tal-Petrosian, USSR Cht (Moscow) 1974.

7 ♝e3

One disadvantage of 6...♝g4 is that it has allowed this move without White having to bother about ...♞g4. Instead, 7 h3 ♝xf3 8 ♝xf3 has never given Black serious problems after 8...e5. White has the two bishops but his position is hampered by the knight on c3, which allows Black to sink his knight in on d4 and exchange a bishop, or otherwise play a well-timed ...f5. The tempo lost by h3 is meaningful; otherwise perhaps White could reorganize and gain the advantage. Instead of 8...e5, Black also has the more ambitious move 8...♞c6, again taking advantage of his extra tempo. Then 9 ♗e3 e5 10 dxe5 dxe5 11 ♘d5 is well-answered by 11...♘xd5 12 exd5 ♘d4, but of course there's oodles of theory to look at.

7...♘c6 *(D)*

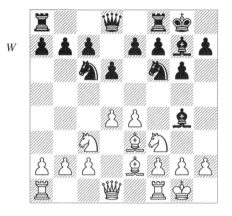

8 ♕d2

Logical: White connects rooks, contemplates ♗h6, and challenges Black to advance in the centre. The other important main line is 8 d5, and then:

a) 8...♘b8 can lead to the characteristic manoeuvre 9 ♘d4 ♗xe2 10 ♕xe2 c5 11 ♘f3 ♕b6 12 ♖ab1 ♕a6!, either exchanging queens in a position with no weaknesses or mobilizing the queenside pawns. This may be Black's best line.

b) 8...♗xf3 9 ♗xf3 ♘e5 10 ♗e2 c6! *(D)*.

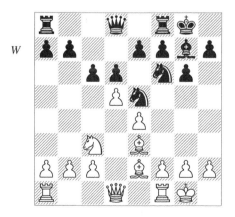

Black has to strike quickly before White consolidates the two bishops. His plan includes moves like ...♕a5, ...cxd5, a rook to the c-file, and perhaps ...♘c4. A typical line goes 11 a4!?

(11 f4! is probably good, but some players may find it too loosening; one line among many is 11...♘ed7 12 dxc6 {or 12 ♗d4} 12...bxc6 13 ♕d3 ♕b8 14 a3 with a small edge; play what works!) 11...a5!? (11...♕a5 12 ♖a3 aims for ♖b3, but 12...♖fc8 13 ♕d2 cxd5 14 exd5 ♘c4 15 ♗xc4 ♖xc4 16 ♖b3 b6! is equal, and illustrates a common plan for Black) 12 ♗d4 ♘ed7 13 ♕d2 ♕c7 14 ♖ad1 ♖ac8 15 ♖fe1 ♖fd8 and White has difficulty playing for advantage because Black's pieces are so well-placed, Rozentalis-Ftačnik, Manila OL 1992.

We now return to 8 ♕d2 *(D)*:

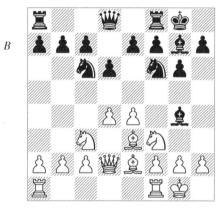

8...e5

8...♖e8 used to be played, a useful move that waits for White to commit before playing ...e5. But White has a *more* useful move in 9 ♖fe1! a6!? (to prevent ♘b5 in view of the line 9...e5?! 10 d5 ♗xf3 11 ♗xf3 ♘d4 12 ♗xd4 exd4 13 ♘b5; note that 9 ♖fe1 protected the e-pawn in this variation) 10 ♖ad1 (every white piece is centralized) 10...e5 11 dxe5 dxe5 (11...♘xe5 12 ♘xe5 dxe5 13 ♕c1 ♕c8 14 ♗xg4 ♕xg4 15 f3 ♕e6 16 ♕d2 ♗f8 17 ♘d5 and White captures with pieces on d5, winning the d-file) 12 ♕c1 ♕e7 13 ♘d5 ♘xd5 14 exd5 ♘d8 15 c4 f5 16 c5. White is in control of the game, Geller-Přibyl, Sochi 1984.

9 d5

The endgame 9 dxe5 dxe5 10 ♖ad1 has given Black problems but a good line is 10...♕c8! 11 ♕c1 ♖d8 12 ♖xd8+ ♘xd8! followed by ...♘e6, aiming at d4 and f4; e.g., 13 ♖d1 ♘e6 14 h3 ♗xf3 15 ♗xf3 c6 16 ♘e2 ♕c7 17 c3 a5 18 ♕c2 ♗f8! intending ...♗c5, Kaidanov-Wolff, USA 1990. ...♗f8 is a nice move to remember, getting rid of both White's good bishop and Black's bad one!

9...公e7 *(D)*

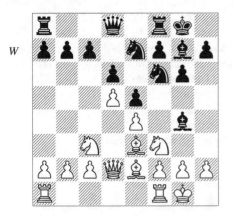

Now the question is whether White can make something of his space advantage. The examples seem to indicate that he can.

Donaldson – Felecan
Kona 1998

10 罩ad1!

It's odd, but this position seems the least promising that we have seen thus far for White. He has made no progress on the queenside, Black still has his bishops, and with the knight on e7, the idea of ...f5 has gained force. However, White has achieved something that he hasn't been able to do in any other line. So far Black has always successfully traded White's d-pawn after ...c6, allowing him to take over good posts rapidly before White could reorganize. With threats and piece activity, White's bishops didn't have time to find good positions. But here Black doesn't get ...c6 in because the d-pawn will fall. And ...f5 is still to be discussed, but has its problems. This means that White has time to put his pieces on the appropriate squares and make a pawn-break, either with f4 or c5.

10...兔d7!

Instead of waiting around, Black embarks upon a new idea: queenside expansion. A game of Spassky's is a model of how White should handle the exchange on f3: 10...兔xf3 11 兔xf3 公d7 12 g3!? (a little odd-looking, but the move is very flexible; White may be interested in

h4-h5, 含g2 and 罩h1, or he may want to support the pawn-push f4, or he can do what he does in the game) 12...f5 13 兔e2! 公f6 14 f3 (that's the end of Black's kingside attack) 14...營d7 15 兔b5 營c8 16 罩f2 a6 17 兔f1 公h5 18 兔h3 營e8 19 公e2 含h8 20 c4 (after all that we get two bishops and a standard-looking queenside formation) 20...b6 21 罩df1 營f7 22 f4 and White had too much firepower in Spassky-Parma, Havana OL 1966. An excellent positional demolition.

11 公e1 b5

Some noteworthy play follows 11...公g4 12 兔xg4 兔xg4 13 f3 兔d7, because Black has the two bishops but he isn't well organized to meet 14 f4! *(D)*.

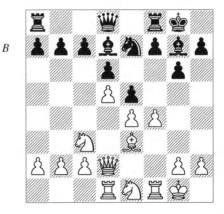

This seems to grant Black an outpost on e5 but he can't get to it, whereas White will win more than his share of the centre. For example, 14...兔g4 15 公f3 f5 (15...營d7 16 fxe5 dxe5 17 兔c5 f5 18 營g5 兔f6 19 營h6 罩f7 20 d6, Gligorić-Pfleger, Moscow Echt 1977) 16 h3! 兔xf3 17 罩xf3 with the ideas 罩df1 and 罩de1.

12 a3 a5 13 b4

The bottom line is that White has space and a better grip on the position. A different order is 13 公d3 營b8 14 f3 c6!? (14...b4 15 公b1! bxa3 16 公xa3) 15 dxc6 兔xc6 16 b4 d5 (16...axb4? 17 公xb4! 罩xa3 18 公xc6 公xc6 19 公xb5 罩a2 20 兔c4 and Black is in big trouble, Vogt-Bernard, Wildbad 1990; 16...罩c8!?) 17 兔c5 罩e8, Kuczynski-Chernin, Budapest Z 1993, and now White could play 18 exd5 公exd5 19 公xd5 公xd5 20 bxa5. It seems that White keeps the advantage in a number of ways, which is a good sign for 10 罩ad1 and his opening as a whole.

13...axb4 14 axb4 ♕b8 15 f3 *(D)*

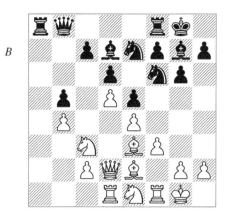

15...♖d8

15...♖a3 *(D)* has two good answers:

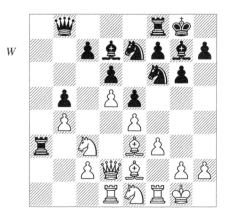

a) 16 ♘b1 ♖a8 17 c4! bxc4 18 ♗xc4, and now the only freeing move, 18...c6, would open up the c4-bishop: 19 dxc6 ♘xc6 20 ♘c2!.

b) 16 ♘d3 c6 17 dxc6 ♗xc6 18 ♘c1! (or 18 ♖a1, or 18 ♘f2) 18...♖d8 19 ♘b3 d5. This is a transposition to Thorsteins-Kasparov, Saint John blitz Wch 1988. It looks as though White will win a clear pawn after 20 ♗c5! ♖d7 (or 20...♘c8 21 exd5 ♘xd5 22 ♘a5) 21 ♗xe7 ♖xe7 22 exd5! ♗e8 (22...♖d7? 23 ♕c1 ♕a7+ 24 ♔h1 ♘xd5 25 ♘xb5 ♗xb5 26 ♗xb5 ♖d6 27 ♗c4) 23 d6 and ♘c5.

16 ♘d3 c6 17 dxc6 ♗xc6 18 ♘f2!? ♖d7

White still stands better after 18...d5 19 ♗c5 ♘c8 20 exd5 ♘xd5 21 ♘xd5 ♖xd5 (not 21...♗xd5?? 22 c4) 22 ♕e3 ♖xd1 23 ♖xd1 ♕c7 24 ♘e4!.

19 ♘g4!?

Going for the f-file. Perhaps White had a better move, but he foresees the promising sacrifice ahead.

19...♘xg4 20 fxg4 d5 21 exd5 ♘xd5 22 ♘xd5 ♖xd5 23 ♕xd5! ♗xd5 24 ♖xd5 *(D)*

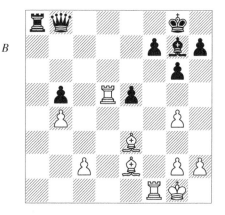

If the b-pawn falls, White gets two passed pawns, and f7 is also a target. But his pieces are loose on the kingside, so Black gets counterplay. Although one feels that White should have a way to combine attack and defence, the position can probably be assessed as dynamically equal. Since the opening is long over, I'll just show the moves of this fascinating game:

24...♕c8 25 ♖c5 ♕b7 26 ♗f2 ♖c8 27 ♗f3 ♕d7 28 ♖d1 ♕e6 29 ♖d6 ♕e8 30 ♗c6 ♕e7 31 ♗xb5 ♖a8 32 ♖d1 ♗h6 33 h4 e4 34 g5 e3 35 ♗g3 ♗g7 36 ♗e2 ♖d8 37 ♖f1 ♖d2 38 ♗c4 ♗d4 39 ♖xf7 ♕xf7 40 ♗xf7+ ♔xf7 41 ♖c7+ ♔e6 42 ♔f1 ♔f5 43 ♖c4 ♔e6 44 c3 ♗a7 45 ♖c6+ ♔f5 46 ♖a6 ♔g4 47 ♖xa7 ♔xg3 48 ♖e7 ♔f4 49 b5 ♖d1+ 50 ♔e2 ♖d2+ 51 ♔e1 ♖c2 52 b6 ♖xc3 53 b7 ♖b3 54 ♖xh7 ♖b2 55 ♖e7 ♔g4 56 ♖e4+ ♔h5 57 g3 ♖xb7 58 ♖xe3 ♖b2 59 ♖e2 ♖b3 60 ♔f2 ♖xg3 ½-½

Index of Players

Numbers refer to pages. When a player's name appears in **bold**, that player had White. Otherwise the FIRST-NAMED PLAYER had White.

Index of Openings

Numbers refer to pages. Codes are ECO codes.

Other Books from Gambit Publications

Chess Strategy in Action
John Watson
Here Watson fleshes out the theory presented to enormous acclaim in *Secrets of Modern Chess Strategy*. He illustrates the modern practice of chess with examples from imaginative players such as Kasparov, Kramnik, Anand, Ivanchuk and tempestuous innovators such as Shirov and Morozevich.
288 pages, 248 mm by 172 mm
$29.95 / £19.99

Creative Chess Opening Preparation
Viacheslav Eingorn
Grandmaster Eingorn is a chess opening trendsetter. Here he reveals the methods by which he prepares his openings, and shows the reader how new systems can be pioneered from scratch.
160 pages, 248 mm by 172 mm
$26.95 / £15.99

Garry Kasparov's Greatest Chess Games Volume 2
Igor Stohl
Stohl's detailed annotations explain the reasoning behind Kasparov's decisions, and the powerful principles and concepts embodied by his moves.
352 pages, 248 mm by 172 mm, hardback
$35.00 / £22.50

Foundations of Chess Strategy
Lars Bo Hansen
Grandmaster Hansen presents some systematic techniques that enable a player to evaluate his own strengths and weakness. Original and thought-provoking.
176 pages, 248 mm by 172 mm
$27.50 / £15.99

Winning Chess Explained
Zenon Franco
This book will improve your all-round chess strength. Topics include: Pawn Sacrifice, The Art of Manoeuvring, The Second Weakness, Permanent vs Temporary Advantages, Regrouping, 'Strange' Exchanges, Denying the Opponent Squares, and The Central Breakthrough.
192 pages, 248 mm by 172 mm
$26.95 / £15.99

Secrets of Modern Chess Strategy
John Watson
In a profound but thoroughly practical manner, this classic work explores how chess concepts have evolved over the past 75 years. Acclaimed double-winner of the 1999 British Chess Federation and 1999 United States Chess Federation 'Book of the Year' awards.
272 pages, 248 mm by 172 mm
$29.95 / £19.99

Beating the Fianchetto Defences
Efstratios Grivas
A comprehensive and detailed repertoire for White against five important openings: the Grünfeld, King's Indian, Benoni, Benko and Modern.
192 pages, 248 mm by 172 mm
$26.95 / £15.99

How to Calculate Chess Tactics
Valeri Beim
Experienced trainer Beim shows how intuition and logic can be used hand-in-hand, to solve tactical problems at the board.
176 pages, 248 mm by 172 mm
$26.95 / £15.99

About the Publisher: Gambit Publications Ltd is passionate about creating innovative and instructive chess books. Gambit specializes in chess, and the company is owned and run exclusively by chess masters and grandmasters.

www.gambitbooks.com